PLANNING WAR, PURSUING PEACE

MODERN WAR STUDIES

Theodore A. Wilson
General Editor

Raymond A. Callahan
J. Garry Clifford
Jacob W. Kipp
Jay Luvaas
Allan R. Millett
Dennis Showalter
Series Editors

PLANNING WAR, PURSUING PEACE
THE POLITICAL ECONOMY OF AMERICAN WARFARE, 1920–1939

PAUL A. C. KOISTINEN

UNIVERSITY PRESS OF KANSAS

© 1998 by the University Press of Kansas
All rights reserved

Published by the University Press of Kansas (Lawrence, Kansas 66045), which was organized by the Kansas Board of Regents and is operated and funded by Emporia State University, Fort Hays State University, Kansas State University, Pittsburg State University, the University of Kansas, and Wichita State University

Library of Congress Cataloging-in-Publication Data

Koistinen, Paul A. C.
Planning war, pursuing peace: the political economy of American warfare, 1920–1939 / Paul A.C. Koistinen.
p. cm. — (Modern war studies)
Includes bibliographical references and index.
ISBN 978-0-7006-2115-6 (pbk. : alk. paper)
1. War—Economic aspects—United States—History—20th century.
2. United States—Defenses—History—20th century. 3. Industrial mobilization—United States—History—20th century. I. Title. II. Series.
HC110.D4K645   1998
338.4'76233'0973—dc21
                                                                97-47716

British Library Cataloguing in Publication Data is available.

10 9 8 7 6 5 4 3 2 1

The paper used in this publication meets the minimum requirements of the American National Standard for Permanence of Paper for Printed Library Materials Z39.48-1992.

For the Northridge Six

Shiva Bajpai
John J. Broesamle
Ronald L. F. Davis
Sheldon H. Harris
Ronald Schaffer
Reba N. Soffer

To every thing there is a season, and a time to every
purpose under the heaven:
A time to be born, and a time to die; a time to plant,
and a time to pluck up that which is planted;
A time to kill, and a time to heal; a time to break
down, and a time to build up;
A time to rend, and a time to sew; a time to keep
silence, and a time to speak;
A time to love, and a time to hate; a time of war,
and a time of peace.

Ecclesiastes 3:1–3, 7–8

CONTENTS

Preface	xi
Part One—Planning War	1
1 Procurement Planning, 1920–1939	5
2 Industrial Mobilization Planning, 1920–1939	42
3 Military-Business Relations, 1920–1939	72
4 Commodity Committees	97
5 Steel	105
6 Aluminum and Rubber	116
7 Petroleum, Copper, and Lead	129
8 Manganese, Tin, Mica, Wool and Woolen Goods, Machine Tools, Optical Glass, and Medical Supplies	138
9 Lumber, Coal and Coal Products, Cotton and Cotton Textiles, and Leather and Leather Goods	160
10 Explosives and Aircraft	170
11 OASW Planning: Conclusion	199
Part Two—Pursuing Peace	209
12 The Graham Committee	211
13 The American Legion, the Office of the Assistant Secretary of War, and the War Policies Commission	220
14 The Nye Committee	253
15 The War Resources Board	305

Epilogue	319
Notes	323
Bibliographical Essay	409
Index	415

PREFACE

This volume is the third in a five-volume study of the political economy of American warfare—the means the nation has employed to mobilize its economic resources for defense and hostilities. In this book, I examine the years from 1920 through 1939. Volume 1, *Beating Plowshares into Swords: The Political Economy of American Warfare, 1606–1865* (Lawrence: University Press of Kansas, 1996), covers the colonial period through the Civil War; volume 2, *Mobilizing for Modern War: The Political Economy of American Warfare, 1865–1919* (Lawrence: University Press of Kansas, 1997), focuses on the Gilded Age, the Progressive Era, and World War I. In volume 4, I shall deal with World War II and in volume 5, with the Cold War period.

My goal in this multivolume study is to provide scholars and other readers with a source that is now unavailable: a comprehensive, analytical, and interdisciplinary study of the economics of America's wars from the colonial period to today. In doing so, I demonstrate the impact of the political economy of warfare upon domestic life and explore what economic mobilization for defense and war reveals about the nature and operations of power within society. I also seek to expand on the study of military history by examining in depth and breadth an aspect of warfare that is often ignored or treated in a perfunctory manner. This different perspective leads to different insights and conclusions about civilians, soldiers and sailors, and warfare. If I raise as many questions as I answer, I will have more than accomplished my purpose.

Analyzing how America has mobilized its economic resources for war and defense is important for a number of reasons. Logistics are basic to warfare and depend upon the nation's ability to marshal effectively its economic might. Over the centuries, economic mobilization has followed a discernible evolutionary pattern that illuminates the study of warfare and the military. Furthermore, how the United States has mobilized its economy reveals a great deal about institutional and power structures. Indeed, the stress and demands of warfare make manifest social patterns that are less evident or are obscured during years of peace.

The political economy of warfare involves the interrelationships of the political, economic, and military institutions in devising the means to mobilize resources for defense and to conduct war. In each war, the magnitude and duration of the fighting have dictated *what* the nation had to do to harness its economic power, but prewar trends have largely determined *how* this mobilization took place. Four factors are essential in determining the method of mobilization. The first is economic—the level of maturity of the economy; the second is political—the size, strength, and scope of the federal government; the third is military—the character and structure of the military services and the relationship between them and civilian society and authority; and the fourth is the state of military technology.

Patterns of economic mobilization for war have passed through three major stages over the course of American history. The Revolutionary War, the Civil War, and twentieth-century warfare best characterize these stages, which I have labeled preindustrial, transitional, and industrial. Altering the four factors—economic, political, military, and technological—modifies each stage of mobilization. The factors have seldom changed at the same time or pace, but over time each has had to keep up with the others so that viable patterns of economic mobilization could be maintained.

The preindustrial stage of economic mobilization for war extended from the colonial period to approximately 1815 and included the Revolutionary War and the War of 1812. During the American Revolution, economic, governmental, and military institutions were in an embryonic state and were not clearly distinguished from one another. Military technology was rather primitive and varied little from production in the peacetime economy. Hence, economic mobilization involved increasing civilian output and diverting products from civilian to military use in order to supply the armed forces without converting the economy. Nonetheless, to maximize output, comprehensive regulation of the emerging nation's economic life became essential. Yet the undeveloped nature of economic, political, and military institutions not only prevented such regulation from ever working well but also resulted in private and public, civil and military activities becoming inextricably intertwined. Merchants simultaneously served as public officials and military officers while they continued to conduct their private affairs.

The effects of harnessing the economy for war carried over into the years of peace. By highlighting the weaknesses of the Articles of Confederation, economic mobilization helped to create the momentum for the ideas underlying the Constitution. And, during the early national period, intense conflict grew between the factions that became the Federalist and Republican parties over the strength and policies of the national government under the new charter.

This strife weakened the federal government and stunted the growth of the armed services, a major source of dispute. Consequently, although the economy was much stronger in 1812 than in 1776 and military technology had changed little during that period, economic mobilization for the War of 1812 did not improve measurably over what it had been for the Revolutionary War.

The second, or transitional, economic mobilization stage extended from 1816 to 1865. During this period, the economy developed enormous productive capacity; it became diversified and quite industrialized, and specialized functions emerged in manufacturing, marketing, banking, and the like, although the size of firms was comparatively small. The federal government was limited in size, scope, and activity, but it was capable of expanding in order to handle economic mobilization effectively and efficiently. Both the army and navy, for their part, had professionalized to the point where they had definable structures and missions. But military technology still had not experienced any dramatic change. Since weaponry remained basic, economic mobilization required only expanding and diverting civilian production, not economic conversion.

Harnessing the economy for war was more readily accomplished in the transitional stage than in those stages that preceded and followed it. The pattern was evident in the Mexican War but was best demonstrated by the Union during the Civil War. Operating under the direction of the president, the War, Navy, and Treasury Departments acted as the principal mobilization agencies. They relied on market forces in a strong, competitive economy, not on the elaborate regulation of the preindustrial and industrial stages, to maintain economic stability while meeting the enormous demands of war. Moreover, institutional barriers were not breached. In the economic realm, little mixing of activities or personnel occurred among private and public, civilian and military affairs. The only major exception involved the railroads, which had begun to organize modern corporations before hostilities. The telegraph system followed a similar trend.

Union success contrasted sharply with the Confederacy's failure. The South was closer to the preindustrial than to the transitional stage. Like the colonies/states during the revolutionary years, the Confederacy experimented with comprehensive economic regulation without much success. Weak economic and political systems consistently undermined the Confederacy's economic mobilization effort and played an important role in the South's defeat.

Modern warfare in the twentieth century represents the third, or industrial, economic mobilization stage. By 1900 the United States had become a mature industrialized nation with a modified capitalist system. Although market forces remained significant in the production and distribution of goods, the administered decisions of several hundred modern corporations exercised strong, at times dominant, influence over the economy's direction. In order to make concentrated and consolidated economic power more responsible to the public and to stabilize an enormously complex economy, the federal government began to act as economic regulator. The growth of huge bureaucracies in the corporate and governmental spheres began to blur the institutional lines between both. Businessmen often staffed the government's regulatory agencies, and, as during the preindustrial stage, the affairs of government and business touched or merged at many points. A government-business regulatory alliance began to emerge during the Progressive Era.

For a time during the late nineteenth century, the military services entered a period of relative isolation in America as the nation became absorbed in industrialization, the threat of war receded, and the army and navy became intensely involved in professionalizing their functions. A technological revolution in weaponry in the later years of the nineteenth century, however, drew the civilian and military worlds back together. The consequences of this revolution were first manifest with the navy. In order to build a new fleet of steel, armor, steam, and modern ordnance, a production team consisting of political leaders, naval officers, and businessmen was formed. Although the composition, responsibilities, and operation of such a team have varied over the years, it has continued to exist. The army was slower to feel the impact of technology, but it eventually experienced the same needs, and a relationship developed with industry and civil authorities similar to the navy's.

By the eve of World War I, therefore, the federal government, the industrial community, and the military services had developed complex, modern, and professionalized structures, each dependent upon the others in terms of national defense. Economic mobilization for World War I (unlike the brief and limited Spanish-American War) forcefully demonstrated this institutional interdependence. The quantity and sophistication of military demand meant that increasing and diverting civilian production was no longer adequate; market forces could not be relied upon. Production had to be maximized and industries had to be converted in order to manufacture the often specialized military hardware. Priority, allocation, price, and other controls had to be introduced. Existing governmental departments and agencies were unequal to the task. New mobilization bodies had to be created, the most important being the War Industries Board (WIB). Through the board, centralized control over a planned economy was established and carried out by representatives of the government, the business community, and the military. The process obscured institutional lines. Civilian and military, private and public activities combined. For very different reasons and with quite different results, the first and the third mobilization stages are strikingly similar.

World War I mobilization left an indelible imprint on national life. During the interwar years, direct and indirect economic planning patterned after the WIB was tried. Congress and other governmental bodies repeatedly investigated the methods and consequences of harnessing the World War I economy in order to understand better what had taken place, to prevent future mobilization abuses, and to head off the perceived threats of modern warfare. Moreover, close ties between the civil and military sectors of the government, the industrial community, and other new and old interest groups were maintained in order to design, produce, and procure specialized munitions and to plan for industrial mobilization. During World War II, a modified form of the World War I model was used to mobilize the economy for meeting the astronomical and often highly specialized demands of the armed forces and America's allies. As the Cold War followed World War II, the nation for the first time in its peacetime history supported a massive military establishment, one that became inordinately expensive because of its size and because of a continuing transformation of weaponry through scientific and technological advancement. As a result, a defense and war "complex" included and affected most private and public institutions in American life.

Economic mobilization has been carried out largely by political, economic, and, ultimately, military elites. Economic and political elites are closely related and comprise the nation's upper classes. In the late eighteenth and early nineteenth centuries they included merchants, planters and large landowners, and professional elements. As the economy matured, the people involved with banks, railroads, and manufacturing gained in importance, and the twentieth-century economic elite is based primarily on the vast corporate and financial communities.

Military elites as a distinct group did not work in close association with economic and political elites until the industrial stage. In the preindustrial period, no clear line separated the military from the civilian world. During the transitional stage, both the army and the navy distanced themselves from civilians as they began to professionalize and to acquire separate identities. But in the industrial stage, military leaders out of necessity had to join their political and economic counterparts in order successfully to mobilize the economy for war.

Elites shaped economic mobilization in a number of ways. The federal executive—or what approximated it during the Revolution—devised and implemented the methods for harnessing the economy for war. Throughout American history, the highest appointed officials in the executive branch have been drawn predominantly from among the wealthy or those associated with them. Moreover, the federal government has turned to the nation's business leaders to assist in economic mobilization. They have acted as temporary or permanent advisers to government mobilizers, served in established or newly created federal agencies with or without pay, or engaged in some combination of these activities.

Harnessing the economy for war has generated a great deal of political controversy in America. Much of the conflict grows from the fact that economic mobilization highlights the nation's most basic contradiction: an elitist reality in the context of a democratic ideology. During years of peace that dynamic contradiction tends to be obscured; during years of war it is magnified by elitist economic mobilization patterns. Excluded interest groups and classes inevitably challenge the legitimacy of mobilization systems run by the few as unrepresentative and as failing to protect larger public interests. This resentment is exaggerated by the widespread aversion to and fear of government at the national level. Moreover, economic mobilization for war elevates the armed services to positions of central importance, which intensifies the strong antimilitary strains in American thought. Opposition to war among nonelites also often leads to adverse critiques of economic mobilization policies. There is a close correlation between antiwar and antielite attitudes.

Controversy over the political economy of warfare was greatest in the preindustrial and industrial stages. By requiring a form of planning, underdeveloped and highly developed economies have made elites quite visible. Market economies do not have as exaggerated an effect because mobilization agencies combining political and economic elites are unnecessary. Consequently, economic mobilization caused less political turmoil in the transitional stage.

Throughout the course of American history, the role of political, economic, and military elites in economic mobilization for defense and war can be understood fully only within the four-factor, three-stage paradigm. If the preindustrial stage is dated from 1765 to 1815 (instead of including the entire colonial era), it lasted only about fifty years, approximately the same duration as the transitional stage. Accelerated physical and economic growth quickly modified institutions and power operations, altering in the process the stages of economic mobilization. Rapid industrialization after the Civil War ushered in the last mobilization stage, one that has had a permanence of sorts to it. Since the late nineteenth century, political, economic, and military elites have been absorbed in creating and refining planning structures to cope with the ongoing weapons revolution, a revolution that has comprehensively affected how America prepares for and conducts warfare.

This volume is the most challenging for the reader of the three that have been published to date, and it is also perhaps the most significant. It is difficult because it deals with planning for and investigation of war mobilization rather than with the actuality of harnessing the economy for hostilities. Planning for future contingencies raises the question of what needs to be included in order to do the topic justice. Answering the question would be easier if I could refer readers to other studies. In most instances that option is unavailable because related publications are limited in quantity and quality. That is precisely why the volume is significant. In some areas, and for the topic as a whole during the interwar years, my work stands alone.

As the title indicates, this volume is divided into two parts, dealing with war and peace. Part One is longer and more demanding. It describes and analyzes at length the War Department's (and to a lesser degree the Navy Department's) procurement and economic mobilization planning for war. The planning played a vital role in preparing the armed services for World War II. Yet it has never been examined in its entirety, and parts of the planning have not been studied at all. Much of this planning, and particularly that dealing with the work of commodity committees, will be more familiar to students of economic and business history and political economy than to military historians. Many of the army and navy officers who carried out the planning felt a sense of strangeness, even bewilderment and resentment, as they struggled to understand the operations of the economy in general and various industries in particular that had become essential for fulfilling the modern military mission. Throughout the 1920s and 1930s, civilians stepped in to assist the armed services in dealing with the enormity of the task they faced. I assist the reader in understanding the planning through summaries before and after detailed treatment. In chapter 4 I briefly outline the salient aspects of commodity committee work. In chapters 5 through 10 I then examine this planning in detail for readers who will benefit from more extended analysis. In chapter 11 I present an overview of the aspects of the military's economic planning and its significance for the armed services and the nation.

Part Two is easier to grasp and is inherently more interesting than Part One. It deals with America's struggle to understand the effects of modern warfare and to work out solutions for mitigating the adverse consequences of war. This material has a clarity to it that requires fewer signposts for the reader; it also has a dramatic quality that the bureaucratic planning of Part One lacks.

As with aspects of Part One, I take the reader into new terrain with Part Two. The House Select Committee on Expenditures in the War Department has been totally neglected by historians, and nearly the same can be said of the War Policies Commission and its antecedents. Although the Senate Special Committee Investigating the Munitions Industry, chaired by Sen. Gerald P. Nye (R-ND), has received a great deal of attention, it has never been studied in depth—from the standpoint of World War I economic mobilization, the military's interwar procurement and economic mobilization planning, or preparedness for World War II. Only within that rich and complex context can the importance of the Nye Committee's investigation be fully understood.

I have benefited greatly from the assistance of others in putting this third volume into its final form. My son and daughter, David J. Koistinen and Janice H. Koistinen, combined their excellent critical and copyediting talents to help turn a rough and long manuscript into one that was briefer and more readable. Later, Terry J. Woulf proved equally valuable as an assistant. At California State University, Northridge, John J. Broesamle and Ronald Schaffer read the entire manuscript and provided me with invaluable insights and advice. Russell F. Weigley used his unequaled expertise and keen analytical skills to point out errors on my part and to suggest textual revisions that improved the volume. Finally, Theodore A. Wilson's assessment of the work was helpful. I could not ask for more from a publisher than the services provided by the University Press of Kansas. Michael Briggs, editor-in-chief, oversees the project with a sure but gentle hand, and his capable and dedicated staff—including Susan Schott, marketing manager, and Rebecca Knight Giusti, production editor—go about the wonders of converting manuscripts into published volumes with a high level of professionalism.

My debt to these people is matched only by my appreciation for their labors and contribution. Needless to say, I, not they, am responsible for all that is and is not said in this book.

Much precedes the review and publication of a manuscript. John Taylor and Wilbert Mahoney, Textual Reference Division, National Archives, and numerous other archivists in other divisions, provided me with invaluable assistance in coping with the voluminous records of the interwar years and World War II. Nancy Bressler of the Princeton University Library helped guide my work in the Papers of Bernard M. Baruch and Frank A. Scott. The staff of the Franklin D. Roosevelt Library facilitated my study of the Franklin D. Roosevelt Papers, as did the archivists at Carlisle Barracks with the Army War College Collection. Without the Oviatt Library at California State University, Northridge (CSUN), especially its interlibrary loan services, I would have been hard-pressed to complete this work. Charlotte Oyer, Donald L. Read, Michael Barrett, and Felicia Cousin worked endlessly on my behalf. For word processing of the various drafts, I appreciate the skill and good humor of Marcia M. Dunicliffe, formerly of the History Department, and Pamela Fowell, formerly with the College of Social and Behavioral Sciences. Finally, the continued support, encouragement, and love of my wife, Carolyn Epstein Koistinen, is crucial to what I do.

For financial support, I have had many benefactors over the years, including research fellowships from Harvard's Charles Warren Center for Studies in American History, the American Council of Learned Societies, and the National Endowment for the Humanities. Furthermore, CSUN's History Department, College of Social and Behavioral Sciences, and the university as a whole have assisted me in numerous ways for many years.

The volume is dedicated to a remarkable collection of academics and friends at Northridge. They have made the History Department an outstanding center of scholarship and instruction; individually and together they have encouraged, supported, and challenged me. Without them, the university and I would be diminished.

PART ONE
PLANNING WAR

The political economy of warfare during the interwar years was shaped largely by the War Industries Board (WIB) of World War I. In its final form, the board was a gigantic planning partnership of government and business that inextricably combined public and private interests.

Worked out in various stages between 1915 and 1918, the WIB was patterned roughly after the American economy. Serving for a dollar a year or without compensation, businessmen and professionals directed the board through its commodity section–war service committee system. Commodity sections oversaw major industries or economic sectors, such as steel, chemicals, and finished products, and were staffed by businessmen on temporary government service. War service committees existed for most industries and were made up of industry representatives, trade association officials, and various experts. Unlike commodity sections, these committees were not technically a part of the WIB; they were set up only to advise commodity sections on production, priorities, and other economic mobilization functions. In actuality, however, commodity sections and war service committees usually operated as one.

Although crude, the War Industries Board proved to be an effective means for harnessing the economy for war. The greatest obstacle facing the board was the War Department, the major claimant on the economy. It intensely resisted adjusting army supply operations to those of civilian agencies. The results were dire. By winter 1917–1918, the economic mobilization machinery began grinding to a halt. Under the threat of losing control over supply, the War Department was forced to adapt its economic functions to those of the WIB. Although considerable progress was made along these lines by the time of the armistice, a great deal remained to be done before America's mobilization future was secure.

Interwar planning by the army continued its adjustments to the dictates of modern warfare. Legislation passed in 1920 authorized the War Department to plan for procurement and economic mobilization. Procurement planning was intended to rationalize army supply operations so that the service could respond better during an emergency; economic mobilization planning was intended to familiarize the War Department with developments that had occurred during World War I and to help keep the nation prepared for future hostilities. The Navy Department ultimately joined in the planning, although the War Department was always in the lead.

The armed service required extensive civilian assistance in carrying out this planning. Help came first from World War I mobilization figures, new organizations like the Army Ordnance Association, and engineering societies. Gradually support broadened to include most business, industrial, and financial associations and representatives from virtually every industry in the United States.

Underlying the economic planning by the army was that carried out by commodity committees. The War Department created committees for raw materials, semifinished products, and finished goods critical to a war effort, such as rubber, steel, and machine tools, or goods that could be in short supply during hostilities, like manganese.

The military's commodity committees continued the operations of the WIB's commodity section–war service committee system in a limited way during the interwar years. In that sense, the War Industries Board was never totally disestablished. The postwar commodity committees were as important to military planning as the commodity section–war service committees had been to the operations of the War Industries Board. Familiarizing the armed services with America's economic system, the committees helped make the military palpably aware of its dependence on civilians for fighting a modern war. Committee work also brought army planners into contact with the full range of American businessmen. In turn, commodity committee activity gave the army and navy the opportunity to explain military requirements and operations to the business community.

The War Department's planning in one way or another centered on the War Industries Board's legacy. Four Industrial Mobilization Plans (IMPs) written by the military services between 1930 and 1939, for example, came successively closer to duplicating patterns that had been followed during World War I. The individuals advising the army reinforced this trend. As the only federal agency planning for economic mobilization, the War Department attracted close attention from World War I mobilizers such as Bernard M. Baruch and Frank A. Scott. In their eyes, preparedness demanded that the World War I approach be followed.

Civilians not associated directly with military planning also acted to perpetuate World War I mobilization patterns. During the 1920s, Republican administrations attempted to achieve the benefits of wartime planning informally through the encouragement and guidance of concentrated economic power and trade association activity. In the throes of the Great Depression, the Franklin D. Roosevelt administration opted for direct economic planning under the National Recovery Administration, which closely resembled the War Industries Board. These developments validated War Department planning and made it relevant to civilian life.

Interwar planning, like World War I mobilization, involved great complexity and grave risks for the nation. Modern warfare was breaking down barriers among public and private, civilian and military institutions, thus opening the door to endless abuses. More significant, it threatened to create forces that encouraged war.

Various civilian groups became acutely aware of the dangers. During World War I, agrarian advocates of small government had opposed the War Industries Board because it concentrated power further in Washington and because it was rife with conflicts of interests, profiteering, and other malfeasance. In the 1920s and 1930s, critics went beyond their wartime counterparts to voice alarm that WIB mobilization methods, combined with the current military procurement practices and army economic planning, were creating the basis for what the next generation would call a military-industrial complex (MIC).

No MIC per se existed in the interwar years. But as a continuation of World War I mobilization methods, elaborate ties were growing between the armed services and the industrial community. Organizations like the Army Ordnance Association lobbied for the army and worked to increase industrial-military contacts. Emerging industries like aircraft and mature ones like shipbuilding demonstrated nearly every pattern and practice later associated with the MIC of the Cold War years. Missing in the interwar years, however, were decades of multibillion-dollar military budgets that inevitably created powerful domestic interest groups requiring war, or its threat, to protect their power, profits, and prestige within the nation's political and economic structure.

Levels of military spending aside, no military-industrial complex could have sprung full blown into existence without decades of institutional adjustment. That process started in the late nineteenth and early twentieth centuries with the building of a modern navy. It was vastly accelerated by mobilizing the World War I economy; it made steady progress with the War Department's planning in the interwar years; and it came to maturity during World War II and the Cold War.

During the interwar years, therefore, among the economic, political, military, and technological factors shaping the political economy of warfare, civil-military relations revealed the most significant changes. The armed services adjusted their systems to relatively stable economic and political structures. Although differing to some degree between the boom times of the 1920s and the depression of the 1930s, economic power remained highly concentrated. Several hundred giant corporations constituted the economic hub around which thousands of lesser corporate entities turned. Although the federal government's role of economic regulator and social welfare agent diminished somewhat in the 1920s only to burgeon during the distress of the 1930s, Washington continued to operate along lines already established in the Progressive Era. The War Industries Board, after all, was only an extension and an elaboration of the government-business regulatory alliance that began emerging during the Progressive years as the principal, elitist mode of twentieth-century American political economy.

Weapons technology was significant in the interwar years without being the principal force shaping the political economy of warfare. The quantity of military demand, more than its specialized nature, necessitated economic mobilization for World War I. Nonetheless, the tools of war were becoming industrially more demanding as the tank, the airplane, and the submarine indicated. Unlike that of World War I, the economy during World War II was prodigious in both the sophistication and quantity of weaponry produced. That achievement was made possible by the procurement and economic mobilization planning of the army and the navy in the interwar years.

1
PROCUREMENT PLANNING, 1920–1939

THE NATIONAL DEFENSE ACT OF 1920

Congress attempted to prevent a disorganized army from disrupting future economic mobilization through key provisions of the National Defense Act of 1920. In a major innovation, the nation's legislators strengthened the assistant secretary of war to oversee the supply bureaus' current purchasing and, more important, to initiate and supervise procurement and industrial mobilization planning. These changes were intended to prevent a repetition of the pattern that had occurred during World War I. By refusing to cooperate with the War Industries Board and its predecessors, the army had undermined economic mobilization until basic reforms required it to work with the board beginning early in 1918.

The 1920 legislation divided the War Department into two spheres: one headed by the chief of staff, the other by the assistant secretary of war. The former would plan for and direct the fighting forces; the latter would do the same for the supply bureaus. By law and theory, the assistant secretary of war was the chief of staff's equal. Since the bureaus—designated "supply arms and services" (SA&S) in the interwar years—were responsible for supplying the troops as well as for producing, procuring, storing, and transporting goods and munitions, they reported to both the chief of staff and the assistant secretary of war, depending on the functions performed.[1] The secretary of war coordinated the two sides of the department through a newly created War Council, consisting primarily of himself, the chief of staff, and the assistant secretary of war.[2]

These reforms were based principally on the recommendations of Assistant Secretary of War Benedict Crowell. He had attempted to implement a similar setup during the winter crisis of 1917–1918 but lost out in a power struggle to Gen. George W. Goethals, who ultimately created the Purchase,

Storage, and Traffic Division of the General Staff.³ After the armistice, the assistant secretary of war reintroduced his proposal, which had been revised with the advice of prominent industrialists temporarily serving in the army during the war years, supply bureau chiefs, and other civilian and military personnel.⁴ The Military Affairs Committees of both houses of Congress were enthusiastic about Crowell's recommendations. They helped to focus and sharpen congressional thought in a way that was instrumental in producing Section 5a—and related Sections 5 and 5b—of the National Defense Act of 1920, dealing with supply.⁵

World War I, argued Crowell, had demonstrated that modern warfare made industrial production as important to military success as tactics and strategy. Supply and procurement, therefore, must receive the same emphasis in War Department affairs as traditional military functions. That would not take place, Crowell insisted, under the old system in which the chief of staff, aided by the General Staff, served as the secretary of war's major adviser. The staff would neglect supply because it knew little about the subject. The Purchase, Storage, and Traffic Division had been an emergency arrangement with no lasting impact on the General Staff. Testimony of staff and line officers before the House and Senate Military Affairs Committees on measures that became the National Defense Act of 1920 validated Crowell's point. Most knew little about supply, were ignorant of what had transpired during the war, and believed procurement would present no problems in the future. A vital lesson of the war had been missed, adding weight to Crowell's insistence that the army place the bureaus under a qualified civilian, preferably an outstanding industrialist. The secretary of war, then, would have two principal advisers, not one as had been the case prior to 1920.

Conflicting advice on army supply structures created problems for Congress in 1919 and 1920. The General Staff proposed, in effect, continuing the Purchase, Storage, and Traffic Division. This would have meant staff control of supply and the virtual end of the supply arms and services. The chief of staff and the General Staff argued that such a course was essential for rationalizing the department and preventing the supply chaos of World War I. Not surprisingly, the bureaus fought furiously against a plan that called for their own demise. They insisted that they had performed well during the war under intolerable conditions, that this wartime experience would eliminate many future problems, and that the General Staff control would resolve no supply problems.

A perplexed Congress remained uncertain about what to do until Benedict Crowell presented an apparently reasonable compromise. The legislators' move in the assistant secretary's direction was eased by the support of Secretary of War Newton D. Baker and by Gen. John J. Pershing's belief that middle ground existed between the conflicting positions of the SA&S and the General Staff.

Crowell's proposal was difficult to implement, and neither the assistant secretary of war, his advisers, nor Congress thought through how the changes could best be made. The result was a flawed statute, made worse by the inevitable bargaining of the legislative process. Consequently, the supply reforms of 1920 ended up as inadequate in almost every way.

The 1920 bill violated several cardinal rules of command and leadership. The assistant secretary was given statutory authority over the operations and planning of the bureaus without emphatically placing him under the supervision of the secretary of war. That arrangement reduced the secretary's options and created conditions in which the assistant secretary during an emergency could have responsibilities and power greater than his superior. Secretary of War Baker argued that the assistant secretary should perform his duties only at the discretion of his chief. Baker's protests went unheeded, although Henry L. Stimson, after being appointed secretary of war in 1940, moved quickly to have the law changed along the lines Baker had favored.

As egregious as the assignment to a subordinate of powers possibly exceeding those of his superior was the act's requirement that the bureaus report to two masters, the assistant secretary of war and the chief of staff. That blunder was compounded by failing to apportion supply responsibilities between the two spheres. An already quarreling War Department was left to fight the matter out for itself.

Moreover, the 1920 law did not create an office for the assistant secretary of war. In order for the assistant secretary to match the chief of staff's authority and carry out his duties, he needed a statutory agency as powerful as the General Staff. The statute noted only that the assistant secretary could draw required personnel from the bureaus. Various War Department and army orders and regulations eventually set up an office for the assistant secretary. However, the office's highest ranking officer, the director of procurement and commandant of the Army Industrial College, was only a colonel. By contrast, the chief of staff was ordinarily no less than a major general, his principal assistants major and brigadier generals, and the head of the Army War College a major general. Statute aside, the assistant secretary's office was inevitably viewed as inferior to the General Staff.

The assistant secretary and his lieutenants also lacked clout with the bureaus, most of which were headed by major generals. An early version of Section 5a of the 1920 legislation provided the assistant secretary with a high-powered office that would distribute responsibilities among the bureaus as necessary. With such authority, the assistant secretary might have bent the bureaus and the General Staff to his will. But neo-Jeffersonian elements in Congress insisted on excising those crucial powers from the act.

Thus although the National Defense Act of 1920 intended to make the assistant secretary the chief of staff's equal and place him in charge of the bureaus, the realities of power in the extremely rank-conscious army made those goals unattainable. Not fully accustomed to military mores and thought, Congress might be excused for this naivete. Crowell and his military advisers, however, should have been fully aware of what they were doing. Apparently, some advisers from the SA&S who had a role in drafting the 1920 law intentionally worked for a weak assistant secretary of war so as to free the bureaus from the General Staff and any other source of authority.

There was little the assistant secretary of war could do to strengthen his position. The General Staff originated and commented upon legislation involving the army, and the bureaus had political weight through their close congressional ties. In 1927 the assistant secretary was allowed one representative on the Advisory Council on Legislation but with little effect. The General Staff also had authority over budgets, even though the bureaus spent the major share of appropriations in the interwar years. It was not until 1939 that the assistant secretary was given responsibility for supervising budgetary estimates for procurement planning. Furthermore, subject to bureau influence where supply personnel were concerned, the General Staff determined the selection, assignment, transfer, and promotion of all commissioned officers, including those assigned to the assistant secretary's office. The latter was even denied an official voice in selecting the bureau chiefs, who were critically important to virtually everything he did.

Largely excluded from legislative, budgetary, and personnel decisions, the assistant secretary of war had enormous responsibilities without much authority. Congress tacked the assistant secretary's position on to the existing War Department structure without otherwise altering the department to accommodate this basic change. Repeatedly throughout the 1920s and 1930s, assistant secretaries, their staffs, bureau heads, and others tried statutorily to give the assistant secretary the organization, rank, and office he needed to act effectively. Success always eluded them.[6]

Furthermore, the legislation of the National Defense Act of 1920 was vague and contradictory about what planning would be done and who would do it. Congress, Crowell, and their advisers intended the assistant secretary of war to plan for wartime procurement. Such planning without larger blueprints for mobilizing the entire economy would be difficult, probably impossible. Yet no agency existed for this major task. Congress suggested that the assistant secretary of war might carry out industrial mobilization planning but offered no details. To complicate matters further, the 1920 legislation appeared to grant the General Staff the authority to plan for economic mobilization, and some members of Congress seemed to support that interpretation when the bill was debated. Again, however, clarity was missing. Obscure references and afterthoughts were no substitute for forthright declarations.

With the National Defense Act of 1920, Congress appeared anxious to rid itself of the chronic wrangling between the General Staff and the bureaus and to try to prevent another military supply muddle in a future war. It grabbed at Crowell's proposal as an easy way out, thereby avoiding the strain of fundamental change that had characterized the creation of the chief of staff–General Staff system at the turn of the century. The General Staff opposed Crowell's initiative without waging a major fight against it, apparently secure in the belief that rank and status could be used to ward off incursions from the assistant secretary of war. On their part, the bureaus looked upon Crowell's proposition as a godsend. It ended the Purchase, Storage, and Traffic Division, freed them of General Staff control, and created an assistant secretary who would not impinge excessively, even substantially, upon their prerogatives. For those in the SA&S and the General Staff who were serious about the need for procurement planning, the task could be carried out to some degree without the prestige and power of rank and position.

Continuing World War I patterns, the Woodrow Wilson administration, Congress, and the military used the National Defense Act of 1920 to dodge the vexatious issue of military supply and the related and larger matter of economic mobilization. In the short run the legislation benefited the SA&S; in the long run it favored the chief of staff–General Staff. During peace the War Department could tolerate fragmented power; during war, centralized direction by the General Staff was imperative to prevent chaos. When the United States entered World War II, the chief of staff moved quickly to take control of supply operations.

This is not to say that the Crowell reforms were without merit. On the contrary, as a result of procurement and economic mobilization planning carried out by the assistant secretary of war's office, the army, and the navy as well, gradually recognized that modern, industrialized warfare had made them dependent on the civilian economy for carrying out their mission. Henceforth, all military strategic plans had to be based on the potential of a mobilized economy. Once that basic change occurred, the General Staff could assert control over supply during World War II without disrupting the army or the economy.

THE OFFICE OF THE ASSISTANT SECRETARY OF WAR

The supply reforms of the National Defense Act of 1920 had no immediate effect. Little planning took place during most of 1920 and the early part of 1921 as the General Staff and supply arms and services maneuvered for position in their ongoing conflict.[7]

General John J. Pershing moved quickly to end the impasse when he took over as chief of staff in July 1921. He appointed Maj. Gen. James G. Harbord—a protégé who had served successively as his chief of staff and commanding general of the Services of Supply in the American Expeditionary Forces (AEF)—to head a board of officers to study and make recommendations on the War Department's organization and distribution of responsibility and authority, including supply operations, under the 1920 legislation. After several false starts, the Harbord Board proposed an equitable division of supply duties that became incorporated in War Department General Orders no. 41, August 16, 1921. The General Staff would set requirements for supplies and weapons—what, how much, and when—and the assistant secretary would handle production and procurement. The two shared decisionmaking on research and development, specifications, and storage, but with the General Staff having an edge. This proposal opened up new areas of dispute, which an army regulation of 1932 finally settled in favor of the assistant secretary. Of critical importance, the Harbord Board recommendations and a clarifying order and directive made procurement and economic mobilization planning the exclusive preserve of the assistant secretary of war.

General Orders no. 41 set the guidelines for War Department operations in the interwar years. The Harbord Board's most important long-range impact, based on Pershing's convictions and the AEF experience, was in creating a strong General Staff with five main sections, G-1 through G-4 and the War Plans Division.[8]

J. Mayhew Wainwright was the first assistant secretary of war to serve under the 1920 act. He began organizing an office late in 1921. Colonel Harley B. Ferguson was released several months early from the Army War College to aid the assistant secretary, and he served as head of the Office of the Assistant Secretary of War (OASW) until 1927. While the OASW underwent numerous reorganizations between 1921 and 1942, its functions basically divided between a branch for supervising current procurement and a Planning Branch (PB) for directing procurement and economic mobilization planning. Since peacetime purchasing was routinized and took place on a relatively small scale, the more important duties of the OASW were performed by the latter branch. Consisting of seven officers at first, the OASW slowly grew to fifty officers by

1939. In 1941, when it had become more a mobilization than a planning agency, the OASW had 1,200 officers and civilians working in a complex bureaucratic structure. While the OASW was in the planning stage, no officer on regular assignment ever exceeded the rank of colonel.[9]

In 1922 a War Department general order provided for an Army-Navy Munitions Board (ANMB). The assistant secretary of war took the initiative in creating this agency from the realization that without the Navy Department's cooperation, procurement and economic mobilization planning would be seriously limited. Consisting of the assistant secretaries of war and navy and their staffs and subordinate bodies, the ANMB was considered to be the supply and economic counterpart of the Army and Navy Joint Board, created in 1903 to coordinate the military operations of the two services. At no time did the ANMB achieve either the level of activity or the degree of coordination between the services that its authors had intended. The principal difficulty stemmed from the Navy Department's lack of interest in planning. During World War I the navy's requirements had been relatively limited, and it had an outstanding supply organization for fulfilling them.[10] Failing to anticipate World War II's high level of demand over an extended period of time, the navy remained confident that it could handle all emergencies.

Even if committed to planning, the Navy Department would have encountered difficulties since, unlike the War Department, it lacked statutory authority. Furthermore, the navy had no office for planning comparable to the assistant secretary of war. The chief of naval operations, the Office of the Secretary of the Navy, and the material bureaus had jurisdiction in the area without clearly defined parameters, which put a damper on initiative. Complicating matters further, the Navy Department, which was always in a state of at least semipreparedness, preferred to concentrate on specific strategic war plans—e.g., War Plan Orange against Japan—in which it would have a dominant role. By contrast, the War Department, starting from nearly zero, emphasized general mobilization plans to prepare for as many contingencies as possible.[11] The Navy Department in the interwar years narrowly concentrated its supply efforts on immediate operations, shipbuilding, and ordnance rather than on future hostilities, industry, and the economy.[12]

Since the two services had such different outlooks, common ground was difficult to find. Consequently, the ANMB atrophied during the 1920s. The board was reorganized in 1931 for a new start, but the effects were less than those anticipated. Even though plans were published under the imprimatur of the ANMB, the OASW continued to do most of the work. A substantial change occurred only at the end of the decade. In mid-1939 Pres. Franklin D. Roosevelt by executive order placed the board directly under his supervision, and Congress granted it statutory recognition. With new power and legitimacy, the ANMB began to act more as a mobilization agency than as a planning body. Its responsibilities continually expanded until early 1942 when the creation of the War Production Board and a major reorganization of the War Department caused the ANMB to slip into insignificance.[13]

In 1924 the Assistant Secretary of War rounded out his planning structure by establishing the Army Industrial College (AIC). The OASW required a formally trained staff to plan for procurement and economic mobilization. At first, the few officers who made up the office relied on an apprenticeship system, consisting principally of studying War Department supply records and the voluminous papers of the War Industries Board and predecessor agencies deposited with the War Department. Recognizing the limitations of this approach, various officers persuaded the assistant secretary of war to organize the AIC, intended to become in purpose and prestige the counterpart of the Army War College (AWC). As with all other aspects of supply and economic mobilization planning, the college got off to a slow start. The first class consisted of only nine officers drawn from the bureaus and the OASW. Thereafter, classes grew in size until they had reached approximately sixty members in the late 1930s. By 1940, just before the AIC went on an emergency and accelerated schedule for pending war, it had graduated a total of 804 students. At first, the classes were made up exclusively of army officers; later, as the navy became more interested and involved in the planning activities, its officers became regulars, constituting about one-third of the students. A few marine officers also attended.

In terms of operation, the college was really more an extension of the Planning Branch than a separate entity. Besides lectures by prominent businessmen, previous war mobilizers, and experienced or informed military officers, the AIC worked mainly through case studies and independent projects that were closely related to or actually a part of Planning Branch activity.[14]

Throughout the interwar years, the AIC constantly faced hard times. Always inadequately funded and staffed, the college was also plagued by low-grade students because it lacked minimum standards and the prestige for advancing careers. The AIC competed with but was adversely compared to the high-powered AWC. Nonetheless, like the OASW as a whole, the college gradually had an impact on military planning. By the end of the 1930s, many important OASW and bureau officers were AIC graduates. The principal weakness of the college, reflecting the larger shortcomings of the OASW, was its failure to train enough supply personnel, not to mention staff and line officers, to make the army fully aware that the industrial revolution had permanently reshaped the military mission.[15]

The Planning Branch and the Army Industrial College, as subdivisions of the Office of the Assistant Secretary of War, constituted, along with the supply arms and services, the core of the interwar planning structure. It was mostly a military operation. Civilians, however, often played an important part. Of the six secretaries of war between 1921 and 1940, Patrick J. Hurley (1929–1933) was the most dynamic and forceful, though probably less talented than John W. Weeks (1921–1925). Hurley, who was assistant secretary of war for almost a year, took an active role as secretary in guiding the department through presenting publicly its first economic mobilization plan to the War Policies Commission from 1930 to 1932.[16] Dwight F. Davis, who served as assistant secretary of war from 1923 to 1925 and as secretary of war from 1925 to 1929, played an important though unspectacular part overseeing procurement planning. Louis A. Johnson (1936–1940) was unquestionably the most determined and resourceful assistant secretary of war, although ambition warped his judgment at key times. Nonetheless, Johnson assisted the army during the wrenching transition from planning to mobilization, often doing more than his superior, Secretary of War Harry H. Woodring (1936–1940).

Though turnover occurred among the War Department's civilian leaders from 1921 to 1940, the interwar years were comparatively stable. Six secretaries and eight assistant secretaries are lower figures than for most similar periods. Moreover, three of the assistant secretaries became secretaries of war: Davis, Hurley, and Woodring. Hence, for seventeen of the twenty years under consideration, the War Department experienced more continuity in civilian leadership than it was accustomed to. This was particularly true for the crucial years at the beginning (1923–1929), when Davis was successively assistant secretary and secretary of war, and at the end (1933–1940) when Woodring was assistant secretary and secretary of war. Without the direction of experienced leadership, the OASW might have faced greater difficulties than it did in procurement and economic mobilization planning.[17]

CHALLENGES OF PROCUREMENT PLANNING

For most of the 1920s the Office of the Assistant Secretary of War by necessity concentrated on planning for procurement, not for economic mobilization. The pre–World War I years provided no meaningful precedents for how planning for supply, let alone for economic mobilization, should be carried out in the modern era, and the war years did little more than confirm the need for planning. Entering uncharted territory, the military planners wisely began with the army, which they knew best, rather than with the entire economy.[18]

It took the army planners a full ten years to work out and partially apply effective procedures for procurement planning. This planning entailed preparing the army to purchase or have manufactured the munitions and supplies needed for wars of varying magnitudes. By necessity, procurement plans were based on the General Staff's war plans.

War planning by the General Staff was a source of constant irritation within the War Department throughout the interwar years.[19] At the outset, no such plans existed. The OASW in 1921, therefore, focused on general economic potential rather than on actual requirement figures. This situation changed gradually as the General Staff produced by stages between 1921 and 1924 "the first mobilization plan worked out in the United States by the General Staff in time of peace."[20] The War Department General Mobilization Plan, 1924, which was subsequently revised about every three years, was a radical departure for the General Staff. Previously, the army had concentrated on strategic plans involving specific enemies and regions, the so-called colored plans—e.g., War Plan Orange aimed at Japan and the Pacific. By contrast, the General Mobilization Plan laid out procedures for raising an army of approximately 4 million, considered to be the maximum the nation could support. Such a plan could be adjusted to meet any strategic situation or a smaller-scale mobilization effort. The army, unlike the navy, favored general mobilization plans over the strategic ones because its state of preparedness was so rudimentary, its mobilization task so huge, and its potential combat role so varied and demanding.[21]

The army's reliance on general war plans grew partly out of pressure from procurement planners. Since World War I had established the primacy of supply in military matters, the procurement planners needed reasonable goals to guide their work, which required years of effort. The general mobilization plan allowed the General Staff and the OASW to carry out extended, complex planning without working in lockstep with each other.[22]

Once the General Staff established the outline of a general mobilization plan, the OASW could begin procurement planning. The first stage involved calculating requirements, that is, what the army would need in terms of munitions and supplies in an emergency. Setting tables of organization, equipment, allowance, maintenance, and replacement and of rates of mobilization launched the process. Additionally, equipment had to be designed and specifications for materials and production established. With those jobs finished—or at least started, since no part of procurement planning proceeded in a neat, orderly pattern—the OASW could finally oversee the computation of requirements by the bureaus. When the OASW had approved the requirement figures and they had been accepted by the General Staff, the first stage in procurement planning was completed.[23]

Setting requirements was the easiest phase of procurement planning. The assistant secretary of war reported in 1923 that when his office received the first rudimentary general mobilization plan from the General Staff, fifty officers came up with total requirement figures in about nine months. Complete procurement plans for all items, he warned, would take another five years. His prognosis was quite accurate. Even when planning had become routinized in the mid-1930s, a complete cycle of procurement planning based on a revised general mobilization plan still took three years of intense work.[24]

Procurement planning was so taxing that the OASW in 1923 created a new supply appendage to facilitate its work—the Procurement District system. Though new for the War Department as a whole, the system had originated with the Ordnance Department during World War I. By 1918 Ordnance had concluded that centralized purchasing in Washington created more problems than it solved. Consequently, it decentralized operations to first eleven, later thirteen, Procurement Districts, into which it divided the nation. Each district had a headquarters in a leading city. Prominent industrialists headed the districts in order to maximize the assistance of businessmen while freeing them of the numerous restraints on military men. Ordnance phased out its wartime structure during demobilization in 1918 and 1919, then revived it in 1922 to aid in procurement and economic mobilization planning. Once again, civilians headed each of the districts, by then fourteen in number.

In 1923 the Office of the Assistant Secretary of War directed all bureaus to create a similar decentralized structure with the proviso that a bureau could operate with only a few districts in peacetime; the truncated system would then be expanded during a national emergency. The War Department delineated fourteen districts and headquarters of its own that closely paralleled those of the Ordnance Department so that the OASW could coordinate the multidistrict system and bring about uniform structures and policies. The approach never worked. Various supply arms and services, and especially the Quartermaster Corps, rebelled at the prospect of having their localized operations shaped and controlled by higher authorities. Bowing to pressure, the OASW in 1933 replaced the fourteen War Department Procurement Districts with four amorphous Procurement Zones. In 1938 even the latter went, leaving the bureaus to run their own affairs.

Decentralization resulted in bureau districts that were completely devoid of system. No two SA&S had the same geographic lines, and modes of operation varied even among the districts of the same bureau. Ordnance's system stood alone. The other SA&S had from three to nine areas, fair to poor in quality of operations. The Air Corps and the Chemical Warfare Service, as new bureaus, had to set up district operations from scratch; the Quartermaster Corps, Corps of Engineers, Medical Department, Signal Corps, and Coast Artillery Corps, like the Ordnance Department, built upon existing units like the Quartermaster Corps depots.[25]

The Procurement Districts often assisted the SA&S with procurement plans. After determining requirement figures, the bureaus distributed the hypothetical load among the various districts to avoid the excessive contracting in certain cities, states, and regions that had occurred repeatedly during World War I. The district chiefs and their staffs reviewed the apportionment for their districts and advised the bureaus as to its feasibility and pointed out what, if anything, was essential to prepare a district for meeting its production schedule.[26]

After apportionment came the allocation of facilities by the OASW, that is, assigning business firms to various bureaus for their exclusive use. To leave adequate production capacity for civilian needs and other claimant agencies, 50 percent of the normal peacetime output of each firm was reserved for these uses. Since expanded wartime production was calculated as 250 percent of normal output, 200 percent of peacetime capacity was assigned to the military.[27] If two or more SA&S or the army and navy designated any firm or group of firms as indispensable, then "joint allocations" could be made. These were always kept to a bare minimum because of the complexities and conflicts involved. Giant corporations like the General Electric Company, Eastman Kodak Company, and United States Steel Corporation and specialty firms like machine tool producers were usually kept as "reserve facilities." Most military contractors wanted to use the enormous capacity or specialized capabilities of these firms. In such cases, the OASW or the Army-Navy Munitions Board apportioned the productive potential of the firms among the various military claimants. Allocated and reserve facilities for both services numbered about 5,500 in 1923, rose to 20,000 in 1927, and dropped to around 12,000 on the eve of World War II. Included in these lists were all of the largest manufacturers in the country. To apportion and allocate facilities, the OASW relied not only on the information gathered by the bureaus, the districts, and their business, industrial, and financial contacts but also on such agencies as the Commerce Department and the Bureau of the Census. In its 1925 survey, the bureau included a form devised by the OASW to elicit maximum data on potential military contractors.[28]

Allocations usually were made only for products with which important problems were anticipated or for which significant amounts of strategic or critical materials would be needed. The planners also allocated plants if total anticipated military need exceeded 50 percent of an industry's normal peacetime output. Whatever criterion was used, allocations included the American corporate elite. The 10,000-plus plants ultimately selected by the army planners for allocation included the cream of the American industrial system.[29]

After facilities had been allocated or reserved, they were surveyed to determine their suitability for procurement needs of the bureau to which they had been assigned. Firms found to be suitable were earmarked for the surveying bureau; those that were not went back into a general pool. Procurement District personnel executed most of the plant surveys. The next step involved negotiating "accepted schedules of production" between firms that were agreeable and the supply bureau. These nonbinding estimates of wartime production included calculations of the necessary quantities of inputs. At this stage, production was scheduled only for commodities that were commercial or close to commercial in nature and, hence, required minimal plant conversion. In instances where noncommercial items such as munitions were involved, "factory plans" had to be drafted first. These were plans to expand, convert, or build new facilities, particularly for goods needed by the SA&S such as the Ordnance Department, the Air Corps, and the Chemical Warfare Service. After the factory plans had been completed, then schedules of production could be drawn up. Since funding for the armed forces was quite limited in the interwar years, industry often donated substantial time and money to assist OASW procurement planning.[30]

While the process of moving from requirements to accepted schedules of production was going on, the OASW steadily improved contract forms to avoid a repetition of World War I practices. During hostilities, over 400 different types of contracts had been used by the bureaus, creating great confusion and inefficiency and leading to the use and abuse of cost-plus contracting, the absence of meaningful termination clauses, and other deficiencies. By the end of the 1930s, the army had devised four basic contract forms that it believed would handle virtually all contingencies while reducing substantially the failings of World War I methods.[31]

Had these various functions—requirements, apportionment, allocation, survey, factory plans, and accepted schedules of production—been the sum of procurement planning, that process could have been completed within a period of perhaps two years. Matters were not that simple. These planning steps related to "primary requirements," or finished products. Restricting planning to that realm would have been easier but extremely shortsighted since there was no assurance that primary products could be delivered. "Secondary requirements," or the goods and services essential to the production of primary requirements, such as raw materials, semifinished goods, machine tools, power, transportation, and labor, had to be included in the planning. Consequently, while getting under way in planning for primary production, the OASW simultaneously had to broaden its purview to include secondary demand.[32]

The OASW concentrated its planning for secondary requirements on raw materials, semifinished products, and a few finished goods like machine tools.

Since all bureaus depended on a broad range of these goods, the OASW approached planning for secondary requirements through "commodity committees." These were patterned in idea, if not in structure, on the committees of the same or similar name organized during World War I within the War Industries Board and eventually within the Division of Purchase, Storage, and Traffic of the General Staff.[33] The bureaus that required a certain commodity for their production programs had a representative on the appropriate commodity committee; an officer from the bureau with the greatest wartime demand chaired the committee. The commodity committees also included a technical adviser who was an officer from the OASW, although in some instances a reserve officer or a civilian acted in that capacity.[34]

As it ultimately worked out, a commodity committee thoroughly familiarized itself with the product or products for which it was responsible. To do so meant acquiring maximum information on military, civilian, and allied demand and domestic and foreign sources of supply; rating the essentiality of the product for the bureaus and other claimant agencies; and establishing substitutes and conservation measures, tentative prices, proposed emergency controls, and other pertinent information. Using this data, the commodity committee then wrote a plan for procuring or controlling the product, or both, in wartime.[35] By 1936, anticipating the Controlled Materials Plan instituted by the War Production Board in 1942,[36] the OASW devised a scheme in which the commodity committees allocated to each bureau available raw materials, semifinished goods, and other products required to meet wartime production needs. The bureaus would then make allocations to their contractors, contractors to subcontractors, and so on. Hence, the flow of inputs in short supply would follow the pattern of contractual commitments. This allotment program was devised for the first three months of an emergency with the supposition that it would be continued throughout the years of hostility. Most commodity committee planning, though, was projected for a period of twenty-four months to match the mobilization plans of the General Staff.

The OASW divided raw materials into strategic, critical, and essential categories to facilitate the work of the commodity committees. Strategic raw materials were those indispensable to national defense for which domestic supply was either absent or deficient and no satisfactory substitutes existed. Critical raw materials would be in short supply but more plentiful than strategic materials, either because demand was less or the dependable supply greater. Essential materials had no current procurement problems, but their importance required close monitoring in the event reclassification became necessary. Commodity committees wrote procurement plans for all strategic materials, authored monographs for critical materials to facilitate planning if necessary, and collected enough information on essential materials for checking their status from time to time.

Once the commodity committees were in operation, the OASW worked to reduce the number of products in the three categories for greater efficiency. With the discovery of new sources for raw materials, the development of new or improved processing techniques, and the availability of substitutes, numbers declined. Between 1929 and 1939 the strategic list dropped from twenty-six to seventeen, including in the end nickel, tin, and rubber. By 1939 there were also twenty critical materials, such as graphite, titanium, vanadium, and thirty-five essential materials, such as chlorine, iron and steel, and petroleum.

Starting from a rather modest base, commodity committees constantly grew in proficiency, playing an important role in War Department mobilization for World War II. In 1922 Assistant Secretary of War Wainwright officially created the first two committees for chemicals and machine tools. By 1925 the OASW had regularized commodity committee procedures and placed them under a newly created Commodities Division. Fifty-two committees existed in 1929, with nineteen being fully active; by 1936 the numbers had fallen to forty-three and seventeen.

With the reorganization of the Army-Navy Munitions Board in 1931, that agency, and the Navy Department as well, became increasingly active in commodity committee work. The board organized committees of its own that were patterned after those of the OASW, staffed by the chairmen of the War and Navy Department committees, and acted as final reviewing agencies for the commodity plans written in the subdivisions of the two armed services. Actually, the OASW, not the ANMB, continued to do most of the work until the national emergency of the late 1930s. Both of those agencies maintained a skeletal structure that could be expanded when economic mobilization began. The expansion began in 1939 and continued past America's entry into World War II. From July 1939 through March 1942, the ANMB, working directly under the president, became a significant mobilization body, with the commodity committees assuming crucial functions. The ANMB was virtually phased out as a mobilization board late in 1942 and early in 1943 when the War Production Board and a reorganized War Department began to function effectively. Nonetheless, the OASW continued to function in a reorganized form, and its commodity committees became part of the Commodities Branch, Resources Division, Army Service Forces.

Despite their growing importance in the interwar period, commodity committees created special difficulties for the OASW. Although most other OASW functions were fairly well stabilized by 1929–1930, commodity committee activity did not take final shape until the mid-1930s. The principal trouble stemmed from the anomalous position of the OASW vis-à-vis the supply arms. Congress intended the OASW to be a supervising and coordinating body, not, like the Purchase, Storage, and Traffic Division of World War I, an operating agency that took over bureau functions. That reality, combined with the bureaus' fiery independence, led the OASW initially to proceed cautiously to avoid even the appearance of commodity committee activity violating the SA&S' prerogatives. The Commodity Division head, for example, was called "coordinator" instead of "chief," as was true with the other divisions. More important, the committees were to "collect, collate, and evaluate" information about commodities and the chairman was to act as the department's technical expert on the subject, but the commodity committees were not to write the commodity plans. That responsibility was reserved for the bureau with the greatest demand for the product, a stipulation that was most significant where strategic raw materials were involved.[37]

This system never worked. The bureaus assigned a low priority to the commodity committees because the supply arms and services emphasized primary, not secondary, requirements and suffered from a chronic shortage of officers. Consequently, the officers assigned to commodity committees, including the chairman, not only carried the committee load in addition to their other duties but were also often of limited ability. The OASW ended up rejecting most of the first procurement plans written under the direction of the commodity committees. Trying to improve the quality of the planning by upgrading the caliber of and the time available to the commodity committee officers was not very successful. Gradually, the OASW took over the commodity committees. The OASW staff from the bureaus having the major interest in the wartime use of the commodities chaired the committees. Hence, an Ordnance officer headed the Commodity Committee on Steel and Iron, a Quartermaster Corps officer the committee on Hides, Leather, Leather Goods, and Tanning Material, and so on. Decisions involving commodity committee work could go as high as the assistant secretary of war himself. For a time, the OASW held on to the fiction that the SA&S had an important role in the commodity committees, but eventually even that charade was dropped. By the mid-1930s, the commodity committees were clearly OASW operations.

This outcome was practical. The bureaus were unprepared for conducting the research and formulating the plans that secondary requirements necessitated. That function was closer to economic mobilization planning than procurement planning and was appropriately executed by an agency representing the whole War Department, not a part of it. In the case of commodity committees, the OASW's fears of antagonizing the bureaus were misplaced. The supply arms did not resent losing control of commodity committee planning, and the Quartermaster Corps had been trying to rid itself of the chore for a number of years.[38]

Commodity committee activity brought army planners into contact with a broad range of industrial firms, business and professional organizations, and other governmental agencies, which acted to raise OASW sights from military supply to emergency procurement as it related to the larger economy. Trade associations were especially important to commodity committee work. Army planners also turned to general business organizations, like the National Association of Manufacturers, to seek support for planning, to encourage business cooperation, or to make contact with specific firms. Quite often, the best source of information on a commodity was another government agency, such as the U.S. Bureau of Mines. Sometimes the OASW found professional organizations to be particularly helpful. Beginning in 1922 and continuing into the 1930s, the American Institute of Mining and Metallurgical Engineers conducted studies for the army planners on nonferrous metals like manganese as well as on petroleum and other raw material indispensable to conducting war.[39]

By the mid-1930s, commodity committee work was well advanced, a situation that strengthened overall procurement planning substantially. Indeed, various commodity committees performed so well that in the eyes of Congress and other public and private groups the army became the recognized authority on some strategic materials. As this occurred, industry more readily assisted the War Department with its work, thereby further enhancing planning quality.[40]

Secondary requirements not covered by commodity committees included power, fuel, transportation, labor, and finance. Plans for these goods and services were made by various sections that operated under an Industrial Division, later called the Contributory Division. These secondary requirements could not be handled by commodity committees because they encompassed the entire economy and were often politically charged. Contacts with industry, business, finance, labor, government agencies, and various experts became imperative. Planning for those inputs began early in the 1920s but proceeded slowly because specific procurement and commodity committee plans had to be reasonably advanced beforehand. Only in the 1930s did the plans begin to take shape, and even then they were usually embryonic or undeveloped. Eventually, these plans became appendixes to the OASW's Industrial Mobilization Plan, which provided for harnessing the entire economy for war.[41]

On a planning spectrum, the work of the commodity committees stood somewhere between procurement and economic mobilization plans; on the same spectrum, the plans for power, labor, and the like were closer to economic mobilization planning. Invariably, the more army planning diverged from procurement, the more general it became.

Once both primary and secondary requirements either had been calculated or sufficient progress in that direction had been made, bureaus wrote plans for selected supplies and the common items they procured. These plans minimally contained, first, primary requirements—how they were calculated, monthly projections usually for a two-year period, and a cumulative demand curve; second, full information on projected production—including apportionment of load, accepted schedules of production, building and conversion programs to meet demand, stock on hand, and a cumulative supply curve; third, details on specifications, cost and price, and inspection and packing; fourth, a summary of possible procurement difficulties and proposed steps to remedy them; and last, an analysis of secondary requirements. Plans ranged from the simple to the intricate, depending on the significance and complexity of the items involved, the magnitude of requirements, and the level of sophistication in OASW planning.[42]

When the OASW was created, the staff considered writing plans for every item procured by the War Department. The astronomical scope of army purchasing quickly changed such thinking. During World War I, the army bought almost .75 million different items. In 1940 the Signal Corps alone had 50,000 products slated for purchase. Even without the restraints of personnel and money, the OASW faced the need to choose a relatively few items for planning. With time and experience, army planners became increasingly efficient in determining which goods needed plans. Between 1933 and 1938, the OASW gradually adopted a system for dividing emergency procurement into three categories: Section I included items presenting difficult procurement problems and for which formal plans were required, Section II involved goods with fewer procurement problems for which informal plans were necessary, and Section III covered commercial products in ample supply for which no plans were needed but for which procuring officers maintained at least elementary data on requirements and supplies.[43]

Abstracts of the plans for Section I articles had to be filed with and approved by the OASW and, like commodity committee plans, revised every three years at a minimum. After 1939, when OASW activity was accelerated to meet the international crisis, plans were reviewed and modified annually. For Section II items, the bureaus needed only to file data on which the informal plan was based. In 1939, out of procurement lists that probably exceeded 1 million items, the supply planners selected only 7,268 items for Sections I and II. Of that figure, 1,143, or less than 16 percent, were Section I articles, and of those, Ordnance claimed slightly over 50 percent. The Medical Department accounted for

44 percent of the 7,268 figure, and the Quartermaster Corps for another 26 percent. By 1940 the planning list had increased to only 7,400 items, and Section I goods stood at 1,200. The classification system reduced the number of formal and informal plans to manageable proportions. Nonetheless, due to the extreme complexity of planning for primary and secondary requirements involving even the most rudimentary articles, the task was still enormous.[44]

The OASW's review of the bureau plans was not pro forma. Through its oversight, the office determined if the bureaus' progress was adequate, their approach and information current, and their overall program balanced. The procurement plans collectively allowed the OASW to assess whether anticipated emergency supply operations were distributed nationally on a rational basis and whether the entire wartime procurement load and hence the General Staff's war plans were feasible.[45]

Even though the classification and review systems promised to make army wartime procurement more rational, they were a small part of a much larger process. In time of war, effective industrial mobilization depended less on guaranteed output of a relatively few crucial items than on an uninterrupted supply of steel, lumber, oil, rubber, and aluminum—the bone and sinew of an industrial system. The OASW personnel recognized this reality through commodity committee planning, and they looked to the civilian mobilization agencies in the Industrial Mobilization Plans to ensure the orderly flow of basic materials through priority, allocation, price, and other such controls.[46]

By 1929 procurement planning had come a long way. An elaborate planning structure had been built up in the OASW, and each bureau had a planning office. These offices were intended to expand during an emergency. Moreover, policies and procedures had been worked out for wartime procurement (with refinements continuing to take place throughout the 1930s). Within a decade, then, the War Department had gone from virtually no planning system to quite an effective one.

THE OASW AND INTERWAR PROCUREMENT

The Office of the Assistant Secretary of War's progress in procurement planning was not matched by the office's success in controlling the supply arms and services's current procurement. In and of itself, this development was not serious since interwar buying was limited. But as the army's basic supply units, the bureaus were critical to wartime operations. Without establishing effective direction over the SA&S' procurement in the interwar years, the OASW was unlikely to do so during hostilities, jeopardizing its war plans.

The OASW's failure in the area of current procurement resulted from matters of priority and power. Military buying was as old as the army; planning for procurement and industrial mobilization was a wholly new endeavor. Priority dictated that the OASW concentrate on the latter function. Assistant Secretary of War J. Mayhew Wainwright assigned only one officer to current procurement and eight to planning. That pattern continued until the national emergency of the late 1930s, leaving the bureaus' peacetime buying largely unsupervised.[47] Moreover, because planning, unlike procurement, was new, the SA&S had little investment in it, allowing the OASW to claim the planning territory without stepping on supersensitive bureau toes. Trying to bend the SA&S to its will over current procurement while simultaneously launching planning, the OASW would have threatened the latter without making much headway in the former.

Beginning in 1922 and continuing through 1941, assistant secretaries regularly reassured the SA&S that their office constituted no threat to established procurement prerogatives.[48] Indeed, the National Defense Act of 1920 left the statutory power over buying in bureau hands, restricting assistant secretaries to the nebulous area of "supervising" procurement. Assistant Secretary of War Hanford MacNider in 1927 argued that for his office to carry out the assignment it required a voice in budgets, surveys to ensure efficiency, uniformity, and legality in buying, and reliable statistical services. Organizational changes and reforms designed to accomplish those ends produced few positive results.[49]

The SA&S operated after World War I much as it had before the war. At the end of hostilities but before the OASW's creation, most bureaus reorganized their structures, and those systems continued largely unchanged until the World War II years. Policymaking was centralized at headquarters, with divisions for administration, supply, production, and so forth; operations were decentralized among subunits like depots and arsenals. The SA&S used a type of commodity structure in which unified activity centered on one item. The Quartermaster Corps, for example, assigned one commodity to a depot, and that unit bought, stored, and distributed the article. All sorts of variations, however, occurred within this general pattern. The Signal Corps eventually turned procurement over to its districts. Diverging from all norms, the Air Corps between 1926 and 1933 had its own assistant secretary and located the Supply Division at Wright Field, Dayton, Ohio, separated from the other staff divisions in Washington. To complicate matters further, each bureau after 1933 had dissimilar Procurement Districts.[50]

This eclectic system functioned reasonably well in peacetime when the load was light. The interwar army averaged around 140,000 men, 50 percent of the regular army provided for in the National Defense Act of 1920. Between 1922 and 1940, the army as a whole spent $6.4 billion, which made purchasing steady and unhurried. By comparison, the rate of mobilization even before the United States entered World War II was furious, totaling more than $6.6 billion for the first quarter of fiscal year 1941. According to law, most interwar buying was done by competitive bidding. Over 80 percent of all contracts fell into that category between 1937 and 1940. Open market buying, purchases from other agencies, and negotiated contracts for special items accounted for the rest.[51] Beginning in 1933 relief activities, public works programs, and operations of the National Recovery Administration increased army buying considerably. With the deterioration on the international scene and expanded army budgets, more traditional military spending also stepped up, beginning in 1936. Its ability to handle this varied activity with success convinced the War Department that its supply system was sound.[52]

Statutes governed most interwar buying. It was within that legal framework that the OASW was supposed to direct current procurement. The Current Procurement Branch of the OASW generally interpreted the law, established policy when essential, and oversaw procurement to the degree it could. Moreover, the OASW put out publications such as the *Current Procurement News Digest* to help rationalize bureau buying. From 1920 through 1941, the OASW worked for efficient, uniform, and legal supply practices without many positive results. The assistant secretaries, for example, failed at repeated efforts to codify the laws, rules, and regulations under which army buying was conducted. Codification waited until 1942, when the wartime load made it imperative. The OASW had some impact on bureau operations involving procedures for bidding and contract forms. It also worked steadily to reduce contractor complaints about army procurement methods, an activity closely related to procurement planning. Yet none of this had much effect on overall procurement operations.

Perhaps the OASW's hand in procurement was most visible in the area of interbureau and interdepartmental buying. As an outgrowth of World War I reforms, the National Defense Act of 1920 charged the Quartermaster Corps with purchasing all supplies of standard manufacture or those commonly used by two or more bureaus. The OASW also sought to work out policies for mutual buying with the Navy Department. Further, the office coordinated activity with the Treasury Department's Procurement Division, which bought standard commercial products for government agencies, arranged interdepartmental purchasing where possible, and set general guidelines for government buying. These efforts at coordination had little effect. On the eve of World War II, government buying, and especially army procurement, was as much a decentralized function as in 1920. The OASW had surprisingly little impact on the War Department's current procurement operations.[53]

THE TRANSITION FROM PLANNING TO MOBILIZING FOR WAR

Procurement and industrial mobilization planning, not current procurement, always held first place with the Office of the Assistant Secretary of War. The office's labors led to a string of plans. The divisions of the OASW, every bureau, and their subdivisions were required to have plans for wartime operations.[54] These plans were based on M-Day or Mobilization Day, a major emergency—most likely war—requiring general mobilization. A massive merging of planning and operating agencies would take place from the bottom to the top of the War Department. All plans would be patterned on the OASW, which reflected those of the Army-Navy Munitions Board, which would be based on the civilian mobilization agency. With uniform, integrated procurement and mobilization entities, the theory ran, the War Department would be ready for the economics of war.[55] But no M-Day as such ever occurred. Instead, the United States began girding incrementally for war in 1938. This approach threw off the planning, with mixed results among the supply bureaus.

The Ordnance Department implemented its pre-emergency procurement plans with a sharp break occurring between planning and mobilization in June 1940. The bulk of War Department Educational Orders (contracts awarded to firms to prepare them for quantity production of specialized military goods, such as rifles and gas masks) from 1938 went to Ordnance. When large defense appropriations began in 1940, the department knew what it wanted and where to get it. One month after those funds were available, 70 percent of all Ordnance orders had been placed and 95 percent of that figure went to facilities previously surveyed by the department. Beginning in 1938, procurement districts gradually began operating according to plan and played an important part in the Ordnance Department's supply operations. With actual war, regular army officers serving as assistant chiefs or other army officers replaced the civilian Procurement District chiefs. Businessmen and industrialists were too busy for the full-time work the districts demanded. Only a few civilians serving districts in the interwar years were called to active district duty, but many businessmen continued to serve the districts through civilian district advisory boards. Overall, unlike in World War I, the Ordnance Department executed a relatively smooth transition to World War II.[56] Although much smaller in size and less advanced in planning, the Signal Corps approximated the Ordnance Department's accomplishment.[57]

The Quartermaster Corps' record was dramatically different. At no time before or after America's entry into World War II were corps planning and current procurement systems integrated. Both planning, which was based on centralized functions, and operations, which were decentralized, continued separately after 1939, despite emergency conditions. This absurdity ended only in October 1942, when procurement planning was finally shut down. Planning in the 1920s and 1930s obviously had not prepared the Quartermaster Corps for wartime expansion.[58]

The experience of the Air Corps resembled that of the Quartermaster Corps, with current operations and planning going in different directions, never to merge. Separating the Supply Division at Wright Field, Dayton, Ohio, from the other staff divisions in the nation's capital aggravated these conditions. The Air Corps was unready when the Franklin D. Roosevelt administration expanded airplane production as it began to rearm late in the 1930s. Since Air Corps procurement involved special products unavailable on the civilian market, its failures were more consequential than those of the Quartermaster Corps.[59]

The other bureaus—the Corps of Engineers, the Chemical Warfare Service, the Coast Artillery, and the Medical Department—were closer to Quartermaster in terms of procurement planning than to Ordnance. The results were less adverse, however, because they bought comparatively few items.[60]

Outstanding interwar planning explains the Ordnance Department's preparation for World War II. In order for the planning to work, the bureau chief and his staff had to be behind it. Ordnance officers enthusiastically supported planning from the outset.[61] Indeed, Ordnance deserves much of the credit for Section 5a of the National Defense Act of 1920 and the achievements of the Office of the Assistant Secretary of War. General Palmer E. Pierce, an Ordnance officer who served in the War Department and in civilian economic mobilization agencies during World War I, was a chief architect of Section 5a. The assistant secretary of war in 1921 organized the Planning Branch based largely on proposals of the chiefs of Ordnance and the Corps of Engineers. Numerous Ordnance officers served with distinction in the OASW. Probably the most important was Col. (later general) Charles T. Harris, Jr., who as head of the Planning Branch from 1933 to 1938 was instrumental in bringing the army's procurement and industrial mobilization planning to maturity. Harris became one of the two principal assistants to the chief of ordnance during the national emergency and early World War II years; the other assistant was Gen. Earl McFarland, who also put in valuable service with the OASW. General James H. Burns was another officer of great importance to both the OASW and the Ordnance Department. In 1922 he led in convincing the assistant secretary and the chief of the Planning Branch to set up the Army Industrial College. He authored Ordnance's program for expanding munitions production in 1940 and after, and he served with distinction as the executive officer to the assistant secretary of war and in World War II civilian mobilization agencies. General Harry K. Rutherford, the last of the Planning Branch chiefs, was also an Ordnance officer. Finally, Dwight F. Davis, who served as assistant secretary and secretary of war from 1923 to 1929, was an Ordnance reserve officer.

The Ordnance Department had such a prominent place in OASW affairs that the Quartermaster Corps accused it of dominating the office at the expense of other supply arms and services. Ordnance's influence stemmed from its numerous contributions to the office. Planning received more attention from Ordnance than from any other supply arm. Early in 1940 the Ordnance Department had 231 officers and civilians engaged in procurement planning, compared to 264 for the other bureaus combined, including the Air Corps. The year before, Ordnance accounted for $8 million of the $9 million spent by the War Department on procurement planning. Between 1938 and 1940, the Ordnance Department, which began pushing for educational orders in the 1920s, consistently received most funds appropriated for that purpose. The intensity and quality of the department's planning prepared it better for World War II than any other supply service.

Ordnance's dedication to planning grew from World War I reforms. With the supply shakeup in late 1917 and early 1918, Gen. Clarence C. Williams, who replaced Gen. William B. Crozier as chief of ordnance, almost immediately began reorganizing the Ordnance Department for purposes of efficiency. He turned for help, among others, to Guy E. Tripp, chairman of the board of Westinghouse Electric and Manufacturing Company, who was serving as a reserve colonel, and later as general, in the department, and who acted as a principal Ordnance adviser. Tripp proposed to bring Ordnance into closer contact with industry by decentralizing procurement to local areas. This approach was the origin of the Ordnance District system, eventually ordered into effect for all bureaus in the interwar years by the OASW. Besides the district system, the Ordnance Department kept the military-industrial bonds of World War I intact through the Army Ordnance Association, organized in 1919 by leading individuals in the Ordnance Department and industry. With Williams serving as chief of ordnance from 1918 to 1930, the department had the benefit of continuity through the crucial years from World War I until procurement planning became an established fact. Other talented leaders followed Williams. General Charles M. Wesson, chief between 1938 and 1942, guided the department through the transition from planning to war production. General Levin H.

Campbell, Jr., as wartime Ordnance chief, took great pride in the efficiency and productivity of what he dubbed the "industry-ordnance team."

The supply and economic mobilization failures of World War I left an indelible imprint on the Ordnance Department. Never again, its officers realized, could the department afford to drift. Ordnance had to face the harsh fact that unlike other nations, the United States had neither government-sponsored monopolies such as Vickers Limited, huge munitions reserves, nor elaborate arsenals. Its arsenals, modest in number and size, could be used for small-scale output, research, and production of patterns and prototypes. But to meet the demands of war, Ordnance had to rely on industry to manufacture most of its munitions. That reality required good relations with industry and knowledge about plant facilities and relevant technology. Even then, under favorable circumstances a minimum of eighteen to twenty-four months was necessary to achieve full-scale production of Ordnance items. Accepting its dependence on private industry, the Ordnance team worked closely with such prestigious individuals as Guy E. Tripp and Frank A. Scott as well as hundreds of others to win and keep industry's support.

That task was not an easy one. Industrialists were put off by the red tape involved in military contracting, and they resented the army's crude and unplanned cancellation of contracts at the end of World War I. Moreover, antimilitary sentiments and "merchants of death" critiques made business cautious about associating with the army. Despite the obstacles, Ordnance's courtship of industry gradually paid off. When the rearmament began, the foundations for the World War II "industry-ordnance team" were already established.

Ordnance's attitudes toward planning and the OASW were never free of some ambivalence. The independent tradition of the bureaus was too deeply entrenched for any quick change. At the conclusion of World War I, the department was as intent as any in the SA&S on freeing itself from General Staff control. During congressional hearings on what became the National Defense Act of 1920, Chief of Ordnance Williams unfairly insisted that the Purchase, Storage, and Traffic Division had grievously harmed, and in no way helped, Ordnance. Like the other bureaus in the SA&S, Ordnance initially resisted OASW control, and a residue of prewar attitudes continued throughout the interwar years. Unlike some bureaus, however, Ordnance rose above its suspicions to cooperate fully with the OASW for a larger good.

The Signal Corps was similar in many ways. Like the Ordnance Department, the corps' heavy dependence on private industry for manufacturing its specialized equipment made it receptive to planning. It also played an influential role in the founding and evolution of the Office of the Assistant Secretary of War, although less so than Ordnance because of its age, size, and mission. General Charles McK. Saltzman of the Signal Corps wrote the preliminary draft of Section 5a of the National Defense Act, 1920, and he was among the handful of officers who organized the OASW. Saltzman served as chief signal officer from 1924 to 1928. General Irving J. Carr also contributed meaningfully to the growth of the OASW and eventually acted as the Signal Corps' chief from 1931 to 1934. The Signal Corps reached out to industry without hesitation. Its three principal Procurement Districts were located in New York, Chicago, and San Francisco and were purposely built around General Electric, Westinghouse, and Western Electric Company. Like Ordnance, the Signal Corps worked out good relations with skeptical industrialists and helped shape and ensure the existence of the OASW.[62]

The Quartermaster Corps followed the opposite direction.[63] Quartermaster generals and their staffs neglected planning. Consequently, the corps never functioned as intended after it was reorganized in 1920. The staff gradually absorbed the operating units, separated them from planning entities, and starved the latter for personnel, resources, and prestige. Actually, the Quartermaster Corps had not begun the interwar years in this manner. Planning agencies were created in 1920 and the Quartermaster Corps, first on its own and later under General Staff direction, initiated procurement studies, surveyed facilities, and engaged in other activities that set the pattern for some of the Planning Branch's activities. That early momentum, however, was not sustained.

The most significant factor shaping the Quartermaster Corps' dim view of planning was that about 90 percent of the items it procured were commercially produced. Unlike Ordnance, it faced no huge task of industrial conversion; industrial expansion would meet most of Quartermaster's wartime needs. In that regard, the corps compulsively kept itself informed about the actual and potential capacity of industries manufacturing required goods. These conditions convinced Quartermaster that it would not benefit from most of OASW planning, a negative outlook that affected all areas. Quartermaster commodity committee work was among the weakest in the bureaus. The corps even pressed the OASW to release it from various planning responsibilities, a move the office refused to make.

The Quartermaster Corps also opposed the OASW as a rival for power. As the oldest and largest of the supply arms and services, assigned common purchasing among other duties, the corps had the most to lose from a strong assistant secretary. Quartermaster's initial support for planning and the OASW from 1919 to 1921 was short-lived. It soon began actively and passively to resist the OASW and to participate only minimally in the office's activities. More than any other supply arm, the Quartermaster Corps seemed intent on using Section 5a and the OASW to break free from General Staff control while ensuring that the OASW's supervisory duties were nominal. The opposition of the biggest, most powerful bureau cost the OASW a great deal in lost prestige and forced it to expend valuable time and energy trying to persuade the Quartermaster Corps to carry its weight. Quartermaster was the most debilitated supply arm during World War I, which, among other factors, nearly cost the War Department control of supply. In the interwar years, the corps continued its destructive behavior, weakening itself and the War Department and again jeopardizing army supply operations as World War II approached.

For different reasons, the Air Corps' response to planning was comparable to that of the Quartermaster Corps.[64] Among the newest procuring branches, the Air Corps depended most heavily on private industry to fulfill its mission, which made it similar to the Ordnance Department, except that aircraft manufacture was in the infant stage. Like Quartermaster, the Air Corps favored planning at the outset. General William (Billy) Mitchell joined General Saltzman in negotiations leading to the adoption of Section 5a of the National Defense Act, 1920, and the Air Corps created agencies for planning. Interest soon waned, though. Planning units suffered from neglect and were ultimately isolated at Wright Field from the staff. That breakdown occurred despite the embryonic aircraft industry's enthusiasm for working with the government in general and the military in particular to boost an otherwise restricted market.

A number of factors overwhelmed the Air Corps' efforts to plan. An unstable, emerging industry with constantly changing technology made planning a nightmare. The airframe and motor industries were so small and potential wartime demand so great that the gap seemed unbridgeable in terms of either expanding existing industries or converting automobile firms. Planners became so distressed that they even looked upon educational orders as useless or unrelated to Air Corps needs.

Other reasons help explain the planning failures. The dismal World War I airplane production record, which reflected gross incompetence and corruption, made Air Corps leaders and planners so defensive that they all but froze when facing the demands of planning. The problem was magnified by the lack of a useful history of World War I production and procurement for guiding the corps officers as they struggled to fulfill their duties.

Also figuring into the Air Corps' bleak planning performance was the incessant controversy surrounding it—controversy that distracted leaders and made estimating requirements nearly impossible. Throughout the interwar years the corps engaged in an intense struggle over its combat role and the related battle to become an independent service. Additionally, Congress subjected Air Corps procurement to more investigations and statutory regulations than any other supply service, partly because of World War I developments and the controversial nature of airplane technology. Under such circumstances, the Air Corps for a time took on a siege mentality unconducive to planning. Moreover, until its combat role was defined, the Air Corps had extreme difficulty in even trying to determine wartime demand.

These adverse circumstances undermined Air Corps leaders' enthusiasm for planning. It therefore took on a rarified quality in which internal criticism was unwelcome and outside review unsought. Isolated planners plodded away at piecemeal matters, ignoring larger problems. Predictably, the Air Corps contributed little to overall army planning. Its officers appeared infrequently in the counsels of the OASW and usually in minor roles. The consequences of the Air Corps' failed planning were severe. Airplane production became the top priority in the mobilization program beginning in 1938. With the Air Corps unprepared for such contingencies, aircraft manufacturers and other civilian and military mobilization agencies had to step in to provide the initiative and imagination for the corps to meet the enormous demand suddenly thrust upon it.

The other supply bureaus resembled the Quartermaster Corps in their response to interwar planning. With almost all of its procurement items produced commercially, the Corps of Engineers showed little interest in planning. Although the Chemical Warfare Service faced almost total dependence on private industry, unlike Ordnance and the Air Corps, its products were relatively uncomplicated and rather easily manufactured. Although most of the Medical Department's buying was specialized, civilian industries made what it needed. Since these three services were so small in size, their impact on general procurement and procurement planning was not great. (The Coast Artillery Corps never played any discernible role in planning, and its procurement activities were absorbed by Ordnance during World War II.) Further, none played significant roles in shaping the OASW, even though Col. Harley B. Ferguson, the first director of the Planning Branch and one of the pioneers in procurement and industrial mobilization planning, came from the Corps of Engineers.[65] Still, planning had some positive impact on these bureaus and prepared them to a degree for World War II.[66]

The generally negative response of the SA&S to the OASW had an adverse effect on the overall performance of the office. On the eve of World War II, the army was unprepared for hostilities in terms of supply; an integrated supply system did not exist. This lack was most readily apparent in the calculation of requirements, the beginning step in all procurement planning. Despite OASW efforts in behalf of uniformity, eight different approaches existed.[67] Even within some bureaus differences reigned. The Quartermaster Corps was the worst. As late as mid-1941, the corps had three different sets of requirement figures. The one that it relied on was based on the pre–World War I system. No change occurred until the Army Service Forces, set up in March 1942, forced the corps to adopt a consolidated system.[68]

The OASW's problems only began with the calculation of requirements. The entire informational foundation upon which the office's procurement planning was based was fundamentally flawed. Major David C. Cordiner of the Planning Branch complained bitterly in October 1934 that the army was hostile to a statistical approach, despite its indispensable value. Two principal difficulties plagued procurement planning calculations, the major contended. First, the SA&S approached the subject at best casually, at worst irresponsibly. Second, the OASW would not or could not either compel the bureaus to be more responsible or use the information the supply arms provided in a meaningful way. "A study of statistics in this office in 1932," Major Cordiner continued,

> furnished convincing proof that they had become meaningless, and either lost all the elements or had never had the elements which would insure that this office [the Planning Branch] controlled the situation insofar as rapid and consistent progress of procurement planning was concerned. It is true that they contain some information, but in such form as to be entirely inconsistent, or so voluminous that no practical analysis had ever been made or, I doubt, even attempted. The reports came in, were consolidated, glanced at and filed.

The reports from the bureaus the Planning Branch used to guide and evaluate procurement planning, Cordiner argued, were so sloppy, dated, inconsistent, and erratic that they were useless. Not infrequently, the SA&S dusted off old reports in an attempt to satisfy the assistant secretary. One bureau refused to do even that, making no effort to submit requested information over a three-year period. More positively, the major cited the Ordnance Department as an example of good statistical technique.[69]

Because of statistical deficiencies, the OASW was unprepared to guard against conditions in which some sections of the nation were overloaded with contracts while others nearly starved. The office lacked the system and the information to prevent the contract maldistribution that had created such chaos during World War I.[70]

In 1933 and 1934 the OASW introduced a new and rationalized reporting system intended to provide reliable statistics. The office was particularly intent on evaluating the feasibility of proposed wartime contract placement for specific regions and for the nation as a whole. Although it seemed auspicious at the outset, the new approach fared no better than its predecessors. Within a year it was jettisoned. So many different bases were used in making calculations that the information could not be collated, rendering the reports nearly worthless.[71] Primary to the failure was the OASW's unwillingness or inability to impose common standards and methods on the bureaus.

The weaknesses and flaws of procurement planning became more exaggerated after 1938–1939 as America began to rearm. Despite the urging of staff members and a growing volume of procurement, the OASW at no time before World War II initiated a clear transition from planning to mobilization. Instead, planning tied to the concept of an M-Day continued alongside the burgeoning procurement effort. Inevitably confusion grew. The M-Day concept, however, was more an effect than a cause of flawed planning. An Army Industrial College committee pointed out that enemies do not necessarily proceed as expected; a worthy plan must be adaptable to differing circumstances.[72] Even if based on M-Day, a sound plan could have been adjusted to guide mobilization between 1938 and 1941.

After being appointed assistant secretary of war (now the Under Secretary of War) Robert P. Patterson in April 1941 called upon the management consultant firm of Booz, Fry, Allen, and Hamilton to advise him in reorganizing his office for purposes of efficiency. After months of study, the Booz group in December 1941 found that the OASW (now the Office of the Under Secretary of War—OUSW) had functioned better before 1939 than after. Years of planning had not adequately prepared the office for its principal role. Booz and his associates were particularly concerned about the OUSW staff, which they generally characterized as untrained, poorly trained, or incompetent. They even charged, albeit discreetly, that the under secretary's executive officer was unqualified for his key position and did not inspire confidence within and outside the OUSW. In its most searching indictment, the Booz group pointed out that the staffs of the OUSW and the SA&S did not clearly understand the purpose of the under secretary's office. To remedy the deep-seated problems they uncovered, Booz and his associates proposed a fundamental restructuring of the OUSW.[73] Before Patterson could fully act on the recommendations, the chief of staff and General Staff in March 1942 instituted a thorough reorganization of the War Department for World War II.[74]

The Booz group's analysis failed adequately to analyze the crucial role the SA&S played in keeping the OUSW weak. The bureaus thwarted the General Staff's attempt in 1919 and 1920 to extend its power over them through the Purchase, Storage, and Traffic Division. Thereafter, they used statutes, rank, budgets, and personnel to minimize OASW influence over supply. In large bureaucracies, organization and structure tend significantly to influence, even to determine, policy. With short terms of duty and high turnover rates, that tendency becomes even more exaggerated in the military.[75] Less subject to personnel turbulence, the bureaus also had the advantage of organizational longevity over the OASW. Moreover, the assistant secretary's office lacked a crucial element of staff loyalty for establishing its authority. Throughout the interwar years, OASW officers came from and returned to the bureaus and generally continued to identify with them. The OASW was extremely cautious not to offend the bureaus' sense of prerogative. It usually requested and consulted rather than emphatically ordering. The OASW became somewhat more assertive in the 1930s, compared with the 1920s, but not to any great extent.[76]

The supply arms and services, which had helped create the Office of the Assistant Secretary of War, could have best protected their long-run interests by assisting the office in carrying out its duties. Reasonable uniformity in bureau operations and planning and a system for merging the two functions during an emergency would have enhanced the SA&S' efficiency and preparedness immeasurably without threatening the supply services' existence. Supporting the OASW meant assigning the office well-qualified officers, working for appropriate rank in the office and a strengthened hand for the assistant secretary in budgets and promotions, and cooperating in improving office and bureau policies and techniques. The Ordnance Department and the Signal Corps came close to such support, but that was not enough. The OASW needed the Quartermaster Corps' backing. A united stand by Ordnance and Quartermaster in favor of the assistant secretary would have forced the lesser bureaus into line, with the exception of the Air Corps, which was already moving outside the OASW's orbit toward independence.

The situation of the OASW in the interwar years was not dissimilar to that of the General Staff in the pre–World War I period. Between its creation in 1903 and 1917, the staff drifted without clearly established authority or duty, ultimately failing to prepare the army for World War I. The staff's failure stemmed partly from its status as a new agency with inexperienced personnel but also from the bitter opposition that the SA&S directed toward it.[77]

In fairness to the bureaus, trying to build up the OASW could be a thankless and frustrating endeavor. Supersensitive about War Department positions of power, various secretaries and assistant secretaries avoided directly and boldly seeking increased authority for the OASW and favored indirect, timid approaches that did not work.[78] A weak OASW encouraged bureau parochialism because the office could not defend vital SA&S interests against General Staff ambitions.

THE OASW, THE GENERAL STAFF, AND WAR PLANS

The Office of the Assistant Secretary of War's troubles in planning and supervising the supply arms and services adversely affected its relations with the chief of staff–General Staff. An adversarial relationship had existed between the General Staff and the OASW from the outset.[79] Losing control over supply with the National Defense Act of 1920, the General Staff sought to isolate, ostracize, or ignore the assistant secretary of war and his office. But it could not carry the antipathy too far since the chief of staff and his subordinates played important parts in supply functions. General Staff responsibility and authority in the supply area, like those of the OASW, however, were unclear in key areas. Some SA&S used that ambiguity masterfully to play off the OASW against the General Staff to maximize their own independence.[80]

If the OASW had managed to establish firm control over the bureaus, it might have had an ally in the General Staff. After all, the fighting forces had been threatened directly by the supply failures of World War I, and that threat remained as long as the SA&S operated without adequate supervision. Moreover, in peacetime the bureaus accounted for the largest share of appropriations and exercised enormous power in a fragmented way. Centralizing authority over the badly divided SA&S promised greater efficiency and reliability both in war and peace. Though not welcoming a rival for power in the War Department, the General Staff might have at least accepted a strong OASW.[81] An ineffective OASW invited General Staff disdain since it complicated the staff's relations with the supply bureaus without improving them.

As a multidivisional bureaucracy, the General Staff was not monolithic. The OASW's relations were closest with the G-4 Division (Supply). That was not the case when the OASW was created since the assistant secretary's office took over duties G-4 and its predecessors had been performing. The rivalry between the two was resolved over time because each needed the other's cooperation in fulfilling its duties. The Supply Division had responsibility for translating war plans into requirements and for distributing finished goods to the troops. The OASW's duties covered buying, producing, storing, and transporting the required supplies. By 1929 and 1930, the OASW and G-4 had reached reasonable agreement on the division of responsibilities, and their working relationship in the 1930s was generally good.[82]

The OASW's interaction with the General Staff as a whole, though, and especially with the G-3 Division (Operations and Training) and the War Plans Division, was bad. For complicated reasons, relations tended to deteriorate for most of the 1920s and into the 1930s. The General Staff knew little about supply and tended to ignore or downplay its significance. Furthermore, it looked upon the OASW as a tool of the bureaus, which were its archrivals. This outlook strengthened, rather than diminished, in the 1920s and early 1930s as the memories of the supply crises of World War I faded. The General Staff had difficulty accepting its dependence on supply for fulfilling the military mission. As long as such views predominated, the OASW was looked upon as an interloper.[83]

Growing tension between the General Staff and the OASW and coinciding improvement in relations between the assistant secretary's office and G-4 are best exemplified by interwar struggles over the staff's war plans. Until the late 1930s, these plans were unrealistic. The size of the army was not the problem. In the War Department's General Mobilization Plan, 1924, the General Staff set the figure at 4 million men. This number was based on World War I levels, and the plan was continued with some variation until World War II. A consistent goal for guiding procurement and economic mobilization planning was a great asset for both the OASW and the bureaus.[84]

The projected rate of mobilization, however, caused trouble for the OASW. The General Mobilization Plan, 1924, called for mobilizing 1.4 million men within four months of the outbreak of war, and in 1928 the figure was increased to 1.6 million.[85] In the 1930s, the projected mobilization rate was reduced somewhat, but the General Staff's proposals were still so far beyond supply potential that war planners as late as 1936 seriously proposed requiring "enrollees" to report to camp with items of basic use. The Quartermaster Corps would have been unable to provide common, commercially produced goods to the troops under the existing mobilization rates.[86]

Arming the troops under such time frames was even more problematic. General Staff plans called for the heaviest procurement load in the first months of war, when industry was not far enough along in converting to munitions production.[87] The vital lesson of World War I, that arming men for combat took at least a year longer than raising and training them, was ignored.[88] Recognized at first, that rule was lost as memories of the war grew older. In the General Mobilization Plan, 1924, the General Staff, at least in theory, recognized that all war plans had to be geared to supply as the primary factor of any mobilization scheme. By 1928, however, a very different set of priorities existed. Concern with manpower took on obsessive proportions, with General Staff officers averring that supply was subordinate. Late in 1928 a highly placed General Staff planner, Col. James K. Parsons, insisted:

> Deficiency in supply may seriously impair the fighting efficiency of a nation, but most defects are caused by a shortage of men. In the last analysis, manpower is the primary factor, and its importance is supreme.

Supply is secondary, and is of value only in direct proportion to the extent which it may be used.[89]

Although the specifics of the 1928 General War Plan differed from 1924 only in degrees, the shift in outlook was dramatic.

The OASW and the supply arms criticized the unrealistic war plans from the outset. By 1925 they had adequate information about the economy's potential to substantiate that supply in crucial areas could not meet the manpower mobilization rates of the 1924 plan.[90] Only huge reserves would make up the deficiency. Yet World War I surplus diminished through use and deterioration, and the political climate of the 1920s denied the military renewed reserves or even stockpiles of strategic raw materials.

The OASW and the SA&S were not alone in questioning war plans. Over time, opposition came from within the General Staff. First G-4 and much later the G-1 Division (Personnel) challenged the G-3 Division and the War Plans Division for their flawed General Mobilization Plans. Based on students' studies, the Army War College also became a critic.[91]

Growing, at times heated, criticism of General Staff war planning gradually paid off. Conditions for fundamentally reordering the process developed between 1935 and 1936. In September 1936 Harry H. Woodring became secretary of war after serving as assistant secretary from 1933 to 1936. He was determined to change the seriously unbalanced plans.[92] Late in 1935, Gen. Malin Craig had become chief of staff. A protégé of Gen. John J. Pershing, Craig had wide experience as both a line and a staff officer. He had commanded troops at home and abroad and had headed the G-3 Division and the AWC.[93] That broad experience, combined with a fine and open mind, convinced Craig that the staff's General Mobilization Plan was hopelessly and dangerously unfeasible. "The problem I encountered on my entry into office . . . was the lack of realism in military war plans," he wrote in 1939. Those plans "comprehended many paper units, conjectural supply, and a disregard of the time element which forms the main pillar of any planning structure."[94] "Without the supplies necessary for our forces," Craig had observed some three years earlier, "trained personnel, however numerous, will be of little avail in time of conflict." Craig, like his predecessor as chief of staff, Gen. Douglas MacArthur, insisted that all war planning must be consonant with supply potential and be carefully geared to the realities and constantly changing character of the industrial community.[95]

Supported and encouraged by Secretary of War Woodring, General Craig in December 1936 abruptly ended updating the General War Plan of 1933. He then ordered into effect a wholly new planning approach that ultimately led to the Protective Mobilization Plan in 1937 and 1938. It was refined and improved until a reasonably complete plan existed by 1939.[96]

Though Woodring and Craig shared in redirecting war planning, Craig's overall contribution was probably greater. "The profound influence which General Craig during his tour as Chief of Staff had on preparing the Army of the United States for World War II," Lt. Col. Marvin H. Kreidberg and Lt. Merton G. Henry have observed, "has never been widely known or appreciated except by the professional soldiers who were closely associated with him during these years."[97] Equally unknown or unappreciated is the fact that MacArthur, as chief of staff from 1930 to 1935, helped break the ground that Craig so successfully tilled.

MacArthur's predecessor, Gen. Charles P. Summerall, chief of staff from 1926 to 1930, had abruptly and rancorously rejected adjusting General Staff planning to economic considerations. In 1930 he boasted:

> One of my first actions upon assuming the duties of the office of Chief of Staff was to direct the restudy of mobilization plans which had been based upon the view that rate of mobilization is governed by the rate of supply.... The revised plans resulting from this restudy are based upon the principle that the mobilization rate is governed by the hostile strength which can be brought against our territory within given periods....
>
> The only supply factor that in our present situation seriously affects our ability to maintain troops in the field is ammunition supply. The contention that the supply rate governs mobilization therefore reduces itself to the proposition that mobilization plans should be made to accord with ammunition supply and anticipated rates of production.[98]

In a spirited and bitter diatribe that became his final report to the secretary of war in 1930, Summerall came across as almost a caricature of the military man's deep resentment that modern warfare had made him inordinately dependent on supply, and with supply, dependent on civilians. He demanded that the bureaus be subordinated to the General Staff as Elihu Root's reforms had intended; he insisted that outside of procurement, most supply matters should be reserved for the combat units; and he argued vehemently that economic mobilization should be carried out by expanded and revamped regular departments of the government instead of by new agencies, with the War Department in general, and the General Staff in particular, dominant. The departing chief of staff proposed three pieces of legislation designed to achieve these aims.[99] In retrospect, Summerall's report was the loud and mournful swan song of the old army.

Once MacArthur took over change was dramatic and swift. A cardinal rule of his years in office was that all war plans

> must be supported by carefully devised procurement plans, and by programs for mobilizing the industrial resources of the Nation. These two latter, in the War Department, are prepared by the Assistant Secretary of War. This whole coordinating process is one of the most important features of war planning.

Moreover, the chief of staff insisted on close War Department coordination with Navy Department planning, and, to further intramilitary and intermilitary relations, worked to organize what he called a "Joint Army-Navy-Industrial Proposal for National Organization in War."[100]

The Protective Mobilization Plan (PMP) that took shape under Craig called for the immediate mobilization of a small, well-equipped defensive force (essentially the established regular army and the National Guard) with troop quotas in the event of an emergency far below those set by the preceding General Mobilization Plan. At the end of the first three months of fighting, a 400,000-man army would exist, to be increased to 800,000 within eight months, and to 1 million at the end of a year. Eventually, the army would have between 3.75 and 4 million men. At these rates of mobilization, the military planners were convinced, incoming troops could be adequately supplied.[101]

With the PMP, the army for the first time in its peacetime history had plans for full and realistic mobilization. The PMP grew from the concept of "feasibility," the idea that the size of the armed forces could increase only at a rate that matched the productive capacity of the economy. Otherwise the stability of the economy would be undermined and the war effort threatened.

The army was introduced to the feasibility concept during World War I, the first total, industrial war.[102] But the idea had been neither fully developed nor comprehended by the War Department by the end of hostilities. Only the procurement and economic mobilization planning of the OASW during the interwar years, combined with the insight, flexibility, and courage of staff officers such as Craig, made feasibility a fully understood and integrated part of overall War Department planning. Without OASW planning, the vital mobilization lessons of World War I would most probably have been ignored instead of studied and absorbed. Such an outcome would have produced incalculably adverse consequences for America immediately before and during World War II. Realism, first in supply and then in general mobilization planning, prepared the nation as never before for major hostilities.[103] Despite its numerous and fundamental weaknesses—including serious and chronic statistical lapses—procurement planning in the interwar years played a vital, indeed indispensable, role in adjusting the army to the dictates of modern warfare.

During the interwar years, military supply and the roles of civilian mobilization agencies in military affairs became intertwined in struggles for power, prestige, and position within the army and the War Department. The complexity of crucial issues was, therefore, magnified manyfold, which produced conditions of a Catch-22 perversity. As bitter rivals, both the bureaus and the General Staff would have more willingly lent their support to a beleaguered Office of the Assistant Secretary of War had it been stronger and more effective. Yet the office needed the backing of one or both to gain more power and to improve its performance, and it could not afford heedlessly to alienate either. Nonetheless, over time plans for procurement and economic mobilization were ultimately worked out because they were essential for preparedness. All parts of the War Department gradually came to recognize the critically important role of the OASW. The assistant secretary of war and his staff modified meaningfully the War Department's collective thought about the imperatives of mobilizing for modern warfare.

That modification was accomplished without significantly changing power relations in the War Department and, as assistant secretaries of war constantly complained, with a pool of officers devoted to economic mobilization planning that was less than 8 percent of the number of officers engaged in planning for manpower mobilization.[104] By any measure, that accomplishment was no mean feat.[105]

2
INDUSTRIAL MOBILIZATION PLANNING, 1920–1939

The National Defense Act of 1920 charged the assistant secretary of war with planning for economic mobilization as well as for army procurement. Authority for the larger planning was vague, and the process was slow to be initiated. Although the assistant secretary of war's office produced some plans for mobilizing the economy between 1922 and 1928, they were always rudimentary. Finally, after a year of concerted effort, the office completed and ultimately published its first significant blueprint to harness the American economy for hostilities—the Industrial Mobilization Plan, 1930.

Several reasons account for the sluggish start of the Office of the Assistant Secretary of War (OASW) toward economic mobilization planning. War Department personnel, civilian and military alike, shied away from a task they considered to be a civilian responsibility. Only gradually, as planners studied World War I mobilization and established widespread ties in the civilian economy, did they begin to see the necessity for economic mobilization planning and gain confidence in their ability to do it. Even then, pressure from such World War I mobilizers as Bernard M. Baruch was essential to launch full-scale planning.[1]

Also interfering with the OASW's progress was a lack of clarity about the aspects that distinguished planning for the entire economy from planning for army procurement. Procurement planning, unlike industrial mobilization planning, clearly fell into the military area. Having become aware of the need for industrial mobilization planning, the OASW initially thought that it was already performing this function through commodity committee studies; plans for power, fuel, transportation, labor, and finance; and Procurement District activities. Although no absolute lines set off procurement from economic mobilization planning, the OASW members had to develop a clear sense of the elements that the latter planning involved before they could do it.[2]

Finally, and most important, the OASW was simply unprepared for the larger planning until the more limited job of procurement planning had been mastered. Most of a decade went into working out the details of emergency procurement. For the OASW to have tried economic mobilization planning while struggling with procurement planning would have jeopardized both. By 1929 the OASW was finally ready to turn its attention to planning for the whole economy.[3]

THE CROOKED PATH TO INDUSTRIAL MOBILIZATION PLANNING

Virtually no one during World War I or in the immediate postwar years intended for the War Department to plan for economic mobilization. The principal civilian and military movers behind Section 5a of the National Defense Act of 1920 had in mind only procurement planning. "Industrial preparedness" was almost always associated with civilian, not military, institutions.[4]

The logical civilian agency to carry on industrial mobilization planning in the interwar years was the Council of National Defense (CND) and its companion body, the National Defense Advisory Commission (NDAC). From early 1918 into 1921, the CND–NDAC strove mightily and unsuccessfully to win a role for itself in reconversion and then in long-range planning for economic mobilization. The last concerted effort by a civilian body to carry on economic planning was the aborted Industry Board of the Department of Commerce, which came and went between February and May 1919.[5]

Varied proposals for economic mobilization planning followed the Industry Board's demise. Late in 1919, for example, Baruch, in a preliminary report to the president on the War Industries Board (WIB), recommended a skeletonized postwar WIB he later called the Industrial Strategy Board. Including representatives of the military services and all other claimant agencies, this body would meet at least annually to review plans and to consider staffing for mobilization. In an emergency, it would have the authority to mobilize the economy. World War I mobilization leaders would make up the board, each grooming an understudy to take over when he was no longer capable of or available for service. Baruch also proposed, along with a program for stockpiling strategic raw materials, an expansible munitions industry to work with the armed services.[6] His ideas met the same fate as all the other proposals.

Neither the Woodrow Wilson administration nor Congress appeared interested in creating new or continuing existing agencies for economic mobilization planning.[7] Yet wartime conditions made clear the need for such planning, particularly as it involved the military services. Consequently, Congress in the National Defense Act of 1920 ambiguously authorized the assistant secretary of war to carry out economic mobilization planning in addition to planning for procurement. Assigning the task to one of the oldest departments in government, traditionally responsible for war preparation, avoided political controversy.[8]

Placing economic mobilization planning in War Department hands turned out to be a positive step. The planning prepared the armed forces for future hostilities by helping them fully absorb the lessons of World War I. Business did not need such assistance. Republican efforts at informally planning the economy in the 1920s and direct planning by the National Recovery Administration in the 1930s served to prepare industrial America for war mobilization.[9]

Assigning the War Department the task of planning for a wartime economy nevertheless created serious problems. It generated great tension both within and outside the department. The initial difficulty in the War Department involved competition between the OASW and the General Staff. The National Defense Act of 1920 obliquely granted the General Staff, as well as the OASW, the authority to plan for industrial mobilization. Through the Harbord Board's recommendations, procurement and economic mobilization planning was assigned to the assistant secretary of war in 1921. Although bowing out of procurement planning, General Staff subdivisions continued to intrude on economic mobilization planning.[10]

The Army War College (AWC) was the major offender in this regard. It began offering courses on industrial mobilization in 1920, and in 1924 the college further emphasized the subject by establishing an Assistant Secretary of War Division. Major General Hanson E. Ely, the AWC commandant, personally guided the division's work. For a time, he and other General Staff officers favored economic mobilization carried out principally by the existing executive departments. That approach would have made the War Department, and within it the General Staff, key to any system for harnessing the economy. After studying World War I mobilization, Ely and the AWC switched to advocating a modified form of the wartime model for future hostilities. In the process, General Ely and the college lavished attention on Bernard M. Baruch, Frank A. Scott, and others with the obvious intent of recruiting their support for AWC planning. Even as early as 1925, the AWC's work on economic mobilization was astute and sophisticated. By comparison, the output of the OASW was primitive and unaccomplished. One reason was that the AWC attracted more talent than the OASW; another was that it focused on economic mobilization planning without bogging down in procurement planning, an option not open to the assistant secretary of war's office.[11]

At any rate, the AWC's planning infuriated the OASW. Pressure from the office led to the AWC's abolishing the Assistant Secretary of War Division in 1928. Thereafter, procurement and economic planning were incorporated in an abbreviated form in the G-4 (Supply) course. Under the changed circumstances, AWC and General Staff knowledge about the subject declined perceptibly, an outcome anticipated by advocates of economic mobilization in the college.[12]

Outside pressures exacerbated the War Department's internal planning tensions. As the sole source of industrial mobilization planning, the War Department attracted the attention of various individuals and groups dedicated to preparedness. The first group of importance included Frank A. Scott, an early chairman of the WIB, and Palmer E. Pierce, a retired army general who had served in the highest echelons of the War Department and civilian mobilization agencies during World War I, along with Newton D. Baker and Benedict Crowell, secretary and assistant secretary of war during World War I. These individuals were familiar with and friendly to the army. Initially critical of the OASW for its slow start and halting progress in planning, they came to realize that the assistant secretary's office had to proceed carefully in the new assignment, completing procurement planning before moving forward seriously with economic mobilization planning.

With patience and perseverance, Scott, Crowell, and the others played an almost indispensable role in guiding the OASW in the early stages. Critical to their influence were the Procurement Districts and the Army Ordnance Association (AOA). Working with the War Department on a day-to-day basis, these institutions bridged the military and business worlds.[13] They included in their organizations representatives from the corporate and financial elite as well as big, medium, and small businesses. Individuals such as Scott and groups like the Procurement Districts were so pervasive in the OASW work throughout the 1920s that procurement and early economic mobilization planning could not have proceeded as it did without them.

Bernard M. Baruch also looms large in the assistant secretary of war's planning, both in negative and positive ways. The former chairman of the WIB was uninterested in and unimportant to the early phases of the OASW's efforts. Fully developed economic mobilization plans became virtually an obsession with him. Turning to the War Department to fulfill this end, Baruch encountered repeated frustration, especially in the 1920s.

Baruch's role in War Department planning requires attention for a number of reasons. Harry B. Yoshpe, an official War Department historian, has called Baruch the "civilian godfather of the military M-Day Plan," and this judgment has been accepted by most scholars writing on the subject.[14] Yoshpe's assertion requires revision because it exaggerates the influence of the former WIB chair. Moreover, as a leading war mobilizer, Baruch was a logical person to advise the OASW. But the OASW could not have avoided Baruch even if it had wanted to, which at times was the case. The former chairman of the WIB became the self-appointed expert on industrial mobilization for war.

Baruch knew no limits in his interwar drive for economic mobilization plans based on World War I experience. His efforts included an unending stream of lectures on the subject to civilian and military audiences, articles for prestigious magazines like the *Atlantic Monthly,* close contacts with influential legislators interested in the subject such as Cong. John McSwain (D-SC) and Sen. Arthur H. Vandenberg (R-MI), and proselytizing for the cause with whoever would listen and could help, including presidents.[15] Baruch's most successful venture involved secretly financing Grosvenor B. Clarkson's *Industrial America in the War: The Strategy Behind the Line, 1917–1918,* published in 1923, which became the standard source on the subject for over half a century. Although a useful survey, the book is a sophisticated and distorted publicity tract for the WIB and its chairman.[16] Baruch also helped finance another study of the war economy by Prof. Alvin S. Johnson of The New School for Social Research, which apparently never reached the publication stage.[17] Moreover, the former WIB chair tried to make himself the international authority on the economics of warfare. In an involved series of negotiations conducted primarily through Owen D. Young, Baruch endowed a lecture series at the Johns Hopkins University's Walter Hines Page School of International Relations to further the cause of socially equitable economic preparedness. Baruch aimed at having the American effort duplicated in Great Britain, France, Germany, Italy, and Japan. To his chagrin, this project was portrayed as an effort to analyze the relationship between war and profiteering.[18]

Key to Baruch's success in pursuing economic preparedness was his shrewd cultivation of public figures, especially Southern senators like James F. Byrnes (D-SC) and Joseph T. Robinson (D-AR). He was a regular contributor to their campaign coffers, entertained them grandly at his baronial estate in South Carolina and at times on trips abroad, and dispensed to them lavish gifts, praise, investment advice and assistance, and loans, which were not regularly repaid. Franklin D. Roosevelt claimed that Baruch "owned" up to sixty members of Congress.

Perhaps of equal significance were Baruch's connections with the media. Columnists and newspaper moguls Frank Kent and David Lawrence of the *Baltimore Sun,* Arthur Krock of the *New York Times,* and Mark Sullivan, to mention only the most prominent, received the same attention as politicians. When desiring publicity, Baruch turned to one of his highly placed press contacts. Moreover, a bevy of talented journalists, writers, and analysts were periodically on the Baruch payroll, including Hugh S. Johnson, Herbert Bayard Swope, Marquis James, and Samuel Lubell. They analyzed and drafted legislation, summarized congressional hearings, wrote speeches, reports, and proposals, and performed numerous other tasks.[19]

Baruch's influence allowed him to open doors virtually anywhere, including the White House. A better publicist for industrial preparedness could not be found. Few individuals could enjoy the privilege of having an appearance before the Army Industrial College elaborately covered in the *New York Times*.[20] Nor could many hire Richard H. Hippelheuser to collect his "comments" on the subject of industrial mobilization, arrange for their publication with a foreword by Gen. John J. Pershing, and distribute gratis copies throughout the nation's network of power and publicity.[21]

Complex motives powered Baruch's obsession with economic mobilization. Most forthrightly, he was dedicated to preparedness. More obliquely, he was determined not to lose the fame he had won during World War I. By becoming the self-appointed expert on economic mobilization for war, he staked out territory few others would challenge or care to pursue in terms of time, money, and effort.

Baruch was also committed to portraying the War Industries Board in a favorable light. A good press for the WIB meant a secure reputation for its chairman. Protecting the board's image was no mean feat; it was vulnerable to attack on many levels.[22] Congressional investigations of war mobilization began soon after hostilities ended and continued throughout the interwar years. Political partisans, pacifists, populists, radicals, antiwar advocates, and others also zeroed in on the WIB.[23] Baruch skillfully maneuvered around the numerous critics. The WIB proponents, not its detractors, won the battle of how posterity viewed the board. (By way of contrast, at least partly because they lacked such a dogged and well-heeled defender, the economic mobilizers for World War II are much less esteemed.)

By defending the WIB, Baruch simultaneously defended corporate America, the model on which the board was based. Corporate capitalist America made Baruch wealthy; the WIB made him famous. The system and the board were inseparable. On corporate capitalism Baruch became as zealous an ideologue as he was on the WIB.[24]

Motivation aside, without a civilian board for economic mobilization planning, Baruch had to work with the War Department. At first his efforts involved the Army War College more than the OASW. The AWC showered attention on Baruch and unquestioningly followed his lead. Baruch began lecturing before the AWC as early as 1920. From then until World War II, he was virtually an annual speaker at the college.[25] With only slight variation, his message for twenty years was the same—so much so that by 1927 he proposed that the students need only read his 1926 address and question him on key points.²⁶ Baruch maintained that World War I had shown that economic preparedness was at least as important a prerequisite as military preparedness for fighting a modern war. The wartime mobilization model, with modifications and a new taxation system, was nearly perfect for handling an emergency. But plans had to be put on paper while war mobilizers were available and the experience fresh in mind.²⁷

To Baruch's delight, the AWC in the mid-1920s was writing outstanding critiques of OASW procurement planning and, more important, proposing astute plans for industrial mobilization.²⁸ Early in 1926 Baruch reported that an AWC work was "the best thing that I have seen from the War Department on this general subject and it shows a thorough understanding of it."²⁹ After the AWC was forced to downgrade economic mobilization planning in 1928, its relations with Baruch cooled. The two had been using each other and had already maximized their gain. Nonetheless, the AWC experience demonstrated that proper instruction could persuade staff and line officers that industrial mobilization was crucial for conducting war.

Baruch's initial success with the AWC did not meet his goal of officially sanctioned plans for economic mobilization. Such plans had to emanate from the Office of the Assistant Secretary of War. The former chairman of the WIB never established cordial, open relations with that office at any time in the interwar years. As late as September 1937, Baruch complained to Assistant Secretary of War Louis A. Johnson that OASW members still viewed him suspiciously because he had been "captured" early by the AWC. Baruch was convinced that this attitude explained why the OASW neglected wartime economic mobilization figures.³⁰

Baruch's difficulties with the OASW stemmed from multiple causes. The office was slow to appreciate the realities of economic mobilization, a matter that angered and disappointed the war mobilizer. In 1927, for example, Maj. R. R. Nix, a talented Ordnance officer, suggested that the Procurement Districts could replace an agency like the War Industries Board.³¹ A year later the head officer in the assistant secretary's office proposed that procurement planning in general eliminated the need for civilian superagencies.³²

Rivalry between the Office of the Assistant Secretary of War and the Army War College also soured Baruch's relations with the former. Frank A. Scott, Newton D. Baker, and many others worked with both institutions without appearing to favor one over the other. Baruch, however, seemed to identify with the General Staff, perhaps because it had been more flexible in resolving World War I mobilization crises than the supply arms and services (SA&S). Hugh S. Johnson, his chief adviser and a major figure in army supply operations during the war, thought the bureaus were still in the Dark Ages.³³ Furthermore, the AWC readily accepted Baruch's directions about industrial mobilization, a move the OASW would not match.

Baruch's approach to the OASW lacked sensitivity. He failed to appreciate that the assistant secretary of war could proceed no faster than the tradition-bound SA&S were willing to go. Begrudgingly acknowledging that procurement planning was important, the former WIB chair insisted that such work without simultaneous advances in economic mobilization planning could create conditions more threatening even than those that had occurred during World War I. A military better prepared to handle supply could overrun or dominate a civilian economy with disastrous consequences.[34] Baruch also seemed unable to grasp that the OASW's planning was as much an educational experience as a means of preparing for war. A plan drawn up, pigeonholed, and periodically reviewed, as Baruch advocated, accomplished little. Day-to-day work on procurement and economic mobilization planning left the indelible mark. AWC officer-students made rapid headway when force-fed and aping Baruch, but progress dropped off when the force-feeding stopped.

Politics likewise played a role in Baruch's tense interaction with the OASW. The War Industries Board was engulfed in controversy after the war with a sharp partisan edge to the differences.[35] As a new agency, facing challenges from every side, the OASW was in no position to embrace the WIB and its chairman. That would have been the case if Baruch had been a Republican; it was more so since he was a highly placed Democrat associated with Wilson. Consequently, neither Baruch nor his chief WIB lieutenants were invited to visit the OASW during the first two years of operations.[36]

Baruch harshly complained about this state of affairs to Secretary of War John W. Weeks, General Pershing, Sen. James W. Wadsworth, Jr. (R-NY), and other prominent figures. The OASW's planning was inadequate, he explained, because the planners were not consulting the people who were experienced and informed. These protests paid off in time. In December 1922 Baruch and Alexander Legge met informally, away from the War Department, with Assistant Secretary of War J. Mayhew Wainwright. Wainwright in January 1923 tapped Legge, a Republican, to act as liaison in arranging for WIB leaders, except Baruch, to assist the OASW. With Hugh S. Johnson in the lead, George N. Peek, Legge, and others refused to cooperate in what they considered a petty partisan act unless Baruch participated and assumed the customary role of chief.

Bowing to this pressure, Wainwright and his successor Dwight F. Davis cautiously tried to work out a way to tap the knowledge of the war mobilizers. The task was never easy because Baruch was high-handed. In assessing the OASW's work, Legge, seconded by Senator Wadsworth, General Pershing, and others, thought that the OASW had made impressive progress within a few years and that the office had to be allowed to proceed at its own pace. Baruch paid lip service to OASW gains but insisted that the office must draft plans for economic mobilization along the lines of a more centralized WIB. Unlike the AWC, the OASW, though desiring the approval of the World War I mobilizers, could not churn out plans simply to suit Baruch. Nor would the assistant secretary of war and his lieutenants surrender their prerogatives to outsiders, as Baruch in effect proposed. In 1923 Davis suggested to Baruch that by arranging for businessmen to assist OASW commodity committees he could achieve his goal of training younger industrialists for future mobilization service. Baruch seized upon the idea to push for an Industrial Strategy Board, headed by himself and staffed with his wartime assistants, to keep the nation economically prepared for hostilities. The OASW let the matter die, losing an opportunity for integrating industrialists into the top levels of the OASW's operations on a regular basis.

Wainwright's and Davis's failure denied the OASW the advice of Baruch and his talented associates for most of the Dollar Decade, which complicated further the tangled OASW–business relationship. Scott, Baker, Crowell, and their group, unlike Baruch's, had close working relations with the OASW. The interaction between Scott's group and the Baruch coterie had grown rather adversarial during World War I; the animosity continued into the postwar years, and it now spilled over to affect interwar planning. Although the two groups subordinated their differences whenever possible to the larger good of economic preparedness, Scott's group had the greater impact on the OASW in the 1920s; Baruch's influence did not begin to be felt fully until the 1930s.[37]

INDUSTRIAL MOBILIZATION PLANNING IN THE 1920S

The Office of the Assistant Secretary of War wrote several plans for economic mobilization between 1922 and 1928, but these were preliminary, halfhearted efforts. The planning did not begin seriously until 1929. A few months after its creation in February 1922, the OASW began working on economic mobilization. By December, the first War Plan for Industrial Mobilization was completed. Subsequent versions appeared in 1924 and 1928, with revisions of the latter coming out in 1929 and 1930 as Industrial Mobilization, the Assistant Secretary of War, Basic Plan and Basic Procurement Plan.[38]

These early plans reflected OASW confusion over the procedures that constituted procurement as distinguished from economic mobilization planning and the proper role of the office in each sphere. The plans concentrated on procuring military goods, though they at least mentioned the larger aspects of economic mobilization. In the 1922 plan, for example, subdivisions of the OASW were assigned to cover priority, price control, and foreign relations as well as power, labor, and fuel. The SA&S were also charged with calculating their needs for raw materials, facilities, power, transportation, and labor to facilitate coordination at higher levels. Most directly related to economic mobilization, the 1922 plan contained a legislative section that included provisions for superagencies like the War Industries Board.[39] The 1924 plan went even further, setting forth some principles to guide economic mobilization and listing superagencies that might be created. Moreover, by 1924 the Legislative Appendix included drafts of bills and executive proclamations for creating mobilization bodies.[40] Finally, (although not in the 1924 plan) the OASW was becoming quite sophisticated about when superagencies should be created, whether one should be dominant, and how they could be coordinated.[41]

By 1928 the OASW planners were beginning to discriminate more clearly between procurement and economic mobilization planning. The plan of that year and its revisions were given the more correct label of "procurement plans," and to make the contents more consistent with the title, all references to superagencies were deleted and the Legislative Appendix excluded. Yet confusion persisted. The 1928 plan proposed active roles for the War Department in wartime labor, transportation, and power policies, and more significantly, introduced the concept of war service committees reminiscent of WIB operations during World War I. Also included in the 1928 plan were proposals for the OASW to act as a transitional mobilization body until the necessary civilian agencies could be created.[42] In contrast to its advances in procurement planning, the OASW obviously had not made much progress with economic mobilization planning by 1928.

The OASW's attempts to write plans between 1922 and 1928 are not a reliable guide to the office's progress in the area of economic mobilization. Legislation sanctioning economic mobilization is a better measure. When the OASW in 1922 started writing its first plan for controlling a wartime economy, it also began searching for statutes to authorize economic mobilization. It turned up little more than the 1920 National Defense Act's authority for the president to place compulsory orders and to commandeer facilities. Since that would not support economic mobilization, the OASW decided to write new legislation.[43]

The American Legion accelerated the OASW's efforts. The legion was committed to creating a legal base for equalizing the burdens of war and reducing or eliminating war profits. It asked for the OASW's assistance in writing the legislation; the latter did most of the work, and a committee made up of OASW, General Staff, and American Legion members completed the draft.

Very brief and general, the bill provided, in the event of an emergency or war, for military conscription and authority for the president to control capital and labor through existing or newly created agencies and to stabilize wages and prices. Congressional action was essential to trigger the draft, but the president could move on his own to harness the economy if he perceived an imminent threat to the nation. From 1922 through 1941, the Legion bill was repeatedly introduced in Congress, and it had the War Department's support throughout the 1920s.[44] Writing to the chairman of the House Military Affairs Committee in February 1923, Secretary of War Weeks declared: "If these principles were now enacted into law they would furnish the War Department for the first time in our history a legal basis on which to formulate plans in time of peace for mobilizing all of our resources as contemplated in the National Defense Act."[45] The bill, or legislation resembling it, was included in all economic mobilization plans written between 1922 and 1928 as the potential legal foundation for all future mobilization.

While supporting the American Legion bill, the OASW continued to work on its own legislation for economic mobilization after 1922. To aid this effort, the Judge Advocate General's Office assigned Lt. Col. Edwin O. Saunders to the OASW in May 1923. At the outset, the OASW thought Saunders could quickly complete the task, but it took nearly a year to accomplish. Before writing legislation, the Judge Advocate's Office and the OASW had to have some idea of what economic mobilization entailed. The more they studied the subject, the more complex and nearly overwhelming it appeared. To avoid numerous pitfalls and to permit maximum flexibility, the planners concluded that they should keep the proposed legislation concise and vague.[46]

Completed in March 1924, Saunders's draft, like the American Legion bill, was very general. In the event of war or emergency, the president was authorized to create a selective service system; establish agencies for mobilizing and controlling resources, industry, capital, and labor; and stabilize prices and wages. Including a military draft in the bill transpired only after considerable debate and some reluctance as part of a larger program for regulating labor supply.[47]

Throughout the preliminary stage of economic mobilization planning, the OASW rewrote Saunders's proposed legislation and added new bills to the legislative package. By 1928 five bills and three executive proclamations were included in the Legislative Appendix to the embryonic economic mobilization plan. The first and primary legislation was Saunders's modified bill, which established the legal base for mobilizing the economy. Other bills specified what mobilization agencies would be created and, along with the executive proclamations, provided detail on the exercise of presidential powers in specific areas. Most of the proposed legislation was patterned after World War I practices.[48]

Working on the legislative package reinforced for the OASW the conviction that bills must be kept as general as possible. Thus they could be adjusted to a war of any magnitude and to almost any economic, political, and social circumstance. Additionally, and of equal importance, the more general the legislation, the easier it was to defend and the more difficult to attack. Army planners grasped a valuable lesson that World War I mobilizers had only gradually and painfully learned. Because it involved crucial matters of political economy, the military, national defense, and war, industrial mobilization was exceptionally controversial. Disputes could be avoided or mitigated while still getting the job done by staying away from detail and close definitions. Generally delegating powers to the president, with specifics left to him and his advisers to spell out in executive orders where necessary, seemed the best solution.[49]

The OASW ultimately elected not to advocate the passage of general legislation for economic mobilization. With periodic reservations, the War Department supported the American Legion bill from 1923 through 1930; it reversed itself during most of the 1930s. The Legion bill and numerous other legislative proposals had been before Congress for almost eight years without a real chance of passage, emphasizing how divisive the matter was. Because Congress would so modify and encumber any bill before passage, the military mobilizers concluded, it would be better temporarily to avoid the legislative halls. That approach allowed them the opportunity to refine the intended legislation as necessary. In an emergency, the appropriate bills could be enacted expeditiously and with only minor modifications.[50]

The OASW also evidenced growing sophistication about how a mobilized economy would function. Although the bill that the OASW helped the American Legion write, and some of its own drafted legislation, contained proposals for a "total draft" of capital and labor, the label was misleading. By 1923 the OASW had concluded that "universal conscription"—drafting labor, industry, and capital in the same way as military personnel—was impossible. The economic system had to be used as it existed. When employed, "conscription," therefore, meant "utilizing" industry, finance, and business in conjunction with price controls and taxation measures designed to avoid inflation and profiteering. Some officers in the General Staff, the OASW, and elsewhere in the War Department continued to advocate universal conscription in a literal sense, but not many.[51]

Such gentle persuasion did not extend to labor. Although rejecting the expediency of a labor draft, or national service legislation, as early as 1922, the OASW throughout the 1920s flirted with indirect methods of controlling the labor force. Under political pressure in the 1930s, the War Department denied that it intended to coerce workers, but that was not exactly the case. Furthermore, in contrast to its widespread and harmonious relations with business, the OASW contacts with organized labor were late in developing and usually were strained.[52]

The OASW in the 1920s also had the opportunity to work out plans for economic mobilization of a more limited nature. In spring 1924, the assistant secretary of war requested that the American Association of Railway Executives appoint a committee for determining how the railroad system would operate in an emergency. Within a year, the association, the War Department, and the Calvin Coolidge administration had ratified a policy. Government control would be implemented only if absolutely essential. In such an eventuality, an executive assistant to the secretary of war would direct rail lines in conjunction with an executive committee of railroad presidents. Even then, all lines would remain in private hands. Compensation to owners would be based on the average of the three years preceding the emergency. Beginning in 1925, the American Association of Railway Executives appointed representatives to assist the OASW and other army planning subdivisions in preparing for war and emergency duty.[53]

The OASW's planning efforts included electrical power as well, although the outcome was less successful than with the railroads. The Corps of Engineers completed a rather thorough survey of generating facilities by 1925. As this was one of the country's most rapidly changing industries, the information was updated annually. Based on this data, a plan for wartime coordination of power industries was completed in 1927 and presented to the National Electrical Light Association. Despite repeated requests, the association appeared unable or unwilling to endorse the plan. Nonetheless, the OASW included the blueprint in its economic mobilization plans.[54]

By 1928 the assistant secretary of war's office had made a respectable start on economic mobilization planning. Progress was more evident in proposed mobilization legislation than in the crude plans drafted between 1922 and 1928. Perhaps the most important development was the OASW's recognition that plans for economic mobilization had to be based on the nation's existing political economy. That, after all, had been the outstanding lesson of harnessing the economy for World War I. The preliminary work on economic mobilization, combined with procurement planning, laid the foundations for the rapid progress the OASW made with the industrial mobilization plans in the 1930s.

INDUSTRIAL MOBILIZATION PLAN, 1930

The War Department's economic mobilization planning began in earnest when Herbert Hoover assumed the presidency and Patrick J. Hurley became first assistant secretary of war (1929) and then secretary of war (1929–1933). Characteristic of the focused energy of the early Hoover administration, the dynamic Hurley organized a series of conferences and other programs to accelerate economic mobilization planning.[55] Of key importance, Brig. Gen. George Van Horn Moseley in summer 1929 became executive assistant to the assistant secretary of war in charge of industrial preparedness, a temporary post he filled for about sixteen months. A talented officer, Moseley brought new vitality to the councils of the assistant secretary.[56] Writing to Bernard M. Baruch in November 1929, Hugh S. Johnson observed that Moseley "is the first man they have had on this job who will bring matters to a clear issue and fight hard for his point of view."[57] Moseley got the OASW off to a fast start in writing a full-fledged economic mobilization plan.

Moseley's first effort, "Plan for Governmental Organization for War," completed in November 1929, was a false start, however. Economic mobilization would be carried out by three coordinate agencies: an Administration of National Resources, an Administration of Manpower and Labor, and a Department of Munitions. The first would perform duties similar to the War Industries Board; the second, plans for which would be written by the General Staff, would control the flow of manpower to the military and civilian economy; and the third, a newly created executive department, would take over the procurement functions of the War and Navy Departments. The heads of the three new agencies, along with the secretaries of war and navy, the army chief of staff, and the chief of naval operations, would serve as a War Council to the president. Moseley was a proponent of unifying the military under a Department of National Defense. The Department of Munitions was a first step in that direction.

A Munitions Department was the most novel, but not the most crucial, aspect of the plan; more important was the dominant position of the military. The Manpower Administration would be controlled by the General Staff, the Munitions Department by the combined armed forces, and the two new agencies together could be at least the equal of the National Resources Administration. Additionally, military representatives would essentially hold six of the seven seats making up the War Council. The plan was unclear or uncertain on exactly how policy would be made and executed.[58]

The plan was widely circulated within the War Department and selectively outside it. It was subjected to harsh criticism, especially the proposal for a Munitions Department. Creating such an agency during a national emergency, dissenters argued, could be disruptive to military and economic mobilization in general. Other criticisms were leveled at the plan's vagueness or silence about existing government policies and agencies.[59]

The most comprehensive critique came from Baruch. Johnson wrote to Baruch in November 1929 that "Moseley's paper is very authoritative," but "of course, this is all wrong." Johnson continued, "I think that it is highly important to hit this one on the nose and I will have, by Monday, a suggested draft of a letter to Moseley."[60] Telling the military planners that they were totally right in intent, Baruch asserted that they were totally wrong in execution. The plan gave the military too much power in the mobilization scheme; a refined World War I system must be adopted instead.[61]

Despite its weaknesses, Moseley's plan—actually called the Hurley Plan after the assistant secretary—was a giant step forward for the OASW compared to the fragmentary blueprints produced between 1922 and 1928. As a complete plan, it could be circulated for review. For the first time, the OASW work was scrutinized. Only in that way could the planners be assured that their work was realistic.

Once the critiques were in, the OASW began an intensive process of redrafting the Hurley Plan to meet objections, incorporate new insights, and produce a generally better work. By February 1930 a new version had been written; it went through a number of revisions and was ready early in December 1930.[62] Completing an acceptable plan took on greater urgency for the OASW in mid-1930, when Congress created the War Policies Commission (WPC) by Joint Resolution to study and make recommendations on equalizing war burdens and formulating war policies. The commission gave the War Department the first opportunity publicly to unveil its work.[63]

The plan submitted to the WPC was not a finely honed product. Important information was scattered throughout more than 100 pages, and the mobilization structure was described in a piecemeal fashion. If studied carefully, numerous charts and graphs often gave a clearer view of what the OASW had in mind than the frequently opaque text. Moreover, crucial information missing from the plan had to be presented to the WPC by Chief of Staff Gen. Douglas MacArthur as official spokesman for the War Department. Nonetheless, the pieces of the plan were present, even if the reader had to fit them together.

Hurley's redrafted plan was labeled the Industrial Mobilization Plan (IMP), 1930. The Department of Munitions and the Manpower Administration were scrapped. The new plan was centered on a director of War Industry. This agency was comparable to the War Industries Board except that it would be divided into a coordinator of War Industry and a coordinator of Requirements. The latter would bring together the armed services and other claimant agencies; the former, structured along commodity section–war service committee lines, would mobilize industry. With supply and demand organized by the two wings of the same administration, the director was expected to manage economic mobilization effectively.[64]

The OASW plan finessed the controversial issue of other superagencies and their relationship to the principal mobilization authority. It provided for Labor, Selective Service, and Public Relations Administrations, although only the director of War Industry and the Labor Administration were fully outlined. The heads of these agencies, along with the director of War Industry and the secretaries of war and navy (advised by the chief of staff and the chief of naval operations on military matters), would serve as the president's Advisory War Council.

Technically, therefore, the other superagencies had the same level of power as the director of War Industries. Few planners intended this to be the case since the agency mobilizing industry would clearly be more important than other administrations. Nonetheless, with strong disagreement over centralized control of a wartime system, planners left the president the option of integrating lesser agencies into the major one, leaving them independent, or some position in between. Proposing excessive centralization would diminish the plan's chances of adoption. The OASW was even more uncertain about other sectors of the economy. War finance, shipping, power, and so forth were to be controlled by National Service Corporations. Exactly what these agencies were and how they would function were points left undefined.[65]

The IMP, 1930, also failed to establish how economic controls such as priority, allocation, commandeering, and pricing would operate. The last function caused the most dispute as adherents divided between the Baruch-favored system of a total, across-the-board price freeze on or before the outbreak of a national emergency and a system of selective, gradual price-setting once wartime inflation began. The IMP again veered away from dissension, but MacArthur indicated that the army favored the more flexible approach. Taxation and other policies for holding down war profits and attempting to equalize war burdens were at least mentioned in the plan, the chief of staff once more providing specifics and warning that whatever was done should not hamper war production.[66]

The Legislative Appendix was changed somewhat from earlier versions, but not fundamentally so. It now had six, instead of five, bills. The keystone bill, besides sanctioning a selective service system, made available to the president the nation's material and human resources, authorized him to set prices and wages, and allowed him to create agencies to carry out these functions. A new, modified title, along World War I lines, gave the chief executive the authority for reshuffling his administration to facilitate military procurement and granted him power to suspend restrictive legislation inhibiting the war effort.

Other proposed legislation involved mobilization specifics. The new, sixth bill, written by the General Staff, dealt with a selective service system and duplicated provisions of the first bill, partly because the staff claimed conscription as its domain.[67]

The IMP, 1930, also included a proposal for keeping the nation prepared for hostilities. These provisions grew from the planning of 1922 to 1928 but went beyond it. In peacetime, OASW subdivisions, personnel, and files would match those of the proposed war mobilization structure. In an emergency, they would serve as a mobilizing nucleus until civilian agencies were up and running. The OASW would maintain up-to-date rosters of qualified industrialists to staff various administrations as a way of facilitating mobilization.[68]

To avoid controversy, the IMP treated labor with extreme care. The work force, especially organized labor, was assured that it faced no coercion, that labor would be represented throughout the mobilization structure, and that equitable policies would be used for directing manpower and settling disputes between employer and employee. Nevertheless, the IMP was replete with provisions that could be threatening to labor. Suspending laws for purposes of war production, for example, could adversely affect working conditions and industrial relations.[69]

The IMP, 1930, opened by declaring that economic mobilization must be achieved without radically changing the economy. Public support was crucial, and "the attempt should be to guide and influence the operation of natural forces rather than to attempt opposing them by arbitrary and unfair regulations."[70] Baruch and others had rejected earlier plans because they did not support the status quo. Another objection to previous plans had been the prominence of military controls. Throughout the IMP, 1930, military influence was reduced, but as the plan noted, not eliminated. The General Staff, for example, was responsible for writing plans for the Selective Service System and the Public Relations Administration. Although the armed services needed a major voice in determining the quantity and quality of their manpower, that did not qualify them for operating a selective service system. General Staff preeminence in public relations could be a hazard to national traditions. The IMP proposed that public opinion at least partly would be "molded by the presentation of proper information."[71]

Military presence in the proposed mobilization structure was by necessity systemic, not isolated to parts. The IMP, 1930, incorrectly claimed that the director of War Industries "follows in its general lines that developed by the War Industries Board of 1918."[72] By dividing the agency into two areas, one for supply and the other for demand, and by giving the armed forces control of the demand side, the IMP increased significantly the power of the military and created horrendous organizational tangles. The War Department was even unsuccessful in reorganizing itself or the Navy Department to match the system proposed in the IMP. The WIB had functioned as a multidivisional structure directed by Baruch and his assistant at the top; the military services and other claimant agencies were integrated into most parts of the bureaucracy, not set off by themselves, directing half the agency in a structurally awkward and almost dysfunctional way.

Numerous flaws aside, the OASW made enough progress with the IMP, 1930, to mollify critics. In writing to Moseley in February 1930, Baruch declared, "I feel that your revised plan is the first indication I have seen since the war that the essence of the principles used by the War Industries Board has been grasped."[73] What appeared to please Baruch most was Moseley's assertion that a mobilized economy would, "as in the last war," be run by "the prominent business men of the country."[74] Before and during the WPC hearings, Baruch gave the Industrial Mobilization Plan, 1930, his cautious endorsement, even though disagreements persisted over price controls, other mobilization methods, and Baruch's concerns about the War Department's planning for the economy and the threats of excessive military controls during wartime.[75]

Baruch's endorsement defused controversy and helped gain the backing of the War Policies Commission, a major accomplishment for the OASW. Although not as strongly or as unequivocally as Assistant Secretary of War Hurley and others wanted, the WPC nonetheless gave the IMP its blessing.[76] The Office of the Assistant Secretary of War was now the officially recognized authority on economic mobilization for war. Since it previously had had no public standing, the OASW acquired a new respectability and legitimacy. The office had come a long way within a decade.

INDUSTRIAL MOBILIZATION PLAN, 1933

The next edition of the Industrial Mobilization Plan appeared in 1933. The Office of the Assistant Secretary of War began reworking the 1930 plan after the War Policies Commission hearings. Although the general outline of the earlier plan was maintained, the IMP, 1933, was much more accomplished. The planners integrated the scattered parts of the 1930 plan into a smoothly unfolding whole.

The IMP, 1933, made three significant changes from the previous version. These involved the structure of the principal mobilization agency, the role of the Army-Navy Munitions Board (ANMB), and important modifications in the Legislative Appendix. There were also some minor alterations.

The principal mobilization agency, labeled the War Industries Administration, was patterned more explicitly after the War Industries Board, and its operations were simplified and centralized. Dividing the agency between supply and demand, as proposed in the 1930 plan, was so unworkable that it threatened the success of any mobilization program. To correct this basic defect, the two parts of the War Industries Administration were combined, with all functions placed directly under the director. The administration would operate through various divisions—e.g., commodities, facilities, power, and transportation—based on a commodity section–war service committee system. The OASW and the ANMB and their subdivisions were reorganized to match this pattern so that the process of coordinating and integrating institutions during an emergency or a war would be facilitated.[77]

Much more emphatically than in earlier plans, the War Industries Administration was designated as the primary mobilization agency. It was, the IMP, 1933, declared, "the industrial pivot about which war-time control turns; the most powerful arm of the President for converting the industries into war uses."[78] Although the administration would control fuel, food, and transportation at the outset of a war, those and other functions might require separate superagencies later, and the planners left room for this eventuality. The IMP also made it clearer than before that the War Labor, War Trade, Public Affairs, and Selective Service Administrations would function as autonomous bodies. Although ambiguity remained on the vital issue of whether there would be one major mobilization agency or several coordinate ones, the IMP, 1933, appeared to be aiming for a compromise. Several superagencies would exist, but the War Industries Administration would clearly be in a dominant, not just a coordinate, position.

The OASW planners made a number of less important changes involving autonomous mobilization bodies. An agency for War Trade, for example, was elevated in status. More significantly, a Price Control Committee was added to the prospective mobilization system. The Advisory War Council of the 1930 plan became the Advisory Defense Council and included the chairmen of the superagencies, the head of the Price Control Committee, and the secretaries of war and navy, again advised on military matters by the chief of staff and the chief of naval operations.

By creating a Price Control Committee and writing an appendix on its structure and duties, the IMP, 1933, for the first time highlighted this critical issue. The war mobilizers left it to the committee to choose between selective and total price controls. The OASW also proposed that most important wartime and many peacetime agencies be represented on or consulted by the committee, which would have broad authority to meet its responsibilities. To ensure adequate authority, the planners drafted legislation and an executive order providing price control the legal base missing during World War I. Though spelling out general guidelines for the Price Control Committee, the OASW stressed that it needed to be flexible so as to maintain economic stability with production protected, equity maximized, and abuses reduced.[79]

Next to the War Industries Administration, the War Labor Administration changed the most in the IMP, 1933. Trade unions were treated less favorably than before. All mention of "organized labor" was excised from a plan that put an "outstanding industrial leader" in charge of the work force. The OASW planners neither emphasized the need for a voluntary approach to manpower nor made assurances against the use of coercive techniques. And the 1933 blueprint insisted that protective labor legislation would have to be waived during an emergency. An elaborate War Labor Administration bureaucracy would have regional subunits, but centralized direction of labor supply and labor relations would be centered in Washington. The plan left few duties for the Department of Labor.[80]

The latter point contradicted another new direction of the 1933 plan. To counter criticism that the earlier version had neglected or threatened the peacetime system of government, the 1933 plan declared that "the existing executive structure is maintained for carrying on, under necessary restrictions, the usual statutory duties."[81] Especially important were those departments and agencies authorized to deal with national emergencies, such as the Interstate Commerce Commission and various bureaus of the executive departments.

The next of the three major modifications in the IMP, 1933, dealt with the Army-Navy Munitions Board. Barely mentioned in the 1930 plan, the board had a central role in the 1933 edition. It coordinated the activities of the two services in procurement and economic mobilization planning. An appendix spelled out in detail the structure, operation, and responsibilities of the board. Henceforth, all Industrial Mobilization Plans would be written under the aegis of the ANMB, and the board was organized to parallel the structure of the OASW and the War Industries Administration.[82] These were not changes simply tacked on to the IMP. Nearly every section explained how the ANMB interacted with the War and Navy Departments.

The place of the ANMB in the IMP, 1933, reflected the shifting conditions the assistant secretary of war faced. As long as the OASW concentrated on procurement planning in the 1920s, it could tolerate the navy's lack of interest in planning by ignoring the ANMB.[83] Once economic mobilization planning became central during the 1930s, the board was no longer expendable. The two services had too great a stake in economic mobilization not to work together. In 1931, therefore, the ANMB was reorganized, and it functioned after a fashion. Although the OASW continued to do most of the work, the Navy Department became more active in planning activities.

Nevertheless, the ANMB was made key to the OASW's entire planning scheme. Responsibilities only vaguely outlined in previous plans became explicit in 1933. Serving as the nucleus for the War Industries Administration and other superagencies, the ANMB would carry out economic mobilization functions until civilian agencies were fully active.[84] Still missing from the plan, however, were concrete proposals on how this process would be accomplished.[85] Details were finally provided in a Transition Plan, written and approved in July 1934. During a national emergency, the president would create a War Industries Administration by executive order based on Section 120 of the National Defense Act of 1916. Until such an agency could be organized and staffed, the ANMB would execute all mobilization functions. The board's transitional role would end as civilian agencies took over, but ANMB plans, records, and personnel would constitute the foundation for the system of harnessing the economy. The OASW planners recognized that setting up a War Industries Administration without legislation was probably illegal, but a major emergency made the act tolerable for a relatively short period of time.[86] The ANMB was expected to protect military interests. As the Transition Plan made clear,

> In order to make the War Industries Administration responsive to the needs of the Army and Navy, it is proposed to take from the Army and Navy Munitions Board and from the Army and Navy Departments a limited number of seasoned officer personnel . . . to assist the Administrator of the War Industries Administration and to act as advisers to him.[87]

The last of the three principal changes in the IMP, 1933, involved the Legislative Appendix. Because of a change in political strategy, the OASW recast the legislation granting the president broad, undefined powers over the nation's material and human resources. Until 1930 the OASW favored the passage of legislation in peacetime enabling the president to inaugurate a program of economic mobilization during an emergency or war. The subject bill was purposely kept brief to make it adaptable to varying emergency circumstances and to minimize controversy by avoiding specifics. In 1930 the OASW decided against supporting further bills in the belief that Congress would not pass them during peacetime. Even during an emergency, the legislators would balk at general grants of power. To facilitate congressional action in a crisis, the planners concluded that bills for economic mobilization had to be detailed in nature. In 1933 the secretary of war went further by advocating that proposed legislation be regularly revised and reviewed by appropriate committees of Congress.[88]

The principal bill of the Legislative Appendix opened with a general grant of authority for the president to mobilize the economy "during the present emergency and until such time as Congress shall declare the emergency at an end." It then provided specifics about mobilization agencies, economic controls, and modifications of existing governmental structures and statutes. Additionally, provisions of the keystone bill dealing with a military draft were transferred to the General Staff legislation that set up a selective service system. The latter bill was then made the first one of the Legislative Appendix, perhaps because it was considered to be less controversial than bills dealing with economic mobilization. The rest of the Legislative Appendix remained unchanged except for minor matters.[89]

Although more detailed than before, the omnibus economic mobilization bill was still exceptionally broad in conception and could be interpreted as sanctioning a presidential dictatorship. That quality, along with the dominant role spelled out for the military in the ANMB Transition Plan, guaranteed that the IMP would face intense opposition at most levels.

In terms of procurement as opposed to economic mobilization planning, the IMP, 1933, also manifested progress. The 1930 plan had incorporated a reduced version of the 1928 Basic Procurement Plan as an appendix. Procurement was incorporated in the text of the 1933 IMP in an even more abbreviated form, and at the same time the Basic Procurement Plan was phased out. This important step indicated that by distinguishing fully between procurement and economic mobilization planning the OASW was able to take the necessary step of integrating the two functions. The 1930 plan claimed that procurement planning was "really an included part" of economic mobilization planning; the 1933 IMP more clearly demonstrated that reality.[90]

The Industrial Mobilization Plan, 1933, was an improvement over 1930, especially in terms of the restructured War Industries Administration. Reactivating the ANMB was practical and necessary. Revising the main bill of the Legislative Appendix, despite major flaws, signaled a growing realism among army mobilizers. War Department planners generally seemed more confident about themselves and their work.

INDUSTRIAL MOBILIZATION PLAN, 1936

There were fewer modifications in the Industrial Mobilization Plan between 1933 and 1936 than had been the case between 1930 and 1933. Throughout the 1936 version the most consistent change involved evidence of growing cooperation between the War and Navy Departments. Even more than the 1933 edition, the 1936 plan detailed how the Navy Department would be a fully integrated partner in the mobilization scheme. The Army-Navy Munitions Board was concretely and emphatically identified as the author of the industrial mobilization plans. Moreover, navy supply operations received equal billing with those of the army, and the ANMB's authority was extended to coordinate the procurement of the two services. Nonetheless, the Office of the Assistant Secretary of War continued to do most of the planning.

Based on the Transition Plan of 1934, the IMP, 1936, also designated the ANMB more systematically as the nucleus and transitional economic mobilization body. (Some ambiguity continued because the board's functions were scattered throughout 120 pages of text.) Attempts were made, however, to downplay excessive military influence. In 1933 and earlier, the ANMB would initiate and execute economic mobilization until civilian agencies took over. With the IMP, 1936, the board would act only after the civilian mobilization chief, or the War Resources administrator, was appointed. Despite the change, the ANMB would still have substantial influence in the early days of mobilization, which could be decisive in shaping patterns in harnessing the economy for war.[91]

The general mobilization structure of the IMP, 1936, remained about the same as that of 1933 with some minor variations. A new and final name was adopted for the principal mobilization agency—the War Resources Administration. The price control agency was upgraded in status. The War Labor Administration also was reworked slightly to make it appear less threatening to labor because of criticism from the Senate Special Committee Investigating the Munitions Industry, chaired by Gerald P. Nye (R-ND). Further, the IMP, 1936, envisioned a greater role for Washington in financing or actually performing various economic mobilization functions previously assigned to the private sector. These changes mirrored the shifting conception of government brought about by the New Deal.[92]

Several modifications affected the War Resources Administration. Most important, as introduced earlier in the ANMB Transition Plan, the agency could be established by the president's implied powers without statutory authority. Gaining confidence and facing the real possibility of war, the mobilizers became more determined to have alternative approaches to economic mobilization should Congress stall on the matter. The OASW, however, still held back from giving the War Resources Administration explicit, instead of implicit, authority to regulate and coordinate the other superagencies. Leaving decisions to the president created certain risks. In the heat of an emergency or a war, administrative fragmentation could threaten the economy's stability.

The IMP, 1936, rekindled old rivalries between the General Staff and the OASW that had cooled considerably in the early 1930s. In redrafting the plan in 1936, the OASW and the ANMB rewrote the appendix on selective service. This contravened an informal agreement dating from the 1920s in which selective service as well as public relations were the General Staff's domain. To protect its turf, the staff not only rejected the rewritten appendix but also insisted that the Joint Army-Navy Board (created in 1903 to coordinate strategic planning between the two services) have formal jurisdiction in all areas "not strictly pertaining to the mobilization of industry," i.e., "public relations, publicity, censorship, and the Selective Service system."[93] Moving quickly to resolve the conflict, the OASW negotiated an agreement with the General Staff in which the staff agreed that it would no longer review "the Industrial Sections of the Industrial Mobilization Plan,"[94] in exchange for having the selective service and public relations appendixes turned over to the Joint Board. The board passed the assignment along to its major subdivision, the Joint Planning Committee. A member of the OASW was designated to work with this committee and did so for the next few years with generally good results.

After studying the matter, the Joint Planning Committee concluded that only industrial, not military, manpower should be included in an economic mobilization plan. The question of why public relations belonged to the General Staff remained unaddressed. By not completing drafts of the appendixes on selective service and public relations in 1936, the Joint Planning Committee deferred final decisions of these subjects. The IMP, 1936, noted that these appendixes were being "revised by the appropriate agencies" and would be included in later versions of the plan.[95] No progress was made between 1936 and 1939, leaving the OASW to declare in the Industrial Mobilization Plan, 1939, that the selective service system and public relations were outside the jurisdiction of the OASW and the ANMB.

By far the most sweeping change in the IMP, 1936, occurred in the Legislative Appendix, which was cut from seven bills to two, one of which was inconsequential. The other was HR 5529, passed by the House of Representatives in 1935, totally rewritten by the Nye Committee, and revised and reported out by the Senate committees on Military Affairs and Finance. The legislation as reworked by the Nye Committee would have established rigorous taxation measures to curb wartime profiteering and to finance war costs. It also allowed the president to draft management, granted the chief executive authority for "price fixing, licensing, rationing, requisitioning, priorities, and other measures for directing and unifying the industrial war effort," and gave him the power to create agencies for accomplishing those functions. After excluding the section on war financing, expressing reservations about a draft of management, and modifying a few other parts, the OASW replaced its previous omnibus bill with HR 5529 as rewritten by the Nye Committee.[96]

By including HR 5529 in the IMP, 1936, and endorsing, albeit reluctantly, the measure, the OASW reversed its decision of the late 1920s against supporting industrial mobilization legislation. The military planners would have created more controversy by remaining neutral on HR 5529 than by going along with the prevailing sentiments in Congress and the nation. Generally, the OASW tried to avoid divisiveness and sought the most expedient path for advancing economic preparedness.

With intense scrutiny by the Nye Committee and heightened concern over war, the IMP came under greater attack. The State Department objected to the War Department's proposals to control war trade as encroaching on its territory. Bernard M. Baruch and Hugh S. Johnson quibbled with the OASW plans and fretted about the threats of military control in a mobilized economy. Radicals, pacifists, and isolationists damned the planning and plans as warmongering, fascism, and militarism.[97]

Critics notwithstanding, the Industrial Mobilization Plan, 1936, with the few changes made from 1933, indicated that the Office of the Assistant Secretary of War's planning had achieved a new level of continuity and maturity.

INDUSTRIAL MOBILIZATION PLAN, 1939

The last Industrial Mobilization Plan appeared in 1939. Rewriting began early in 1938. For the first time since 1930, the IMP was totally recast in form and language. In 1933 and 1936, the planners had merely modified what had been written before. The Office of the Assistant Secretary of War was intent on making the final edition as concise and clear as possible. Compared with the 122-page IMP, 1936, that of 1939 was twenty-five pages and stripped of all unnecessary detail. With war all but declared in Europe and American entry likely, the military planners wanted wide publicity for the IMP in order to enhance its chances of adoption.

To further that end, the OASW tried to mollify its past critics. Although written by military officers, the plan noted that civilians had assisted in the work and would run the mobilization agencies. The planners also emphasized the need to create the principal mobilization agency, the War Resources Administration (WRA) as soon as possible, with the Army-Navy Munitions Board playing only a brief, transitional role. As soon as the WRA was inaugurated, the ANMB would return to its intended purpose of representing the military services. To avoid alarming various interest groups, the general public, or both, the IMP, 1939, deemphasized, euphemized, or passed over wartime controls and particularly dire measures like commandeering. For the same reason, the plan addressed for the first time or highlighted civilian demand, economic balance through distribution of contracts, the use of small business, and the need for agencies to plan for and implement reconversion policies.[98]

The OASW made three fundamental changes in the 1939 plan. First, the WRA was finally and explicitly given authority to direct and coordinate all other superagencies.[99] Serving directly under the president and acting as his executive assistant, the War Resources administrator would centrally control the entire mobilization program. More directly than in 1936, the president could draw upon his war powers and existing statutes to establish the WRA, with legislation coming later. Moreover, the WRA would at first perform all economic mobilization functions through subdivisions, with other agencies created only when necessary. The WRA would be staffed by "patriotic business leaders of the nation" and assisted by an advisory council consisting of representatives of all other superagencies, major divisions of the WRA, and the secretaries of state, war, and navy, the last two advised by the chief of staff and chief of naval operations (who were full-time advisory members, not merely available for military matters as in past plans).[100]

In the event that the president balk at centering authority in one agency, the OASW offered the alternative of coordinate superagencies. To stress its preference for centralization, the WRA was the only one sketched out in the text of the IMP. The others were merely mentioned in the plan and then developed fully in annexes.[101] Only superagencies for selective service and public relations were left outside the orbit of the WRA. Since the General Staff was responsible for their functions, the IMP only noted that selective service would be determined in large part by legislation.[102]

A second change fell short of its major billing. Whenever possible, existing governmental agencies would be used for mobilization. The War Finance Administration, for example, would operate largely through the Treasury Department, the Federal Reserve Board, the Reconstruction Finance Corporation, the Securities Exchange Commission, and the Export-Import Bank, with the secretary of the treasury acting as ex-officio chairman. Moreover, the War Trade Board, the Price Control Authority, and the WRA Advisory Council would include other existing departments and agencies. In general, this was a modest departure intended to silence critics, and the IMP, 1939, made clear that mobilization would be carried out mostly by new and temporary bodies.[103]

The third modification of importance involved excluding appendixes, now called annexes, from the published version of the IMP. OASW planners argued that it was impractical to publish annexes that required constant modification to meet changing circumstances.[104] But another reason for excluding the annexes, now classified SECRET, may have been that they were more likely to stir controversy since, unlike the IMP proper, they set out in detail how a mobilized economy would operate.

Withholding the annexes denied general readers crucial information about the IMP, 1939. The annexes, for example, basically altered the rigid M-Day concept. Mobilization could take place under three varying scenarios: preparing the United States as a neutral for a major war that was imminent or had broken out, initiating overt or covert mobilization for an emergency, or instituting full-scale mobilization for a declared war.[105] This vital adaptation resulted from the phased mobilization schedule of the Protective Mobilization Plan (PMP), approved in December 1938. (The PMP, in turn, grew from the OASW's ten-year struggle for realistic mobilization plans based on the economy's potential.)[106] Additionally, President Roosevelt had had the Industrial Mobilization Plan, 1936, reviewed late in 1938 as a result of the Czechoslovak crisis and had rejected the M-Day concept as too limiting because international realities and domestic politics might require gradual, partial, or even secret mobilization.[107]

The IMP contained eight annexes (Price Control, Power and Fuel, Transportation, Labor, War Trade, War Finance, Facilities, and Commodities), with two others (Priorities and Transition) either being prepared or revised. Compared with the appendixes of the past, the 1939 annexes were more detailed, varying from eighteen to eighty-nine pages, and covered a wider range of subjects.[108]

The Price Control Agency was designed to begin operating as soon as practical, although the OASW still declined to choose between an across-the-board or a piecemeal approach to pricing since a consensus on the subject was still lacking.[109] For power and fuel, the annex indicated that the OASW had done its homework on surveys, requirements, distribution of loads, financing of new facilities, and coordination with other agencies.[110] On transportation, the military planners continued to prefer that government leave management in place even when regulation became necessary. Nevertheless, war mobilizers were offered choices that varied from virtually no controls to governmental operation of transportation facilities, with added advice on what legislation would be required.[111] For labor, controls were further centralized in Washington. Over the objection of some military spokesmen, the annex provided for exempting from the draft skilled workers in essential industries. Although military planners still rejected compulsory manpower systems, they favored stronger indirect controls over the work force through implementing a "work or fight" program, registering all males between eighteen and forty-five and imposing graduated levels of punishment for noncompliance. Labor laws restricting production would also be suspended during hostilities. Unlike previous appendixes, however, the 1939 annex placed a greater emphasis on avoiding or ending strikes and other management-labor conflict through agencies designed to settle disputes equitably.[112]

The IMP, 1939, contained no legislative annex as such. A number of annexes included an omnibus bill, however, that made available to the president the manpower and material resources of the nation. It was similar to legislation included in mobilization plans from the 1920s through the IMP, 1933, and dropped by the IMP, 1936, in favor of HR 5529. To placate adherents of Sen. Gerald P. Nye, the bill claimed to share HR 5529's goals of discouraging war and curbing its economic evils through rigorous taxation.[113]

With the IMP, 1939, the OASW gradually moved back to its position between 1929 and 1934 of not endorsing mobilization bills. Military planners feared that pushing for major legislation would give isolationist, anti-interventionists, and others the opportunity to castigate the Industrial Mobilization Plan and charge them with warmongering. In the process the measures for lesser preparedness that Congress appeared ready to pass could be jeopardized.[114]

Several other aspects of the IMP, 1939, are noteworthy. Other than the War Resources Administration, the Army-Navy Munitions Board was the only economic mobilization agency fully described in the text of the plan. And, reversing the IMP, 1936, the board could now move to set up the War Resources Administration. Disclaimers to the contrary, the armed services intended to maximize their influence in a mobilized economy. While doing so, however, the OASW demonstrated a better sense of priority than in its earlier work. The IMP, 1939, opened with economic mobilization planning and closed with procurement planning, not vice versa as had been the case in all other plans.[115] The planners recognized fully that military supply was only part of a much larger economic scheme, overcoming a strong measure of military parochialism.

Despite the planners' ten years of experience, the IMP, 1939, was not well integrated. Key proposals appeared in some of the unpublished, secret annexes, not in the IMP proper. The principal legislation intended as the legal foundation for the whole mobilization system, for example, appeared in three annexes. All annexes contained the critical three-stage, as opposed to M-Day, mobilization procedure, but it was unstandarized and varied from one annex to the other.[116]

The piecemeal quality of the IMP, 1939, probably stemmed more from sloppy, hurried composition than from desires for secrecy. Some of the unpublished material would have benefited the military had it been known. The War

Trade Board Annex, for example, provided for the War Resources Administration acting as a coordinate, not a superior agency,[117] a position Roosevelt favored.[118] The War Finance Annex urged that the War Resources Board be established expeditiously so as to preclude a possibly unqualified ANMB serving as the transitional agency or serving for only a short period before returning to its military duties.[119] Furthermore, the Facilities Annex emphasized protecting civilian uses in wartime and using the full production potential of small business.[120] And measures for preventing profiteering, equalizing war burdens, and rationalizing war finances appeared in the bill for creating the War Resources Board.[121] Even if preferring to keep the annexes unpublished, the OASW could have incorporated into the IMP proper the concepts from the annexes that were significant to mobilization and beneficial to the reputation of the armed services' planning.

Perennial problems of personnel shortages, constant and rapid turnover, and the pressure of time probably account for the flaws. The OASW personnel also declined in quality in the late 1930s. In light of the importance of the IMP to the armed services and to the nation, the War Department should have moved to correct these long- and short-term problems plaguing the planning. It could ill afford to turn out a final Industrial Mobilization Plan that was less than first-rate.

Despite flaws, economic mobilization planning by the Office of the Assistant Secretary of War, assisted by the Army-Navy Munitions Board, had reached a significant level of accomplishment. With the War Resources Administration, the OASW not only recreated a counterpart of the World War I War Industries Board but also improved upon and more fully rationalized the general mobilization program that had existed at the end of 1918. In the Industrial Mobilization Plan, 1939, to use OASW language, the WRA was the "pivot" around which all other mobilization agencies turned. Although an alternative existed in having other superagencies act as coordinate, not subordinate bodies, a wartime economy would function best with the WRA in a position of dominance.

A weak spot in OASW planning was turning selective service and public relations over to the General Staff. Both the staff and the OASW needed a voice in selective service, but neither should have been involved with public relations. War planning would have been better served had the General Staff and the OASW shared decisionmaking over selective service, with planning for public relations handled by nonmilitary sources. The OASW appeared to be moving in that direction, but its troubled relations with the General Staff limited what the office could do.

Civilian contributions to the planning were of great importance. Frank A. Scott and his associates made their greatest contribution in the 1920s with procurement and initial economic mobilization planning. Bernard M. Baruch and his coterie were most influential in the 1930s with the writing of the industrial mobilization plans. This followed the pattern of World War I, in which the former group held sway in 1916–1917 as mobilization methods were worked out and the latter became dominant in 1918 once the War Industries Board took its final form and acquired significant authority. Both stages were important to economic mobilization and planning for it.

Stages aside, Scott and his circle institutionalized and gave continuity to their contribution through organizations like the Ordnance Procurement Districts and the Army Ordnance Association. Baruch and his supporters depended more on political influence, publicity, and personal contacts. Though leaving a deep imprint, Baruch's group lacked a vehicle for perpetuating its presence and goals. Baruch always operated more as an individual leading lieutenants than as a full participant in the operations of the corporate-financial world. He was an associate, more than a member, of America's economic elite. By comparison, Scott and Benedict Crowell were much more traditional figures, well integrated into the economic system with its numerous associations and groupings.[122] The different approaches surfaced in mobilizing the World War II economy as they had during World War I.

The OASW's industrial mobilization planning by necessity followed and gave perspective to the office's procurement planning. Together the two forms of planning prepared the armed services for warfare better than had ever before been the case.

Procurement planning was principally a military function continuously evaluated by the supply arms and services' interaction with the industrial and business community. That was not the case with the industrial mobilization plans, which involved the entire economy. Earlier versions of the IMP had been scrutinized and criticized by the War Policies Committee and the Senate Special Committee Investigating the Munitions Industry. As the OASW's last blueprint, the Industrial Mobilization Plan, 1939, required civilian review for validation. That final act was performed by the War Resources Board late in 1939.

3
MILITARY-BUSINESS RELATIONS, 1920–1939

Interwar procurement and economic mobilization planning by the Office of the Assistant Secretary of War (OASW) drew the military and business worlds closer together than ever before in American peacetime history. The planning broadened and deepened the relations between the armed services and business which had taken on a new level of importance during World War I and which reached maturity during World War II. The interwar years, therefore, were a significant period of transition in civil-military relations.

The army, and particularly the Ordnance Department, led the way in basically revising relations between the military and industry. Contacts with business began in a slow and hesitant manner in the 1920s and then grew steadily until actual mobilization began late in the 1930s. At first, prominent war mobilizers such as Benedict Crowell, assistant secretary of war during World War I, constituted the OASW's primary link to the economic community. Crowell and others had close ties with the Ordnance Department, and they advised and assisted the army planners either as individuals or through such organizations as the recently founded Army Ordnance Association, the Ordnance Districts, and similar groups. Engineers, associated with the Ordnance Department and other supply arms and services (SA&S), and their organizations, such as the American Society of Mechanical Engineers, also provided valuable assistance in procurement and economic mobilization planning.

The OASW relied on business federations to advance the cause of economic preparedness in general. In that regard, Ordnance Department connections facilitated relations with the National Industrial Conference Board and the National Association of Manufacturers. Military ties to the U.S. Chamber of Commerce were largely absent, which explains in part why that organization was slower than other business groups to support OASW planning.

Army relations with the business community were closely attuned to prevalent trends in the political economy. Attempts at economic rationalization by the

Republican administrations during the prosperity decade and by the Democratic administration in the depression decade acted to facilitate OASW planning.

The War Department's interaction with industry gave a maturity to its planning that otherwise would have been lacking. In the long run, the extensive contacts with business and the basic knowledge about the economic system resulting from planning were as important as, perhaps even more significant than, the plans themselves. The contacts and knowledge convinced the army planners that the economy's potential was key to fulfilling the twentieth-century military mission.

THE ECONOMY IN THE INTERWAR YEARS

The structure of the economy in the interwar years was somewhat different from that which existed in the early years of the twentieth century, but not in any far-reaching way.[1] In 1919, 1929, and 1939, as in 1903, 1909, and 1917, the strength and growth of the economy depended primarily on oligopolistic industries (defined as six or fewer firms accounting for 50 percent or twelve or fewer firms accounting for 75 percent of total product value in a given industry). Roughly three out of ten industries were concentrated in this way between 1909 and 1939, but they had a rising importance in the economy, accounting for 16 percent of total product value in 1909 and 28 percent in 1939. The oligopolistic industries tended to be the newer ones and included chemicals, petroleum, rubber, primary metals, electrical machinery, and transportation equipment and vehicles. Firms such as E. I. du Pont de Nemours and Company, Standard Oil Company of New Jersey, B. F. Goodrich Company, United States Steel Corporation, General Electric Company, and the Ford Motor Company were prominent.

A second tier of older industries experienced moderate concentration along oligopolistic lines, but the largest companies seldom accounted for more than 25 percent of total value produced. This group included textiles, paper, fabricated metal products, machinery, and food.

The last tier, and in some instances the oldest industries, experienced negligible concentration, the biggest firms never producing more than 3 percent of total output. Here were found leather, publishing and printing, lumber and wood, furniture, and apparel. The second tier included giant firms like Armour and Company, and the third Weyerhaeuser Timber Company, but they were a minority in the former and exceptional in the latter.

The concentrated industries were fairly well established after the massive merger movement between 1897 and 1903. From then until the 1920s, the giant corporations in these industries followed a path of growth through vertical integration in which they incorporated in one firm all or most inputs of production and marketed their own goods. Simultaneously, these firms developed a full line of products—i.e., commodities made by comparable production technologies for quite similar markets.

By 1920 America's industrial giants in the oligopolistic industries were adopting a new growth strategy through diversification, meaning the use of approximately similar technologies to produce commodities for very different markets. Thus, the major corporations in the 1920s and 1930s operated in five different industries. General Motors Corporation, for example, began producing and selling diesel locomotives, household appliances, tractors, and airplanes. This process was accelerated by the pressures of the depression, which forced sharp reductions in existing lines of goods. The diversification process would not reach full maturity until around 1960, when many major firms in the concentrated industries produced in ten or more major industries and had become truly multi-industrial. Corporations in the most technologically advanced industries—chemicals, rubber, and electrical and transportation machinery—led the way in diversification; industries of less sophisticated technology, like metals, food, other machinery, and oil, also diversified, but at a slower pace. In the interwar years, Du Pont, U.S. Rubber Company, General Electric, and General Motors continued to lead in shaping the modern American economy.

Big business achieved and maintained its status partly because it possessed or had acquired the research and development funds and skills to invent, use, or adapt new technologies for making new products. Growth of new product lines, however, was not enough. New management and administrative systems were also essential. To run the emerging multi-industrial firms, corporate managers gradually devised the decentralized structure in which different lines of production were handled totally by autonomous corporate divisions, with a general office evaluating them and allocating resources among the firm's parts.

The interwar years, then, saw the beginning of rapid diversification of the giant firms in the oligopolistic industries. Around 200 corporations constituted the muscle of the gigantic American economic machine. Not only did these firms provide the basis for growth and strength of the economy, but they also constituted the wherewithal for it to wage war. The huge corporations in the consolidated industries were the prime government contractors in World War II and after.

The emergence of diversified corporations with decentralized managerial structures in the concentrated industries facilitated coordination and planning within the industrial community and between it and the government. It was through this structure that the Republican administrations in the 1920s sought indirectly to plan the economy. Coordination of the same system dominated the National Recovery Administration (NRA) during the early years of the New Deal and continued to be the basis of any recovery program after 1935 even without a formal planning structure. Trade associations had also become a significant feature of the business community. The commodity section–war service committee system of the War Industries Board (WIB) had provided the stimulus for bringing the modern trade association movement to maturity. In the 1920s the Republican administrations encouraged trade association growth, especially in the competitive industries. Some large, consolidated industries had such groupings, as was the case with steel and oil, but they were less essential for coordination and planning than was the case in the smaller, unconcentrated fields. The NRA also served to stimulate the growth and strength of trade associations, as did the pressures and tensions of the depression.[2]

The government played a significant role in the growing rationalization of industry. In the 1920s no government agency was more dedicated to business than the Commerce Department. Under Herbert Hoover, the department was restructured to match the business community, and its representatives were integrated into the department in official or advisory capacities reminiscent of the WIB. The New Deal's NRA was patterned quite explicitly on World War I's planning venture, with antitrust laws overlooked and a form of cartelization in operation.[3]

If changes of significance occurred within the industrial community and in its relations with government, the same was true of other interest groups. A decade of depression for farmers in the prosperous 1920s led in the late 1920s to hesitant planning and in the 1930s to full-blown planning for agriculture, sponsored and carried out by the federal government. As a result of these efforts, dealing with millions of farmers in an organized way was thereafter much more possible.

No economic group experienced more dramatic changes in the interwar years than the blue-collar workers in the mass production industries. Starting first with the American Federation of Labor and later the Congress of Industrial Organizations, and with the encouragement and protection of the 1935 National Labor Relations Act, the primary work force was organized into industrial unions in the depression years. Union membership had stood at around 3 million in 1933; it had tripled to about 9 million by 1939.

Interwar prosperity and depression in no way altered the essential shape of the economy. But in numerous areas changes of substance had taken place. Generally speaking, the business community was more organized and more organizable in 1939 than it had been in 1919, the government's size and responsibilities were much greater, and other economic interest groups were also better structured for centralized direction. Those developments made the economic system more subject to coordination and planning than had been the case at the outset of the interwar period.

THE ORDNANCE DEPARTMENT, THE ORDNANCE DISTRICTS, AND THE ARMY ORDNANCE ASSOCIATION

Relations between the Office of the Assistant Secretary of War and business in the 1920s largely grew from activities and organizations associated with the Ordnance Department. That made sense since Ordnance was the most active and accomplished bureau of the supply arms and services in procurement and economic mobilization planning.[4]

The fourteen Ordnance Procurement Districts were key to the Ordnance Department's elaborate ties with corporate and financial America. Prominent businessmen acted as chiefs of the districts with staffs that could be expanded in an emergency. Civilians serving in this capacity often were or became reserve officers. Frank A. Scott, for example, was chief of the Cleveland Ordnance District from 1924 to 1928 and had a staff drawn from firms like Ohio Bell Telephone Company and National Malleable Casting Company, and a group of attorneys. Districts also created advisory boards of varying size composed principally of businessmen from the region. The New York District, headed by James L. Walsh, associated with the Bankers Trust Company of New York, featured a large advisory board with representatives from giant firms, including U.S. Steel, General Electric, and Westinghouse Electric and Manufacturing Company. From time to time the Ordnance Districts created subsidiary bodies such as the Ordnance District Contract Boards to study contracting in wartime. Assigned to each Ordnance District was a regular army officer from the Ordnance Department, who, as the only full-time official and executive officer to the chief, was indispensable to the district's operation.[5]

The Army Ordnance Association (AOA) was organized by the Ordnance Department and civilians on active duty with the bureau during the war. Walsh, at the time a regular army Ordnance colonel who served as executive assistant to the chief of ordnance from July 1, 1918, to January 2, 1920, oversaw the creation of the AOA in 1919–1920. In doing so, he worked closely with business executives like Guy E. Tripp, chairman of the board of Westinghouse, Samuel McRoberts, vice-president of the National City Bank, and Scott, vice-president of the Warner and Swasey Company. Tripp, who had become a brigadier general during the war and served as chief of the Ordnance Department's Production Division, had been instrumental in establishing the Ordnance District system during the war. McRoberts, also a temporary brigadier general, had headed the Procurement Division in Washington and had served with the American Expeditionary Forces (AEF); Scott chaired the War Industries Board and its predecessor. The three businessmen became longtime members of the association's Board of Directors. Benedict Crowell, chairman of Crowell and Little Construction Company of Cleveland, was elected president in 1919 and continued in that post until 1945.[6]

Once the AOA was under way, the Ordnance Department continued to play a crucial role in its operations. Walsh acted as the first secretary (later, and more accurately, designated as executive secretary) and editor of the AOA's journal, *Army Ordnance,* from 1919 to 1922. Until the end of 1929 Walsh's successors as secretary/editor were regular army Ordnance officers. That practice ended when Congress moved to prohibit military personnel from working on publications in which government contractors advertised. Moreover, the job of running the association became too demanding for a regular army officer expected to fulfill other duties as well. Thereafter, the position of executive secretary and editor was filled by Leo A. Codd, a reserve Ordnance officer, who had served for a number of years as the associate editor of *Army Ordnance* and assisted the executive secretary. In 1940 Codd became executive vice-president and secretary of the AOA, and during World War II he returned to active duty as a member of the executive staff of Gen. Levin H. Campbell, Jr., chief of ordnance from 1942 to 1946. After the war, Codd returned to his AOA posts and served until his retirement in 1963. As the only paid and full-time officer, the executive secretary was the drive wheel of the association.[7]

An intricate web of personal and institutional ties bound the Ordnance Department, Army Ordnance Association, and Ordnance Districts together. The AOA established local posts that paralleled the boundaries of the Ordnance Districts, and the same personnel frequently staffed the two structures; Ordnance District chiefs often served simultaneously as directors of the AOA; and the regular Ordnance officers assigned as executive secretaries to the districts recruited for the AOA and acted to keep the two organizations synchronized. Many Ordnance officers were AOA members, most AOA officials were or became Ordnance reserve officers, and the chief of ordnance and subordinate officers took an active part in AOA affairs. When retiring in 1930 after twelve years as Ordnance chief, Gen. Clarence C. Williams became an AOA director. Additionally, the Ordnance Department arranged for the AOA to hold its annual meetings at the Aberdeen Proving Grounds in Maryland. The yearly affairs usually demanded considerable time and attention from the staff and line.[8]

With its close Ordnance ties and support, the AOA had an easier time getting started than did similar organizations. In the early years, it operated on a lean budget of $15,000–$20,000 annually. Membership stood at about 2,500 in 1921, with active army officers making up about 15 percent of that number and the rest coming from those involved (or potentially involved) in munitions production or engineering and military preparedness enthusiasts. In the next few years, membership remained stable or dropped. Once the Ordnance Districts were reestablished and the AOA had local posts, however, the association's membership began to rise again. Growth was facilitated by the creation of company memberships in 1929. This move enabled a firm involved or interested in munitions production or preparedness to join the AOA for a set fee with special privileges, including ten free membership slots for selected employees. Various AOA officials worried that company members would associate the organization with the "merchants of death."[9]

By 1926 the Army Ordnance Association had passed through its initial stages of organization, was on a sound footing, and was entering a new period of activity and vitality. By 1930 its membership was up to nearly 3,500, its finances were sound, and its influence and prestige were enhanced. Despite the financial impact of the Great Depression and growing antagonism to war and the military in the 1930s, the AOA managed to survive and even to grow in strength, though its membership dropped.[10]

Actually, the AOA's influence was greater in the 1920s than in the 1930s. The Office of the Assistant Secretary of War needed all the help it could get in the earlier decade. Also, the depression and the institutional upheavals in Washington during the 1930s reduced the impact of organizations like the AOA that were dedicated to conservative values. Moreover, association members were mostly Republicans and, hence, exercised more influence in the Republican decade of the 1920s than in the Democratic years of the 1930s.

The first and most sustained work of the AOA and the Ordnance Districts with the OASW involved procurement planning. Industrialists with Ordnance connections created special committees to advise the War Department on general and specific production problems, wartime contract forms, and critical and essential products.[11] Additionally, in 1928 Ordnance Districts set up a program of study involving private plants such as Warner and Swasey and government arsenals to familiarize Ordnance officers with the design and production of munitions so as to improve procurement practices.[12]

These were workaday functions, but they could not be carried out effectively without the support and cooperation of industrialists in the Ordnance Districts and the AOA. Had the army approached manufacturers without the introduction or backing of these men, many doors would have remained closed. Assistant Secretary of War Hanford MacNider observed that while about 125 officers involved in procurement planning performed 50 percent of all military preparedness activity, their numbers were augmented manyfold by volunteers in the Ordnance Districts. "If we did not have those District Chiefs putting in that effort in the industrial districts of this country," he declared, "we could be in a sad way indeed."[13]

The AOA and the Ordnance Districts also played an often crucial part in initiating economic mobilization planning. Beginning in 1921 Scott, Palmer E. Pierce, and others persisted in the face of discouraging prospects in helping the OASW to see the need for going beyond procurement planning.[14] From the outset, two Ordnance officers—Maj. Morgan L. Brett, who served first in the OASW and later as executive officer of the San Francisco Ordnance District, and Maj. Richard H. Somers, who was executive secretary of the AOA from 1922 to 1925 and later on the OASW staff—had an excellent grasp of what economic mobilization entailed. They combined their efforts with those of Scott and others to move the assistant secretary's office toward the larger planning.[15] Somers originated the concept of an Army Industrial College (AIC), and he and Brett worked with Scott, former Secretary of War Newton D. Baker, and others to perfect the idea, win support for it within the army, and secure bipartisan political backing for what they considered to be "one of the most important steps taken by the War Department since the Armistice."[16] Scott joined Bernard M. Baruch, Elbert H. Gary, Walter S. Gifford, Robert S. Brookings, Daniel Willard, and other prominent figures as honorary advisers to the AIC.[17] These individuals and numerous other officials involved in wartime economic mobilization lectured before the college. First Scott and later Baruch virtually became standard parts of the college's curriculum, appearing almost annually and consulting regularly about industrial mobilization matters.[18]

At almost every stage of the OASW's development in the 1920s, businessmen played some role, if only by lending their prestige through serving on various advisory boards. In 1926, for example, the War Department organized a Business Council to help introduce modern business techniques into army operations and to familiarize industrialists with army procurement and planning methods. Sitting on this council were such luminaries as John J. Carty, vice-president, American Telephone and Telegraph Company, Edward C. Delafield, president, Bank of America, Gerard Swope, president, General Electric, William C. Spruance, vice-president, Du Pont, and James Bonner, sales manager, U.S. Steel. Most of these men were members of or associated with the AOA, Ordnance Districts, and the economic preparedness movement. Leonard P. Ayers, vice-president of the Cleveland Trust Company, also a member of the Business Council, and a World War I mobilizer, had been called upon earlier to advise and assist the OASW with statistical work.[19]

The AOA and Ordnance District members also involved themselves in the selection and promotion of leaders they favored. Without the efforts of Scott and his associates, Assistant Secretary of War Dwight F. Davis probably would not have been elevated to secretary of war in 1925. In that year, the very talented but physically ill John W. Weeks retired.[20] Davis had served as assistant secretary since 1923 and had demonstrated capability for and dedication to the job that appeared to warrant his promotion to the higher slot. With a secretary of war who had served for over two years as the civilian chief of procurement and economic mobilization planning, the preparedness advocates believed that they would have nearly an ideal leader. To achieve their goal, the AOA and Ordnance Districts turned to Elbert H. Gary, chairman of the board of U.S. Steel, and William F. Durand, a past president of the American Society of Mechanical Engineers and a prominent economic mobilization figure since World War I, to persuade the Calvin Coolidge administration to tap Davis for the post.[21]

Less than a year after becoming secretary of war, Davis experienced the same type of political pressure that had landed him his job. The circumstances grew from the future status of an assistant chief of ordnance, Brig. Gen. Colden L'H. Ruggles, who had responsibilities for the Ordnance Districts and the production of Ordnance materiel. Ruggles would complete his four-year appointment in March 1927 and could expect reappointment, except that Davis was instituting a new policy prohibiting continuous service. By all accounts, Ruggles's performance was outstanding, and he was held in especially high regard by the Ordnance Districts for his efforts in bringing the civilian and military worlds together. Ordnance District chiefs quickly stepped in to point out to Davis that his no-reappointment policy would undermine the entire bureau structure. For Ordnance the move would be particularly distressing because over six years of hard work by military and civilian personnel was just beginning to show results. Any successor to Ruggles would be unable to match for some time, if ever, his experience, level of understanding, and dynamic leadership. The secretary of war rather quickly backed off and arranged for Ruggles to be redetailed.[22]

The AOA and the Ordnance Districts had less success in influencing War Department personnel decisions in the 1930s. In late 1932 and early 1933, Leo A. Codd, then executive secretary of the AOA, could not persuade the Franklin D. Roosevelt administration to appoint a designated preparedness enthusiast as assistant secretary of war.[23] In 1934, with Codd again assuming the initiative, AOA leaders were also unsuccessful in accelerating the advancement of Col. Charles M. Wesson in the Ordnance Department hierarchy.[24] Throughout the 1920s and 1930s, however, the AOA continued to exercise considerable influence in the selection and promotion of reserve officers.[25]

The OASW depended on Army Ordnance, the Ordnance Districts, reserve officers, the Reserve Officers Association, and other preparedness advocates to lobby in and outside the War Department for policies to further industrial preparedness that had to be approached cautiously. Of particular importance were rank for OASW officers comparable to that of the General Staff and the SA&S, more equitable distribution of funds and personnel within the department for procurement and economic mobilization planning as opposed to manpower planning, and a greater voice for the assistant secretary of war in budget and personnel matters. Movement in these areas was blocked or took place only gradually and incrementally.[26]

A greater measure of success occurred with educational orders. The Ordnance Department took the lead in reversing statutes that prohibited such orders since it required a long lead time in producing weapons and faced pressures of constantly advancing technology.[27] Finally, in 1927, the War Department had a bill authorizing educational orders introduced in Congress, but the department felt that it could neither lobby for such legislation nor sanction a publicity effort in the bill's behalf. However, Ordnance District chiefs stepped in to mobilize their forces, along with those of the American Legion and the National Association of Manufacturers, to win the support of business for educational orders as part of a larger preparedness package.

Although the 1927 measure for educational orders never reached the floor of Congress, it was reintroduced almost annually until finally becoming law in 1938. During the 1930s, the AOA also advocated educational orders as part of a larger plan for using military spending as an antidote to the depression. In this regard the army was, to the distress of AOA elements such as Codd, less aggressive than the navy in securing such funds.[28]

Industrialists working with the military through the Ordnance Districts, the AOA, and other institutions often became frustrated by what they considered hidebound military regulations and meaningless or counterproductive procedures. Limits on the number, rank, and training of reserve officers were especially irksome.[29] Moreover, Ordnance could be insensitive and irritating, as was the case when it transferred Scott's Ordnance District executive officer without consulting him.[30]

Keeping businessmen, manufacturers, engineers, and other professionals committed to preparedness was no easy task. Most were willing to participate on an intermittent, ad hoc basis. When it came to the regular, continuous, and long-run service in the Ordnance Districts and as reserve officers, troubles mounted. Throughout the documents of Scott and others runs a constant refrain that visits to the districts by the secretary and assistant secretary of war, the chief of ordnance, and other high officials, along with more frequent meetings and communications, were needed to stir greater interest in military concerns. Part of the problem grew from the inevitably tight schedules of exceptionally busy executives. But the slow-moving, apparently inefficient, and bureaucratic military put off or dampened the interest of many professionals dedicated to preparedness.[31]

These immediate matters were compounded by the inclination of many businessmen to dismiss the possibility of a future war. B. F. Franklin, chief of the Bridgeport District, described this attitude when writing to the secretary of war in early 1927:

> The whole development of this Industrial Preparedness has been a matter of considerable thought and interest to me, because I saw the great difficulties of inertia on the part of a body of reserve officers, and on the part of a body of manufacturers who were asked to actively believe that a war was likely to take place some time in the future, when according to their human nature, whether rightly or wrongly, they do not believe that any such thing is liable to happen in their time.[32]

Despite the obstacles to procurement and economic mobilization planning that originated in and outside the military, the job did begin.[33] The most significant role of the Army Ordnance Association, Ordnance Districts, and other preparedness organizations and advocates in that planning was bringing substantial business elements and their organizations into contact with army planners.

Shortly after its creation, the Army Ordnance Association began reaching out to include other organizations in its activities. This move was most evident in the annual meetings held at the Ordnance Department's Aberdeen Proving Grounds. At first the association invited technical and professional organizations like the American Society of Mechanical Engineers. Soon, however, it began to broaden its approach to include business and industrial organizations such as the American Iron and Steel Institute and the Chamber of Commerce. The annual meetings constantly grew in size, importance, and in the prominence of the individuals and organizations participating. By 1927 around 6,000 people attended the annual meeting, almost twice the membership of the AOA itself.[34]

Army Ordnance's annual meetings in the interwar years were the largest and most frequent national gatherings devoted to industrial preparedness.

They provided the various branches of the army with the opportunity to demonstrate their weapons and procedures and also permitted them to join with AOA leaders in setting forth the importance of procurement and economic mobilization planning. Military and civilian leaders alike realized the value of constantly reminding businessmen about the importance of keeping the nation economically prepared for hostilities.[35] In February 1930, in arranging for the Twelfth Annual Meeting at Aberdeen, Benedict Crowell, long-time president of the AOA, wrote to Secretary of War Patrick J. Hurley: "I believe I am accurate in saying that these gatherings and demonstrations have been one of the most influential factors in sustaining interest in industrial preparedness and in the characteristics of munitions design."[36]

As least as important as the annual meetings of the AOA were the activities of the association's local posts. In that regard, no local post was more important than the one in New York, organized in 1921. Guy E. Tripp served as president of the New York Post for a number of years, and John Ross Delafield, who replaced Henry L. Stimson as counsel to the AOA in 1929 and in October 1923 assumed the presidency of the Reserve Officers Association of the United States, was also an officer. James L. Walsh, however, was the real moving spirit behind the New York Post. Along with Scott, Pierce, and a few others, he became one of the top civilian economic preparedness advocates.[37]

The New York Post's location in the nation's leading city gave it an enormous advantage. It was no accident that in November 1922 the secretary and assistant secretary of war and deputy chief of staff chose to give their maiden public speeches in behalf of industrial preparedness at the New York AOA Local.[38] Walsh's success stemmed as well from his ability to recruit a high-powered, prestigious advisory board to the New York Ordnance District that operated in close association with the local post. The board was chaired by Gary and included Patrick E. Crowley, president, New York Central Lines, James G. Harbord, president, Radio Corporation of America, Charles M. Schwab, chairman of the board, Bethlehem Steel Corporation, and Tripp.[39]

Walsh knew how to use the high profile of these names to gain maximum publicity for preparedness. For example, in September 1924 the New York Ordnance District staged an economic war game to test its procurement plans during National Defense Day. With men like Gary and Harbord involved, the event received a great deal of favorable press coverage.[40] Walsh constantly called upon Gary for assistance. In March 1925 Walsh arranged for the head of U.S. Steel to host a luncheon for Gen. Charles P. Summerall, who would serve as chief of staff from 1926 to 1930, and other preparedness figures, to introduce them to "a fair cross section of down town New York business life."

The guest list was based on an expanded list of New York AOA and Ordnance District members and read like a who's who of the business world.[41]

Walsh also either headed or was closely involved in efforts to have the New York Post involve the major engineering societies in the industrial preparedness movement. On February 5, 1924, the New York Post, in cooperation with the War Department, joined forces with five leading national engineering societies to sponsor an Industrial Preparedness Dinner in New York City. Gary presided over the affair, at which Assistant Secretary of War Davis was the featured speaker. This was probably the largest and most prestigious post–World War I industrial preparedness event up to that time.[42]

THE OASW AND ENGINEERING SOCIETIES

The American Society of Mechanical Engineers (ASME) was among the major engineering societies most active in economic mobilization activities. The society had a membership of 17,500 and had assisted the Ordnance Department's procurement planning as early as 1921–1922 through its Ordnance Division, which in 1924 was expanded into the Ordnance and Aeronautical Division and in that same year finally became the National Defense Division. In mid-1923 the society's longtime secretary, Calvin W. Rice, insisted that the ASME should play a major role in the planning of the assistant secretary of war's office. He maintained that his organization could be structured to parallel the War Department's Procurement Districts and that the society could aid all bureaus, not just the Ordnance Department and the Air Service. The ASME had been especially successful in persuading engineering societies to cooperate with the military on the local level. The same accommodation, Rice proclaimed, could be accomplished for procurement and economic mobilization planning at the national level. Moreover, Rice constantly warned, preparation for war faced great opposition. In order for the OASW to fulfill its tasks, widespread support for and understanding of its functions would have to be generated nationally and in Congress. He proposed that the ASME, along with other leading engineering societies, help mobilize that support. Rice appears to have been motivated primarily by patriotism. He resembled Howard E. Coffin in his enthusiasm, energy, and devotion to organization, formulated and directed by engineers, as the key to success in modern societies. Like most preparedness advocates, Rice had served in World War I and sought to perpetuate the war's sense of purpose and community.[43]

Close personal affiliations bound the ASME to the Army Ordnance Association and the Ordnance District system. Frank A. Scott headed the National

Defense Division from 1924 through 1926, and his executive committee included the assistant chief of the Cleveland Ordnance District, James B. Dillard, and Brig. Gen. Colden L'H. Ruggles, an assistant chief of ordnance. The other committee members were reserve officers, with Lt. C. W. Whitney, executive officer of the Cleveland Ordnance District, acting as secretary. To further its work, the National Defense Division strove to create local committees throughout the nation. James L. Walsh headed up the effort in New York. The ties also ran the other way. Rice, for example, was an Ordnance reserve officer, a charter member of the AOA, and active in Ordnance District affairs.

For a time it appeared that the ASME would become a leading private mobilization organization. Engineering groups were prepared to join the War Department in conducting a census of engineers and business executives and in determining who desired reserve or regular military service or might serve successfully in various mobilization structures. In late 1924 ASME personnel worked out procedures for representatives of principal army and navy supply bureaus to serve as "cooperating members" of the National Defense Division. The division also sketched out proposals for educating engineers and the general public about the virtues of economic preparedness.

The National Defense Division held frequent meetings with the armed services to further the goals of industrial preparedness. Special sessions of the division were held at the spring meetings of the ASME in 1924 and 1925. For the annual convention in December 1925, the National Defense Division gathered engineers and industrialists to hear Secretary of War Dwight F. Davis deliver a nationally broadcast speech on industrial preparedness. The highlight of the National Defense Division's efforts came at an Industrial Preparedness Meeting in New York City on December 4, 1925. Once again Elbert H. Gary was tapped to officiate, and he also hosted a private dinner for notables, including the secretary and assistant secretary of war, army generals, chiefs of the bureaus' Procurement Districts and their advisory boards, presidents of all the major engineering societies, mobilization leaders from World War I, and representatives from principal banks, manufacturers, railroads, and public utilities. At the meeting itself, Secretary of War Davis, Assistant Secretary of War MacNider, and James G. Harbord, former chief of staff to Gen. John J. Pershing's Army Expeditionary Forces, were the featured speakers. Just prior to the event, Scott observed:

> We have succeeded, for this occasion, in uniting a number of the great engineering interests and organizations in a gathering which we hope will be of national significance. . . . The whole scope and purpose of the

gathering is to emphasize our work of Industrial Preparedness upon the engineering and industrial minds of our country.[44]

The grandiose plans of Rice and the ASME never materialized. Even the limited goal of classifying engineering and other talent proved overly complicated and expensive. The OASW proceeded cautiously with Rice and his assistants since Rice seemed almost intent on taking over or duplicating the office's work. Even if army planners were not protective of their turf, procurement and economic mobilization planning was not far enough advanced between 1923 and 1926 for engineering societies to do much good. Further, supply bureaus besides Ordnance were not sufficiently interested in either planning or in the help of engineers to make the effort worthwhile. Each of the supply bureaus had organizations like the AOA, and they, not the ASME and other engineering groups, were the logical organizations to aid the supply arms and services.

Engineers differed over the role of their organizations in preparedness. William C. Spruance and Coulter Craig, for example, Du Pont executives, members of the ASME and AOA, and Ordnance reserve officers, argued that engineering societies should leave planning to the AOA and associations affiliated with other supply bureaus in order to concentrate on reversing antimilitary and antipreparedness attitudes and on creating a positive image for the armed services. Engineers were ideal for this approach since, unlike munitions manufacturers and trade associations, they were viewed as disinterested parties. Scott and Walsh disagreed. By attracting leaders like Gary to planning, the engineering societies helped persuade other large manufacturers to follow suit. Moreover, Scott insisted, distinguished engineers involved in procurement and economic mobilization activities helped validate the claim that planning was intended to guarantee peace, not prepare for war.[45] Moreover, although the AOA was of great help to Ordnance Department planning, that was not true of organizations associated with the other bureaus. They were small, rather nominal groups, and the SA&S did not need or want that much assistance.[46]

Middle ground between Spruance and Scott was found by the American Institute of Mining and Metallurgical Engineers (AIME). Relations between the AIME and the OASW became a model of civil-military links in the interwar years. In part this resulted from the outstanding leadership qualities of Arthur S. Dwight, president of the AIME and a reserve officer in the Corps of Engineers. Also of significance was the sensible response of the assistant secretary of war's office. The society was among the first private groups to approach the OASW about assisting in the planning, and the army planners were eager to work out good relations with the society so as to set a positive pattern for other organizations. Dwight offered the services of his society to the OASW with the idea that the latter should determine what the former could and should do.[47]

The OASW at first flirted with vague and impractical schemes similar to those put forward by the American Society of Mechanical Engineers. They were ultimately scrapped in favor of having the AIME assist the OASW in devising plans for dealing with strategic metals. Between January and March 1922 the AIME and the OASW set up committees to work out details for the enterprise. At first the army planners thought the society could write the plans, but proposals for shifting responsibility were quickly abandoned. Instead, AIME studies of various metals for the OASW would include sources of supply in and outside the United States during wartime and projected wartime demand. "For our immediate purposes this is all that is necessary," Dwight observed, "but later it may prove desirable to supplement this statement of facts by an analysis, based on our war experience, on the specific steps and machinery necessary to make sure of an adequate supply."[48]

The committees operated under a high-powered body, the Committee on Industrial Preparedness, chaired by Dwight and consisting of George Otis Smith, director of the U.S. Geological Survey, H. Foster Bain, director of the U.S. Bureau of Mines, Josiah Edward Spurr, editor of *Engineering and Mining Journal* and, earlier, of *Political and Commercial Geology,* Pope Yeatman, consulting mining engineer, and Charles K. Leith, professor and chair, Geology Department, University of Wisconsin. Spurr and Yeatman had played key roles involving metals and minerals during economic mobilization for World War I. Under the Committee on Industrial Preparedness, six subcommittees were set up to study chrome, manganese, mercury, tin, tungsten, and vanadium. Later, graphite, petroleum, and platinum were added to this list, and finally, a Subcommittee on Nonferrous Smelting and Refining was created to study copper, zinc, lead, and brass.

As it turned out, the AIME's Industrial Preparedness Committee paralleled almost identically in structure, personnel, and function the Committee on Domestic and Foreign Mining Policy of the Mining and Metallurgical Society of America, although the second committee focused more on peacetime conditions and the first had a wartime slant. To avoid duplication of effort and rivalry between the two societies, which shared a largely identical membership, the subcommittee studies became a joint venture, although the AIME clearly remained the dominant institution. Due to the well-connected membership of the AIME's Industrial Preparedness Committee and the fact that many people belonging to the institute worked for the government, the subcommittees had access to often unequaled archives of the federal government and especially to those of the Geological Survey and the Bureau of Mines.

Writing high-quality reports turned out to be much more demanding than anyone had expected, requiring extensive effort and often considerable expense from the AIME and its members. The biggest source of difficulty often turned out to be conflicting information about manganese and other raw materials supplied by industry and directly or indirectly involving America's largest corporations. Most of the subcommittees completed their reports in 1923 and updated them later in the decade at the request of the War Department.

Acting on the suggestion of J. W. Furness—chief, Minerals Division, Bureau of Foreign and Domestic Commerce, Department of Commerce, and later chief, Economics Branch, Bureau of Mines—the War Department in 1928 created a Mineral Advisory Committee. Made up of members from the AIME, the Mining and Metallurgical Society of America, and the War Department, the committee was intended to go beyond the narrowly focused research of the minerals subcommittees. It examined larger issues such as changes in domestic supply of minerals and the impact of new uses for certain metals. As the war approached, the Mineral Advisory Committee late in 1938 was placed under the restructured Army-Navy Munitions Board with some changes in membership and with the Navy Department represented. Under this arrangement, the Mineral Advisory Committee set aside larger issues of industrial mobilization to focus on more immediate and detailed information necessary to prepare for war. Subcommittees were again created to study strategic minerals and metals.[49] As the transition from planning to economic mobilization began in 1939, the Mineral Advisory Committee of the Army-Navy Munitions Board (ANMB) became a part of the mobilization structure.

The American Institute of Mining and Metallurgical Engineers related exceptionally well to the OASW in a new area of war preparation. With a minimum of red tape and suspicion, the army and then the navy joined civilians in working for a common cause. In a straightforward manner and apparently without ulterior motives, civilians offered their valuable abilities to the armed services. The two sides allowed the process of cooperation to develop naturally and adapt to changing circumstances and needs.

Civilian and military preparedness advocates believed that there was more to the planning than the plans themselves. An OASW officer appeared to be reaching for that dimension when addressing the AIME in February 1922:

> Industrial mobilization means the combined efforts of some *one hundred million people* of the United States. There is less value in plans which are carefully typewritten and then filed away, then there is in a *mental* attitude of *preparedness* on the part of the various leaders in industry. We

will accomplish much if we can get *one hundred* or *two hundred* mining engineers to give a little consideration from time to time as to the means and methods by which they can contribute their maximum effort for winning the next war, if we should have war.[50]

The military was after more than increasing the public's receptiveness to preparedness. It also wanted business leaders to assist it in determining how best to use economic power during hostilities.

THE OASW AND BUSINESS FEDERATIONS

The National Industrial Conference Board (NICB), the National Association of Manufacturers (NAM), and the U.S. Chamber of Commerce helped to advance the goals of the Office of the Assistant Secretary of War. Typical of interwar preparedness activity, personal ties bound the NICB and the NAM to the Army Ordnance Association and the Ordnance Districts. Again, the Chamber of Commerce was the exception.

The National Industrial Conference Board was organized in 1916 as an effort by the National Association of Manufacturers to combat unionism. Having learned from the bitter intrabusiness fights and failures of the past, the new group tempered its approach in order to attract large corporations and to create a positive image within the business community and the nation at large. Focusing on the economy and business, the NICB boasted that its diverse membership benefited from the "largest private economic research staff in the world" and "the most widely used economic information bureau."[51]

In November 1926 the NICB devoted its regular monthly meeting to Industrial Preparedness. This was a first for the board. It apparently resulted from Guy E. Tripp and William H. Woodin, president of the American Car and Foundry Company (who were members of the advisory board of the New York AOA Post) serving in the NICB'S governing structure. The board invited the Ordnance Department to conduct the meeting, and Gen. Colden L'H. Ruggles headed the effort. The Ordnance District chiefs were invited, along with leading bureau heads of the army and navy, the chief of staff, the secretaries and assistant secretaries of war and navy, AOA President Benedict Crowell, and Elbert H. Gary. Ruggles labored long and hard to ensure that the meeting was a success. Writing to an Ordnance District chief, he observed:

> The National Industrial Conference Board is probably the most influential body of industrial executives in the country and this is an oppor-

tunity to do a very fine piece of missionary work to aid us in our contact with manufacturers in developing our factory plans to the greatest extent possible. . . .

I hope the District Chiefs will bring out the favorable attitude of some of the leading manufacturers in their Districts. I think there is no doubt that the fact that certain of our leaders of industry consider this movement good enough to justify their cooperating with us generously as they have done makes a great impression upon other manufacturers who have not yet shown a like cooperation.[52]

Scott, never one for exaggeration, seemed to agree with Ruggles's assessment. He wrote to the general: "I am anticipating that it will be one of the most valuable moves made thus far to acquaint a very important group of American manufacturers with the real significance of the work now under way."[53]

By all reports, the November meeting was a success, initiating an ongoing relationship between the NICB and the military services. Members of the OASW became regular members of the board, keeping abreast of its activities and making board members aware of the progress of military planning. This association served to create a new level of awareness in civil-military relations among NICB officials. Board President W. W. Alexander told Assistant Secretary of War Frederick Payne in 1930:

I would merely suggest that you point out that it is not only necessary for the military leaders and the industrial leaders of the country to work together in time of strain and stress of war, but that it is equally important that they work together all the time in order that there might be a mutual understanding and, therefore, an adequate appreciation of the necessities of our defense forces, and that the military leaders may have at all times the moral backing of the business leadership in carrying out defense program [sic] and securing Congressional approval for it.[54]

Relations between the OASW and the NICB took on new urgency toward the end of the 1930s as the threat of war grew. During 1938 and 1939, the OASW from time to time briefed the board and reviewed with it the army's procurement and industrial mobilization plans and its general state of economic preparedness. By 1939, with the nation passing from planning to mobilization, the army's relations with the NICB, as with all other private and public institutions, entered a new phase.[55]

The War Department's ties with the National Association of Manufacturers were closer, more formal, and more institutionalized than those with the

NICB. In mid-1923 one of the founders of the OASW, Col. Charles McK. Saltzman, reported that the NAM

> is probably the most powerful industrial organization of its kind in the world.... If the industrial plans and problems of the War Department could be presented at one of these annual meetings by a competent and tactful speaker, the maximum good results would be obtained because the desires of the War Department would then be brought directly to the heads of the great manufacturers of the country.[56]

That year the OASW managed to have a resolution introduced and adopted at the annual convention of the NAM that backed the OASW's work and pledged to support it.

Further work by the OASW led to greater commitment from the NAM. In November 1926 the association's executive committee created what later was designated the Industrial Preparedness Committee to explore industry-military relations. The committee was chaired by Guy E. Tripp and included as members Frank A. Scott, Howard E. Coffin, Gerard Swope, and Eugene Grace. It met on December 15, 1926, and quickly wrote a report that James L. Walsh (who was not a member of the committee) helped put into final form. The NAM Board of Directors unanimously approved the report and Frank A. Scott personally conveyed its contents to Pres. Calvin Coolidge.

Although important for the military's economic planning, the report highlighted the distortions occurring when the individuals associated with the Ordnance Department spoke for the OASW as a whole. The findings and recommendations of the NAM committee focused excessively on Ordnance concerns instead of on those involving the entire War Department.

The report emphasized that much more time was needed to prepare industry for war than to increase the army's size. Yet only twenty-four officers were assigned to mobilizing the economy while 1,700 were detailed for mobilizing manpower. Two industries were particularly important, aircraft and ordnance. The first was receiving adequate attention, but the second was not. To remedy this situation and protect the otherwise excellent planning of the OASW, steps had to be taken to increase the size and training of the Ordnance officer corps and to modify existing statutes to permit the use of educational orders.[57] To give added weight to these measures, Walsh arranged for the Army Ordnance Association to endorse them.[58]

Of the NAM recommendations, only that involving educational orders was acted upon. On December 7, 1926, Sen. James W. Wadsworth, Jr. (R-NY), introduced a bill sanctioning the practice. From then through 1929, the NAM, at the urging of the Ordnance Department, Walsh, and others, worked continuously though unsuccessfully to persuade Congress to adopt legislation authorizing educational orders.

Relations between the NAM and the OASW remained low-keyed throughout the 1930s but became quite active as the threat of war grew in the latter years of the decade. Seeking to further industrial preparedness, the National Association of Manufacturers in September 1938 appointed an official to serve in Washington, DC, as its coordinator with the Office of the Assistant Secretary of War. A year of negotiations followed in setting up in October 1939 an NAM committee to work with the Army-Navy Munitions Board on mobilization. Association president Charles R. Hook headed the committee, indicating the importance the organization attached to its work. The NAM ultimately concentrated its mobilization energies on advancing apprenticeship training, disseminating and awarding educational orders, assisting the War Department in placing munitions orders through production studies or factory plans, and coordinating efforts among industrial and trade associations to facilitate the operations of the ANMB. The work of the NAM was well received by the armed services since some 50,000 manufacturers could be tapped through the organization, particularly small-to-medium-sized firms that might otherwise remain out of reach. To facilitate this work, the NAM in 1939 began issuing bulletins on the Industrial Mobilization Plan and sending out copies of the plan itself.

As the workload grew heavier toward the end of 1939, the NAM added a National Defense Bureau in Washington to supplement and coordinate a growing staff. On its part, the OASW kept abreast of and facilitated NAM activities and accommodated the association's frequent requests for speakers at its various meetings.

A sudden chill overtook army–NAM relations after Henry L. Stimson and Robert P. Patterson took over as civilian leaders of the War Department in July 1940. With the defense program growing in 1940 and 1941, small business began to suffer as the output of civilian goods was cut back. The War Department attempted to ameliorate the problem through a program headed by Col. Ray M. Hare for distributing defense work as widely as possible. Various associations affiliated with the NAM and composed principally of smaller firms initiated efforts of their own in assisting members to cope with the threatening conditions. In September 1941 they called a meeting in Chicago to work out more effective responses. In requesting that Hare attend the meeting to explain military procurement policies to representatives of small business, the president of the NAM appealed to Under Secretary of War Patterson:

I am sure you will agree that it offers an excellent opportunity not only to enlist their informed cooperation, but to get over to them, and through them to their member manufacturers all over the country, a firsthand knowledge of the program, with its full implication to the smaller manufacturer.[59]

Patterson did not see it that way. Hare, he claimed, was absorbed in the urgent reorganization of the under secretary's office. Even a substitute was not offered.

Two developments account for the abrupt shift in the War Department's relations with the NAM. First, Stimson and Patterson brought in new staff who ignored or remained ignorant about past planning policies and structures in directing what was now the Office of the Under Secretary of War. Second, since harnessing the economy for war depended on big, more than small, business, and since actual economic mobilization was under way, the War Department refocused its attention on giant corporations. The NAM was left to adjust to the new circumstances.[60]

The OASW's relations with the U.S. Chamber of Commerce were more distant than those with the NICB and the NAM, which is somewhat surprising in light of the chamber's active role in mobilizing the World War I economy.[61] Perhaps that record gave the Chamber of Commerce a sense of security about dealing with future emergencies, which the NICB and the NAM lacked because they had played an insignificant part in wartime economics. Moreover, unlike other business federations, the Chamber of Commerce had no direct connections with the Army Ordnance Association or the Ordnance Department.

The OASW attempted to involve the Chamber of Commerce in its planning activities as early as 1923. Reserve officers in the organization and other individuals showed some interest and suggested various ways in which the chamber could be helpful, but without tangible results. From the outset, local chambers of commerce were much more receptive, regularly offering to assist in surveying plants and industries.[62]

Educational orders proved to be the OASW's successful opening with the Chamber of Commerce. The office began seeking chamber support on the issue in 1927, and early in 1929 the Chamber of Commerce created a special committee made up of the people involved in World War I munitions production to join the National Association of Manufacturers and others in lobbying Congress on behalf of educational orders.

Early in 1928 the Chamber of Commerce took its most forthright step in the direction of industrial preparedness by setting up a Special Committee on National Defense. The committee spent over a year and a half on industrial mobilization matters. By October 1929 it completed a rough-draft report unfavorable to the OASW. In reviewing the War Department's work, the committee relied heavily on the views of Bernard M. Baruch. It reported that the military should be restricted largely to matters of combat and supply, with planning for economic mobilization carried out by a civilian Board of Economic Strategy. The committee waffled on proposed American Legion legislation for universal conscription. Using contacts within the Chamber of Commerce, the OASW succeeded in modifying the draft report's harsh response to its planning, an important accomplishment since the War Policies Commission hearings would begin soon. The final report of the Special Committee on National Defense, completed in February 1930, turned out to be quite favorable to the War Department's work.

Except for educational orders, the chamber committee opposed peacetime legislation on economic mobilization. Such legislation constituted a "grave danger" since it could place the nation in a "legislative straightjacket," much worse than any delays resulting from passing legislation to handle an emergency. A Council of National Defense and its Advisory Commission had initiated industrial mobilization in the past, and authority still existed for them to do so in the future. The chamber committee emphasized, however, that planning was essential and by law this responsibility rested with the OASW. Concerning the planning, the committee observed:

> As experience has been gained and trained personnel developed, there has been a decided improvement in this planning work of the War Department, particularly noticeable perhaps in ordnance supply. It is to be remembered that the most serious of all causes of confusion and delay in the last war was the lack of knowledge of what was wanted. This essential feature of any sound industrial preparedness program is in very much better shape as a result of the large amount of work which has been done and is daily being carried forward through the office of the Assistant Secretary of War.[63]

The committee reported that it had consulted World War I mobilization figures, including Walter S. Gifford, Baruch, Alexander Legge, Palmer E. Pierce, Howard E. Coffin, and Benedict Crowell, as a part of its study. Pierce and Coffin appeared to have played an important part in the committee's final work. At least indirectly, therefore, the Ordnance Department and its allies were influencing the Chamber of Commerce. The OASW, of course, was pleased with the Special Committee on National Defense's ultimate report.[64]

Throughout the 1930s, relations between the Chamber of Commerce and the War Department remained reasonably cordial but not close. In 1933 the chamber appointed a new nine-member Special Committee on National Defense and requested the War, Navy, and State Departments to appoint nonvoting ex officio members. The War Department selected the director of the Planning Branch as its representative; he was later joined by a deputy chief of staff. The final report of the committee late in 1933 was again well received in the War Department. According to the deputy chief of staff,

There appeared to be no sign of hostility nor of the pacifism which seems to have permeated conferences of a few years previous. Rather there was conviction of the necessity for an adequate defense establishment, and they wanted to know what the Departments considered that to be.[65]

Giving lip service to the "renunciation of war" and the general principles of the "limitations of armaments," the report recorded the Chamber of Commerce as in favor of a navy and an army of a size and modernity needed to defend American interests and also as backing government support for a merchant marine that would serve as a naval auxiliary in time of war. Moreover, it supported the continuous building of an air force. In regard to the OASW, the committee recommended "the maintenance of necessary reserves of war materials and systematic planning for industrial mobilization; it reaffirms the National Chamber's position urging amendment of the National Defense Act to permit educational orders for equipment, munitions, and accessories."[66] All parts of the report were overwhelmingly approved in a Chamber of Commerce referendum in April 1934. The chamber's second Special Committee on National Defense continued in existence for several more years and was generally supportive of the armed services.

More than ever before, the Office of the Assistant Secretary of War in the interwar years established extensive and regular relations with industrial, business, and professional organizations. In doing so the office began to modify civil-military relations significantly. World War I mobilization figures, retired officers, former officers, those on temporary wartime duty with the armed services, and reserve officers led in bridging the military and economic worlds. Civilians and officers associated with the Ordnance Department, such as Frank A. Scott, Guy E. Tripp, Palmer E. Pierce, and Benedict Crowell, were particularly important in that regard. They constituted a relatively small industrial preparedness vanguard that helped shape the national defense policies of military associations, engineering societies, and business federations. That the vanguard was inordinately identified with the Ordnance Department is predictable since that bureau both led and dominated the OASW. In the long run, the Ordnance group had a profound effect on American policies for defense and war.

The OASW's contacts with the Army Ordnance Association and Ordnance District affiliates were the closest and the most important, but various engineering societies, such as the American Institute of Mining and Metallurgical Engineers, were not far behind. These organizations played an instrumental role in initiating and sustaining procurement and economic mobilization planning, assisting the OASW in its struggles for place and power in the War Department, and winning support for OASW activity within the corporate community. Business federations like the National Association of Manufacturers helped popularize and legitimize OASW planning, assisted in educating the military planners about the economy, joined the AOA in supporting such legislation as that for educational orders, and started to prepare themselves for wartime mobilization functions.

The most sustained interaction between the military and economic communities, however, took place through the operation of commodity committees. These committees drew up detailed plans for mobilizing key industries in the event of hostilities. Their activity was broad, deep, and enormously complex, giving a new dimension to civil-military relations in the 1920s and 1930s.

4
COMMODITY COMMITTEES

Commodity committees were at the center of economic planning by the Office of the Assistant Secretary of War (OASW).[1] At the outset, the office attempted to reconstitute the commodity section–war service committee system of the War Industries Board as a means for initiating procurement planning. That approach, however, was beyond OASW planning competence, and it was too formal for industry during years of peace. Consequently, the office created military commodity committees to plan for raw materials, semifinished products, and some finished goods critical to any war effort. In doing so, the OASW worked with numerous trade associations and industries ranging from rising chemical firms to declining shellac companies and with industries that included giant businesses along with small ones. By combining commodity committee planning with that for services like transportation, the OASW included most of the economy in its activities.

The OASW classified raw materials and semifinished products as strategic, critical, and essential. Commodity committees prepared plans for all strategic goods—those indispensable for national defense but with serious deficiencies in domestic supply. Commodity committees were discretionary for critical and essential products. The former involved materials also vital to national defense but for which supply problems were less pressing; for the latter, ample domestic supply existed, but they still required careful monitoring because of their importance to wartime production. Commodity committees were also established for a few finished goods, such as machine tools, which were considered to be imperative for the success of any mobilization program but for which production capacity was limited.

How army planners classified a raw material or semifinished product was not necessarily an accurate guide to the quality of planning for it. Steel, for example, never rose above the essential category, yet plans for it were better than for most strategic items. The attention devoted to a product depended in part on the supply bureau directing the planning. Committees headed by the Ordnance Department generally performed well. Those under the Quartermaster Corps were often weak. Other supply arms and services (SA&S) performed somewhere between these poles. The industries involved naturally influenced the planning. Positive attitudes among those involved in steel contributed immeasurably to the high-quality plans that resulted. In contrast, the surgical instruments industry obstructed planning because it was incapable of working effectively with the army.

Instead of depending on strategic, critical, or essential labels, one can better understand commodity committee planning if it is divided into six categories. First were heavy, large, oligopolistic, and nonstrategic industries with active trade associations for which the War Department took the initiative in planning. The second category dealt with heavy, large, oligopolistic or potentially oligopolistic, and strategic industries for which trade associations could be of some significance; here the War Department and industry shared responsibility for committee work. The third involved heavy, large, oligopolistic, and nonstrategic industries whose members, trade associations, or both pursued the War Department in behalf of planning. The fourth included small-to-medium-sized firms in small-to-medium-sized strategic industries, with or without strong trade associations, in which the OASW and the industry members combined efforts to plan. The fifth was characterized by small-to-medium-sized companies in small-to-medium-sized nonstrategic industries, with active, often aggressive trade associations intent on pressuring the OASW to be more active and assertive in planning. And the final category was composed of large, or potentially large, oligopolistic industries, with or without strong trade associations, which were major peacetime contractors for the army. In the last category, planning was an extension of ongoing procurement (see Table 4.1).[2]

Commodity committee planning reflected the complexity of both the vast American economy and the highly bureaucratized armed services. The richness and importance of this planning can be grasped only through detailed analysis (presented in chapters 5 through 10). A number of generalizations set forth here nonetheless highlight the most salient aspects of commodity committee work. In chapter 11 there is a summary and an evaluation of what the commodity committees did within the context of overall procurement and economic mobilization planning.

The best commodity committee planning took place when the industry involved was stable, well organized, rationalized, and fully willing to work with the military. The army also had to be committed to and flexible about

TABLE 4.1. Categorization of Industries for Which OASW Commodity Committees Planned

Category	One	Two	Three	Four	Five	Six
Characteristics of industries	heavy, large	heavy, large	heavy, large	small to medium	small to medium	large or potentially so
Market conditions	oligopolistic	oligopolistic	oligopolistic	small-to-medium firms	small-to-medium firms	oligopolistic or potentially so
Classification of product	nonstrategic	strategic	nonstrategic	strategic	nonstrategic	contracted with War Dept. in peacetime
Trade association activity	active	varied	varied	varied	active	varied
Initiative for planning	War Dept.	War Dept. and industry	industry	War Dept. and industry	industry	planning as extension of procurement
Industries	steel	aluminum, rubber	included petroleum, copper, lead	included manganese, tin, mica, wool and woolen goods, machine tools, optical glass, medical supplies	included lumber, coal and coal products, cotton textiles, leather and leather goods	included explosives, aircraft

the planning for the effort to succeed. Conditions were optimal in steel. A commodity committee led by the Ordnance Department combined forces with the United States Steel Corporation and the American Iron and Steel Institute in writing superior plans.

Other commodity committees besides steel carried out accomplished planning, despite different circumstances. The commodities they represented, in contrast to steel, were classified as strategic. Working in tandem with the OASW, Ordnance planned for some ferroalloys in an excellent manner, especially manganese and nickel. Ordnance likewise carried out planning for nonferrous metals like tin in a commendable way, and the same was true for optical glass.

Ordnance did not have a monopoly on good planning. The Signal Corps performed exceptionally well with mica and the Quartermaster Corps did well with rubber. Besides being strategic, these commodities usually received extensive attention from government agencies besides the War Department. Such activity proved invaluable, perhaps indispensable, to OASW preparations for an emergency.

The planning for other commodities was of a decidedly mixed nature, even though all were either designated as strategic or were considered to be so by military planners. Hence, the strategic classification alone did not ensure good plans. The Quartermaster Corps and the Ordnance Department worked hard and achieved some positive results with wool and woolen goods and machine tools, yet their planning was basically flawed. Industries were not at fault. The bureaus were responsible for weakening the planning by protecting their parochial interests. Such an outcome was predictable for the Quartermaster Corps, but it was out of the ordinary for Ordnance. Planning for shellac was also undistinguished, but that was because this commodity increasingly lost its importance as advances occurred in synthetic products.

Planning for many commodities was a failure. Aluminum and petroleum products stand out in this regard. The first was classified for a time as strategic, and the second was always only in the essential category. Consequently, classification does not account for the breakdown. War Department planners deserve much of the blame. The Air Service's leadership for the committee on aluminum was wanting. The Quartermaster Corps, which chaired the Commodity Committee on Petroleum, also performed poorly. Culpability rests not alone with the military, however. Although quite eager to cooperate with military planners, aluminum and oil were almost constantly involved in controversy over their monopolistic and similar practices. This dissension prevented them from focusing effectively on planning, directing the OASW properly in handling their products, and winning its confidence. As concentrated industries, aluminum and oil were easier to mobilize than small-to-medium, competitive industries like machine tools and wool, making planning in some respects less pressing.

Planning for copper and lead was also weak. Since the Ordnance Department headed the Commodity Committee on Non-Ferrous Metals, the outcome appeared unusual. But Ordnance was being prudent in not making an all-out effort for industries designated only as critical and essential. Moreover, though the copper and lead industries were eager to work with the OASW, their opportunistic and exploitative ways put planners on guard.

Various small-to-medium industries categorized no higher than critical or essential also experienced poor commodity committee work.[3] Wood products, cotton and cotton textiles, and leather and leather goods stand out in this regard. They favored planning and attempted to cooperate with the military, even though divisions within industry often thwarted unity. Their efforts were not reciprocated by the military. An obstructionist Quartermaster Corps headed commodity committees for these products. Having procured textiles, leather, and lumber for centuries, the corps opposed outside interference. Also, because lumber was involved in continuing controversies over World War I cantonment and military construction programs, the OASW was more cautious than usual.

Explosives and aircraft were also handled unsatisfactorily. The first was assigned to a committee, the second was not, although the planning for it was much like the work done by commodity units. Neither of these finished products had an exact label, although both were looked upon as strategic. The Ordnance Department, which had the strongest planning record, handled powder and explosives. In this instance, the bureau relied on its close relations with explosives firms (especially E. I. du Pont de Nemours Powder Company) and on its continuous peacetime procurement to substitute for effective planning. The Air Service/Air Corps carried out planning for aircraft in a weak manner. It depended on high levels of research and development on and procurement of planes to take the place of reliable plans. Although not an ideal solution, this approach worked to a degree. The Quartermaster Corps also used ongoing buying as a way of trying to stay on top of wool, cotton, and leather.

Coal and related products emphasized an important characteristic of commodity committee planning. The OASW depended on the World War I model to guide its work. If a commodity diverted from the standard wartime pattern, as was true with coal, military planning was thrown off.

In certain industries, a high level of activity by nonmilitary governmental agencies in promotion, regulation, or rationalization tended to fill the void left by weaknesses of OASW planning. This was not uniformly so, as the planning for rubber indicated, but it took place for wool, leather goods, and wood products, cotton goods, and coal and coal products, commodities ranging from the highest to the lowest planning priority. When substituted for OASW planning, peacetime military procurement or activity of other governmental agencies could be negative if it discouraged military effort. Otherwise, OASW planning was strengthened.

Several additional major aspects about commodity committee planning need to be stressed. If the supply bureau heading a commodity committee resisted planning, the outcome would inevitably be flawed. The Office of the Assistant Secretary of War could try pressuring or persuading a bureau to perform better, as it did with some success for wool, but if resistance continued, as happened with lumber, then planning suffered. Conversely, a bureau dedicated to planning and carrying out its commodity committee functions with ability could, with OASW support, move other supply bureaus in the right direction. Ordnance's handling of steel and Quartermaster's treatment of rubber amply illustrate the point. Ambivalence by a supply bureau unmistakably showed up in the planning, as machine tools demonstrate. The assistant secretary of war depended on the SA&S for fulfilling his mission.

Another point involves the relationship between planning and technological change. Progress in technology was so rapid in some industries that planners had trouble keeping pace. The explosives and the aviation industries are outstanding examples in this regard. Ordnance and the Air Service, however, tended to use constant flux as an excuse, more than a reason, for planning deficiencies. The Quartermaster Corps' work with rubber established that the planning could remain abreast of technological change and even influence its application.

An additional facet deals with the degree to which industries participated in planning for opportunistic or exploitative purposes or both. The topic is as elusive as it is critical. Industries can be placed on a spectrum with the ends representing the least and the most exploitative tendencies. Steel, machine tools, optical glass, and others would be at the least exploitative end; copper, lead, manganese, and others at the most exploitative. Neither steel, machine tools, nor optical glass stood to reap immediate and direct gains from OASW planning. These industries, however, had experienced the tumult, even chaos, of World War I mobilization and would benefit from more effective efforts to harness the economy in a future emergency. But these industries differed in other ways. As an oligopolistic industry, steel could protect its interests under most conditions. Composed of small firms, machine tools could greatly benefit from or be severely harmed by mobilization. Optical glass, principally one firm, only reluctantly participated in war and preparations for it. The responses of these industries to the OASW obviously stemmed from enlightened self-interest blending with national interests. Ulterior motives are not evident. Since these industries varied from strategic to essential, classification alone did not determine action.

In contrast, copper, lead, and manganese were among the most opportunistic and exploitative industries. Representatives from copper companies labored incessantly to gain special treatment for their product, and those from lead crudely attempted to influence military planners. The fact that these industries were classified only as critical or essential appeared to strengthen their attempts to benefit from the national defense rationale. By placing manganese at the top of the strategic category, the War Department ended up encouraging its industry spokesmen in persistently, ruthlessly pursuing a favored status.

The War Department was usually cautious in aiding any industry. Genuine need had to exist; demand for a product could not be based on false claims. Despite industry resistance, military planners dropped shellac from the strategic list and subsequently ignored the product when substitutes were developed. Silk, though maintaining the strategic label, was treated similarly because of ample supplies and ready substitutes. Furthermore, the military, with or without industry's cooperation, could not manipulate national policy if the promise of return was too slight or the price too high, as was the case with surgical instruments.

Most industries fell somewhere between the extremes on the exploitation spectrum. Aluminum and petroleum were closer to manganese than to steel. Rubber was close to the middle, as was lumber. Wool and cotton textiles and leather goods were closer to the enlightened self-interest end. Unless products were at the extremes, distinguishing the lofty or practical from the crass or shortsighted is very difficult.

On the whole, industrialists participated in OASW planning, and made considerable sacrifices to do so, with little promise of immediate or even long-run gain. Most Americans in the interwar years viewed warfare with repugnance; military budgets were relatively small; and, World War I notwithstanding, military spending had not yet become associated with prosperity. Indeed, many people considered World War I and the financing for it to be a principal cause of the Great Depression.

Whatever motivated industry in OASW activities, political more than the military structures determined the impact of national security spending on the economy in the interwar years. Republican administrations in the 1920s showed considerable willingness to grant industry special favors under the mantle of national defense, even though these administrations were stringent with armed forces' budgets and had an antimilitary cast. Democratic administrations of the 1930s, in contrast, were more sympathetic to the armed services but less permissive toward industry in areas related to national defense, as is evident with natural rubber, manganese, and other products. In the late 1930s the Franklin D. Roosevelt administration repeatedly vetoed an aggressive stockpiling policy, even after Congress had became more accommodating toward it. The hard times of the Great Depression of course shaped Roosevelt's policies to some degree. Also involved was an attitude of lessened solicitude toward business and economic strategies that stressed demand over supply in seeking recovery.

The final point about commodity committees relates to the larger one that together industry and the military would dominate the World War II economy. As a vital part of procurement and economic mobilization planning, the armed services' work with commodity committees began preparing them for that inestimably important role. The commodity committees of the 1920s and 1930s highlighted many of the critical wartime mobilization developments. Steel, aluminum, and copper, for example, formed the foundations for the Controlled Materials Plan, among the most important means for managing the wartime economy and one that OASW planning anticipated. The services' work on commodities focused on most areas of scarcity during World War II, including rubber and machine tools; and OASW commodity committees acted to head off wartime problems with a number of products and materials, including optical glass, manganese, tin, and mica.

Despite the severe limitations and failures of commodity committees, their planning was of the highest significance. In both detailed and general ways, the planning familiarized the armed services with the principal contours of America's economy and brought them into close association with the nation's corporate structure and the people who ran it. More than any other part of procurement and economic mobilization planning, commodity committee activity acted as a bridge, connecting the military and the industrial worlds and leading to the mobilization partnership that would grow during World War II.

5
STEEL

Steel is the best example of the first commodity committee category that included nonstrategic, oligopolistic industries.[1] The industry was among the earliest with which the Office of the Assistant Secretary of War (OASW) established a working relationship. Steel and the military remained in close contact for most of the interwar period. The interaction between the two was interrupted at several points in the 1930s as personnel changes occurred in both the OASW and steel firms, only to be reestablished at even more productive levels. Since steel was the framework around which economic mobilization for World War I was built and would play the same role in another major war, the army planners quickly perceived the need to write reliable plans for it. On their part, steel companies had fresh memories of the disarray of World War I mobilization and were willing to assist the OASW in avoiding a repetition.

The first significant contact between the military and the steel corporations in the post–World War I period came from the Army Ordnance Association (AOA) rather than from the OASW. The AOA invited the American Iron and Steel Institute to its annual meeting in October 1922. After that, the institute and its members played an active role in the affairs of the AOA, Ordnance Procurement District, and reserve officers that related to economic preparedness. Elbert H. Gary, chairman of the board of the United States Steel Corporation, was the most prominent representative from steel participating in these events.[2]

In the early 1920s, while still putting together its planning structure, the OASW opened up its own communications with steel. Between July and December 1924 the office created a Commodity Committee on Steel and Iron that remained active throughout the interwar years and was ordinarily chaired by an officer from the Ordnance Department. From 1923 through 1929 the OASW worked principally with James B. Bonner, who until January 1927 was U.S. Steel's representative in Washington and thereafter served as sales manager for U.S. Steel Products Company in Philadelphia. During

World War I Bonner had served on the Cooperative Committee on Steel and Steel Products to the National Defense Advisory Commission (NDAC) and then acted as vice-chairman of the Steel Distribution Committee of the War Industries Board's (WIB) War Service Committee on Iron and Steel.[3] He knew the steel industry and wartime mobilization patterns exceptionally well.[4]

After the armistice, the steel industry led, albeit unsuccessfully, in the move to continue some form of WIB planning.[5] Not surprisingly, therefore, it was receptive to OASW planning overtures. According to Bonner, during the war the military's ignorance of requirements, insistence upon fulfilling its own demands regardless of others' needs and priorities, lack of standardized specifications and contract forms, and overly bureaucratized supply procedures created havoc. Planning could avoid similar disorder during another conflict. U.S. Steel, which dominated the American Iron and Steel Institute, could provide the army planners with virtually all the information on steel that they needed. The corporation accounted for 42 percent of all industry output, thirteen other firms produced an additional 40 percent, and the remaining 18 percent was manufactured by numerous small firms about which U.S. Steel had full information. Moreover, in 1926, the corporation, according to an OASW officer, was "making a broad study of mill capacities, the transportation factors and commercial demands by districts throughout the United States in order to gauge better the trend of industries depending upon steel and the necessity for planning for new steel mills in specific localities."[6]

Between 1922 and 1926, the steel industry and the OASW worked out procedures to plan for the wartime use of steel. At the industry's insistence, all contacts were centralized. The industry would not tolerate numberless questionnaires and requests for information from supply bureaus and their subdivisions as had occurred during and after World War I. Also, it was agreed that nine classifications of steel worked out by the WIB during World War I would be used in interwar planning. For classes that involved standard commercial usage, no plans were essential since capacity was adequate. In cases involving specialized steel products or in the few instances where commercial-grade steel was actually or potentially in short supply, special planning was necessary between steel firms and the Ordnance Department and the Signal and Air Corps.[7]

The most important outcome of the OASW–steel industry work was a plan for the industry written between 1925 and 1927. This blueprint first established projections of the military's wartime requirements for steel, including the building of a merchant fleet. These requirements were classified into the nine steel categories. In an unusual display of cooperation and efficiency, the OASW acquired requirement figures from both the army and the navy by 1925. Commerce Department and wartime records were used to set requirements for an emergency fleet. All demand figures were checked against WIB records to give greater accuracy to OASW calculations. Army planners estimated that the military, including the Emergency Fleet Corporation, had absorbed 25 percent of steel output during World War I; their current plans proposed using 20 percent of existing capacity, leaving ample amounts for civilian and allied needs. Second, the plan established existing and projected wartime output in the nine categories of steel based on military surveys, manufacturing censuses, American Iron and Steel Institute reports, publications of various associations, and contacts with industry. These figures were again checked against those on wartime steel consumption. Last, through modifications in what had been implemented in the final months of the war, a system of allowances was developed in which the SA&S were assigned output from various firms with provisions for constantly adjusting demand to production and shipment schedules. For steel, this allowance approach replaced the accepted schedules of production or factory plans used in other industries.[8]

The steel plan was circulated among the supply bureaus for criticism, corrected or amended, and prepared for submission to the American Iron and Steel Institute for approval in 1928. For various reasons, the last step never occurred. Nonetheless, informal consultation with steel representatives took place at each stage of the planning. Revisions of the plan would be worked out every two years.[9]

In order to improve the process that produced the Steel Plan of 1927, the OASW and industry considered various proposals for exchanging personnel, ultimately settling on an informal approach. The OASW's officers met with Bonner and his associates quite frequently to exchange information and review work. Bonner arranged for Dr. John S. Under of Carnegie Steel Company's Division of Research to spend several weeks at the OASW going over procurement and planning procedures, and he selected experts to assist the military on the use of specialized steel. On Bonner's initiative, OASW officers also visited various steel plants.[10] In general, relations between the steel industry and the OASW from 1923 through 1928 were ongoing and productive.

The steel industry's cooperation with the military in the 1920s exhibited strengths and weaknesses. In a positive sense, it reinforced on both sides the need to plan for hostilities. Negatively, both steel and the OASW viewed planning in a narrow, parochial way. They became convinced that industry and the military could plan for and execute economic mobilization without a coordinating agency like the World War I WIB. This outlook by the OASW is explicable since the army was new to the planning. It is more curious for industry, perhaps reflecting steel's confidence in being able to protect itself under most circumstances.

Bonner advised OASW officers that all requirements should be as close to commercial demand as possible:

> Get a "Going Organization" in time of peace. Tie this organization in with industry by intimate contact in time of peace so that both the Government and Industry will talk in the same terms and it won't be necessary to ask industry to revolutionize its practices and methods in the event of war.

Bonner also observed "that much superior results would be accomplished if industry could deal with Army and Navy officers in preference to dealing with a large group of civilians from every walk of life." During World War I, Bonner complained, many of these civilians had been competent but unfamiliar with the industries with which they worked and ended up causing more problems than they solved. Of particular interest to the steel companies was the problem of overexpansion. They maintained that proper use of existing capacity would eliminate the need to build new plants. "A going organization of officer personnel in time of peace with reasonably stabilized plans and policies," Bonner averred, would go far in preparing the nation for hostilities without the numerous failings of the World War I mobilization experience.[11]

Throughout its planning for steel, the OASW was especially concerned that military requirements be "expressed in terms intelligible to industry," that its planning appear businesslike and efficient, and that it not offend or antagonize the business community. Bonner made clear that such conditions were essential for winning and keeping industry's respect and cooperation.[12] With industry satisfied and its own house in order, the OASW, like steel, operated under the impression that little or no "overhead coordination and control" would be necessary in the event of war. Procurement would be decentralized to the fourteen Procurement Districts. When a higher level of decisionmaking was necessary, it would be carried out on the military's side by the commodity committees.[13]

Planning by steel and the OASW may have had an indulgent quality to it because neither side actually anticipated war. Assistant Secretary of War Dwight F. Davis appeared to be offering a generally held belief when he noted, "It seems to me that our efforts are really directed to the training of the next generation and that we must set up some system by which the war time experience, not only of the War Department but of the steel corporations may be handed down to it."[14]

The OASW's relations with the steel industry in general and with Bonner and U.S. Steel in particular went through a dramatic transformation in 1928 and 1929. From 1923 to 1928 Bonner spoke and acted for what the OASW called the Corporation, the rest of the steel industry, and the American Iron and Steel Institute (AISI) as if they were one. This attitude was possible because of Elbert H. Gary's dominant position as head of U.S. Steel, founder and president of the AISI from 1909 to 1927, and senior spokesman for the industry. Gary's death in August 1927 led to significant change. A former president of U.S. Steel and a rival of Gary's, Charles M. Schwab of the Bethlehem Steel Corporation, assumed the presidency of the AISI and became the steel industry's most important executive. Schwab had been alarmed for some time about steel making lower returns on capital investments than most other industries. He attributed this to uncontrolled competition among firms, resulting in excess plants and equipment, price wars, and other practices leading to inefficiency. The Great Depression, of course, aggravated exponentially the conditions disturbing Schwab. Moreover, Gary, Schwab, and their corporations had been squabbling and engaging in disturbing court battles since 1926 over charges of patent infringements. With Gary's demise, Schwab's rise, and the onset of the depression, power within the steel community shifted away from U.S. Steel and toward the AISI, which now acted for the entire industry rather than closely reflecting the views of Gary and U.S. Steel.[15]

Modified industry politics disrupted OASW planning for steel. Early in 1928 Bonner for the first time felt compelled to explain to the AISI his relations with the OASW, to play down what he and his associates had done to assist the military planners, and to ask the institute officially to approve his continued role as OASW adviser.[16] Moreover, the Steel Plan of 1927 was never formally submitted to the institute for approval. The AISI sanctioned Bonner's efforts, and he continued to work with the OASW for several months. Before the end of the year, however, his liaison role with the assistant secretary's office had abruptly and inexplicably ended. This change occurred just about the time that the bureaus, and especially the Ordnance Department, were mounting a strong challenge to the Steel Plan as interfering with their right to deal directly with corporations, a prerogative they considered vital to efficient procurement. Moreover, key personnel changes during 1928–1929 in the army's planning structure destabilized the military's relations with the steel industry.[17] This turmoil threw OASW planning for steel into a state of disarray from which it did not recover for a number of years.

Between 1929 and 1931 the OASW had virtually no direct contact with the steel industry. By late 1931, however, army planners appeared to have settled quarrels between the OASW and the SA&S over jurisdiction. At that point, they unsuccessfully attempted to have U.S. Steel executives, and particularly W. A. Mace, who had served as assistant to J. Leonard Replogle, director of steel in the War Industries Board, resume assisting them along the lines of Bonner in the past. Although reaffirming interest in procurement planning, U.S. Steel informed the OASW that it could no longer participate in OASW activity

> except upon request from the American Iron and Steel Institute, preferring that all actions shall be the actions of the institute which represents the entire industry rather than as an employee of the Steel Corporation whose actions might be subject to misinterpretation by other companies of the Steel Industry.

The OASW was told, furthermore, that the office, rather than the AISI, would have to select specific companies for contracts because "no trade association can afford to place itself in the position of discriminating among its members—in favor of one and against the other."[18] The AISI clearly had assumed a substantially different place in the steel industry after Gary's death.

Another significant change occurred between 1929 and 1932 in OASW–steel industry relations. Operating from the perspective of a trade association rather than as a corporation and with a greater emphasis on cooperation than competition, steel spokesmen emphasized the need for an overall mobilization body like the WIB instead of proposing that industry and the military proceed alone. On their part, having completed their first Industrial Mobilization Plan, which was reviewed by the War Policies Commission, army planners also realized the imperative value of so-called superagencies.[19]

Beginning in late 1931 army officers encountered repeated frustration in approaching the steel industry. After careful and cautious work with the AISI in behalf of a modest steel survey between October 1931 and March 1933, for example, OASW planners turned up empty-handed when their principal contact, the institute's secretary, was suddenly forced into retirement because of ill health. The negative impact of such blows was magnified manyfold for the OASW by constant turnover in its own staff, creating untimely delays as newly assigned officers tried to educate themselves about steel.[20]

The year 1934 was key in reestablishing communication between the OASW and steel. In mid-1933 Col. Charles T. Harris, Jr., took over as director of the Planning Branch, and several months later Maj. H. C. Minton of the Ordnance Department became head of the Commodity Committee on Steel and Iron. Harris revitalized procurement and economic mobilization planning, and during his five years in the Planning Branch for the first time put them on a solid base. Minton proved to be an exceptionally resourceful planner. Under the leadership of the two, the OASW reconstructed and built upon what their predecessors had done between 1923 and 1929 instead of discarding or remaining ignorant of the past, as had occurred between 1929 and 1934. Steel officials, the most important of whom was Walter S. Tower, executive secretary of the American Iron and Steel Institute, were also outstanding. With talented, continuous leadership on both sides, industry and the military were able to put steel on a planning track leading directly to mobilization for World War II. The OASW's efforts were assisted to some degree by the fact that the Army-Navy Munitions Board (ANMB) had been reorganized in 1931 and was more active than before.[21]

Once Harris, Minton, and their associates reviewed and understood OASW steel planning of the 1920s, they were ready to revise the Steel Plan of 1927.[22] Before starting, they negotiated agreements with the AISI between February and September 1934 to facilitate their work. These accords were approved by the institute's Board of Directors and hence had a greater degree of authority than had ever before been the case.

The 1927 Steel Plan required basic revisions because substantial changes had occurred in both the army and the steel industry over a period of almost ten years. The 1927 plan was based on the War Department Mobilization Plan of 1924 and involved outdated requirement figures. For industry, the 1929 depression had forced a much greater amount of change than average. Additionally, large increases had taken place in the output and use of alloyed, stainless, and high-speed tool steels, as opposed to plain carbon steel. Minton elected to revise the 1927 plan rather than write a new one. According to the proposed revision, the first part of the plan involving requirements for the War and Navy Departments and an agency comparable to the Emergency Fleet Corporation would be updated according to recent mobilization plans. Revisions would also distinguish more clearly between plain carbon and specialized steels. The second part of the plan would record the transformations and modifications that had taken place in the steel industry. In the third part of the plan, steel output would be distributed according to class and grade, procurement agency, and producing unit, indicating which corporations would provide what percentage of industry's total wartime production.

To satisfy disgruntled supply bureaus, the OASW in the revised plan proposed an elaborate allocation program that would allow the SA&S to work indirectly with steel corporations. This change turned out to be nominal. Steel was so concentrated that it never made sense to have other than a centralized system, as implemented by the 1927 plan. Thus in the 1930s the OASW did most of the work with steel, but it left the door open for the SA&S to deal with individual steel firms when practical. This more fluid approach appeared to assuage the bureaus without significantly changing past operations.

Once completed, the Steel Plan would be revised every four years by the OASW. Since the revised version would be a statistical study more than an operational plan, further changes could be made with relative ease. To facilitate revisions of the 1927 plan, Minton was stationed in New York City so that he could be in close contact with the AISI headquarters located there.[23]

Revisions of the 1927 Steel Plan began in July 1934, and a preliminary draft was done by April 1936, with copies sent to the SA&S, the Navy Department, and the AISI for review. By December 1936 the final draft was completed. It was approved by the War Department, the Navy Department, the Army-Navy Munitions Board, and, most significantly, the AISI. Institute assistance was recognized in the plan, and Tower signed it as the official representative of the AISI.

Without the AISI, the OASW could not have written the Steel Plan of 1936. The institute's *1935 Iron and Steel Works Directory of the United States and Canada* was the principal source for establishing steel production capacity. In key areas the publication cited aggregate figures on actual or potential production instead of output by firm, which the OASW needed to distribute companies among various bureaus and Procurement Districts. To obtain firm-by-firm figures, the institute and the OASW worked out an arrangement whereby steel companies were asked to allow the AISI to release classified information to the OASW. Almost all corporations agreed. The AISI's Statistical Division also reviewed and corrected Part 2 of the plan, and institute personnel helped the OASW convert data from other sources into forms consistent with military usage. All parts of the Steel Plan were ultimately reviewed by the AISI. Finally, the institute informed the OASW that a special version of future editions of the *Directory* would be prepared for the military to facilitate planning. Although willing to help the OASW, the AISI insisted that it, not the steel corporations individually or collectively, would be the contact point for all planning.[24]

Several aspects of writing the Steel Plan, 1936, stand out. Meager military budgets, and especially those for the OASW, created constant obstacles for the planners. In November 1934 Minton faced extraordinary difficulties in acquiring a long-carriage typewriter to prepare the plan for reproduction in a way that was accurate and professional in appearance. He also had to beg for travel funds so that he could do his job properly, acknowledging at one point that seventy dollars was a "large" expenditure. The military's practice of constantly transferring its officers also added to the tribulations of the planners. In July 1935 Minton was moved from his special assignment in New York, close to the AISI, to the Pittsburgh Ordnance District. The revision of the Steel Plan was at that time less than half completed. Despite the changed assignment, Minton directed the revision through to the end, but his task was inevitably made more difficult, and only his commitment and ingenuity, along with the support of Harris and the AISI, ensured that the job was done well.[25]

Once the 1936 Steel Plan was completed, communication between the OASW and the steel industry dropped off dramatically. Early in 1939, however, with war approaching and defense preparations increasing, the U.S. Steel Corporation and its affiliates contacted the OASW with the aim of surveying the steel industry, inquiring about educational orders, and reviewing the 1936 Steel Plan. For a time, it appeared as if a type of 1920s' conditions would be duplicated, with military planners working directly with the steel corporations. Colonel Harry K. Rutherford, Harris's replacement as director of the Planning Branch, suggested to U.S. Steel representatives that it might be wise to form an advisory committee from steel for revising the Steel Plan and creating closer relations between the industry and the OASW. Fortunately this approach, which would have entailed restarting the planning anew, was not followed. Although Harris was gone, Minton was still available to relate what had been done previously and to start modifying the 1936 Steel Plan in line with past work. This revision began in December 1939 and was completed in October 1940. Major W. E. Becker of the Ordnance Department took charge of the planning while still a student at the Army Industrial College (AIC) and continued this work after he graduated in June 1940.

The 1936 Steel Plan had been so well done that reworking it in 1940 took place with relative ease. The basic format was maintained and made current. The army's updating was based on requirements of the Protective Mobilization Plan, 1939. Instead of using World War I and projected figures for an Emergency Fleet Corporation, as was done in 1927 and 1936, the 1940 version included the Maritime Commission as a claimant agency. As with the 1936 plan, the AISI, and particularly its *1938 Steel Directory*, which the institute updated for 1939, remained the chief source of information on production capacity. Work with the institute went smoothly since Tower was still executive secretary (in mid-1940 he became the organization's president). Tower's usefulness was enhanced by the fact that he served with the National Defense Advisory Commission in 1940. For the War Department to obtain figures on individual companies producing alloy, stainless, alloy tool, and high-speed tool steels, the OASW and the AISI used the device employed in 1936 of seeking permission from corporations for the institute to release confidential data to the military planners. The OASW sought out the information directly from those firms that did not belong to the AISI. Through its own efforts and the exceptional cooperation of the AISI, the War Department probably had more complete data on steel production than had been true in 1927 or 1936.[26]

The AISI had a lesser role in the 1940 revision than earlier only because the level and quality of its assistance in shaping the 1936 plan had been so great. Nonetheless, the AISI reviewed all aspects of the updated plan, aided the OASW whenever possible, created or offered to establish special review agencies when problems arose, and gave the completed plan its seal of approval. Furthermore, Tower stepped in to prevent the army from undermining the planning by following routine practices. At the end of June 1940, Becker, who was directing the revision, was to be reassigned upon graduation from the Army Industrial College even though the Steel Plan was still months away from completion. Tower's plea to the War Department to allow Becker to finish what he described as an "outstanding" performance on a "very important job" apparently kept Becker in charge until his task was finished.[27]

The completion of the 1940 Steel Plan served as part of the War Department's transition from planning for economic mobilization to actually mobilizing the economy. By the end of 1940 military budgets and procurement were growing rapidly, the War and Navy Departments and the ANMB were acting as mobilization agencies, and the NDAC had been reactivated. Through its work on the steel plans, the OASW's information about and relations with steel were at least as good as with any other industry.

The OASW's interaction with the steel industry highlighted certain characteristics of interwar planning. Based on the World War I experience and emphatic insistence by steel executives, the military planners accepted the need for procurement agencies to adapt their requirements and operations to those of the steel industry. Although the supply bureaus' fight for autonomy, shortages of personnel and funds, and endless shuffling of officers complicated the OASW's work, the planning continued and generally improved.

The steel industry's motivations for participating in planning were quite straightforward. Without extensive and ongoing assistance from the steel community, military plans would be of limited value. Poor plans could lead to a repetition of the World War I mobilization muddle, fundamentally threatening steel and most other industries. In this sense, the steel executives were being practical. On another level they were being high-minded, or at least thinking of long-run as opposed to short-run gains. The idea of war in the 1920s was remote and in the 1930s unpopular and repugnant. But War Department planning fitted well into the informal and formal efforts to plan industries and the economy that were prevalent in the 1920s and 1930s. Without this peacetime planning, the steel industry might have been less willing to devote the amount of time and effort to military affairs that it did. Assistance to the OASW was better, broad-based, and more reliable under the auspices of the American Iron and Steel Institute in the 1930s than as an extension of the U.S. Steel Corporation in the 1920s.

Throughout the records there are scattered instances of steel companies or collections of firms offering to serve the OASW or attempting to manipulate the War Department for reasons that were clearly selfish. Invariably these incidents occurred during the depression years of the 1930s, not in the prosperous years of the 1920s. In 1934, for example, an Infantry reserve lieutenant colonel clearly used Ordnance Department connections to try to stir up government interest in possible iron and sulphur deposits in Alaska in which he was commercially involved. In 1937 the Institute of Scrap Iron and Steel, Incorporated, and similar associations began unctuously pressing their devotion to national defense before the OASW as international tensions rose, although they had never expressed similar concern before or bothered with the military planning.[28] On the whole, however, instances of such opportunism and attempted exploitation were relatively rare in the steel industry and showed up mostly among rather small, even marginal, elements.

In general, steel presented almost ideal planning conditions for the OASW. Plans and planning for other giant industries suffered by comparison, as was the case with aluminum and rubber.

6
ALUMINUM AND RUBBER

The second type of commodity committee work by the Office of the Assistant Secretary of War (OASW) involved strategic, heavy, large industries composed of big or potentially big corporations. Particularly notable were aluminum and rubber. The OASW and the industry, which had either no trade associations or weak ones, were equally responsible for initiating and maintaining the planning. Neither commodity had created serious problems during World War I, but both headed the list of severely troubled industries during World War II.

Aluminum was virtually unique as a heavy industry in that it was a monopoly. The Aluminum Company of America (Alcoa) accounted for almost all production of the metallic element, although other firms were involved in fabrication. The OASW showed some interest in the early 1920s, but aluminum was not taken seriously until the 1930s. Lieutenant Colonel Alfred H. Hobley of the Army Air Corps provided the army with the first extensive information about the industry. Hobley served in the OASW from 1928 through 1932 and then studied at Harvard's School of Business Administration during 1933 and 1934. While there he wrote a study, "Aluminum Company of America, Its Operations and Capacities."[1] Alcoa provided Hobley with a great deal of secondary literature about aluminum and, more important, prepared for him a confidential report about the company that included extensive statistics. In 1934 Hobley sent a copy of the paper to the OASW, which made it available to all the supply arms and services (SA&S). Hobley considered Alcoa's report so important that the director of the Planning Branch observed that his study was written "in collaboration with the officials of [the] Aluminum Company of America."[2] Hobley's work probably made the OASW more knowledgeable about the national and international status of aluminum production and use than any other government agency.[3]

The report appeared to have both a positive and a negative effect on OASW planning: positive in that it gave the army as much or more information about aluminum as any other commodity, negative in that the data took away the urgency to plan. After filing his study, Hobley served as contact man with Alcoa for a few months until his transfer back to the Air Corps in mid-1934. For the next two years, relations between the aluminum industry and the army remained rather casual. As the principal user of aluminum, the Air Corps arranged meetings with Alcoa to consider the industry's ability to meet emergency requirements. The OASW also went on record as recognizing the importance of aluminum for defense and war production. More formal steps were needed, however, to write plans for aluminum.[4]

In 1936 the OASW finally began to act more decisively. It designated aluminum as a strategic material and created a commodity committee to plan for it. (Previously, the Commodity Committee on Non-Ferrous Metals had periodically reviewed the aluminum situation.) This action was precipitated by a growing realization that "military and civilian requirements for aluminum are increasing at a tremendous rate, particularly in relation to aircraft." Output of the quality and quantity the military required was significantly dependent on imports and one company. "In summing up the aluminum situation," chief of the Planning Branch Col. Charles T. Harris, Jr., noted in late 1936, "it is only in high strength alloys, and in the fabrication, casting, and other shaping processes that a shortage may exist." Earlier in that same year, a commodity committee, which included an Alcoa official serving as a reserve officer, had concluded that a shortage in capacity for producing and shaping aluminum could arise during a national emergency. Only plans that included demand for specific types of aluminum, not simply gross tonnage, would settle the matter conclusively.[5]

Despite greater interest about aluminum in the mid-1930s, OASW planning never got very far. Industry was not to blame. Alcoa officials, including top-level management, met frequently with OASW members and other military groups between 1936 and 1939 to assess production potential, establish categories to facilitate calculating military demand, and estimate civilian requirements. Under protest, Alcoa even allowed the SA&S to deal individually with the company, something steel and other industries would not tolerate.

Trouble originated on the military's side. Planning was divided between an OASW Commodity Committee on Aluminum and an Army-Navy Munitions Board (ANMB) committee that also dealt with the metal. The former committee was passive, in contrast to committees dealing with other goods; the latter was more active. Navy Department aluminum requirements were large, and the service could best protect its interests in the shared power structure of the ANMB instead of letting the War Department work alone. But even the ANMB commodity committee was not very effective. It was chaired by an

Army Air Corps officer, and the corps' planning was among the weakest in the War Department. Moreover, the Air Corps' Material Division, which provided representation for the ANMB's commodity committee, was located at Wright Field, Dayton, Ohio, far from Washington and the Eastern centers of planning and industrial activity. At one point, Lt. Col. H. V. Hopkins, the army's principal spokesman on the ANMB committee, missed an important planning meeting in Washington because inclement weather precluded flying.[6]

Under such conditions, progress was slow. Hopkins reported in 1938 that the ANMB was concentrating on requirements. Yet the committee had neither received existing figures from the navy, the Air Corps, or other SA&S, nor did it have data made available by Alcoa to the OASW and the ANMB. The committee continued meeting with Alcoa and various governmental agencies without much result. Finally, in 1940, the War Department reported that "after several years of research, and continued technical developments in the aluminum industry a thorough survey of materials and facilities matched against requirements reveals that no particular problem is presented."[7] Furthermore, with changed conditions, aluminum was dropped from the strategic list. At that point, commodity committee planning came to a halt.[8]

Despite the planners' blunder of failing to anticipate the vast increase in the demand for aluminum during World War II, interwar planning still made some gains. It acquainted the military with a relatively new industry of importance and made aluminum executives aware of military operations and requirements. To some degree these modest steps assisted economic mobilization for World War II.

OASW–Alcoa relations in the 1930s led to consequences anticipating the Cold War years. In 1937 the Justice Department filed an antitrust suit against Alcoa as a monopoly restraining trade. Attorney General Homer S. Cummings requested a copy of Hobley's paper from the War Department in 1938 to support the department's case. OASW and Air Corps officers initially agreed to comply, and Cummings reasoned that a study completed at Harvard and filed with the university involved no military secrets or confidential data. However, in June 1937, the OASW had returned copies of Hobley's reports to Alcoa for updating and was unable to make the paper immediately available to the Justice Department.[9] Quite suddenly, the War Department reversed itself, arguing that cooperating with the Justice Department would jeopardize its planning by alienating industry. The director of the Planning Branch explained:

> Our relations with industry in preparing procurement plans have been on the basis that it should talk freely to us, even confidentially, and that any confidential data furnished would be safeguarded and protected.

If now this position should be reversed and data requested should be furnished to the Department of Justice for use in a lawsuit, industry would soon learn that the War Department had committed what it would consider to be a breach of faith and our future industrial planning would be very seriously hampered.[10]

The secretary of war argued that Hobley's report was confidential, that all copies, including Harvard's, had been returned to the War Department's custody, and that the report could not be surrendered without compromising public interest. Since copies of the report were actually in Alcoa's hands at the time, Justice subpoenaed a copy from the company in April 1938. Alcoa turned to the War Department for advice. Assistant Secretary of War Louis A. Johnson personally took charge of the matter, informing Alcoa that it was not to comply with the subpoena, that the War and Justice Departments would work out a settlement based on the War Department's position. Johnson offered to show Cummings a copy of the report when it was available to verify that national defense was indeed involved. The court ultimately accepted the War Department's arguments, as did the Justice Department. Hobley's report never went either to the Justice Department or the court. In July 1938 the OASW finally received from Alcoa a revised form of the study and collected all other extant copies to ensure confidentiality.[11]

This episode is revealing for a number of reasons. A Federal Bureau of Investigation agent hit upon the crux of the matter in addressing a member of the OASW: "We want to know something about whether or not Alcoa, which the Government is sueing [*sic*] as a monopoly, is one of the main sources on which you are dependent."[12] The answer, of course, was yes, and this led both Alcoa and the War Department, by acts of omission and commission, to be less than candid with the Justice Department. Both the company and the army called Hobley's report a mobilization plan for aluminum when that was not the case. Hobley's study had much to do with OASW relations with industry; it had nothing to do with national defense per se. Moreover, although the evidence is conflicting, the War Department appeared to treat the Hobley report as unclassified until the Justice Department sought access to it. And, even if Hobley's study was classified, that protection did not cover the Alcoa study upon which Hobley's work was largely, perhaps exclusively, based. The War Department and Alcoa appear to have kept Justice intentionally ignorant about Alcoa's report.

The Alcoa incident touched on some of the intractable problems warfare creates for a modern state. The military wittingly allied itself with private industry against other branches of government and the public in the name of national defense. Candor quickly went by the board. Other institutions could not escape the corrosive effects of industrial-military relations. Once agreeing to train military officers, Harvard soon found itself compromising canons of academic freedom, open inquiry, and free access to information. The OASW, Alcoa, and Harvard were entering a new world in which old guidelines were inadequate and new ones were difficult, even impossible, to define as long as a primary function of the state was preparing for and conducting modern warfare.

In assisting OASW planning activities, Alcoa was not simply motivated by patriotism and goodwill. Unlike steel, Alcoa was too willing to let the army set planning terms and too eager in devoting the time and energy of high-level management quickly to meet War Department requests. As a monopoly, Alcoa was vulnerable. War Department connections and the mantle of national defense provided excellent protection in the 1930s when the political climate was hostile toward business. This turn of events was demonstrated by the antitrust suit controversy and by Alcoa's looking to the War Department for support in its fight for favorable tariff policies.[13] Perhaps more important, as a relatively new industry, Alcoa executives realized that military hardware and especially aircraft would be a growing source of future demand. George R. Gibbons, Alcoa's senior vice-president, articulated that outlook to Secretary of War Harry H. Woodring in 1934.[14]

RUBBER

Unlike aluminum, rubber was classified as strategic by the Office of the Assistant Secretary of War from the outset of planning and remained in that category until World War II. The reasons were obvious. Approximately 90 percent of the world's rubber supply came from plantations in the East Indies. In the early 1920s Britain controlled 80 percent of rubber output, and between 1922 and 1928, through what was called the Stevenson Plan (after Sir James Stevenson, commercial adviser to the Colonial Office), it cut back the quantity of crude rubber marketed. The formation of the British cartel in conjunction with increasing demand caused prices to rise as high as $1.21 a pound in 1925. Intense American opposition, market forces, and other developments forced the British to abandon restrictions in the late 1920s. That action, combined with the onset of a worldwide depression, resulted in a drastic price drop. By 1928 rubber had fallen to forty cents a pound, went down to sixteen cents later that year, and in 1931 hit a low of seven cents.

The United States was the principal consumer of crude rubber. In 1925 it used 74 percent of world output and in 1938, 52 percent. The huge rubber corporations like Goodyear Tire and Rubber Company bought 80 percent of the rubber imported into the United States, principally for the production of tires. The American rubber industry had two trade associations: the Rubber Manufacturers Association, Incorporated (previously the Rubber Association of America) representing nearly 75 percent of rubber manufacturers and reclaimers, including the biggest rubber firms like B. F. Goodrich Company, and the Rubber Trade Association, made up of rubber importers and dealers. Tire manufacturing in the United States was quite concentrated, with ten producers accounting for about 90 percent of output.

The problem that concerned OASW planners was that virtually no rubber was grown in the United States, only a small portion came from Latin America, and alternate sources or substitutes were nonviable. During war, America would be in a precarious position if cut off from its supply, thousands of miles away. Army planners considered rubber to be among the most threatened strategic commodities.[15]

The OASW's sense of urgency resulted in an ongoing study from 1921 through 1939 with industry and other governmental departments for ways to mitigate national dependence on Asian imports. By 1924 army planners had organized a Commodity Committee on Rubber and Rubber Goods. It remained among the most active of OASW committees.

War Department efforts, like those of all other private and public sources, focused on alternate sources of rubber. The endeavors fell into three categories: finding a form of rubber-producing vegetation besides the Hevea tree that could be grown in the American Southwest, Mexico, or both; cultivating Hevea in other locations, preferably Central America and the Caribbean; and developing a synthetic rubber to match or exceed the qualities of natural rubber, producible at a reasonable price.

In the early 1920s the War Department was instrumental in pushing the Agriculture Department into experimenting with rubber production. By the early 1930s the department was experimenting in Arizona, California, and Florida with fifty varieties of shrubs and plants containing rubber. Next to the Agriculture Department, Thomas A. Edison was the most active in searching for Hevea substitutes at his Edison Botanic Research Corporation laboratories in New Jersey and Florida.[16]

Guayule was the most promising established substitute for Hevea. It was virtually the exclusive reserve of Intercontinental Rubber Company, which also owned Hevea plantations in Sumatra. The dynamic, exceptionally well-informed George H. Carnahan was president of the company. Intercontinental's work in guayule took place through subsidiaries in the United States and Mexico. Guayule is a hardy, deciduous shrub that lives indefinitely in the temperate zone and requires heavy frost for a dormancy period. A guayule shrub reaches maturity after four years and can be harvested at that point or simply allowed to grow indefinitely without any loss of rubber-harvesting capacity. For a number of years, guayule was second only to Hevea as a source of commercial rubber, constituting 19 percent of consumption in 1910. Its use declined thereafter, but it was still in demand because of unusual qualities. Intercontinental Rubber began experimenting with guayule in 1912, and by 1931 it had extraction plants in Mexico and California.

Along with the Department of Agriculture, the OASW kept a close eye on guayule as an alternate source of rubber during a national emergency. The Bureau of Foreign and Domestic Commerce and the National Bureau of Standards, Department of Commerce, also maintained close contacts with Intercontinental and experimented with and kept statistical data on guayule. Secretary of Commerce Herbert Hoover led in America's determined drive to free rubber from Britain's domination under the Stevenson Plan. Hoover's interest carried over to the White House, and at his urging the OASW in 1930 conducted its own survey of guayule. In April of that year, the office sent Majors Gilbert Van B. Wilkes and Dwight D. Eisenhower to the Southwest and Mexico to investigate guayule, possible areas for further cultivation, and Intercontinental's facilities. By June 1930 the two officers had concluded that production of guayule rubber in the United States and Mexico should be promoted by the government in the event that war cut the nation off from its Asian supply.

Despite favorable reports by governmental departments and others, market forces undermined the economic feasibility of guayule. With Hevea going at seven cents a pound in 1931, guayule could be sold only for specialty purposes. Carnahan became desperate, insisting that unharvested guayule plants provided America with a ready reserve. The argument was cogent, but a Congress uninterested in any stockpiling was not about to purchase growing shrubs. Despite its continuing interest in guayule, the OASW had to turn down Carnahan's cry for help in combating import duties[17] and Roosevelt administration policies of encouraging rubber imports to support American exports.[18]

Cultivating Hevea trees in the Western Hemisphere was the other major search for an alternate rubber supply. Rubber output was not new to Latin America. The area had produced most of the world's crude rubber until 1907, when a series of market and man-made calamities struck.[19] Supported and encouraged by the War and Commerce Departments, the Agriculture Department in the early 1920s began investigating the feasibility of rubber culture in Latin America, and in the mid-1920s it established experimental stations in the Panama Canal Zone and Haiti.[20] By 1926, Agriculture tentatively reported that cultivated Hevea could be grown throughout Latin America and even as far north as southern Florida. However, various diseases and insects were a risk, a suitable labor force was probably unavailable, and political and economic instability remained a threat. These findings, in addition to a shortage of funds for further research, made the Agriculture, War, and Commerce Departments cautious about advocating private rubber investment in the area.

Despite the caution, the OASW never wavered in its quest to strengthen America's position concerning natural rubber. It followed carefully and supported the rubber plantations of Firestone Tire and Rubber Company and the Ford Motor Company in Liberia and Brazil. Between 1923 and 1926 the office lent its name to endeavors of Firestone and others to counteract Britain's Stevenson Plan. And in 1926 the War Department backed the Agriculture Department's projects for experimenting with rubber cultivation in the Philippines.

Economic forces undermined attempts to grow Hevea commercially other than in Asia. The Stevenson Plan encouraged production outside British-controlled areas, especially in the Dutch East Indies. Furthermore, the use of reclaimed rubber in the United States increased dramatically. It remained in demand even after the price of crude rubber fell to seven cents a pound. These forces combined to create a situation in which rubber prices in the late 1920s were exceptionally low, supply exceeded demand, and huge visible and invisible reserves of rubber existed throughout the world. The depression, of course, reduced the demand for rubber further. In July 1932 the War Department estimated that the United States had on hand almost a year's reserve of crude rubber and a three-year supply of scrap for producing reclaimed rubber. In terms of national defense, the country was in good shape. Several years later, conditions had improved further. By the 1930s public and private anxiety about rubber had dissipated.

Another significant change took place in the 1930s. The Roosevelt administration was less interested than the Republican administrations in working directly with and subsidizing private industry. Moreover, the Roosevelt administration remained convinced that rubber purchases from Southeast Asia supported U.S. exports. Hence, in the mid-1930s, despite strong backing from the War Department and obvious excitement in the Agriculture Department, the administration refused to cooperate with Goodyear's experiments designed to remove the last major obstacle to Hevea cultivation in Latin America. In 1939 a disappointed Assistant Secretary of War Louis A. Johnson felt compelled to turn away from crude rubber users' organizing efforts for promoting the growth of rubber in Latin America.[21]

The failure in finding alternate sources of natural rubber served the nation's long-run interests. Synthetic rubber provided the solution to American problems. Processes for producing synthetic rubber were known as early as 1879. The rise in the price of natural rubber to $2.90 a pound in 1910 triggered extensive experimentation. Germany actually produced small amounts of synthetic before World War I. With lower prices after World War I, experimentation with synthetic rubber continued with less urgency. The United States had a marketable product late in 1931 with Duprene (later called Neoprene), invented and perfected by E. I. du Pont de Nemours and Company. Neoprene cost much more than natural rubber at the time, but special qualities made it profitable for use in hoses and tubing for solvents and in various gas containers.

The War Department and Du Pont almost immediately began working together on potential applications of Neoprene for military uses. Almost every SA&S used Neoprene. However, 80 percent of rubber purchased by the War Department went into tires, and this use was logically the department's chief interest. At the suggestion of Du Pont, the Quartermaster Corps and the OASW early in 1932 arranged for the U.S. Rubber Company to manufacture and test tires made from Neoprene. Although the project never materialized, Firestone made an experimental airplane tire from Neoprene in the mid-1930s for the Air Corps to test, and in the late 1930s Du Pont arranged to have a few smaller automobile tires manufactured, with uncertain results.

The breakthrough in synthetic rubber occurred in 1937. By then, three products other than Neoprene were on the market: Koroseal by Goodrich, Thickol by the Dow Chemical Company, and Buna by Germany's I. G. Farbenindustrie A. G. (I. G. Farben). The three American companies were working closely with the Chemical Warfare Service in testing products. By 1938 the United States manufactured about 500 tons of synthetic rubber monthly, with Neoprene accounting for five times the output of Koroseal and Thickol combined. Synthetics ranged in price from a low of $.65 cents to a high of $1.00 a pound. The major problem of tire production had not been solved, but progress was being made. I. G. Farben manufactured tires from Buna in 1938, which it declared to be superior to those of natural rubber, a claim later substantiated by Goodrich.

Even before the major breakthroughs, the War Department begun focusing on synthetics as an answer to the critical rubber problem. In 1935 it started a program for testing synthetics as opposed to natural rubber in tires and made sure that it stayed abreast of all developments.

Matters began to move even more quickly with synthetic rubber in 1939 and 1940. In 1939 Standard Oil Company of New Jersey obtained patent rights to I. G. Farben's Buna N, a synthetic rubber similar to Neoprene, and

Buna S, reputed to be capable of producing tires superior to those of natural rubber. Buna N could be manufactured profitably. However, Standard maintained that it could not develop the full potential of Buna S without a guaranteed market. No other company was willing to act as a pioneer for Buna S since the low price of natural rubber made synthetic competition prohibitive.

Standard approached the OASW for help in dealing with the situation. Exactly why the company approached the army is not documented but can be inferred. The War Department's interest in synthetic rubber made it more current on developments than any other federal agency. Further, the department's relations with Standard, rubber companies, and business America in general were better than those of most other departments in the Roosevelt administration. Moreover, and perhaps most important, war had broken out in Europe and Nazi Germany had control over I. G. Farben. The growing power of the War Department provided Standard with the cloak of national security in its controversial relations with the German firm.

Standard of New Jersey sketched out to the War Department several ways for handling German synthetics. Standard could issue licenses for Buna N only to companies willing simultaneously to develop Buna S, which would involve small experimentation and production programs until a marketable product at a competitive price was reached. Standard was dealing with Goodyear, Goodrich, Du Pont, U.S. Rubber, Firestone, and the Rohm and Haas Company, all but the last of which were the giants of their industries. These companies would welcome access to Buna N but would resist any tie-in with Buna S because of the uncertain investment involved. "A Government subsidy, guarantee, or some sort of outlet for tires fabricated from Buna S," Standard informed the War Department, "would help carry the burden and ameliorate this restrictive contractual clause." If that approach would not work, Standard asked whether for purposes of national defense the War Department preferred that it license Buna N to companies individually and require them to work separately on Buna S as well, or that it issue licenses for Buna N to those companies agreeing to a "joint development and experimental facility for development of Buna S."

The OASW quickly concluded that no funds for developing Buna S were available. Besides, no money would ever be used without first assessing Buna S independently and then determining "what may be behind this proposition other than the facts as here represented." Nonetheless, the department maintained interest in Buna and continued to offer any aid it could. Since that response meant Standard would proceed on its own, the OASW suggested that the corporation pursue the alternative, involving joint and centralized experimentation and development of Buna S.[22] By mid-1939, however, and apparently without Standard's consent, numerous nonrubber corporations were experimenting with what was essentially Buna S, including Universal Oil Products Company, Phillips Petroleum Corporation, Shell Oil Company, and Dow Chemical.

By mid-1940 Standard Oil made another big leap in successfully developing its own synthetic rubber, Buna X or Butyl, apparently a variation of Buna S. It was operating a small pilot plant and hoped to achieve large-scale production by mid-1942. Butyl cost less than Buna N to produce, would probably be cheaper than other synthetics, and might be the best synthetic rubber for making tires. (Butyl ultimately turned out to be useful only for making inner tubes.) The OASW was so impressed with Butyl that it made a commitment to recommending a government subsidy in an emergency if progress continued and private industry could not carry the financial burden, a rare move by that office. To test the product before enough material was available for all companies, Standard and the OASW worked out a solution in which the latter requested the former to choose the most qualified firm for experimenting with Butyl. Within days, Standard turned to Firestone, a company well qualified for handling almost any synthetic rubber project.

World events and developments within the synthetic rubber field moved so fast that new solutions were necessary before earlier ones could be applied. By mid-1940 Goodyear had also come up with a synthetic, a variation on German Buna. In June 1940 Standard reported to Edward R. Stettinius, Jr., of the National Defense Advisory Commission, that based on consultation with the OASW and leading rubber companies,

> no solution of this [synthetic rubber] problem satisfactory from a national standpoint appears to be possible, save one which involves the broadest possible cooperation along the lines of finance, technical development and patents, between the leading units of the rubber industry and ourselves. It might also prove to be necessary to add other interests in the oil and chemical industries to any such cooperative group in order to insure that the objective is attained.

Furthermore, government financing was indispensable. Without such assistance, mass production of synthetic rubber would not get off the ground. With financial help, a superior synthetic could probably be produced at twenty cents a pound, about the going rate for natural rubber. But everything remained uncertain until experimentation was completed and production under way. Even though government financing was discretionary, cooperation among oil, rubber, financial, chemical, and other firms, many of which Standard was already contracting with, probably required legislation to exempt such practices from antitrust laws.[23]

Standard was beginning to dictate terms for synthetic rubber development. Working closely with the War Department served the corporation well, for it had an ally as negotiations began in 1940 with economic mobilization agencies. Synthetic rubber created a furor within government circles before any resolution was worked out. Ultimately, courts, congressional committees, and most industrial mobilization agencies became involved in a controversy in which private industry was accused of blackmail and aiding Nazi Germany at the expense of the United States, and the federal government was criticized for incompetence. As the government agency most concerned with strategic materials, the military was at the center of this imbroglio.[24]

Army planning for rubber was carried out by a commodity committee headed by a Quartermaster Corps officer because the bureau was the principal consumer of rubber. In contrast to its record in other planning areas, the corps did an excellent job with rubber. By 1925 the committee managed to get reasonably accurate requirement figures from War Department bureaus, the Navy Department, and the Marine Corps. Its first plan of 1925 was uninformed, but revisions between 1926 and 1935 improved steadily. Representatives of the rubber industry reviewing the 1928 plan gave it their "unqualified approval."[25] The commodity committee always stayed abreast of developments involving substitutes, alternate sources, and synthetics. Its last plan was written in 1935 for a three-year period. Planning stopped at that point since synthetic rubber was changing so rapidly that no plan could be kept current.

As a new departure for the Quartermaster Corps, industry and rubber specialists were consulted from the outset and they reviewed the planning and plans. For example, Francis R. Henderson, president of Henderson, Helm, and Company, Incorporated, an expert on rubber and other products in international trade and founder of the New York Rubber Exchange, was recruited in 1926. Even earlier, the Commodity Committee on Rubber and Rubber Goods made contact with the Rubber Manufacturers Association, which included in its membership major rubber corporations as well as many medium-to-small-sized firms. The association continued to serve the OASW until the nation entered the war. For synthetic rubber, the committee dealt with large rubber corporations and other big businesses associated with its development and production.

The Commodity Committee on Rubber and Rubber Goods performed so well and received such unaccustomed cooperation from all military departments and their subdivisions for a number of reasons. With the growing importance of motor vehicles and airplanes to the conduct of warfare, rubber became not only a strategic material but also one that was exceptionally vulnerable.

Under those conditions, accomplished planning became imperative.[26] Other executive agencies and various industries shared the military's concerns.[27] That interest encouraged War Department planners and provided them with a rich body of material and numerous checks to ensure that their planning was realistic and accurate.

Furthermore, OASW planning was affected by peculiarities, making the rubber industry especially dependent on the government. Asian Hevea involved international economics, politics, and diplomacy which in some instances only Washington could handle. Companies attempting to find alternate natural rubber sources in the United States and Latin America also relied heavily on the federal government for research and experimentation and as a potential customer. Without warfare forcing the federal government to act as financier and contractor, the synthetic rubber industry, involving America's industrial giants, would have developed in a very different way. The War Department was included in Washington's extensive ventures with rubber, making OASW activity as much policymaking as planning. That aspect heightened the interest and maximized the performance of even Quartermaster officers, who otherwise tended to be detached.

Rubber, like aluminum, illustrated that national security affected basic federal policies, such as those involving the antitrust statutes. Standard Oil's relations with I. G. Farben pointed to the fact that the interests of multinational corporations could clash with those of national security. Few institutions or policies escaped the impact of modern warfare.

More mundanely, the need for rubber and aluminum indicated the OASW's ability to respond flexibly to strategic industries facing different circumstances. The army planners took a leading role in seeking to resolve a potential rubber shortage under emergency conditions. Their reaction to aluminum was much more passive. Although the OASW underestimated wartime demand for the metal, it realized that aluminum requirements could be met by increasing the nation's productive capacity. Hence, the sense of urgency concerning aluminum was always less than that concerning rubber.

This same flexibility was also evident in the OASW's handling of petroleum and nonferrous metals. These industries further illustrate the multiple complications created by national security in a capitalist economy.

7
PETROLEUM, COPPER, AND LEAD

The third category of the Office of the Assistant Secretary of War's (OASW) commodity planning included petroleum, copper, and lead. These were heavy, large, oligopolistic industries that were nonstrategic. Because of their classification, the industries were often as active, in some instances more active, in pursuing planning than the War Department. The three industries selected for analysis hardly exhaust the list in this grouping.

Petroleum and petroleum products were naturally of great concern to the military since military demand was expanding by leaps and bounds. The use of petroleum products as a source of lubricant and, more important, of fuel, constantly grew as the army became increasingly mechanized and technically advanced. The navy was at least as concerned about oil as the army. Before World War I, the navy had switched almost completely from coal to oil. This led the William Howard Taft and Woodrow Wilson administrations to create naval oil reserves in Wyoming and California and to calls from the Navy Department for tougher regulation of the petroleum industry, perhaps even nationalization. Civilian demand also grew dramatically before and after the war, with the dieselization of the railroads, farm mechanization, the substitution of oil and gas for coal in heating, and most important, the rise of motor-vehicle transportation.

Army planners were fully aware that the United States was better off in terms of oil supply than any other industrial country. In the mid-1930s OASW studies indicated that the United States accounted for 60 percent of world oil output, and when Venezuela and Mexican production were combined with that of the United States, the total reached 80 percent. Nonetheless, during World War I shortages had occurred as a result of distribution problems, transportation being especially troublesome. The huge and intricate system of pipelines for delivering crude that was built after the war appeared to relieve that limitation. During World War II regulation of the oil industry was troubled, although petroleum shortages occurred only in specialized areas such as high-octane gasoline.

What concerned the War Department planners most was the turbulent nature of the industry. After World War I widespread fears existed that the United States would run out of domestic oil. As the decade wore on, rising crude production abroad and a series of dramatic oil strikes at home turned fear of scarcity into intense concern about a flood of excess oil. This reaction led to a controversial but ongoing private-public attempt to stabilize the industry by controlling the output of crude.

The oil industry was divided among various groups. The most important and powerful faction was the "majors," consisting of approximately twenty large, vertically integrated firms, such as Standard Oil Company of New Jersey, which were also the principal importers of crude. These firms and their government allies were instrumental in organizing the American Petroleum Institute (API) in 1919 to continue wartime cooperative patterns. Although the institute's membership included firms from throughout industry, it usually spoke for the big companies. Below the majors were the "independents," made up of smaller, usually unintegrated producers. Though most independents were affiliated with the Independent Petroleum Association of America (IPA), they were far from a united group. Various companies went their own way; some broke from the IPA to set up organizations like the Independent Petroleum Association Opposed to Monopoly, and others operated through state or specialized associations. The oil producing states were also involved in policy formation, and regional splits occurred among Eastern, Southern, Southwestern, and Western producers and states. Independents were generally domestic operators opposed to petroleum imports; the majors divided on the issue, depending on their foreign operations. Further divisions occurred among domestic- as opposed to foreign-based corporations. The major point of difference among the various factions was whether output should be controlled, how this should be done, and who should do it.

Once surplus crude became the main problem, most firms looked to the government for price stability. Republicans in the 1920s and the Democrats in the 1930s proved to be cooperative. By slow stages between the late 1920s and the years of the National Recovery Administration and after, the oil companies joined forces with state and federal governments to limit domestic oil output through a quota system that continued into the post–World War II years. This move constituted all but a cartelization of the industry as an extension of the international oil cartel worked out between 1928 and 1934. Despite ongoing and strong opposition from many sources, the arrangement continued because most private and public interests involved in oil benefited from it.

Because of the World War I experience and the chaotic state of the oil industry in the interwar years, the OASW planners recognized the need to keep abreast of petroleum developments in order to ensure adequate supply at a reasonable price in the event of a national emergency. To accomplish that purpose, a Commodity Committee on Petroleum and Products, chaired by a Quartermaster Corps officer, was created in 1925 even though the industry was classified only as essential. By 1926 the committee had calculated requirements for the various army supply arms and services (SA&S) and had begun coordinating its efforts with the Navy Department. At no time did the committee draw up a detailed plan for petroleum, but it did draft a Resource Study in 1926 that set forth the realities of supply and demand.

To increase its understanding of petroleum, the commodity committee arranged for reserve officers from oil firms to serve for several weeks in the OASW; consulted with oil company executives and other experts such as Mark L. Requa, who headed the Oil Division of the U.S. Fuel Administration during World War I; attended conferences dealing with oil; and availed itself of as many publications as possible. Such exposure, along with revised military mobilization plans, allowed the commodity committee knowledgeably to revise its Resource Study from time to time. Additionally, the committee considered means for regulating the petroleum industry in the event of an emergency, and in 1938 the committee even had a sales manager of Pure Oil Company, who was a reserve major in the Chemical Warfare Service, rework the study to make it easily adaptable to changing circumstances. About the same time the Army-Navy Munitions Board (ANMB) joined in the planning. Its commodity committee on petroleum, drawing on a study made for the board in May 1939 by the Petroleum Subcommittee of the Mineral Advisory Committee, finally wrote a plan for oil that the ANMB approved in January 1940.[1]

Throughout the interwar years, OASW contacts with the oil industry always involved matters other than industrial mobilization planning, especially in the late 1930s and early 1940s after war had broken out. In November 1939, for instance, Standard Oil of New Jersey, as leader of the industry, worked out with the War and State Departments procedures for denying Japan access to the processes for manufacturing high-test aviation gasoline. In other matters, national defense blended much more directly with self-interest. In 1939 and again in 1940, the corporation led representatives of War and Navy Department bureaus on tours of the Esso Laboratories in Bayway, New Jersey, to get the armed services' advice on the direction its research should take.

Despite considerable contact with the petroleum industry, OASW planning was fundamentally flawed. Only at the insistence of the National Defense Advisory Commission in 1940 did the army and navy begin standardizing fuels and lubricants so as to reduce the variety of military usage and to make possible reliable calculations of demand. As things stood, military requirements were stated in amounts of crude. Both civilian and military personnel recognized in the late 1920s that the oil industry's centralized structure required a similar approach within the armed services for efficient operation. Resistance to change stemmed from the traditional War Department problem of independent-minded SA&S going their own way. Also, the Quartermaster Corps' planning for petroleum was typically casual and uninspired.

A more fundamental problem was involved, however. The OASW lacked the forceful, enlightened business guidance essential to plan effectively for a mature industry. In steel, assistance came first from the industry's dominant corporation and then from its powerful trade association.[2] Neither came forth in the oil industry because it was badly divided, subject to legal scrutiny, and constantly under a cloud of suspicion.

Intraindustry strife encouraged political attacks on and governmental action against the oil industry. Despite the government-sanctioned arrangement that virtually cartelized the industry, late New Deal rhetoric was antimonopolistic, antitrust suits were filed and won against petroleum companies for price fixing in the late 1930s, Congress debated legislation for breaking up oil firms, and the Temporary National Economic Committee zeroed in on oil as a primary target. Having to keep an eye on other companies and the federal government while seeking market stability prevented major oil firms from focusing properly on OASW activity.

The American Petroleum Institute was the logical agency for assisting the OASW. With the institute taking an active role in research in 1926, the Commodity Committee on Petroleum and Products assumed that this would lead to a larger role in army planning. The belief was strengthened when Paul Foley, a retired navy captain who had served on the petroleum industry's World War I War Service Committee and was currently on the API staff, proposed creating an agency within the institute to facilitate OASW activity. Despite support from some of the biggest oil firms, the idea was rejected. Various majors, like Union Oil Company of California, foreign-owned firms such as Shell Oil Company, and big independent and small-to-medium-sized companies apparently feared that planning for war would lead domestic giants to tighten their grip on the industry. When Standard of New Jersey offered to set up its own committee on industrial mobilization, the OASW felt compelled to say no.[3] The director of the Planning Branch explained that the War Department preferred working with reasonably representative organizations like the API so as not to antagonize other firms.[4]

Widespread distrust of big oil kept the OASW constantly on guard. Army planners suspected that Standard of New Jersey and other majors were using national defense for ulterior motives, which could end up tainting OASW planning and, during the late 1930s, putting it at odds with antitrust sentiment in the Franklin D. Roosevelt administration and the nation. In the late 1920s William F. Paris, a technical adviser to the Commodity Committee on Petroleum and Products, warned the OASW that if the API sponsored research, big oil firms would exploit the results for commercial benefit.[5] The chair of the petroleum commodity committee in 1934 fretted that Standard Oil of New Jersey's habit of manipulating the gasoline market and other practices of big oil all but invited government control.[6]

Needing the majors, but concerned about associating with them, the OASW turned instead to independent consultants, government officials, or representatives from smaller oil companies for advice. Its contact with leading firms in the industry was at best piecemeal. The situation began to change in 1939 under conditions of a national emergency, but by then civilian mobilization agencies were beginning to be created. When reviewing the OASW oil study in 1940, the National Defense Advisory Commission (NDAC) found it to be grossly inadequate.

Without the guidance of the majors, the study could be nothing else. The American Petroleum Institute and big oil, for example, were fully aware that the military had to centralize its planning and standardize its requirements, but unlike big steel, they were not in a position to impose their will. The needed change took place only when the NDAC, taking signals from the oil majors, insisted on it.

The Commodity Committee on Petroleum and Products constantly chafed under the circumstances it faced. It remained well informed about the oil industry at home and abroad but never wrote a plan. Besides, planning seemed unnecessary since industry had the ability to handle any emergency. Throughout the 1920s, the committee sought to disband or to be placed on inactive status. The OASW regularly said no, with the result that the committee continued to function in a desultory manner.

The Quartermaster Corps, which headed the commodity committee on oil, failed to grasp the reason for planning. Planning was intended to facilitate industrial mobilization by adjusting the military to the patterns of industry. The Quartermaster Corps resisted such change, and a divided and defensive industry was unable to push it in that direction.[7] Oligopolistic industries required direction from major firms in order for OASW planning to succeed. Hence, planning went well with steel, but not with oil.

COPPER

The copper industry resembled that of petroleum in various ways. As an oligopolistic industry indispensable to any war effort, copper could also provide ample supply during hostilities. But copper was free from constant threats of antitrust action because it was not regarded with the same public suspicion as petroleum.

During the war years, the United States produced about 62 percent of the world's supply of refined copper at extraordinarily high prices. On the eve of hostilities, the industry was just beginning to integrate mining, smelting, and the fabrication of semifinished goods. After the war, integration quickened, as did industrial consolidation. The copper industry was well on the way to being dominated by the so-called Big Four: Phelps Dodge Corporation, Anaconda Copper Corporation, American Smelting and Refining Company, and Kennecott Copper Corporation. In the late 1930s these four firms accounted for 80 percent of America's copper, and their subsidiaries processed 50 percent of the copper they produced.[8] During World War II copper deficits were serious, especially in the early years of hostilities.

Washington's interwar policies facilitated further integration and consolidation. With huge copper surpluses threatening to paralyze the industry during the Great Depression, the Herbert Hoover administration pushed through Congress in 1932 an excise tax of four cents on imported copper, just slightly below the cost of output for the principal producers. The National Recovery Administration went further, allowing a code authority to set quotas and prices and to regulate all aspects of production and distribution. A government-backed oligopoly at home allowed American copper giants to participate in a cartel abroad. Under these circumstances, prices rose, domestic output fell below demand in 1936 and 1937, and copper fabricators without their own mines were threatened with extinction. Operations of the copper industry began to concern the people responsible for national defense as America began to prepare for war.[9]

For a good part of the interwar period, copper was classified as critical; then it dropped to the essential category in 1939. The Office of the Assistant Secretary of War estimated in 1933 and 1936 that two years of war would leave the United States with almost a full year of surplus after meeting all military and civilian requirements.

Nonetheless, as was true for all critical and essential commodities, the OASW began preparing studies on copper in the mid-1920s and periodically reviewed and updated the data. Military planners worried only about the location of most copper refining plants, which were on the East Coast, especially around New York City. These centers could easily be knocked out by saboteurs or military attack without the opportunity to rebuild plants before hostilities ceased. Facilities built on the West Coast and in the Southwest in the late 1920s and 1930s modified only slightly this geographic concentration. The OASW's studies led by the Signal Corps and the Signal Corps Industrial Defense Association confirmed these realities, recommended protecting further plants on the East Coast, and suggested that facilities might be relocated at public expense. Since war was remote in the 1920s and relocation complex, expensive, and an unwanted precedent, the recommendation never went far.[10]

By 1933 the OASW Commodity Committee on Non-Ferrous Metals concluded that although copper needed only monitoring, action was necessary to ensure fair pricing. Four years later, planners changed their thinking by declaring that few controls were needed and pricing was not a problem. As its planning progressed, the OASW increasingly accepted the consequences of oligopoly in copper.[11]

The copper industry in the interwar years rather blatantly attempted to use national defense to further its own interests. Industry members had proposed relocating refining facilities at government expense, and in 1933 they pressed the War Department to stockpile the metal even though the need was nonexistent. Firms also lobbied to maintain the excise tax on copper and even to cut off all copper imports to further national security.[12]

The OASW did less planning for copper than for any commodity yet considered. Ample supply and control of the industry by a few firms explains why. Industry's representatives willingly assisted OASW studies, were as active as the War Department in promoting planning, and would have had even closer relations with the planners except for the low priority of copper. The aspect that stands out in the interwar years is the copper corporations' attempts to manipulate the military for their own purposes.

LEAD

Lead, like copper, was classified as a critical commodity for most of the interwar years and then downgraded to the essential category in 1939. Lead was among the first industries to be consolidated in the late nineteenth century under the leadership of the National Lead Company, a vertically integrated firm with an extensive national and international sales organization, a diversified product line, and a high-powered research staff. More stable than either the petroleum or copper industries, the lead industry was also much smaller in size. Despite the importance of the metal for munitions output, the United

States had a plentiful supply. No shortages occurred during World War I, and civilian usage was not seriously curbed.[13] In the early years of World War II, however, the supply of lead presented some problems.

Because of World War I and interwar conditions, the Office of the Assistant Secretary of War never paid much attention to lead. Military planners prepared studies of the industry and reviewed the findings from time to time. In 1933 the Commodity Committee on Non-Ferrous Metals concluded that "lead offers no serious difficulties in time of an emergency and that observation and trouble-shooting only would be necessary." An update in 1936 found conditions to be the same.[14]

The OASW's contacts with industry representatives were virtually nonexistent for most of the interwar period. Then in 1938, apparently because of the war threat, National Lead suddenly began courting the OASW. In February 1938 John J. Dooley, a reserve colonel and a Special Representative for the company, arranged for Col. Charles T. Harris, Jr., director of the Planning Branch, to meet with Fletcher W. Rockwell, president of National Lead, and with other executives. National Lead managers began advising the OASW on lead and other products it handled. Dooley sent the OASW, supply bureaus, and Procurement Districts data and samples of National Lead's line of goods. The OASW was deluged with studies and information on lead, tin, antimony, zinc, and other products from the company's files and from the International Tin Research and Developmental Council and the American Tin Trade Association, organizations in which company executives served as officers. National Lead quickly became well informed about the OASW planning system. It offered to work with the Procurement Districts, accept schedules of production, and so forth. In March 1938 Dooley told Harris that "our concern stands ready to do everything we possibly can to aid in the planning work which you are doing."[15]

National Lead's interest went beyond planning. The company pressed the bureaus and the OASW for contracts, using its military connections to protest when it failed to win competitive bids. More blatantly than most corporations, National Lead plied the OASW with favors. Colonel Harris had standing invitations for lunch, and Dooley sent him courtesy cards from the Commodore Hotel and the Waldorf Astoria. Harris left the Planning Branch in 1938, and Col. Harry K. Rutherford, his replacement, was less than enthusiastic in accepting Dooley's blandishments. Relations between National Lead and the OASW terminated early in 1939 as abruptly as they had started a year earlier.

With critical or essential nonferrous metals besides copper and lead, including zinc, cadmium, rhodium, cryolite, and uranium, the OASW did no more and usually less than it had done with lead. The War Department's contacts with firms in those industries were also limited at best.[16]

Petroleum, copper, and lead highlighted a significant aspect of commodity committee planning. The less strategic a commodity, the greater the tendency for industry to use national security for special gain, such as tariff protection and stockpiling. This tendency usually resulted in lessening the quality of planning because the military was put on guard, and industry, from fear of alienating the planners, would not insist on standardizing usage among supply bureaus and other necessary practices.

Since petroleum, copper, and lead were concentrated industries, relatively easy to regulate, planning was less essential for an emergency than was the case with competitive industries, which were difficult to control. The OASW's work with smaller industries was both more essential and difficult, as its relations with producers of manganese, machine tools, and a host of other commodities made clear.

8
MANGANESE, TIN, MICA, WOOL AND WOOLEN GOODS, MACHINE TOOLS, OPTICAL GLASS, AND MEDICAL SUPPLIES

The fourth category of the Office of the Assistant Secretary of War's (OASW) commodity planning consisted of small-to-medium firms in small-to-medium industries facing an intensely competitive market either at home, abroad, or both. These industries frequently found themselves at odds with industrial giants like steel over national economic policy. Some of the industries in this fourth category had exceptionally strong, active trade associations, but others had weak ones or none; most fell somewhere in between. Because many of these industries were strategic, the OASW was especially interested in them. The industries reciprocated since they frequently used the national defense rationale as a key element in their struggle to survive or grow in a hostile environment. Consequently, OASW personnel and industry leaders shared in the process of initiating and sustaining the planning effort. The enormously rich and varied nature of the fourth category of planning, which included dozens of industries, can be adequately portrayed by focusing on manganese, tin, mica, wool and woolen goods, machine tools, optical glass, and medical supplies.

Except for machine tools, none of these commodities presented critical difficulties during World War II, partly because of interwar efforts to improve supply. The OASW often played an important role in the remedial activity, particularly for manganese, tin, mica, and optical glass.

MANGANESE

The military consistently ranked manganese as the most important strategic commodity throughout the interwar years. The metal was indispensable for making steel, without which no economic mobilization was possible. Approximately fourteen pounds of metallic manganese went into each ton of steel in order to eliminate oxygen and sulfur and to impart desirable qualities. Manganese was also used in the foundry business, including the production of forgings for the military, and in making high-manganese steel alloys. Of less importance, manganese was used in the chemical industry, particularly for the manufacture of dry cell batteries. The steel industry alone consumed 95 percent of the manganese used in the United States.

No substitutes for manganese existed. Moreover, the nation had virtually no ferrograde deposits—i.e., ore containing a minimum of 35 percent metallic manganese used to produce ferromanganese, an alloy of 70 to 82 percent manganese. Prior to World War I, the United States had imported virtually all ferrograde ore or ferromanganese. It possessed nearly boundless deposits of relatively low-grade manganese, but it was uneconomical to process under normal conditions.

With the outbreak of World War I, foreign sources outside Latin America were largely cut off because of the interruption of shipping or the shortage of ships. Manganese shortages became even more exaggerated as demand increased after the United States entered hostilities. Consequently, the price of ferrograde ore and ferromanganese increased by five to six times or more between 1913 and 1918. With such high prices and governmental encouragement, a manganese industry began growing in the United States in 1916. By 1918 it was producing more than 30 percent of overall domestic demand.

When the war ended and trade patterns returned to normal, however, the domestic manganese industry could no longer compete. As a result, the ferroalloy mining interests managed to persuade Congress in early 1919 to amend the War Minerals Stimulation Act of October 1918 so that Washington through early 1926 granted relief funds exceeding $7 million to various mining firms that had expanded operations for war purposes and that had had to cut back at the end of hostilities. Moreover, those same interests pressured Congress into protecting domestic manganese in the 1922 tariff and increasing the strictures against imports in the tariff bill of 1930. Such protection, the manganese producers promised, allowed them to meet or to better foreign prices and to provide a domestic source for this strategic commodity.[1]

To further the cause of controlling raw materials internationally, the American Institute of Mining and Metallurgical Engineers (AIME) and the Mining and Metallurgical Society of America made a comprehensive study of the world's minerals after World War I. In 1922 the OASW arranged for these groups to set up committees of specialists to report on strategic metals and other commodities as an extension of their earlier work.[2]

Manganese was among the metals studied by a group the engineering societies called their Committee on Industrial Preparedness. In its 1924 report to the OASW, the Sub-Committee on Manganese spoke as a detached neutral in the highly charged debate over manganese. Its principal finding was that the United States had no high-grade manganese ores able to compete with foreign sources; it had at most a five-year supply of rich ore. Under the best peacetime conditions, including assistance, domestic producers could account for only 7 percent of demand. These realities led the subcommittee to recommend that the United States slowly build up a two-year stockpile of ferrograde manganese ore so that it could begin domestic production and seek alternate sources if cut off from foreign markets.[3]

The engineering societies updated their report on manganese in 1932. With that work, supplemented by investigations by Naval Intelligence, the Interior Department's Bureau of Mines, the U.S. Geological Survey, and by the Commerce Department's and its own planning, the OASW had information on manganese as complete as was possible. All parties agreed that the United States could never be self-sufficient in high-grade manganese. New or existing processes for concentrating manganese ores were either unproven or of limited applicability.[4]

These findings reflected the views of the steel industry. About nine of the major American steel corporations manufactured or used, and usually both, about 90 percent of the ferromanganese consumed in the United States. These firms, along with the steel industry in general, opposed tariff protection for manganese because it would not result in a reliable domestic supply, and it would deplete peacetime, in-ground reserves in the event of war and a manganese shortage.

Manganese markets were determined abroad, not at home. The four major suppliers were Russia, India, Africa, and Brazil. Each had huge reserves, and their combined production exceeded international demand, which made the industry intensely competitive and not particularly profitable. Russian manganese was the best in quality and the most extensive in quantity. In order to earn foreign currency, the Soviets attempted to out-compete others through price cuts. American steel firms, and particularly the United States Steel Corporation, continued to purchase most of their manganese from the USSR, as they had previously from Czarist Russia, based on long-term contracts and good relations with the existing government.

U.S. Steel also owned and worked the principal manganese mine in Brazil. However, it preferred to buy manganese from other sources so as to hold the Brazilian ore—which was expensive to market—in reserve.[5] When the Franklin D. Roosevelt administration in 1935 signed a reciprocal trade agreement with

Brazil reducing the existing tariff on manganese by 50 percent, the action caused an uproar in domestic manganese circles and an upset in the War Department, but the consequences were hardly dire.[6]

The OASW never settled on a firm manganese policy, despite reliable data from authoritative sources. In part this stemmed from reluctance to accept dependence in such a critical area. Of even greater importance was the manganese industry's unremitting lobbying and promise of national self-sufficiency.

The manganese producers demonstrated considerable political clout in the subsidies and tariff protection they won after World War I. Determined to increase their influence in what they perceived as a fight for existence, the small producers characteristic of the industry organized in August 1927 the American Manganese Producers Association (AMPA). The organization's driving force was its president, J. Carson Adkerson, who was also vice-president of the Virginia-based Hy-Grade Manganese Company.

The AMPA used national defense as its principal rationale. Adkerson proved to be an energetic, shrewd, and ruthless advocate for his cause. He focused on the War Department as the federal agency most concerned about manganese, maneuvering in 1927 to make it appear as if the department endorsed AMPA policies.[7] Adkerson also quickly launched a major campaign to locate and survey all possible manganese deposits in the United States. Between 1927 and 1933 he periodically announced the number of states with reserves as the totals climbed from twenty to thirty-five. State officials, representatives in Congress, and geologists could then be called upon for support and ultimately for votes. The AMPA also encouraged and fully publicized the development of new methods for treating and concentrating low-grade ore. When the Great Depression all but wiped out domestic production of manganese, Adkerson added jobs as a principal argument for supporting the industry.

In fighting to save manganese producers, Adkerson sought funding from a host of governmental agencies, pushed legislation requiring that steel used in government projects be made from domestic manganese, and advocated numerous similar measures. If given a chance, he vowed, American manganese firms would make bonded commitments to meet all domestic demands with higher grade products than those coming from abroad at a competitive price. Standing in the way, according to Adkerson, were giant steel firms and an ideologically motivated Soviet Union using "convict labor" to dump manganese on the world market. To support his claims, the AMPA president mustered elaborate statistical data that was at best manipulative, at worst grossly deceptive.[8]

For the Office of the Assistant Secretary of War, manganese was as controversial as it was important. Late in 1926 an OASW officer warned his colleagues about being made "a cat's paw of the 'Interests'" or others seeking to manipulate national policies for manganese.[9] Several years later, the secretary of war explained that he could not comment on tariffs because "manganese ore is so involved with conflicting commercial interests."[10] The department regularly turned away from requested backing for subsidies, loans, and price supports.[11]

Throughout the interwar years, however, the War Department pushed stockpiles of manganese more than any other commodity. But even here it encountered endless conflict. The AMPA unrealistically argued for stockpiling from domestic supply and vehemently opposed exchanging excess American farm products for manganese or having war debts paid off in strategic commodities. Fearing that stockpiles might come from its own limited funding, the War Department late in 1934 desperately but unsuccessfully tried to persuade steel companies to set aside part of their manganese holding as a reserve. The OASW made little progress with manganese before Pearl Harbor, even after the Roosevelt administration rather reluctantly agreed to a congressionally sanctioned program of stockpiling strategic materials beginning in 1938.[12]

The OASW's most extensive effort in behalf of domestic manganese involved concentrating low-grade ore. The so-called Chamberlain, South Dakota, reserves stand out in this regard. In 1932 the American Institute of Mining and Metallurgical Engineers recommended that the federal government explore the possibility of having the extensive Chamberlain deposits concentrated and commercially exploited as a way of ending America's manganese dependence.[13] By early 1933 the Bureau of Mines and the General Manganese Corporation, which controlled large acreage in the Chamberlain area, had conducted preliminary explorations but lacked funds to complete the job. Desperate for the work to go on, the War Department sought the steel industry's financial support.[14] When that failed to materialize, the OASW then tried to tap National Industrial Recovery Act money and even promised to commit up to $.5 million of departmental funds to keep the project going. Tight budgets all around delayed and then ended progress. Nothing came of the Chamberlain deposits.

That was not true for new technology in concentrating ores. Ongoing work by the Bureau of Mines perfected the electrolytic process for extracting metallic manganese from lean ores between 1936 and 1939. As a spin-off of bureau accomplishments, the Electro Manganese Corporation was organized in 1939 and began producing electrolytic manganese at a facility built in Knoxville, Tennessee. By 1942 the company had become commercially viable, and it expanded through wartime demand and the government's financial assistance. The company established, however, that no domestic manganese ores were suitable for the electrolytic process, denying the United States the desired self-sufficiency. Imported low-iron, high-manganese ores had to be used.[15]

Other ferroalloys were classified as strategic, although none had the urgency of manganese. Of great importance was nickel, which increases substantially the tensile strength of steel and, when combined with copper and small amounts of cobalt, produces monel, an alloy resistive to salt water and corrosion. Nickel is also crucial to the production of many munitions. Army planners never worried much about nickel. The International Nickel Company (switching its incorporation from the United States to Canada in 1929) had a virtual monopoly on world nickel output. The company had cooperated fully with the War Industries Board during World War I, and it assisted OASW planning throughout the interwar years.[16]

Chromium and tungsten also remained on the ferroalloys strategic list throughout the interwar years. The first was used in making stainless steel and high-strength, high-elastic steels for munitions and numerous civilian uses as well as serving in the manufacture of refractories and in the tanning of leather. The second was needed for making high-speed cutting tools and specialized munitions. These metallic elements concerned the OASW even less than nickel because of supply sources in the United States, Alaska, Canada, or Latin America and because of available substitutes.[17]

The group that became the Commodity Committee on Ferro-Alloys was, along with the steel committee, among the best of the OASW subdivisions. It established an elaborate system of advisers drawn from government agencies, leading engineering societies, and representative industrial firms. Before approaching such experts, the committee usually familiarized itself with the literature on the subject. It was able to operate effectively even when a commodity as controversial as manganese was involved. By 1925 the committee had guided the writing of procurement plans for manganese, nickel, tungsten, chromium, and vanadium (which in 1938 was dropped from the strategic to the critical category) and periodically reviewed and updated them. Moreover, the commodity committee stayed abreast of technological advances and worked with arsenals and private industry in searching for substitutes.

This work was accomplished despite the usual problems of officers coming and going with regularity or being distracted by other, higher-priority duties and despite the bureaus resisting planning. Nevertheless, through persistence, the commodity committee managed by the mid-1920s to receive fairly good requirement figures from the supply arms and services (SA&S) and the Navy Department; it then began refining calculations by introducing standardized methods for computing demand and by insisting that gross figures on ferroalloys be broken down to indicate specifics on types and uses.

The quality of planning stemmed largely from the Ordnance Department's direction. It was the best of the supply bureaus in planning, and the other supply units followed its firm, consistent, and intelligent lead.[18]

TIN

As with ferroalloys, some nonferrous metals also fell into the strategic category. The most important of these was tin, but mercury and antimony also demanded attention.

The United States has no significant tin deposits. Yet before World War I the nation consumed more than 50 percent of total world output. Britain dominated the international tin market through its control of Malaya (the principal source) and other areas. Most of the metal went to the tin plate (sheet iron or sheet steel covered with tin) industry, with large quantities also used in making solders, bearings, and brass and bronze. Tin also had other uses, with some applications in munitions.

At the outbreak of World War I, demand for tin escalated, with the supply interrupted for various reasons. Prices skyrocketed. By May 1918 tin sold for $1.38 a pound as compared with $.31 in August 1914. Through national and international efforts, the United States managed to bring the price down to about $.70 in late 1918. In August 1918 an International Tin Executive, formed in London, directed all Allied purchases of tin. The War Industries Board (WIB) linked its efforts with those of the London executive.

In addition to working out a system for obtaining foreign tin at a reasonable price, the WIB's Tin Section managed to reduce demand through conservation and substitution measures. The war also stimulated the detinning industry. Then in 1916, American Smelting and Refining Company and another firm built modest tin-smelting plants in New York and New Jersey. In the last year of war about 10 percent of total national tin consumption was produced in the United States, with recovery methods accounting for an additional 25 percent. The rest was imported. In general, the nation suffered no tin shortages, although the total supply declined.[19]

Through export taxes and other devices, the British moved quickly after World War I to shut down America's new tin smelting industry. The War Department supported tin firms in seeking tariff protection in 1922, but the effort failed because the industry was weak and divided and steel was opposed.[20]

The Office of the Assistant Secretary of War, therefore, turned to other approaches. Its first and continuing emphasis was on stockpiling, as part of a broad-based program for building up reserves of strategic materials, which the office pushed throughout the interwar years and for which it received backing in the mid-1930s from a subdivision of the National Resources Board (created in June 1934 by Pres. Roosevelt to consider national planning for all natural resources), the State Department, and some elements in Congress. Nothing significant occurred until 1938. In the early stages of stockpiling, though, tin received a high priority, with 40 percent of appropriations going for its purchase.[21]

With prospects slight for restarting a domestic smelting industry or for storing adequate reserves, the OASW ultimately turned to the detinning industry. Secondary tin recovered from scrap was not an especially large enterprise, but it had received a big boost during World War I. For a ten-year period stretching from 1925 through 1934, secondary tin recovery accounted for nearly 27 percent of total national usage. Over opposition from the White House, the Commerce Department, tin plate producers and users, and metal and scrap exporters, the OASW was instrumental in Congress' authorizing the secretary of state to regulate the export of tin plate scrap. In doing so, he was advised by a National Munitions Control Board, created under the Neutrality Act of 1935 and consisting of representatives from the State, War, Navy, Treasury, and Commerce Departments. The War Department used the board to reduce and then cut off the export of tin plate. By 1940 military planners also advanced from verbally supporting new detinning firms to considering using departmental funds in their behalf.[22] The OASW additionally stayed abreast of and encouraged research on substitutes for tin, although this approach had limited results.[23] At all times, conservation actually appeared more promising than substitution, where tin was involved.[24]

Tin planning had a slow start because the metal had a separate commodity committee between 1924 and 1926, chaired by an officer from the Quartermaster Corps, among the weakest of the supply arms and services for economic planning. Lacking knowledge and without industrial contacts, the committee produced useless plans in the 1920s, and its efforts were saved from total failure by Ordnance officers taking the initiative to inform themselves about tin. In mid-1926, the Commodity Committee on Tin was abolished and responsibility for the metal given to the Commodity Committee on Non-Ferrous Metals, headed by an Ordnance officer. From that point, the quality of planning improved greatly, based on extensive study and wide consultation with industry, engineering societies, and other governmental agencies. By the mid-1930s the War Department was considered to be an expert on the subject.[25]

Mercury and antimony as strategic commodities also required planning. Since the demand for both could be met through national sources or those in Latin America, and since various substitutes could be used in an emergency, planning for these commodities lacked the urgency of tin. In the nonferrous field, the commodity committee also focused on platinum and zinc, but they received even less attention because the former was listed only as critical and the latter as essential.[26]

MICA

Mica, a generic term for various mineral silicates, remained classified as strategic throughout the interwar years. Its virtually unique qualities as an insulator against electricity and heat, its durability and toughness, and its ability to be worked into almost any shape gave this mineral numerous industrial uses, especially for all aspects of the growing electrical industry. The use of mica increased steadily along with the sophistication of the economy, doubling every seven years in the twentieth century. With the use of electricity in automobiles, airplanes, radios, and the like, the armed forces also used growing amounts of mica either directly or indirectly.

Most high-grade mica came from India; Canada was a principal source of a lower-grade variety, which the United States also produced in quantity. During World War I, the United States joined Great Britain in controlling imports and distribution and indirectly in setting prices. Through foreign supply and increased domestic output, America avoided a crisis in mica during hostilities, although serious shortages of high-grade mica existed at the war's end. Prices went up rapidly for a time, but the American-British control mechanisms kept them reasonably stable once implemented. Prices that ranged from $.25 to $5.00 per pound in 1913 stood at $.50 to $15.00 in 1918.[27]

The Office of the Assistant Secretary of War classified mica as strategic as soon as planning began and the office played as important a role in formulating national policy for the product as it did with tin. Lacking readily available, reliable data on mica, the OASW between 1924 and 1928 consulted widely with miners, producers, importers, dealers, users, and trade associations, including the Asheville Mica Company, the General Electric Company, and the National Electrical Manufacturers Association.[28] Requiring even more facts,[29] the War Department prevailed upon the Bureau of Mines to conduct a full-scale survey of domestic mica between 1928 and 1930. The accumulated information established that the United States had enough mica deposits to be self-sufficient in an emergency, although at least a year would be necessary to establish substantial production. Furthermore, with foreign sources plentiful, imports were unlikely to be cut off entirely.[30]

To improve peacetime output of mica, the OASW worked with producers and users and the Bureau of Mines, the Bureau of Standards, and other governmental agencies. Although results were disappointing, the War Department succeeded in persuading Washington to adopt standards and grades for mica that would help the industry and assist military calculation of requirements and procurement. By 1934 the OASW concluded that although mica required close attention, it was not as serious a concern as other strategic materials.[31]

The Commodity Committee on Mica was an excellent planning body because the Signal Corps (next to Ordnance, the best of the supply arms and services in planning) directed activity, and Majors Alfred H. Hobley and William H. Crom of the Air Corps—two of the OASW's outstanding officers—served as technical advisers and coordinators during critical years. Through its diligence and insistence on performance, the mica committee won the cooperation of the other SA&S. By 1925 it had complete mica requirements from the War and Navy Departments, and those figures were periodically updated. Unlike some committees, the mica committee carefully examined statistics coming from the SA&S. The committee was also one of the few systematically to clear bureau requirements and to push the SA&S in placing accepted schedules of production.[32]

WOOL AND WOOLEN GOODS

Wool is the most important animal fiber, of critical importance to the military. Any substantial increase in the size of the fighting forces converts immediately into a sizable jump in demand for wool and woolen products to clothe the troops. In 1934 the OASW estimated that during the first year of war, military requirements per person would be about twenty times that of average civilian usage and around ten times that amount in the second year of hostilities. The industry simply could not meet such a sudden surge in demand with domestic output. The choke point would be in the availability of raw wool, not in preparing the fiber for processing or in actual manufacturing, since significantly increasing the sheep population required a long lead time. Military requirements could be met if the entire output of wool went to the armed forces, but this was unacceptable because the civilian economy would be left with nothing.

To deal with these realities, the OASW established a Commodity Committee on Wool and Woolen Goods in 1924 that remained active until the nation began mobilizing for World War II. During those years, the OASW classified wool as strategic. In 1934 the director of the OASW's Planning

Branch observed that wool would require "the closest control of any commodity" in the purview of planners.[33]

During World War I, the War Industries Board and its predecessors, the War Trade Board, and the War Department worked with Great Britain to regulate the importation of Australian and New Zealand wool, and they gradually took control of all domestically produced and imported wool, including its distribution and price. Conservation measures, policies to curb speculative abuses, and related programs were also implemented to protect the civilian sector.[34]

The OASW's concern about wool centered on two areas. With the military services absorbing an extraordinarily high percentage of total wartime supply, and particularly so during the first year, mobilization would have to be exceptionally efficient. Only then would the armed services' needs be met, with adequate amounts left for civilians.

The second factor involved the complex and volatile nature of the domestic industry. Raw wool output depended on weather conditions, slaughter rates, and the like. Its marketing took place through an intricate network that was vulnerable at a number of points. Making raw wool into manufactured cloth involved numerous stages, including yarn-making, weaving, knitting, and dyeing. The United States had quite a few integrated mills that performed these functions. The largest was the American Woolen Company, which accounted for 18 percent of total production but was unable to dominate the industry because it operated in a buyers' market. Small, mostly privately owned, and specialized firms predominated. Wool was still an old-fashioned, outdated industry that had not standardized products or costs, had no large customers other than the automobile industry and the government, and had crude marketing methods. Generally unprofitable, the industry was ravaged by intense competition.

Rightfully concerned about the instability of an industry upon which it was so dependent, the army turned to a number of public and private organizations to facilitate planning and ultimately mobilization. For the first stage of gathering and purchasing wool, there was the National Wool Marketing Corporation, created under the Agriculture Marketing Act of 1929. Through its financial functions, the Farm Credit Administration of the New Deal years also had considerable influence over wool markets. Two trade groups, the National Wool Growers Association and the National Wool Trade Association, represented most wool producers.

An organization also existed for the next major stage, which included processing the wool and manufacturing wool products: the National Association of Wool Manufacturers (NAWM), one of the nation's oldest trade associations. It represented around 75 percent of all wool manufacturers, who accounted for about 90 percent of marketed wool products. The association worked quite effectively with various governmental agencies to maintain excellent trade statistics and to improve trade practices. The National Recovery Administration (NRA) had been a definite plus for the industry, regulating hours and conditions of work and attempting to limit production capacity to the level of demand. Other business groups also aided the Commodity Committee on Wool and Woolen Goods. Further, the OASW drew heavily on the expertise of various subdivisions of the Agriculture Department, consulted with the Bureau of Standards, and sought the assistance of former members of the War Industries Board and other World War I mobilization agencies.

Planning for wool reached maturity by the mid-1930s. The plans were based on a principle, repeated time and again, that "the existing marketing machinery must be utilized, since an entirely new organization could not be set up in time," and attempts to create one would mean that "we will fail in handling the problem."[35]

The Quartermaster Corps headed the Commodity Committee on Wool and Woolen Goods and did a reasonably good job, perhaps because wool played such a large part in the corps' activities. By early 1925 Quartermaster had obtained complete figures on requirements from the supply arms and services and had written the first procurement plan for wool. It was revised and updated every few years. In addition, the commodity committee allocated plants to the various bureaus and surveyed facilities when possible.[36]

Several fundamental and interrelated flaws marred the otherwise sound planning of the commodity committee. Constant turnover of personnel deprived it of the continuous leadership essential for first-rate planning. Consequently, the planning went through periods of inactivity between 1925 and 1939 that became most serious when the War Department began the transition to war in the late 1930s.

More consequentially, the Quartermaster Corps intended to dominate the wool industry during wartime. In its plans, the corps would operate virtually alone, not as part of the OASW, the War Department, the Army-Navy Munitions Board, or civilian mobilization agencies. Such parochialism by the SA&S had all but wrecked army supply operations in 1917. Without much success, the ANMB insisted that Quartermaster operations had to be consistent with the Industrial Mobilization Plan. When the Quartermaster Corps also refused to formalize the advisory role of the National Association of Wool Manufacturers and others in the military's planning, an exasperated ANMB in 1939 joined the NAWM in providing for a series of advisory bodies.

Mixed motives account for civilian advisers assisting the military. Self-interest was evident in the industry's request for assistance with tariff protection and expanding sheep husbandry. Moreover, a number of wool manufacturers sold to the government in peacetime, particularly to the army. On a different plane, a decentralized, destructively competitive industry, which benefited from forms of government planning in the 1920s and 1930s, looked positively on OASW activity. More directly, aiding the army could help avoid repeating the chaotic mobilization of the early World War I period.[37]

Along with wool, the OASW classified silk as strategic throughout the interwar years. But military uses were limited, involving mainly cartridge bags and parachutes for personnel and pyrotechnical devices. Ample reserves of silk, and of rayon and nylon as substitutes, reduced the importance of the commodity further. The OASW came close to removing silk from the strategic list, but it never did so.[38] Despite the lack of urgency, the Ordnance Department's planning for silk was always excellent. Dedicated to helping the military and themselves, the industry and its principal trade association proved to be exceptionally cooperative. Manipulating the national defense rationale for commercial gain showed up only with those individuals who were trying to create a raw silk industry in this country.[39]

Unlike silk, shellac was removed from the strategic list in the interwar years.[40] Before that happened, however, the Commodity Committee on Shellac, which was one of the first to be created by the OASW, set important precedents for the use of civilian advisers. After nearly stumbling badly over this crucial practice, the OASW decreed that advisers had no official War Department status and should be representative of industry. This move allowed the War Department readily to shift advisers, as lacquers and synthetic resins replaced shellac in nearly every instance. Representatives of the shellac industry cooperated readily with the commodity committee, at least in part to help save their market position. Actually, shellac spokesmen were more impressive than the military planners, led first by the Air Service and then by the Quartermaster Corps, both of which were often lax in commodity committee work.[41]

MACHINE TOOLS

The other industries in the fourth category of commodity committee planning were unusual in that they manufactured either finished products or goods essential to their output. Nonetheless, these industries were of such importance to the military that they were labeled as strategic or were the subject of intensive planning or both throughout the interwar years. Machine tools, optical glass, and surgical instruments were particularly significant in this regard.

Machine tools, used to work metal for the purpose of making other goods, are basic to the operations of any industrial society. The United States led the world in the quality and quantity of machine tools produced. The specialized nature of munitions made machine tools critically important to the military. In fact, the origins of the industry in the United States were closely related to the production of firearms. During World War I, machine tools created problems that would have grown in severity had hostilities continued. Nonetheless, good management by a subdivision of the War Industries Board handled the situation effectively.[42]

The OASW's interwar work on machine tools illustrated some of the best and worst features of the military's economic planning. Beginning early and continuing until 1940, army planners never flagged in their effort to be prepared in the area. But War Department politics undermined the planning. Because machine tools were so important, the supply bureaus thwarted the OASW's goals for the industry.

The machine tool industry had qualities that both facilitated and complicated planning. It was a small industry of modest-sized companies concentrated in the sector east of the Mississippi and north of the Ohio Rivers. Major producers were owner-managed family firms of generational depth. If the necessary skilled labor and stock of machine tools were available, the industry had great elasticity in production.

Machine tool manufacturing was not especially profitable, and it was highly competitive in terms of quality, originality, and ingenuity of output. Patents and trade names were less important than company labels and reputations, such as Pratt and Whitney Corporation and Brown and Sharpe Company. Within a competitive atmosphere, a cooperative spirit existed among firms that were big purchasers of each others' specialized machines. This relatively friendly attitude was reflected in the industry's principal trade association, the National Machine Tool Builders' Association (NMTBA), which, its president boasted in 1937, was "one of the finest trade associations in the U.S."[43] The association's statistical and forecasting services were excellent, as were its educational, promotional, and legislative functions.[44]

Planning for machine tools began virtually with the creation of the Office of the Assistant Secretary of War. After some organizational juggling, a commodity committee was created for machine tools in 1926. For the OASW, "practically the whole of the industrial mobilization must be based on the capacity for obtaining special tools," giving them "precedence over practically all other items."⁴⁵ Machine tools, however, never had the strategic label because theoretically they could be manufactured as needed.

Pushed by the National Machine Tool Builders' Association, the Commodity Committee on Machine Tools conducted the first national, peacetime survey of machine tools between 1926 and 1928. The planners then moved on to requirements. The supply arms and services were asked to establish their needs as rapidly as possible, the Navy Department was invited into the planning, and, most important, all planning staffs were encouraged to complete factory plans expeditiously so as to facilitate determining machine tool needs.⁴⁶

The crash of 1929 brought machine tool planning to a sudden halt. The depression wrecked the industry and reduced military planning to little more than gestures. Years passed before any measurable progress was made. Early in 1934 the head of the OASW again assembled army and navy personnel to restart machine tool planning.⁴⁷ By then, the industry had slowly returned to reasonable levels of production.

The National Recovery Administration, the National Machine Tool Builders' Association, and the Army Ordnance Association (AOA) played key roles in reactivating the planning. The chairman of the Commodity Committee on Machine Tools served on the NRA code authority for machine tools and forging machinery, and the NMTBA was active in NRA affairs. At the same time, the Army Ordnance Association began acting as liaison between the NMTBA and the OASW. Personal ties helped. Individuals such as Walter W. Tangeman, vice-president of the Cincinnati Milling Machine Company, were simultaneously members of or advisers to the Ordnance Procurement Districts, the AOA, and the NMTBA.⁴⁸

R. E. W. Harrison, in 1934 and 1935 chief of the Machinery Division, Bureau of Foreign and Domestic Commerce, Department of Commerce, did more than most in improving relations between the machine tool industry and the government. A nationally recognized authority on machine tools, Harrison resumed his practice as a consultant to metal working industries after leaving government, and he served as an officer of the Hydraulic Machinery Manufacturers' Association. Harrison was also a reserve officer and a member of the AOA.⁴⁹

Ironically, the Ordnance Department was the biggest obstacle to restarting machine tool planning. With machine tools basic to so many of its operations, the Ordnance Department in the 1930s became uncharacteristically protective in the area, opposing any outside interference. This attitude violated many of the planning principles Ordnance had helped to author and implement. Disharmony between the OASW and Ordnance—which controlled the Commodity Committee on Machine Tools and had a dominant voice in the assistant secretary's office—virtually paralyzed the former. For several years, the OASW, the NMTBA, and machine toolmakers attempted to proceed with the planning, but Ordnance consistently dragged its feet.

In February 1936 Capt. D. N. Hauseman, Ordnance chair of the Commodity Committee on Machine Tools, ultimately moved to break the stalemate.[50] Under his leadership, the Navy Department joined the planning, and a full-scale program for governing machine tool use during war was proposed. It set forth the principle of centralized control of machine tools during an emergency. In 1937 and 1938 the military and civilian planners worked more closely together on requirements than had ever before been the case.[51] Most immediately, they initiated and oversaw a new survey of the machine tools between February and October 1938 to guide policymaking.

As military planners entered their most intense period of activity with the NMTBA, they also participated in a similar, small-scale project with the Hydraulic Machinery Manufacturers' Association. Unlike machine tools, the hydraulic machinery industry depended rather heavily on the sale of its products to the armed services and military contractors in peace and war for the manufacture of powder, explosives, and shells. Since the OASW's work with the Hydraulic Machinery Manufacturers' Association began only in 1938, progress was slow.

Abrupt changes clouded the OASW's relations with both the National Machine Tool Builders' Association and the Hydraulic Machinery Manufacturers' Association by late 1938. Military planners cut off communication with industry spokesmen, rejected or avoided their initiatives, and appeared uninformed about or uninterested in what had recently transpired. Most important, industry advice in critical matters was ignored. The ANMB, for example, began instituting a system for allocating machine tools contrary to policies that had been agreed upon.

Several developments explain this sudden and dramatic turnabout. As the military began shifting from planning to procurement in 1938, different priorities prevailed as the services focused on producing munitions, not on preparing to do so. Of even greater significance, the OASW in 1938 and 1939 lost some of its best officers, who had directed the most productive stages of planning in the mid-to-late 1930s, when their bureaus recalled them for duty. Their replacements were inferior in almost every way. Finally, with mobilization starting, the Army-Navy Munitions Board took on greater responsibility and authority, seriously disrupting the continuity and quality of planning. These changes encouraged rigidity on the part of the armed services, strengthening earlier and negative proclivities in machine tool planning that had been slowly modified between 1936 and 1938.

The machine tool industry was furious with the new turn of events. Late in 1938, R. E. W. Harrison admitted to a sense of

> frustration and futility. I feel that we have gotten precisely nowhere. I have a major over-riding interest in seeing that the Services get what they ought to have, even though the way the Services go at buying their machinery at times gives me a heartache and headache, and a lot of other pains which are indescribable.[52]

Overall, planning for machine tools was erratic at best, a failure at worst. That the Ordnance Department, backed by the Air Corps and the Navy Department, would undermine the planning indicates the enormous difficulty the OASW faced at all times in fulfilling its responsibilities.

The machine tool industry's participation in planning resulted from both self-interest and national interest. The NMTBA assisted the OASW's activities at least in part to strengthen its position, attract more members, and rationalize the industry. With some success, the industry worked for greater military appropriations, for legislation authorizing educational orders, and the like. These activities, however, were not tied to any special gain, since machine toolmakers sold little to the military during peacetime. The hydraulic machinery manufacturers did; yet their cooperation with planning did not begin until 1938. Planning activity was lowest in the early 1930s when machine toolmakers most needed orders. Ample evidence exists for patriotic motives on the industry's part.[53] Beyond question, the industry and the NMTBA wanted to avoid the disorganization and distortions of World War I. Their part in preparedness planning was closer to the high level of the engineering societies than to much of the rest of the manufacturing sector.[54]

The OASW suffered by not maximizing relations with the machine tool industry, which became clear in 1939 and 1940. The Army-Navy Munitions Board found itself competing unfavorably for machine tools with newly created civilian mobilization agencies. Late in 1940 the Ordnance Department pleaded for a prestigious, high-powered civilian assistant to enable the military to hold its own in machine tools against the National Defense Advisory Commission.[55] These problems would have been lessened greatly by implementing the centralized control over machine tools advocated so adamantly by the NMTBA.

Failures notwithstanding, interwar planning for machine tools had positive results. The OASW fully understood the importance of machine tools for mobilization, the need to work closely with private industry, the necessity for reducing requirements to a minimum and standardizing and simplifying demand, and using existing plants and tools before building new ones. In one way or another, interwar planning for machine tools anticipated almost every meaningful problem encountered during World War II.[56]

The OASW did some work on hardware and hand tools from the mid-1920s to the early 1930s. A commodity committee was established for these products, but it never became active. These goods were too numerous, too easily produced, and too readily substituted to create any special concern among military planners. Nonetheless, the office studied the industries, sought the advice of experts, and analyzed market conditions before concluding that no particular effort was required. Consequently, the OASW allocated facilities to the various SA&S and the latter were left to deal with the industries as they chose, an approach that avoided any serious problems.[57]

OPTICAL GLASS

Optical glass, a critical component for various finished goods, was a subject of extensive study in the interwar years, and it carried the strategic label.

Prior to World War I, the United States had almost no optical glass industry and few optical instrument producers. (Germany was the leader in both fields, holding the patents and, for optical glass, the secret formulas.) With the outbreak of war, most nations had to scramble to provide their forces with optical glass and instruments. In modern militaries, these products had critically important direct applications as fire-control instruments, field glasses, sextants, and photographic and projecting equipment, and various indirect uses, such as in microscopes and surveying equipment.

Once the United States became a belligerent, it launched a program for creating or enlarging the optical glass and instrument industries, with the federal government central to the activities. Actually, Bausch and Lomb Optical Company of Rochester, New York, moved before the war started. Anticipating hostilities and adverse effects on its civilian markets, the company established the nation's first plant for making optical glass in 1912. Experimental work became frantic when America entered the war. Washington arranged for the Carnegie Institution's Geophysical Laboratory to send a team of scientists to Bausch and Lomb to speed the production of optical glass. The Bureau of Standards also played a significant role, combining its own efforts to perfect optical glass-making with those of Bausch and Lomb and other firms. To help provide the needed work force, Rochester Mechanics' Institute—a trade school—supervised a training program. The Mount Wilson Observatory joined forces with the Ordnance Department to expedite the grinding of precision optical glass.

In March 1918 the War Industries Board created a Military Optical Glass and Instruments Section, which established control over the placement of all orders and generally directed the industry.

The concerted wartime drive for self-sufficiency in optical glass and instruments ultimately paid off. The United States entered hostilities producing a few thousand pounds of optical glass a month; late in 1918 it had a monthly output of 80,000 pounds. Bausch and Lomb emerged as the major optical equipment-maker, producing 65 percent of wartime output. Official histories claim that the glass was excellent, but Carl L. Bausch, vice-president of the company, said that it was distinctly of inferior quality compared to German products.[58]

America continued to produce optical glass in the interwar years but never to the point of self-sufficiency. Most of the wartime producers were forced out of business by European competition. Only Bausch and Lomb continued as a major producer, making glass for the lenses and prisms of the high-quality scientific apparatus and military instruments it turned out. The Bureau of Standards also continued to produce and experiment with glass. A small part of its output went to War Department arsenals; most went to Navy Department optical shops.

The Commodity Committee on Optical Glass (first called Optical Glass and Instruments) became active only in February 1927, delayed by resistance from the supply arms and services and the Navy Department. Since it was the major claimant, the Ordnance Department headed the planning for most of the 1920s and 1930s. Ordnance, the Air Corps, and the Navy Department were the principal users; the other War Department bureaus were of only incidental importance.[59]

The committee made no substantial gains until the early 1930s when the hesitant Bausch and Lomb was almost literally integrated into the planning process. Between 1934 and 1937 the Commodity Committee on Optical Glass combined its efforts with the company—assisted by the Rochester Ordnance District, the Bureau of Standards, and various military and naval users—to devise solutions for the major issues affecting the production of optical glass and instruments. Under new formulas for estimating requirements, the planners concluded that if Bausch and Lomb maximally expanded its optical glass output, other firms matched the company's production, and the Bureau of Standards operated at capacity, wartime requirements could probably be filled.[60] To facilitate that goal, the commodity committee and industry worked out policies to ensure the availability of raw materials, specialized equipment, and trained workers. Even then, six months would pass before full production was under way. To cover that period, the War Department ingeniously drew on current funding to stockpile optical glass, quantities that took up less space than that of a railroad box car.

To rationalize the procurement of optical instruments, Ordnance and Bausch and Lomb reduced optical glass used by the military to fourteen types and also standardized and minimized the number of shapes. Under pressure, the armed services agreed to accept Bausch and Lomb's high-quality field glasses and other commercial products for official use. So as to put military contracting within reach of more companies, Bausch and Lomb also persuaded the services, particularly the Army Air Corps, to ease permissible tolerances for camera equipment. Moreover, Bausch and Lomb generally convinced the OASW that optical glass production and optical instrument manufacturing were closely related. The military thus would be heavily dependent on the company for instruments as well as for glass.[61]

The value of planning was proven when war mobilization began. Between mid-1939 and mid-1941 optical glass output increased by about 700 percent. Moreover, smooth transitions in mobilization took place first from the OASW to the Army-Navy Munitions Board, and then from the military services to civilian agencies. Optical glass and instrument manufacturers consistently produced on or ahead of schedule, with new facilities emerging as necessary. War mobilizers felt sufficiently confident even to allow export of optical glass in special cases.

Though slow to start, planning for optical glass turned out to be very good. The Ordnance Department was largely responsible for this result, and the War Department carried the Navy Department. The latter proved especially negligent, perhaps because the Bureau of Standards supplied its optical glass. The government provided unusual leadership in initiating the optical glass industry during World War I, and it continued to play a crucial role in the interwar years.

The optical glass industry had obvious commercial motives for participating in the planning. Throughout the 1920s and 1930s Bausch and Lomb repeatedly insisted that the military increase purchases from the company, forgo foreign buying, and support its drive for tariff protection. The War Department usually complied, fully aware that "the cooperation and good will of Bausch and Lomb are especially to be desired."[62] But the army refused to be used by the individuals exploiting the national defense to push new and untried technology.[63]

With the production of optical glass, self-interest and national interest blended well. Dedicated to professionalism and manifesting high standards,

Bausch and Lomb resisted planning for years because it believed the army was unprepared to operate on its demanding level. Optical glass and instruments were only a small part of the company's peacetime business, involving, as the firm reminded the OASW, sacrifice and dedication on its part.[64] When agreeing to assist the OASW, the company did so with great energy and keen insight. The Bausch and Lomb Company deserves a good deal of credit for the success of planning.[65]

MEDICAL SUPPLIES

The production of surgical instruments resembled that of optical glass in that not much of an industry existed before the war. The industry was also like the machine tool industry in that it was never labeled as strategic.

Prior to World War I, the United States produced only about 20 percent of its surgical instruments; the rest were imported from Germany. With that source cut off, America greatly expanded its output between 1914 and 1917 to supply its own needs and those of the Allies. The prewar industry consisted of small shops staffed by skilled and semiskilled workers who did much of the work by hand. Production was increased principally by converting related industries. Manufacturers of household scissors, for example, made surgical scissors. Voluntary groups and mobilization agencies also standardized surgical instruments, reducing varieties by almost 95 percent. Under these changes, the United States met military and civilian demands, although adequate supplies were fully ensured only at the war's end.

Although the Office of the Assistant Secretary of War created a commodity committee dealing with medical and dental supplies, most planning was done by the Medical Department. The department became alarmed in 1922 when the expanded surgical instrument makers, rapidly losing ground to German and Japanese imports, proved inept in their fight for tariff protection. After reviewing possible remedies, the OASW concluded that only reviving the waning industry would protect army interests in an emergency. Lacking confidence in the surgical instrument producers, the OASW took the lead in pressing for increased tariffs. By 1926, however, the OASW had to back off after the Tariff Commission insisted that surgical instruments would not benefit from protection, and even if they did, industry, not government agencies, had to seek redress.[66]

At that point the OASW dropped its quest. The crisis had been met during World War I largely through the exceptionally alert and resourceful medical profession in and outside the military, and it would have to be depended on again to grapple successfully with any further emergency.[67]

Planning for relatively small, competitive industries was much more challenging for the Office of the Assistant Secretary of War than it was for larger ones. Manganese, for example, pulled the army planners into bitter conflict between small producers and giant corporations, the complexities of foreign supply, and national mineral and trade policies. Though less complicated, tin and mica still required working with numerous sectors of the industries as well as with various other government agencies. Wool was so critical to the Quartermaster Corps and machine tools to the Ordnance Department that the bureaus never managed to free themselves fully from parochial interests in order to plan effectively for these goods. In contrast, first-rate planning by the OASW could not make up for the deficiencies of a surgical instrument industry unable to protect its own interests. The OASW had unusual success with optical glass because it was determined to overcome numerous obstacles to expanding output, and it had an indispensable, committed informal partner in Bausch and Lomb, the one firm that virtually made up the industry.

There was also a greater tendency by small, vulnerable industries to use national defense in their struggle to survive. Substitutes allowed the OASW to walk away from silk and shellac, but not from manganese. In the instance of manganese, as with tin and even more so with mica, army planners led the federal executive in devising policies and practices for coping with anticipated shortages of strategic goods in an emergency. With wool, the army planners fell back on numerous public and private organizations in preparing for a crisis. Optical glass was almost unique. Military need virtually created the industry. While becoming increasingly involved in national policies outside the usual military realm, the armed services at this point were still quite effective in thwarting industry from exploiting national defense for its own advantage.

Most of the complicating characteristics the OASW encountered with small, strategic industries also showed up with lesser ones that were nonstrategic. Lumber, coal, cotton textiles, and leather clearly illustrate the point.

9
LUMBER, COAL AND COAL PRODUCTS, COTTON AND COTTON TEXTILES, AND LEATHER AND LEATHER GOODS

The fifth category of commodity committee planning by the Office of the Assistant Secretary of War (OASW) involved mainly small-to-medium-sized firms in small-to-medium-sized, highly competitive industries. Most of these industries had one or more effective trade associations; none was strategic, and most were not even listed as critical or essential because the United States had an ample supply of the goods they produced. Nonetheless, as crucial to any war effort, they demanded attention because numerous competing firms made emergency management difficult. The military assigned commodity committees to study them, but some of these committees remained inactive for a large part of the interwar period. Generally, these industries stood to benefit from being associated with national defense, and their leaders tended to be aggressive in seeking participation in military planning, a situation that made the OASW cautious, even suspicious. Four representative industries illustrate well the attributes of this category: lumber, coal and coal products, cotton and cotton textiles, and leather and leather goods. In the last years of World War II, lumber, cotton textiles, and leather became scarce. Tumultuous labor relations plagued coal throughout the years of hostilities.

LUMBER

America always had enough lumber, especially Southern yellow pine, the standard construction wood. Nonetheless, early, elaborate, and effective controls over the industry were implemented during World War I by the National

Defense Advisory Commission and the War Industries Board to avoid market distortions, including skyrocketing prices, because huge quantities of lumber were necessary to build cantonments and other facilities.¹

For a number of reasons, OASW planning for lumber in the interwar years experienced a slow and confused start and realized few notable achievements. Most obviously, a commodity in plentiful supply did not create a sense of urgency among planners. Moreover, the War Department's enormous construction programs during World War I were racked by jurisdictional disputes and charges of corruption, which inevitably carried over into the postwar years to affect planning adversely.² Further, the Quartermaster Corps directed most of the planning, with expectably poor results.

Planning began after a number of false starts in January 1926 when the OASW activated what became a Commodity Committee on Building Materials, of which lumber was the most important. A host of troubles plagued the committee's work. Supply arms and services (SA&S) were slow with requirements, and coordinating efforts with numerous other government agencies in an emergency was nearly impossible. When the navy joined the planning in 1933 with competing demands and dissimilar specifications, circumstances grew worse. Additionally, Civilian Conservation Corps building projects set off jurisdictional conflicts and administrative tangles in the War Department reminiscent of World War I. Virtually no planning took place between 1933 and 1939.

Without plans for centrally directing construction programs at the onset of an emergency,³ the commodity committee comforted itself with notions of ample supply precluding a crisis, trade associations directing events, and the Army-Navy Munitions Board taking over. As mobilization accelerated in 1939, the OASW veered between panic and false reassurance. Under such conditions, much of the World War I chaos in cantonment and other construction was repeated. In mid-1940 the National Lumber Manufacturers' Association offered to help the War Department untangle the mess, but the army was uninterested.⁴

Industry was in no way responsible for the failed planning. As early as January 1924 lumber offered its services to the OASW. In mid-1926 the National Lumber Manufacturers' Association organized to work with the military. The association's membership accounted for approximately 70 percent of production of lumber in peace and almost 90 percent in an emergency. It had provided the leadership for mobilizing the industry during World War I and looked forward to playing a similar role in the planning of the 1920s and 1930s. Economic planning, the association forthrightly told the OASW, would be mutually beneficial. By adopting standard sizes and lengths as well as accepting the most recent lumber and timber grading rules, for example, the government would not only facilitate procurement in peace and war but also help the industry.

The lumber trade's eagerness to work with the War Department was part of a widespread public-private effort to rationalize a highly competitive industry made up of thousands of small-to-medium-sized firms and a few giants. Herbert Hoover's Commerce Department was in the forefront. It organized in the mid-1920s a National Committee on Wood Utilization to popularize wood uses and to systematize the industry. The committee worked primarily through trade associations and depended on them for staffing and funding its programs.

Alex H. Oxholm directed the National Committee on Wood Utilization from the mid-1920s into 1933. A dynamic and creative leader, he went out of his way to court the War Department. "The United States Army," he declared, "is one of the largest single purchasers of forest products, in peacetime as well as in wartime." In an emergency, it consumed "20 percent of the annual lumber production."[5] Oxholm regularly addressed the Army Industrial College, met with the Commodity Committee on Building Materials, and in 1929 served in the OASW as a reserve officer. After leaving the Commerce Department, Oxholm continued to advise and assist the planners in numerous ways. He persuaded the War Department in 1927 to endorse the use of short lengths of lumber as a major step in having the practice accepted nationally.[6]

Going beyond the National Committee on Wood Utilization, the Commerce Department also held annual General Standardization Conferences to achieve uniformity in the lumber business. Similar activity was pursued by the Forest Service and the American Society of Mechanical Engineers. Kept informed of these activities and usually asked to participate, the OASW, atypical for military planners, seldom did so.

The course of events with lumber in the 1920s was part of the larger Republican effort to plan the economy indirectly. The level of civilian planning activity dropped noticeably once the Great Depression hit, however, and planning virtually came to a halt in 1933. It resumed at a level lower than its earlier apogee in the late 1930s as war approached.

The OASW never took full advantage of the cooperative endeavors involving the industry. Corruption in military construction during World War I partly explains why. Army planners were exceptionally suspicious of the lumber industry. An officer warned the Commodity Committee on Building Materials that lumber companies had placed Oxholm at the head of the National Committee on Wood Utilization and that "he was more concerned in making money for the manufacturers than he is in wood conservation."[7]

Concerning the lumber association's offers to aid in planning, an OASW member expressed his doubts about "anything coming from this association" since its officials are "undoubtedly more interested in results right now than they are in war time preparedness."[8] A ranking officer of the OASW characterized trade associations in general as untrustworthy.[9]

There was truth to these allegations. During World War I lumber interests had often acted rapaciously, and serious charges of bad judgment or wrongdoing arose about construction work. In the interwar years, the lumber trade was admittedly motivated by a mixture of self-interest and national interest. This attitude was true for many, even most, industries, but it did not paralyze military planning. The solution was not to keep industry's organizations at arm's length but to use business advisers in a way that guarded against abuse. Not to plan, to drift toward war unprepared, almost ensured future exploitation and incompetence.

Lumber highlighted the reality that if strong leadership did not come from the SA&S, the OASW was limited in advancing plans. Between 1933 and 1938 Col. Charles T. Harris, Jr., director of the Planning Branch, acted to focus and stimulate commodity committee planning. New approaches in steel and optical glass serve as good examples of the improvements that were made, but no comparable advances occurred with lumber.[10]

COAL AND COAL PRODUCTS

Coal was of greater significance to national defense than lumber because it had a more central place in the twentieth-century industrial economy. In that regard, the United States was extremely fortunate, since it produced approximately 35 percent of the world's coal in 1929, furnishing its own coal and exporting the excess.

Nonetheless, the coal industry was troubled. A rich endowment of coal led to an extremely, at times destructively, competitive industry under fiercely independent, often reactionary, mining executives. A few coal firms were industrial giants, but no corporation, combination of companies, or association controlled the industry or dictated prices. Mechanization strengthened competitive pressures, with employment steadily falling after 1923. And coal faced growing competition from natural gas, fuel oil, and hydroelectric power. Prior to the 1930s, coal stood almost alone in facing a strong, effective industrial union—the United Mine Workers of America (UMW), organized in 1890.

Because of the complexity and importance of coal, it was treated as a special case during World War I. In August 1917 Congress passed legislation that led to the creation of the U.S. Fuel Administration, which focused most of its attention on coal. There was never a coal shortage at any time during hostilities. Transportation, particularly the railroads, limited the amount of coal brought to market and caused some extreme shortages to users. However, the Fuel Administration, the Federal Trade Commission, and other government agencies instituted firm but fair regulations over the coal industry.[11]

The OASW carefully restricted its planning for coal, for reasons both obvious and subtle. With America having the world's largest coal deposits, the commodity was hardly strategic or even critical. Other reasons were also involved. Although the Office of the Assistant Secretary of War held the records of the War Industries Board (WIB) and predecessor agencies, it was not the depository for the Fuel Administration files and therefore lacked information for proper planning. Since coal had been treated as a separate case during World War I, the OASW responded similarly. Although a Commodity Committee on Coal and Coke and another on Coal Gas Products were created in the 1920s, they never became active. Instead, the OASW handled coal and its by-products under the Fuel Section, which dealt with industry in only broad and general ways.

Two additional reasons accounted for the OASW keeping its distance from coal: the unstable nature of the industry, and extensive private and public planning, which made the OASW's work seem superfluous. Extreme tensions in the coal industry during the 1920s and 1930s made army planners wary about dealing with it. A major and bitter strike by the United Mine Workers hit the industry immediately after the war, and brutal UMW organizing campaigns continued in the 1930s. Even more important, the industry struggled throughout the period with excess capacity, made more severe by the Great Depression.

Coal's troubles were matched by industry and government programs for stabilizing it. In 1924 the National Coal Association (NCA) organized a Bituminous Operators' Special Committee to plan for emergencies, based largely on World War I operations and including representatives from the American Railway Association, the National Retail Coal Merchants Association, and the American Wholesale Coal Association. The NCA informed the OASW that its special committee could serve army planning needs.[12] In 1922, as part of his drive to advance corporatism, Secretary of Commerce Herbert Hoover led in creating the U.S. Coal Commission for recommending policies to rationalize the industry. Recalcitrant coal operators resisted government interference, but even the most reactionary among them were willing to allow Appalachian Coals, Incorporated, to try regularizing coal marketing in the depth of the depression. Before that experiment got very far, leaders at all levels pulled together to write a code for the coal industry under the National Industrial Recovery Act (NIRA), which regulated prices, production, and employment. After the NIRA was declared unconstitutional in 1935, management, labor, and government joined together in that year and again in 1937 successfully to persuade Congress to continue a form of NIRA controls.[13]

Ongoing attempts to plan the coal industry took care of the OASW's work for it. Anticipating that existing private and public planning agencies would be established during an emergency, the OASW kept its approach to coal very general.

In the mid-1920s, however, the OASW almost allowed itself to be drawn into the coal vortex. Between 1924 and 1926 the OASW consulted broadly with industry members, government agencies, and other experts on how it should proceed with the industry. The chief authority for the military planners turned out to be the National Coal Association, the principal organization of the bituminous industry, established during World War I and representing about 60 percent of bituminous output. The association eagerly joined the War Department in actively planning for coal. Begun in 1924, this activity abruptly ended in 1926. Reactionary Southern elements took control of the NCA, dampening the cooperative spirit. Moreover, the director of the Planning Branch, Col. Harley B. Ferguson, reined in his subordinates. Ferguson understood the hazards of the military becoming too closely involved in the tumultuous coal scene.

No meaningful contacts occurred between the coal industry and the OASW between 1927 and 1939. In the latter year, the National Bituminous Coal Commission, created in 1935 to continue some of the rationalizing activities of the NIRA, asked the OASW to work with it on planning. A protective Quartermaster Corps guarding its turf wanted to say no, but the OASW insisted on extending a friendly hand. Cooperation with the commission was hardly under way when civilian mobilization agencies of World War II took charge.

The coal industry was erratic at best in cooperating with OASW planning, but related industries were much more enthusiastic in seeking an advisory position with the military. Standard Oil Company of New Jersey, Union Carbide and Carbon Corporation, and Universal Oil Products Company in the 1920s and 1930s rushed to share information with the military planners on coal-tar products, aviation gasoline, and other commodities that would help a war effort.

Even though limited, the OASW's work with coal was good. The effort contrasted rather sharply with the planning for lumber, which was always marred by serious contradictions. The positive record for coal stemmed partly from recognizing the product's importance, complications notwithstanding, and partly from the bureaus involved, principally the Corps of Engineers, to a lesser degree the Ordnance Department, and occasionally the Quartermaster Corps. Even more important, the less parochial and more imaginative top-level OASW planners had greater direct control because work on coal and coal products did not take place under commodity committees. Finally, more directly with coal than with most industries, other government agencies carried out the OASW's planning objectives.[14]

COTTON AND COTTON TEXTILES

Cotton and cotton textiles were much like wool and woolen goods except that the latter products were strategic and the former were only essential. America grew about three-fifths of the world's supply of cotton and exported over half of what it harvested. Except for crucial differences in supply of raw material, the cotton textile and knit goods industries closely resembled those of wool textiles. Excess productive capacity plagued these industries in the interwar period. Most were composed of small, owner-operated units, with a few large mills controlling only one-thirteenth of the market. Cotton textiles were concentrated in New England and the South, the former declining and the latter rising in significance.

These conditions, as in wool textiles, made for an intensely competitive industry, which suffered from long periods of little or no profits. Standardization of costs, methods, and the like simply did not exist. Different types and qualities of cotton goods were produced in different regions, encouraging the growth of regional trade associations. The Cotton-Textile Institute, dating to 1926 and representing around three-quarters of the operating machinery in the industry, was the most significant organization and the first one that was genuinely national. As with so many industries, cotton textiles and knit goods experienced a greater measure of cooperation during World War I than ever before under the National Defense Advisory Commission and the War Industries Board.[15]

The military limited its interwar planning for cotton textiles and knit goods. Commodity committees on cotton, cotton goods, and knit goods were designated on paper, but only the Committee on Cotton Goods was activated for a brief period in 1929. The committee's tenure was short and its accomplishments few because the supply arms and services, led by the Quartermaster Corps, almost unanimously insisted on dealing with firms on their own, which restricted the efforts of the OASW and industry. Although planning never went far, the OASW nevertheless obtained fairly good information on the textile industry by consulting with war mobilizers, industrial specialists, government agencies, and trade associations. At least in the 1920s, the office insisted that the SA&S keep it informed of requirements and planning activity. Late in 1935 a former president of the Cotton-Textile Institute singled out the War Department as a rare example of a government agency readied for emergency measures. Just getting under way and trying to consolidate its power, the institute wanted to act as a clearinghouse for the textile industry's relations with the OASW, but opposition from the SA&S blocked the way.

Despite minimal planning, army relations with the industry in the interwar years were mostly positive. Continuous peacetime procurement took place and memories remained fresh of World War I procurement, which, after initial confusion, had been sound and accomplished. Textile firms and cotton goods associations eagerly cooperated with the military whenever possible under conditions in which self-interest and national interest blended well. Virtually no attempts were made to manipulate the military for crass gain. Actually, the industry was too competitive and the firms too small for that type of behavior to succeed or to go undetected.

With cotton textiles and knits, as with coal, the military benefited from government efforts to stabilize a troubled industry. The industry was more important to the economy perhaps than wool, because a whole region was tied to cotton, textiles and knits were among the nation's largest employers, and the industry was crucial to export trade in finished products and raw materials. Hence, Republicans in the 1920s and the New Deal supporters in the 1930s participated in planning that related directly and indirectly to the relations that the OASW sought to achieve.[16]

LEATHER AND LEATHER GOODS

Leather and leather goods are almost as important to the military as wool. Even though wool had a strategic classification, leather was only essential because of actual or potential national self-sufficiency.

The United States produced and consumed more leather than the countries of Europe combined. To sustain the industry, the nation imported hides of all kinds from around the world and exported finished leather goods, particularly shoes. In its multiple stages the leather industry had few giant corporations and consisted mostly of small-to-medium-sized firms with often individualistic methods of production and marketing similar to those of cotton and woolen textiles.

During World War I an elaborate regulatory structure for leather evolved under the National Defense Advisory Commission and the War Industries

Board.[17] After hostilities, the leather industry was eager to cooperate with the military, principally through the Tanners' Council of America, a national trade association of the tanning industry whose membership accounted for about 90 percent of leather produced in the United States. The group was founded in 1917 to facilitate war mobilization.

Planning for leather began in 1924 when the Office of the Assistant Secretary of War created a commodity committee eventually designated as Hides, Leather, Leather Goods, and Tanning Material. In 1925 the OASW held a series of conferences on leather with experts from industry and government. With national use of leather dropping, tanning no longer a problem, and most leather coming from domestic sources, supplemented by imports from Canada and Latin America, the United States was close to self-sufficiency. The Tanners' Council and others, however, maintained that accurate requirements, uniform and flexible specifications close to commercial lines, and reasonable, efficient inspection methods were essential for avoiding the chaotic conditions of World War I. Those goals, it insisted, were achievable through continuous planning by military and industrial elements.

The Quartermaster Corps agreed with these points and worked with the leather representatives to implement them through an advisory committee. The intensity of planning slowed by 1926, and by 1930 industry-military contacts were few. Increasingly, the army emphasized leather substitutes—textiles, treated textiles, or imitation leather. This shift provided the Quartermaster Corps with an excuse to neglect leather. Under pressure from the OASW, it paid only lip services to planning.[18]

Almost no planning for leather occurred between 1934 and the beginning of mobilization around 1939, and relations with industry were almost nonexistent. When the Tanners' Council of America tried to restart planning in 1939, the OASW was unprepared to do so. Mobilization of the leather industry for World War II was more advanced than that during World War I, but the inactivity and neglect of the 1930s seriously weakened the preparations made in the 1920s.

Industry's motivation for joining in the activity of the OASW appeared to be quite straightforward. World War I had introduced a new level of cooperation that industry wanted to continue in years of peace. The national defense rationale could also be used to pressure the Agriculture Department and other government agencies to perform better in areas such as statistics, important to the leather industry. Unlike coal, leather wanted as much government assistance as possible, as long as cooperation did not threaten the industry's independence.[19]

Although somewhat better than the planning for wood and cotton textiles, the planning for leather reemphasized that without a supply bureau's able and committed leadership, commodity committee planning in general inevitably suffered. The Office of the Assistant Secretary of War was always restricted on what it could do alone.

Lumber, coal, cotton, and leather highlighted a number of important characteristics about the OASW's interwar planning. The imprint of World War I planning was indelible. In most instances the planning continued in one form or another during the 1920s and 1930s. This trend made the OASW's work both easier and consistent with the times. It also meant that on the eve of World War II industry collectively was better prepared for economic mobilization than it had been before World War I. Indeed, when the OASW's planning faltered, other government agencies, assisted or pressured or both by private organizations, were active in working to stabilize industries, as was especially the case with coal and with cotton textiles.

10
EXPLOSIVES AND AIRCRAFT

The sixth and final commodity committee category involved industries that were or would become large and oligopolistic, that might or might not have strong trade associations, and that were tied to the military as substantial contractors in peace and war. In such conditions, interwar planning merged with current procurement much more than was the case in the numerous industries that made only limited sales to the armed services during peacetime.

Two very different industries are involved in this category: explosives and aircraft. The first was undergoing a major transformation in the interwar years from simply producing explosives to manufacturing a wide range of technologically advanced chemicals. It included some of the world's largest chemical firms. The second industry was just beginning to take shape in the 1920s and 1930s and would come fully of age during and after World War II. (Other industries, such as shipbuilding, are relevant to this category and will be briefly analyzed here and then considered at greater length in chapter 14). Aircraft, along with shipbuilding, would be among the first industries whose relations with the armed services would manifest many of the characteristics that the Cold War generation would see as features of the military-industrial complex.

Beginning in 1940 the federal government built or largely paid for a virtually new ordnance industry and a vastly expanded one for aircraft. The latter had almost full peacetime utility, which the probably overbuilt former one lacked.

EXPLOSIVES

Explosives and propellants were of overwhelming importance to the American military. On the eve of World War I, the E. I. du Pont de Nemours Powder Company, despite the dissolution order resulting from an antitrust suit of 1907 to 1912, had a preponderant market position in military powder and explosives in general. As a wartime supplier, first for the Allies between 1914 and 1917, and then for the United States from 1917 onward, the industry expanded its output exponentially. In 1914 American firms produced approximately 450,000 pounds of smokeless powder a *month*. This was a product the United States had led in developing. At the time of the armistice, they were manufacturing 2.5 million pounds a *day* and had nearly completed a plant for upping the figure to 3.5 million pounds in 1919. The increase in the output of high explosives—ammonium nitrate, picric acid, and trinitrotoluene (TNT)—was nearly of the same magnitude. In dollar terms, American output of explosives jumped from $50 million in 1913 to $500 million in 1917, reached an annual rate of almost $1 billion in October 1918, and could have exceeded $2 billion in 1919. The United States ended up supplying more than one-half of all Allied explosives and propellants used during World War I.

Most of the new and expanded plants for producing explosives and propellants were publicly financed. Allied purchases were priced so that new plants were often paid for with production for the first contract. When the United States entered the war, it chose to rely principally on building additional facilities at government expense rather than through amortized private financing, at a cost of between $300 to $400 million for about fifty-three plants. For nitrocellulose powder, Du Pont and the Hercules Powder Company expanded their existing plants and the government built two new factories, the Old Hickory plant at Nashville, Tennessee, with Du Pont as agent, and a facility at Nitro, West Virginia, with Hercules acting as operator. Additionally, toluol output, essential for the production of TNT, increased greatly at new, expanded, or modified facilities. Du Pont and Hercules also enlarged their TNT plants, and the government contracted to build three new ones at Racine, Wisconsin, Giant, California, and Perryville, Maryland. To increase ammonium nitrate capacity, Washington began the construction of two huge nitrogen fixation plants at Muscle Shoals and Sheffield, Alabama, and completed a plant using a different process at Perryville, Maryland. The federal government also built three plants for producing picric acid, with 90 percent of the output going to France and Italy and 10 percent to the United States. Finally, a program was launched to expand the output of phenol.

The production of explosives and propellants was always under close government supervision once America entered the war. Nonetheless, considerable continuity existed between the programs undertaken between 1914 and 1917 and those inaugurated with the onset of America's belligerency. Leland L. Summers served as a technical adviser on explosives in J. P. Morgan and Company's purchasing operations for the Allies from 1915 to 1917. Summers then became a key adviser to Bernard M. Baruch in the National Defense Advisory Commission (NDAC). Under that agency and its successor, the War

Industries Board (WIB), he and Charles H. MacDowell, who had been president of the Armour Fertilizer Works and who became head of the board's Chemicals Division, played instrumental roles in putting together the explosive and propellants program. That program was largely outlined in mid-1917 by a special committee consisting of Summers, Gen. Palmer E. Pierce of the army, and Adm. Frank F. Fletcher of the navy.[1]

The Chemicals Division, which included subdivisions for explosives and other chemicals, evolved during 1917 and 1918 as a part of the NDAC and the WIB. The division always maintained close coordination with the War and Navy Departments, and the Ordnance Department played a more direct and ongoing role in the mobilization of explosives than for any other civilian-made product. Ordnance, in turn, drew heavily on the corporate structure and personnel of Du Pont, and to a lesser extent on other firms, in carrying out its duties. Mobilization of the American explosives industry had to be carefully synchronized with that of the Allied countries. This was particularly true of nitrates and cotton linters. In late 1917 and early 1918, the United States, Great Britain, France, and Italy worked out a scheme for purchasing Chilean nitrates through an international operation that was centered in London and had elaborate private-public structures in the United States. In August 1918 an even more complex, worldwide Cotton Linter Pool was set up and continued to operate until July 1919.

When war broke out in 1914, the United States faced a harsh reality. Although the nation had a powder industry of long standing, America and the Allies possessed only limited modern, organic chemical industries producing high explosives, as well as artificial dyes, many pharmaceuticals, photographic chemicals, and numerous other products. Coal tar is the starting point for manufacturing these goods. Fractional distillation and other processing of coal tar yields hundreds of chemicals, first as crudes such as toluol and then, by further chemical treatment, as intermediates like phenol, which are made into final products.

Explosives are virtually identical in chemical composition to artificial dyes. In 1914 Germany produced over three-quarters of the world's supply of artificial dyes and almost all intermediates used in their manufacture. The United States manufactured only 10 percent of dyes it consumed, with 90 percent of the intermediates for this limited output coming from Germany. By ruthless price wars and the manipulation of patents and licenses, Germany maintained almost a world monopoly on chemicals and had the world's only centrally controlled and integrated chemical empire.

The outbreak of war cut off America from German supply, forcing the domestic chemical industry to expand to meet national needs. Though the nation produced only $3.5 million worth of dyes in 1914, by 1917 numerous firms produced hundreds of intermediates with a total value of $69 million. The entire chemical field received an enormous boost when the government seized all German patents under the Trading with the Enemy Act of October 1917 and licensed American firms to manufacture the patented products. During the war most areas of chemical output, such as explosives, pharmaceuticals, and dyes, were regulated to varying degrees by the WIB or other government agencies or both. American productive efficiency increased enormously during the war. For example, before 1914 the nation wasted almost 65 percent of its coal resources by extracting only coke from the dry distillation of bituminous and neglecting the other by-products, of which coal tar is among the most important. The use of coal tar as an input opened new fields for American enterprise. In 1914 the United States had had very little modern chemical output, but by 1917 it had a substantial industry producing dyes, fertilizers, explosives, and numerous other products from the same or similar crudes and intermediates.[2]

The newly developed American chemical industry faced almost immediate threats once the war ended and Germany began to reconstruct. Germany could reestablish its prewar international dominance in the chemical field unless the United States and other industrial nations moved to check it, which they did to some degree. The Treaty of Versailles and America's treaty with Germany in 1921 ending belligerency between the two countries included unprecedented provisions legalizing the Allies' seizure of German patents during the war and, under the right circumstances, authorizing continued possession in peacetime. Attempting to buy time to develop a strategy for protecting its war-induced industry, the United States in 1921 placed an embargo on all organic chemical imports and transferred, for a nominal sum, numerous, critical German patents from the Alien Property Custodian to the Chemical Foundation, Incorporated. The latter was a stock company chartered in Delaware that paid no dividends and was headed by the former Alien Property Custodian. The company was formed to prevent the federal government from being forced to return the patents to Germany, since Washington faced enormous legal problems if it granted licenses to private firms for production or engaged in manufacturing itself.

No effective public policy was ever devised to guard the nation's chemical firms. The tariff of 1922 provided protection, but it was ineffective in the face of German experience and industrial organization, the dollar-mark exchange rate, and comparative labor costs in Germany and the United States. Moreover, Congress refused to extend the 1921 embargo for another year. Consensus on a chemical policy was lacking in American industry. Giant firms such as General Electric Company, the United Shoe Machinery Corporation, Singer Sewing Machine Company, and the International Harvester Company opposed stringent action against Germany on patents and tariffs. They had factories in Germany to take advantage of cheap labor and accessible patents for producing competitively in foreign and American markets. Certain textile firms and large wholesale dyers also opposed excessive restraints on Germany.

The resolution to America's chemical situation vis-à-vis foreign competition and Germany in particular came about when the chemical firms, acting on prewar patterns, created worldwide combinations. An elaborate and comprehensive system of international cartels, based on the exchange of patent rights and technical information and involving the division of world markets, grew in the interwar years. Giant American, British, and German firms lay at the foundation of this international order, Du Pont working closely with Britain's Imperial Chemical Industries, Limited, and Standard Oil Company of New Jersey in close partnership with Germany's I. G. Farbenindustrie A. G. (I. G. Farben). American firms like Du Pont were able to negotiate such agreements because they used huge wartime earnings and expanded corporate structures to transform themselves into diversified chemical firms—companies initiating and using the most up-to-date research and technology.

In the interwar years and after, the chemical industry was among the fastest growing and most profitable industries in the United States. It was also oligopolistic. Du Pont, among the largest chemical firms in the world, headed the list but shared dominance with other massive corporations such as Union Carbide and Carbon Corporation, Dow Chemical Company, Hercules Powder Company, and Monsanto Chemical Company as well as with nonchemical firms with substantial assets in the chemical field: Standard of New Jersey, Eastman Kodak Company, and B. F. Goodrich Company. At home, as abroad, corporations involved in chemical production negotiated widespread and elaborate agreements to protect specialties, divide markets, guard technologies, and maintain prices—practices designed to maintain as much stability as possible in an industry at the cutting edge of change.[3]

After the close of World War I, the War Department in general and the Office of the Assistant Secretary of War (OASW) in particular were intensely interested in explosives and hence in the whole organic chemical field. World War I had dramatically demonstrated the nation's great vulnerability and Germany's enormous advantage in explosives and propellants. The department vigorously supported the embargo on organic chemicals in 1921 and again in 1922 and, pitting itself at times against the State and Justice Departments, led in seeking legislation to ensure the United States maximum latitude in handling the seized German patents. Those efforts failed, with Congress rejecting a renewed embargo in 1922 and never passing legislation on patents. The War Department then used its own intelligence sources and those of other government agencies to keep itself posted on Germany, its relations with British, French, and American firms, its international sales practices, and its efforts to rebuild the prewar chemical empire. In this regard, the War Department found various chemical trade associations, such as the Synthetic Organic Chemical Manufacturers Association and the Chemical Division, Bureau of Foreign and Domestic Commerce of the Department of Commerce, to be helpful. Once it became clear that the American organic chemical industry would not go under but would instead burgeon in strength and importance and that Germany could recover its international chemical power only through cooperation with firms of the former Allies, the War Department ceased to be alarmed about the organic chemical situation both at home and abroad.

Although its activity would later decline, the OASW began an early and well-conceived planning effort for explosives. Late in 1922 the office created a Chemical Commodity Committee designed virtually to duplicate the Chemicals Division of the War Industries Board. The committee immediately began consulting with experts, such as Charles H. MacDowell, and also with the American Chemical Society and major chemical explosives firms such as Du Pont, Union Carbide, Hercules Powder, and Atlas Powder Company. By 1925 the committee had overseen the writing of a procurement plan for nitrates, which was thoroughly reviewed by Du Pont's technical expert on the subject. It was in fact the first of the numerous commodity committee plans to be approved and was even praised by the office for its qualities. The plan was revised in later years and reviewed by Du Pont and the Fixed Atmospheric Nitrogen Corporation. Other plans for explosives and related products were also written, approved, and revised.

Throughout the 1920s the commodity committee managed to stay on top of the rapidly changing technology in chemicals through its own efforts and with the assistance of industry and other government agencies such as the Agriculture Department's Fixed Nitrogen Research Laboratory and the U.S. Bureau of Mines. In 1933, after conducting a broad review of explosives and propellants, the commodity committee, now designated as the Committee on Powder and Explosives, concluded that a number of manageable problems existed:

> There would undoubtedly be deficits in the production of the following: Smokeless powder, T.N.T. and tetryl; that these deficits would occur in the early months of an emergency but would be wiped out after possibly the sixth to ninth month. No shortage was apparent in fixed nitrogen.

Shortages were apparent in nitric acid and possibly sulphuric acid but the sulphuric acid facilities to be erected at explosives plants would convert this probable deficit into a surplus.[4]

The committee, which was headed first by an officer from the Medical Corps and later and much more logically by one from the Ordnance Department, demonstrated perspective unusual among military planners. At all times it insisted that planning for explosives required the proper context:

> A powder policy is only part of the Ordnance Munitions Policy and this in turn is only part of a general munitions policy. If the last is made effective the first as a part thereof will also be effective. Our goal should, therefore, be to assist in the adoption and execution of a General Munitions Policy.[5]

With such an outlook, the committee was well positioned to advise the War Department on crucial matters such as reserves, budget distribution, and the like.

Perspective was critical for the OASW, not only because powder and explosives were so important to the military but also because the War Department was subjected to intense pressure from industry. In the early 1920s, as the War Department attempted to shape policy on German patents and American tariffs to favor the chemical firms, the American Chemical Society and chemical firms like Zinsser and Company insisted that the department be more aggressive; at the same time, representatives from the textile industry were vehemently denouncing the War Department's stand. Later in the 1920s greater tariff protection was sought to maintain small firms that could produce potassium nitrate and potassium chlorate, and pressure was exerted to maintain the existing protection for smokeless powder. In the early 1930s a cry was raised to protect the war-born American potash industry against Russian imports. Constant proposals were also made to stockpile nitrates and various explosives, propellants, and their ingredients. Moreover, private industry, in ways ranging from the direct and blatant to the indirect and subtle, consistently attacked the government's nitrate plants at Muscle Shoals.

Du Pont presented the greatest challenge to the War Department while also providing it with the most assistance. Du Pont threatened to shut down its operations in the early 1920s. It charged that the federal government had purchased none of its smokeless powder between 1914 and 1917, had returned to that practice after the armistice, and was currently rejecting its current bids. The War Department reacted with alarm because the firm was its chief private supplier, carried out extensive research and development that was unmatched and unmatchable by the government, had access to foreign technology and information, and constituted the best base for expansion in an emergency. The Navy Department had a facility for producing smokeless powder at Indian Head in Maryland and the War Department had one at the Picatinny Arsenal in Dover, New Jersey, but private output was essential for national defense.

The War Department, and especially the Ordnance Department, was sympathetic to Du Pont's position and eager to placate the company. The department correctly believed, however, that Du Pont did not want to stop producing smokeless powder and would maintain output, facilities, and research with a minimum of encouragement. Moreover, Du Pont's lines of commercial, as opposed to military, powder acted to keep it prepared to produce for the armed services. Since smokeless powder had an estimated life of about fifteen years, the wartime surplus the military was using in the 1920s would eventually run out, and the services would again constitute a regular market. An Ordnance officer argued that an appropriation of a little over $3.5 million annually would allow the War Department to adopt a reasonable powder policy: about $.5 million would be spent at the Picatinny Arsenal and the rest would go to commercial firms so as to keep all facilities ready for emergency expansion, ensuring that technology was up to date. Du Pont and the War Department settled their conflict along these lines. And as Du Pont increasingly diversified to become a general chemical producer, explosives were less important to its operations, creating more flexibility on the company's part.

Actually, the War Department, and especially Ordnance, worked closely with Du Pont and had done so for many years. For example, in 1912, during antitrust deliberations over breaking up the company, army and navy Ordnance officers provided crucial support for the corporation's retaining all smokeless powder production facilities as essential for national defense. This closeness continued during the interwar years in planning and in procurement. In 1925, for instance, Du Pont shared with the Office of the Assistant Secretary of War the results of its recent survey of America's nitrate resources. Ordnance went so far as to lend explosives to Du Pont illegally and through subterfuge when the company needed them, though the army's reserves were low. Such activity went beyond strictly military affairs. This relationship was illustrated when Gen. Clarence C. Williams, a retired chief of ordnance and active in the Army Ordnance Association and other industrial-military affairs, headed the Chemical Code Authority as a deputy director of the National Recovery Administration. Du Pont was vitally interested in that agency. So intertwined did the activities of the Ordnance Department and Du Pont become that the Senate Special Committee

Investigating the Munitions Industry, chaired by Sen. Gerald P. Nye (R-ND), in the 1930s concluded that the two functioned virtually as one.[6]

As it turned out, the War Department's exceptionally close relations with Du Pont involving current procurement were more important for powder and explosives than the OASW's planning effort, not only because of Du Pont's preeminent position as a chemical firm but also because only limited planning took place after 1925 once the pattern emerging in America's chemical industry became evident. The urgency to plan that had existed right after the war diminished significantly when America's future as a chemical producer was secured. A major review conducted in 1933 by the Office of the Assistant Secretary of War revealed no major problems. Moreover, rapid technological change in the chemical industry quickly made any plans obsolete, and most problems appeared resolvable then or in the near future. When the Universal Oil Products Company in the late 1930s attempted to persuade the War Department to underwrite its new process for producing toluene, for example, the department confidentially rejected the proposal, knowing that the Pure Oil Company and Standard of New Jersey had made significant advances on similar techniques for fabricating the product.[7] By 1939 no explosives, propellants, or their ingredients were labeled as strategic. Phenol, picric acid, and toluol carried the critical classification, and other products indispensable to powder production, such as cotton linters, were only in the essential category.

On the eve of World War II, the military planners' neglect of chemicals quickly became evident. Few plans were available, and a Chemical Advisory Committee had to be established quickly to write procurement plans for crucial products like sulphuric acid that were basic to any mobilization program. The military's contacts with civilians had also suffered. In 1939, as an example, the American Institute of Chemical Engineers sought information from and offered assistance to the OASW in mobilizing the chemical industry. The office, in a revealing manner, had little to offer and responded as if it were in the early stages of planning instead of facing the possibility of war. Nonetheless, the oligopolistic nature of the industry made adapting it to conditions of warfare relatively easy, especially since chemicals had been in a constant state of change and development since at least World War I.

Thus, to the degree that it was done, planning for explosives and powder under the Ordnance Department's direction was quite accomplished. Industry and its associations—none of the latter was especially strong—cooperated with the military for a mixture of motives that ranged from self-interest to patriotic commitment. Industry and the military had sound relations based on long association and the recognition of mutual need.[8]

AIRCRAFT

The aircraft industry in the interwar years presented the most complex set of economic and political problems involving national defense and war preparation for several reasons. First, the industry was a relatively new one, which began to take on significant size and output only with the massive demand of World War I. Aircraft firms experienced unusual challenges as they fought to survive in the 1920s, were hit hard during the Great Depression, and achieved some stability near the end of the 1930s. Only during World War II and after did the industry become the giant it is today. Second, for most of the interwar years, the industry relied heavily on government demand in general and on the military services in particular. Thus it was almost unique among American industries, and the relations that developed between the evolving industry and a growing government anticipated in many ways practices associated with the so-called military-industrial complex of the Cold War period. Third, because of its peculiarities, the aircraft industry and its interaction with government created a source of constant conflict in the interwar years. The discord began during World War I and never fully subsided until the United States was fully mobilized for World War II. The intensity of the conflict was multiplied many times by the related and acrimonious issue of the role of air power in warfare and the organizational place of the air services in the traditional military structure.

From the initial flight in 1903 of Wilbur and Orville Wright until the outbreak of World War I, the American aircraft industry was little more than an odd collection of makeshift firms. In 1914 the Census Bureau listed sixteen companies with a total output of forty-nine planes. Entry into World War I quickly and dramatically reversed those conditions. Between April 1917 and November 1918, under a forced government program designed to supply the American armed forces and those of its Allies, American firms produced almost 14,000 aircraft and more than 30,000 engines, even though, to the nation's chagrin, only a small percentage ever got to Europe. Some 300 firms, most of which had not been involved in aeronautics before the war, employed thousands of persons in order to achieve these records.

Government stimulus stopped more rapidly than it had begun once the armistice was signed. Contracts totaling more than $100 million were suddenly canceled, plunging the bloated industry into a severe crisis in which 90 percent of the wartime producers either returned to prewar output such as automobiles or went bankrupt. The few survivors included the Curtiss Aeroplane and Motor Company, Incorporated, the Wright-Martin Aircraft Corporation, and the Boeing Airplane Company. Despite overwhelming odds, a few new firms directed by experienced leadership even started up in the early 1920s, as was the case with the Douglas Aircraft Company, Incorporated, and the Consolidated Aircraft Corporation.

From the armistice into the late 1920s, the aircraft markets were exceptionally weak. With the war over, military demand all but stopped. There was little desire to expand further a new military arm that was embroiled in controversy over procurement practices and combat missions. Besides, so many surplus aircraft existed from the war that the army and navy could be supplied for years to come. There was no meaningful civilian demand prior to World War I, and none suddenly came into existence after hostilities. None of the necessary conditions for civilian transport and passenger traffic was present, including reliable and fast aircraft, airports, and federal regulation and licensing. Immediately after the war, as before it, civilian usage was confined to a small circle of aircraft enthusiasts, individuals and firms involved in invention, research, and development, and those seeking to establish regularized air routes.

In addition to the military, the Post Office Department was continuously involved in aviation. In mid-1918 the Army Air Service had inaugurated air mail service for the Post Office between some of the major cities of the Northeast. Before the year was out, the Post Office Department took over the operations itself and by 1925 had established transcontinental delivery with numerous feeder lines that fairly well covered the nation. The Post Office proved to be a good promoter of aeronautics, but not a good customer for aircraft. It relied principally on World War I planes, showed little interest in purchasing new aircraft except when necessary, and did not act to advance technology.

The total demand for aircraft from all sources just after World War I was simply not very great. Between 1920 and 1925, about 3,000 planes were produced, 80 percent of which went to the military and the remainder to various civilian sources. This proved to be enough barely to keep the fledgling aircraft industry going.

The years 1925–1926 proved to be a watershed for the American aircraft industry. By then war surplus aircraft had been absorbed or were obsolete. Much more significantly, four critically important statutes placed American aeronautics on a sound footing. These bills included the Air Mail (Kelly) Act of 1925, the Air Commerce Act of 1926, the Air Corps Act of 1926, and the Naval Aircraft Act of 1926.

The Air Mail Act of 1925 gradually turned over to private industry the task of carrying air mail. As it was implemented, the legislation brought into being the first regular, civilian, and privately operated air transportation system in the United States. Here was the basis for the current airline system. By contracting out air mail delivery to private firms under lucrative terms, the federal government indirectly—as opposed to the direct method commonly used in Europe—subsidized the growth of American airlines and the development and production of aircraft. Moreover, the Post Office Department from the outset dealt only with companies having extensive capital resources. Small, independent firms were squeezed out by companies that became the giant airline corporations—corporations in effect favored by negotiated, as opposed to competitively awarded, contracts. Legislation for air mail services in 1930 acted to concentrate power even further among a few airlines. By 1934 three airline companies serviced 65 percent of air mail routes, carried 90 percent of air mail, and received 88 percent of government payments for air mail delivery. Between 1928 and 1938 the number of domestic airline operators declined from thirty-four to sixteen.

By fostering oligopoly in the airline industry through mail contracts, government practices created a scandal when exposed. The result was a restructuring of the entire system with the passage of the Air Mail Act of 1934. Henceforth, contracts had to be awarded to low bidders, regardless of responsibility, reliability, or capital worth, thereby ending government subsidies. Had this act been passed in 1925, the entire airline and aircraft industries might have been substantially different. Coming in 1934, the legislation was too late to alter patterns significantly. The giants were already entrenched and could meet most competition, even though airline income from air mail was cut in half between 1933 and 1935. But in future years, as the amount of air mail increased, the airline companies made greater income than before 1934. And more important, passenger traffic took on growing significance. In 1925 passengers on the airlines were unusual and a nuisance. By 1934, as the airlines' reputation for reliability, safety, and comfort improved and they lowered their fares substantially, passengers and scheduled routes grew in prominence. Indeed, between 1928 and 1934 passenger traffic increased tenfold. In the latter year, income from passengers exceeded that from the mails and in 1938 stood at almost 60 percent of carrier profits, with vast new markets just beginning to be tapped.

The Air Commerce Act of 1926 was as important as the Air Mail Act in getting the aeronautics industry fully under way. Passed as a result of lobbying by the various groups and firms involved with air flights, the act created within the Department of Commerce a Bureau of Air Commerce (partially incorporated into the Civil Aeronautics Board in 1938) to regulate the aircraft and airline industries by establishing uniform traffic and safety codes and licensing, registering, and inspecting air services. The act also codified existing laws involving air carriers. Further, under the 1926 law the Bureau of Air

Commerce established and maintained radio stations, teletype communications, beacons, and emergency landing fields. It also established airways and encouraged the growth of airports. The Weather Bureau assisted by issuing regular reports on weather conditions.

By regularizing air services, the act enhanced the safety and reliability that the industry required for growth but could not provide for itself. By directly and indirectly financing facilities and services, such as radio stations and air fields, the federal government allowed the strapped airlines to invest in aircraft and airline development that otherwise would have been neglected. Moreover, municipalities throughout the nation began building airports and providing other facilities and services to aid private carriers. In 1925 the United States had a makeshift series of rather poor airports, with facilities and services of widely varying quality. By 1931 thousands of airports, ranging from rudimentary to first-rate, existed to serve airways that had become common. These indirect facility subsidies were less dramatic than those stemming from the air mail contracts, but they were still of great importance in promoting modern air traffic.

The Air Corps Act of 1926, along with the Naval Aircraft Act of the same year, was as important to military aircraft development as the Air Mail Act and the Air Commerce Act were to civilian aeronautics. Since air power was more important to the army than to the navy, I will focus on the first without unnecessarily violating the significance of the second. The Air Corps Act grew from the constant investigation of air power and production for it that had occurred since World War I and that involved such timely and controversial issues as the role of air power in military affairs, proper procurement methods, and the level of appropriations necessary to maintain an adequate military air arm. The Billy Mitchell (Brig. Gen. William Mitchell) imbroglio was a part of this ongoing turmoil.

Basically, the Air Corps Act of 1926 had three parts. First, as a compromise between air radicals and traditional military elements, organizational autonomy or preeminence for the air arm among the armed services was rejected in favor of making the Air Service, redesignated as the Air Corps, a combat arm of the line. Second, to end the neglect of the postwar years, a five-year program provided for increasing aircraft and personnel, including both officers and enlisted men, to adequate levels. Third, Congress instituted an intricate procedure combining both negotiated and competitive features for designing, testing, developing, and processing aircraft. The measure was to ensure aircraft of the latest and best design, create and sustain a healthy aeronautical industry, and avoid the alleged corruption and inefficiency of the war years. The last part of the statute was ambiguous, however, reflecting the complexity and controversy involving the industry.

The 1926 legislation was only partially successful in its second and third parts. Both the Calvin Coolidge and the Herbert Hoover administrations used their discretionary powers to delay and then to retard the implementation of the five-year program. The War Department also acted to ensure that the Air Corps did not get all that it wanted. Air Corps policies involving the use, repair, and counting and categorizing of aircraft also slowed the pace of acquisition, and adequately trained personnel were not easy to acquire. By mid-1932 when the five-year expansion program should have been completed, goals for equipment and personnel had not been met. Nonetheless, by comparison with the rest of the army, the Air Corps was well off in terms of manpower and weapons.

The failure to meet the goals of the Air Corps Act of 1926 caused much less protest than did the Air Corps' procurement policies. Indeed, some individuals charged that the failure to meet the 1926 quotas or to achieve an air arm of excellence was a direct result of procurement practices.

With few exceptions, and based principally on existing army regulations, the Air Corps interpreted the 1926 law in such a way that the design, development, and production of aircraft took place through negotiations, not competitive bidding. Air Corps officers, most experts on air power, and nearly all aircraft manufacturers and their trade associations insisted that the high technology of airplanes made competitive bidding virtually impossible. Experimental airplanes could be handled only through negotiations with the designers. If, when the production stage was reached, the contract did not in whole or in part go to the designing and developing firm, the company could not recoup costs and was discouraged from future effort. Moreover, low bidders might be inexperienced, incompetent, or corrupt. Even if thoroughly qualified and adequately financed, a contractor other than the developer would have to adapt the new design to the firm's manufacturing methods, which took time and modified the end product. Industry was especially disturbed by any contracting system that failed to respect the designer's proprietary rights—a practice that occurred with the military. These realities led the Air Corps to favor negotiations over competitive bidding, based on the argument that stability and dependability were essential in an industry indispensable to its operations. This line of reasoning and the practices it fostered opened the door to charges of favoritism, profiteering, price-setting, encouraging oligopoly, inhibiting inventiveness, and other irregularities.

These accusations took on special significance when Public Works Administration funds in the 1930s were used to keep Air Corps spending up to predepression levels. That practice allowed the peace and isolationist advocates to sharpen their attacks on all military spending. Business practices in general were under attack. More specifically, the Air Corps appeared to perform badly in 1934 when the Roosevelt administration tapped it for carrying air mail after abruptly canceling private contracts over alleged scandals.

Several congressional investigations of military aircraft procurement ensued, the most important of which was conducted by the House Military Affairs Committee. These were often sensational events, producing glaring headlines of gross procurement irregularities, profiteering, and so forth. So much heat was generated by the congressional hearings, reports, and recommendations that Congress came close to amending the Air Corps Act of 1926 to make competitive practices mandatory in all or most aircraft procurement. Such rigidity was avoided and the Air Corps Act of 1926 left intact only because in 1933 Assistant Secretary of War Henry H. Woodring moved before the congressional uproar to mollify critics. Woodring instituted intricate procedures for designing, testing, and producing aircraft that reinstated competitive features; but he did so under conditions ensuring the quality the Air Corps wanted, protecting the aircraft manufacturers, and allowing the assistant secretary to use negotiations if necessary to guarantee government interests.

The furor that developed in 1934 over procurement policies diverted the War Department from what it considered to be the more important task of increasing the number of aircraft for its air arm. After several investigations by the army, executive boards, and Congress, the Air Corps in mid-1936 was increased in size to 2,320 planes, a goal about 30 percent higher than that set in 1926. This figure remained the official ceiling on army aircraft until the rapid expansion for war began in 1939.

The aircraft industry, and along with it the military air services, were constantly under public scrutiny because directly or indirectly the federal government financed the development of this new industry and the revolutionary technology that was an inherent part of it. Throughout the interwar years, private and public, civilian and military institutions and personnel interacted in dynamic and complicated processes for developing and producing what became the modern airplane in the mid-1930s.

Among the public institutions dedicated to aeronautical research, none was more important than the National Advisory Committee for Aeronautics (NACA). Created in 1915 to further aeronautical research along the lines major European nations followed and to help prepare the nation for war, this organization remained active until 1958, when it became the nucleus for the National Aeronautics and Space Administration. Composed of a mix of private and public representatives, the NACA helped guide all aviation and aeronautical activities until 1926, when the Bureau of Aeronautics was established within the Department of Commerce. Thereafter, the committee confined itself almost exclusively to research activities, which had absorbed a good part of its energy before 1926. Although the NACA stressed fundamental research, it almost inevitably became involved in applied research as well. Indeed, the chief authority and historian writing about the agency affirms that "in one way or another NACA was involved in the design, development, or refinement of virtually every airplane produced in the United States during its lifetime."[9] This work was carried out at the committee's sophisticated research facilities at Langley Field in Virginia, Moffett Field in California, and what was eventually called the Lewis Flight Preparedness Laboratory in Cleveland, in addition to the army and navy research and development centers. Operating principally through a series of subcommittees, the NACA conducted high-quality research and used conferences, publications, and observers to encourage further research, propagate knowledge, and stay abreast of virtually all relevant aeronautical and aircraft developments both at home and abroad.

Within a short period of time the National Advisory Committee for Aeronautics became prestigious, and membership within the organization was a coveted goal. To maintain impartiality, the NACA's principal committees at first banned all representatives of the aircraft industry. Gradually, however, industry's members gained seats on the NACA technical subcommittees, and by World War II they had been fully integrated into the agency's structure. Whether they came from private or public institutions, almost every prominent name in American aeronautics eventually served on or was associated with the NACA. Beginning with a meager budget of $5,000 in 1915, a membership of twelve (increased to fifteen in 1929 and then to seventeen in 1948), and one paid staff member, the NACA by the end of World War II consisted of numerous subcommittees of highly trained professionals numbering in the hundreds, a staff consisting of thousands, annual budgets in the millions, and research facilities valued in the hundreds of millions. In the late 1930s and during World War II, as the NACA devoted increasing time and effort to the military, it was dominated by the armed services. Among the numerous volunteer federal agencies established on the eve of World War I to mobilize the economy, the NACA was clearly among the most important in maintaining a significant role after the war and almost the only one to maintain its institutional integrity.

On a much more limited scale compared with the NACA in terms of time, money, and resources, the Daniel Guggenheim Fund for the Promotion of Aeronautics also made a significant contribution. Between 1926 and 1930, millions of dollars went toward funding research and educational programs involving aeronautics at various universities and schools. Additionally, the fund financed programs to elevate knowledge about and improve the image of aviation in the public's mind as well as to further research on projects like blind flight and to underwrite an experimental passenger service in California. Since funds and programs in these areas were scarce, this philanthropic endeavor was of considerable importance.

Although fundamental research was indispensable for any programs in aircraft development, it was applied research that produced the airframes and power plants for what became the modern airplane. Most of this research and development was financed by the federal government: directly through procurement by the armed services, indirectly through negotiated air mail contracts. Statistics on military versus civilian markets indicate the importance of military purchasing for the evolution of the modern airplane. Between 1926 and 1936 the military bought almost 4,700 planes for a total outlay of about $83 million. In these same years, some 9,000 planes were sold to civilians at a price of approximately $55 million. Clearly, much more money went into designing, developing, and manufacturing aircraft for the military than for civilian usage.

The high-powered aircraft engine, basic to the modern airplane, resulted almost exclusively from military specifications, design requirements, developmental contracts, and procurement. Nearly all of the fundamental work was done by private industry through contractual arrangements. The army made some contributions at McCook (later Wright) Field and the navy at the Philadelphia Naval Aircraft Factory, but the armed services only supplemented (and underwrote) the work of the engine manufacturers. The NACA also did some work directly or indirectly related to power plants; however, rather than engines, its most important contributions involved airframes.

A major breakthrough in aircraft power plants occurred around 1925 with the perfection of the radial air-cooled engine. Thereafter, regardless of the source of finances or sponsorship, no major innovation came about except by refining well-known and existing types until the advent of jet propulsion supplanted air-cooled engines. The air-cooled engine made possible the dramatic flights of the 1920s—the most important of which was the Charles A. Lindbergh Atlantic crossing of 1927—that did so much to popularize and stimulate interest and investment in aviation.

Between 1925 and 1935—again with public money critical for advancement, but with the government playing a less direct role than with engine development—industry step by step produced the modern airframe. The culminating product came in 1935 with the Douglas Aircraft Company's DC-3. Representing a synthesis of over a decade of invention, design, development, and refinement, this plane was an all-metal monocoquel, low-wing monoplane that incorporated the controllable-pitch propeller, retractable landing gear, and wing flaps. It set the design for civil and military planes for the next twenty, perhaps thirty years. Most immediately, it made possible profitable passenger traffic. With the DC-3, the modern airplane had come of age.

The decade of airframe innovation from 1925 to 1935 opened with private firms taking over air mail contracts, the Bureau of Air Commerce getting under way, and the army and navy beginning five-year development programs. Hence, though private industry designed and developed what became the modern airplane, the financing, and often the requirements, and the services, facilities, and regulation essential for airline operations came principally from the federal government. By 1935 private airlines were able to carry on without air mail subsidies; they could not have done so in 1925, 1928, or even 1930.

The aircraft industry demonstrated a definite tendency toward consolidation even in its early phases, and on the eve of World War II it was well on the road to oligopoly. Nevertheless, since the industry was subject to rapid and continuous technological change and constantly under public scrutiny, legislative enactments, and regulation, control by corporate giants was neither as secure nor as clear-cut as was the case with America's other huge industries.

Between the outbreak of World War I in 1914 and America's entry into hostilities in 1917, three firms emerged in a dominant position, based on Allied war orders and the anticipated demand from the United States entering hostilities. Large financial interests and automobile firms led in a series of mergers that created the leading aircraft producers. First, the Wright-Martin Aircraft Company consisted of a merger of the Wright brothers plant, the Glen L. Martin Company, and the Simplex Automobile Company put together between 1915 and 1916 by financiers including the Manufacturers Trust Company and the Chase National Bank. Second, in 1916 Glenn H. Curtiss turned to the Willys Car Company and other automobile interests to expand production capacity of the Curtiss Aeroplane and Motor Company to fill foreign orders. Then the Dayton Wright Airplane Company was established between 1916 and 1917. This corporation was the most important in the field during the war and was dominated by automobile interests from Dayton and Detroit. Among the former group, Edward A. Deeds of the Dayton Engineering Laboratories Company (Delco) was key, and among the latter Howard E. Coffin of the Hudson Motor Car Company was the most significant. H. E. Talbott, Senior and Junior, Charles F. Kettering, and others who became dominant aviation figures were also involved. Since Coffin and Deeds held key posts in the wartime mobilization of the aviation industry, the Dayton Wright Airplane Company found itself in a favored position for war contracts, a situation that helped produce major scandals involving World War I aircraft production and forced the departure from public office of both Coffin and Deeds in April 1918.

The end of the war threw the aircraft industry into a period of enormous turmoil, with numerous firms leaving the field or driven out of business. The Curtiss Aeroplane and Motor Company emerged from the war years the strongest, with the Wright-Martin Aircraft Company—reorganized in 1919 as the Wright Aeronautical Corporation—also doing reasonably well. Other firms managed to hang on, and a few other companies even got started in the starved years of the early 1920s.

Only after the crucial developments of 1925 and 1926, including the Air Mail Act, the Air Commerce Act, and the five-year expansion programs for the army and navy, was the aircraft industry able to get back on its feet and grow. That accomplishment, the popularity gained from the Lindbergh flight, and the need for capital led the aviation firms for the first time on a significant scale to sell stock in the soaring market of the late 1920s. This triggered another round of mergers, which dwarfed that of the pre–World War I period. During these years of consolidation, the modern airline and aircraft industry began to take on its final shape. The process of merging was usually led by executives with long experience in aircraft management, production, and flying and was backed, guided, and dominated by major financial banking houses or existing corporate giants or both.

The first mergers began in 1927. Frederick B. Rentschler and William E. Boeing, underwritten by National City Bank of New York, led in creating United Aircraft and Transportation Company (United). This merger was a vertical combination that included firms making airframes, engines, propellers, and parts and semifinished goods. It also put together air routes that spanned the continent. The second giant to emerge was North American Aviation, Incorporated (North American), Clement M. Keys playing the leading role but with the firm falling under the control of General Motors Corporation in the 1930s. A third consolidation, the Aviation Corporation (AVCO), was founded in 1929 by W. Averell Harriman and Lehman Brothers. Finally, in 1929 the biggest and best of Detroit's automobile producers, looking forward to doing for aircraft what they had done for cars, organized the Detroit Aircraft Corporation with the Lockheed Aircraft Corporation as a base.

Even with these massive mergers, the aircraft industry never achieved the desired goal of secure and stable oligopoly. Major firms such as Consolidated Aircraft Company, Glenn L. Martin Company, Douglas Aircraft Company, and numerous smaller corporations remained unaffected or only minimally affected by the hectic activity surrounding them. Moreover, the Great Depression abruptly ended the merging mania. That trauma put an end to Detroit Aircraft. But United, North American, and AVCO managed to survive and even in time grew under the harsh conditions of the 1930s. Airplane output did not again match the 1929 record until rearmament was under way in 1940.

The mergers of the late 1920s were facilitated by the Air Mail Act of 1925 and were strengthened significantly by Hoover's Postmaster General, Walter Folger Brown. Out to build a formidable national aviation industry, Brown in an arbitrary and dictatorial manner used the amended Air Mail Act to subsidize handsomely and visibly the consolidated firms while attempting to squeeze out the small, independent companies. Under the Franklin D. Roosevelt administration, the outcries against Brown's blatant methods by smaller or excluded units, or both, forced Washington to reverse its policies. The Air Mail Act of 1934 mandated competitive bidding for mail contracts and, more important, required legally separating manufacturing from transporting functions among aviation firms. Consequently, the United Aircraft and Transportation Company was divided into two parts: United Airlines for transportation and United Aircraft Corporation for manufacturing, with the Boeing Airplane Company resuming its independence. North American Aviation divided its airlines into two companies—Transcontinental and Western Air (TWA) and Eastern Air Lines—and ultimately reorganized North American Aviation, Incorporated, as a company devoted exclusively to the design and production of military aircraft. From AVCO, American Airlines, Incorporated, eventually emerged, but its manufacturing subsidiaries remained comparatively small and were not totally devoted to aircraft production.

Hence, the federal government acted to break up the consolidation in the industry that it directly and indirectly had fostered. Most industry representatives and aviation specialists considered the divestiture inaugurated in 1934 to be desirable so that competitive forces would keep the industry dynamic and technologically advanced. As a result, the aviation industry in the interwar years was well on its way to becoming among the nation's giant industries with mammoth corporations. But the nature of the industry and the government's policy toward it prevented oligopoly from emerging.

Nevertheless, patterns of dominance existed in the aviation field by the 1930s. In the military aircraft sector, for example, with high developmental costs and rigorous production requirements, only about twelve firms competed effectively, with the lion's share of contracts going to four airframe companies—Douglas, Boeing, Curtiss-Wright, and North American—and two engine manufacturers—Curtiss-Wright and the Pratt and Whitney Corporation. Nonetheless, two new firms entered the field in the 1930s. What became Republic Aviation Corporation got started in 1931, and Bell Aircraft Corporation was founded in 1935. Some new entrants also appeared in engine manufacturing and light civilian aircraft. Even in civilian aircraft, which the DC-3 made virtually interchangeable with military planes, a few of the dominant firms led in the transition from the two-engine DC-3 to four-engine planes, with Boeing, Douglas, and Lockheed heading the list. Moreover, by the late 1930s, Southern California had emerged as the principal airframe center in the United States; engine and propeller output remained in the Northeast.

Corporate turbulence aside, more continuity than change characterized the aviation industry between 1914 and 1941. Close study of corporate structures and their control is necessary to establish the point. Elsbeth E. Freudenthal, in a book published in 1940, has provided the most complete and detailed analysis of power relations within the aviation industry.[10] After surveying the results of the merger movement of the late 1920s, Freudenthal concluded:

> The names of the new holding companies . . . may be unfamiliar, but they were merely continuations of the war and prewar companies. These groups—General Motors, Curtiss-Wright, Aviation Corporation, and United Aircraft and Transport—controlled the industry in all its phases.[11]

After the mid-1930s' division of transport and manufacturing within the aviation industry, Freudenthal saw some definite changes:

> The separation of manufacturing and transport companies into two industries weakened, even if it did not entirely destroy, the strangle hold of the large, monopolistic holding companies. A good deal of actual, as well as formal, separation of interests resulted, with a simultaneous improvement in the competitive position of the smaller, independent units.[12]

In Freudenthal's eyes, however, little changed with manufacturing. She summarized the situation, as new prosperity and growth began transforming aviation into one of America's giant industries:

> This metamorphosis has affected everything in the industry except two essentials: the same three groups dominate it now as in the past, and these groups show the same financial interests that have controlled them throughout their history. . . . General Motors–North American, Curtiss-Wright, United Aircraft—these three forces have been active, in various corporate forms or through the activities of important individuals, since before the war. Their position as the principal producers is due to the fact that each is an integrated group.[13]

The market for aircraft naturally had done much to shape the industry in the interwar years. Demand for aircraft came from three sources: domestic military, domestic civilian, and the export of both. From 1928 to 1938 military demand was less in numbers of planes but greater in overall price. In 1928 the armed services bought 1,219 planes for $19 million; in 1937, 949 for $37 million. By comparison, civilian figures for the same years were 3,542 for $17 million and 2,281 for $19 million. Because of the high unit cost of military aircraft and the exceptionally rigorous performance and quality requirements, this market was limited to about a dozen firms out of approximately seventy-five active manufacturing companies. Sales for the domestic civilian market were high because they consisted of single-engine, small planes that were relatively inexpensive to produce. Only the technological revolution that produced the DC-3 made civilian sales important. By the mid-to-late 1930s the United States had the world's most advanced and substantial airline industry, which purchased multiengine aircraft that were expensive to produce and approximated those made for the armed services. Without a hefty civilian trade in the large transport field, the American aviation industry would not have made the progress that it did.

The export trade was also of major importance, especially when sales were slow in the 1930s. Because major nations were subsidizing their own aircraft and cutting out American products, the United States had to turn to the lesser powers of Latin American and Asia as markets. Moreover, national security required a two-year delay before new military aircraft could be exported, and the neutrality legislation of the mid-to-late 1930s restricted exports further. Despite these obstacles, the nation exported in 1937 about $39 million in aircraft, engines, parts, and accessories. In aircraft, alone, that meant that one-third of output went abroad, accounting for about 50 percent of net profits. The same held true for spare parts and accessories. Engine sales abroad accounted for an even greater share of American production.

Although not all scholars agree, Irving Brenton Holley, Jr., after a careful analysis of the statistical information has concluded, "Clearly, military sales, whether for domestic or export destinations, constituted the most important element of the aircraft market even during the years of peace from 1928 to 1938."[14] It was the massive military demand during and after World War II that made the substantial, but still developing, aviation industry among the largest industries, not only in the United States but also in the world.

The highly competitive nature of the aviation industry, the constant technological pressure and change under which it operated, and its essentially unintegrated quality made for endless divisions and discord among the numerous firms. This dissension became clear when the various aircraft and airline companies could not agree on a National Recovery Administration code before the demise of that ill-fated institution in 1935. Nonetheless, the industry did have several associations. The most important was the Aeronautical Chamber of Commerce, organized between 1919 and 1921; by 1935 it included in its membership over 90 percent of firms involved in aircraft manufacture and air transport. Actually, this group was preceded by the Manufacturers Aircraft Association (MAA), founded in 1917. This association was specifically created to administer a cross-licensing system patterned after that of the automobile industry, which would allow any producer joining the association to use patents under a fee system. The military services joined forces with the National Advisory Committee for Aeronautics to push through such a procedure in order to free the aviation industry from the interminable litigation and turmoil over patents that plagued it and that would paralyze any war mobilization program. Once created, the MAA as spokesman for the aircraft industry played an important role in most aspects of aircraft production during World War I.

The Aeronautical Chamber of Commerce was actually an outgrowth of the MAA in an effort to create an organization that represented all aspects of aviation, not just manufacturers. Until 1929 the chamber and the association were virtually one, sharing the same facilities and the same general manager, Samuel S. Bradley. Thereafter, they became recognizably separate entities, the MAA mainly implementing cross-licensing agreements and the Aeronautical Chamber of Commerce fulfilling the larger role of a general business and industrial association.

Aviation and aircraft were the source of constant investigation and study during the interwar years. The scrutiny began during the war years when the aircraft production program appeared to be little more than broken promises and was riddled with inefficiency and conflicts of interest. To head off an unwanted Senate investigation, Pres. Woodrow Wilson in May 1918 swallowed his pride and appointed Charles Evans Hughes to review the entire wartime aircraft program. In a report released late in 1918, Hughes laid bare the mismanagement and irregularities that had plagued the production effort, pinpointed criminal behavior, and recommended disciplinary action against Edward A. Deeds.[15] After the armistice, inquiries and reports on aircraft continued, which reviewed and damned the war record and sought to find the proper place for the airplane in civil and military life. The investigations hit a high point in the mid-1920s, tapered off thereafter, and flared up again in the 1930s. The executive vice-president of the Aeronautical Chamber of Commerce of America asserted in 1935:

> During the past two years the industry has been the subject of investigations by fifteen major government committees or groups. The indus-

try has itself . . . conducted eighteen major meetings. . . . Further, during this period of two years some 230 separate pieces of legislation affecting aviation were introduced in Congress.[16]

Governmental study and analysis of aviation slowed once more in the later years of the 1930s, only to pick up again and become a major source of attention and concern as the United States began harnessing its resources for World War II.

Investigations involving aircraft were numerous and frequently intense in the interwar years because vital issues of political economy, civil-military relations, and the nature of modern warfare were involved. The federal government had to devise policies for civil and military aircraft without precedent or consensus and in a political climate charged with acrimony, uncertainty, and confusion. Almost inevitably the decisionmaking was piecemeal, ambiguous, and shifting.

Aircraft was a new, high-tech industry that required government regulation and support to develop and grow. During World War I Allied and American demand acted quickly to create a substantial industry from the mere outlines of the one that had existed in 1914. Washington also created various agencies to mobilize the aircraft industry. With the end of hostilities it was clear that the future of the industry depended on governmental regulation and subsidy, but no consensus and a great deal of controversy existed within the aircraft industry and government over what Washington's role should be.

By 1925–1926 the federal government had enough information and experience involving aircraft and the conflicting parties had narrowed their differences sufficiently to produce the compromises incorporated in the Air Mail Act, the Air Commerce Act, and the Air Corps and Naval Aircraft Acts. As a result, the federal government provided the necessary level of regulation, facilities, and services to allow airlines to grow and indirectly subsidized those firms and the aircraft industry through air mail contracts and substantial expansion of the army and navy air arms. Federal government policies and practices growing from the 1925–1926 legislation favored the largest airline and aircraft manufacturing firms and over time fostered oligopoly in the industry, as was particularly the case for air mail contracts and military procurement. The practices also occurred through the operations of the National Advisory Committee for Aeronautics.

Aviation created enormous challenges to the nation's political economy. There were no precedents to guide policy. A relatively small and inactive federal government subsidized the railroads in the late nineteenth century and later stepped in to regulate them as a developed, consolidated industry. An expanding government in the twentieth century gained experience in regulating the banking and industrial sectors, but again it was dealing principally with large, mature institutions. Moreover, railroads, banks, and manufacturers had evolved over an extended period of time and employed technology and practices that were or became familiar. Aviation, by comparison, was revolutionary in terms of technology and performance. Consequently, a governmental system struggling to define its political economy was simultaneously forced to deal with a wholly new and multifaceted industry that was still emerging and about which there was nearly endless disagreement. Whatever policies Washington worked out for aircraft and aviation would have a definite impact on the industry and would inevitably be controversial.

The complexities of aircraft and aviation were compounded manyfold because civil-military relations were involved. Economic relations between the armed forces and society had entered a new stage with the building of a modern navy in the late nineteenth century, and the process of change was greatly accelerated by World War I. More than any other tool of war, the airplane bound industry and the fighting forces together. From World War I through World War II, civil and military aviation were nearly inseparable. Military demand launched the industry in 1914, sustained it during the interwar years, and brought it to maturity during World War II. Military contracting with industry produced the high-powered aircraft engine. That engine, combined with the airframe developed by manufacturers, provided the basis for the modern airliner and the military bomber. The National Advisory Committee for Aeronautics had the army and navy prominently represented in its principal governing body and considered military needs to be its first priority but believed that its research benefited private firms and worked with the industry whenever possible. Although the NACA predictably supported the traditional military viewpoint of keeping the air arm subordinate within the army, significant numbers of aircraft manufacturers favored an independent or united air arm, partly from the belief that such an outcome would lead to greater prominence and larger appropriations for military aviation and to more orders for them.

The movement for an independent or united air service raised the crucial issue of the airplane as a weapon of war. During World War I, the airplane advanced from performing scouting and observing functions to serving as a tactical fighter and then as a strategic bomber. Although air power was not used in an unlimited way during hostilities, Giulio Douhet, the Italian air power theorist, and other experts graphically set forth in the interwar years the airplane's destructive potential. The ugly and bloody face of modern warfare was never far from the ongoing debate about aviation during the interwar years. Separating the airplane as a major transition for civilian transportation from that of a revolutionary weapon of war usable against civilians as well as soldiers was never possible. This reality was made clear by the intense emotions generated over the campaign in behalf of air power by Billy Mitchell, his eventual court-martial, and the maneuvering for position by a host of advocates and critics of the cause he represented and symbolized. The nearly intractable philosophical and ethical issues raised by the airplane as a weapon of war greatly complicated deliberations about policies involving its political economy.[17]

The complexity surrounding the airplane in the interwar years was related to the larger issue of what the Nye Committee labeled an "unhealthy alliance." A later generation used the term military-industrial complex. Senator Nye and his colleagues pointed out that modern warfare was eroding the barriers between private and public, civilian and military institutions. Various industries depended on military contracts, and the armed services depended on industry for developing and producing weapons. Reflecting a mutuality of interests, industry favored and worked for increased military appropriations, and the armed services granted industry special favors, encouraged monopoly where it served their interests, financed research, and displayed little concern about profit restraints. Munitions firms joined with the military services and other governmental departments to compromise national policies for disarmament, arms limitation, arms sales, and arms embargoes. Furthermore, a web of institutional and personal ties bound industrial and military elements together.

The Nye Committee spent some time with aircraft, but it relied primarily on the navy and on shipbuilders to illustrate the major points of its analysis. In that regard, the Army Air Corps and aircraft firms were even better examples. Nye and his committee appeared to prefer the navy and shipbuilders because the patterns of their relations were well established, reaching back to the late nineteenth century. By comparison, the Air Corps and aircraft firms were both relatively new creations whose relations were still evolving and uncertain, making an analysis of them more difficult. The uncertainty aircraft engendered surfaced when the Nye Committee, like its numerous interwar predecessors, could not make up its mind about how to deal with this new weapon of war that fostered "unhealthy alliances." Should the federal government force the military to deal with aircraft firms through competition, should the government impose regulation, or should Washington nationalize the entire aircraft industry? The Senate Special Committee Investigating the Munitions Industry concluded, in effect, that none of these solutions would solve the problem. After nearly two decades of examination, the role of the state in aviation still remained unresolved on the eve of World War II.[18]

The Air Corps naturally did the procurement planning for aircraft. The corps' Material Division located at Wright Field near Dayton, Ohio, was assigned the planning and created an Industrial Planning Section to fulfill it. Generally, the planning was not very successful. Indeed, the Air Corps, along with the Quartermaster Corps, was among the weakest bureaus where procurement and economic mobilization planning was involved.[19]

The Air Corps' problems that led to weak planning were legion. To begin with, confused organizational structure and lines of command rendered effective planning nearly impossible. With the Material Division separated from the chief of the Air Corps and his office in Washington, coordination, let alone communication, became extremely difficult. In 1937 the chief of the Material Division moved his headquarters to Washington in order to be at the seat of power but inexplicably left supply operations, including procurement and economic mobilization planning, behind without establishing clear lines of authority and responsibility between Washington and Ohio. The troubles of physical separation were compounded by the Air Corps having its own assistant secretary from 1926 to 1933. This arrangement gave the corps direct access to the secretary of war and circumvented the chief of staff and the General Staff, whose resentment of the Air Corps grew in intensity. To complicate matters even further, in 1935 the War Department created a General Headquarters, Air Force, as an air command reporting directly to the chief of staff, not through the chief of the Air Corps or his subordinates. The system divided authority and left fighting forces uncoordinated with Air Corps units that handled supply and planned for logistics.

Organizational confusion was exacerbated because the Material Division was always understaffed and unable to focus properly on planning. In 1938, for example, with war approaching, the Air Corps planners were still trying to adapt the 1933 Industrial Mobilization Plan to the new and recent plans for mobilizing troops. The rotation of officers also tended to undermine any work that was done. For a new service coming into existence, these unsettled conditions were especially disruptive.

The Air Corps' Industrial Planning Section (IPS) did plan, despite the weaknesses. But it never had adequate requirement figures, which were indispensable for fulfilling its responsibilities. The entire army suffered from this deficiency to some degree. But conflict over the role of air power made the condition more consequential for the Air Corps. Very different requirement figures would be necessary, for example, if the airplane was intended primarily as a tactical as opposed to a strategic weapon or if the corps stressed heavy over light bombers. None of these issues was settled in the interwar years, a situation that was exaggerated by rapidly changing technology. At best, the procurement planners depended on educated guesses, which had to be constantly adjusted. When it came to the detailed planning, the IPS turned responsibility over to the six Air Corps Procurement Districts. They surveyed plants, negotiated or drew up schedules of production and factory plans, and so forth.

If requirement figures were inadequate, the same held true for information on industrial capacity. As late as November 1938 when rearmament was under way, the assistant secretary of war admitted that his office did not know what industry could produce. The fault did not rest with industry. Recognizing the significance of planning and the importance of military procurement for the industry, most aircraft firms cooperated with the IPS in gathering plant statistics. This contribution did not produce the desired results because the IPS failed properly to collate, review, and analyze the data.

The greatest limitation of the planning was the failure to determine policies for vastly increasing industry's output in an emergency. In the 1920s and early 1930s the Air Corps vacillated between proposals for expanding the existing plants or converting the automobile industry to aircraft production. By the mid-1930s conversion became the favored approach. Yet efforts to work with aviation and automobile executives to prepare for such an exigency never got very far, in effect leaving this critical matter to be worked out during a crisis. Attitudes about conversion reflected potentially disastrous assumptions. Air Corps planners believed that full mobilization could effectively take place *after* the outbreak of war, would require fewer planes and economic controls than during World War I, and could be accomplished with few restraints placed on industry, which should be left to do the job largely on its own. Even foreign experience with mobilization, and particularly that of Great Britain in the late 1930s, failed to impress the Air Corps planners.

When mobilization began in 1938, the Air Corps responded lethargically. It failed to see the importance of educational orders for preparing the automobile industry to produce aircraft and other industries to manufacture standardized airplane parts. Although Air Corps planners and leaders grasped some of the fundamentals of mobilization, they appeared unable to convert insight into action.

The Air Corps' hand was forced in 1939 when the president and Congress settled on expanding the Air Corps to about 6,000 planes. The deficiencies of procurement planning prevented the corps from effectively handling the expansion; it had to turn to industry for solutions to the numerous problems. Theodore P. Wright, of the Curtiss-Wright Corporation, ultimately devised an effective method for calculating industrial capacity. With that accomplished, the Air Corps in effect allowed industry to write the plans and establish the patterns for increased aircraft output. Industry did so, but in a way that avoided the threat of excess capacity, even at the price of inadequate plant expansion for basic commodities like aluminum, airplane parts, and finished aircraft.

Despite enormous obstacles, the aircraft and related industries met the challenge of greatly expanded demand after 1938–1939. This accomplishment cast some light on procurement planning in the interwar years. The Air Corps could not meaningfully plan as long as its status was uncertain, its mission undefined, and its technology constantly changing. However, the ongoing research and development and procurement involving airplanes in the interwar years partly compensated for the inadequacy of the planning. Without years of working together, the Air Corps and the aircraft industry could not have met the extreme challenges of World War II.

Weak as it was, the Air Corps planning was not in vain. The Procurement Districts kept key industrialists involved in Air Corps problems and procedures. And despite disappointing results, the planning forced the Air Corps to focus on requirement figures and industrial capacity. Although the Air Corps was among the weakest of the supply arms and services in terms of economic planning, it was among the most active in terms of procurement. Planning and procurement combined prepared the Air Corps to some degree for the enormous complexities it faced.[20]

For both explosives and aircraft, substantial procurement during the interwar years made up in part for weaknesses in procurement planning. The close association between the military and industry in developing and producing aircraft in the 1920s and 1930s also anticipated many of the controversial policies and practices that in the post–World War II years would be attributed to a military-industrial complex.

11
OASW PLANNING: CONCLUSION

Economic planning by the Office of the Assistant Secretary of War (OASW) was an exceptionally intricate and tangled process. Nonetheless, planning for military procurement, for industrial mobilization, and for individual commodities blended together into an integrated although uneven whole. That planning became the means by which the War Department, and the entire military, absorbed the lessons of World War I in order to adjust to and prepare itself for fighting another wholly modern war.

THE MILITARY'S ECONOMIC PLANNING

Two major points stand out about economic planning by the military: It was guided by World War I mobilization patterns, and it was thoroughly consistent with the political economy of the 1920s and 1930s. Mobilization for World War I served as the point both of departure and reference for all planning in the 1920s and 1930s. The commodity section–war service committee structure had been the backbone of the War Industries Board (WIB), and the military planners adapted it to meet their needs with commodity committees. Those committees relied heavily on World War I economic mobilization figures to guide their work. In instances where the interwar planning varied from what had been done during World War I, the OASW's planning was thrown off, as was the case with coal. Wartime quirks tended to be carried over into the interwar years. For example, the Quartermaster Corps exercised unusual control over textiles and leather goods in the war years, and that pattern distorted corps planning for those commodities in the interwar years. Even more consequential was aircraft. The Air Service planning in part was defective because, unlike almost all other commodities, no coherent historical record of war mobilization existed to guide the planners' work.

World War I introduced the concept of scarcity under conditions of modern warfare. Civilians led in working out the mobilization schemes for dealing with conditions where demand exceeded supply. The military services, and especially the army, were moved by events during the war more than they controlled them. In the interwar years, the armed services used the planning process first to understand wartime developments and then to prepare for future hostilities so as to be on top of events. Through planning, the past merged with the present and even with the anticipated future. For the military, civilians and civilian institutions held the key to World War I mobilization, and therefore their assistance was indispensable for meeting the demands of modern warfare.

The consistency of OASW planning with the nation's political economy is evident at every turn. Economic planning by the army blended well with Republican efforts in the 1920s informally to plan the economy through incentives, regulation, and encouragement of and cooperation with trade associations. Herbert Hoover, first as secretary of commerce and then as president, personified enlightened business Republicanism. Inspired by the World War I mobilization model, Hoover as secretary of commerce attempted to further economic rationalization by restructuring key subdivisions of his department to match the patterns of the industrial community, with business representatives integrated into these subdivisions. On a small scale the Department of Commerce functioned like the War Industries Board and its commodity section–war service committee system.

Seeking new or adapted tools of economic management, Hoover became the source of a veritable whirlwind of governmental activity. Experts were consulted, conferences called, and government agencies organized or proposed to improve business operations, collect statistics, eliminate waste, deal with unemployment, and seek solutions for troubled industries like the railroads and for new industries like aviation. Under the banner of the "associative state" or a similar label, Hoover looked to voluntary organizations, and especially to trade associations, to provide the economic, social, and political controls essential for an industrial society and to correct business abuses without the necessity of an overbearing federal government. Although the Great Depression forced Hoover to adopt new priorities and to try different means, as president he continued to seek many of the same goals he had set for himself as secretary of commerce.[1]

The OASW in the 1920s worked closely with the Commerce Department because the activities of the two agencies were so similar in key areas. Both the Commerce and War Departments used the War Industries Board as their model for economic rationalization. Like Hoover, the OASW planners appeared to be more comfortable working with engineering and professional societies than with strictly business associations. Nonetheless, the trade associations that Hoover and his department favored were indispensable to OASW planning. Moreover, the hand of Hoover and his department was directly evident in commodity committee work for aviation, rubber, mica, coal, cotton, wool, wood, and other products.

Republican attitudes and policies toward business in the 1920s probably helped to make industrial America more willing to cooperate with the OASW. The idea of war may have been remote, but the concept of economic rationalization was not. The OASW's planning in the 1920s, and particularly the work of the commodity committees, highlighted major trends in the American political economy.

During the 1930s OASW's planning remained basically consistent with the times. Initially, of course, the depression had a devastating impact on OASW work, with the worst years occurring between 1929 and 1933. Industries struggling to survive lacked the time and the inclination to focus on remote contingencies. With the nation unable to sell a good part of what it produced, planning for scarcity also made OASW efforts appear surrealistic. And the War Department had its own problems, given its reduced budgets and added responsibilities such as the Civilian Conservation Corps. Moreover, between 1929 and 1932, the OASW concentrated on writing the Industrial Mobilization Plan and participating in the War Policies Commission hearings, which pulled it away from industrial contacts.

Once under way, the Roosevelt administration acted to stimulate, not retard, OASW planning. As a peacetime equivalent of the War Industries Board, the National Recovery Administration (NRA) experiment gave army planners firsthand exposure to actual, not past or prospective, planning. Various military officers served as NRA executives or as public members on code authorities, and the OASW studied carefully how the administration operated. Despite being declared unconstitutional, the National Industrial Recovery Act benefited army planners in terms of experience gained, data collected, trade association activity stimulated or sustained, and planning in various forms continued.

After the NRA's demise in 1935, OASW planning, and particularly commodity committee activity, increased significantly in quantity and quality. The improvement was due in part to new leadership under Col. Charles T. Harris, Jr., and the fact that the army's Industrial Mobilization Plan had been tested and endorsed by important governmental elements. Just as important was the approach of another world war. Economic mobilization planning was no longer an academic exercise as it had been in the 1920s; it had become a necessity.

The Roosevelt administration altered the form, if not the substance, of the nation's political economy. Changed circumstances created new demands for the army planners. They had to align their attitudes, plans, and studies to a more activist state in terms of regulatory and welfare functions and to a growing federal bureaucracy staffed with more nonbusiness personnel than before. Other interest groups besides industry and finance also had to be considered, especially organized labor. The OASW began paying more attention to unions in 1928, and that emphasis grew during the New Deal years.

Growing antagonism between the Roosevelt administration and corporate and financial America eroded the cooperative spirit between business and government, thereby making the OASW's job both more difficult and more essential. Economic planning by the military was also under greater attack in the 1930s than in the 1920s because of strengthened peace, isolationist, antimilitary, and antibusiness attitudes and movements. Contrast the treatment, for example, of the OASW's procurement and economic mobilization planning by the War Policies Commission from 1930 to 1932 with the Senate Special Committee Investigating the Munitions Industry from 1934 to 1936.

Despite the challenges, OASW planning continued to improve in the 1930s. The imperatives of approaching war were more compelling than the movement for peace or the moderate reforms of the New Deal. Economic mobilization for World War I laid bare the power structure in America and the dominant position held by the corporate-financial elite; World War II would reveal that little had changed, despite New Deal reforms. Since OASW planning reflected the realities of power, only fundamentally altering the nation's political economy would significantly modify the nature of the military's plans. No such change occurred during the depression decade.[2]

The two major points—that OASW planning was patterned after World War I methods and reflected the existing political economy—are actually one. Mobilization for World War I accelerated the emerging Progressive political economy based on a government-business regulatory partnership. In the 1920s the Republican administrations attempted to achieve the benefits of wartime planning through a small state and indirect means. The Great Depression ended that experiment, forcing the Roosevelt administration in the 1930s to seek recovery through direct planning, economic stimulation, and a moderately expanded welfare and regulatory state. Nonetheless, World War I remains the twentieth-century watershed. By focusing on the wartime mobilization model, the armed services concentrated on the salient points of the nation's political economy. That perspective made their planning both contemporary and astute.

Prior to World War I a certain distance characterized civil-military relations. World War I demonstrated that such separation was no longer possible. During the war years, military attitudes about and institutions concerning civilians began to change. But the transformation was incomplete at the end of hostilities. Interwar economic planning by the military continued the process of adaptation. At the same time, civilian America was absorbing the wartime changes in political economy and adapting its institutions accordingly, as the NRA most directly demonstrated. Under such circumstances, military planning could fail only if the nation's political economy did so, a fate the New Deal averted by modestly modifying capitalism.

Significantly altered civil-military relations created the basis for what would later be labeled the military-industrial complex (MIC). Exploitative and opportunistic behavior by industry was only a manifestation of what was taking place. The important development was the need for the military services to plan with most American industries in order to prepare themselves for war—planning that was joined by the U.S. Chamber of Commerce, the National Association of Manufacturers, and the National Industrial Conference Board. Professional groups such as engineering societies also became seriously involved. New organizations emerged to facilitate war preparations, like the Army Ordnance Association, the Ordnance Procurement Districts, and similar groups for other supply bureaus. Although thousands of businessmen and professionals participated in the planning, a limited number of individuals and institutions on the business side constituted the close web of personal, corporate, financial, and other organizational ties developing in the interwar years around the cause of national defense. To an unusual degree they were associated with the Ordnance Department and groups related to it.

Modern warfare was drawing most economic elements into military preparedness. The armed services' relatively small budgets in the interwar years obscured the significance of OASW planning. World War II and the Cold War years demonstrated that the planning was of the utmost importance. Substantial-to-heavy expenditures for the armed services over a sustained period of time created a warfare state with far-reaching consequences for the United States. But the nation required institutional preparation for dealing with a rising military and the vast spending for it. The process of adjustment began with the building of a modern navy in the late nineteenth century; it was accelerated manyfold by economic mobilization for World War I; and it continued with the military's economic planning in the interwar years.

The outlines of an emerging MIC in the interwar years, although faint, are visible in ways more concrete than through planning. The chemicals/explosives and aviation industries in the 1920s and 1930s illustrate a development that would become commonplace in the post–World War II years.[3] The airplane industry is especially important. Interwar spending on aviation was comparatively high and military involvement substantial. New and rapidly changing technology required extensive governmental subsidies, regulation, and promotion. Influential institutions such as the National Advisory Committee for Aeronautics indicated the intricate personal and institutional ties involved in manufacturing modern weapons. Enlightened, selfless acts by private and public persons and institutions abounded in the aviation field. But so too did the darker side of exploitation and manipulation that national defense engenders. As a continuation of the war years, the aviation industry during the 1920s and 1930s manifested in microcosm most of the patterns and practices that future generations would attribute to a military-industrial complex.

More immediately, the consequences of a military-industrial complex were fully evident during World War II. Bernard M. Baruch had worried that the military would use the experience and knowledge gained from economic planning to dominate a mobilized economy in the future.[4] The elder statesman anticipated only part of the problem. Rather than trying to break free of civilian control—which would have been enormously damaging to themselves and to the society—the armed forces instead joined industry in an alliance of mutual benefit. That pattern was obvious in decisions involving industrial conversion and expansion and military demand and procurement during the early phase of mobilizing the economy for World War II. Once America entered hostilities the practice continued in every facet of harnessing the economy, including assessing the feasibility of military requirements, the distribution of contracts, the protection of the economy's civilian sector, the fate of small business, the policy for handling labor, and the method for reconverting the economy.

The armed services were never able or even inclined to work alone in economic mobilization. Interwar planning, however, provided the indispensable training for the armed services to work in harmony with industrial America for meeting the economic demands of modern warfare in ways consistent with American traditions.

OASW PLANNING IN HISTORICAL PERSPECTIVE

Scholarly studies of the Office of the Assistant Secretary of War's procurement and economic mobilization planning have been written principally by official military historians associated with what is now called the U.S. Army's Center of Military History. Their principal contribution has been detailed accounts of procurement planning by the various supply arms and services. Many of the authors treating with the planning in general, and the industrial mobilization planning in particular, have been critical of the army's work. They have argued that the War Department was ill-equipped to handle or benefit from the planning; that the army was out to avoid or dominate civilian agencies; that it was unprepared for the problems of mobilizing the World War II economy; and, most important, that it did not adapt effectively to the political conditions of the late 1930s preceding America's entry into World War II.[5]

There is at least some validity to these charges. But to focus on the negative aspects of the planning misses the central point. The overall result was positive. Through twenty years of planning, the War Department, and to a lesser degree the Navy Department, learned the lessons of World War I, and in 1940, as opposed to 1917, was ready to participate as a willing partner in harnessing the economy for war. The confused and chaotic mobilization scene from 1939 to 1943 and beyond originated as much or more from civilian sources as from military ones.

The major flaw of the interwar planning involved internal military operations more than the armed services' interaction with the civilian world. The biggest failure was the inability of the War Department to put together an integrated supply system. Caught in a power struggle between the bureaus and the General Staff, the Office of the Assistant Secretary of War remained weak throughout the interwar years. Without an integrated supply and planning system, centralized and uniform statistics, reliable requirement figures, and proper methods for contracting and for distributing wartime contracts were impossible to achieve.

Indeed, an effective transition from planning to mobilization did not occur. War Department supply and mobilization conditions even deteriorated around 1939, just when greater strength was essential. The bureaus recalled their best officers from the OASW, leaving the office in inexperienced and less talented hands. This drain occurred while the secretary and assistant secretary of war engaged in a running feud with each other and with the White House over preparedness matters, wreaking havoc with the entire mobilization program and further injuring an already badly damaged OASW. To get the War Department back on track, a new secretary and assistant secretary took office in mid-1940. Unfamiliar and unimpressed with the OASW, the new civilian heads brought in their own advisers and executives to handle economic mobilization. The OASW ultimately was bypassed. Army supply and mobilization functions, therefore, were tumultuous and confused between 1940 and 1941. Once the United States entered the war and full industrial mobilization began, the General Staff early in 1942 reorganized the army–War Department structure. It placed supply operations under its jurisdiction and virtually excluded the assistant secretary of war (upgraded then to under secretary of war) from active control in this area.[6]

Numerous scholars writing on the OASW have criticized the inflexibility of various plans since they were based on the concept of M-Day (a general mobilization date).⁷ No clear demarcation ever occurred, and the United States made a gradual, haphazard transition to a mobilized society from 1938 to 1942. (Although in the Industrial Mobilization Plan of 1939, the OASW modified significantly and made much more flexible the M-Day-approach.)⁸ Although there is some validity in criticizing the military for a rigid M-Day concept, as the years from 1914 to 1917 should have made clear, that point can be pushed too far. A well-structured and integrated planning-procurement-mobilization system could have adjusted to the ambiguities America faced in the late 1930s and early 1940s. The Ordnance Department did so. It was the lack of an integrated supply system and inadequate coordination between the army and navy that was the principal source of difficulty, not the plans or the concept of M-Day. The M-Day idea revealed the weaknesses of the supply/planning structure; it did not create them. Furthermore, in evaluating the planning, the commodity committee work could have been better. Concerning the Industrial Mobilization Plans themselves, the planners should have been more sensitive to the political realities that existed.

Nonetheless, these are minor, not major, matters. Interwar planning made the military fully aware of the concept of feasibility, a reality reflected in the Protective Mobilization Plan, which was the most significant development of the 1920s and 1930s. Without it, any mobilization program would quickly fail. Once feasibility was accepted by the armed services, they could then make the necessary adjustments in their internal structures to participate in a basically sound mobilization effort. That step was an enormous accomplishment, which made planning by the Office of the Assistant Secretary of War in the long run fundamentally sound and successful.

Recasting the interwar years along the lines of the four-factor paradigm shaping the political economy of warfare is instructive. In the 1920s the second factor—the maturity of the economy—temporarily became all-important as the industrial-financial community achieved unexampled power and prestige during the Dollar Decade. Then the Great Depression quickly subordinated the second factor to the first—the size, strength, and scope of the federal government. Washington became dominant as the nation struggled to deal with the devastating consequences of economic collapse and attempted to find a way out of the depression.

Although warfare did not affect the social system directly until the late 1930s, civil-military relations—the third factor—were the most important force shaping the political economy of warfare in the interwar years. The armed services were undergoing a profound transition as they adjusted their thought and institutions to dependence on a mobilized civilian economy for fulfilling the military mission in wartime. The adjustment took place principally through the army's economic planning; it was complicated by the shift in emphasis from the corporate community in the 1920s to the national government in the 1930s. That shift was manageable because it occurred within a context of continuity. Throughout the interwar years the long-run trend was toward the ongoing refinement of the government-business regulatory alliance as the principal mode of twentieth-century political economy. Different emphases occurred within that development according to the short-run needs of the social system.

Technological developments—the fourth factor—had some impact on the political economy of warfare, as exemplified by the airplane; and they suggested the far-reaching implications for future civil-military relations of high-technology weapons, combined with large expenditures on them by the armed services. Nevertheless, at this juncture, the sheer magnitude, more than the specialized nature, of military demand in a mature capitalist system during a major war remained the principal concern for the political economy of warfare.

PART TWO
PURSUING PEACE

Civilian groups were as interested in mobilizing the World War I economy and economic planning for future conflicts as were the armed services. Their motivation, however, was quite different. They perceived in modern warfare a comprehensive threat to American civilization. By analyzing how the economy was harnessed for World War I and how mobilization would be handled during another major war, civilian groups hoped to devise the means for avoiding or tempering the adverse consequences of wartime economics.

These civilians came principally from two overlapping constituencies: a revived and strengthened peace movement, and neo-Jeffersonians from agrarian sectors of the Midwest, West, and South. Before the Great War, neo-Jeffersonians had opposed big business and big government. During hostilities they chafed at economic mobilization policies that accelerated the growth of a government-business regulatory partnership as the dominant mode of twentieth-century political economy. After the war, they set about exposing the abuses of mobilization and attempting to devise methods for harnessing the economy that were less threatening to the Republic. Advocates of peace and antimilitary and isolationist elements, opposed to war and mobilization for it, joined the neo-Jeffersonians. By the 1930s these forces constituted a formidable opposition to modern warfare and its political economy. Their ranks were strengthened further by veterans' groups agitating for more equitable wartime economic policies.

Congress was largely responsible for documenting how the economy had been harnessed for war through hearings and investigations conducted in the 1920s and 1930s. Beginning between 1919 and 1921 with the House Select Committee on Expenditures in the War Department, gaining momentum with the War Policies Commission (1930–1932), and culminating in 1934 to 1936 with the Senate Special Committee Investigating the Munitions Industry, chaired by Sen. Gerald P. Nye (R-ND), the nation learned not only about what had occurred during World War I but also about the military's interwar procurement and economic mobilization planning.

Building on the work of its predecessors, the Nye Committee explicated the broad dynamics of modern warfare. It established that weaponry was drawing together economic, political, and military institutions into an association that it labeled an unhealthy, elitist alliance, which was abusive of the public interest and treasury, and more important, which could encourage and perpetuate warfare. With remarkable clarity and insight, Senator Nye and his colleagues anticipated today's so-called military-industrial complex. The only way to deter the growth of such a complex, the Nye Committee concluded, was to avoid excessive spending for defense and participation in war.

12
THE GRAHAM COMMITTEE

Throughout the interwar years, groups opposed to war and its consequences repeatedly forced Congress to investigate war mobilization and to consider legislation to avoid the drive for war or the alleged economic evils of war if hostilities occurred again. Washington moved slowly and reluctantly in creating investigatory bodies, with the hope of minimizing the political fallout from a persistent issue that demanded attention. The subject of modern warfare was so sensitive that nearly all highly-placed political leaders preferred to keep it out of the spotlight.

The political economy of World War I also engaged the attention of numerous scholars, journalists, and other analysts in the interwar years. Charles A. Beard, Seymour Waldman, and Grosvenor S. Clarkson published numerous articles and books on the subject. These publications can essentially be divided into two categories, although the actual separation was never so neat. Writers like Clarkson spoke for the elite corporate war mobilizers, of whom Bernard M. Baruch was the most prominent. They sought to claim the past for the present and future by recording the wartime mobilization experience in a light as favorable as possible.[1] The second group was made up of critics, such as Beard and Waldman, who saw the political economy of World War I as a grave threat to America and attempted to warn the public of perceived dangers.

In the short run, the Beards won the battle, as antimilitary, antiwar, and isolationist sentiments grew in strength during the 1920s and 1930s. But the Clarksons, as surrogates for the Baruchs, eventually won the war by persuading the public and the scholarly community to accept their version of World War I mobilization. World War II and the Cold War were instrumental in deciding who the victors would be. One measure of their victory is the present state of scholarship on the subject. Two points stand out in that regard. First, despite its importance, the topic has not commanded much scholarly attention. Second, although the 1960s opened up a critique of World War I similar to that of the interwar years in terms of scholarship, the ferment did not last long. A more balanced view of harnessing the economy for World War I emerged, but the interwar years and World War II remained neglected.

The critique of the political economy of American warfare was more profound and persistent during the 1920s and 1930s than in any previous period. This attention becomes amply clear by focusing on the numerous investigations of the subject. In doing so, the motivation and rationale of the foes and the defenders of war are clarified. So too are the policies and procedures of the War Department as the government agency most involved in the economics of warfare. The debate over mobilizing the economy for war moved out of government circles to include historians, political scientists, economists, and other social critics. Their analyses, which continues to the present, add both insight and perspective to the effects of warfare on the American social system.

The House Select Committee on Expenditures in the War Department, despite its misleading title, conducted the first full-scale investigation and analysis of World War I mobilization methods. Both during and immediately after hostilities, various congressional committees had examined the role of the War and Navy Departments in economic mobilization, but their scrutiny was brief or narrow or both.[2] Established in June 1919, the Graham Committee, named after William J. Graham (R-IL), who led in creating the committee and later acted as its chair, continued examining and reporting on the war mobilization process for about two years. This was the most comprehensive investigation of a war effort that the nation had ever experienced. Its hearings produced over 20,000 pages and its reports alone exceeded 700 pages.

The Graham Committee has not fared well in the assessment of historians. Indeed, little work of substance has been done on the committee.[3] In part this lack of attention stems from the fact that scholars have tended to neglect the economics of warfare. Moreover, the work of the Graham Committee has been dismissed as the hatchet job of an excessively partisan and parochial group of legislators.

The Graham Committee was unquestionably an intensely partisan and, in some respects, unsophisticated body. It carried out its work while the American political scene was highly charged over the war, the Treaty of Versailles, and the transition that both major parties were undergoing. These conditions were further aggravated by the nature and composition of the committee. Had the committee been a joint committee, rather than just a House committee, as some people desired, it would probably have had greater breadth and sophistication. Moreover, a committee of ten Republicans and five Democrats, which conducted most of its affairs through five subcommittees composed of two

Republicans and one Democrat each, could only heighten rather than temper political identification. This tendency was further exaggerated because Republicans on the committee were not well seasoned and respected. Graham, for example, was only in his second term in Congress. Some of their Democratic counterparts, by contrast, were highly regarded. The leading Democrat was Henry Flood of Virginia, who had been in the House since 1901 and, among other distinctions, had chaired the Committee on Foreign Affairs. The minority party, therefore, was better served than the majority.

This experience showed up in the operations of the committee. For reasons that are still unclear, the committee conducted its affairs without counsel and without much of a staff. As a result, and especially at the outset, the committee or subcommittees tended to be discursive, as obviously unbriefed committee members sought basic information. If the committee as a whole suffered from the lack of a counsel, the subcommittee dealing with the American Expeditionary Forces weakened its credibility by having as counsel a former acting judge advocate general who had been constantly at odds with the secretary of war and other War Department personnel during World War I. Further, the Republican leaders of the committee tended toward neo-Jeffersonian, isolationist, rural values; they represented Illinois, Wisconsin, Nebraska, and South Dakota, not the neo-Hamiltonian, urban, internationalistic wing of the party. That outlook had the effect of prejudicing committee leaders against the subject of their investigation, which both narrowed their purview and increased the partisanship of minority members.[4]

Partisanship is evident throughout the committee's work. Most of the investigating was done by subcommittees, which submitted majority and minority reports that followed party lines with predictable regularity. During the hearings, the Republicans attacked the war record, and the Democrats defended it. The same pattern held when the committee occasionally operated as a whole.

Despite its numerous weaknesses, the Graham Committee does not deserve the oblivion to which it has been consigned by scholars. The thousands of pages of hearings and reports it compiled are a gold mine of information. Furthermore, the fact that the committee largely acted without counsel and staff had some advantages. The committee members themselves had to do much of the work, which, although a disadvantage at the outset, made them better informed in the long run. And without careful preparation of either witnesses or committee members, the hearings had a rough quality but one that was spontaneous and genuine. The attitudes of committee members and witnesses came through at times with alarming candor. Readers can join committee members in gradually putting together the pieces of the World War I economic mobilization puzzle.

During two years of investigation, the Graham Committee laid a solid foundation for all future debate over the political economy of World War I. It looked at and commented on every major economic mobilization development from 1915 through 1919.

On the War Department's program of cantonment construction, the majority of the subcommittee on military camps was appalled at what had taken place. The Emergency Construction Committee, a remote subdivision of the National Defense Advisory Commission (NDAC), essentially staffed and run by civilians and ultimately headed by William A. Starett, had taken over the building of cantonments for all intents and purposes from the Quartermaster Corps in 1917. Cost-plus contracts distributed to chosen firms were pioneered by this committee in place of the usual competitive bidding for lump-sum contracting. Although the subcommittee's minority stressed the dire emergency faced, the majority emphasized that duly constituted and tested procedures were figuratively thrown out. They were replaced by methods devised by businessmen working without any meaningful guidance from established agencies like the War Department or new ones like the NDAC and without reasonable safeguards against abuse. The predictable results were favoritism, gross conflicts of interest, subcontracting abuses and waste, inefficiency, profiteering, and fraud.[5]

Similar charges were made by the Graham Committee about the army's procurement system. Under NDAC procedures, a civilian-directed Committee on Supplies took over numerous Quartermaster procurement functions, with many of the same results that occurred with the Emergency Construction Committee. Comparable developments transpired with the Ordnance Department and the purchase of leather and leather products.[6]

Some of the most impressive work of the Graham Committee was done by the subcommittee on Ordnance expenditures. Its principal target was Bernard M. Baruch, who first headed the NDAC's efforts on raw materials, minerals, and metals and later chaired the War Industries Board (WIB). In one of the most thorough, even-handed, and damning reports of the Select Committee on Expenditures in the War Department, Graham and his associates laid bare the operations of the Cooperative Committee on Copper, which Baruch, Clarkson, and others had held up as the arch example of industrial statesmanship. Wartime copper policy, the committee established, was dominated by the major copper corporations. They directly or indirectly controlled copper policy, first, under the rather crude arrangements of the NDAC, and then through the more sophisticated structure of the War Industries Board. The result was the sale of copper to the government on terms and under formulas for production dictated by the major firms in the industry. Profits were enormous. Based on capital stock, net profits ranged from 40 to 800 percent for corporations on which information was available. Elevated prices were justified on the grounds that they allowed high-cost mines to operate in order to maximize production, but production actually declined because of manipulation by the major copper corporations. This profiteering took place, the subcommittee argued, with the cooperation, and even the encouragement, of the mobilization agencies. Moreover, those agencies, from their own studies and those of the Federal Trade Commission, were fully aware of prices, profits, and production patterns within the copper industry. The Democratic subcommittee minority, pleading lack of time for a detailed answer, cried foul about the majority's methods and attitudes, reminded it of emergency conditions, and cited the production record to establish that wartime practices achieved the desired results.[7]

Although the report on copper was among the most detailed studies made by the Ordnance subcommittee, it reviewed and found wanting almost all aspects of Ordnance Department operations. According to the subcommittee, no preparations had been made for war, and when hostilities arrived, confusion reigned supreme. American tanks never got to the front despite great need; powder, artillery, and ammunition programs were fraught with waste, excess production, and various abuses approaching fraud; and plants the Allies had paid to build before the nation entered the war went unused. Similar charges were leveled at the largest steel and oil corporations over by-product coke ovens and toluene production. The committee was especially critical of the nitrate plants built at Muscle Shoals as an unnecessary waste of public funds and a threat to private enterprise. Conversely, Graham and his colleagues criticized the War Department for deferring to business by not using government facilities to the full in producing Quartermaster equipment. The attempted rebuttals in the minority report were hardly more convincing than those on copper.[8]

The subcommittee on aviation drew upon the wartime investigations of the Senate Military Affairs Committee and especially the work of Charles Evans Hughes, who headed the Justice Department's study, to bolster its own scathing indictment of the wartime aircraft production program. The nation's disastrous production effort stemmed from more than inexperience and incompetence; gross manipulation and conflicts of interest involving the large corporations that had taken over the existing aviation firms were involved, as well as criminal behavior. The subcommittee insisted that directly or indirectly, the trail led to Secretary of War Newton D. Baker, who bore responsibility by acts of omission and commission. Since the aviation record was so bad and the fault so clearly laid out by the earlier investigations, the minority in defense pointed to "the excusable incompetence of inexperience" and "causes that were inevitable and for which no just condemnation will lie."[9]

The one relatively positive report of the Graham Committee came from the subcommittee on the American Expeditionary Forces (AEF). After a period of confusion, the subcommittee found that the command structure abroad, with the aid of civilian advice and assistance, achieved good results by creating an efficient, responsible organization that established centralized direction over supply operations.[10]

Such was not the case, the subcommittee on the AEF argued, in the disposal of surplus property, contract termination, and salvage. In this area, the Graham Committee found the Woodrow Wilson administration to have performed badly abroad and at home. So solicitous was the administration of business interests that it let food spoil before selling it if markets would be disturbed, and it let industry set the terms for the cancellation of contracts and the disposal of surplus property.

In attacks on War Department behavior in these areas, the Graham Committee hurled charges that it believed applied to the entire mobilization program. The committee asserted that a system had been allowed to grow in which fixing responsibility was almost impossible and government officials too often dealt in areas where they were unqualified and faced experienced businessmen. Under such circumstances, the public interest could not be properly protected. Evaluating the overall mobilization process was almost impossible because adequate records were simply unavailable on expenditures of public funds reaching billions of dollars. For demobilization, in cases where contractors and business and industrial representatives were honest, final settlements followed suit. In instances where they were not, the government was too often fleeced or at least failed to achieve an equitable settlement. The entire demobilization process smacked of a hurried and unplanned effort to end a rather dismally executed program of mobilization.

Hence, in the eyes of the majority members of the Graham Committee, abusive economics continued for about a year and a half during the war and ended much as they had begun. For the minority, the majority findings and conclusions simply highlighted the basic flaws in the entire investigation. The minority asserted that the majority's facts were often wrong, its methods unfair, and its criticisms unsound. The government had worked out policies to dispose of surpluses in a systematic way, with various alternatives available to meet differing conditions so that the public was protected while various industries and the economy were not needlessly harmed. The minority's report on reconversion was its best effort, the Democratic members marshaling their strongest arguments and presenting a reasonable defense of administration policies.[11]

Had the Graham Committee stopped with findings on the different parts of the economic mobilization effort, its contribution would not have been outstanding. It would have documented abuses, ranging from opportunism to criminal behavior, that inevitably accompany economic mobilization for warfare. Moreover, during the war years, other investigations had examined in whole or in part the ground that Graham and his colleagues covered.[12]

The committee stands out, however, because it was the first systematically to establish how the nation had mobilized the economy for modern warfare. This outline was not constructed in a fully coherent fashion or in a logical order. Indeed, vital information on the general pattern of mobilization was often mixed in with details, for instance, about the operations of the Emergency Construction Committee or the industry advisory committees. Nonetheless, the basic outline of World War I mobilization is there if the reader spends the time to extricate it from the thousands of pages of hearings and reports.

The committee first traced the course of developments in the War Department from the virtual collapse of the decentralized bureau system of supply in 1917 to regeneration under the centralized Division of Purchase, Storage, and Traffic structure in 1918. Since the War Department was at the center of all war mobilization, the committee's focus and emphasis were the proper ones.[13] However, the Military Affairs Committees of both houses of Congress covered some of the same ground in preparing to write the legislation that became the National Defense Act of 1920.[14] Hence, the Graham Committee's contribution in this area, though valuable, was not indispensable.

The committee's work was indispensable though in setting forth how the civilian mobilization structure began with the Naval Consulting Board, took on greater coherence under the Council of National Defense–National Defense Advisory Commission, and reached the concluding stage with the War Industries Board. The Graham Committee examined with particular care the evolution of industry's role in mobilization from the cooperative committees of the NDAC to the commodity section–war service committee approach of the War Industries Board and the emergence of the dollar-a-year-man practice. In pursuing these topics, the committee examined many key documents and heard the testimonies of numerous chief mobilization figures. The hearings occurred while memories were relatively fresh and before conscious and unconscious distortions obscured the events that actually had taken place.[15]

The quality of the committee's investigation was weakened by its attitudes, naivete, exaggerations, and discursiveness. For example, as the committee minority protested, the majority operated on the assumption that if wrongdoing was possible, wrong took place. Graham breathlessly announced at a hearing in July

1919 that the committee had discovered that the Council of National Defense had secretly been running the government. The majority insisted that through the civilian mobilization agencies, *all* of the nation's industries had been slated for consolidation. Then the committee, while scrutinizing the American Expeditionary Forces' expenditures, still found time to damn Wilsonian internationalism as exemplified by the American expedition in Siberia.[16]

The committee's work was also marred by the highly questionable conclusions it repeatedly reached. The evidence often did not back up or at times even contradicted these conclusions. The committee insisted, for example, that adequate preparation by the War Department could have prevented the mobilization muddle. It then declared that the Quartermaster Corps had plans for handling all construction demands and that the Purchase, Storage, and Traffic Division of the General Staff could and should have been created immediately upon the outbreak of war, not well over a year after hostilities erupted. It further asserted that since the Muscle Shoals nitrate plants had never operated, they should never have been built. It also claimed that the federal government's power to commandeer industrial plants and to coerce the business community negated the need for seeking industry's voluntary cooperation in the mobilization program when resistance was encountered.[17]

Weaknesses in the Graham Committee's work distracted, and have continued to distract, from its solid achievement. The committee's judgments were often astute. For example, it repeatedly made the point that mobilization methods denied the government the information it needed for reliable decisionmaking, especially where benefits to business were involved. The Senate Special Committee Investigating the Munitions Industry and scholars later studying the World War II economy reached the same conclusions. Moreover, the committee majority made the valid point that although modern warfare required new methods of mobilization, this circumstance did not necessitate jettisoning the safeguards of the past, such as the antitrust laws; and even if such action was necessary, constitutionally prescribed methods existed for instituting change, including the participation of Congress.[18]

The majority recommendations of the House Select Committee on Expenditures in the War Department reflected clearly the committee's strengths and weaknesses.[19] The majority insisted that in the future no cost-plus contracts be used.[20] It maintained that the power of mobilization authorities to waive competitive contracting must be prohibited or checked. The committee further supported the passage of legislation instituting a type of military discipline over economic mobilization functions—legislation that would make available to the government at existing or determined prices, wages, and salaries the goods and services essential to prosecute a war. All mobilization functions must also be carried out by *existing* agencies, not by new ones, under guidelines written during peacetime. Only then, the Graham Committee majority argued, would the nation be prepared for war, with clear lines of responsibility and accountability maintained. In pressing its case, the majority continued:

> The vagueness and looseness with which it [economic mobilization] was carried on in the past war through the indiscriminate, irresponsible calling into a sort of semiservice, of the interested parties themselves, to control their own industries and activities, must never be repeated.

The fact that some War Department officials favored World War I methods alarmed the committee. The majority insisted that avoiding such an outcome required peacetime mobilization legislation including severe safeguards against its repeal during a national emergency. Moreover, the committee argued, all nonmilitary personnel participating in economic mobilization should be temporarily commissioned, thereby eliminating many of the World War I practices that had enriched the few. The majority went on to demand legislation that would prevent numerous subcontracting abuses and "evils." Finally, Graham and his Republican colleagues advocated that the Constitution be amended to make wartime profiteering treasonable behavior.[21]

The Graham Committee proposed draconian measures to ensure that existing institutions and practices be used to provide stability and continuity in the face of modern warfare. In an attempt to prevent World War I mobilization patterns during another conflict, the committee majority embraced cures that it recognized could be worse than the disease. The legislation proposed by the Graham Committee could be used to implement universal service in which all or most citizens and institutions could be subject to rigid, probably military, control. Ironically, a quest for neo-Jeffersonian ends could ultimately employ dictatorial means.

Although the Graham Committee had not thought through vital issues involving the political economy of modern warfare, it nevertheless wrote the agenda for decades of debate about the topic. The American Legion, the War Policies Commission, and the Nye Committee would travel down the path first blazed by Congressman Graham and the majority and minority members of the House Select Committee on Expenditures in the War Department.

13
THE AMERICAN LEGION, THE OFFICE OF THE ASSISTANT SECRETARY OF WAR, AND THE WAR POLICIES COMMISSION

Some of the major issues raised by the House Select Committee on Expenditures in the War Department (the Graham Committee) became part of the American Legion's interwar drive for equalizing the burdens of war and eliminating the promise of riches as an inducement to war. Ironically, the Legion's advocacy of such goals ultimately ended up as an effort to support war preparation. The American Legion's composition and its relations with the Office of the Assistant Secretary of War (OASW) explain why.

The American Legion received a national charter from Congress on September 16, 1919. Its antecedents, however, were in an organization of the same name founded in 1915 as an elite preparedness society with a membership including Theodore Roosevelt, Henry L. Stimson, and Elihu Root. After the war, American officers in Europe, with Theodore Roosevelt, Jr., playing a leading role, revived the prewar organization. Their effort was sanctioned by the General Headquarters of the American Expeditionary Forces and, although the evidence is far from complete, it was apparently financed by business, and probably big business. Legion leaders sought to bolster the sinking morale of the troops remaining in Europe and to combat among them any threats of radicalism. A patriotic organization par excellence, the American Legion dedicated itself to God, country, Constitution, and law and order. Its first national convention was held in November 1919. A year later, its membership stood at about 840,000. Thereafter, the ranks thinned until they bottomed out at 610,000 in 1925 and then slowly rose again, reaching over 1 million in 1931, which constituted 27 percent of the potential membership.[1]

Democratic rhetoric and image notwithstanding, the American Legion was an elite-oriented, conservative organization. Retired, reserve, or active-duty officers, particularly from the army, dominated the body. The Legion's top leadership was from the upper strata, and its membership was generally better off financially than the typical ex-serviceman, coming heavily from business and professional circles rather than from wage earners. Some conflict always existed between the rank and file and the leaders, but the latter usually had their way.

Although the American Legion was nationalistic and favored war preparation, its leaders had to recognize the often deep-seated ambivalence that such advocacy created among the membership by at least acknowledging that maintaining peace was a group goal. The Legion's complexities and contradictions became evident in the politically tumultuous interwar years as it struggled with the issues of war and peace.[2]

The idea of "universal service"—a "total draft" of capital and labor during war—became an American Legion commitment beginning with its first national convention in 1919. A total draft was intended to deal with charges of profiteering, high wages, indiscriminate draft exemptions, and other wartime abuses. Why should draftees sacrifice, suffer, and die, the argument ran, while others benefited from the economic opportunities created by hostilities? Although the concept of universal service was vague, several themes remained constant: monetary gain should be removed as a temptation to commencing hostilities; and, if war occurred, its burdens should be equalized.[3]

At the 1921 convention the American Legion directed its national commander to appoint a committee to study and report on the proposal for universal service. This committee was entirely composed of officers, two of whom were on active duty (a practice the Legion permitted from the outset in the face of some dissent): Maj. Gen. Hanson E. Ely, at the time head of the Army Service Schools at Fort Leavenworth and later commandant of the Army War College, and Brig. Gen. John McA. Palmer, a protégé of General of the Armies John J. Pershing and an influential adviser on what became the National Defense Act of 1920. Almost immediately the legionnaires turned to the War Department for advice. The Office of the Assistant Secretary of War, consulting with the General Staff and the Navy Department, assisted and carefully guided the Legion's work.

Ultimately the Legion's National Military Affairs Committee recommended to the national convention in 1922 a bill essentially written by the OASW's director of Procurement, Col. Harley B. Ferguson. The proposed legislation was brief and comprehensive: upon the declaration of a national emergency by Congress, the president could institute a military draft in which no male between the ages of twenty-one and thirty (or as determined by the president) could be exempted because of industrial occupation. In the event of war or need, the president could conscript through agencies of his choosing all of the material resources, industrial organizations, and services essential to meet an emergency. And finally, the president could act to stabilize prices and wages. Versions of the bill were included in the OASW's Industrial Mobilization Plans, and it was used to launch the American Legion's nearly twenty-year crusade for a so-called universal draft.[4]

Shortly after the American Legion convention, Cong. Royal C. Johnson (R-SD), a member of the Graham Committee and a legionnaire, introduced the Legion–OASW bill in the House of Representatives virtually as it came out of the study committee. It became known as the Capper-Johnson bill in 1924, after Sen. Arthur Capper (R-KS) introduced a companion measure in the upper house. On December 6, 1922, the day that Johnson introduced his bill, Cong. John J. McSwain (D-SC) placed in the House hopper a joint resolution to create a commission charged with writing legislation to take the profits out of war, to equalize the burdens of war, and to provide for mobilizing the economy in wartime. Also a legionnaire, McSwain was acting for that organization. He argued that he and Johnson proposed different means to the same end. The brevity of Johnson's bill rendered it half-baked and, if it intended to "draft" capital, unconstitutional. McSwain insisted that no proposed legislation, including a competing bill he had authored, dealt adequately with the crucial issues raised by the American Legion. Hence the need for the commission he favored. Such a body, with the time and detachment lacking in Congress, could study the matter properly and carefully craft legislation that would be effective, popular, and constitutional, qualities expediting the ends sought.[5]

The Capper-Johnson, McSwain, and related measures were constantly before Congress between 1922 and 1928. None ever came to a vote in either house, although hearings were occasionally held on them, the most important of which took place before the Senate and House Military Affairs Committees between 1924 and 1928. Analyzing each set of hearings is unnecessary, but a significant pattern emerges from them.

First to appear were the spokesmen for the American Legion, who included John Thomas Taylor, the Legion's chief lobbyist; D. John Markey, chairman of the committee that ultimately produced the American Legion bill introduced by Johnson; and Edward E. Spafford, national commander of the American Legion in 1928. Legion spokesmen varied to a degree in style and message, but their broad message was clear. While paying lip service to promoting peace, eliminating war profits, and equalizing war burdens, they stressed a "reasonable state of preparedness" and mobilization policies based on a refined World War I model. When pressed as to how this constituted a total draft, Legion witnesses evaded and filibustered. Defensively, more by suggestion than statement, they ruled out a draft of capital but not of labor. Either to satisfy numerous advocates of universal service in their constituency or the critics of World War I mobilization methods, American Legion representatives were simply unwilling to admit their intent. Whatever the case, the Capper-Johnson bill was so ambiguous that it could be called a measure for peace, for war, for defense, or for social justice.[6]

The second set of witnesses fall into the category of true believers. It included individuals such as Congressmen Charles L. Richards (D-NV), John M. Evans (D-MT), Morton D. Hull (R-IL), and Daniel E. Garrett (D-TX), and to some degree, Stanley High, speaking for the *Christian Science Monitor* (which was campaigning for action in behalf of peace and eliminating the economic abuses of war). Almost all elected officials among the true believers were neo-Jeffersonians from rural districts, as had been the case with the Republican leaders of the Graham Committee. This group was as direct as the American Legion was evasive. It was genuinely for peace, believed profiteering had been or would be an inducement to war, was outraged by World War I mobilization abuses, and was determined to avoid a repetition if war should come again. Unlike the Legion representatives, these people wanted a total draft and one that was aimed more at capital than at labor. Like Graham and his colleagues, they would chance a constitutionally prescribed dictatorship to halt warmongers and war profiteers. The true believers were angry, militant persons who tended to be discursive or fixated in their thinking. Hull, for example, was obsessed by the idea that profits would never be eliminated from war until they were first removed from peacetime munitions production. To achieve that end, he introduced a bill enabling the government to produce all munitions and related products in peacetime. The true believers obviously generated much of the heat involving the movement for universal service; they did not, however, cast as much light on the subject.[7]

A third group included House members such as McSwain, John C. McKensie (R-NY), who had been a member of the Graham Committee, and J. Mayhew Wainwright (R-NY), also a legionnaire, who had been the first assistant secretary of war under the National Defense Act of 1920. Without the fervor of the true believers, although at times displaying their proclivity for meandering thought, these individuals seriously sought to reduce war profiteering as an evil practice and as a cause of war. But they feared the goal might be unattainable. It was a stupendous undertaking that involved critical constitutional issues related to individual and property rights, presidential versus congressional responsibilities, and like considerations. They denounced as dangerous and simplistic loose talk about dictatorial powers in wartime and calls for the wholesale drafting of people and capital. Instead, careful study was essential. Although this group was distinct for its warnings about how to approach war profiteering and related subjects, it had little to offer in the way of resolving the momentous problems created by the economics of modern warfare.[8]

Baruch himself constitutes the fourth category of testimony. The former chairman of the War Industries Board (WIB) insisted that he and his World War I associates had achieved or were in the process of achieving methods for eliminating wartime profiteering. According to Baruch, the Capper-Johnson bill and others like it would suffice because they were brief and general, granting the president broad powers to implement a program that would resemble the World War I approach. While arguing for the status quo in economic mobilization planning, Baruch mouthed slogans for drafting labor and capital, agreeing that he favored crude forms of compulsion applied to labor.

During the years in which he testified Baruch corresponded widely about industrial mobilization and published several articles on the subject. His line was generally the same, although he was willing in private to admit that business profiteering during the war had been great. Moreover, he revealed that war mobilization, not peacekeeping, was his primary concern. To Samuel Gompers, he insisted that no labor draft was possible, contrary to what he had said before a congressional committee. When former wartime colleagues, such as Alexander Legge, seemed to wander from Baruch's approach, the former WIB chief moved quickly to try to bring them in line. Baruch's most astute adviser on "taking the profits out of war" was Hugh S. Johnson. The former general asserted that controlling capital, industry, labor, and the other economic elements was essential in war but that trying to draft them would be "mad," a form of "national hari-kari." Baruch, the War Department, the American Legion, and others in less colorfully phrased ways soon picked up Johnson's argument.[9]

Robert S. Brookings, another war mobilizer, represents the fifth point of view. His reasoning was not that much different from Baruch's, but his approach and attitude were. Despite highly questionable assertions—e.g., that industry had not influenced wartime pricing—Brookings was less intent on creating a legend about past mobilization and setting a mold for future efforts and more interested in relating what had taken place. The president, Brookings argued, must have virtually dictatorial power for mobilizing the economy for war. Paradoxically, however, the secret to success was in knowing the limits of such power and how and when to use it. Thus, the antitrust laws had been ignored during wartime but the constitutional rights of property and the structure and operations of the economy were left alone. Brookings insisted that the people determining prices had to balance carefully the need for checking inflation with the imperative for increasing production. He argued that by necessity the nation's political economy had to be used as it existed. Any law that allowed that to occur was acceptable, but no law could guarantee its intelligent application or cover any and all contingencies. Any mobilization policy in one way or another relied on the talents of the individuals implementing it. "In the last analysis," maintained Brookings, any future president, if he is to succeed, "will get around to doing just exactly what we did during the war."[10]

The sixth outlook is also represented by a war mobilizer, William B. Colver, who was the wartime chairman of the Federal Trade Commission and a member of the Price Fixing Committee. Unlike Baruch or Brookings, he was a dissenter concerning World War I methods, and he displayed expert knowledge about the operations of the wartime economy. Colver insisted that the only justification for wartime policies was the terrible pressure of time and inexperience, not the results that had been realized. Single pricing with excess profits taxes to recapture riches from the low-cost producers did not maximize production but instead fed inflationary fires, encouraged waste, enormously enriched corporate coffers, and burdened the public with higher prices and unnecessary government spending. A system of variable prices would be much more effective. If such a practice were combined with various governmental devices for rewarding and encouraging efficiency and discouraging waste, the outcome would be even better. Colver, however, promised no quick fixes. The matter was extraordinarily complex and required intensive study by the best minds available.[11]

The final stance involves the military, and particularly the Office of the Assistant Secretary of War. Since the OASW was the principal author of the main bill before Congress on war profiteering, the War Department naturally supported it. However, the department was divided on the matter, and the differences became evident to some degree during congressional hearings. As chief spokesman for the War Department, the assistant secretary of war, along with his assistants, favored the Capper-Johnson bill, but principally as a mobilization measure. In private more than in public, they maintained that checking war profiteering and equalizing war burdens interested them only to the degree that doing so made economic mobilization more efficient. The OASW officials also at first put themselves on record in favor of the highly controversial notion of financing a war through taxation, rather than through borrowing or the use of monetary devices, so as to control inflation. The most divisive issue within the War Department involved labor. Rather intensely antilabor attitudes abounded throughout the department. Nevertheless, the OASW modified its antagonism toward the working population when, in cooperating with the American Legion, it studied the matter of a labor draft and found the proposal to be totally infeasible. Moreover, once procurement and economic mobilization planning got under way, the OASW, joined by elements of the General Staff, realized that the categorical denial of exemptions to an age group was excessively rigid and could threaten a mobilization program. Other General Staff officers favored a system of no deferments as part of a larger and harsher "labor draft" system. Where industry and capital were concerned, however, there was never any systematic support in the War Department for a so-called draft.

More emphatically than other witnesses, military spokesmen questioned the constitutionality of controlling, particularly of drafting, people and property during wartime. They did so because their ranks were divided on key issues, and they appeared uncomfortable dealing with essentially civilian issues. Along the same lines, even though the assistant secretary of war went on record in favor of general legislation like the Capper-Johnson bill, others from the War Department warned that such crucial powers should be defined in detail. By the end of the 1920s, the War Department was beginning to take a more united stand in regard to economic mobilization. It recognized the need to avoid numerous political pitfalls by leaving to civilians the matter of constitutional rights, degrees of governmental control, and related issues. Finally, in 1929, the War Department decided that henceforth it would comment upon, but no longer endorse, proposed legislation dealing with war mobilization. The entire subject was becoming too controversial and complex. The decision was a sign of the department's growing maturity about and experience with a volatile subject.[12]

The preceding seven positions do not exhaust the responses to legislation on the economics of war. Frank A. Scott, for example, supported drafting general bills to authorize mobilization but opposed considering and adopting them during peacetime because of the controversy they would generate. Hence, he never testified in the hearings.[13] On the other hand, labor, and especially the American Federation of Labor (AFL), rushed forward to damn the various bills such as the Capper-Johnson measure as hoaxes aimed at regimenting workers. The federation announced that it would gladly support a total draft when industrialists and public officials joined labor in registering for national service. In the meantime, the AFL would work for peace and the control of profits, ends best reached through an in-depth study by a special commission.[14] For the War Department the idea of a commission was not especially appealing at first. But the more the OASW learned about the intricacies of the subject, the more favorably it viewed the prospects of a study group.[15] Capper and Johnson virtually defy classification. Despite glaring contradictions, they appeared to incorporate the views of the American Legion, the true believers, and individuals such as McSwain.[16]

Attitudes on legislation like the Capper-Johnson bill shifted rather dramatically in the 1920s. In 1924 the bill appeared attractive to many observers. President Warren G. Harding in 1921 and after voiced general support for universal service, and the two major parties followed suit in 1924.[17] During the congressional hearings in 1924, references to a wartime presidential "dictatorship" were commonplace, even by such an opponent of an oppressive state as Herbert Hoover. Apparently believing they reflected a national consensus, Hoover, Ely, Baruch, and others seemed unconcerned about the constitutionality of proposals like the Capper-Johnson Bill.[18] After the bill was carefully scrutinized and criticized, a much more cautious approach was evident by 1928. After 1924, the authors of the Capper-Johnson bill excised "conscript" from their work, the War Department and others explained that they had always meant "control" instead, and the American Legion witnesses in 1928 found themselves on the defensive about the legislation their organization backed. Commander Spafford protested that he was being unfairly harassed and pleaded with the House Military Affairs Committee to halt the divisive scrutiny and to pass the legislation. Rhetoric about dictatorship was also dropped in favor of attempts to protect constitutional rights during wartime.[19]

By 1928 it was clear that efforts for legislation to check profiteering, equalize war burdens, and sanction economic mobilization were going nowhere. The American Legion's drive, backed at least tacitly by the War Department, had been stymied. A different approach had become necessary.

THE WAR POLICIES COMMISSION: HEARINGS

The energy and effort devoted to the economics of warfare in the 1920s ultimately produced the War Policies Commission in 1930—which constituted until then the most detailed consideration of economic mobilization for war ever undertaken in America during peacetime. The commission resulted from the American Legion's switching tactics, and the War Department's following suit. Until 1928 the legion had supported both the Capper-Johnson bill and Cong. John J. McSwain's joint resolution, though preferring the former. In 1928 Legion leaders made war economics their first priority. That led legionnaires in Congress to decide in 1929 that although they could not get a bill passed on the issue they could get a commission formed to study it. Even establishing the commission required full unity in Congress. McSwain, who had been sponsoring the call for a commission since 1922, allowed a Republican to lead the effort so as to further the chances of success. After an aborted effort in 1929, the goal was finally achieved in 1930 with the so-called Snell resolution (for Cong. Bertrand H. Snell, R-NY).[20]

Creating a commission was not easy. The Snell resolution was amended eleven times in the House and twice in the Senate before ratification. One of the major amendments in the House, authored by George Huddleston (D-AL), forbade the commission from considering the conscription of labor. It was probably intended to protect workers against "work or fight," "national service," and other forms of compulsion since they lacked the constitutional protection of property under the Fifth Amendment.[21]

The Snell resolution mirrored the contradictions always involved in the movement for a universal draft. As some observers suggested, the investigating body created under it should have been called the Universal Mobilization Commission, not the War Policies Commission (WPC). To compound the irony, the resolution creating the WPC declared that it was intended "to promote peace."[22]

The WPC consisted of the secretaries of war, navy, agriculture, commerce, and labor, the attorney general, and four members from each house of Congress. These public officials were to study amending the Constitution so that private property could be taken for public use by congressional action during war. They were also to consider "methods of equalizing the burdens and to remove the profits of war, together with a study of policies to be pursued in event of War." Congress did not intend the commission to be a high-powered body, despite its prominent membership. It had no subpoena power, and its funding was minimal. Office space and clerical assistance came principally from the War Department.[23]

In its day-to-day operations, the War Policies Commission was largely a War Department affair. The department not only provided the commission with its basic needs but also with its leadership. Secretary of War Patrick J. Hurley was elected chairman. He was among the most dynamic of the secretaries of war during the interwar years, and he had served as assistant secretary before being appointed head of the War Department in December 1929. The department also played a leading role in selecting the commission's executive secretary, Robert H. Montgomery, a prominent New York attorney-accountant, who had served off and on in the army since the Spanish-American War. During World War I, he had, among other things, represented the War Department on the Price Fixing Committee and was in the upper echelon of the Purchase, Storage, and Traffic Division. Montgomery was well known to and highly respected by Bernard M. Baruch and his advisers. In fulfilling his tasks, Montgomery was served by a team of officers from the Office of the Assistant Secretary of War, headed by Gen. George Van Horn Moseley, of whom the most active and important participant was Maj. Dwight D. Eisenhower. Eisenhower for a time served as the assistant executive secretary of the WPC.[24]

Hurley and the OASW had great ambitions for the WPC. They saw it as an opportunity for popularizing and legitimatizing their work. The War Department prepared diligently to work with the commission, coordinating the OASW and the General Staff to present a united front. To ensure that the WPC did a thorough job, the OASW proposed organizing an elaborate secretariat staffed by personnel drawn from existing departments. Shortly after the WPC was authorized in June 1930, Hurley attempted to have a temporary secretariat set up in order to get the commission off to a fast and sound start. Lacking unanimous agreement, he was reluctant to proceed. It was not until late January/early February 1931, that the WPC met as a body and began functioning. Hurley was then able to get approval for a secretariat consisting of sections for legal affairs, military policy, manpower, industry, agriculture, and war finance and trade, in addition to the staff and a committee of the whole, with appropriate governmental departments providing the personnel.

Had the secretariat performed as set forth on paper, the WPC would have made a far-reaching study of the economics of warfare. But it did not. The only sections that actually functioned were the legal section and those assigned to the OASW. The latter body served as the principal staff to the executive secretary, the former concentrated on, and bogged down in, the constitutional aspects of economic mobilization for war. Other departments resisted or ignored the War Department's ambitious goals. Consequently, except for the hearings, little occurred other than the activities that the OASW could undertake or had already performed. The Great Depression may have distracted most people; others seemed to suspect that the WPC was little more than an elaborate charade. Whatever the case, outside of a rather small circle, the WPC did not stimulate others to work, even though its activities at times captured headlines.[25]

Of the six cabinet members only Secretary of War Hurley consistently participated. The secretary of labor was reasonably active during early hearings but not thereafter, and the secretaries of navy, agriculture, and commerce were rarely heard from. The attorney general played a major role in the last few months of the commission's life but not before. The WPC did spur the Navy Department on to greater activity involving industrial mobilization and by persuading it to work more closely with the OASW through the Army-Navy Munitions Board (ANMB), restructured in 1931 for that purpose.

Congressional members made a much greater contribution. Although Sen. David A. Reed (R-PA), elected vice-chairman, was a silent member, Senators

Joseph T. Robinson (D-AR), Claude A. Swanson (D-VA), and Arthur H. Vandenberg (R-MI) played reasonably active roles. The most important and persistent congressional voices, however, came from the House of Representatives. Ross A. Collins (D-MS) almost always participated. He and Hurley were by far the most attentive of the commissioners, even though Collins criticized war preparation and Hurley defended it. Congressmen Lindley H. Hadley (R-WA), who was secretary, and John J. McSwain (D-SC) were also quite active. Congressman William P. Holaday (R-IL) matched Senator Reed for his lack of contribution.[26] Congressional members perhaps were much more active than cabinet members not only because they were elected but also because they were principally from rural-oriented, small-town America, which tended to be more agitated about the political economy of warfare. Vandenberg asserted to Hurley early in 1930 that the principle of a "'Universal Draft' has powerful enemies—particularly in a large section of the metropolitan press."[27]

As it turned out, the War Policies Commission was the appropriate title for the agency created under the Snell resolution, a predictable outcome since the War Department dominated it. The WPC concentrated on how to mobilize the economy for another war, not on how to avoid war, eliminate war profits, or equalize the burdens of war. Differences over the need for amending the Constitution to harness the economy effectively for war, however, almost scuttled the commission.

The WPC ended up as a superficial study. Nevertheless, in its own way the commission represented progress. Much more than the Graham Committee or the hearings and reports of the Senate and House Military Affairs Committees in the 1920s, the War Policies Commission began to reveal the dynamics of an emerging military-industrial complex. Exactly why the commission produced such insights is difficult to discern. Perhaps the perspective of time played a part. The Great Depression, a deteriorating international scene, and the threat of another war no doubt also were relevant. Two developments were probably the most important. First, the maturation of the OASW's planning produced a full-fledged Industrial Mobilization Plan (IMP) in time for the WPC hearings. This action made much clearer to many people what had happened during World War I, what was taking place after the war, and what would occur during another worldwide conflagration. Second was the growth of a revived, and in a sense new, peace movement, which not only agitated against war but also began to zero in on the institutional aspects of modern warfare and their consequences for the future.

The various witnesses appearing before the WPC can be narrowed down from the seven positions represented in earlier hearings to five. The first group was made up of Baruch, the OASW, and their supporters who, for the most part, were World War I mobilizers. They are placed first because they were the only ones to make specific proposals for future war mobilization. Hence, their plans became the hub around which the WPC turned.

Baruch testified early in the hearings, appearing with Hugh S. Johnson and Herbert Bayard Swope, both of whom had served with him during the war. His statement, largely the work of Johnson, by then his chief adviser on industrial mobilization, was his best to date and the most polished presentation made to the commission. After most of the others had testified, Baruch answered his critics, modified his recommendations, and proposed legislation to accomplish his goals. Baruch's second appearance was arranged with the cooperation of the OASW. Montgomery, the War Department, and Senator Robinson joined together in assisting the former chair of the War Industries Board by ensuring that Johnson had full access to the stenographic record of the hearings, tentative reports, and other relevant documents. Johnson was also allowed to work with the legal section of the secretariat in writing a legal defense of Baruch's proposals.[28] Baruch and the War Department intended that his testimony would shape the WPC's work.

Baruch maintained that modified World War I policies and structures could handle any future crisis. During the Great War, Baruch remembered angels in human forms:

> Only a telegraphic request was ever necessary to bring immediately to Washington the busiest heads of the greatest industrial concerns in the country. Responses to any suggestion were instantaneous and the final result was a solidarity and cooperation the effects of which remain in our industries to this day. . . . Industry mobilized itself. The great bulk of accomplishment must be credited to spontaneous enthusiasm and self-abnegation and not to artificial control.[29]

That reality made any scheme for conscripting industry "crazy," "absurd," and "impossible."[30] Baruch did not damn a labor draft in such unequivocal terms, but he labeled it as unconstitutional and unwise. Besides, work-or-fight requirements as implemented during the last months of World War I would achieve the necessary measure of control. Baruch repeatedly warned that no constitutional amendments to facilitate economic mobilization or to make it more just were necessary or desirable.

The new twist, which Baruch claimed came out of World War I, was comprehensive price controls. When war threatened or erupted, the former WIB chairman argued, the president should select a date prior to the emergency when prices were determined by the laws of supply and demand without the distorting effects of a major conflict. With such a "norm," all prices, including "rents, wages, interest rates, commissions, fees—in short, the price for every item and service in commerce," would be frozen and could not rise above the ceiling imposed. A price control agency would make essential adjustments.[31]

Baruch asserted that reinstituting the World War I mobilization methods with a strict price-fixing scheme was "a plan to mobilize effectively the resources of the Nation for war which shall eliminate war profiteering, prevent war-time inflation, and equalize war-time burdens," although naturally "common belief" dictated the avoidance of war whenever possible. What he proposed was "neither dream nor theory";[32] it had been done in the Great War.

Baruch's proposal for freezing prices attracted the most attention, a tactic that appeared to be purposeful. He argued that inflation was the primary economic culprit, implying that any wartime abuses were attributable to it. By emphasizing how to deal with this problem, he diverted others from the larger mobilization scheme and focused their thought on price controls. In attempting to persuade Newton D. Baker to accept his reasoning, Baruch argued:

> There is a very general popular feeling that the knowledge that there would be no profiteering in the next war would in itself be a great deterrent of war. This has translated itself into a demand for confiscation. Believing thoroughly in the correctness of the plan I proposed, I felt very strongly that the presence of a law supporting price fixing would appeal to the public as having all of the benefit of a confiscatory statute and would result in none of the harm of the latter form of legislation.[33]

Contrived or not, Baruch's approach worked. He was never taken to task on the overall model he proposed for mobilizing the economy. Instead, the questioning was much more limited. For example, since World War I price fixing dealt only with wholesale products, how could he claim experience for the retail level? Or how would he determine the feasibility of military demand? Baruch dodged even these lesser issues, giving answers only in the statement prepared by Johnson that Baruch read at the end of the hearings, when few questions were asked.

Baruch's position during the hearings had changed to some degree from that of the 1920s, perhaps because of the new pressures from the masses he had written about to Baker. He placed much more emphasis than before on economic stability and equity, and he favored the passage of detailed bills in peacetime rather than just general grants of power. Such advocacy was new for Hugh S. Johnson as well as for Baruch and indicated the differing influences shaping thinking about the political economy of warfare.

When pressed to give the War Policies Commission a more full-fledged plan for economic mobilization, Baruch pointed to the War Department's Industrial Mobilization Plan as fulfilling the need in a way that met with his general approval. Yet in his prepared statement, he warned that the armed services could not take on roles properly belonging to civilians during economic mobilization. And he insisted that the military's work had to be reviewed annually or biannually by World War I mobilization executives to ensure its soundness and to begin training younger talent for future hostilities. When questioned about the possibility that the IMP sanctioned a labor draft, Baruch pleaded lack of knowledge, saying that he had only read the OASW work in a cursory fashion. Military planning for economic mobilization was as potentially volatile as the matter of war profiteering, and Baruch approached both subjects with extreme care.

Characteristic of his appearance before the WPC, Baruch was being less than candid with the commission. Almost two years of negotiations had taken place between Baruch and the Office of the Assistant Secretary of War to ensure their basic agreement before the WPC. Secretary of War Patrick J. Hurley and Gen. George Van Horn Moseley directed the writing of the first complete Industrial Mobilization Plan between 1929 and 1931, with Baruch consulted at every step of the way.[34] Hence, his plea of ignorance about the IMP was disingenuous. Baruch was using the IMP, as he had used the proposal for freezing prices, to divert attention from World War I mobilization methods and to focus it on military planning and the threats the OASW posed to civilian control of the economy.

Any fundamental disagreement between Baruch and the War Department could have seriously damaged the cause of economic preparedness. Disputes would have made public information best kept in limited circles. Consequently, a bargain was struck. Baruch gave the OASW his blessing, despite basic disagreements with the agency's work. In exchange, the War Department accepted the World War I model and a more limited role in running a mobilized economy than it desired. Throughout the WPC hearings an intricate minuet took place. Secretary of War Hurley skillfully persuaded Baruch to endorse the OASW's role as planner and its plan. By pleading ignorance about the military's work, Baruch left enough room for himself to differ with the War Department in case of conflict or to distance himself from the IMP where it was controversial. At no point did Baruch or the OASW ever publicly clash. Indeed, close ties among Baruch, the OASW, and the WPC minimized chances of an open dispute.

The War Department's presentation of its Industrial Mobilization Plan before the War Policies Commission was of equal significance with Baruch's testimony. Army Chief of Staff Gen. Douglas MacArthur was the department's principal witness. He was preceded by Assistant Secretary of War Frederick H. Payne and followed by the Deputy Chief of Staff (earlier executive assistant to the assistant secretary of war) General Moseley. Hurley as secretary of war and chairman of the WPC deftly stepped in to assist witnesses in avoiding trouble, elicit information the department wanted on record, and ensure that key matters were emphasized. The War Department witnesses repeated that the mobilization apparatus proposed by the OASW would be run by civilians in an emergency, the army and navy providing only interim direction. Furthermore, with the assistance of business and its associations, the OASW was in the process of compiling rosters of talented executives to run the apparatus, and it wanted such individuals and Congress frequently to review the Industrial Mobilization Plans.[35]

The Industrial Mobilization Plan, 1930, was modeled after the mobilization apparatus worked out for World War I, with some refinements and drafted legislation for implementing it.[36] After first indicating a preference for selective price controls, the OASW by the end of the WPC deliberations endorsed Baruch's approach as the better one. The IMP's proposal for a military draft included provisions for industrial and humanitarian deferments, a sign of growing harmony within the military over this contentious issue, even though some differences continued to be aired before the commission. Although methods for mobilizing manpower were intended to assuage labor, some clauses were either so vague or seemed to threaten unions so much that they came under attack by organized labor and its advocates. The War Department also supported registering wealth and additions to it during a national emergency, and MacArthur expressed the belief that government contractors should be limited to 6 percent profit during wartime. These provisions addressed to some degree the issues of war profiteering and equalizing war burdens, but MacArthur insisted that the War Department's first priority was fulfilling the military mission:

> In our attempts to equalize the burdens of and remove the profits from war, we must guard against a tendency to overemphasize administrative efficiency and underemphasize national effectiveness. The objective of any warring nation is victory, immediate and complete. It is conceivable that a war might be conducted with great regard for individual justice and administrative efficiency as to make impossible those evils whose existence in past wars inspired the drafting of Public Resolution No. 98, Seventy-first Congress. It is also conceivable that the outcome of such a war would be defeat.... We must never overlook for one moment the fact that while efficiency in warmaking is desirable, effectiveness is mandatory.[37]

For some reason, Hurley denied that the War Department approved of any legislation for economic mobilization, despite the inclusion in the IMP's Legislative Appendix of a number of bills.

Generally, the War Department's presentation of its plan was a success. The OASW proved to be flexible, and it finessed effectively controversial issues. The department benefited from the fact that the IMP was so bulky that it was hard to analyze without expertise, which the WPC collectively lacked. Hurley, the press, and others constantly repeated that there were two formal plans before the WPC: Baruch's price freezing proposal and the IMP. In effect, these two approaches were complementary, not different or supplementary. Nonetheless, the appearance of variety obscured the agreement and collaboration between the OASW and Baruch.

The Baruch–OASW position was supported by the Navy Department through the brief testimony of Capt. H. K. Cage, director of the Materiel Division, Office of the Chief of Naval Operations, whom the secretary of the navy had appointed to make up the navy section of the WPC secretariat. The Navy Department expressed its approval of the OASW work, based on the General Board reviewing the IMP. Moreover, the two services restructured and revived the Army-Navy Munitions Board to facilitate coordination between them and to stimulate greater effort by the Navy Department on procurement and economic mobilization planning.[38]

Much more important for political purposes was the endorsement of the Baruch–OASW work by a host of prominent World War I mobilization figures. These included Daniel Willard, George N. Peek, Eugene Meyer, Jr., Augustus H. Griswold, Homer L. Ferguson, Benedict Crowell, and J. Leonard Replogle. They expressed their desire for peace but advocated preparedness for war. Most placed a greater emphasis on excess profits taxes than had Baruch, a matter the latter corrected in his second appearance before the War Policies Commission. Almost all favored a price freeze, some with reservations. Some, such as Willard, stressed their support for OASW planning; others, like Replogle, emphasized their dedication to Baruch's guidance, although all endorsed the necessity to prepare industrially for hostilities. All opposed amending the Constitution to facilitate wartime mobilization and the quest for equity.[39] Conspicuous by his absence, despite Montgomery's plea for support, was Alexander Legge, the former vice-chairman of the WIB. Never comfortable in the role of disciple, Legge found Baruch's obsession with economic mobilization to be tedious.[40]

The War Department also called specialists to testify before the commission on various aspects of economic mobilization. This group included Philip A. S. Franklin, president of the International Mercantile Marine Company and the Atlantic Transport Company, who had served as chairman of the Shipping Control Committee during World War I and who advised the WPC on shipping. Clyde B. Aitchison, an Interstate Commerce Commission member, informed the WPC about transportation. Arthur N. Ballantine, assistant secretary of the Treasury Department, from the law firm of Root, Clark, Buckner, Howland, and Ballantine, was the best of the expert witnesses. He provided the commissioners with elaborate information on World War I taxation and the difficulties of recapturing all profits due to war. And Herbert Bayard Swope offered up virtually dictatorial solutions for managing public opinion during hostilities.[41]

The views of the second set of witnesses before the WPC resembled those of Robert S. Brookings in the 1924–1928 hearings. They too were war mobilizers, but they looked upon the war years somewhat differently from Baruch and his coterie, and hence their prescriptions for the future also varied. Their quarrel was not with the Office of the Assistant Secretary of War. For the most part, they favored both War Department planning and the Industrial Mobilization Plan.

Included in this group were Newton D. Baker, Walter S. Gifford, Howard E. Coffin, Leonard P. Ayers, John M. Hancock, Palmer E. Pierce, Clarence C. Williams, and John Ross Delafield. They had played leading roles in World War I mobilization, the first four acting primarily as civilians and the last four involved in supply as highly placed military officers. Some of these individuals carried over World War I economic mobilization rivalries and animosities that tended to center on Baruch.[42] All of them took about the same position on questions of policy as the first group, with one major exception: they were opposed to a price freeze, supporting instead selective and partial price controls. (That the OASW initially favored this approach and later shifted to Baruch's position was one measure of the latter's influence before the WPC.) Generally, this group had less fear of military influence during economic mobilization than Baruch's cohort. Indeed, Baker voiced the opinion that extending the military's power was inevitable during a war. Further, these witnesses were more willing to stress that inflation, war profiteering, and inequalities were unavoidable costs of war. There were limits to how much they would gild the war lily. Some members of this group, particularly Gifford and Coffin, felt the Council of National Defense–National Defense Advisory Commission system should be revived in order to further industrial preparedness.[43]

The differences between the first and the second category of witnesses were not great but were nonetheless significant. Unsuccessful in getting Baker to follow his lead, Baruch, and later Montgomery, minimized the divergence of the groups by acknowledging the positions taken by the men associated with the former secretary of war. Hurley also treated them deferentially during the hearings.[44] Generally, the testimonies of the first and second groups of witnesses did not vary greatly and never touched on the fundamental issue of whether the World War I model should be used for future mobilization. The Baruch–OASW contingent smoothed over the limited differences between themselves and influential witnesses without any substantial damage to their cause.

The third group of witnesses consisted of American Legion representatives. Compared with its role in earlier hearings, the Legion played a much less prominent part in WPC deliberations, even though six of the fourteen commissioners were legionnaires. By achieving a major goal with the creation of the WPC, the Legion lost its drive and concentration. The first American Legion witness was the national commander, Ralph T. O'Neil. His performance hurt the cause more than it helped. In his prepared statement, O'Neil insisted that universal service served the purposes of peace, preparedness, and equity and that during hostilities it meant the use of agencies and controls similar to those of World War I. O'Neil's text was confused and his answers to questions worse, despite a helping hand from sympathetic members of the WPC. He could not make up his mind as to whether the states, the federal government, or the military should control economic mobilization. If he had his preference he would draft labor, but not capital, which would be entitled to around a 7 percent wartime profit. A universal draft, he averred in an attempt to give some meaning to his testimony, was only a symbol, not a system, which the Legion used because it was popular.[45]

Perhaps to repair O'Neil's damage, Hurley asked Paul V. McNutt, a former American Legion commander and currently dean of the Indiana University Law School, to testify. McNutt turned out to be an excellent witness, but not what the War Department had in mind. He supported taxing away all war profits, and he insisted that the Capper-Johnson bill or similar legislation required amending the Constitution to permit taking property without full compensation. Despite pleas by Hurley and others that a constitutional amendment was unnecessary and would have the effect of limiting governmental options, McNutt refused to budge from his convictions.[46]

The WPC turned next to Charles B. Robbins to try straighten out the Legion's message. Robbins was commander of the Iowa Department of the American Legion, chairman of the Legion's National Defense Committee, and a former assistant secretary of war. His testimony also had mixed results. Clearly and candidly he explained the American Legion's thinking on war mobilization. Universal service meant a type of World War I control over industry as set forth in the Industrial Mobilization Plan. For labor, all able-bodied men and women would be required to register with manpower agencies for assignment to civilian duties. To the embarrassment of Hurley and others, Robbins suggested that industrial mobilization could mean military control of the economy, and he favored limited, as opposed to total, price control.[47] Thomas Kirby, national legislative chairman of the Disabled American Veterans, and Paul C. Wolman, commander in chief of the Veterans of Foreign Wars, also testified in behalf of universal service.[48] Kirby's performance was as confused as that of O'Neil; Wolman's was sensible, but he was not questioned by the commission.

The WPC leadership made one last effort to give some coherence to the American Legion's position. O'Neil, McNutt, and Robbins submitted a memorandum to the commission in which they defended and explained how the Capper-Johnson bill would work, emphasizing three points: no constitutional amendment was necessary; taxation would limit wartime profits to about 6 percent; and prices would be frozen and adjusted according to need. (McNutt shifted his position considerably from his earlier testimony without explanation.)

Even this statement did not end the Legion's travail. Insisting that American Legion spokesmen did not speak for the rank and file, Congressmen Ross A. Collins and John J. McSwain tried polling the membership. The result was resounding silence. Either the local leaders fully supported the national leadership, or, more likely, they and the membership were ignorant, apathetic, or both about what was taking place in Washington.[49] After the War Policies Commission wound down, the American Legion was no longer the major player involving the economics of modern warfare.

The fourth group of witnesses resembled the true believers of the earlier hearings, but no zealots sat on the WPC. Instead, various individuals carried the message to the commission. Among them was (retired) Adm. Samuel McGowan, former paymaster general of the navy, who had headed procurement and supply operations for the Navy Department during World War I. To preserve peace and avoid the "cupidity" and "sordidness" of war, McGowan proposed that the Constitution be amended so that, unless the country was attacked, war could be declared only by national referendum. If the people opted for war, then all able-bodied males between eighteen and thirty-five would be drafted and all prices and wages frozen.[50]

Congressman James A. Frear (R-WI), who had been a member of the Graham Committee, fell into the true believer category. His presentation to the WPC was a combination of shrewd insight and incoherent rambling. Frear argued that the nation should not be allowed to go to war, short of repelling an invasion or putting down a rebellion, unless a majority of the states gave their approval. In case of war, no draftee could serve outside the North American continent. If men were drafted, Frear insisted on amending the Constitution so as to conscript property as well.[51] Dr. Thomas Hall Shastid, an oculist who chaired several small antiwar groups, shared Frear's outlook. Shastid opined that profits and prices should be rigidly controlled during hostilities, but his main concern was maintaining peace by constitutional limits on declaring war and financing belligerents.[52]

And there was Cong. Royal C. Johnson, the old warrior who had first introduced the American Legion bill in 1922. Tired and ill, Johnson held to his faith that the Constitution should be amended to allow the conscription of all people and things in the event of hostilities since war itself could not be abolished. With the "bolsheviks" of capital and labor blocking such an approach, he would settle for what he could get, including freezing prices and wages, steep taxation, and the like. In contrast to his testimony during the hearings in the 1920s on equalizing the burdens of war, Johnson, although more discursive, this time seemed more sincere. His appearance before the WPC made it look as if the American Legion, Baruch and his coterie, and the other industrial preparedness advocates had used the guileless Johnson to advance their cause.[53]

The last group of witnesses was not new but was greatly strengthened since the hearings of 1924–1928. A composite group, they principally represented three elements: peace advocates, speaking for a revived movement that was growing in numbers and influence; radicals, who had been under severe attack in the 1920s but who had regained a voice with the distress of the Great Depression; and the people beginning to perceive that modern warfare was creating an institutional juggernaut with potentially grave consequences for the future. No rigid lines separated these three groups, and some individuals fit into several of them. These people shared common ground in their opposition to Hurley and his colleagues using the WPC inquiry to further war preparation and to legitimize that cause. In this sense, the dissidents, next to the preparedness advocates, were the most significant group participating in WPC affairs. Their arguments forced the War Department, Baruch, and others to modify their tactics, if not their strategy.

The dissidents did not get much support from organized labor. Only William Green, president of the American Federation of Labor, and Arthur J. Lovell, vice-president and national legislative representative of the Brotherhood of Locomotive Firemen and Engine Men, testified. The latter stressed that labor would gladly support a universal draft, but it knew well that only the working force would be called. Green indicated that the World War I methods appeared to be just about right. In general, labor's representatives knew little about the subject and manifested little interest in it.[54]

Dr. Arthur Deerin Call stood out as a peace advocate. He served as secretary of the American Peace Society and as editor of the *Advocate of Peace*, among other posts.

It has been said that it is quite impossible to equalize the burdens or remove the profits of war. That is in error. There is one solution of all the problems facing the War Policies Commission, probably the only solution. Every policy to be pursued in time of war can be perfectly clarified. Every burden of war can be lifted. Every war profiteer can be subverted. Every property can be secured. Every principle of law and every section of the Constitution can be protected. Every one of these highly desired ends can be achieved by avoiding war. The excuse for calling attention to this simple reminder lies in the fact that the title of the act under which the War Policies Commission is set up begins with these words: "Joint resolution to promote Peace."

Call was the most moderate representative of the various peace groups appearing before the WPC. He recognized that the mobilization methods of the last war, with some improvements, were about the best that could be expected, and this approach did not require additional legislation or constitutional amendments. Call even admitted that after twenty years of study he was uncertain as to whether moderate preparedness promoted or undermined peace.[55]

Other spokespersons for peace groups were more strident. Dorothy Detzer, executive secretary of the Women's International League for Peace and Freedom, advised the WPC to abolish conscription in every form instead of extending the practice to property if it truly wanted peace. Labeling modern munitions makers and sellers as people without a country, Detzer argued that the entire industry should be nationalized. But such an act, she said, was no peace panacea, as the Soviet Union proved. Furthermore, the promise of riches in no fundamental way contributed to the drive for war. Just as certainly the efficient prosecution of war and preparation for it did not further the chances for peace. Only the repudiation of war would end the horrors and distortions of hostilities.[56]

Tucker P. Smith, secretary of the Committee on Militarism in Education, insisted that war grew from long, deep, and broad national policies of imperialism and militarism over which few people had control. War profits did not cause war, equalizing war burdens would not avoid war, and military and industrial preparedness were not peace measures. But the League of Nations, the World Court, and revising the nation's international economic policies would reduce the chances of hostilities. Words and deeds, Smith maintained, had to match. The War Policies Commission, rhetoric notwithstanding, was obviously dedicated to war, not to peace. Smith was a formidable witness who could not be shaken by the invidious analogies and non sequiturs that Secretary of War Patrick A. Hurley, Sen. Claude A. Swanson, and others had used to sidetrack those disagreeing with them.⁵⁷ The Reverend John Nevin Sayre, executive secretary of the Fellowship of Reconciliation, also gently explained to the commissioners the principled stand of his organization.⁵⁸

The peace spokespersons provided an impressive record. They spoke to deaf or unlistening ears, however, for few commissioners were there to hear them, and few or no questions were asked. At best, they were tolerated. Most came on their own initiative or through the efforts of Congressmen Ross A. Collins or John J. McSwain.⁵⁹

Radicals were close to the peace advocates. Among the first of this group to testify was Benjamin C. Marsh, secretary of the People's Lobby (of which John Dewey was past president) and associated with other similar organizations. Marsh insisted that an economic system dominated by "unscrupulous exploiters" at home and abroad was a primary cause of war and had to be changed. Focusing on ending war profiteering and on equalizing war burdens, he said, was ill-advised since those ends could not be achieved without a fundamentally reordered social system. Marsh's aggressive stance and radical proposals agitated members of the WPC, particularly Hurley and Swanson, producing a verbal free-for-all in which the secretary of war hurled the epithet "Bolshevist" at the People's Lobby spokesperson.⁶⁰

Hurley did not quarrel with Norman Thomas, director of the League for Industrial Democracy; instead, he unsuccessfully attempted to prevent Thomas and others of similar beliefs from testifying. Like Marsh, Thomas argued that socialism promised the best path to peace. But war socialism always threatened to end in fascism. Thomas, therefore, was skeptical of universal conscription and doubted that prices could be frozen. If the burdens of war had to be faced, then the best way to do so was to ensure that the total cost of hostilities came from current income through rigorous taxation. Thomas concluded by observing that having industrialists in the Reserve Officer Corps, placing educational orders, and using other modes of industrial preparedness were distasteful to him. These measures constituted an attempt to sweeten the war pill and to encourage the psychology and philosophy of militarism—situations and attitudes to be avoided at all costs.⁶¹

Norman Thomas's opinions about industrial mobilization and its potentially insidious effects reflected the major concern of the last group of dissidents, who began to see growing institutional adjustments dedicated to war. These individuals were not necessarily pacifists or radicals, and Cong. Ross A. Collins, a member of the commission, was among them. Grappling with a new phenomenon, this group appeared to be uncertain about its target. Nonetheless, it vaguely began identifying threatening institutional consequences of modern, industrialized warfare.

The institutional critics directed their first line of attack the War Policies Commission itself. Like the American Legion, they insisted, the commission in the name of peace was following paths leading to war. Modern warfare had already begun to replace truth with "doublespeak." Throughout the hearings, an agitated Collins constantly pointed to the contradictions. Congressman Frear, Mercer G. Johnston, director of the People's Legislative Service (which Sen. Robert M. La Follette had led in founding in 1920), Cong. Fiorello H. LaGuardia (D-NY), and others joined Collins in a spirited, at times scathing, attack on the commission as a study in hypocrisy and manipulation.[62]

If war could not be avoided, LaGuardia, Robert M. Lovett (a University of Chicago English professor associated with the *New Republic*), and others maintained that the economics of warfare then became a prime priority. Dollar-a-year men, industrial self-regulation, and the promise of freezing prices had to give way to a total draft of all economic resources and services designed genuinely to equalize the burdens of war both to further justice and to discourage future aggression. Amending the Constitution would be essential for accomplishing these purposes, and the drastic measures involved had to be overseen closely by Congress, not left simply to the president.[63]

Congressman C. William Ramseyer (R-IA) argued that total conscription was a desirable but politically impossible goal. Hence, along with Benjamin C. Marsh, Norman Thomas, and Sen. Smith W. Brookhart (R-IA), he advocated a solution he thought to be feasible: drastic taxation, which would finance totally the costs of war while maintaining economic stability and deterring future hostilities.[64]

Collins was sympathetic but philosophical, even about Ramseyer's more modest approach: "I think some of your proposals are excellent; but I fear that if we merely resolve something it is not going to amount to a row of pins, and I seriously doubt if Congress will pay attention to it if we should have war."[65] The WPC member was hitting upon a basic truth. The institutional critics of war seldom mustered any enthusiasm for policies designed to make war more just and equal. They doubted that such policies would be enacted; if enacted, enforced; and if enforced, effective. Avoiding war was the real answer.

Yet these dissidents feared that the chances of avoiding war were growing remote. They sensed an institutional buildup perpetuating the forces that made for war. This view introduced a new theme in the debate over war that had been suggested by the Graham Committee but never pursued or developed. Mercer G. Johnston, picking up on a Baruch term, condemned "atmosphering" the nation for war with romanticized notions of military service, the

National Guard, organized reserves, citizens' military training camps, the Reserve Officers' Training Corps, military programs in the schools, the National Rifle Board, and the like. Benjamin C. Marsh complained that the concept and practice of Universal Military Training helped produce war. Such developments fed the instincts of individuals in the general population and public officials who were drawn to warfare.

Some of the institutional critics were even more specific. Industrial preparedness was a major concern of Norman Thomas. In his attack on war "atmosphering," Johnston struck out at "our procurement agencies, which really run their fingers back into all the recesses, especially the industrial recesses, of everyday life and leave almost no phase of our industrial life untouched by militarist fingers."[66] Detzer, eschewing some simplistic notions of munitions makers as the cause of war, still singled them out as requiring close attention and study.

It was Collins, however, who probed the deepest and most consistently in this area. Day after day, witness after witness, and in repeated exchanges with Secretary of War Hurley, Senator Swanson, and other commissioners, he pursued the consequences of "militarizing industry or industrializing the military"—terms first used by Baruch. He insisted that the hypocritical nature of the War Policies Commission was part of this dual development, along with the Office of the Assistant Secretary of War and the Industrial Mobilization Plans. In an often clumsy manner, Collins berated the military for intruding into civilian life and civilians for welcoming the military ethos.

The Mississippi congressman, however, was never able to articulate clearly why modern warfare so deeply bothered him; he seemed to be shadowboxing with an unknown. Seymour Waldman, a journalist covering the hearings and whom Collins and others inspired, came closer than anyone else in identifying the institutional consequences of modern warfare:

> The hearings revealed a gigantic machine, whose intricate parts touch the entire nation, which is being constructed by the War Department and industrial magnates for use in the event of war. . . . They reveal the dangers inherent in a militarization of industry, an industrialization of the military forces, or a combination of the two. . . .
>
> I would feel rewarded and gratified if this book should be the precursor of a much needed diagnosis of the whole problem, a study of the interlocking of our war mechanism and our economic system. . . . Such a work . . . is imperative if we are to be effective in preventing more national and international bloodshed.[67]

THE WAR POLICIES COMMISSION: REPORT

The War Policies Commission's principal work consisted of the public hearings that took place on March 5–18 and May 13–22, 1931. Thereafter, the commission did not meet until early November 1931, and a quorum could not be convened until December.

During the hearings, Congressmen John J. McSwain and Lindley H. Hadley suggested rather elaborate procedures for drafting a commission report and recommendations.[68] Nothing ever came of them. Early in November Chairman Hurley was informally asked to put together a report that would be circulated to the commissioners and based partly on their suggestions.[69] This request was only pro forma. Shortly after the public hearings, Robert H. Montgomery began drafting a report and noted reasonable progress late in July 1931. By early November, with assistance from Maj. Dwight D. Eisenhower, he had finished the First Tentative Draft and made it available to commission members. Montgomery and Hurley believed that only Collins would oppose their work, without effect since he was isolated within the WPC. A few changes in the report, they believed, would allow the commission to conclude its work by the end of the year.[70]

This Tentative Draft of about fifty pages served as the basis for the final report of the WPC. In it, the commissioners recommended against any constitutional amendment to achieve the goals under consideration. But they supported legislation for immediate introduction in Congress to fix or freeze prices before or during a war. Wartime legislation should also be prepared to tax away from individuals and corporations 90 percent of all income in excess of averages for the three years preceding hostilities. Further, the industrial mobilization planning of the War and Navy Departments should continue. Their plans should be revised continuously and experts regularly consulted. A permanent committee made up of representatives from the government, the U.S. Chamber of Commerce, the War Industries Board, and others should be created to review the War Department's work at least biannually. This committee should prepare a list, also revised every two years, of individuals for staffing the mobilization system.[71]

In justifying these recommendations, Montgomery summarized arguments for taking the profits out of war, along with the testimony, findings, and conclusions of the War Policies Commission and other investigating bodies. In the summary, he emphasized several major points. First, despite the dissent of a few people, promoting peace and preparing for war were not incompatible and were often complementary, and planning to improve the economic conduct of war had to take place during peacetime. Second, for most people, including the American Legion, conscripting capital was actually a catchphrase for holding war profits to peacetime levels. Taking property without compensation, which only a few individuals seriously advocated, Montgomery claimed, would create chaos. But prices had to be fixed, and Baruch's proposal for a freeze was the most promising technique, in Montgomery's view, even though some individuals favored a more limited method. Fourth, although interpretations differed, Montgomery believed that most people opposed a constitutional amendment to fix prices. The inherent powers of the president appeared in his eyes to be adequate for implementing such a program, but the issue should be resolved by legislation as soon as possible. Last, although fast, efficient, and, if need be, retroactive price fixing and freezing would be the principal approach to profit limitation, Montgomery proposed that excess profits taxes would be an effective second line of defense. Moreover, devices such as cost-plus contracting should be eliminated or modified to avoid abuses.

In his Tentative Draft, Montgomery insisted that no evidence existed to connect war with profits. Nonetheless, legislation should be passed in peacetime authorizing all aspects of mobilization. Thus, the nation would be put on notice that war profiteering would henceforth be prohibited. Such legislation would also prepare America for war better than ever before. The War Department's Industrial Mobilization Plan would further that goal by avoiding the slow and fumbling process of harnessing the economy for the last war.[72]

Montgomery's Tentative Draft mirrored the War Department–Baruch point of view and the status quo in general. It did not reflect the depth of feelings against the injustices and inequalities of war or the strength of the peace movement manifest at the WPC hearings. Montgomery glossed over the dissenters, quoting peace advocates and even some radicals in highly selective and distorted ways. He did not even mention the institutional critics of war. The individuals challenging the central thrust of the WPC did not have a genuine voice in the Tentative Draft. Moreover, contradictions abounded. At one point, for example, he claimed that profiteering during World War I had been great, only later to insist that major contractors had nothing to do with that outcome.

The principal difficulty with the First Tentative Draft was that it did not do justice to differing positions within the commission, to say nothing of those testifying before it. Minimal participation by commission members accounts for this development. When the WPC was organizing and getting under way late in January through early March 1931, it always had a quorum (eight out of fourteen for doing business). Despite repeated attempts, it never again managed to gather eight commissioners at once until December 1, 1931. As a result, the leaders and staff of the WPC lost contact with a majority of the commission, which created great difficulties in writing a final report.[73]

With a quorum finally assembled on December 1, 1931, Secretary of War Hurley, Executive Secretary Montgomery, and the Office of the Assistant Secretary of War intended to wrap up matters quickly. However, major disputes arose over the Tentative Draft report that postponed conclusions for almost four months.

In critiquing Montgomery's work, Cong. John J. McSwain stressed that it was much too biased in favor of the OASW's work. Senator Joseph T. Robinson agreed, also objecting to Montgomery's associating the WPC with the Graham Committee's partisan attacks on the Wilson administration and to the suggestion that Congress at once take up legislation implementing the War Policies Commission's recommendations. Hurley and Montgomery readily accepted these criticisms, along with other minor ones, and agreed to modify the report accordingly. But trouble grew from McSwain's curious request to exclude all references to excess profits taxes because the subject was too controversial. With Robinson acting as mediator, Hurley and Montgomery persuaded McSwain to drop his objection, arguing that the commission would lose credibility if it ignored such a critical issue. The WPC also agreed to a few insubstantial changes offered by Congressman Hadley. Thus far, Montgomery's Tentative Draft had survived without basic change. Most other commissioners appeared to be satisfied.[74]

But Attorney General William D. Mitchell, who became the source of the extended delay, was not. Mitchell had played virtually no role in WPC affairs since the early organizational meetings in January and February 1931. According to McSwain, however, the attorney general had said that he could arrange for leading constitutional authorities to address critical legal questions facing the WPC. Despite McSwain's entreaties, the WPC never pressed the attorney general to make good on his offer. Mitchell delegated his responsibilities to Alexander Holtzoff, a special assistant to the attorney general and later an assistant attorney general. Holtzoff, together with Maj. George P. Hill of the Judge Advocate General's Office and Lt. Comdr. Robert A. Lavender of the Navy Department, constituted the legal section of the WPC secretariat. Holtzoff led the section's in-depth examination of the constitutionality of price fixing. Montgomery and the secretary of war strongly influenced the section in their insistence that prices could be controlled without amending the Constitution. Hugh S. Johnson, acting for Baruch, also pressured the legal section along the same lines, and particularly so in the case of Baruch's price-freezing plan. Holtzoff, Hill, and Lavender concluded that the issue was controversial, subject to varying interpretation, but if approached correctly could be done within the existing constitutional framework. They cautiously supported Montgomery and others.

At the December 1, 1931, meeting, the attorney general protested that since he had never seen the legal section's opinions, he could not support the Tentative Draft's position on price fixing. Only a constitutional amendment would place price fixing beyond question, Mitchell averred, and he requested time to study the matter further and to consult experts in his department. Mitchell's declaration was an unexpected bombshell that shattered the careful consensus Hurley, Montgomery, and the OASW believed they had achieved.[75]

McSwain disturbed the December 1 meeting further by supporting and going beyond Mitchell. He argued that the WPC was wrong in trying to dodge vital constitutional issues involved in economic mobilization; it was better to face them during peace when there was time for deliberation rather than during the legal chaos of war. He proposed that the following amendment be submitted to the states:

When the Congress should declare war or a national emergency to exist, it shall have power to prevent profiteering by controlling prices or by other appropriate measures, and to equalize the burdens of defending the nation.

The amendment, McSwain argued, would lay to rest all constitutional doubts, enable the WPC to meet fully its charges, and ensure equity and justice in the event of war. The debate over the amendment would focus public attention on a critical subject, he continued, committing the people and its representatives to results different from those of World War I. McSwain confidently declared that the amendment would be easily ratified: "There is practically no division of sentiment in the country on this great question."[76]

McSwain went beyond Mitchell, but Collins went beyond McSwain. He proposed creating an Advisory National Economic Council to further economic equity at home among agriculture, industry, business, and the general population and to work with other nations in promoting international trade as a means for advancing the cause of peace. Collins further recommended two amendments to the Constitution: during a time of war, Congress could provide for taking private property without compensation; and the nation could neither make nor renew loans to a government at war when the United States was not a belligerent. Congress would be empowered to enforce this prohibition with appropriate legislation.[77]

McSwain and Collins could be ignored with ample votes to spare. Such was not the case with the attorney general. His objections threatened the adoption of Montgomery's Tentative Draft. To complete its work, the WPC negotiated a modus vivendi. It made an Interim Report to the president asking for a ninety-day extension to resolve constitutional issues about unspecified War Policies Commission recommendations. This request was preceded by the introductory remarks from Montgomery's report, including a declaration that the quest for peace and preparation for war were compatible, a description of the commission's approach to meeting its charges, and a list of those testifying. A record of the WPC's *Minutes* and *Hearings* was also included. The members of the commission signed the Interim Report except for Collins and McSwain, who, although not publishing their dissenting proposals, would do no more than concur in the request for a ninety-day extension.[78]

The December 1 meeting threw the WPC into a state of disarray from which it never fully recovered. Montgomery immediately began rewriting the First Tentative Draft to meet the modest changes wanted by McSwain, Robinson, and Hadley. To circumvent the objections of the attorney general, Hurley, at Montgomery's suggestion, proposed that Mitchell forgo a written opinion in exchange for inserting into the report the attorney general's recommendation for a constitutional amendment to resolve all legal doubt about wartime price fixing, with a draft amendment included. The arguments against an amendment would remain, and the report would encourage Congress to act on a legislative program for industrial preparedness since constitutional revisions would be long in coming. Otherwise, Montgomery maintained, two months would probably pass before the attorney general rendered a final opinion. Mitchell rejected this end run.

Montgomery, therefore, rewrote the report to recommend a constitutional amendment for price fixing, with the attorney general's decisions to be included in whole or part. At this point, the secretary of war dug in his heels. He refused to go along because of his adamant opposition to a constitutional amendment, threatening to issue a minority report if necessary. Montgomery's revised report, therefore, was never circulated. As the executive secretary had feared, the WPC began drifting. Montgomery himself returned to New York, and Eisenhower took over as assistant executive secretary. Under Hurley's direction, the latter reworked and expanded Montgomery's report, prepared the files for retirement, and dispersed the office staff.[79] In late December Eisenhower lamented to Montgomery, "Everyone appears to have lost interest in the Commission." At the end of February Eisenhower told Montgomery that nothing had occurred for months except for the sudden rush required to meet the extension deadline.[80]

The commission met again on February 26, 1932, after the attorney general delivered his opinion. His findings were not complimentary to the War Policies Commission's legal section and staff. He argued that they had confused price fixing in general with the government's fixing prices on its own purchases, had failed to distinguish between presidential and congressional authority in these areas, and had mistaken price controls for effectively prosecuting a war with those intended to further social justice. All price fixing was challengeable in the courts on the grounds that it was unnecessary for war purposes or that the prices set were unreasonable. Freezing prices was unlikely to survive court review. Prewar legislation authorizing wartime price fixing would probably do little better since need would not be obvious at the time the law was passed. If the WPC were willing to rely on established constitutional powers and procedures for fixing prices, amending the Constitution was unnecessary. Certainty required an amendment.[81]

Before acting on Mitchell's memorandum, the WPC decided to poll its membership by mail on whether a constitutional amendment was essential to fix prices and enforce decisions. With Sen. David A. Reed not voting and Sen. Claude A. Swanson out of the country, the vote was 7 to 5 against an amendment; Secretary of Labor William N. Doak, Sen. Joseph T. Robinson, and Congressmen Ross A. Collins, William P. Holaday, and John J. McSwain voted for it. Among the no votes, astonishingly, was the attorney general, who also had the proxy of Senator Vandenberg. Had Mitchell voted for an amendment, the large minority favoring this decision would have been converted into a narrow majority.[82] Divisions had become so great that either a stalemate would have to be declared or a compromise worked out.

A carefully drawn compromise of March 3, 1932, enabled the WPC to complete its work.[83] A report with final recommendations was submitted to the president on March 5. It proposed a constitutional amendment authorizing price fixing. Until that was done, the government should adopt policies for minimizing war profits and equalizing war burdens, including a congressionally sanctioned program for the president to set prices and eliminate war profits. Congress should additionally authorize the president to reorganize his administration for wartime economic mobilization. It should also continue presidential power for compelling contracts and commandeering property during war. Wartime taxes should deny corporations and individuals 95 percent of all gains exceeding averages of the three years preceding hostilities. Moreover, economic mobilization planning, particularly by the War and Navy Departments, should continue, with appropriate committees of Congress reviewing the Industrial Mobilization Plans at least biannually to ensure that they were sound. Finally, the commission recommended against a constitutional amendment permitting property to be taken in time of war without compensation.

The members of the WPC signed the report, except for Collins. He filed a minority report in support of amending the Constitution to fix prices so as to minimize or eliminate war profits but opposed all military planning as a threat to civilian institutions.[84]

The report was clearly the result of careful negotiations. Otherwise, the commission would have ended without any report or with majority and minority reports that revealed its serious divisions. Most likely, Hurley, Robinson, Hadley, and McSwain worked out a compromise. The majority accepted a recommendation for a constitutional amendment on prices. On their part, dissenting or wavering members such as McSwain and Robinson agreed to support War Department planning and to oppose an amendment to take property without compensation in wartime. Even Collins had to have participated in the bargain that was struck. His minority report was tepid. It said nothing about his proposed Advisory National Economic Council to further economic justice and peace or about constitutional amendments to take profits without compensation and to limit loans to belligerents.

The individuals who were serious about curbing wartime profiteering and equalizing wartime burdens, such as Collins and McSwain, had their priorities emphasized in the final report. Hurley and the Office of the Assistant Secretary of War achieved a firm endorsement of the Industrial Mobilization Plan and military planning. Those in the middle, such as Robinson and Vandenberg, who also had a congressional image of moderation and responsibility to uphold, could feel gratified with the final product. The marginal participants, a substantial bloc of votes including Secretary of the Navy Charles F. Adams, Secretary of Commerce Robert P. Lamont, Secretary of Agriculture Arthur M. Hyde, Reed, and Holaday, were no doubt happy to agree to any reasonable solution that would end an obligation they did not want and to which they had contributed little. Mitchell, on his part, seemed mostly interested in protecting his legal credentials, and the report certainly did that.

The apparent WPC bargain included one last element. The principal antagonists, Hurley and Collins, seemed to agree on forthrightly supporting their positions outside the commission's formal proceedings. On March 9, a few days after the WPC's final report was filed, Collins inserted into the *Congressional Record* his full recommendations involving an Advisory National Economic Council and two constitutional amendments. The next day Hurley, under his own signature but according to the "desires" of the WPC, submitted as supplementary documents the Tentative Draft that Montgomery had worked on for at least six months and that Hurley had directed Eisenhower to expand and revise in the last months of the commission's life. Neither Collins nor Hurley passed up the opportunity for publishing and distributing under the government's imprimatur their final word on the WPC's work. This move was especially important for the OASW, for Montgomery's report had been carefully crafted as a sophisticated justification of its planning.[85]

Several points about the War Policies Commission stand out. First, its study was superficial. For the most part, the commission covered familiar ground. As several dissident witnesses made clear, little could be done without a large and dedicated staff, ample time and funding, and subpoena powers. Certainly the Office of the Assistant Secretary of War could not act as an effective secretariat because its experience was too limited and its presence too controversial. Second, the War Department benefited from having its work reviewed and publicly endorsed. Few people knew about the OASW and the IMP before 1930. By 1932 they had become the subject of major news coverage for at least a brief period. Third, the individuals who did not testify at the commission hearings were as important as those who did. Other than war mobilizers, the business community was absent. The Chamber of Commerce was invited to testify but begged off because it could not poll its members. In general the business community steered clear of industrial preparedness because universal conscription was controversial, movements for war and peace generated strong emotions, relations with foreign businesses could be adversely affected by emphasizing national security, and similar considerations.[86] Industrial and financial America responded to the WPC in a manner consistent with its position throughout the interwar period.

A fourth point is that the War Policies Commission, unlike earlier investigatory bodies, revealed the growing strength of the people opposed to war, a group consisting of hardheaded realists, humanists, peace advocates, pacifists, radicals, and the like. When they combined their numbers with those seeking more equitable wartime economic policies and limits on exploitation, they could not be ignored by the advocates of preparedness and war. One measure of their influence was the fact that Bernard M. Baruch and his coterie proposed detailed schemes for making economic mobilization more just; earlier they had advocated only brief and general powers for the president to carry out economic mobilization.

A fifth point is that the forces for peace and equity began stressing the institutional consequences of modern warfare, which they dimly perceived as increasing the chances of further war. They feared the military's expanding presence in society in general; more specifically, they became alarmed by the growing ties between the industrial community and the armed services. To illustrate their concerns Cong. Ross A. Collins, Seymour Waldman, Norman

Thomas, and others pointed to economic mobilization for World War I, procurement and munitions patterns of the interwar years, and the War Department's industrial mobilization planning.

Finally, the War Policies Commission demonstrated that the political economy of American warfare could not be approached directly without threatening fundamentally to rend the nation, as had happened with World War I. The War Department and Baruch were unable to manipulate the commission for the purpose of unequivocally endorsing their position. Yet the varied elements opposed to preparedness or determined to make warfare equitable could not push too far without isolating themselves as Collins did and as McSwain chose to avoid doing. When the opposing sides threatened to create a stalemate and to unloose a national debate over economic mobilization for war, moderate elements such as Robinson and Vandenberg stepped in to craft compromises that dodged, more than faced, the nearly intractable issues raised by harnessing the economy for hostilities.

No one realistically expected Congress or the public to act on the War Policies Commission's recommendations. The final report served the purpose of terminating the commission's tenure and an unresolved and probably unresolvable debate. The WPC grappled with and then elected to avoid the fundamental issue of how to manage the immeasurably powerful and distorting consequences of modern warfare. The majority affirmed that preparedness and peace were not incompatible and proposed a constitutional amendment few people truly believed in or wished pursued. The WPC argued that its charge did not involve the quest for peace, which was essentially correct. Yet Collins concluded that peace was the only way to avoid the results of war he found so distressing, results he would try to prevent through an advisory, populist agency and restrictive, even draconian, constitutional amendments. Unwilling to follow his lead, the other commissioners ended up supporting preparation for war, preparation they hoped would be conducted in a way that was economically and socially just at home. Few people actually believed that those goals could be achieved through the means proposed. But unrealistic proposals were more attractive than advocating basically reoriented national and international policies to further peace. The War Policies Commission, consequently, ended unsatisfactorily for all members who were serious about its inquiry.

14
THE NYE COMMITTEE

The Senate Special Committee Investigating the Munitions Industry, named after its chair, Sen. Gerald P. Nye (R-ND), conducted incomparably the most complete and astute interwar study of the political economy of warfare.[1] The committee drew upon but rose far above its predecessors. Unlike the House Select Committee on Expenditures in the War Department (the Graham Committee), the Nye Committee did not allow partisanship to distract from its work; and, in contrast to the members of the War Policies Commission (WPC), Nye and his colleagues represented the critics, not the advocates, of war preparedness and elite mobilization practices. Although reflecting some of the confusion and uncertainty about economic mobilization demonstrated by previous investigating bodies, the Nye Committee faced squarely, rather than dodging or becoming trapped by, the complexity of modern warfare. Most committee members concluded that the nation could escape a system that a later generation called a military-industrial complex only by maintaining peace.

The Senate Special Committee Investigating the Munitions Industry was created by dual movements that were conflicting yet interacting: the American Legion–War Department–war mobilizers' drive for industrial preparedness and the peace movement, which was brought to maturity by World War I and reached flood tide in the 1930s. The peace movement included pacifists, adherents of peace, isolationists, internationalists, and others sharing a fervent desire to avoid another world conflagration. Although the industrial preparedness enthusiasts often cloaked their advocacy in terms of avoiding war and equalizing its burdens, their first priority remained national security. Nevertheless, the American Legion's involvement in war mobilization (upon which the War Department and economic preparedness enthusiasts heavily depended) actually began as a movement for peace and for equalizing war burdens, and that intent continued as an undercurrent in the interwar years, growing quite strong in the 1930s. The two forces uniting to produce the Nye Committee curiously shared some common ground.

253

But the peace movement was the more important.² A deteriorating international situation, antibusiness sentiments spawned by the depression, and revelations about the machinations of the munitions makers before, during, and after World War I combined to strengthen enormously the opponents of war. When they joined their strength with that of churches, labor, and other institutions, peace groups could force even the White House to heed their message.

Dorothy Detzer, the shrewd and tenacious executive secretary of the Women's International League for Peace and Freedom, led the drive for setting up the Nye Committee. Working principally with Sen. George W. Norris (R-NE), she settled on Senator Nye to head a congressional investigation of munitions makers for the purpose of curbing the contagion of war. Nye and Detzer joined forces with Sen. Arthur H. Vandenberg (R-MI), a member of the WPC who in 1934 revived efforts to implement the recommendations of the commission. Vandenberg was supported by the American Legion and other preparedness advocates. A national campaign for a munitions investigation and careful parliamentary maneuvering ultimately produced the Senate resolution in April 1934 that created the Nye Committee.³

The committee was charged with investigating all aspects of the munitions business, including manufacturing, sales, exports, and imports, and relevant legislation and treaties. It was also to study and report on the desirability of nationalizing the munitions industry. Moreover, Nye and his associates were to review the findings of the War Policies Commission.⁴

The Nye Committee reports stand alone among the interwar studies of the economics of modern warfare. Indeed, the committee is among the most significant congressional investigating agencies in American history. Its members never shrinking from their charges, the committee's examination of war mobilization led it to probe the nature of America's political economy and the impact of modern warfare upon it. In doing so, the Nye Committee uncovered and explicated the dynamics of an emerging military-industrial complex in the United States. Its contribution did not stop there. The committee published key governmental records involving World War I mobilization, and it reproduced invaluable documents of the J. P. Morgan and Company's wartime operations before the financial house destroyed its archives.

The committee's accomplishments were based on almost two years of investigations begun in 1934 and concluded in 1936. Unlike the Graham Committee and the WPC, the Nye Committee had what amounted to a chief counsel or investigator—Stephen Raushenbush, son of the noted theologian, Walter Rauschenbusch. He directed a dedicated staff of around twenty, which was augmented from time to time by personnel from New Deal relief agencies. Other voluntary groups and individuals also assisted the committee's work. Unlike the War Policies Commission, the committee had subpoena powers. In a relatively short period of time it gathered extensive documentation from companies, individuals, and government agencies, using it to guide its examination of witnesses. The heart of the committee's work is contained in thirty-nine volumes of hearings, totaling about 14,000 pages, and in eight reports, adding hundreds of pages.

By any measure, the membership of the Nye Committee was unusual. In a Senate dominated by Democrats, a Republican headed the committee. The other members consisted of four Democrats and two Republicans: Bennett Champ Clark (D-MO), James P. Pope (D-ID), Homer T. Bone (D-WA), and Walter F. George (D-GA), and Vandenberg and W. Warren Barbour (R-NJ). Committee members were selected not only on a partisan basis but also to reflect the nation's and the Senate's ideological spectrum, ranging from Western radicalism to Eastern and Southern conservatism.

Nye, Clark, and Vandenberg, along with Raushenbush, were the drive wheels of the committee. Despite the committee's diversity, its findings were unanimous, although some differences existed on recommendations. In light of the committee's often dramatically revealing and morally damning reports, unanimity was remarkable. Harmony prevailed because the Nye Committee was unfailingly thorough, judicious, and fair. Virtually all witnesses affirmed that they were treated in an evenhanded, courteous, and respectful manner, a reality amply supported by the published hearings.

Yet the committee has been painted in negative tones by most scholars and writers since. In part this stems from Gerald P. Nye's often intemperate and hyperbolic speeches on the stump, which differed from his performance in the Senate and in the committee room. More significantly, judgment of the committee took place during the Cold War, when questioning American foreign policy, political economy, and a huge military establishment was not only unwelcome but also looked upon as close to disloyal. Seldom has a conscientious and accomplished investigating body been treated as shabbily by history as the Senate Special Committee Investigating the Munitions Industry.

Although the committee contained a New Deal and a conservative internationalist Democrat in Pope and George and a regular Eastern Republican in Barbour, Midwestern, Southern, and Western isolationists and neo-Jeffersonian agrarians shaped its course in the persons of Nye, Clark, and Vandenberg, supported by Bone. Moreover, Raushenbush and his staff were New Deal liberal, with perhaps even a radical tint, and definitely devoted to peace. With the Nye Committee, therefore, neo-Jeffersonians continued to lead the debate over the political economy of warfare that they had begun during World War I. The strain of radical pacifism, or at least dedication to peace, was also stronger than before. This combination produced nearly inexplicable paradoxes in the Nye Committee's work. It added further to the distorted image of the committee since neo-Jeffersonians and liberal-to-radical peace advocates, supported by New Dealers with a populist bent, ran counter to the elite strains shaping twentieth-century America.

From the outset, the Nye Committee was almost bound to be cast in the role of pariah. The committee would deal with such sensitive subjects that Senator Norris and Detzer concluded that of the Senate's entire membership only Nye was fully qualified and able to lead the investigation they wanted. Even before the committee began to publish its evidence and analysis, major elected officials realized that an investigation of munitions makers and the economics of warfare would lead to the highest levels of government and reveal policies and practices contrary to declared national principles, threatening in the process the conduct of domestic and foreign affairs.

The parts of the Nye Committee's inquiry can be divided into three related areas. The first involved the munitions industry and its web of business, governmental, and extragovernmental ties at home and abroad. The second dealt with the role of American financial houses, and particularly J. P. Morgan and Company, in financing the Allied cause between 1914 and 1917 and in organizing the American economy to produce munitions and materiel for belligerents. The committee was particularly interested in the effects of these activities on America's neutrality and eventual entry into the war. The third area was the Office of the Assistant Secretary of War's procurement and economic mobilization planning and its actual and implied consequences for the nation. The first subject was the principal charge of the committee and the one for which it is mainly known. The third part grew from its assignment to review the work and recommendations of the WPC. Had the committee been timid or politically prudent, it could have avoided the second area entirely, denying its numerous opponents the eventual opportunity abruptly to cut the ground from under its feet.

The Nye Committee was neither timid nor politically prudent, establishing an extraordinary record. This record rested on a guiding principle that appeared to direct the committee's work from the outset: munitions makers, foreign policy during peace and war, and industrial preparedness were only pieces of a larger whole that involved the American political economy. To give meaning to the pieces, Nye and his colleagues placed them in the context of the United States as a mature industrial society and as a major world power in an international system in transition and prone to warfare. Grappling with a principal trend of twentieth-century life, Nye and his colleagues came extraordinarily close to determining what caused and what would result from a military-industrial complex unless America fundamentally altered its domestic and foreign policy.

In that sense, the committee was radical. It brought to full articulation and logical conclusion the neo-Jeffersonian critique of American society that had been growing since the late nineteenth century. World War II and the Cold War eventually overwhelmed the neo-Jeffersonians' dedication to decentralization at home and a modest presence abroad. As a result, much of their vitality turned toward negative, even destructive, paths. Before that occurred, the Nye Committee was their triumph.

THE MUNITIONS MAKERS

Members of the Senate Special Committee Investigating the Munitions Industry neither individually nor collectively embraced the vulgar concept of a tight-knit, international combination of arms makers and traders whose conduct put them in league with Lucifer.[5] The committee expended considerable effort examining the munitions trade without much result. As John E. Wiltz—the author of a full-scale study of the committee—rightly maintains, Sen. Gerald P. Nye and his colleagues found some evidence for all of the charges leveled at the munitions industry, but it was spotty and thin.[6] In support of the principal allegation about a worldwide munitions trust, the committee turned up agreements between the Electric Boat Company, E. I. du Pont de Nemours Powder Company, and some American companies and British and other foreign firms, such as Vickers-Armstrong and Imperial Chemicals Industries. They conspired to share patents, divide markets and pool profits, circumvent embargoes, oppose arms control measures, and rely on notorious international arms brokers. The committee also documented some of the very worst suspicions about the munitions makers. It showed that they tried to undermine peace by working against disarmament, arms control, negotiations to end conflict, and arms embargoes; that they evaded or ignored laws and treaties by gun running, selling illegally through intermediaries, and falsifying documents; that they perpetuated war scares and played belligerents off against each other to further funding for the military and to advance the quantity and the price of their sales; that they relied on bribery in all underdeveloped areas as a standard business device; that they hid behind a facade as honest, neutral brokers by selling on the basis of ability-to-pay, regardless of moral or legal considerations; and that they insisted by word and action that their products were like any other commodity and should be treated similarly. Many of these practices were episodic rather than clearly established, long-term patterns.[7]

That the Nye Committee could not document fully widespread beliefs about the munitions firms is not surprising for a number of reasons. As some committee investigators suspected, the firms under scrutiny had probably sanitized their files or had never put into them evidence that would substantiate questionable, embarrassing, immoral, or illegal behavior. Certainly the firms inhibited the committee's work through various obstructionist tactics.[8] Moreover, since arms races were viewed as at least partly responsible for World War I, munitions makers were under close scrutiny from major investigations in the United States and Great Britain and under careful monitoring by the League of Nations. This circumstance made munitions executives defensive, cautious, and much more subtle in pursuing their ends. Furthermore, the arms trade was down in the interwar years after the vast production of munitions for World War I and the distress of the worldwide depression. Most important, the modern munitions business launched in the nineteenth century was undergoing a major transition. Private firms and international brokers such as Sir Basil Zaharoff were surrendering center stage to governments that directly purchased or produced the increasingly lethal and technologically sophisticated weapons.[9]

In its investigation of shipbuilders, the Nye Committee illuminated the key role government was beginning to play in the modern arms trade. Unlike firms dealing in guns and ammunition, which sold most of their wares abroad, Washington was the single largest customer of the shipbuilders. Moreover, the Navy Department had played a decisive role in the creation of a modern shipbuilding industry in the late nineteenth and early twentieth centuries.[10]

Naval shipbuilding was the subject of the first of a seven-part series of reports by the Nye Committee and was issued in May 1935. The committee's overall finding was that an interdependence had grown between private shipbuilders and the Navy Department, which was not in the national interest. The economic welfare of corporations loomed much too large in the navy's decisions about the size and manner of building its fleets. This consideration not only strained the national budget but also affected foreign affairs. Modern navies were by nature offensive as well as defensive and consequently always threatened to trigger or exacerbate an arms race.

> Since the Navy is an instrument of national policy, this closeness in financial interests of the private shipbuilding yards to the Navy becomes a matter of national concern. . . . These private shipbuilders are part of the private system of national defense which has grown up. Their activities ultimately have a bearing on our foreign policy.[11]

In exploring private naval profits, the Nye Committee emphasized that a so-called Big Three had come to dominate shipbuilding for the navy: Newport News Shipbuilding and Drydock Company, Bethlehem Shipbuilding Company, and New York Shipbuilding Company. Throughout the period of substantial building in the 1920s and 1930s, they acted in a way that ensured that Navy Department contracts for ships were divided among them, often to the detriment of other qualified firms. Such practices were facilitated by the Marine Engineering Corporation, a jointly created and owned firm designing ships for the three companies. In an unpublished document, the committee insisted that the companies had colluded to eliminate competition in dealing with the Navy Department.[12] Overwhelming circumstantial evidence supported the charge, but inconclusive direct evidence led the committee to soft-pedal its published accusations:

If there was no prearrangement . . . there was, at least, amazingly fortuitous coincidence.

If there was no collusion, there was a sympathetic understanding among the big companies of each others' desires.

If there were no conversations about bidding among them, there was telepathy.[13]

Even more disturbing to the committee was the fact that the Navy Department obviously knew about the collusion, indirectly participated in and at times encouraged it, and that corporations and the navy used governmental agencies, such as the National Recovery Administration, to help circumvent laws governing military contracting. The result of the rigged bidding was exorbitant profits for industry based on creative accounting and a type of cost-plus contracting that could exceed even the generosity of World War I. The government also ended up heavily dependent on private firms as opposed to public navy yards for designing its ships. The Navy Department, for instance, turned over to the Electric Boat Company results of fifteen years of research and development to keep the firm building submarines and to protect its monopoly. Contrary to the economies of scale, shipbuilding firms were in the enviable position of charging the Navy Department more, not less, when government contracts were plentiful because the navy was dependent on them. In a year-by-year, ship-by-ship analysis of bidding and awards in the 1920s and 1930s, Nye and his committee demonstrated that either total irrationality ruled or a careful division of what one corporate official called "the plunder" was taking place.[14]

The Nye Committee established that shipbuilding firms placed an exceptionally high priority on preventing contracts from going to navy yards. Here again the companies had the active and passive cooperation of the Navy Department. For example, the department in 1935 submitted to Congress a study of comparable costs between private and public yards based on the calculations of the National Council of American Shipbuilders, which set private yard profits at about one-third the level the Nye Committee obtained from other sources. Such maneuvers obscured the fact that navy yards could build ships for millions of dollars less than private corporations. Moreover, the Navy Department was uninterested in using its shipbuilding facilities as a yardstick for measuring private companies' costs, prices, and profits, assessing their efficiency, and providing itself with some independence in planning, designing, and building its fleet. Realizing that government facilities could not meet wartime demand, the armed services willingly sacrificed their peacetime procurement autonomy. Hence, the Navy Department claimed to have no figures on the comparability of private versus public yards—lacking even rudimentary information on such things as wage rates—and made no effort to obtain such data to assist in the awarding of contracts. The Nye Committee observed, "The Navy has never examined the underlying costs or profits of the private builders. It makes no pretense of doing this. It has no staff for it. The figures studied by the Munitions Committee were all news to it."[15] Yet the hearings revealed that while pleading ignorance, naval officers logically knew all about the economics of shipbuilding.[16]

In truth, the Navy Department was unconcerned about the economics of private shipbuilding. After the passage of the Vinson-Trammell Act of 1934, which limited profits on ships and aircraft to about 10 percent of costs, the Navy Department showed no interest in enforcing the law, passing responsibility to the Treasury Department. But neither Treasury nor the Comptroller General's Office had analyzed shipbuilding profits since World War I. Even if they had, Senator Nye and his colleagues demonstrated that enforcing the law was virtually impossible. Based on its investigation of shipbuilding in general and World War I operations in particular, the committee concluded that the cost calculations of private corporations were thoroughly unreliable. The government needed independently acquired information. If, as appeared to be the case, shipbuilders combined with each other and with subcontractors to present a united front against the government, nothing could be done. A firm usually did not report its final profits on a ship until about four years after a contract was signed. By then accounting was complex to the point of being impenetrable. Accurate figures depended on the government's stationing auditors on site for about three years with authority to review all governmental and commercial transactions.

Even then, costly and time-consuming lawsuits could be expected. Such a cumbersome and expensive approach was out of the question. Attempts at profit controls on government contracts were little more than ceremony.[17]

Other aspects of the navy's relations with private shipbuilders generated concern within the Nye Committee. It spotted a revolving door for personnel in which naval officers left the service to take up high executive positions in private firms contracting with the navy. One of these men was Homer L. Ferguson, president of Newport News. Ferguson had testified in behalf of industrial mobilization before the War Policies Commission. He now uncomfortably explained shipbuilder-navy relations to the Nye Committee. The actions of men like Ferguson could fundamentally compromise the integrity of military contracting. Nye and his colleagues also uncovered examples of inferior products resulting from the favored position of the private contractors. Moreover, the committee was unhappy to find the Navy Department using its contracting powers to assist management in disputes with labor. On a very different plane, the Nye Committee turned up an instance of a naval officer on active duty in Latin America acting as adviser to Colombia on munitions while also in the pay of several private firms.[18]

These matters took on greater significance for Nye and his colleagues because naval contracting had become big business that was being woven into the fabric of the American economy. The navy, the Nye Committee argued, "is one of the largest governmental contractors in the world," dispensing hundreds of millions of dollars annually. Although most contracts went to only a few firms, the overall impact on the economy was substantial:

> The shipbuilding industry is allied in interest with naval suppliers and subcontractors, including the steel companies, the electrical manufacturing groups, the boiler producers, the instrument people. These spread out over the country, and together probably represent several billion dollars of invested wealth. Several of the biggest fortunes in the country are involved in these groups. Connections with the largest banking interests in the Nation, as well as with smaller ones, are involved.

The committee stated that it had neither the time, the money, nor the responsibility to analyze these ties and their significance. Nye and his committee also noted that the same conditions prevented them from pursuing the political activities of shipbuilders and their industrial and financial allies and supporters. Practices that the committee turned up through purposeful investigation and those that surfaced as a matter of course "indicate a far greater activity than has so far been brought to light."[19]

The shipbuilders alone constituted a powerful, well-financed, and effective lobby, spending hundreds of thousands of dollars to influence policies at home and abroad. In reviewing the case of William B. Shearer, Nye and his associates refused to engage in the whitewash of the earlier investigation by the so-called Shortridge Committee (after Sen. Samuel M. Shortridge, R-CA) in 1929. Shearer had been hired as a lobbyist by the Big Three shipbuilders between 1926 and 1929 and claimed credit for undermining the Geneva Naval Conference in 1927, which, if successful, could have cut back the navy's shipbuilding program, hurting shipbuilders badly. The Nye Committee documented the case against Shearer and the Big Three much more thoroughly than before, established that the lobbyist was aided by highly placed navy and even some army officers, and that prominent executives of the Big Three had perjured themselves before the Shortridge Committee. The Nye Committee then demonstrated that shipbuilders strove to create an environment favorable to fleet growth, including the perpetuation of war scares. The shipbuilders had also led in the passage of the Merchant Marine Act of 1928, which contained provisions outlandishly beneficial to shipbuilders and detrimental to the government. Another display of the shipbuilders' clout was in their mobilizing an effort that included organized labor to obtain $238 million of Public Works Administration funds appropriated for naval shipbuilding in 1933, when it was known that $40 to $55 million more would be required to complete the ships contracted for.[20]

The Nye Committee also came across repeated instances of shipbuilders spending large sums in thoroughly bipartisan efforts involving national, state, and local officials to advance the passage of legislation desired by themselves, the Navy Department, or both, to acquire contracts, and to staff influential governmental posts with friendly appointments. This lobbying and influence-peddling was tied to that of other munitions makers such as Du Pont, Remington Arms Company, and Curtiss-Wright Corporation and to those seeking air mail and ocean mail contracts. Moreover, there were corporate ties between the shipbuilding complex and aircraft firms. Lines of influence also ran to the major steel companies, which either owned or supplied the principal shipbuilders. Westinghouse Electric and Manufacturing Company, General Electric Company, and other major corporations were also linked. The committee regretted that it could not investigate the relationship between shipbuilders and shipowners and the activities of the National Council of American Shipbuilders as well as the Steamship Owners Association, along with other relevant subjects. The committee cursorily investigated the Navy League but did not turn up much. By inference, but never directly, Nye and his colleagues indicted the casual or evasive congressional attitudes toward the navy and shipbuilders as represented by the Shortridge Committee.[21]

The Nye Committee argued that what it found was not a simple matter of private industry using and abusing government but a reciprocal and mutually beneficial relationship between the shipbuilders and the navy. While corporations got contracts, high profits, support for oligopoly and monopoly, and so forth, the Navy Department was guaranteed facilities to meet its demand in peace and war, influential support for its growth, and powerful lobbies for what it desired from government. Witnesses from the Navy Department were at least as uncomfortable and defensive before the Nye Committee as the shipbuilders.

It was the navy's hurry to proceed with shipbuilding as soon as appropriations were available that made private builders so attractive and concern about the economics of shipbuilding so slight. This dependency, according to Nye and his colleagues, made investigating the charges of favoritism and fraud difficult because information was being guarded and suppressed at all levels. The navy obviously preferred the existing institutional structure to the system used in Great Britain; there, government facilities designed, developed, and produced prototypes before letting contracts by competitive bidding. Such a system, argued the Nye Committee, would allow the navy to plan and control its destiny and to protect national interests much more effectively than when private interests and motives became almost inextricably mixed with public affairs.[22]

The Nye Committee was not naive. Interest-group influence, even dominance, and clientelism were an inherent part of huge bureaucratic government. But, the committee insisted, naval contracting was fundamentally different from "road or building" arrangements.[23] Although economy, honesty, efficiency, and quality were desirable goals for all governmental expenditures, Navy Department policies and practices affected foreign affairs, including matters of peace and war. Subjecting such decisionmaking to the influence of private interests seeking to maximize profits was totally unacceptable.

The government's role in munitions distressed the Nye Committee the most. In one way or another, Washington was involved in nearly all the abuses or questionable practices Nye and his committee examined. Collusion, deceptive accounting, and other practices of the shipbuilders could not take place or operate effectively without at least the tacit consent of the navy. To discover the Big Three attempting to undermine the Geneva Naval Conference was less surprising than to find the Navy and War Departments assisting in that effort. The 1927 conference, however, was not an isolated example. Nye and his colleagues reviewed every major national and international effort between 1919 and 1932 to embargo, control, and halt the manufacture and trade in arms and to reduce the level of international armaments. Without exception, the munitions firms, in league with the War and Navy Departments, joined at times by the Commerce Department and even the State Department, had worked against these aims. In doing so, the military services often violated existing national policies. Moreover, laws governing the shipment of munitions were weak and poorly enforced, virtually inviting munitions firms to circumvent them.

It was official military policy to encourage and assist the export of munitions so as to ensure existing productive capacity in the event of war. From aircraft carriers to ordnance, the army and navy aided the munitions firms in every way possible to sell their products abroad. This assistance included demonstrating weapons, improving the competitive position of American firms, helping companies meet schedules by lending them aircraft and other munitions or allowing them to divert production intended for American use, sanctioning illegal or unsavory overseas munitions sales, and urging and aiding other nations to buy from U.S. firms. The Commerce Department was active in these matters; and military, naval, and commercial attachés served as salespersons for American munitions producers.

These developments were facilitated by a network of personal ties between the munitions firms and the armed services of the type that the Nye Committee had encountered with shipbuilders. Almost every munitions company had officials and employees who were former members of the army and navy, and the Nye Committee believed agents of the munitions companies worked for the military's intelligence services. Moreover, munitions company officers were often in the reserves and could be in the Military Intelligence Association.[24] Other institutional ties existed:

> Through such organizations as the Army Ordnance Association, the Navy League, the National Rifle Association, the American Council of Shipbuilders, etc., all more or less closely allied in interest with the service departments, the War and Navy Departments have strong allies in securing the passage of their appropriation bills and the allocation of Public Works funds.[25]

The fact that Public Works Administration funds were going to the armed services and that some businessmen favored defense spending as an antidote to the depression further disturbed Nye and his colleagues.

In viewing the full panorama of munitions operations, the Nye Committee carefully avoided charges of conspiracy. It pointed out that plausible reasons existed for what was done and stated that it was not drawing a one-to-one correlation between expenditures for defense and the causation of war. Nonetheless, argued the committee,

> any close association between munitions and supply companies . . . and the service departments . . . of the kind that existed in Germany before the World War, constitutes an unhealthy alliance in that it brings into being a self-interested political power which operates in the name of patriotism and satisfies interests which are, in large part, purely selfish, and that such associations are an inevitable part of militarism, and are to be avoided in peacetime at all costs.[26]

To check the growth of this "unhealthy alliance," the Nye Committee sought a number of reforms. In a May 1935 report on shipbuilding, the committee unanimously recommended two bills: one to prevent shipbuilders from colluding, and the other to curb profiteering on navy shipbuilding. Furthermore, Nye and his committee supported strengthening the Vinson-Trammell Act. Without administration support and with strong opposition from the Navy Department, the Senate Naval Affairs Committee bottled up even these modest recommendations. However, in 1935, as a result of Nye Committee revelations, an appropriations bill for the Public Works Administration prohibited any spending for "munitions, warships, or military or naval matériel."[27]

The Nye Committee held off on a broader approach until it was prepared to render advice on a government munitions monopoly. In a February 1936 report on munitions in general, the committee unanimously agreed on all findings but divided over solutions. The majority (Nye, Clark, Pope, and Bone) favored government ownership and operation of all facilities for the production of principal munitions items. They argued that regulations could be evaded and that the involvement of munitions makers in foreign affairs had to be halted. A modest government plant for peacetime supply, expansible with private firms in the event of war, would provide for the national defense, reduce costs, and halt despicable practices. The minority (George, Vandenberg, and Barbour) opposed nationalization because they believed "that the public welfare, from the standpoint of peace, defense, and economy, can be better served by rigid and conclusive munitions control than by nationalization except in a few isolated instances." Neither the majority nor the minority presented bills to implement their recommendations, partly because the committee had not concluded studying the costs of government production. By the time the committee did so, Congress had shut it down. This outcome was probably inconsequential. The fate of the two moderate bills on shipbuilding indicates that any proposed legislation for rigid control of munitions production, not to mention nationalization, would have gone nowhere.[28]

ECONOMIC MOBILIZATION FOR WAR

The Nye Committee's study of war mobilization was more important than its focus on munitions because its significance was broader and deeper. The committee concluded that modern warfare eroded the barriers between private and public, civilian and military institutions. To fight a modern war and even to prepare for one involved the entire economy. During hostilities, the committee observed, "practically every important industry in the country is necessary for the supply of the armed forces." "Even in time of peace," the committee continued, "the line of demarcation between the munitions industry and other industries is not clear and fixed." The chemical and dye industries, for example, were essential to the production of all explosives. Every development in aircraft had some military significance.[29]

The committee's focus on World War I provided more insight about the economics of modern warfare than any other aspect of its investigation. Although Nye and his associates concentrated on wartime taxation and profits, they initially had to understand how the economy was harnessed for hostilities. From the committee's probing came the first major publication of mobilization documents. Under its imprimatur, the committee printed the minutes of most mobilization agencies and the Price Fixing Committee in addition to a history of the War Industries Board compiled, edited, and introduced by Hugh S. Johnson. Nye and his colleagues then briefly traced the evolution of the mobilization structure from the rough beginnings under the Council of National Defense–National Defense Advisory Commission in late 1916 to the much smoother period under the War Industries Board in 1918. In doing so, they pinpointed the basic dynamic of wartime economics: lacking the experience, information, and personnel for planning the economy, Washington relied on businessmen to design, staff, and operate the mobilization structure. That outcome had enormous potential for rationalizing and maximizing production; it also created great opportunities for abuse.[30]

The Nye Committee concentrated on the possibilities for abuse, particularly "shameless profiteering" and extravagant waste. The war's legacy, it pointed out, included inflation, debt, and increased concentration of economic power. However, the committee did not engage in muckraking. Its analysis of certain aspects of the World War I economy was detailed, thorough, and sophisticated. The committee made the major point that removing war profits and equalizing wartime burdens could not be achieved without drastically altering the nation's political economy during hostilities. Two methods had been offered during and after World War I to deal with the economic abuses: severe taxation and price control. Since neither had worked effectively in the past, they could not be relied upon to do so in the future.

Taxation during World War I had not reduced wartime profits in any significant way. Despite tax rates reaching as high as 80 percent of war profits, a group of the largest manufacturers and mining corporations paid only 23–25 percent and 33–35 percent in total taxes on their net taxable income in 1917 and 1918. Even these figures were suspect since they were based largely on corporation calculations that could be unreliable.

Wartime taxes were ineffective because they involved intractably complex issues. Two bases were usually offered for assessing excess profits taxes: invested capital and average peacetime returns. The first was extraordinarily difficult to apply because a set rate could not measure "degree of risk, geographical location, business skill, patent rights, and any number of other factors" affecting business.[31] Since these circumstances were so varied and subjective, government faced endless challenges in collecting taxes, and business had countless opportunities to avoid them. Newport News Shipbuilding and Dry Dock Company, for example, had a running dispute with the Bureau of Internal Revenue from 1917 to 1931 over invested capital; a settlement occurred only after the government backed off from its position. Even if a figure for invested capital could be set, extended conflict would result from questions of depreciation, depletion, amortization, and accrual of income. These matters were complicated many times over by cost-plus and other government contracts. If Washington allowed its officials wide discretion, to avoid protracted wrangling and court action, past practices pointed to the loss of revenue by decisions favoring industry. Furthermore, old and new methods of avoiding taxes were ever present, the most significant of which was investment in tax-exempt securities. Finally, almost all major tax disputes were settled after, not during, hostilities, when the urge to tax was less, different administrations with varying priorities were in office, and a profitable wartime enterprise was less profitable or even unprofitable—circumstances likely to give business its way. Even if such circumstances did not transpire, government faced overwhelming odds. "The audit of the income, excess-profits, and war-profits tax returns of the United States Steel Corporation and its subsidiaries for 1917 and 1918," the Nye Committee reported, "required, approximately, the services of twenty-two men for a period of five years."[32]

When reviewing the shipbuilding industry, the committee dwelled on the "very considerable profits" that were "close to being disgraceful" during

World War I,³³ the numerous strategies used to increase those profits, and the enormous benefits received as the navy continued wartime building into the postwar years when excess-profits taxes no longer existed. The fact that Charles M. Schwab, chairman of the board of Bethlehem Steel Corporation, was director general of the Emergency Fleet Corporation, and Eugene G. Grace, Bethlehem's president, was on the steel war service committee, highlighted for the committee the rampant conflicts of interest tied up with war mobilization and inevitable war profiteering.³⁴

Some observers, including the War Policies Commission, proposed using an average period of prewar earnings to avoid "the fantastic complications of the invested capital approach."³⁵ The committee made the logical point that prewar earnings could not be used without so many necessary exceptions involving invested capital that the two bases for calculating taxes would actually end up being the same.

The Nye Committee also reminded its readers that wartime taxes, like any taxes, would be passed on by business to the degree possible, thereby adding to inflationary pressure, the major bane of any war. More important, no government could afford to impose wartime taxes that limited production. Contrary to common belief, excess profits taxation was no panacea for curbing war profits or for equalizing war burdens.³⁶

Many of the same observations held true for price control, the other essential wartime device for curbing profits and tempering inflation. During hostilities, a seller's market, increased costs, expanding plants, and the like generated intense upward pressure on prices. To address the issue authoritatively, the Nye Committee analyzed in depth World War I price fixing. "Bulk-line" pricing was the basic method used, which meant setting prices as high as necessary to obtain all necessary production, resulting in prices far above peacetime levels. High cost producers were subsidized, and low cost producers made extraordinary profits, but their abnormal gains were theoretically removed by excess profits taxes. This approach applied only to wholesale prices, with about 40 percent of the commodities in the War Industries Board's Price Index under regulation at the war's end. Retail prices, except for food and fuel, were basically left unattended. In some instances, industrial organizations worked out the details of pricing in line with the general decisions of the Price Fixing Committee (PFC). The American Iron and Steel Institute, for example, set the prices for thousands of finished iron and steel products based on the figures the PFC set for the basic raw materials.

In analyzing World War I price fixing, Nye and his colleagues offered a number of observations. The bulk-line method almost guaranteed high profits for low cost producers, which were usually the major firms in an industry, accounting for most output. By shifting responsibility for handling high war profits from its own aegis to the Treasury Department, which collected taxes, the PFC all but ensured failure in this critical area. (Here the PFC's approach resembled the Navy Department's attitude toward the Vinson-Trammell Act). Moreover, although PFC prices were supposedly maximum rather than set ones, virtually no prices were reduced during the war, regardless of market circumstances. Despite these realities, few alternatives existed to bulk-line pricing. Setting separate prices for firms making the same product based on costs, cost-plus pricing, or pooling production for government sale involved nearly unworkable complexity.

Nonetheless, Nye and his colleagues argued, high wartime prices and profits resulted from more than market conditions and production requirements. The people manning the mobilization machinery were generous to industry. The committee noted:

> In the last war there was a very close connection between business and the price-control administration, either through the actual presence of interested parties in governmental posts, or through the reliance on business representatives for advice and information concerning their own industries. This condition, which must prevail if the persons who are in direction of industry in peacetime are to aid in its wartime control, results in the creation of a powerful counterpoise in the shape of double interest to the elimination of war profits. It is necessary to recognize that such devices as the formal severance of relationships or the discontinuance of company compensation for the duration of the war do not extinguish the real interest of the official in his company since in most cases he will return to it with the coming of peace. Furthermore, there will always be a strong tendency not to antagonize business connections which may have been built up over a long period of years and from which future benefit can be expected. Finally, as was the case in the World War, there is the very direct interest which comes from stock ownership in companies subject to regulation.
>
> These definite interests, combined with the habits of thought and the personal associations of men who have spent their lives in private enterprise, make for a sympathetic attitude toward the complaints of those who remain in charge of industrial operations and a willingness to rely upon the information presented by industry.[37]

Along these lines, the Nye Committee pointed out that prices in monopolistic or nearly monopolistic industries such as aluminum, nickel, and sulfur were usually fixed at levels matching nonmonopolistic industries even though additional production was not at stake. Monopolistic firms successfully argued that all industries should be treated alike for purposes of equity and legality.

Nye and his colleagues also repeatedly documented the Price Fixing Committee's practice of treating industrial representatives as partners, not as the regulated; of joining the Food Administration in using industry spokesmen, instead of neutral experts, to interpret cost sheets compiled by the Federal Trade Commission; of increasing prices to achieve production levels beyond any reasonable need; of discouraging government orders until anticipated higher prices were in effect; and of acting to justify and legitimize businesses' high prices and profits instead of attempting to bring them down. In short, World War I price fixing took place through negotiations between industry and the government, not through the unilateral exercise of government authority.[38] That arrangement eliminated the need for a huge government cadre to determine and enforce the Price Fixing Committee's decisions, for industry enthusiastically cooperated with the government.[39]

Yet the Nye Committee recognized that the PFC did not have many options. It faced such an overwhelming job that reliance on industry for cost figures was almost inevitable. The Federal Trade Commission could provide some independently acquired data, but such information was minuscule compared to the overall task faced and, in a rapidly changing economy, often not up to date. Current audits were even more demanding than those conducted after the fact. Based on the Emergency Fleet Corporation's experience, the committee estimated that one plant required seventy to one hundred persons to do a thorough current audit, assuming the unlikely agreement of auditors on what constituted costs. The nation lacked sufficient auditors and accountants to do the job, without even considering the delays incurred and the animosities created between industry and the government at a time of crisis. Since industry largely supplied the figures, the same problems plaguing taxing also affected pricing. The chances for evading price controls were nearly endless, and if business could not have its way, rules were easily broken. When industries like steel and copper insisted on upward adjustments over the protests of the PFC, the committee reluctantly had to give way.

The Nye Committee hammered at the point that Washington had few effective tools for bending industry to its will on prices and other decisions. Du Pont, for example, with a virtual monopoly on smokeless powder production, held out for three critical months during 1917 until the government agreed to its terms for building the Old Hickory powder plant. Although less dramatic, conditions were not that different in most other industries. Only goods for the army and navy could be requisitioned or commandeered and at prices that could exceed those fixed during the war. Talk of seizing industries like steel or copper was pure bluster since Washington could not run plants without management's cooperation. Using priority power to strong-arm industries necessary for fighting the war was similarly impractical. Cutting off fuel and transportation to, say, the steel industry would grievously damage economic mobilization, an act no sane leader would countenance.

Economic mobilization for World War I was based on the voluntary cooperation of business, serving in and outside government, in an intricate pattern that tailored private property and the profit motive to the needs of war without altering their basic functions. The inevitable results, taxation and price control notwithstanding, were high prices, high profits, and great inequality in sharing the burdens of war.[40]

THE MILITARY'S ECONOMIC MOBILIZATION PLANNING

With the analysis of World War I behind it, the Nye Committee turned its attention to the postwar industrial mobilization planning of the Office of the Assistant Secretary of War (OASW). Compared with past inquiries, the Nye Committee's examination of the army's planning was rigorous, informed, and sophisticated and was carried out by critics of wartime economics.

Senator Nye and his associates believed economic mobilization for war to be the most significant aspect of their inquiry.[41] It unified their work by tying the various parts together. More important, world war was again looming, making the prospects of harnessing the economy more of a reality than a theory. The committee's judgment was validated by the intense response to its study in this area. President Franklin D. Roosevelt attempted to outflank Nye and his associates by appointing his own group to deliberate and write legislation on economic mobilization. This move led to members of Congress, Bernard M. Baruch, and the American Legion conducting counterinvestigations and supporting alternate bills instead of those authored by the Nye Committee.

The Nye Committee's review of the OASW's operations and plans was scattered over a period of almost two years, with most work taking place late in 1934 and early in 1935. Colonel Charles T. Harris, Jr., was the military's principal witness and representative before the committee. As director of the Planning Branch of the OASW, Harris headed the army's economic planning effort between 1933 and 1938, guiding it through the most fruitful period and beginning the transition from planning to mobilization.

The Nye Committee focused its attention on the Industrial Mobilization Plan, 1933 (IMP). Senator Nye and his staff arranged for the seven bills included in the IMP and intended to implement it to be introduced into Congress and referred to the committee for hearings.⁴² The committee also had the IMP, 1933, published, and it included numerous OASW and supply arms and services documents in the hearings and appendixes.⁴³

The Nye Committee then analyzed the OASW's planning, based on its knowledge of how the wartime economy and the interwar munitions business operated. Since the IMP intended to use World War I methods in a future war, it promised to make a fundamentally flawed system work better: industry and the military would be pulling together, rather than apart, as had occurred between 1916 and 1918. But the abuses and distortions of World War I would then be repeated, probably exaggerated, warned Nye and his associates, with a real possibility of weakening the economy to the point of another depression. Even worse, an "unhealthy alliance" dedicated to warfare would be strengthened, threatening every aspect of America's future.

To head off such a bleak prospect, Senator Nye and his colleagues called upon John T. Flynn to devise an alternate method for harnessing the economy for war. A journalist and an economic analyst, Flynn was a liberal reformer dedicated to the decentralized, competitive economics favored by Louis D. Brandeis. Senator Nye had earlier but unsuccessfully attempted to recruit Flynn as the committee's chief counsel. This time Flynn agreed to serve on a three-man committee to assist Nye and his group in investigating the economics of World War I. Some years earlier, Flynn had acted in an advisory capacity to the Pecora Committee (after Ferdinand Pecora, counsel for the Senate Banking and Currency Committee, investigating banking and stock-market practices in 1933–1934). For assistance in drafting a bill for the Nye Committee, Flynn had assembled a collection of prestigious economists and legal experts.⁴⁴

The so-called Flynn Plan, in the form of a proposed bill, consisted of six parts. First was an elaborate wartime taxation program limiting corporate profits to 3 percent of adjusted declared value and individual net income to $10,000. The second part provided for drafting management. Because drastic taxation could dampen businesses' enthusiasm for economic mobilization, all corporate executives had to register with the federal government upon the outbreak of war. If the president declared a plant or an industry essential to the emergency, the managers would be incorporated into the army and subject to military discipline. Those refusing service would be removed from their positions, remain in the army, and be replaced by the firm. Any corporate officer attempting to defraud the government of tax revenue would be subject to court-martial and summary punishment. Flynn insisted that these measures would not fundamentally alter the capitalist institution of private ownership and corporate charters; only managers would be subject to military control. As a third provision, all goods, such as rubber, sugar, and wheat, sold on commodity exchanges would be controlled absolutely by the government. This control would prevent repeating the speculation of World War I that had caused such dire consequences after hostilities. Fourth, the president could by proclamation close all securities exchanges. Fifth, a War Finance Corporation would strengthen efforts to market securities and to help finance production for the war effort but prohibit corporations from writing off such assistance against their taxes. Finally, there was an omnibus section that granted the president the authority to create mobilization agencies that could fix prices, wages, and profits, establish priorities, requisition needed products, property, and the like, license business, and institute other controls. In staffing mobilization agencies, "No one [could] pass upon any matter affecting his own personal interests." The foundation of the World War I mobilization system would be abolished.[45]

Flynn and the Nye Committee insisted that their bill was intended primarily to control inflation. Paying a large part of the war's costs from current tax revenue would hold down prices by drastically limiting mass spending power, something price controls alone would not do. Borrowing to meet the huge capital outlays of modern warfare was a prime contributor to inflation, which destabilized the economy and opened the door to profiteering. Senator Arthur H. Vandenberg summarized the principal argument:

> It is proposed to strike at the economic heart of the war profit by the simple fundamental device of requiring that no future war shall be fought on borrowed money, but shall be paid for substantially by current taxes. It is the process of making war on borrowed money which primarily creates the sinister inflation out of which grows: 1) the opportunity for swollen profits; 2) the economic dislocation of the war era; and 3) the post-war calamity of deflation.[46]

Nye argued that it was best to begin a war with exceptionally harsh legislation, later easing conditions through regulation and litigation as that became possible and necessary, rather than vice versa. Flynn explained further that his system would not allow corporations to defer disputed taxes for years, ultimately settling in ways usually favorable to themselves, as had happened in the last war. Instead, all calculated payments would be due at once, with corporations able to make post facto claims if they had been treated unjustly. Thus the onus would be shifted from the government to the taxpayer.

Other aims were used in defending Flynn's bill, and at times they were given equal weight with inflation controls, depending on circumstances and evidence considered. Nye, Flynn, and others frequently emphasized that taking profits out of war would reduce its attractiveness and discourage talk of war as an antidote to the depression. Equalizing the burdens of war also received attention. Repeatedly the point was made that if life could be sacrificed by some, surely money could be forgone by others. The $10,000 figure for maximum individual income was based on the salary of a major general; no civilian executive should be making more during hostilities. Ultimately, Flynn and others maintained, his approach meant better and fairer mobilization. With legislation written by disinterested parties in peacetime when debate was more possible than during the rush of war, the nation could harness its resources free of conflicts of interest, profit-mongering, and corporate obstruction.

Despite other arguments, protecting the economy by paying for the war from current income remained the principal rationale for Flynn's handiwork. Flynn took what had been only a minor theme of the Graham Committee and the War Policies Commission and made it a central principal of the Nye Committee.

Flynn's bill predictably generated enormous controversy. Actually, the most significant challenge came before Flynn unveiled his bill to the Nye Committee. In mid-December 1934 Roosevelt suddenly announced that he was appointing a committee composed mostly of cabinet officials and former war mobilizers to draft legislation for taking the profits out of war. Bernard M. Baruch and Hugh S. Johnson were on the committee, which was named after them as the only active participants. Roosevelt clearly intended to outflank, if not undermine, a Senate investigation that was already proving to be embarrassing to the administration. If the president intended to put a quick end to the Nye Committee's work, his maneuver failed. Committee members and numerous supporters forced the president to beat a quick retreat, to endorse the committee's work and its continued tenure, and to declare that the so-called Baruch-Johnson Committee would work with Nye and his associates for mutually desired ends. However, if Roosevelt intended, as was more likely the case, to strengthen the hand of men like Baruch, he was more successful. Under the banner of taking the profits out of war and equalizing its burdens, Baruch and his group would act to protect the status quo. Roosevelt's committee never drafted any legislation, but Baruch and Johnson led the move to present a moderate alternative to the supposedly extreme Flynn Plan.[47]

Roosevelt responded characteristically. Facing a volatile issue of great importance, he waited until matters took clearer shape before making final decisions. Since past efforts to pass legislation for economic mobilization had been so unsuccessful, the president could delay until times were more propitious for moving more decisively against the Nye Committee.

The vehicle for Baruch's challenge to the Nye Committee was Cong. John J. McSwain (D-SC), a friend who had sponsored legislation on industrial mobilization and participated in preparedness activity for almost fifteen years.

At the time, McSwain was chairman of the House Military Affairs Committee. In January 1935, he introduced in the House of Representatives a bill, "Taking the Profits Out of War," which was referred to the committee he chaired for hearings. The proposed law resembled the Capper-Johnson bill that in one form or another had been before Congress since the early 1920s. It was a brief bill, authorizing the president to place a ceiling on all prices, commissions, and compensations, at or on a date prior to the declaration of war or an emergency, with a commission making upward or downward adjustments as necessary. The law also empowered the president to determine which public services, industries, and businesses would be licensed for wartime operations, to establish a priority system, and to create or designate agencies, persons, and commissions essential for mobilizing the economy. During the course of hearings and House debate, the bill was altered to exclude wage controls and to add presidential authority for commandeering industrial, financial, and material resources and organizations, and most important, to establish a 100 percent tax on all wartime excess profits.[48]

The hearings on the McSwain bill, held late in January 1935, were both curious and interesting for a number of reasons. These were obviously counterhearings to those being conducted by the Nye Committee. The American Legion, and particularly John Thomas Taylor, vice-chairman of the Legislative Committee, played an exceptionally active role in the hearings, apparently all but directing them. Certain members of the committee manifestly worked hand in hand with the American Legion; and McSwain, Lister Hill (D-AL), and Andrew J. May (D-KY) consistently led witnesses or asked them planted questions. Moreover, Baruch and Hugh S. Johnson, as star witnesses, were touted by themselves and the committee as the principal members of the president's commission to write legislation for taking the profits out of war; and McSwain implied that his committee was linked with White House efforts. Baruch and Assistant Secretary of War Harry H. Woodring also attempted to tie the McSwain bill to advancing preparedness by creating a board to review the OASW's Industrial Mobilization Plan. Frederick J. Libby, executive secretary of the National Council for the Prevention of War, charged that McSwain's activity was no more than a militaristic attempt to implement the IMP.

At this point, McSwain's bill was not even in rough-draft form. The congressman explained that he had literally jotted down some ideas put into a bill rushed to Congress. Given his haste, the anxiety about regaining the initiative from the Nye Committee was obvious. McSwain, Hill, and others virtually pleaded with the American Legion to assist the committee's work by completing the draft of an acceptable bill. Eventually, a subcommittee was appointed to produce a polished product.

Overall, the McSwain Committee suffered drastically in comparison with the Nye Committee. The former operated without a staff, had done no background work, and was unprepared to examine witnesses profitably. Chaos periodically resulted. McSwain, at best discursive, was at his worst, coming across seemingly as demented. Aged and ill, he died in August 1936. Perhaps his health, his debt to Baruch, and Democratic dominance of Washington explain his unabashed support for the status quo in these hearings compared with his nearly radical role in the operations of the War Policies Commission. Witnesses such as Col. Charles T. Harris, Jr., from the OASW tried to get rambling committee members to focus. At one point, Assistant Secretary of War Woodring, present as a witness, began examining Harris, who was there to advise him. Committee members and witnesses were given to making outrageously irrelevant and invalid claims without challenge. And so it went.

The views of the McSwain Committee members and committee witnesses on industrial mobilization for war, however, were significant and revealing. McSwain, Hill, May, and others wanted a bill that most people would support and few would oppose. Here there were some differences with the Baruch-Johnson camp. The critical issue of whether a constitutional amendment was necessary in order to implement the bill was constantly skirted. Any provisions even suggesting wage controls or a labor draft were excised. Unlike similar bills of the past, this one left out controversial provisions on selective service. At the same time, industry would be treated more harshly than in any proposal ever before put forward by moderates. The possibility of a management draft was even entertained. In a dialogue that was all but rehearsed, McSwain and Baruch established that severe wartime excess profits taxation had been left out of the bill on a technicality and would be added later, that any war should be financed from current income to the degree possible, that the munitions industry should be carefully controlled in peacetime and perhaps even nationalized, that policies for maintaining peace must be constantly pursued, and that business profits should be reduced in general to advance the latter end. Obviously, the Nye Committee and the forces that had created it were having an impact on McSwain, Baruch, and others. Baruch and his cohorts used the age-old tactic of co-opting a rival's chief proposals to retain control of events.

Baruch, seconded by McSwain and others, argued that any mobilization legislation should be brief and general, leaving the president the greatest latitude. Backed by Johnson, Baruch claimed that with modifications, the McSwain bill, based on the World War I mode, would prepare the nation for war as never before. Baruch and Johnson endorsed the OASW's industrial mobilization planning, and War Department witnesses stated that the McSwain bill would generally allow civilians to implement the IMP in the event of hostilities. Representatives of the Disabled American Veterans and the Reserve Officers Association endorsed the McSwain bill. The American Legion did, too, in that it had participated in writing the legislation and had more witnesses before the committee than any other organization. However, Legion leaders such as McSwain and Baruch, feeling pressure from their constituents, went on record as favoring the bill as a start but insisted that it had to be strengthened to meet the Legion's long-term goal of universal conscription. Labor's spokespersons were not especially hostile to the McSwain bill but withheld clear support through equivocation and waffling. The Veterans of Foreign Wars had obviously been radicalized by the depression. Their spokespersons expressed extreme bitterness about war mobilization, going beyond the most strident positions taken by anyone on the Nye Committee. A few peace advocates took the Nye Committee's line on the proposed legislation, and one member of the committee, James F. Fitzpatrick (D-NY), seemed to go to the heart of the matter in questioning Johnson: "I have heard much about taking profits out of war . . . for the last ten or twelve years, and yet no action has been taken by our Government, and I am wondering whether or not this is just a lot of talk."[49]

One of the striking aspects of these hearings was the limited range of witnesses. No Navy Department personnel testified, nor did the army chief of staff. The Chamber of Commerce declined to appear. Business was always reluctant to testify on mobilization legislation in the interwar years, and the inquiry of the Nye Committee seemed to make it even more skittish. Individuals willing to challenge the Nye Committee directly were few in number and not well prepared.[50]

McSwain introduced a revised version of his proposed legislation in the House of Representatives early in February 1935 as a new bill, HR 5529. The measure became part of the growing national debate on wartime economics generated by the Nye Committee. Early in April the House took up the McSwain bill. After a raucous session on April 6, when the bill was amended to the point of becoming nonrecognizable, the House restored the measure to a version close to the original and passed it on April 9 by a vote of 367 to 15.[51] Despite over fifteen years of agitation, this was the first substantive bill dealing with economic mobilization for war to pass a house of Congress since World War I.

When referred to the Senate, McSwain's bill was sent to the Nye Committee, which quickly in effect substituted Flynn's bill for McSwain's. Before that occurred, however, the Nye Committee heard an extended debate on the Flynn and McSwain bills.[52] Late in March Flynn testified at length before the Nye Committee, explaining his bill, comparing it with the McSwain measure, and analyzing why the latter was grossly inadequate. Baruch followed Flynn. In testimony and in a later written statement, Baruch defended his position and backed HR 5529.

Flynn argued that the McSwain bill was inadequate because it proposed to duplicate the basically flawed World War I mobilization model. More particularly, HR 5529 depended primarily on price controls to maintain economic equilibrium, an impossibility. Flynn appropriately spent more time explaining his own approach than attacking that of McSwain, the chairman of the House Military Affairs Committee. He asserted that war demand and human greed generated enormous inflationary pressures during hostilities that threatened to wreck the economy. Since those forces could not be curtailed, the government had to limit what he described as the fundamental cause of wartime inflation, borrowing. Through the severe taxation that he proposed, war would be financed wholly or mostly from current income. That approach would eliminate the disruption of war mobilization and its aftermath, which, in Flynn's view, had led to the Great Depression after World War I. Moreover, by eliminating war profits to the degree possible, greater equity and justice would be achieved and further concentration of economic power curbed.

Flynn obviously had not thought through all of the consequences of his plan or resolved apparent contradictions in it. He insisted that he was out to save, not threaten or abolish, the economic system. (Yet at one point he averred that his system was preferable to the profit motive for mobilizing a wartime economy.) When pushed, he admitted that all wartime profits could not be eliminated: capitalism encouraged profits, and they could only be reduced, not avoided. Flynn explained that he would rely on a corporation's adjusted value declared before the war as the basis for reducing all profits to 3 percent. Yet, when members of the Nye Committee and its staff asked for details, he observed that experts were still working on the complex calculations. Flynn unrealistically argued that his proposal was intended to eliminate war profits and inflation, not serve as the basis of a full mobilization scheme. He put little or no emphasis on price fixing, although there was a basis for it in the plan. His declaration that prices and profits could go as high as the market would warrant, with all or most profits then being removed by taxation, never held up well. He could not answer basic questions.[53]

Like all simple, clear-cut proposals for mobilizing the economy, Flynn's plan had numerous pitfalls when carefully scrutinized. But his plan differed from previous ones. It argued that capitalism was open to and encouraged wartime abuses. The bill was out to prevent a repetition of the World War I experience, which was carefully examined and well understood by the Nye Committee. In short, the Flynn Plan was against the status quo. It was cogent, if flawed, and, sponsored by the Nye Committee, the approach received national attention; thus the plan had to be taken seriously. Consequently, Baruch, McSwain, and the others who had previously dominated the debate on war mobilization felt compelled to marshal their might against the work of Flynn and Nye. But they had to proceed carefully, since in 1935 the Nye Committee's views all but represented a national consensus.

Baruch was the chief witness before the Nye Committee supporting World War I mobilization methods. The former chairman of the War Industries Board (WIB) began his testimony with the assumption that he could use his expertise and skills at compromise to win Nye and his associates and staff over to his point of view. Baruch's correspondence indicates that this was a genuinely held belief, not just a tactic or a ploy to get his way. He argued that the McSwain bill with appropriate taxation would be adequate for guiding economic mobilization. More specifically, and consistent with the position he had taken for years, Baruch argued that a ceiling on prices should be set at some point before they had become distorted by wartime demand and then adjusted by a commission as needed. That approach, along with a taxation structure to reduce wartime profits to a practical minimum, would allow the World War I model to be used with efficiency, equity, and justice. Although he had not studied the Flynn Plan in depth, Baruch insisted that he, Flynn, and the Nye Committee differed only on means, not ends, that they could find common ground through exchanging ideas.

The Nye Committee quickly put Baruch on the defensive, a position from which he was never effective. In contrast to past hearings, here Baruch faced people who understood the operations of the World War I economy better than he did and were prepared to challenge virtually every generalization and most details he offered. First, the committee established that price agreements dictated largely by industry, as opposed to prices fixed by the government, were the norm during World War I. Second, profiteering had been rampant. Third, no adequate price or profit controls could be enacted without cost figures; and industry, which could not be trusted, was the only practical source for such information. Fourth, commandeering and other governmental threats were largely futile since the government needed industry for wartime production. Fifth, the World War I model for economic mobilization, price fixing, and profit controls was riddled with conflicts of interest. Specifically, the committee examined at length the handling of copper in which policy was set by those "closely connected personally and financially with the industry . . . (Mr. [Eugene] Meyer, [Jr.], Mr. [Pope] Yeatman, and Mr. Baruch)."[54] Finally, effective and equitable economic mobilization policies depended on amending the Constitution to allow the government to take property without just compensation.

Baruch did not acquit himself well before the Nye Committee. He blamed most war mobilization problems, including industry's holding out for what it wanted ("the strike of capital," in the words of the Nye Committee), on the military's failure to use its commandeering authority. He denied basic facts, claiming, for example, that the dispute over steel pricing lasted two to three days, not three to six months. He insisted that a future war would be different due to the efforts of the Office of the Assistant Secretary of War—even though he knew, as Nye Committee members pointed out, that after years of work, military planners had no basic data on industry costs and emphasized production above all other considerations, including prices and profits. He maintained that not many basic differences divided him and the military, although the OASW had been his favorite whipping boys for years. Finally, he fell back on the defense that he was proposing the best plan he knew; if others had something better to offer, they should do so. This constant shifting from one position to another and his evasion irritated the otherwise even-tempered, rather gentle Raushenbush. At one point, he told Baruch:

> But the question still remains as to whether there is really anything constructive one can do to stop this [manipulating costs and prices to maximize profits], or whether we should stop the pretense of saying—not on your part, sir, but general pretense that might accumulate—that, "As we have done this about fixing prices and have done this about putting on high taxes, that we have therefore taken the profits out of war."[55]

Baruch's testimony ended without his actually conceding any fundamental points. In an attempt to pull things together, Raushenbush summarized the differences between the committee and Baruch just before the latter left the witness chair:

> The Committee did think that no responsible financial or governmental committee could take the responsibility of saying that a price-fixing plan, plus a taxation plan, can really take the profits out of war, unless it has every possible club, including a constitutional amendment. And, as we gather your opinion, you are willing to take the responsibility for standing up, when the occasion comes, and saying that it is possible for the Government to take the profits out of war, without every possible club, that is, without a constitutional amendment.
>
> There is then another line of difference. We think that your ceiling idea, while having a great many advantages, will certainly create larger profits. . . . You admit that the ceiling idea will create larger profits in

certain cases, but it does not seem to make you change your ideas about the necessity for getting the cost figures of the company, and you seem to believe we can get all the company figures through the Security [*sic*] and Exchange Commission. I can say for the staff, Mr. Chairman, that the Bureau of Internal Revenue, with all its facilities and power was not able to get cost figures for fifteen years in some cases, and we doubt if the Security [*sic*] and Exchange Commission will perform the miracle of getting cost figures immediately.

The committee is going on the proposition that taxes of 96 percent or something can be levied, and, as I gather it, you have not exactly formulated your own ideas as to how much the industries of the country are going to need to keep going, but you have to stop at that point where they say, "We need the money to keep going." . . . Under the pressure of war and under the pressure of getting the things out, Mr. Chairman, at least $1,000,000,000 of taxes, including disputes over taxes, are going to be involved at the end of the war, and that will throw the Treasury into politics at the conclusion of the war, and make its capture by the big corporations in a postwar administration inevitable.[56]

This was not the last word in the exchange of ideas between the Nye Committee and Baruch. On April 12, 1935, Baruch filed with the committee a written statement intended to address questions the committee had put to him and to correct a record that was exceptionally garbled because, he insisted, he was wandering around the room while testifying, making record-keeping difficult, and he failed clearly to express himself on vital matters. The statement was written by Hugh S. Johnson, whom Baruch had hired to assist him with the Nye Committee investigation. Lengthy and detailed, Baruch's rejoinder was basically an aggressive, hard-hitting defense of the status quo. The former chairman of the WIB had switched tactics from attempting to co-opt the Nye Committee to attacking it frontally.

Baruch began by arguing that he shared various fundamental goals with the plan advocated by Flynn, including paying for as much of the war from taxation as possible and reducing war profits to an absolute minimum. However, he insisted, the Flynn Plan was intent on destroying the industry at a time when only the economy could ensure military victory. No one was arguing the virtue of the profit motive and capitalism, but attempting to change them in the face of grave national peril was to invite disaster. More specifically, Flynn was wrong on the two assumptions upon which his plan was founded: that wartime inflation stemmed from borrowing and that high taxes could check inflation. Moreover, by downplaying price controls, which could be implemented without elaborate statistical compilations, Flynn was ignoring the most vital wartime control essential for maintaining economic equilibrium. Further, the profit motive had to be used, albeit carefully and in a controlled manner, to direct any wartime economy. Although the controls for the World War I economy were not adequately developed and implemented until well into 1918, they constituted a nearly perfect scheme for industrial mobilization once refined. Contrary to what the Nye Committee believed, "A careful study of the War Industries Board set-up would have shown that no selfish interests could have affected its decisions."[57] Moreover, "with a few temporary exceptions, fully disclosed, no man in a War Industries Board control had any interest in any industry over which he presided."[58] The same ethics and standards held for the Price Fixing Committee. Since the WIB was a proven device, it, not an uninformed experiment, should be recommended for the future. If a constitutional amendment was needed, it could be adopted. Flynn, if he had consulted with Baruch and other informed WIB executives, could have avoided his erroneous and often unfair conclusions.

Baruch's written statement contained elements of meanness and indirect red-baiting, a trend that would grow on Baruch's part. By 1937 he was referring to the Flynn Plan as coming from the "Marxian School of State Socialism"[59] and asserting that by their treatment of the Morgans and "large bankers," Nye and his associates were out to show that they could "cuff around . . . their betters."[60] He also encouraged his highly placed journalist friends to attack "Sly Nye."[61]

Flynn's answer to Baruch covered the now-familiar ground in which he stressed that without controlling inflation all other wartime controls were futile. More impressive than Flynn's memorandum was one written by the committee staff, which laid out more clearly than ever before the fact that although Baruch was right about the WIB and associated mobilization bodies not having conflicts of interests in a formal sense, in actuality conflicts of interests throughout the entire mobilization system had been rife and blatant.[62]

Flynn and Baruch were the key witnesses before the Nye Committee on the war mobilization legislation, but others testified as well. Among the most important were spokespersons for the American Legion and the Veterans of Foreign Wars. Their testimony was much like that before the McSwain Committee, with the Legion using the slogans of universal service yet waffling on key issues, and the Veterans of Foreign Wars militantly pressing for a total draft of all services and resources in wartime. The American Federation of Labor also testified. Even though voicing its opposition to the McSwain bill more clearly than before the House Military Affairs Committee, it still avoided taking a position on the critical issues.

Perhaps the most important witness was Col. Charles T. Harris, Jr., from the Office of the Assistant Secretary of War, who spoke for the War Department. Harris was cautious to the point of being timid about challenging the Flynn Plan. Warning that profit and price controls should not hurt munitions production and that the manufacturing draft could create more problems than it solved, nevertheless Harris indicated that with changes the War Department could live with Flynn's work. The military planners asked for the opportunity to consult with the architects of the bill, however, to seek modifications that would make the proposed legislation more palatable. Harris insisted that by necessity, the War Department could view the bill only through the lens of national defense and its conviction that the economic system in war had to be used as it was in peace, without radical modifications and with the least confusion possible.[63]

After the Nye Committee had essentially turned the McSwain bill, HR 5529, into the Flynn Plan, the measure went to the Senate Military Affairs Committee for consideration. Two members of the Nye Committee also sat on the Military Affairs Committee: Nye and Barbour. This committee appointed a subcommittee to study, hold hearings, and advise the committee on the proposed bill. Nye, Flynn, and another member of the Nye Committee staff also attended the hearings, along with Colonel Harris and his Navy Department counterpart. Actually, Nye and Flynn virtually ran the hearings, even though Nye was not a member of the subcommittee. Senator Robert D. Carey (R-WY) was the only member of the subcommittee critically to probe key parts of Flynn's bill. Rather typically, Flynn did not do well under penetrating examination. He sidestepped or offered unclear or questionable answers, for example, when Carey used the National Recovery Administration experiment to illustrate the difficulties involved in a draft of management. The same was true when Carey inquired about the inflationary implications of excluding wartime wages from governmental regulations.

Subcommittee examination of the Flynn bill was rather perfunctory. Much more important was the bargaining that took place between the Nye Committee representatives and the OASW to persuade the latter to endorse the proposed legislation. Negotiations had begun when the Nye Committee was considering the bill, and they now became more serious. Nye's committee was anxious to get the War Department's approval of the bill to speed its consideration by the Senate and to advance its chances of passage. Since 1936 was an election year, the bill had to get through in 1935; otherwise, its highly controversial nature reduced substantially its chances of adoption. Under the auspices of the subcommittee of the Senate Military Affairs Committee (SMAC), Flynn and a member of the Nye Committee staff met with representatives of the OASW and the Navy Department to revise the bill to the military's satisfaction.

The sessions proved to be fruitful, and the War Department, with qualifications, approved the Flynn bill and ultimately incorporated it in the Industrial Mobilization Plan, 1936. The key provision of the bill involving taxation was left unconsidered, since it was not under the jurisdiction of the Senate Military Affairs Committee and the War Department felt unqualified to pass on its merits. By modifying the maximum profit rate upward from 3 to 4.7 percent, the Nye Committee made the War Department more comfortable.[64] Besides taxation, the principal objection of the OASW to the Flynn bill involved a management draft, which the army considered to be unwise and probably counterproductive. To meet the War Department's objections, the provision was recast to make a management draft discretionary; if implemented, industrial executives would be under the jurisdiction of the War Department, but not actually in the army. These changes ended the military's objection to this section of the bill, although it still declared the provisions to be unnecessary. Under pressure from the OASW, Flynn and his associates also modified their bill to make the mobilization system more rational and effective. But Flynn, Nye, and the subcommittee of the Senate Military Affairs Committee would not agree to the War Department's request for authority to control wages, fearing that such a provision would endanger the bill's passage. With these changes, and a few technical revisions, the Nye Committee and the military services reached overall agreement. The compromise bill was approved by the subcommittee and ultimately its parent body, the Senate Military Affairs Committee. Representatives of the War and Navy Departments endorsed the revised Flynn bill before the subcommittee.[65]

The way in which the Flynn bill appeared in the IMP, 1936, made clear that the military planners had basic reservations about the proposed legislation beyond those involving a management draft and wage controls. Although not including the long and detailed tax section of the bill in their plans, the armed services warned that no taxation should be so onerous as to endanger munitions production. Furthermore, the OASW deleted the absolute ban on conflicts of interest for individuals staffing governmental bodies. The office explained that the prohibition would deny the government the services of virtually all experienced executives, which would create more dangers than having persons pass on mobilization matters in which they had an interest. "The great bulk of business men are, after all, honest and patriotic," the plan stated. Also, the OASW deleted from Flynn's bill a provision banning the use of brokers during war, explaining that procurement agencies should not be needlessly restricted in wartime. Finally, in the section creating a War Finance Control Commission, the OASW struck out provisions making service mandatory for anyone selected to serve on it. The military planners insisted that service unwillingly granted was not worthwhile. In the financial area too the military planners expunged a ban on conflicts of interest, arguing that the prohibition was logical but "unnecessarily drastic."[66]

The Senate Military Affairs Committee reported favorably on the modified HR 5529 in mid-June 1935. However, the bill was held up almost a year as the Senate Finance Committee and a subcommittee it appointed deliberated on the extensive taxation provisions that were the most lengthy and complex part of the proposed legislation. Senator Bennett Champ Clark, a member of the Nye Committee, also served on the Senate Finance Committee. At those hearings, the most detailed examination and modification of the tax provisions of the Flynn Plan took place. The Finance Committee for a time considered passing on the other parts of the bill but ultimately decided that it was restricted to reviewing only the provisions on taxation. In August 1935 the committee asked the Treasury Department and the Joint Committee on Internal Revenue Taxation, both of which had already done some work on the bill for the Nye Committee, to study the tax provisions of the Flynn proposal in depth. The measure was the only detailed tax proposal for a war situation that had been put forward up to that time. Thus, the review by the Treasury and Joint Committee experts, and their interchange of ideas with Flynn and others from the Nye Committee and the Senate Finance Committee, was the most sophisticated analysis of wartime taxation occurring in the 1920s and 1930s.

Lovell H. Parker, chief of staff, Joint Committee on Internal Revenue Taxation, helped shape the Finance Committee's consideration of the Flynn bill by proposing ten questions that needed to be addressed in relation to the taxation provisions. Five were technical matters and need not concern us, but the other five were basic points about wartime taxation proposals:

1. Should the bill be designed so as to take the profit motive away from both the corporation and individual?
2. Should the bill be designed to produce the maximum revenue possible or should the social and economic effects of the bill be deemed more important?
3. If the answer to 1 is in the negative, what maximum rates can be used without destroying the profit motive?
4. Is it sound to adopt the general principle that the most important thing in connection with war legislation is "to win the war"?
5. Should the bill attempt to correct possible defects and to close possible loopholes in existing law when such defects or loopholes are a present problem not directly connected with war revenue legislation?[67]

Directly or indirectly, the witnesses before the Finance Committee's subcommittee, including taxation experts from the Joint Committee and the Treasury Department, Flynn, and members of the committee themselves, addressed those basic questions.

Concerning question one, all agreed that no bill should attempt to abolish the profit motive in any part of the economy, although assessments varied as to the possible consequences of the Flynn bill on the existing system. On question two, most agreed that the primary end of the proposed legislation was raising revenue, not maximizing social and economic justice. In that regard, taxation should be severe during wartime and raise as much revenue as possible to pay for the war. Many, however, believed that the rates in the Flynn bill were too steep and could threaten the war effort, if not the economic system. A consensus seemed to exist around Parker's position that all profits up to the point of diminishing returns should be taxed away. Moreover, Parker seemed to strike the right note with most participants when he observed that the tax rate, which could be changed within a few days, was less important than statutorily establishing as soon as possible in peacetime the principle of maximum taxation in wartime. Disputants then could concentrate on their points of agreement instead of bogging down on less essential details like exact tax rates.

The third question could not be answered with a simple yes or no, although all seemed to agree that the highest revenue possible should be raised without threatening the existing social and economic system. The easiest question to answer was the fourth: of course, winning a war had to have the highest priority. On the last question, which also related to the second one, after considerable debate and uncertainty, the Finance Committee and its advisers unanimously agreed that the bill should not attempt to correct peacetime taxation laws. It was first and foremost a war revenue bill. To make the proposed legislation into a reform measure would load it down with inappropriate provisions that would threaten the ends sought.

The Senate Finance Committee then addressed one more vital question: Should it separate the taxation provisions, as Title I, from the Flynn proposal, leaving the other titles treating with the economic structure in a separate bill? The committee strongly favored keeping the bill intact because the taxation provisions would make no sense unless they were part of a larger proposal for mobilizing the economy for war. The public had to have a clear message about what Congress was doing. With some amendments and rewriting but no fundamental changes, the Senate Finance Committee ultimately approved the Flynn bill as received.[68]

The Senate Finance Committee was under great pressure to report out the Flynn bill so that the Senate could vote on it. The committee did so on June 10, 1936. By then it was too late. The House was in recess, and the Senate adjourned on June 20 without taking up the proposed legislation. In the next Congress, Senators Nye, James P. Pope, and Homer T. Bone reintroduced the Flynn bill as it had left the Senate Military Affairs Committee. Senator Thomas T. Connally (D-TX), who had played a leading role in the Senate Finance Committee's deliberations on the measure, reintroduced the version reported out by the latter committee. The two bills were referred to the Senate Finance Committee and never reemerged. This process or something like it went on year after year until the nation entered World War II.[69] Without the Nye Committee focusing national attention on the issue of war mobilization, the nation's political leadership could again afford to sidetrack legislative proposals that threatened the status quo.

The most astute criticism of the Flynn bill came not from opponents of the Nye Committee but from the committee itself. In the second and fourth regular reports, issued in late July 1935 and early June 1936, in reaffirming its commitment to the Flynn bill, the Nye Committee insisted that three constitutional amendments were essential to enforce the proposed legislation:

1. granting Congress, not the courts, the right to define "fair compensation" when plants, goods, machinery, and the like were commandeered so as to avoid the typical practice of the courts awarding the highest possible price level;
2. allowing Congress to tax war profits in a way that it considered to be fair and just but which could possibly result in inequities among taxpayers;
3. and, permitting Congress to tax the interest of tax-exempt securities during a national emergency.

Only with the first amendment would the commandeering threat be genuine; the other two were essential for implementing the taxation provisions of HR 5529.[70]

The committee was not enamored of these amendments. The first two "contain dangers that may be far worse than the evil of profiteering." They would increase greatly the power of the federal government, making possible countless abuses by industrial or military elements or both out to check competitors, opponents, and critics of the war effort at a time when constitutional guarantees would already be significantly weakened. Nonetheless, checking war profiteering made such amendments essential.[71]

Even laws backed by such constitutional amendments, the Nye Committee argued, did not ensure that wartime economic "evils" would be avoided. They would probably be repealed or ignored during hostilities. The only persons fully qualified to administer a wartime economy were industrialists themselves. It was inconceivable that they would attempt to enforce laws they considered detrimental to the war effort, to the economy, and to their own self-interest and that violated fundamental precepts of their ideology.[72]

The committee's investigation of the World War I economy and the preparations for future mobilization supported its conclusions. When pressed by Stephen Raushenbush about persuading industry to obey mobilization legislation when production for war was the first priority, John T. Flynn responded that he had no confidence that this was possible. Consequently, he was depending on taxes to take profits from industry instead of on regulations to control it. A similar answer was given to Senator Bone when he asked how Congress, responding to inevitable pressures applied in the name of necessity and patriotism, would be prevented from repealing legislation designed to minimize abuses. Flynn admitted that he did not know, that his was a program intended to take profits out of war, not a full blueprint for economic mobilization. He had no confidence in corporate America's providing reliable figures on costs and profits, and without its cooperation there was little that Washington could do. When Bernard M. Baruch was asked how current legislators could prevent future colleagues from repealing legislation to check the economic abuses of war, he could offer no more than the conviction that patriotism would prevent such an action.[73]

The Senate Finance Committee's deliberations on the Flynn bill provided further insights about the economics of warfare. J. S. Zucker, a technical adviser for the Internal Revenue Bureau and temporarily on the staff of the Joint Committee on Internal Revenue Taxation, assisted the committee on technical aspects of Flynn's plan. While doing so, he offered some general observations:

> We function, economically speaking, largely under the impetus of the profit motive. The extent to which other motives, such as patriotism or an appeal to a sense of social justice, equality of contribution, and sacrifice, may shape the determination to remain industrially active, is, to say the least, problematical. Whether, under stress of war and the necessity for preservation of country and family, people might rise to the support of their Government and concede to a levy approximating all of

the profits above a certain minimum is a conjecture which should not be tested at a time of war in view of the dire circumstances of failure.[74]

Bernard M. Baruch, Grosvenor B. Clarkson, and numerous other war mobilizers and industrial mobilization planning advocates had made the same argument against trying to change the economic system during hostilities. The thrust of their argument was quite different, however. They portrayed industry as gladly setting aside the profit motive during World War I to join government in patriotically sacrificing for the national good. Revelations to the contrary, and especially the systematic analysis of the Nye Committee, made a mockery of these claims and proposals for using World War I methods in future wars. By acting as propagandists, rather than as analysts, Baruch and his coterie endangered much of their credibility. When a more detached individual such as Zucker, aside from zealous critics of munitions makers and wartime economics such as Bone and Raushenbush, insisted that the realities of the economic system had to be accepted, then the point could not be easily denied.

The importance of the Nye Committee in illuminating the political economy of modern warfare cannot be exaggerated. Senator Arthur H. Vandenberg, a conservative Republican of isolationist views, perhaps best illustrates this point. He had been a member of the War Policies Commission but not an especially active or influential participant. His role in the Nye Committee was quite different. He played a leading part in its creation, organization, and operation; attended many of the hearings, always making a positive contribution; helped give the committee prestige through the respect with which he was generally held; and was exceptionally thorough and judicious, drawing conclusions only when the evidence so warranted.[75] As the committee dug ever deeper into the economics of war and the intractable problems it caused, the Michigan senator insisted that the clearest way to avoid these results was to avoid war.[76] He later noted that the Nye Committee educated him to the superficiality of the WPC's review. He made this position clear to Baruch, when the latter publicly attacked the Nye Committee for being all but unpatriotic:

> I think your last public statement was exceedingly unfortunate. Perhaps it invited inferences and implications which you did not intend. Certainly it came to me as a distinct shock to have you intimate—as I read it—that our plan [Flynn Plan] to take the profits out of war might precipitate the end of capitalism. . . .
>
> The War Policies Commission did not have the benefit—even remotely—of the type and extent of information which our present Munitions Committee has enjoyed; and I have come to the irrevocable

conclusion that the recommendations of the War Policies Commission were wholly and completely inadequate to equalize the burdens and take the profits out of war.[77]

A few months after the Nye Committee ended, Vandenberg came very close to finding war capitalism to be incompatible with the commonwealth. He wrote to Baruch: "The more I see of the present potential war situation, the surer I am that the 'commercial motive' is not to be trusted in *any* degree."[78]

It was not just Vandenberg who was educated by the committee he served on. The findings of the committee had unanimous support; differences emerged only on recommendations. This was a remarkable achievement for a committee whose members ranged from traditional Republicans to populist, even radical, Democrats. The report in favor of the Flynn bill was unanimous. Besides Nye and Clark, Vandenberg and Barbour were among its most vocal supporters.

Additional information is essential for explaining the Nye Committee's most glaring and revealing contradiction: in May 1935 it favorably reported out the Flynn bill; then, in reports of July 1935 and June 1936—while still supporting the legislation—the committee set forth why Flynn's approach would not work.

Flynn had the support of Nye and others on the committee. Nonetheless, some members of the committee and staff, particularly Stephen Raushenbush and Homer T. Bone, had fundamental objections about the feasibility of Flynn's approach. Raushenbush's basic criticism of the Flynn bill was included in the July 1935 and June 1936 reports. He was able to include it not only because he was chief investigator but also because Nye was an exceptionally democratic and tolerant chair who welcomed divergent points of view. Collectively, the Nye Committee revealed its diverse thought instead of trying to conceal differences.

Raushenbush cast additional light on the seemingly contradictory Nye Committee reports when he testified before the House Military Affairs Committee early in 1937 on proposals for industrial mobilization. He explained that he had had no role in writing the Flynn bill and had little faith in its efficacy for taking the profits out of war and equalizing war burdens. His reasoning was outlined in the Nye Committee reports of July 1935 and June 1936. He stated that he had come to appreciate these truths not from the arguments and analyses of Baruch, Johnson, and others but from members of the Office of the Assistant Secretary of War, especially Lt. Col. Charles T. Harris, Jr. War Department arguments, Raushenbush explained, significantly influenced his thinking. The head of OASW planning insisted that to win a war, the military had to focus on munitions production, not on economic equity and justice; it had to take the economic system as it existed, not as it might want it to be. Thus, the OASW included Flynn's bill in its Industrial Mobilization Plan only after excluding the taxation provisions and prohibitions against conflicts of interest and including warnings against excessive taxes.

Raushenbush explained that though nationalizing the munitions industry might be beneficial, he was not particularly enthusiastic about it as a measure to prevent war. Major wars were caused by trade rivalries, nationalism, and racial conflict involving not only munitions makers but all elements in society.

Raushenbush had several recommendations about HR 1954, or the Hill bill, on industrial mobilization, which the House Military Affairs Committee was considering. (This proposed legislation was much like the initial version of the 1935 McSwain bill but allowed wages to be set during wartime, provided for selective service, and included provisions for a management draft.) The former chief investigator for the Nye Committee argued that the committee should strike from the preamble language describing the bill as intending to prevent wartime profiteering and to equalize war burdens. Such goals, he declared, were unreachable and misled the public. Furthermore, since a management draft was totally unworkable, the provision should be excluded from the bill. He advised that the measure enact as much taxation as financial experts believed to be possible without harming the war effort but not to label such taxation as a draft of capital because that was grossly misleading. Wage setting should be excluded from the bill because, along with a work-or-fight program, it could result in a draft of labor. Last, he recommended that selective service legislation be placed in a totally separate bill.

Raushenbush's final point was the most important. It was basic to the Nye Committee's unanimous conclusion that the only way to avoid the numerous adverse consequences of modern warfare was to place every obstacle possible in the way of entering into hostilities. Provisions for selective service were included along with those for economic mobilization based on the concept of universal service. Drafting management and labor supposedly justified conscripting manpower for the armed services. Such thinking, Raushenbush maintained, was both erroneous and dangerous. Although labor could directly or indirectly be drafted, capital and management could not, rendering the idea of a universal draft at best an unrealistic ideal, at worst a cynical deception. Selective service therefore should be separated completely from economic mobilization so as to be judged on its own merits. The Nye Committee went even further. In June 1936 it unanimously recommended that in 1938 Congress submit to a national referendum the question of whether men could be drafted to serve outside the continental United States. Such a referendum, it was hoped, would trigger a countrywide debate on wartime policies, enlightening the public about the grave dangers and inevitable inequalities of modern warfare.[79]

Avoiding war to avoid its consequences became a central goal of the Nye Committee. It was a goal that had been articulated during the War Policies Commission investigation and earlier. The Nye Committee converted an approach that before had been only a suggestion into a fully formed proposition. It did the same with Flynn's proposal to finance all war expenses out of current income.

WORLD WAR I AND AMERICAN UNNEUTRALITY

The quest to avoid war in part led the Nye Committee to investigate American neutrality between 1914 and 1917 and to play an active role in the passage of the neutrality legislation in the 1930s as another war threatened. Its findings about the Woodrow Wilson administration's unneutral policies during World War I touched sensitive political nerves much more than did other parts of the committee's work. A provoked Congress ended the Nye Committee's tenure abruptly in mid-1936.

The neutrality years became central to the Nye Committee's inquiry. Its charges justified examining the period, and nearly all of the committee's study led back to World War I in one way or another. Furthermore, Nye and his colleagues began to perceive that government, and particularly the executive branch, was responsible as much as or more than business elements for fostering economic policies that could pull the nation into war. Wayne S. Cole has traced Senator Nye's political trek in the 1930s from agrarian liberalism to conservative isolationism. Nye's fears about centralizing power in Washington and the United States assuming a dominant role in world affairs were central to that transformation.

The Nye Committee's investigation of American neutrality policy from 1914 through America's entry into the war, and particularly of the involvement of J. P. Morgan and Company as financier and purchasing agent for the Allies, was of the greatest importance. The inquiry drew upon extended and controversial research in the files of the State, War, Navy, Commerce, and Treasury Departments, the Federal Reserve Board, the House of Morgan, and the papers of Wilson, Robert Lansing, Col. Edward M. House, and others. The documents from J. P. Morgan and Company included in the Nye Committee's work are among the most important that exist. (The firm destroyed its records around 1957 when it merged with the Guaranty Trust Company.)

Committee investigators believed that Morgan and Company placed all possible obstacles in their way and sanitized the files to the degree possible. The committee had to engage in drawn-out negotiations with the State Department and the White House, and indirectly with the British, French, and Italian governments—which objected to their correspondence being examined and perhaps published—to gain access to government documents.[80]

Ultimately, the committee considered its labor to have been fully worthwhile. It brought to light information that is still unsurpassed on the organization, development, and operation of J. P. Morgan and Company's Export Department, which operated as buying agent for the Allies and included in its reach much of the U.S. economy, particularly the American industrial giants. In a relatively short time, the United States went from having a rudimentary munitions industry to having a substantial one. The Morgans guided the process and at times forced the Allies to treat American firms with unexpected favor. To keep this multibillion dollar operation going, indeed, to get it under way securely, the Morgan partners led the way in providing American financial assistance to the Allies. For the first time, the Nye Committee revealed fully the details of the private financing, totaling nearly 3 billion dollars up to April 1917. That investment, Nye and his colleagues established, was ultimately protected and partially paid off when the United States entered World War I and took up the Allies' financial burden. In carrying out its responsibilities J. P. Morgan and Company dealt regularly with political and economic elites on both sides of the Atlantic, including Britain's prime minister and America's president.[81]

The Nye Committee concluded that America was unneutral in the years before it entered hostilities and that economic ties were central to the nation's slant toward the Allies. The unneutrality included a distorted and biased application of neutral rights for the Allies vis-à-vis the Central Powers; unwise, if not illegal, insistence upon rights of American citizens and ships in war zones; questionable policies concerning British merchant ships; and other practices that eventually led the United States to joining the fray. These findings were set forth in the fifth and sixth reports, dated June 1 and June 16, 1936, about the time the committee was forced quickly to wrap up its affairs. Hence, the Nye Committee was unable fully to explore the material, noting that it must "leave to the historians the intricate task of analyzing in detail the evidence which it has made available as public record."[82]

Nonetheless, the committee insisted, certain conclusions for the future were obvious without exhaustive study. First, Congress and the public, unlike their role during World War I, must be kept informed of America's neutrality policy and changes in it, especially if the president were given discretionary authority. Second, for the United States to stay out of war, neutrality laws must be stringent, prohibiting private or public, direct or indirect financial assistance to belligerents, banning the sale of munitions to such countries, limiting exports to nations at war to peacetime levels except for medical and hospital supplies, placing the most severe limits on armed merchant ships entering American waters, and possibly outlawing other aid as well. Third, and most important, America must avoid repeating the wartime experience of a private banking house gradually emerging as a principal financier and supplier of one side, resulting in America's conducting economic warfare and in the stability of the economy becoming dependent on the victory of that side.

Ties to the Allies, the Nye Committee affirmed, had developed step by step, probably without anyone realizing completely their consequences. At least indirectly they affected most interest groups and classes. Inevitably, relations with Great Britain and France greatly narrowed the latitude of America's leaders struggling with conditions of neutrality and war. In following this line of analysis, the committee came close to pinpointing the dynamics of an emerging military-industrial complex:

> Like other leaders in government, business and finance, . . . [Wilson] had watched the growth of militarism in the pre-war years. Militarism meant the alliance of the military with powerful economic groups to secure appropriations on the one hand for a constantly increasing military and naval establishment, and on the other hand, the constant threat of the use of that swollen military establishment in behalf of economic interests at home and abroad of the industrialists supporting it. It meant the subjugation of the people of the various countries to the uniform, the self-interested identification of patriotism with commercialism, and the removal of the military from the control of civil life. After the war had begun President Wilson and a great number of leading Americans became convinced that the war was the logical outcome of militarism, and that the success of militarism anywhere was a constant threat to the democracies of the world. All the members of the Committee and its staff shared that conviction.[83]

Evidence of an incipient military-industrial complex therefore existed in foreign as well as in domestic affairs. But a major point repeatedly made by the Nye Committee was that the effects of modern warfare and armaments were insidious, not blatant. They slowly engulfed most or all of a nation, setting off a process almost impossible to control. A few years after the committee he had chaired closed down, Senator Nye observed:

No member of the Munitions Committee to my knowledge has ever contended that it was munitions makers who took us to war. But that committee and its members have said again and again, that it was war trade and war boom, shared in by many more than munitions makers, that played the primary part in moving the United States into a war.[84]

Raushenbush, testifying before the House Military Affairs Committee in 1937, further explained the Nye Committee's conclusions:

Professor [Philip C.] Jessup, of Columbia University, had made the point that the only way you can take the profits out of war is to take the profits out of neutrality.

This encouragement of a war boom is tied in with the problem of peace. As you sometimes know, a great many of the neutrality proposals before the House and Senate are based upon the belief that when a boom in trade with belligerents starts, once it gets under way, nobody can stop it, not the most idealistic administration in the world and not the most materialistic administration.

Foreign governments throw 5 or 10 million dollars into our economic system and everything starts getting inflated and companies expand, and everybody wants the trade to go on. It is not only the munitions makers and the bankers but you and I who like to see prosperity in the country. We sort of get into that atmosphere and then it is almost impossible to stop the war trade.[85]

In short, modern warfare and even preparation for it through modest defense spending had become "so complex that it spreads its tentacles out over a nation and draws nourishment from its every activity."[86]

The Nye Committee was at the center of the movement that produced the neutrality legislation adopted between 1935 and 1937. John E. Wiltz and Wayne S. Cole, two principal scholars studying the committee, differ about its role in this regard.[87] Wiltz holds that Nye and his associates were unintentionally pulled in the direction of the neutrality legislation by the information they turned up and by international affairs. Cole, however, insists that neutrality was always a crucial part of the Nye Committee's focus. Actually, the two men do not differ that much in terms of ultimate outcome. Both agree that the committee influenced the writing of the neutrality legislation, though Cole is probably exaggerating when he claims that Nye and his colleagues set the agenda on the neutrality issue. The movement for peace and against war preparation—which emphasized the importance of neutrality—created the

Nye Committee at a time when international conflict again threatened and American participation seemed likely if World War I patterns were repeated. Neutrality legislation, therefore, was never far from the committee's concerns. Although the Nye Committee neither created the movement for neutrality nor was it the only or main supporter, it was probably one of the most influential shapers of neutrality legislation.

In 1935 the Nye Committee moved as a body to propose and consider legislation on neutrality, but it was warned away by the Foreign Relations Committee, chaired by Sen. Key Pittman (D-NV). Nonetheless, during the intense legislative battles over the neutrality bills from 1935 nearly until Pearl Harbor, Senators Nye and Bennett Champ Clark played major parts. They were backed at times by Homer T. Bone, James P. Pope, and Walter F. George, with Arthur H. Vandenberg assuming a leading role for the minority party. Furthermore, the Nye Committee investigation helped create a rationale for the neutrality legislation, and the committee provided vital information for those opposing war and seeking to keep America out of it. Committee hearings on World War I neutrality were held early in 1936 when consideration of the neutrality legislation was at a critical juncture. This was in part fortuitous, but the committee juggled some testimony to strengthen the forces of nonintervention. Moreover, the committee's staff assisted the neutrality advocates and participated in writing the legislation. Of crucial significance, and despite the extreme rancor that the Nye Committee's neutrality study caused, the findings and recommendations of its two reports on neutrality had unanimous support, including the backing of Senators George and Pope, who supported Roosevelt's foreign policy at a time when the administration was generally at extreme odds with the Nye Committee on the neutrality issue.

Senator Nye and other committee members sponsored bills as individuals rather than as committee spokesmen. This approach was mostly a formality intended to avoid offending the Senate Foreign Relations Committee, on which sat formidable noninterventionists such as Vandenberg, William E. Borah (R-ID), Hiram Johnson (R-CA), Arthur Capper (R-KS), Robert M. La Follette, Jr. (R-WI), and Henrik Shipstead (Farmer-Labor-MN). Technicalities aside, the Nye Committee was the principal sponsor, advocate, and source of data for the extreme isolationist position in the 1930s.

In the neutrality legislation hammered out between 1935 and 1937, the Nye Committee was probably directly responsible for the prohibitions involving loans and credits. Beyond that, Nye, Clark, and others tried to keep to a minimum presidential discretion in applying the laws and attempted to strengthen the statutes in a way that would reduce trade with belligerents to the vanishing point and remove all points of contact with a world conflict.

Their efforts did not succeed per se; however, through their advocacy, the extreme isolationists doubtlessly moved the middle, compromise position closer to their aims than otherwise would have been the case. Furthermore, without the findings of the Nye Committee, many of the demands of the extreme isolationists would have lacked credibility. Although Nye and others lost most skirmishes with the Roosevelt administration and the interventionists, they succeeded in forcing Americans to face the reality and consequences of their foreign policy and reduced the room for maneuver among the internationalists and interventionists.

It was this last quality that ultimately led to the Nye Committee's demise. The committee had caused unease at best, fury at worst, among a host of groups and interests, including the Roosevelt administration, the political and economic elite, preparedness advocates, business spokesmen, and opponents of the peace and isolationist movements. Despite widespread support for the type of investigation the Nye Committee conducted, careful preparation, skillful political and parliamentary maneuvering, and a fair measure of luck were necessary in getting the committee created. At all times it was vulnerable, but public support provided a mantle of protection, as Roosevelt discovered in December 1934 when he tried to steal the initiative from the committee.

As long as the committee in 1934 and 1935 kept the spotlight on munitions makers, World War I economic mobilization, and interwar planning, it appeared to gain strength among the public. These subjects were not new. They had been investigated since 1920 and in some cases had been the source of heated debate during World War I. Powerful groups like the American Legion and other veterans' organizations were dedicated, at least in name, to the inquiry. And there was an essentially bipartisan aspect to the committee's work. That was the case not only in terms of its membership but also regarding the subjects it looked into. The investigation examined both Democratic and Republican administrations, and, unlike the House Select Committee on Expenditures in the War Department, never stressed party affiliations. Furthermore, prior to the neutrality legislation in 1935, the Nye Committee saw no legislation it favored pass Congress or even come close to doing so.

The investigation of American neutrality policy between 1914 and 1917 and its application to the conditions of the 1930s changed the way the committee was perceived. Nye and Clark played a leading role among extreme isolationists in forcing through legislation in 1935, and their power promised to grow. American unneutrality in the 1914–1917 period had never been so thoroughly documented or made so accessible to the public. The past, through the Nye Committee, was speaking and threatening to dictate policy to the present and the future. This voice was a threat that went beyond embarrassment and revelation; it was beginning meaningfully to affect elite foreign policy formulation that was looking to create the American century abroad.

Senator Nye gave his numerous opponents an opportunity to launch a massive attack on the committee with the intent of ending it. When the committee revealed that Wilson and his Secretary of State Robert Lansing had known about the Allied secret treaties prior to Versailles and had declared otherwise, Nye observed that they had "falsified." The opening had been made. Within two days Thomas T. Connally (D-TX), who had bottled up the Flynn bill for almost a year while professing to be rushing it to the Senate, and Carter Glass (D-VA), secretary of the treasury under Woodrow Wilson and a close associate of J. P. Morgan and Company, launched uncivil, personal attacks against Nye, vowing that the committee he chaired would receive no further funding. Throughout the debate that ensued, no critic of the committee tried denying Nye's irrefutable facts. Instead, they engaged in ad hominem diversions. In his rebuttal, Nye refused to back away from his charge; instead he repeated it. He explained the committee's deep concern about the insidiousness of modern warfare:

> If we find that one of the most idealistic Presidents this nation ever had was unable to stem a flood of munitions orders, is it improper to report on that fact? . . . When we go in search of pertinent truths we ought not dodge them when we encounter them—we ought not let partisan prejudices blind us to those truths, however embarrassing they may be to a mere political party.[88]

Senators Pope and George, as Democratic internationalists, distanced themselves from the committee on this issue. Neither had been present during testimony on the neutrality years. Pope emerged after the blowup to explain that although he and George remained dedicated to the committee's aims, they disavowed all unwarranted attacks on the late president and his secretary of state, and they would rejoin their colleagues when they properly refocused their efforts on munitions practices. Neither Pope nor George dissented from reports five and six, however, issued in June 1936 and covering the neutrality years, including "falsified" statements in high places.

Roosevelt's role in shutting down the Nye Committee is unclear. The committee created great tension within the administration almost from the outset. The president first tried unsuccessfully to outmaneuver Nye and his associates with the appointment of the Baruch-Johnson Committee. By 1936 he was willing to let others pull the rug from under the committee as long as he was not implicated, especially before the election in November. Thereafter, relations between the president and Senator Nye grew increasingly and vocally hostile as the latter went further to the right in terms of domestic policy and isolationism and Roosevelt became increasingly absorbed in America's response to the deteriorating international scene.[89]

Ending the Nye Committee's tenure was not difficult. By the time the imbroglio over Wilson erupted in January 1936, the committee had expended most of its funds. With the congressional Democratic establishment dedicated to shutting it down, the committee negotiated a compromise in which it received an additional $7,369 to complete its work during the current session. February 20 was the last day of hearings. In June 1936 the seventh and final report was issued. It was a disappointment in terms of the committee's earlier work, proposing government ownership and manufacture of munitions during peacetime for a fundamentally defensive military policy, reviewing some economic data on the subject, and reproducing the committee's First Preliminary Report, in which it divided 4 to 3 in favor of public peacetime munitions production.[90]

The quick end to the committee precluded a cogent final report. The absence of such a statement was probably not too significant. Each report stood on its own, constituting a building block in the Nye Committee's edifice against war. A final report could have done little more than summarize effectively the main points of previous reports and set out some general conclusions. The careful reader could do that unassisted. Furthermore, though Nye and his associates had other studies in mind, they had largely completed their agenda. More might have been done with public ownership of munitions facilities. Such an exercise, unlike other committee studies, would have been principally academic. It had no chance of being adopted, it would have said little that was new, and it would have assumed an American foreign policy of isolationism and a defensive posture.

By the time the committee closed its doors, it had held the national spotlight for almost two years, made significant revelations, and presented numerous insights on every topic considered. The public's attention could be held for only so long, and the committee had probably pushed to the outer limits in that regard. After that the committee's influence would be measured by its impact on policies involving neutrality, munitions, and economic mobilization. The debate on these subjects had already begun. The legacy of the Senate Special Committee Investigating the Munitions Industry was no longer in the hands of Sen. Gerald P. Nye or his colleagues and staff.

The Nye Committee offered the nation, perhaps the international community, the most thorough and sophisticated analysis of the political economy of modern warfare it had yet had. (Charles A. Beard observed at the time:

"Respecting no other large phase of American history do we have such a meticulous record of persons and pressures involved in shaping of policies, decisions and events."[91]) Drawing upon World War I and its legacy, the committee established that the term "munitions," as a narrow category, was beginning to lose its significance. Entire industrial economies were becoming machines of warfare that could shape the domestic and foreign policy of nations. Statesmen, businessmen, farmers, workers, critics, reformers, and radicals could still influence events. At some point, however, once the machine of modern warfare, or even preparations for it, got under way, an invisible line was crossed when choices became uncertain. The war/defense machine had a propensity to go beyond the control of its creators.

This insight was disquieting for committee members. They ended up writing reports that basically contradicted one another. America's elected leaders reacted similarly when they chose to shoot the messenger bringing bad news and to cover up the truth with non sequiturs. Senators Pope and George, the dissenters on the Nye Committee, opted to damn the committee for untruthfulness and then, by their silence, endorsed its truth. Senator Bone, given to the most direct, bitter, and radical statements in the committee and the Senate chambers, lamented, "Everyone has come to recognize that the Great War was utter social insanity, and was a crazy war, and we had no business in it at all."[92] In a sense Bone also spoke to the study of the war and its consequences. In its utter rationality, the Nye Committee was exceptional. Too often inquiries involving the political economy of warfare took on a surreal quality, as demonstrated so dramatically by the War Policies Commission.

Nye and his colleagues discovered another major truth. Modern warfare profoundly influenced, and was profoundly influenced by, the political economy of industrial societies. As long as such societies existed, the horrors and insanities of modern warfare were possible. John T. Flynn authored a proposal for managing that reality, but the Nye Committee established better than any critic why Flynn's plan would not work. The government had as much of a role in the new war juggernaut as did industry and finance. Since modern warfare and preparations for it required a vast expansion of the state, Nye came to see Washington as the main culprit and hence joined the extreme conservatives and isolationists by the end of the 1930s. Yet as Stephen Raushenbush explained, not just Nye but all the committee members came to the conclusion that the fires of modern warfare could not be tamed and that its burdens could not be equalized or made just. The only way to avoid the consequences of modern warfare was to avoid war itself and offensive preparation for it. Whether the nation's political economy would allow that the committee members seemed to doubt.

Senator Nye and his colleagues identified an incipient institutional structure dedicated to war. They believed this structure to be an "unhealthy alliance," a form of "militarism" involving business, the military, and the government. With remarkable accuracy, the Nye Committee anticipated the growth of the structure later called the military-industrial complex. It was able to do so through a close examination of economic mobilization for World War I and interwar developments. The committee's investigation was facilitated by the threat of another world war and the fact that the Great Depression stripped away the sacrosanct aura of America's political economy. Those nearly unique conditions allowed the Nye Committee to probe the past and present in which warfare was becoming a principal shaping force. For a short time, the committee had enormous popular support. Ultimately, the committee's truths became too hard to bear; ghosts from the past in the form of Woodrow Wilson and Robert Lansing were used to terminate the investigation. Circumstances resembling those of the Nye Committee would not again occur until the 1960s. By then the institutional consequences of modern warfare far exceeded the worst fears of Senator Nye and his associates. Nonetheless, the fact that the Nye Committee laid the foundations that Cold War generations would build upon, even if those later-day critics of warfare were unaware of their antecedents, stands today as a monument to the Senate Special Committee Investigating the Munitions Industry.

POST–NYE COMMITTEE INVESTIGATIONS

Bills dealing with economic mobilization continued to be introduced in and examined by Congress after the Nye Committee closed up, but the process was anticlimactic at best, pro forma at worst. The Nye Committee had examined the subject well. The nation's legislators could seriously act on the findings and recommendations of Sen. Gerald P. Nye and his colleagues or return to the superficial consideration of proposed legislation that had become ceremony since 1922. Congress chose ceremony. No serious debate occurred, stale hearings were held, and bills stood no chance of becoming law. Legislation written by the Nye Committee was reintroduced with regularity but got nowhere.[93]

After the virtual death of the Nye Committee legislation, the so-called Sheppard-Hill bill (HR 1954 and S 25) became the principal legislation for industrial mobilization. Senator Morris Sheppard (D-TX) chaired the Senate Military Affairs Committee, and Lister Hill replaced the late John J. McSwain as chairman of the House Military Affairs Committee and as the bill's principal sponsor. The proposed legislation was a modified form of the McSwain bill that had been used in an attempt to circumvent the Flynn bill after 1935. Like the McSwain bill, its main author was the American Legion, and John Thomas Taylor, the influential chairman of the Legion's Legislative Committee, played a leading, at times dominant, role in the hearings on the proposed legislation. The Office of the Assistant Secretary of War was closely associated with the bill, worked on it with both the American Legion and its legislative sponsors, and considered it an excellent legislative vehicle for implementing the Industrial Mobilization Plan. With the Nye Committee off the scene, the advocates of the status quo in economic mobilization held the field, as they had before 1934.[94]

Hill introduced the Sheppard-Hill bill in January 1937, and the House and Senate periodically held hearings on the proposal throughout that year. Much like the McSwain bill, the Hill proposal provided for freezing prices and perhaps wages with later adjustments possible, priority power, the necessary mobilization agencies, and a wartime tax of 95 percent of all income above the previous three-year average. It also included provisions absent in the McSwain bill that in effect were drawn from the Nye bill. The president, for example, could require the registration and draft of management during wartime. Additionally, Hill's proposal provided for a selective service system. Provisions for enacting the bill were loosely and inconsistently drawn.[95]

Several points stand out about the proposed legislation and the hearings involving it. First, as in the pre-Nye period, the American Legion continued to play verbal games with the concept of universal conscription. Throughout the hearings, furthermore, members of the Legion, sponsors like Hill and Sheppard, and others stepped in to help those having difficulty explaining the bill's consequences. Also looking backward, the bill promised to prevent war profiteering, equalize the burdens of war, promote the national defense, and advance the cause of peace. The measure was indeed so general that Congress or the president would have wide latitude in determining how it would work. The proposals were quite familiar after more than fifteen years of advocacy.

Second, the Hill bill differed in some ways from past proposals. Provisions for registering and drafting management, licensing businessmen, and severe wartime taxation indicated the impact of the Nye Committee. The congressional sponsors of the bill and the American Legion were also adamantly opposed to a labor draft and even waffled when Bernard M. Baruch, Hugh S. Johnson, and the War Department insisted that the bill provide for wage controls. Baruch and Johnson also argued against conscripting manpower, dodged the issue of management draft, and supported taxes as high as possible. Here they joined a chorus for financing the war from current revenue to the degree possible, another testimony to the influence of the Nye Committee. Even more significant in that regard, neither Baruch, Johnson, nor any other witness held up the World War I model as ideal. Instead, Baruch argued that although Flynn's proposals had gone too far, the "scandalous" profiteering of World War I and the unconscionable gains of cost-plus contracting had to go. Whatever was done, however, wartime burdens could not be equalized; only attempts at a fair and just war mobilization system could be tried. Apparently as a diversionary tactic, Baruch and Johnson continued to take verbal swipes at OASW planning.

A third interesting aspect of the hearings on HR 1954 was that various witnesses, such as Baruch, maintained that the Hill bill complemented the neutrality legislation. A witness for the American League Against War and Fascism argued just the opposite: the neutrality legislation was an illusion; the United States was preparing for war and would enter hostilities if they erupted. In truth, the measure was so ambiguous, open to so many interpretations, and used to support so many causes that defining its intent with finality was virtually impossible. The attempts of Baruch, the American Legion, and others to square the bill with the neutrality legislation and the Flynn bill appeared to be coordinated and intended to shelter Hill's measure from attacks by peace advocates.[96]

Finally, criticism of HR 1954 was more astute than it had been previously, again a tribute to the Nye Committee. Committee members and witnesses from the conservative right to the radical left zeroed in on the ambiguity about implementing the bill, which left the door open to executive abuse. Liberal-to-radical critics, including organized labor's spokesmen, argued that the bill, combined with the Industrial Mobilization Plan, meant a labor draft and other threats to the working population. They pointed out further that the 1933 version of the IMP was so blatant in this regard that it had to be toned down while being considered by the Nye Committee. Probably because of the latter's work, radical critics provided a knowledgeable, if distorted, critique of the IMP, including the fact that the 1936 plan was missing appendixes for Public Relations and Selective Service.[97] Organizations such as the American League Against War and Fascism and the Women's International League for Peace and Freedom, and even more moderate ones such as the National Women's Trade Union League of America, used the Nye Committee analysis to demonstrate that the Hill bill and even the Flynn bill could not achieve their desired aims. Louise Bransten, a member of the National Executive Committee of the American League Against War and Fascism, powerfully articulated the radicals' conviction that world war meant war for America:

> All of us are aware of the fact that the world ties of America will draw us into any general war situation that develops. American goods are sent all

over the world—American ships sail every sea—America depends on the world market for raw materials. American capital is invested in nearly every foreign country. These things are virtually indispensable to our economic life, and aside from any policy that we may pursue at a given moment, armed conflict in any part of the world really involves America. Therefore, it is impossible to maintain neutrality in the event of war that threatens our economic interests; and war trade is not primarily a question of armaments, since highly industrialized aggressor nations can turn secondary war supplies into munitions. No proposal like the Hill-Sheppard bill will serve to keep us out of war, because the causes for our entry into a war lie in the nature of our present economy which needs foreign investments and foreign markets in order to preserve itself.[98]

Hearings on HR 1954, like most other bills that preceded it, had a limited range of witnesses. They were restricted to the American Legion and other veterans' groups, former war mobilizers, some patriotic groups, and radical and peace advocates. Organized business was not heard from, labor had token spokesmen, and consumer groups, farmers, and others were simply absent. The topic, surprisingly, seemed too specialized or too remote for most people.

Also, a mean spirit was on display at the hearings that had only been suggested before. Red-baiting had started. Senator Warren R. Austin (R-VT) loosely spoke of socialism in addressing liberal and radical economic mobilization proposals, and Hugh S. Johnson labeled the Flynn Plan as communism. But it was John Thomas Taylor, speaking for the American Legion, who launched a frontal assault on the American League Against War and Fascism as a disloyal Communist front group and even attempted to tar Stephen Raushenbush with the same brush. With war approaching and ideological passions rising, red-baiting would become a constant feature of the American scene.

HR 1954, like its predecessors except for the Nye Committee–revised McSwain bill, never reached a vote in either house of Congress, although it was reported out by both the House and Senate Military Affairs Committees. Indeed, the subject became more controversial as the likelihood of war grew and the legislation seemed in a sense real rather than theoretical.[99]

Several other congressional hearings were held on aspects of industrial mobilization for war after 1937 and before the outbreak of World War II in 1939, but they were of little consequence.[100] As had been the case before World War I, the initiative began shifting to the executive branch of government.

15
THE WAR RESOURCES BOARD

President Franklin D. Roosevelt's rather sudden and unexpected organization of the War Resources Board (WRB) in mid-1939 was the last significant act of interwar planning and the first meaningful step toward mobilizing the economy for World War II. Over half a century later, the WRB's creation, composition, operation, and ultimate fate are still sources of scholarly confusion and debate.[1]

The process that culminated in the creation of the WRB began after the election of 1936. At that point Roosevelt seriously began to consider reorganizing the executive branch. With international tensions mounting rapidly, preparedness and possible war mobilization figured prominently in the president's thinking.[2] Meanwhile, the War Department entered a period of critical personnel changes. The chronically ill Secretary George H. Dern died in August 1936, and Assistant Secretary Harry H. Woodring was elevated to the secretaryship about a month later with the understanding that his appointment was temporary. Late in June 1937 Louis A. Johnson assumed the post of assistant secretary, insisting that he had been promised the post of secretary of war after a decent interval. A West Virginia attorney who had been active in Democratic politics before World War I, Johnson used the American Legion and veterans' affairs in the interwar years to strengthen his political base. In 1932 he had served as the Legion's national commander.[3]

Extremely ambitious and energetic, Johnson quickly launched a one-man national effort to publicize the Office of the Assistant Secretary of War's (OASW), Industrial Mobilization Plan (IMP), which still remained relatively unknown among the public and even in the highest circles of government. Johnson traveled thousands of miles inspecting plants, arsenals, and air fields and speaking to business, patriotic, and social audiences. He also managed to get extensive media coverage for his office and the job it was doing. In less than two years, Johnson moved the Industrial Mobilization Plan from the shadows into the light of day.[4]

Within a week of taking office, the assistant secretary of war contacted Bernard M. Baruch and Hugh S. Johnson, asking for their assessment of the IMP and the operations of his office. In October 1937 Johnson proposed to Baruch what the latter had been advocating for years: a group of disinterested civilians to review the OASW's plans. Not only would this test the quality of the military's work, Johnson asserted, but it would also give national prestige to the IMP. Baruch jumped at the opportunity. Besides himself, he proposed almost the entire top staff of the World War I War Industries Board (WIB) and its associated agencies, including Hugh S. Johnson, George N. Peek, John M. Hancock, and Robert H. Montgomery. Each of these individuals would appoint a younger understudy to replace him when it became necessary. Assistant Secretary of War Johnson had gently warned Baruch that although some former war mobilizers were welcome, most of the advisory board had to be younger men representative of the industrial community and politically acceptable on a national basis since they might be called upon to take over the economic mobilization duties. Baruch failed to heed the warning, and Johnson repeated it as he diplomatically rejected Baruch's recommendations.[5]

World War I had made Baruch nationally prominent, and the elder statesman looked forward to high office in another war. Experience and prominence were Baruch's greatest assets, but they were also his greatest liabilities: He never grew beyond the World War I experience. Tacking with the political winds when essential, Baruch year after year held up the World War I mobilization model as the only reliable guide to the future. He did so in testimony before Congress and in lectures delivered to the military and whoever else would listen. His campaign made Baruch the acclaimed (often self-proclaimed) authority on economic mobilization, but in constantly looking backward, Baruch paid insufficient attention to contemporary developments and their ramifications for the future.

Baruch in 1936 and 1937 entered an active phase in behalf of preparedness, which continued until Pearl Harbor. Continuously in contact with the White House, leading members of Congress, the civilian and military heads of the army and navy, and corporate executives, he agitated for increased and properly distributed military expenditures, restructured armed services, more air power, modification of the neutrality legislation, and economic mobilization. As usual, Baruch arranged excellent media coverage for his views.[6]

Economic mobilization interested Baruch the most. Early in 1938, he passed the word to Roosevelt that "preparedness necessities will give [the president] the bridge over which business can gladly come in."[7] He preached to corporate executives the necessity of assuming the right attitudes and making the proper statements on war, war profits, and the need for a sense of public responsibility. Baruch went out of his way to compliment Eugene G. Grace and Alfred B. Sloan on their public declarations in this regard and pressed upon them the importance of persuading the Du Ponts to go along.[8] These were the years when the Roosevelt administration made cautious moves in the preparedness area. Military budgets increased in the late 1930s, and programs for educational orders, stockpiling of strategic materials, and production studies finally began with at least minimal funding.[9]

Preparedness was not new for Baruch, but girding for the likelihood of war was. The former chairman of the WIB anticipated either a leading role in industrial mobilization or a major cabinet position such as secretary of state.[10] In 1938 and 1939 his ambitions seemed within reach. Roosevelt had been thinking about establishing a mobilization structure directly under the supervision of the White House as part of his plans for what became the Reorganization Act of 1939. While considering that prospect, the president learned that the statutory authority for the World War I Council of National Defense–National Defense Advisory Commission was still in effect, making that system the easiest mobilization route. He suggested this possibility to Louis A. Johnson in October 1937. Rather typically, Roosevelt then acted on his own without consulting the assistant secretary of war. In June 1938, in response to Baruch's entreaties that war was approaching and preparedness essential, Roosevelt proposed that Baruch head a Defense Coordination Board to study economic mobilization and report to the president by December 1.

Baruch quickly accepted the president's offer and proposed for the board the same personnel he had earlier recommended for a similar assignment to Assistant Secretary of War Johnson. He insisted on bringing in the old WIB crowd, including Hugh S. Johnson and George N. Peek, who by this time were openly at odds with the president and his administration after having headed the National Recovery Administration and the Agriculture Adjustment Administration. Roosevelt rejected Baruch's recommendations, pushed perhaps by the inner circle of New Dealers such as Thomas G. Corcoran and Benjamin V. Cohen.[11] Despite the earlier fiasco with Assistant Secretary of War Johnson, Baruch seemed unable to learn or perhaps believed that desperation in the administration would allow him to dictate terms.

After the rejection of the aborted Baruch board, Roosevelt still faced a major dilemma. War was approaching, yet national attitudes on isolationism and neutrality and against war remained strong. Any actions the president took in the area of defense or war preparation would probably set off a major controversy. This awareness appeared to paralyze the president in selecting high-powered leaders for the Navy and War Departments. The Navy Department was all but lacking in civilian leadership. Harold L. Ickes reported in mid-1939 that Assistant Secretary of the Navy Charles Edison was nearly blind and deaf, and Secretary of the Navy Claude A. Swanson was "only about ten percent alive."

Health was better in the War Department but the politics much worse. Roosevelt had elaborate schemes for reshuffling his administration that hinged on Secretary of War Woodring resigning, a step the latter would not take and one the president characteristically avoided pushing. Woodring lacked prestige, and he was increasingly against preparedness. (The secretary of war virtually forced Roosevelt to ask for his resignation in June 1940, by refusing to approve the president's decision to sell B-17 bombers to Britain.) Assistant Secretary of War Johnson was among the most hawkish members of the administration, but he was unacceptable to the president's closest advisers because of his conservative economic views. He was also a political liability. He crudely grasped for Woodring's job in full public view, the two men fought openly, and each attempted to line up a reluctant officer corps on his side. The discord left the War Department dispirited and drifting.[12]

Roosevelt was clearly allowing Baruch and Johnson to act as point men for preparedness. Had either proceeded with greater finesse, he might have emerged as a dominant figure in economic mobilization for World War II. But Johnson was indiscreet, and Baruch set unacceptable terms for the president. Nonetheless, until he replaced the civilian heads of his military departments, Roosevelt relied on these two politically vulnerable figures to advance preparations for war. Both men played important roles in the quick rise and fall of the War Resources Board.

Despite Assistant Secretary of War Johnson's frustrations in creating an advisory board on economic mobilization in 1937 and 1938, he continued to pursue that goal. In mid-1939 he appointed an Educational Orders Review Committee to report on army procurement practices. The board was chaired by Benedict Crowell, president of the Army Ordnance Association, which included existing and potential military contractors in its organization. Johnson intended to convert the board into an agency for reviewing the Industrial Mobilization Plan, when the president unexpectedly authorized a more direct approach.[13]

THE RISE AND FALL OF THE WAR RESOURCES BOARD

At a cabinet meeting on August 4, 1939, Assistant Secretary of War Louis A. Johnson suggested a review board for economic mobilization. To the surprise of all, President Roosevelt accepted the proposal at the next cabinet meeting on August 8. Roosevelt appeared convinced that the nation could be at war within six weeks, necessitating immediate action. The president appointed Edward R. Stettinius, Jr., chairman of the board of the U.S. Steel Corporation, to head the War Resources Board. Stettinius was a spokesman for a sector of large corporate America that was not avidly and vocally anti–New Deal and that showed some signs of flexibility in areas such as labor relations. The other members of the board were selected by Stettinius, acting as intermediary for the president, Assistant Secretary Johnson, the assistant secretary of the navy, the army chief of staff, and two members of the OASW. The final selection included Walter S. Gifford, president of the American Telephone and Telegraph Company (ATT) and the former executive director of the World War I Council of National Defense; John Lee Pratt, a director of General Motors Corporation; Robert E. Wood, head of Sears, Roebuck, and Company, who had served as quartermaster general during World War I; Harold G. Moulton, president of the Brookings Institution; and Karl T. Compton, president of Massachusetts Institute of Technology. Roosevelt gave the membership his stamp of approval.[14]

Public announcement of the WRB's organization and membership on August 9 created a political storm, triggering a series of events leading to the board's failure. Baruch was described as being "sore as hell" over his exclusion;[15] he unleashed Hugh S. Johnson to attack the board bitterly in private and public. Johnson wrote to Stettinius that he and others were being used, as had been the case with his father, Edward R. Stettinius, during World War I. The board's composition was clearly unacceptable to New Dealers. "Do you suppose the present pack of semi-Communist wolves intend to let Morgan and DuPont men run a war?" Johnson asked. "It is either Louis Johnson's incomparable dumbness or somebody's downright Machiavellism."[16] In syndicated columns, Johnson said the same thing, albeit less colorfully.

The president instructed the War Resources Board at the outset to consult with Baruch and World War I mobilizers, and it moved quickly to do so. However, more concrete steps were necessary to accommodate the Baruch camp. Before the board was fully operational in August, John M. Hancock assumed first a major role in advising it and was then appointed a member. Hancock had been in charge of all navy procurement during World War I and had served in various economic mobilization agencies. After the war, he had been chief of staff for Industrial Organizations in the National Recovery Administration and had become a partner in Lehman Brothers. By 1939 he was a close associate of Baruch. Hancock played as influential a role in the affairs as any other member. Once Hancock was on the board, the old Baruch hands and other war mobilizers, including J. Leonard Replogle and Hugh S.

Johnson, lent the WRB their support and advice. By the end of August 1939, Hugh S. Johnson's syndicated columns handsomely praised Louis A. Johnson for his leadership of the OASW and the Industrial Mobilization Plan as a masterful document. On September 1, Hugh S. Johnson went further by arguing that the War Resources Board should be given a chance to prepare the nation for war.[17]

Opposition to the War Resources Board still remained strong. Anti-Morgan elements on Wall Street such as James Forrestal and business mavericks like Cyrus S. Eaton were furious with the WRB membership. In their eyes, U.S. Steel, General Motors, and ATT were dominated by J. P. Morgan and Company, gaining for the financial house a critically important foothold in the Roosevelt administration at the expense of the White House's other business and financial friends. Eaton and others stressed that Morgan's dominance had already been furthered by the appointment of an emergency advisory committee to the Federal Reserve Board and advisers to the Treasury Department and by the reappointment of J. P. Morgan and Company as fiscal agents for the British Treasury. Organized labor, agriculture, and their spokespersons in and outside of government also damned the business-dominated board and demanded representation.[18]

Opposition within the Roosevelt administration was as strong and as determined as that outside it. Early in September 1939 Ickes recorded in his diary: "Bob Jackson, Tom Corcoran, and Ben Cohen had lunch with me. All of us have been greatly concerned by the inroads into Washington of Wall Streeters and economic royalists since the war was declared."[19] This group had a curious ally in Harry H. Woodring. The War Resources Board had been appointed while the secretary of war was out of town and Johnson was acting secretary. Woodring had not been consulted on the matter and was largely ignored by the WRB. He opposed the board both as a war measure and as another aggressive move by his subordinate and now sworn enemy, Assistant Secretary of War Johnson. Woodring used Johnson's overenthusiastic courting of the business community and his exuberance in promoting the Industrial Mobilization Plan to urge Roosevelt to disavow the WRB.

With opposition on all sides and often in important places, the WRB had to proceed with great caution to have any chance of success. This it did not do. Instead, its members acted as Baruch had when he was asked by both Johnson and Roosevelt to set up advisory committees, insisting on dictating policy in a manner that ensured defeat.

Many of the WRB's blunders stemmed from its subordinate position to the overly ambitious Office of the Assistant Secretary of War. The OASW still controlled industrial mobilization planning, despite the efforts made since at least the mid-1930s to strengthen the Army-Navy Munitions Board (ANMB). The ANMB had become more active in 1938 and 1939 in terms of commodity committees, taking charge of the Mineral Advisory Committee from the OASW, forming a Chemical Advisory Committee, participating in interdepartmental committees on rubber, tin, and other commodities, and also joining the general work in the economic mobilization field. Nonetheless, the board was no more than an appendage of the OASW. Industrial mobilization planning, therefore, continued to be principally a War Department venture, not a joint War and Navy Department effort.[20]

With the appointment of the WRB, Johnson and the OASW began a concerted drive first to have the Industrial Mobilization Plan accepted as the means for harnessing the economy and then to begin the mobilization process. In a staff memorandum to the assistant secretary of war on August 9, 1939, OASW leaders warned:

> Any member appointed to this War Resources Board will be difficult to get rid of for many years if not of the right type, hence should be carefully chosen. The Board, while advisory only in peace, will become an executive agency in an emergency and demonstrated executive ability should be a prime qualification of all its members. Since, in the interest of prompt action in an emergency, the final decision on all matters will rest with the Chairman of the Board, he especially should be carefully chosen. An Army officer familiar with the industrial mobilization plans should be secretary to the Board.[21]

Colonel Harry K. Rutherford, director of the Planning Branch, was appointed secretary of the WRB. Assistant Secretary of War Johnson announced to the nation that the board would review the Industrial Mobilization Plan, 1939, revise it if necessary, and implement it in an emergency.[22] Key to the IMP, 1939, was a type of strengthened War Industries Board, an agency called the War Resources Administration, which was to be organized along commodity section–war service committee lines with military representatives integrated into it. Unlike earlier plans, the 1939 edition moderated proposed military influence in the civilian agencies. While the WRB was being set up, however, the OASW ambiguously proposed a role for the military in the WRB's operations that was contrary to the spirit and letter of the Industrial Mobilization Plan. Had the OASW's intentions been fully exposed, they would have created great antagonism among many civilian elements.[23]

Working hand in hand with the armed services, the WRB, while still reviewing the Industrial Mobilization Plan, began preparing to institute it. In sharp contrast to its attitude toward the War Policies Commission and other government investigations of economic mobilization, the business community was eager to cooperate with the WRB. The National Association of Manufacturers and the U.S. Chamber of Commerce rushed forward to volunteer their services. Through conferences with these organizations, along with former WIB members, the Commerce Department, and other private and public sources, the WRB drew up an industrial who's who to staff the War Resources Administration and also made provisions for the use of war service committees.[24] The most daring move was a memorandum drafted for the president's signature early in September 1939, which would have granted the War Resources Board and the Army-Navy Munitions Board the authority to mobilize the economy, instructing all other government agencies to cooperate with those two agencies.[25]

The memorandum was never sent. The enemies of the WRB within the Roosevelt administration were gathering strength and sought to box the board in. Lauchlin Currie, an administrative assistant to the president, early in September received Roosevelt's authority to block the Brookings Institution from serving as the WRB's primary research center. Instead, Currie himself would coordinate other government agencies and experts in carrying out studies for the WRB.[26] Ickes and Corcoran—the "palace guards," according to the *Milwaukee Sentinel,* and the "Greenwich Village Kibitzers," in the words of Hugh S. Johnson—along with other WRB opponents persistently nipped at the heels of the War Department and the board.[27] Acting on his own or with the encouragement of his advisers, the president forced the WRB to set forth its functions in detail, and he cut Assistant Secretary of War Johnson's request for WRB funding from $125,000 to $50,000. Johnson apparently intended to spend most of this money on the OASW and the ANMB in preparation for economic mobilization functions, with the WRB operating principally through these agencies.[28] The Treasury Department also beat back an attempt by the ANMB in 1939 to assume major responsibility for regulating the export of munitions.[29]

The president himself was the most important influence in undermining the WRB. Roosevelt continued to show interest in the Council of National Defense–National Defense Advisory Commission as a way to begin mobilizing the economy. The furor caused by the War Resources Board seemed to strengthen his thinking along these lines. After agreeing to the appointment of the board and approving of its membership, Roosevelt largely left Johnson and the WRB alone. On August 30, however, the president met with the board and informed it that a centralized agency controlling all economic mobilization functions—the role the Industrial Mobilization Plan proposed for the War Resources Administration—was unacceptable to him, that he was considering reviving the Council of National Defense–National Defense Advisory Commission of which the War Resources Board could be a part, and that the president personally would maintain control over all economic mobilization activity.

Similar to Baruch's behavior in the past, the WRB refused to heed the president. In a memorandum of September 6, 1939, which Roosevelt had requested on the board's proposed role in economic mobilization, the WRB set forth its intentions much as it had from the beginning: It would review and prepare to implement the Industrial Mobilization Plan, at some point becoming the War Resources Administration; and it would exercise central direction over all facets of economic mobilization. A week later, the president again spelled out to the assistant secretaries of war and navy and to Stettinius that the board could be one among several mobilization agencies serving under his direction. Stettinius and his associates then drafted a report they thought was more in line with what the president wanted.[30]

This report, dated October 12, 1939, was largely the work of John M. Hancock; it grew from earlier efforts by Hancock and Harold G. Moulton. Yet it did not begin to conform to Roosevelt's wishes. The one major concession to the president was the proposal that economic mobilization take place through a limited number of agencies that would be coordinated among themselves, instead of one agency dominating all. Under this scheme, ultimate authority would rest with the president, but he would exercise this power only in the event that the various agencies could not agree among themselves. Hence, although the War Resources Administration would clearly be the key mobilization agency, separate agencies could exist for labor, finance, food, price control, and the like, with War Resources Administration members sitting on these other agencies to facilitate coordination. This plan approximated the structure existing during World War I. The IMP, 1939, had proposed that the War Resources Administration be the superagency, incorporating all functions of economic mobilization, with only the Selective Service System and the Public Relations Administration acting independently. Although the War Resources Board favored this system, under presidential pressure it grudgingly opted for the more decentralized and fluid structure.

Hancock's October report insisted that economic mobilization agencies had to be largely staffed and run by "executives having the confidence of industry" and implied that war services committees would again be used. The WRB also pointed out that the confidence of labor, agriculture, and other interest groups had to be won in the mobilization process. But as if to keep those interest groups at bay, the report warned, "No group in the body politic should hope to achieve in time of war a position which it had not been able to obtain under peace conditions." Moreover, New Deal reforms would probably be a casualty of the effort to mobilize the economy: "The efficient conduct of the war may require the temporary abandonment of some peacetime objectives of government as well as of individual and private enterprise." Specifically, the report indicated that some protective labor statutes and the antitrust laws would have to be suspended or modified in an emergency.

The WRB's October 1939 report all but endorsed the Industrial Mobilization Plan and fully accepted its basic assumptions. The report concluded by recommending that the Army-Navy Munitions Board, in conjunction with industry and other government agencies, continue to plan and work on the yet unresolved issues of industrial mobilization. The WRB members also offered to act in an advisory capacity to the ANMB.[31]

The October report could not have come at a worse time for the War Resources Board. Though war had broken out in Europe, Germany quickly went from Blitzkrieg to Sitzkrieg after routing Poland. American entry was unlikely in the immediate future. Moreover, Congress was in the process of revising the neutrality legislation, and Roosevelt had no intention of strengthening the forces of isolation and peace by moving in a direction that appeared to sanction war. The WRB could have that effect. As if to emphasize the point, Leo M. Cherne published a volume in August 1939, *Adjusting Your Business to War*. In it he authoritatively and extensively analyzed the Industrial Mobilization Plan, other military planning, and the consequences of war for the business community. The Office of the Assistant Secretary of War had assisted Cherne, and Louis A. Johnson wrote a foreword to the volume, appearing to endorse the author's work. Those within and outside government who were opposed to Johnson, the War Resources Board, the Industrial Mobilization Plan, and American entry into the war grabbed at the opportunity to attack their opponents. Roosevelt repeatedly insisted that Cherne's volume did not have the administration's endorsement, all but repudiating Johnson and his cause.[32] When the WRB report finally did reach his hands, the president classified it, thanked board members for their services, and never called on them again.[33]

The War Resources Board episode is richly significant in a number of ways. Despite the outcome, Roosevelt's appointment of the board and its membership signaled that during hostilities the president would embrace a modified version of the World War I model for mobilizing the economy. He was fully aware that an industry-military mobilization team was essential for harnessing the economy for war. The Office of the Assistant Secretary of War suffered only a temporary setback with the rejection of the WRB's recommendations. Mobilizing the economy for World War II proceeded essentially along the lines of the Industrial Mobilization Plan.

The IMP, however, could be implemented only under the unique conditions created by hostilities. World War I and nearly twenty years of interwar study, investigation, and debate had established how intensely controversial economic mobilization for war was. Had the United States entered the war late in 1939 or early in 1940, the history of the WRB might have been very different. Since American entry was delayed for two years, the board, through its extreme rigidity, wrote its own death warrant.

Nonetheless, the WRB's fate was virtually preordained. Hurriedly organized to review nearly twenty years of planning by the OASW, the board had little choice but to approve the IMP—a plan that by 1939 represented economic mobilization orthodoxy. For the WRB to have rejected the IMP would have required the board to set off on a course at odds with the OASW, of which it was an appendage. That placed the War Resources Board in an unenviable position. The WRB could not realistically accept a subordinate role for itself within a Council of National Defense–National Defense Advisory Commission structure, as Roosevelt insisted, without rejecting the administrative centralization that World War I, interwar planning, and what common sense showed to be necessary. The Office of the Assistant Secretary of War was convinced that the Industrial Mobilization Plan only needed exposure to receive acceptance. As late as 1939 the office was advocating that Congress review and pass on its plans to advance their adoption. This insistence was political naivete of the worst sort. The OASW seemed impervious to the opposition to World War I mobilization and interwar planning expressed by the War Policies Commission and the Senate Special Committee Investigating the Munitions Industry. The War Resources Board was doomed to failure because in 1939 political realities took precedence over preparation for war.

Furthermore, the extreme difficulties facing the War Resources Board were worsened by Roosevelt's casual administrative style. With war looming, it was irresponsible to leave the War and Navy Departments under weak leaders and to allow the secretary of war and his assistant to continue their political combat. Working together, Harry H. Woodring and Louis A. Johnson could have improved the WRB's chances by focusing on the political as well as on the economic realities of industrial mobilization. And if the War Department faltered, an ably led Navy Department could have stepped into the breach.

But more was involved than neglect by the president. Roosevelt appeared to be moving in the direction of a war council or cabinet to oversee a war effort.[34] Still feeling his way and unable or unwilling to articulate this larger goal, the president left the WRB uncertain about his intentions, probably contributing to the board's inflexibility.

That said, the principal point about the WRB bears repeating: The failure of the War Resources Board and the Industrial Mobilization Plan in 1939 was political. In terms of the political economy of warfare, the board and the plan anticipated the future by sketching out how the World War II economy would be harnessed. That was the ultimate measure of success.

THE MILITARY'S ECONOMIC PLANNING IN HISTORICAL PERSPECTIVE

The implementation of the War Resources Board's recommendations during World War II serves as the best critique of interwar planning. Through the planning, the military services adjusted their thought and institutions to the nation's economy in order properly to conduct warfare. The realities of America's political economy meant that the armed forces saw the necessity of working closely with an elitist, corporate structure in which the federal government played a critically active role. Years of planning by the Office of the Assistant Secretary of War, guided and facilitated by the industrial-financial community, hence proved to be exceptionally productive.

The interwar critics of economic mobilization hardly fared as well. Though their numbers increased and their insight and anxiety about the consequences of modern warfare deepened—exemplified by the investigations of the House Select Committee on Expenditures in the War Department (1919–1921), the War Policies Commission (1930–1932), and the Senate Special Committee Investigating the Munitions Industry (1934–1936)—they failed to influence policymaking significantly. The nation's leaders continued to ignore the critics' truths, and advocates of preparedness and war devised artful defenses against their arguments.

More clearly than other interwar investigations of war mobilization, the Nye Committee demonstrated that once set in motion, the economic forces of modern warfare tended to take on a life of their own. Primarily, those forces left few institutions unaffected and generated powerful, perhaps even irresistible, pressures to continue expanding the machine of war. Though industrialization and technological development accounted in part for this reality, human decisions were also involved. Social systems do not create or run themselves willy-nilly. Basing its conclusions on a thorough study, the Nye Committee laid out for America what modern war and participation in it could do to the country. Many people listened, and some tried to act, as the neutrality legislation demonstrated; but most found drastic measures to reduce the adverse consequences of economic mobilization for war, or the avoidance of war itself, either too fanciful or too radical to embrace.

Because the war critics' insights were not acted upon, the political economy of World War I determined what would happen in another war. That pattern, according to Nye Committee members and some earlier dissenters, almost ensured the future growth of an "unhealthy alliance," or a military-industrial complex, or a "warfare state." Such a consequence was as much a result of human volition, of decisions made or avoided, as a creation of supposedly uncontrollable forces.

Coming after the Nye Committee investigation, the experience of the War Resources Board signaled that America's political and economic leadership, although not necessarily the public, preferred the proven techniques of the War Industries Board for mobilizing the economy. To do otherwise required examination and perhaps meaningful modification of the entire social system, with its intricate patterns at home and abroad. It was easier, no matter how subtle, evasive, or devious the thought process involved, to conclude that there was only one way to harness the mighty American economy for hostilities, regardless of consequences. Such thinking began with mobilizing the World War I economy and, despite ongoing and sophisticated opposition, continued thereafter.[35] To Senators Gerald P. Nye and Arthur H. Vandenberg, to Stephen Raushenbush and John T. Flynn, that outcome pointed to the breakdown of political leadership. For Nye and those accepting his analysis, America had to do its utmost to stay out of hostilities because fighting another modern war would strengthen unhealthy alliances that could threaten even more warfare. Nonetheless, the "no alternative" argument was the loudest and clearest message of the War Resources Board and the profound and disturbing truths it manifested.

My interpretation can be restated in terms of the four factors shaping the political economy of warfare as a way of concluding the analysis. The modern American elite is based on the operations of a large federal government and a giant corporate structure. With Progressive reforms, a government-business regulatory alliance began emerging to adjust the nation to the demands of a new industrial order. This elitist system was fairly well established before World War I. Nonetheless, it had to be refined and advanced in order to mobilize effectively the economy for hostilities under what ultimately became the War Industries Board. The major obstacle to the successful operation of the WIB was removed when the military services, and particularly the War Department, reformed their supply systems and partially integrated them into the board. That process accelerated a transformation in civil-military relations that had begun with the building of a modern navy in the late nineteenth century.

For the federal government—the second mobilization factor—and the business-industrial community—the first one—the adaptations essential for economic mobilization were fundamentally sound and were improved upon in the interwar years by informal and formal economic planning. However, the armed services—the third mobilization factor—in 1918 were still in the beginning stages of adjusting their thought and institutions to the nation's political economy. The major transition took place in the interwar years with the military's procurement and economic mobilization planning. The planning and its results constituted the most crucial development involving defense and war in the 1920s and 1930s. Through it the army and navy prepared themselves for fulfilling their mission and joined the elite as a secondary power group. Elite power patterns allowed the nation to manage the impact of modern technology on warfare—the fourth mobilization factor—as represented by such weapons innovations as modern ships and aircraft.

The political economy of modern warfare did not evolve in a vacuum. It resulted from the United States achieving Great Power status in a twentieth-century world increasingly shaped by war and revolution. From the Spanish-American War forward, a diverse collection of leaders and people in America opposed the nation's active role in world affairs and the probability of belligerency it involved. Increasingly the opposition to expansion, imperialism, and war was centered in the rural areas of the Midwest, West, and South and was associated with the neo-Jeffersonian dedication to small government and competitive economics. Economic mobilization for World War I introduced a new element in the antiwar, antimilitary, and antielite critique: modern warfare was breaking down the barriers between public and private, civilian and military institutions, thus threatening to create an institutional complex dedicated to war and preparation for it. By creating a big military operating in league with big business and big government, the dissidents insisted, twentieth-century warfare imperiled America's constitutional system with a new form of militarism.

The Senate Special Committee Investigating the Munitions Industry, as a creation of and a catalyst for the national antiwar consensus of the 1930s, explicated most fully and convincingly the dynamics of an emerging warfare complex. Despite this extraordinary achievement, the committee's long-term impact on policy and institutions was slight because the individuals opposing modern warfare and the militarism they believed it bred were battling major historical trends and were isolated from centers of power. (In this sense, the neo-Jeffersonians' crusade against twentieth-century warfare resembled their battles against twentieth-century political economy.) Largely excluded from the elite circles of the federal executive, they were restricted at best to the legislative branch. Here they could make their voices heard, but their effect on policy was minimized by the pluralized and dispersed nature of power in Congress. Perhaps the war critics' status as outsiders was an essential condition for seeing so clearly and speaking so forthrightly about the nature and dangers of the political economy of modern warfare.

EPILOGUE

The 1920s and 1930s are aptly called the interwar years. Yet to an unusual degree the period was shaped by warfare, either its aftermath or its anticipation. World War I as the first total war introduced the concept of industrial mobilization: the need to plan mature industrial economies so as to meet the voracious appetite of unlimited conflict. As a longer, broader war with more advanced technology, World War II made the need for preparation and planning even greater.

Without understanding the general and detailed nature of economic mobilization for World Wars I and II, the dynamics of the interwar years cannot be fully grasped. Knowing the middle requires mastering the ends. Mobilization for World War I, in contrast with that of the Civil War, did not stop when the guns fell still. Although the War Industries Board was quickly disestablished, economic planning began virtually with the end of hostilities both to assess the events that had taken place during the war years and to prepare for a future conflict.

The significance of planning is highlighted by comparing economic mobilization for World War I with that of World War II. In 1915 the United States was unaware of how to harness its economy. It had to go through an awkward period of trial and error, which nearly broke down during winter 1917–1918 and which was incomplete when hostilities ended. By 1939 America knew exactly what to do, as the War Resources Board clearly indicated. Politics and interest-group conflict, however, prevented the nation from acting on its knowledge until war was formally declared.

America did not learn about mobilizing its economy in the interwar years through osmosis. Sustained, often conflicted, effort was involved. Attempts of Republicans in the 1920s and the Franklin D. Roosevelt administration in the 1930s to plan a peacetime economy helped, but they were never enough. Modern warfare had elevated the importance of the military in America. Ironically, to fulfill effectively its transformed status, the War Department had to surrender its traditional role of principal economic mobilization agency. Civilian agencies such as the War Industries Board had to assume that function. Otherwise, the army could again obstruct a planned wartime economy as it had during World War I. Through interwar planning, the War Department learned fully why it had to subordinate its supply activities to the authority of civilian administrations and what the role of the armed services would be in a mobilized economy. Those achievements, which were as important as they were difficult, were documented by the plans of the Office of the Assistant Secretary of War. The Industrial Mobilization Plans called for broad-based civilian agencies to mobilize the massive American economy for total war. The armed services would integrate their supply systems into those structures. This solution was both practical and consistent with the nation's ideology and political economy.

Scholars obviously have missed major developments of the interwar years; otherwise, they would not look upon the army's economic planning as an obscure aspect of administrative history. Nor would they ignore, distort, or trivialize the House Select Committee on Expenditures in the War Department, the War Policies Commission, and the Senate Special Committee Investigating the Munitions Industry.

When examined closely, the interwar years provide as much insight into World Wars I and II as those cataclysms reveal about the 1920s and 1930s. Congressional and other interwar investigations cumulatively explained and documented the events that took place in mobilizing the economy for World War I. The Nye Committee went further, warning that modern warfare held grave risks for America's future. The nation did not stumble blindly into the snare of a military-industrial complex during World War II and the Cold War. It went forward with eyes wide open.

In a sense, the interwar years ended an era in the political economy of American warfare. Henceforth, a giant military would become a permanent fixture of American life. The voice of agrarian neo-Jeffersonians would also grow increasingly faint as rural America declined in numbers and changed in nature. Neo-Jeffersonians had been the principal and persistent critics of mobilization policies from 1916 through 1939. In that role, they played a major part in educating the American public about the economics of modern warfare. Congressional critics of World War II mobilization would abound, but they were significantly different from their World War I and interwar counterparts. Basically accepting elitist patterns for harnessing the economy, they aimed at making mobilization less abusive and more efficient, representative, and equitable.

Not until the 1960s would war and its consequences again be subject to the withering onslaught seen in the interwar years. The latter-day critics had an advantage over their predecessors, however. They faced a full-blown military-industrial complex. Senator Gerald P. Nye and those who preceded him had to theorize from limited evidence about what such a complex would be. That insight makes the accomplishment of the neo-Jeffersonians and their allies all the greater, even though their critique failed.

NOTES

CHAPTER ONE. PROCUREMENT PLANNING

1. *U. S. Statutes at Large* 41 (1921), Part 1, pp. 757–812, sec. 5, pp. 762–65. Numerous secondary works treat with the National Defense Act of 1920 in general. A good overall discussion, including the citations of relevant primary and secondary sources, is found in Russell F. Weigley, *History of the United States Army* (New York: Macmillan, 1967), pp. 393–405. I. B. Holley, Jr., *General John M. Palmer, Citizen Soldier, and the Army of a Democracy* (Westport, CT: Greenwood, 1982), pp. 402–79, adds some new and insightful information on the legislation.

2. A precedent for the council existed with the creation of a War Council during the winter crisis of 1917–1918. Although sources on the War Council in the interwar years are somewhat contradictory, the preponderance of evidence indicates that the agency seldom met and quite quickly became all but defunct. For a positive, but unconvincing, view of the council, see address, Assistant Secretary of War F. H. Payne to Army War College (AWC), 10/29/32, file 394-A-3, G-4, no. 3, Army War College Collection, Carlisle Barracks, PA (hereafter cited as AWC). A negative, and more convincing, view is found in James E. Hewes, Jr., *From Root to McNamara: Army Organization and Administration, 1900–1963* (Washington, DC: Center of Military History, 1975), p. 54, and Harold W. Thatcher, *Planning for Industrial Mobilization, 1920–1940* (Washington, DC: Office of the Quartermaster General, 1943), p. 65, n. 20.

3. See Paul A. C. Koistinen, *Mobilizing for Modern War: The Political Economy of American Warfare, 1865–1919* (Lawrence: University Press of Kansas, 1997), chaps. 9 and 10. See also Troyer S. Anderson, "Introduction to the History of the Under Secretary of War's Office" (ms., 1947, Center of Military History, Washington, DC), chap. 2, pp. 15–27.

4. General Charles McK. Saltzman, "Reminiscences of the Battle of Washington," 11/26/35, file 020/2/113.7, Planning Branch (PB), Assistant Secretary of War (ASW), Office of the Secretary of War (OSW) RG 107, National Archives, Washington, DC (hereafter cited as PB, ASW, OSW); Benedict Crowell, "Procurement in War," 12/10/26, file 335 A-4, AWC; Burr to Chief of Staff, 12/11/19, and other correspondence and documents, file, "Organizational Papers from Col. Fair's File," Box 508, Records of the War Department General and Special Staffs, General Staff–Purchase, Storage, and Traffic Division, RG 165, National Archives, Washington, DC;

and Benedict Crowell and Robert F. Wilson, *How America Went to War*, 6 vols. (New Haven: Yale University Press, 1921), 4, *The Armies of Industry: 1*, pp. 8–19.

5. The analysis of the National Defense Act, 1920 is based on "Reorganization of the Army," Senate, *Hearings Before the Subcommittee of the Committee on Military Affairs*, 66th Cong., 2d sess., 1919, vol. 1, pp. 78–84, 215–27, 238–52, 333, 344, 370–73, 394–408, 432–41, 549–53, 634–63, 685–705, 792–93, 826–27, 1025–41, vol. 2, pp. 1133–72, 1234–53, 1374–79, 1394–1415, 1421–23, 1571–1704, 1705–53, 1760–77; "Army Reorganization," House, *Hearings Before the Committee on Military Affairs*, 66th Cong., 1st sess., 1919–1920, vol. 1, pp. 4–5, 41–43, 64–75, 85–87, 142–49, 269–71, 282–83, 309, 324–27, 337–38, 377–78, 441–62, 463–87, 490–537, 557–61, 565, 647–79, 768–71, 789–97, 802, 814–15, 841–42, 899, 925–27, 992–95, 1048–1103, 1116–31, 1180, 1203–6, 1269, 1410–13, 1435–1568, 1772–79, vol. 2, pp. 1801–35, 2105–19; E. O. Saunders, "National Defense Act—Legislative History of Industrial Mobilization Clauses," 10/11/23, file 628, and A. H. Moran, "Legislative History of the General Staff Corps and the Assistant Secretary of War," 2/14/28, and other documents, file 46, PB, ASW, OSW; "Reorganization of the Army," Senate, *Report of the Committee on Military Affairs*, Rept. no. 400, 66th Cong., 2d Sess., 1920; "National Defense Act," House, *Report of the Committee on Military Affairs*, Rept. no. 680, 66th Cong., 2d sess., 1920; "To Amend the National Defense Act," House, *Report of the Committee on Military Affairs*, Rept. no. 1000, 66th Cong., 2d sess., 1920; Frank Scott to Ralph Dravo, 4/19/26, and other documents, file "War Department-Army Industrial College, 1924–1928," Frank A. Scott Papers, Princeton University, Princeton, NJ (hereafter cited as Scott Papers); Assistant Secretary of War to Secretary of War, 12/25/25, and numerous other documents, file 627, PB, ASW, OSW; Anderson, "Under Secretary of War's Office," chap. 3; Marvin A. Kreidberg and Merton G. Henry, *History of Military Mobilization in the United States Army, 1775–1945* (Washington, DC: Department of the Army, 1955), pp. 377–81, 493–96; Weigley, *United States Army*, pp. 395–400; Hewes, *Root to McNamara*, pp. 50–56; and Thatcher, *Planning*, pp. 4–12. Many parts of this complex statute and its tangled legislative history remain obscure. No thorough, scholarly work has yet clarified exactly how, when, and why various key portions of the bill were put together. This is especially true involving the portions that relate to supply and economic mobilization for war.

6. From 1925 through 1929, the Office of the Assistant Secretary of War (OASW) expended considerable time and energy attempting to increase the assistant secretary's authority. Some members of the OASW staff as well as several bureau chiefs favored an outright proposal for statutory authority enabling the assistant secretary of war to meet his responsibilities. Though supportive of such efforts, various assistant secretaries and some secretaries of war preferred to move cautiously and indirectly, basing arguments for augmented authority on military preparedness instead of on the need for harnessing the bureaus or matching the power of the General Staff. A quiet drive for strengthening the assistant secretary's office occurred between 1927 and 1928 after Dwight F. Davis, who had been assistant secretary of war from 1923 to 1925, became secretary of war in 1925. Various proposals of the secretary and assistant secretary of war make little sense unless they are understood to be virtually cryptograms seeking more power for the assistant secretary. See Assistant Secretary to Secretary of War, 12/25/25, and numerous other documents, file 627; and Lt. Col. James D. Fife

to Planning Branch, 9/13/28, and other documents, file 46, PB, ASW, OSW; War Department, *Report of the Secretary of War to the President*, 1927 (Washington, DC, 1927), p. 38 (hereafter cited as *Annual Report of the Secretary of War [ARSW]*); *ARSW*, 1928, pp. 17–18, 45, 49–51, 58; *ARSW*, 1929, p. 71; and Thatcher, *Planning*, pp. 4–12. A study of the OASW by outside management consultants completed in late 1941 recommended many of the same reforms favored by the OASW and some bureaus in the 1920s.

7. Crowell resigned in July 1920. William R. Williams replaced him and served until March 1921, but his was clearly an interim appointment. See *ARSW*, 1921, p. 119.

8. Major Gilbert Wilkes to Chief, Planning Branch, 3/29/28, and other correspondence, file 46; Saunders, "National Defense Act," file 628; and Lt. Col. Earl McFarland, "Organization of the Office of the Assistant Secretary of War," 11/21/34, and other documents, file 020.2/113.11, PB, ASW, OSW; Col. C. T. Harris, "Orientation Conference no. 14," 12/4/34, file 337/203.3-5.3, Records of the Joint Army and Navy Boards and Committees, RG 225, National Archives, Washington, DC (hereafter cited as ANMB); Appendix 1, "Preliminary Inventory and List of File Headings, Planning Branch, Office of the Assistant Secretary of War, 1921–41," Textual Reference Branch, National Archives, Washington DC; John D. Millett, *The Organization and Role of the Army Service Forces* (Washington, DC: Office of the Chief of Military History, 1954), pp. 11–18; Kreidberg and Henry, *History of Military Mobilization*, pp. 493–96; and Thatcher, *Planning*, pp. 4–12.

9. Thatcher, *Planning*, pp. 13–18; Saltzman, "Reminiscences of the Battle of Washington," file 020/2/113.1, PB, ASW, OSW; Wadsworth to Baruch, 2/1/23, with enc. and numerous other correspondence in 1923, Selected Correspondence, Bernard M. Baruch Papers, Princeton University, Princeton, NJ (hereafter cited as Baruch Papers); *ARSW*, 1927, p. 39; and Hewes, *Root to McNamara*, p. 62.

10. For this theme, see Koistinen, *Mobilizing for Modern War*, chap. 3.

11. Additional information on specific vis-à-vis general mobilization plans follows.

12. General Pershing to Secretary of Navy, 6/27/22, and other documents, file 370.26/200-18.00 (1925–1931); "Accomplishments of the Army and Navy Munitions Board," 11/21/41, and numerous other documents, file 370.26/200-18.00 (1932–1942); "Chronological Digest of the Activities of the Army and Navy Munitions Board," 11/8/26, and other documents, file 370.26/200.18 (1925–1931); file 370.26/200.18 and file 370.26/200.18, ANMB Activities, 1940–1943; Harris, "Orientation Conference for . . . Reserve Officers," 11/6/34, file 370.26/213, all in ANMB; Lt. Bullock to Assistant Secretary of War, 12/8/31, file 359, Box 36, PB, ASW, OSW; Appendix 1, "Preliminary Inventory, PB, ASW," National Archives; Robert H. Connery, *The Navy and Industrial Mobilization in World War II* (Princeton, NJ: Princeton University Press, 1951), pp. 31–53; and Weigley, *United States Army*, pp. 405–6.

13. See n. 12 and also Thatcher, *Planning*, pp. 44–52. The ANMB from 1939 into 1942 is covered in the forthcoming volume 4 of this series.

14. Thatcher, *Planning*, pp. 23–42; Terrence J. Gough, "Origins of the Army Industrial College—Military-Business Tensions After World War I," *Armed Forces and Society* 17 (Winter 1991): 259–75; Thomas M. Pitkin and Herbert R. Rifkind, *Procurement Planning in the Quartermaster Corps, 1920–1940* (Washington, DC: Office

of the Quartermaster General, 1943), pp. 26–27; M. L. Brett to Newton D. Baker, 4/10/24, and other documents, file, "War Department, Army Industrial College," Scott Papers; and *ARSW,* 1930, pp. 41–42. See also the appropriate sections of the *ARSW,* 1924–1929, 1931–1941. Peter M. Abramo, "The Economic and Military Potential of the United States: Industrial Mobilization Planning, 1919–1945" (Ph.D. diss., Temple University, 1995), pp. 32–55, provides good information on the founding of the AIC and the office's use of Harvard University and other civilian institutions for training its officers.

15. See n. 14 and also Pitkin and Rifkind, *Quartermaster Corps,* pp. 26–28, and Appendix 1, "Preliminary Inventory, PB, ASW," National Archives.

16. The War Policies Commission is analyzed in chapter 13.

17. The appointment, service, and departure of the secretaries and assistant secretaries of war in the 1920s and 1930s are readily traceable in the *ARSW,* 1920–1941. See also Davis, "Preparations for Procurement," 1/22/25, file 1241, PB, ASW, OSW; Davis, "Procurement," 2/11/24, file 276 A-12, AWC; Baruch to Davis, 3/6/23, and numerous other documents, file 140, PB, ASW, OSW; Keith D. McFarland, *Harry K. Woodring: A Political Biography of FDR's Controversial Secretary of War* (Lawrence: University Press of Kansas, 1975), pp. 140–225; Hewes, *Root to McNamara,* p. 54; and Kreidberg and Henry, *History of Military Mobilization,* pp. 711–15.

18. For a reasonably clear statement of this, see Assistant Secretary of War Davis to General Pershing 6/4/24, file 140, PB, ASW, OSW.

19. This theme is subsequently explored.

20. Kreidberg and Henry, *History of Military Mobilization,* pp. 402–3 (the quotation actually refers to the 1923 plan, which was the prototype for the 1924 plan; see also pp. 377–410); Army War College, "Report of Committee no. 1, The Office of the Assistant Secretary of War," 2/4/25, "Report of Committee no. 2, Analysis of Supply Rates of Six Army Plan," 2/4/25, and "Report of Committee no. 3, General Mobilization Plan," 2/6/25, AWC Unit 8, Box 3, Special Memoranda, Baruch Papers; and J. M. Wainwright, "Mass Procurement," 1/20/23, file 253-18, AWC.

21. General C. L'H. Ruggles, "Industrial Preparedness," 11/18/26, file 345-2, AWC; James A. Huston, *The Sinews of War: Army Logistics, 1775–1953* (Washington, DC: Office of the Chief of Military History, 1966), pp. 406–7; Kreidberg and Henry, *History of Military Mobilization,* p. 387; and Edward S. Miller, *War Plan Orange: The Strategy to Defeat Japan, 1897–1945* (Annapolis, MD: Naval Institute Press, 1991); see also n. 12.

22. *ARSW,* 1928, pp. 50–51; OASW, "Notes on Industrial Mobilization," 11/19/29, AWC, Unit 8, Box 3, Special Memoranda, Baruch Papers (this document, and its various revisions, is one of the best sources on procurement planning); Col. Harley B. Ferguson, "The Present Status of Plans for Industrial Preparation for War," 12/15/27, file 345-A-7, and Col. W. P. Wooten, "The Present Status of Plan for Industrial Preparation for War," 11/7/28, file 353-A-8, G-4, no. 8, AWC.

23. See n. 22 and Ferguson, "Industrial Mobilization," 5/26/22, file 215-114, 228-50; Assistant Secretary of War F. H. Payne, "Mobilization of Industry," 10/29/32, and Wainwright, "Mass Procurement," 1/20/23, AWC; Wainwright to Franklin D. Roosevelt, 8/29/40, with attached "Final Report of the Assistant Secretary of War," 3/2/23, PPF 1678, Franklin D. Roosevelt Papers, Franklin D. Roosevelt Library, Hyde Park, NY (hereafter cited as FDR Papers); *ARSW,* 1936,

pp. 20–22; *ARSW,* 1937, pp. 23–24; *ARSW,* 1938, pp. 20–22; *ARSW,* 1939, pp. 18–19; *ARSW,* 1940, pp. 4–7; and R. Elberton Smith, *The Army and Economic Mobilization* (Washington, D.C: Office of the Chief of Military History, 1959), pp. 35–97 (this is the one best secondary source on procurement planning). The paragraph describes and analyzes the planning process when it was mature around 1929, not when it was being worked out in the preceding years.

24. Wainwright to Roosevelt with attachment, 8/29/40, PPF 1678, FDR Papers; Wainwright, "Mass Procurement," 1/20/23, AWC; and *ARSW,* 1936, p. 21.

25. Ruggles, "Industrial Preparedness," 11/18/26, file 345-2; Wainwright, "Mass Procurement," 1/20/23; Dwight F. Davis, "Procurement," 2/11/24, file 276-A-12; and Army War College, "Report of Committee no. 2, Industrial Preparedness in the United States," 12/21/26, file 335-1, AWC; *ARSW,* 1922, pp. 249–50; Smith, *Army and Economic Mobilization,* pp. 54–55, 91; Pitkin and Rifkind, *Quartermaster Corps,* pp. 24–25, 43–58; Erna Risch, *The Quartermaster Corps: Organization, Supply, and Services,* 2 vols. (Washington, DC: Office of the Chief of Military History, 1953), 1: 246–52; Constance M. Green, Harry C. Thomson, and Peter C. Roots, *The Ordnance Department: Planning Munitions for War* (Washington, DC: Office of the Chief of Military History, 1955), pp. 26–27; Irving B. Holley, Jr., *Buying Aircraft: Materiel Procurement for the Army Air Forces* (Washington, DC: Office of the Chief of Military History, 1964), pp. 153–56; Dulany Terrett, *The Signal Corps: The Emergency* (Washington, DC: Office of the Chief of Military History, 1956), pp. 60–69; Blanche D. Coll, Jean E. Keith, and Herbert H. Rosenthal, *The Corps of Engineers: Troops and Equipment* (Washington, DC: Office of the Chief of Military History, 1958), pp. 5, 234; Leo P. Brophy and George J. B. Fisher, *The Chemical Warfare Service: Organizing for War* (Washington, DC: Office of the Chief of Military History, 1959), pp. 39–43.

Numerous documents in the eight boxes of the Scott Papers present excellent detailed and general material involving the operations of the Ordnance Department Procurement Districts. Of special importance in this regard are the Army Ordnance Association files, 1920–1931, Box 4. See also "Industrial Preparedness Dinner," 2/5/24, file 1206, PB, ASW, OSW. The Army Ordnance Association (AOA) was virtually an extension of the Ordnance Department and was closely tied into the operations of the Ordnance Procurement Districts.

26. See n. 25.

27. Pitkin and Rifkind, *Quartermaster Corps,* pp. 71–72; Smith, *Army and Economic Mobilization,* pp. 56–57; and Holley, *Buying Aircraft,* pp. 152–53.

28. See n. 22 and also *ARSW,* 1925, pp. 26–29; *ARSW,* 1927, p. 31; *ARSW,* 1928, pp. 16–18, pp. 51–52; *ARSW,* 1929, p. 68; *ARSW,* 1930, p. 37; *ARSW,* 1937, pp. 22–23; and Pitkin and Rifkind, *Quartermaster Corps,* pp. 63–74.

29. Smith, *Army and Economic Mobilization,* pp. 57–59.

30. See n. 22 and also Ruggles, "Industrial Preparedness," 11/18/26, file 345-2, AWC, and Holley, *Buying Aircraft,* p. 152.

31. *ARSW,* 1935, p. 35; *ARSW,* 1941, pp. 26–33; Smith, *Army and Economic Mobilization,* pp. 70–72; and Harry C. Thomson and Lida Mayo, *The Ordnance Department: Procurement and Supply* (Washington, DC: Office of the Chief of Military History, 1960), pp. 16–17.

32. OASW, "Notes on Industrial Mobilization," 11/19/29, AWC, Unit 8, Box

3, Special Memoranda, Baruch Papers, and Smith, *Army and Economic Mobilization*, p. 86. Another term used interchangeably with "secondary requirements" was "contributory requirements."

33. For these World War I developments, see Koistinen, *Mobilizing for Modern War*, chaps. 7–10.

34. The paragraphs on commodity committees are based on Major Rogers, "Orientation Conference on the Commodities Division," 11/3/36, file 381.3/129; Lt. Col. C. T. Harris, "Notes on Commodity Committee Operation and Control in War," 7/27/33, and numerous other documents, file 145; Colonel Elgin to Chief of Engineers, 7/9/37, file 400/129.21; General Williams to Assistant Secretary of War, 5/10/29, file 420.1/129.5 (1929–1930); Memorandum, Commodities Division, ANMB, 1/7/39, file 470.1/129.5 (1938–1940); Secretary of War to Charles R. Hook, 9/22/38, file 334.8/246.2; Assistant Secretary of War Davis to General Pershing, 6/4/24, file 140; Colonel Ferguson to Chairmen, War Department Commodity Committees, 12/8/24, file 203; "Report of Meeting of Commodity Committee no. 19," 10/31/33, file 20; Memorandum, "The Nickel Situation," 3/12/29, Commodity Committee no. 198, Ferro-Alloys, Nickel, file 213; Major Nickerson to Major Hobley, 12/31/31, Commodity Committee no. 19, Ferro-Alloys, Tungsten, file 216; MacNider to Chiefs, All Supply Branches, 10/20/27, file 265; numerous pieces of correspondence in Commodity Committee no. 34, Non-Ferrous Metals-Aluminum, file 268; Roy Veatch to Secretary of War, 7/23/34, and other documents, file 289; "Report of Plans for the Procurement of Strategic Raw Materials and Duties and Functions of War Department Commodity Committees," 9/25/25, file 291; Major McCain to Chief, Planning Branch, 12/30/24, file Commodity Committee no. 45, Steel and Iron, 1921–1926; Major Nix, "Work of the War Department Commodity Committee no. 45, Iron and Steel," 5/7/28, file Commodity Committee no. 45, Steel and Iron, 1927–1928; numerous pieces of correspondence in Commodity Committee no. 43, Shellac, files 345 and 346; and "Proposed Plan for Procurement of Wire and Wire Products," 12/12/31, file 357, all in PB, ASW, OSW; Major Crom, "Orientation Conference on Commodities Division," 10/16/34, file 337; Chief of Naval Operations Memo., 9/28/36, and other documents, file 370.261/200.18.0 (5); and ANMB, "Minutes of Meeting of . . . Commodity Committee Representatives," 9/5/39, file 337 (1922–1940), ANMB; *ARSW*, 1937, p. 24; *ARSW*, 1938, pp. 42–43; *ARSW*, 1939, pp. 18–19; *ARSW*, 1941, pp. 22–23; Appendix 1, "Preliminary Inventory, PB, ASW," National Archives; OASW, "Notes on Industrial Mobilization," 11/19/29, AWC, Unit 8, Box 3, Special Memoranda, Baruch Papers; Smith, *Army and Economic Mobilization*, pp. 86–93; and Pitkin and Rifkind, *Quartermaster Corps*, pp. 30–33.

35. At first the OASW intended that the bureau of greatest wartime use would write the plan, but that idea was eventually scrapped.

36. This subject will be taken up in the forthcoming volume 4 of this series.

37. Direct quotation from Major Rogers, "Orientation Conference on Commodities Division," 11/3/36, file 381.3/129, PB, ASW, OSW.

38. The material on commodity committees and their operation in both primary and secondary sources is obscure, fragmentary, and contradictory. A great deal of research in numerous scattered documents is essential to discern commodity committee policy and practice.

39. For more information and substantiation on this topic, see chapter 3. For an excellent early statement about the army's interaction with business and its recognition of dependence on civilians see *ARSW,* pp. 1922, 280–81. See also *ARSW,* 1930, pp. 37–39.

40. These themes are treated more fully in chapters 4–11.

41. This topic is treated more extensively in chapter 2. Introduction to the subject is available in Harris, "Minutes of Meeting of Orientation Conference . . . Planning Branch," 12/4/34, file 337/203.3-5.3, ANMB; OASW, "Notes on Industrial Mobilization," 11/19/29, AWC, Unit 8, Box 3, Special Memoranda, Baruch Papers; *ARSW,* 1927, pp. 32–33; *ARSW,* 1928, p. 53; *ARSW,* 1929, pp. 69–70; *ARSW,* 1930, p. 38; *ARSW,* 1940, pp. 6–7; and Smith, *Army and Economic Mobilization,* pp. 94–97.

42. OASW, "Notes on Industrial Mobilization," 11/19/29, AWC, Unit 8, Box 3, Special Memoranda, Baruch Papers; Pitkin and Rifkind, *Quartermaster Corps,* pp. 75–77; Smith, *Army and Economic Mobilization,* pp. 75–77; and Risch, *Quartermaster Corps,* 1: 56–57.

43. OASW, "Notes on Industrial Mobilization," 11/19/29, AWC, Unit 8, Box 3, Special Memoranda, Baruch Papers; Pitkin and Rifkind, *Quartermaster Corps,* p. 62; Smith, *Army and Economic Mobilization,* pp. 48–50, 65–67; and Risch, *Quartermaster Corps,* 1: 56.

44. See n. 43 and Risch, *Quartermaster Corps,* 1: 56; *ARSW,* 1928, pp. 53–54; *ARSW,* 1929, p. 70; *ARSW,* 1930, pp. 36–37; *ARSW,* 1937, p. 23; and *ARSW,* 1939, pp. 18–19.

45. OASW, "Notes on Industrial Mobilization," 11/19/29, AWC, Unit 8, Box 3, Special Memoranda, Baruch Papers; *ARSW,* 1932, pp. 34–36; and Smith, *Army and Economic Mobilization,* p. 66.

46. The limited nature of procurement planning could be consequential. For some examples, see National Lumber Association to Secretary of War, 5/31/40, file 334.8/246.2, PB, ASW, OSW; Colonel Hines to Pogue, 12/13/40, and numerous other documents, file 470.1/203.2-16.1, ANMB; and *ARSW,* 1929, p. 70. (Civilian mobilization agencies and economic controls are analyzed in chapter 2.)

The Industrial Mobilization Plans, 1930, 1933, 1936, and 1939, had sections that describe and analyze procurement planning. They also demonstrate the progress of the OASW and the SA&S. See the published versions of the 1930 and 1933 plans, "Message from the President . . . Transmitting Report of the War Policies Commission," H. Doc. 163, 72d Cong., 1st sess., 1931 [Hearings], pp. 408–9, 423–27, and *Industrial Mobilization Plan, Revised 1933,* Senate Committee Print no. 2, 74th Cong., 1st sess., 1935, pp. 1–9 [Special Senate Committee Investigating the Munitions Industry]. The 1936 plan is unpublished. See "Industrial Mobilization Plan of 1936," file 120, pp. 8–14, PB, ASW, OSW. For the published 1939 plan, see "Industrial Mobilization Plan Revision of 1939," Senate, *Hearings Before the Special Committee Investigating the National Defense Program,* 80th Cong., 1st sess., 1948, Part 42, pp. 25981–84. For another published version of the IMP, 1939, see chap. 2, n. 98.

47. Wainwright to Roosevelt, 8/29/40, with attachment, PPF 1678, FDR Papers.

48. *ARSW,* 1922, p. 100; *ARSW,* 1928, pp. 16–17; *ARSW,* 1936, p. 24; *ARSW,* 1937, p. 25; and *ARSW,* 1941, p. 28. See also Harris, "Orientation Conference for . . . Reserve Officers," 11/16/34, file 370.26/213, ANMB.

49. *ARSW,* 1927, pp. 25-29, 33; *ARSW,* 1928, pp. 45, 54; *ARSW,* 1929, p. 31; and *ARSW,* 1930, p. 40.

50. *ARSW,* 1921, pp. 131-244; *ARSW,* 1922, pp. 237-312; Green, Thomson, and Roots, *Ordnance Department,* pp. 32-40; Risch, *Quartermaster Corps,* 1: 3-11; Terrett, *Signal Corps,* pp. 70-71; Holley, *Buying Aircraft,* pp. 84-149; Coll, Keith, and Rosenthal, *Corps of Engineers,* pp. 8-12; Brophy and Fisher, *Chemical Warfare Service,* pp. 3-48; Clarence McK. Smith, *The Medical Department: Hospitalization and Evacuation, Zone of Interior* (Washington, DC: Office of the Chief of Military History, 1956), pp. 8-12; Millett, *Army Service Forces,* pp. 11-42; Hewes, *Root to McNamara,* pp. 50-56; and Pitkin and Rifkind, *Quartermaster Corps;* see also n. 25.

51. Smith, *Army and Economic Mobilization,* pp. 121-26, 215-19; Risch, *Quartermaster Corps,* 1: 244-46; *ARSW,* 1939, pp. 15-17; *ARSW,* 1940, pp. 1-3, 7-8; and *ARSW,* 1941, pp. 21-77.

52. *ARSW,* 1934, pp. 28-31; *ARSW,* 1935, pp. 33-40; *ARSW,* 1936, pp. 19-20; *ARSW,* 1940, pp. 7-10; and *ARSW,* 1941, pp. 43-46.

53. Sources on current procurement are especially difficult to locate. The best sources are the *ARSW,* 1920-1941, and especially, *ARSW,* 1921, pp. 11-12; *ARSW,* 1922, pp. 99-100; *ARSW,* 1927, pp. 25-29; *ARSW,* 1928, pp. 45-49; *ARSW,* 1929, pp. 31-35; *ARSW,* 1930, pp. 35-36; *ARSW,* 1931, pp. 22-24; *ARSW,* 1932, pp. 31-32; *ARSW,* 1934, pp. 28-31; *ARSW,* 1936, pp. 24-26; *ARSW,* 1937, pp. 25-27; *ARSW,* 1938, pp. 25-27; *ARSW,* 1939, pp. 15-21; *ARSW,* 1940, pp. 1-10; and *ARSW,* 1941, pp. 21-46. See also "Annual Report of the Executive Committee of the Army and Navy Munitions Board," May 1937, contained in small gray box; and Colonel Hines to Joseph Pogue, 12/13/40, file 470.1/203.2-16/1, and other documents, ANMB; AWC, "Economic and Industrial Support of War," 12/5/38, file A-1939-3 A and B, G4, no. 16, 1939, AWC; Pitkin and Rifkind, *Quartermaster Corps,* p. 4; Risch, *Quartermaster Corps,* 1: 244-46, 262; Holley, *Buying Aircraft,* p. 94; and Smith, *Army and Economic Mobilization,* pp. 45, 215-19, 230-32.

54. Thatcher, *Planning,* pp. 66-67, and Pitkin and Rifkind, *Quartermaster Corps,* pp. 57-58.

55. Pitkin and Rifkind, *Quartermaster Corps,* pp. 57-58, and Smith, *Army and Economic Mobilization,* pp. 81-86, 106-9.

56. Green, Thomson, and Roots, *Ordnance Department,* pp. 57-59; Thomson and Mayo, *Ordnance Department,* pp. 9-23; Levin H. Campbell, Jr., *The Industry-Ordnance Team* (New York: McGraw-Hill, 1946), pp. 10-23; and Chester Mueller, *The New York Ordnance District* (New York: New York Post, Army Ordnance Association, 1947), pp. 6-18.

57. Terrett, *Signal Corps,* pp. 68-69.

58. Risch, *Quartermaster Corps,* 1: 6-7, 246-52, 323-29.

59. Holley, *Buying Aircraft,* pp. 94-112, 146-68, 205-8.

60. Coll, Keith, and Rosenthal, *Corps of Engineers,* pp. 88-102; Lenore Fine and Jesse A. Remington, *The Corps of Engineers: Construction in the United States* (Washington, DC: Office of the Chief of Military History, 1972), pp. 69-74; Brophy and Fisher, *Chemical Warfare Service,* pp. 30-39; Brooks E. Kleber and Dale Birdsell, *The Chemical Warfare Service: Chemicals in Combat* (Washington, DC: Office of the Chief of Military History, 1966), pp. 24-32; Smith, *Medical Department,* pp. 6-7. The

Finance Department and the Chief of Chaplains are not being analyzed along with the other bureaus because they had no direct impact upon supply operations.

61. The analysis of the Ordnance Department is based on Saltzman, "Reminiscences of the Battle of Washington," 11/26/35, file 020/2/113.1; General Williams endorsement, 5/10/29, file 470.1/129.5, Commodity Committee on Iron and Steel, 1929–1930; and Chief of Ordnance to Colonel Jordan, 4/5/35, file 334.8/129.33, PB, ASW, OSW; *ARSW,* 1920, pp. 44–46; *ARSW,* 1921, pp. 157–72; *ARSW,* 1922, pp. 249–56; Anderson, "Under Secretary of War's Office," chap. 3, pp. 30–32; Thatcher, *Planning,* pp. 15–16; Green, Thomson, and Roots, *Ordnance Department,* pp. 27, 52–59; Thomson and Mayo, *Ordnance Department,* pp. 5–6, 9–23; Mueller, *New York Ordnance District,* pp. 3–18; Campbell, *Industry-Ordnance Team,* pp. 1–33; Pitkin and Rifkind, *Quartermaster Corps,* p. 72, n. 48; and Millett, *Army Service Forces,* pp. 11–13.

62. Saltzman, "Reminiscences of the Battle of Washington," 11/26/35, file 020/2/113.1, PB, ASW, OSW; Anderson, "Under Secretary of War's Office," chapter 3, pp. 3–7; *ARSW,* 1920, pp. 47–48; *ARSW,* 1921, pp. 173–78; *ARSW,* 1922, pp. 257–60; and Terrett, Signal Corps, pp. 11, 58–69.

63. The analysis of the Quartermaster Corps is based on Ferguson to Quartermaster General, 6/19/25, and other documents, file 222; Colonel Fife to Quartermaster General, 6/2/25. and other documents, file 291; Assistant Secretary of War to Bonner, 7/17/23, and other documents, file Commodity Committee no. 45, Steel and Iron, 1921–1926; Major Nix memorandum, "Work of the War Department Commodity Committee no. 45, Iron and Steel," 5/17/28, file Commodity Committee no. 45, Steel and Iron, 1927–1928; and "Proposed Plan for the Procurement of Wire Products," file 357, PB, ASW, OSW; *ARSW,* 1920, pp. 32–44; *ARSW,* 1921, pp. 131–56; *ARSW,* 1922, pp. 237–47; Risch, *Quartermaster Corps,* 1: 5–7, 56–57, 208–12, 243–52, 323–29; and Pitkin and Rifkind, *Quartermaster Corps.* See also Erna Risch, *Quartermaster Support of the Army: A History of the Corps, 1775–1939* (Washington, DC: Office of the Quartermaster General, 1962), chap. 16.

64. The analysis of the Air Corps is based on "Army Reorganization," House, *Hearings Before the Committee on Military Affairs,* 1919–1920, 1: pp. 899, 925–27; *ARSW,* 1921, pp. 183–94; *ARSW,* 1922, pp. 261–69; *ARSW,* 1924, pp. 23–25; *ARSW,* 1925, pp. 24–25; *ARSW,* 1927, pp. 41–50; *ARSW,* 1928, pp. 67–75; *ARSW,* 1929, pp. 87–99; *ARSW,* 1930, pp. 57–71; *ARSW,* 1931, pp. 29–36; *ARSW,* 1932, pp. 39–51; Holley, *Buying Aircraft,* pp. 6–329; Terrett, *Signal Corps,* pp. 61–62; Edwin H. Rutkowski, *The Politics of Military Aviation Procurement, 1926–1934* (Columbus: Ohio State University Press, 1966); and Jacob Vander Meulen, *The Politics of Aircraft: Building an American Military Industry* (Lawrence: University Press of Kansas, 1991). The air wing of the army was under the Signal Corps during World War I, achieved independent status as the Air Service with the National Defense Act of 1920, and was further elevated to the Air Corps by legislation in 1926 that also created the position of Assistant Secretary of War for Air, a post that was eliminated in 1933 for purposes of economy. To avoid confusion, Air Corps will be used in the discussion.

65. Ferguson received the usual praise for his stewardship from 1921 to 1927. Nonetheless, his leadership seems indifferent at best. He appeared slow in taking hold, exceptionally deferential to the bureaus, and phlegmatic in grasping and implement-

ing the enormity and importance of the responsibilities he directed. For some sense of Ferguson as a person and for comments on his leadership, see Ferguson, "Industrial Mobilization," 5/26/22, file 215-114, 228-50; Ferguson, "The Present Status of Plans of Industrial Mobilization for War," 12/14/27, file 345-A-7; and Baruch, "The War Industries Board," file 313 A-6, AWC; Gen. Palmer E. Pierce to Frank Scott, 1/26/22, and numerous other correspondence, file, "War Department Preparedness Program, 1921–1928, File Folder 1 to 1923"; and Scott to Dravo, 4/19/26, and other documents, file, "War Department, Army Industrial College," Scott Papers; and *ARSW,* 1927, p. 39.

66. See n. 60 and *ARSW,* 1920, pp. 39–44, 46, 52–53; *ARSW,* 1921, pp. 219–26; and *ARSW,* 1922, pp. 277–90. All bureaus, except the Coast Artillery, have volumes that have been cited and at least touch upon procurement planning.

67. "Report of Meeting of Commodity Committee no. 19—Ferro-Alloys," 10/31/33, file 20, PB, ASW, OSW.

68. Risch, *Quartermaster Corps,* pp. 208–12.

69. Cordiner, "Minutes of Meeting of Orientation Conference no. 5, Subject, Statistics," 10/12/34, file 370.26/200.19, ANMB.

70. Lieutenant Colonel Skelton, "Minutes of Meeting of Orientation Conference no. 1, Subject, Facilities Division-Allocation," 9/5/34, file 337, ANMB, and Pitkin and Rifkind, *Quartermaster Corps,* p. 68, n. 34, and p. 72, n. 50.

71. Cordiner, "Minutes of Meeting of Orientation Conference no. 5, Subject Statistics," 10/12/34, file 370.26/200.19, and Skelton, "Minutes of the Meeting of Orientation Conference no. 1, Subject, Facilities Division-Allocation," 9/5/34, file 337, ANMB; Booz, Fry, Allen, and Hamilton, "Survey of the Office of the Under Secretary of War," vol. 1, 12/20/41, file 310, "Business Methods," General Correspondence of Under Secretary of War Robert Patterson, 12/40–3/43, Under Secretary of War (USW), Office of the Secretary of War, RG 107, National Archives, College Park, MD (hereafter cited as USW, OSW); and Pitkin and Rifkind, *Quartermaster Corps,* p. 53, n. 50.

72. Pitkin and Rifkind, *Quartermaster Corps,* pp. 123–24.

73. Booz Report, file 310, USW, OSW. Key parts of what the Booz group advocated had been espoused by the OASW and bureau personnel since the 1920s (see n. 6).

74. This subject will be discussed in the forthcoming volume 4 of this series.

75. Holley, *Buying Aircraft,* 93.

76. Most documents dealing with the theme of interwar planning make this cautious approach clear. For representative examples, see Ferguson, "Industrial Mobilization," 5/26/22, file 215-114, 228-50, AWC; Harris, "Minutes of Meeting of Orientation Conference no. 14, Subject, Planning Branch," 12/4/34, file 337/203.3-5.3, ANMB; Walter D. Hines to Secretary of War, 11/28/28, and other documents, file 199; and Lt. Col. C. B. Ross to Director, Planning Branch, file 46, PB, ASW, OSW; *ARSW,* 1922, pp. 99–100; *ARSW,* 1928, pp. 16–18; *ARSW,* 1934, pp. 27–31; *ARSW,* 1936, pp. 19–29; and *ARSW,* 1937, pp. 25–27. Some of the bureaus apparently worked with Congress to restrict the number of officers engaged in procurement planning to the 1929 level. At the same time, War Department directives gave the SA&S wide latitude in assigning officers for meeting bureau responsibilities, even if

that occurred at the expense of planning. See Cordiner, "Minutes of Meeting of Orientation Conference no. 5, Subject, Statistics," 10/12/34, file 370.26/200.19, ANMB, and Pitkin and Rifkind, *Quartermaster Corps,* p. 26.

77. The General Staff from 1903 to 1918 is covered in Koistinen, *Mobilizing for Modern War,* chaps. 4 and 7–10.

78. See n. 6.

79. This theme has been discussed (see nn. 1–6).

80. Risch, *Quartermaster Corps,* 1: 209. Occasionally, and untypically, some SA&S would propose that the War Department as a whole would function better if supply and procurement and economic mobilization planning were, in effect, placed under chief of staff–General Staff direction. The motivation and rationale for such propositions were never completely clear. Such proposals were met with swift and final rejection by the OASW. For an example, see Major General Gibbs, "Comments on Industrial Mobilization Plan, 1930," 1/30/31, and other documents, file 381/116.4, PB, ASW, OSW.

81. For the best expression of this attitude, see AWC, "The Office of the Assistant Secretary of War," 2/4/25, AWC, Unit 8, Box 3, Special Memoranda, Baruch Papers; *ARSW,* 1930, pp. 73–154. See also AWC, "Analysis of Supply Rate of Six Army Plan," 2/4/25; AWC, "General Mobilization Plan," 2/6/25; AWC, "Super-Agencies for the Control of Industry in Time of War," 2/5/25; and AWC, "International and Inter-Allied Supply Relations and Dependencies," 2/5/25, AWC, Unit 8, Box 3, Special Memoranda, Baruch Papers; AWC, "Industrial Preparedness in the United States," 12/21/26, file 335-2; AWC, "Industrial Preparedness in the United States," 12/21/26, file 335-2; and AWC, "Mobilization of Material and Industrial Organizations Essential to Wartime Needs," 12/21/27, file 345-2, AWC. See also other AWC files, 345-4, 345-5; 4-1935-3, G-4, no. 12, no. 12A; 4-1937-2, G-4, no. 12, no. 12A, 1937; 4-1938-3; 4-1939 A and B, G-4, no. 16, 1929; 4-1940-3 A and B, G-4, no. 15, 1940; and Kreidberg and Henry, *History of Military Mobilization,* p. 390. See notes 1–6 for further background and documentation on the OASW–General Staff conflict in the interwar years.

82. The best secondary source on this subject is Anderson, "Under Secretary of War's Office," chap. 3, pp. 3–29.

83. Paul A. C. Koistinen, "The 'Industrial-Military Complex' in Historical Perspective: The Interwar Years," *Journal of American History* 56 (March 1970): 825–26.

84. Pressure from the supply planners was significant in leading the General Staff to devise the General Mobilization Plan—a plan theoretically adjustable to all emergencies, instead of specific, or colored, war plans. See Kreidberg and Henry, *History of Military Mobilization,* p. 387; Weigley, *United States Army,* pp. 404–6; *ARSW,* 1922, p. 153; *ARSW,* 1927, pp. 29–30; and *ARSW,* 1930, pp. 40–41.

85. Kreidberg and Henry, *History of Military Mobilization,* pp. 388, 402, 406, 446, specifically—for a full and general treatment, see pp. 377–492; Smith, *Army and Economic Mobilization,* p. 53; and Green, Thomson, and Roots, *Ordnance Department,* p. 53.

86. Pitkin and Rifkind, *Quartermaster Corps,* p. 23.

87. Smith, *Army and Economic Mobilization,* p. 54.

88. Green, Thomson, and Roots, *Ordnance Department,* p. 3.

89. As quoted in Kreidberg and Henry, *History of Military Mobilization*, p. 417.
90. Ibid., pp. 413–14.
91. The General Staff subdivisions are explained in Weigley, *United States Army*, p. 405. For staff opposition to the war plans, see Kreidberg and Henry, *History of Military Mobilization*, pp. 390, 421, 438–39, and 457–59. The students' work at the AWC and the General Staff College often influenced significantly General Staff policy. The involvement of the General Staff in economic planning is analyzed in detail in chapter 2. A number of recent dissertations are useful for enlightening army war planning: Henry G. Gole, "War Planning at the U.S. Army War College, 1934–1940: The Road to Rainbow" (Ph.D. diss., Temple University, 1991); Philip C. Cockrell, "Brown Shoes and Mortar Boards: U.S. Army Officer Professional Education at the Command and General Staff School, Fort Leavenworth, Kansas, 1919–1940" (Ph.D. diss., University of South Carolina, 1991); and William C. Odom, "The Rise and Fall of U.S. Army Doctrine, 1918–1939" (Ph.D. diss., Ohio State University, 1995).
92. McFarland, *Woodring*, pp. 117–37; Green, Thomson, and Roots, *Ordnance Department*, p. 53; *ARSW*, 1937, p. 23; and *ARSW*, 1938, pp. 1–3.
93. Kreidberg and Henry, *History of Military Mobilization*, p. 467, and Weigley, *United States Army*, p. 414.
94. *ARSW*, 1939, p. 23. See also the full chief of staff's report, pp. 23–36.
95. Direct quotation, *ARSW*, 1936, p. 40. See also, *ARSW*, 1936, pp. 31–41; *ARSW*, 1937, pp. 29–37; and *ARSW*, 1938, pp. 29–36.
96. Kreidberg and Henry, *History of Military Mobilization*, pp. 424–26, 438, 466–67, and Weigley, *United States Army*, pp. 406–7, 415–16.
97. Kreidberg and Henry, *History of Military Mobilization*, p. 476.
98. *ARSW*, 1930, pp. 101–2.
99. Ibid., pp. 73–191.
100. *ARSW*, 1931, pp. 38–39. See also *ARSW*, 1931, pp. 37–72; *ARSW*, 1932, pp. 53–104; *ARSW*, 1933, pp. 3–50; *ARSW*, 1934, pp. 33–66; *ARSW*, 1935, pp. 41–74; and n. 96. MacArthur's open-mindedness about the role of supply and economic power in military affairs was not unalloyed. In 1931 he made a curious proposal for a General Council to achieve greater harmony, coordination, and communication within the War Department. The idea apparently never reached fruition. But if it had, the assistant secretary of war clearly would have been subordinated to the chief of staff (see *ARSW*, 1931, pp. 37–72). D. Clayton James, *The Years of MacArthur*, vol. 1, 1880–1941 (Boston: Houghton Mifflin, 1970), pp. 461–70, explores other contradictions of MacArthur and planning.
101. Fine and Remington, *Corps of Engineers*, p. 72; Smith, *Army and Economic Mobilization*, pp. 53–55; Green, Thomson, and Roots, *Ordnance Department*, pp. 53–54; and Kreidberg and Henry, *History of Military Mobilization*, pp. 476–92.
102. On this subject, see Koistinen, *Mobilizing for Modern War*, chaps. 7–10.
103. In one way or another, all major primary source collections cited in this chapter at least touch upon this theme. For secondary sources, see Kreidberg and Henry, *History of Military Mobilization*, pp. 377–492; Smith, *Army and Economic Mobilization*, pp. 53–54; Green, Thomson, and Roots, *Ordnance Department*, pp. 51–54; and Fine and Remington, *Corps of Engineers*, pp. 65–73.
104. *ARSW*, 1927, p. 33, and *ARSW*, 1928, p. 54.
105. For the larger theme of the paragraph, see nn. 1–6.

CHAPTER TWO. INDUSTRIAL MOBILIZATION PLANNING

1. Bernard M. Baruch, "War Industries Board," 1/15/25, file "Lecture-AWC-1/15/25," Box 2, and Baruch, "The Joint Congressional and Cabinet Commission on War Policies," 4/11/31, file "Lecture, AWC-4/11/31," Unit 8, Box 4, Special Memoranda; Baruch, "Second draft of article for *Army and Navy Journal* on industrial preparedness and mobilization," 1921, and correspondence between Baruch and Sidney Ballou (Commonwealth Club of San Francisco), 1929, Selected Correspondence, Bernard M. Baruch Papers, Princeton University, Princeton, NJ (hereafter cited as Baruch Papers); Baruch, "The War Industries Board," 12/2/25, and "Industrial Preparedness," 12/14/26, file 011.2, Records of the War Production Board, RG 179, National Archives, College Park, MD (hereafter cited as WPB); Baruch to Davis, 3/6/23, and numerous other documents, file 140, Planning Branch (PB), Assistant Secretary of War (ASW), Office of the Secretary of War (OSW), RG 107, National Archives, Washington DC (hereafter cited as PB, ASW, OSW); Col. Ferguson, "The Present Status of Plans of Industrial Preparation for War," 12/15/27, file 345-A-7; and Baruch, "Control of Our Economic and Industrial Resources in War," 2/28/29, file 343-A-24, G-4, no. 24, Army War College Collection, Carlisle Barracks, PA (hereafter cited as AWC).

2. Indistinct lines between procurement and economic mobilization planning are well illustrated in OASW, "Notes on Industrial Mobilization," November 1929, file AWC, Unit 8, Box 3, Special Memoranda, Baruch Papers. See also Davis, "Procurement," 2/11/24, file 276 A-12, and Wainwright, "Mass Procurement," 1/20/23, file 253-18, AWC.

3. War Department, *Report of the Secretary of War to the President*, 1931 (Washington, DC, 1931), p. 25 (hereafter cited as *Annual Report of the Secretary of War [ARSW]*); Davis to General Pershing, 6/4/29, file 140, PB, ASW, OSW; Col. Ferguson, "The Present Status of Plans of Industrial Preparation for War," 12/15/27, file 345-A-7, AWC.

4. On the origins of Section 5a, see chapter 1.

5. On proposals for reconversion and proposals for economic planning, see Paul A. C. Koistinen, *Mobilizing for Modern War: The Political Economy of American Warfare, 1865–1919* (Lawrence: University Press of Kansas, 1997), chap. 12.

6. Bernard M. Baruch, *American Industry in the War: A Report of the War Industries Board* (Washington, DC: U.S. Government Printing Office, 1921), pp. 9, 37, 96–100; Baruch, "The War Industries Board," 1/15/20, file 011.2, WPB; Baruch, "The War Industries Board," 2/12/24, file "Lecture-AWC," Unit 8, Box 2, Special Memoranda, Baruch Papers; Baruch to Davis, 3/6/23, and other correspondence, file 140, PB, ASW, OSW. Baruch's proposals were constantly repeated during the 1920s and 1930s in lectures before the AWC, the Army Industrial College, and other military and civilian audiences. Copies of these lectures are in PB, ASW, OSW; Special Memoranda and Selected Correspondence, Baruch Papers; file 011.2, WPB; and AWC.

7. On this point, see Koistinen, *Mobilizing for Modern War*, chap. 12.

8. For a further discussion of this topic, see chapter 1.

9. Developments in the 1920s and 1930s on rationalizing the economy will be discussed further and documented in chapters 4 and 11.

10. On this topic, see chapter 1.

11. The AWC–OASW relationship is discussed in chapter 1.

12. Ely to Adjutant General, 2/17/27, and other correspondence, file 020/255.24; and Capts. Hanley and Elliot to Col. Fife, 3/12/25, file 91, PB, ASW, OSW; extensive correspondence between Ely and Baruch, 1924–1927, and Baruch to Col. Roberts, 3/6/26, and other documents, Selected Correspondence; Baruch, "War Industries Board," 1/15/25, file "Lecture-AWC-1/15/25," Unit 8, Box 2, Special Memoranda, Baruch Papers; numerous other Baruch addresses designated in note 6; Benedict Crowell, "Procurement in War," 12/10/26, file 335-A-4, AWC; Col. Taylor to Scott, 1/5/27, and numerous other documents, file "War Dept.–Army War College, 1928–1929," Frank A. Scott Papers, Princeton University, Princeton, NJ (hereafter cited as Scott Papers); AWC, Rept. of Comm. no. 4, "Super-Agencies for Control of Industry in Time of War," 2/5/25, file 295-4; AWC, Rept. of Comm. no. 2, "Industrial Preparedness in the United States," 12/21/26, file 355-2; and AWC, Rept. of Comm. no. 2, "Mobilization of Material and Industrial Organizations Essential to War Time Needs," 12/21/27, file 345.2 and other similar reports, AWC. One member of the AWC proposed in 1922 what he termed a "wild" scheme for amending the National Defense Act, 1920, Section 5b, so that with a war, the General Staff could implement a total draft of capital and labor. See Col. C. E. Kilbourne to J. McA. Palmer [circa] 4/11/22, and for similar ideas expressed in AWC circles, see Col. Fife to Col. Ferguson, 4/20/22 and 5/24/22, both in file 555, PB, ASW, OSW.

The OASW faced a challenge to its authority from the Joint Army and Navy Board while simultaneously defending its prerogatives against the AWC. The board and its principal subdivision, the Joint Planning Committee, in various colored plans proposed creating economic mobilization agencies that they would dominate, subordinating the OASW and the ANMB to their structures, and controlling or directing procurement by the board or committee. Strenuous objections by the OASW, which were supported by the secretary of war, forced the Joint Army and Navy Board to back off. The struggle was most intense in 1928 when the Joint Planning Committee produced a draft of the Basic War Plan, Orange.

With less intensity and hostility, basic differences between the OASW and the Joint Army and Navy Board continued into the 1930s. Planning at times became secondary to maneuvering for power and prestige within the military services. On this subject, see Major Gilbert Wilkes et al. to the Assistant Secretary of War, 4/26/28, and numerous other documents, file 370.01/184; Woodring to Chief of Staff, 5/11/36, and other documents, file 334.8/172; and Lt. Col. A. J. Stuart, Memorandum to Director, War Plans Division, 5/2/36, file 381/146, PB, ASW, OSW. See also Woodring to Chief of Staff, 5/11/36, and other documents, file 370.26/210-10; and "Annual Report, Executive Committee," ANMB, 5/1/37, file, "Joint ANMB Annual Reports," small gray box, Records of the Joint Army and Navy Boards and Committees, RG 225, National Archives, Washington, DC (hereafter cited as ANMB). For background information on the Joint Army and Navy Board and the Joint Planning Committee, see Mark Skinner Watson, *Chief of Staff: Prewar Plans and Preparations* (Washington, DC: Historical Division, Department of the Army, 1950), pp. 79–81, and Russell F. Weigley, *History of the United States Army* (New York: Macmillan, 1967), p. 420; see also nn. 65, 71, 93–95.

13. Gen. Pierce to Scott, 1/26/22, Major Brett to Scott, 12/27/21, and numerous other correspondence, file, "War Dept.-Preparedness Program, 1921–1928, File

Folder 1 to 1923"; Scott to Gen. Ruggles, 11/12/26, and numerous other correspondence, file, "War Dept.-Preparedness Program, 1921–1928, Folder 2, 1924–1928"; Major Brett to Newton D. Baker, 4/10/24, Scott to Col. I. L. Hunt, 7/9/26, and numerous other correspondence, file "War Dept.-Army Industrial College"; memo, "The Cleveland Ordnance District," 1/28/26, and numerous other documents, "War Dept.-Cleveland Ord. Dist., 1926," Box 4; B. A. Franklin to Gen. Williams, 2/17/27, "Minutes of the Eighth Meeting of the Ordnance District Chiefs," 10/4–5/27, and numerous other documents, file, "War Dept.-Cleveland Ord. Dist.-1927"; Scott to Gen. Ruggles, 6/19/27, and other documents, file "War Dept.-Cleveland Ord. Dist.-1928"; Col. Carr to Scott, 1/31/30, 3/20/30, Payne to Scott, 12/22/30, file, "Correspondence with War Dept. (Ord.), 1921–1927," Box 4; Scott to Asst. Sec. of War, 4/8/25, Dravo to Scott, 5/1/25, and numerous other correspondence, file, "War Dept.-Gen'l, 1922–1926"; Col. Taylor to Scott, 1/5/27, AWC, "ASW, Orientation and Outline of Course," Dec. 6–24, 1924, and numerous other documents, file "War Dept., AWC, 1928–1929"; "Comments of District Chiefs on Basic Chart for District Office," 11/18/24, and other documents, file "War Dept.-Cleveland Ord. Dist., 1925," all in Scott Papers; and Crowell, "Procurement in War," 12/10/26, file 335 A-4, AWC. The involvement of the Procurement Districts, the AOA, and individuals such as Scott in War Department planning will be explored more fully in chapter 3.

14. Harry B. Yoshpe, "Bernard M. Baruch: Civilian Godfather of the Military M-Day Plan," *Military Affairs* 30 (Spring 1965): 1–15. See also Yoshpe, "Economic Mobilization Planning Between Two World Wars," *Military Affairs* 15 (Winter 1951): 199–204, and 16 (Summer 1952): 71–83. The most elaborate application of Yoshpe's idea is found in Harold W. Thatcher, *Planning for Industrial Mobilization, 1926–1940* (Washington DC: Office of the Quartermaster General, 1943), although the author, p. 19, appears to have coined the approximate phrase of Yoshpe's title. Marvin A. Kreidberg and Merton G. Henry, *History of Military Mobilization in the United States Army, 1775–1945* (Washington, DC: Department of the Army, 1955), pp. 493–540, offer a similar interpretation of Baruch and industrial mobilization, as do Albert A. Blum, "Birth and Death of the M-Day Plan," in *American Civil-Military Decision: A Book of Case Studies*, ed. Harold Stein, pp. 61–70 (University: University of Alabama Press, 1963), and E. Elberton Smith, *The Army and Economic Mobilization* (Washington, DC: Office of the Chief of Military History), pp. 35–97.

15. The sources for various speeches by Baruch to military audiences are cited in note 6. Many of his addresses to civilian groups are scattered throughout his Selected Correspondence, Baruch Papers. His speeches, papers, and the like on the subject were collated and edited for private publication by Richard H. Hippelheuser, *Taking the Profits Out of War: A Program for Industrial Mobilization* (New York: privately printed, 1936)—both the date and place of publication remain uncertain. See also Baruch, "Taking the Profit Out of War," *Atlantic Monthly* 137 (January 1926): 23–29. Baruch's relations with the McSwains, the Vandenbergs, and others can be traced through the years in the chronologically and alphabetically arranged Selected Correspondence, Baruch Papers. These matters, with varying degrees of detail and insight, are also covered in the biography by Jordan A. Schwarz, *The Speculator: Bernard M. Baruch in Washington, 1917–1965* (Chapel Hill: University of North Carolina Press, 1981). For an example of Baruch's correspondence with presidents, see Baruch to Coolidge,

1/22/26, 11/15/26, Coolidge to Baruch, 2/9/26, Selected Correspondence, Baruch Papers. Baruch's work with other presidents and especially with Franklin D. Roosevelt will be treated in chapters 14 and 15.

16. Grosvenor B. Clarkson, *Industrial America in the World War: The Strategy Behind the Line, 1917–1918* (Boston: Houghton Mifflin, 1923). Clarkson's relations with Baruch on the nature, publication, and consequences of the volume are covered in intriguing detail in Selected Correspondence of 1923, Baruch Papers, including modifying the text to avoid a possible lawsuit by the Du Ponts, distributing the volume, and arranging for reviews and the content of reviews by such people as Gen. John J. Pershing. Clarkson's sycophantic qualities and the tone of his volume as it involved Baruch are revealed in the following statement to Baruch (Selected Correspondence, 3/27/23), when Clarkson and Roger L. Scaife, a member of the executive staff of Houghton Mifflin, were trying to convince Baruch to allow Clarkson to ghostwrite an autobiography for him: "You are not only the most significant figure of your type in the country, but in many ways there is really no other figure like you in the social evolution of America." Additional information about the Clarkson volume, its relationship to the volumes of Benedict Crowell on World War I mobilization, and the efforts of Newton D. Baker and Frank A. Scott to "hire" their own less-biased historian are covered by Robert D. Cuff, "Bernard Baruch: Symbol and Myth in Industrial Mobilization," *Business History Review* 42 (Summer 1969): 115–33, and Cuff, "Newton D. Baker, Frank A. Scott, and 'The American Reinforcement in the World War,' *Military Affairs* 34 (February 1970): 11–13.

17. Johnson to Baruch, 5/17/26, 5/5/27, and other correspondence, Selected Correspondence, Baruch Papers.

18. The negotiations are recorded in correspondence filed under Arthur Krock, John J. Pershing, and Owen D. Young for the year 1925, Selected Correspondence, Baruch Papers. Concerning Baruch's pique over what he perceived as a misinterpretation of his intent, see John W. Scott to Baruch, 7/11/25, and Baruch to Scott, 9/25/25, also in Baruch Papers.

19. Baruch's relations with political leaders, the media, and advisers and assistants can be traced through the Selected Correspondence, Baruch Papers. These connections, furthermore, are treated in Schwarz, *The Speculator.* See also Arthur Schlesinger, Jr.'s review of Schwarz's volume in *New York Review of Books* 28 (October 8, 1981): 12–14.

20. *New York Times*, 6/24/34, p. 20, and Speaker of the House Rainey to Baruch, 6/25/34, Selected Correspondence, Baruch Papers. Another example involves the *Louisville* [KY] *Courier-Journal and Times.* The president and publisher, Robert W. Bingham, was a friend of Baruch, and the paper frequently devoted coverage to him. In November 1931, the *Courier-Journal* printed an entire speech Baruch delivered at a WIB reunion and commented on it on the editorial page. Bingham told Baruch that if he had had an advance copy of the address, it would have been front-page news. See Bingham to Baruch, 11/21/31, with enclosed news clipping, Selected Correspondence, Baruch Papers.

21. See Hippelheuser, *Taking the Profits Out of War.* There was an initial attempt to have Adm. Cary J. Grayson, Woodrow Wilson's White House physician, write the foreword. See Hippelheuser to Grayson, 4/18/35, Selected Correspondence, Baruch Papers. Hippelheuser in 1941 also edited a new edition of Baruch's *American Indus-*

try in the War (the original publication is cited in n. 6). See also 11/35 Memorandum of printed card to be inserted in privately printed volume for those attending WIB reunion, Selected Correspondence, Baruch Papers.

22. On World War I economic mobilization, see Koistinen, *Mobilizing for Modern War*, chaps. 8–12. See also Baruch, second draft of article on industrial preparedness and economic mobilization for the *Army and Navy Journal*, 1921, Selected Correspondence, Baruch Papers. This article manifests most elements of Baruch's motivation for involvement in the interwar planning.

23. These matters will be treated fully in chapters 12–14.

24. Schwarz, *The Speculator*, builds his volume around the notion of Baruch as "corporatist." Robert D. Cuff in his numerous publications on the WIB examines Baruch's dedication to corporate capitalism. See Cuff, *The War Industries Board: Business-Government Relations During World War I* (Baltimore: Johns Hopkins University Press, 1973). One of Clarkson's attributes that made him so compatible with Baruch was his crusading, ideological commitment to corporate capitalism. This is fully evident in his *Industrial America in the World War* and U.S. Council of National Defense, *Third Annual Report* (Washington, DC: U.S. Government Printing Office, 1919), and U.S. Council of National Defense, *Fourth Annual Report* (Washington, DC: U.S. Government Printing Office, 1920), when Clarkson was director of the CND–NDAC.

25. See n. 6 for the sources for these lectures.

26. Baruch to Gen. Ely, 9/15/27, Selected Correspondence, and Baruch, "The Control of Our Economic and Industrial Resources and Activities in War," 12/13/27, file, "Lecture-AWC-12/13/27," Unit 8, Box 2, Special Memoranda, Baruch Papers. Actually, Baruch had begun to skip over the formal lecture for the question and answer approach as early as 1924. See Baruch, "The War Industries Board," 2/12/24, file, "Lecture-AWC," Unit 8, Box 2, Special Memoranda, and Col. Simmonds to Baruch, 2/8/24 (with enclosure), Gen. Ely to Baruch, 10/31/24, and Baruch to Ely, 11/3/24, Selected Correspondence, Baruch Papers.

27. This presentation is a composite of various lectures. The basic message is set forth briefly and clearly in two places, however: Baruch to Davis, 3/6/23, Selected Correspondence, Baruch Papers, and Baruch, "Taking the Profits Out of War," *Atlantic Monthly* (January 1926): 23–29. Baruch's ideas on price control are set forth clearly in Baruch, "The Economics of Modern Warfare," 4/22/29, file "Address, R.O.A.-4-22-29," and Baruch, "Economic Mobilization of the United States," 3/6/30, file "Address-AWC-3/6/30," Unit 8, Box 3, Special Memoranda, Baruch Papers.

28. See n. 12 for sources on these points and see also numerous AWC studies of economic mobilization and analyses of OASW work located in AWC, Unit 8, Box 3, Special Memoranda, Baruch Papers. For a sharp contrast between the response of the AWC and the OASW to Baruch's entreaties for economic mobilization, see the statements of General Ely and Colonel Ferguson during the question and answer period to Baruch's address, "The War Industries Board," 12/2/25, file 313 A-6, AWC.

29. Baruch to Col. Roberts, 3/8/26 (direct quotation), Roberts to Baruch, 3/15/26, and AWC, Rept. of Comm. no. 4, "General Industrial Mobilization Plan," 12/19/25, Selected Correspondence, Baruch Papers. See also Baruch to Ely, 3/8/26, Davis to Baruch, 3/23/26, and Ely to Baruch, 3/12/26, Selected Correspondence;

AWC, Rept. of Comm. no. 3, "General Mobilization Plan," 2/6/25, file AWC, Unit 8, Box 3, Special Memoranda; Baruch to Col. Taylor, 1/20/27, with enclosed, AWC, Rept. of Comm. no. 4, "War Plans of the Asst. Sec. of War," 12/23/26, Taylor to Baruch, 4/9/27, and Baruch to Taylor 4/18/27, Selected Correspondence, Baruch Papers.

30. Baruch to Secretary of War Johnson, 9/20/37, Selected Correspondence, Baruch Papers.

31. Baruch, "The Control of Our Economic and Industrial Resources and Activities in War," 12/13/27, file, "Lecture-AWC-12/13/27," Unit 8, Box 2, Special Memoranda, Baruch Papers; and Major Nix to Chief, Planning Branch, 1/13/28, with enclosure, file 140, PB, ASW, OSW. See also Major Nix, "Work of the War Department Commodity Committee no. 45, Iron and Steel," file, "Commodity Committee no. 45-Steel and Iron," PB, ASW, OSW.

32. Col. Wooten address, "The Present Status of Plans for Industrial Preparation for War," 11/7/28, file 353-A-8, G-4, no. 8, and Baruch address, "Control of Our Economic and Industrial Resources in War," file 353-A-24, G-4, no. 24, AWC.

33. On World War I mobilization developments, see Koistinen, *Mobilizing for Modern War*, chaps. 8–10. Johnson's attitudes on the General Staff vis-à-vis the SA&S are evident throughout his lectures to the AWC and the Army Industrial College and his correspondence with and work for Baruch. These thoughts are touched upon briefly in Johnson's volume, *The Blue Eagle from Egg to Earth* (New York: Doubleday, Doran, 1935), pp. 88–89. See also John K. Ohl, *Hugh S. Johnson and the New Deal* (Dekalb: Northern Illinois University Press, 1985), chap. 5. For Johnson's most forthright statement that the General Staff, "aided if not directed by the best civilian talent in the nation," should do the economic mobilization planning and for his lack of confidence in the SA&S, see Johnson address, "Industrial and Man-Power Mobilization," 12/11/22, file 250-10, AWC.

34. Baruch's attitude toward the OASW planning is evident throughout his addresses to the AWC and the Army Industrial College and numerous pieces of correspondence. Specifically, see Baruch, "The War Industries Board," 12/2/25, file 313-A-6, and Crowell, "Procurement in War," 12/10/26, file 335-A-4, AWC; and Baruch to MacDowell, 10/17/26, Baruch to Vauclain, 1/8/26, and Baruch to McSwain, 12/17/27, Selected Correspondence, Baruch Papers. Baruch's attitudes toward AWC planning, as opposed to that of the OASW, were inconsistent. At times he criticized the AWC for many of the same charges he leveled at the OASW, as is indicated in some of the preceding sources.

35. See chapter 12.

36. The account of Baruch, economic mobilization planning, and the policies of the 1920s is based on Baruch to Boyle, 2/6/23; Baruch to Davis, 3/6/23; Davis to Baruch, 3/14/23; Baruch to Davis, 6/18/23; Davis to Baruch, 6/26/23; Baruch to Davis, 6/28/23; Davis to Baruch, 8/20/23; Baruch to Davis, 10/14/23; Davis to Baruch, 10/16/23; Baruch to Davis, 10/23/23; Baruch to Johnson, 3/2/23; Legge to Baruch, 2/9/23, 2/16/23, 2/26/23; Baruch to Legge, 3/2/23, 6/29/23; MacDowell to Baruch, 1/4/23; Baruch to MacDowell, 1/6/23; Parker to Baruch, 3/8/23; Peek to Legge, 1/12/23; Baruch to Peek; 1/20/23, 2/8/23, 3/2/23; Peek to Baruch, 3/8/23; Pershing to Baruch 2/13/23; Baruch to Persh-

ing, 3/6/23, 5/31/23; Pershing to Baruch, 10/18/23; Baruch to Wadsworth, 1/23/23; Wadsworth to Baruch, 2/1/23; Baruch to Wadsworth, 2/3/23, 2/6/23; Baruch to Weeks, 1/22/23; Weeks to Baruch, 2/2/23; and Summers to Baruch, 3/3/23, Selected Correspondence, Baruch Papers. See also memo, "Mr. Baruch's Recommendations," 3/2/34, J. L. H. to H. B. F., undated, Major Brett to Baruch, 6/22/23, Baruch to Davis, 10/30/23, Baruch to Pershing, 5/19/24, Davis to Pershing, 6/4/24, file 140, PB, ASW, OSW; and Davis to Baruch, 12/8/24, Baruch to Davis, 12/11/24; Baruch to Pershing, 5/19/24, Pershing to Baruch, 6/7/24; Baruch to MacDowell, 10/17/26. Selected Correspondence, Baruch Papers. For some good insights involving the differing perspectives of Legge and Baruch, see also Baruch to Legge, 5/6/26, and Legge to Baruch, 5/24/26; Legge to Baruch, 6/3/29, with enclosure and Legge to Chamber of Commerce, 6/3/29, all in Selected Correspondence, Baruch Papers; and Forrest Crissey, *Alexander Legge, 1866–1933* (Chicago: privately printed by the Alexander Legge Memorial Committee, 1936).

37. Scott, "Organization of the War Industries Board," 1/15/25, enclosure, Baruch to Scott, 3/28/25, Selected Correspondence, Baruch Papers. The World War I conditions leading to interwar tension are covered in Koistinen, *Mobilizing for Modern War,* chaps. 8–12. The interwar relations among Baruch, Scott, Baker, and Crowell are recorded in the Selected Correspondence, Baruch Papers. The Scott Papers are also helpful, but unlike the Baruch Papers, they are not well cataloged and organized, making them more difficult to use. For a representative example, see Scott to Baruch, 5/17/24, 6/3/24, and Baruch to Scott, 5/29/24, file, "Baruch, Bernard M."; Scott to Major MacMoreland and numerous other documents, file, "War Dept.-AWC, 1928–1929"; Scott to Wainwright, 6/27/23, and Baker to Scott, 6/27/23, file, "War Dept.-Preparedness Program, 1921–1928, file folder 1 to 1923." See also citations in n. 13. For further good insights on this subject, see Cuff, "Newton D. Baker, Frank A. Scott, and 'The American Reinforcement in the World War.'"

38. The best and most detailed secondary account of the OASW economic mobilization planning in the interwar years is Thatcher, *Planning;* other principal secondary sources are cited in n. 14.

39. "War Plan for Industrial Mobilization," 12/1922, file 95, and Memorandum for Planning Branch, 9/20/22, file 90, both in PB, ASW, OSW.

40. Ibid., "Industrial Mobilization, the Assistant Secretary of War, Basic Plan," 1924, file 96.

41. Ibid., OASW, "War Time Procurement, Principles, and Organization," 12/1/25, file 122.

42. Ibid., "Basic Plan for the Procurement of Military Requirement, 1924, 1928–1930," and "Basic Plan for the Procurement of Military Requirements-1928-Revised 1929, 1930," file 94.

43. Ibid., "Memorandum for the Planning Branch, Basic War Power Law-Prices-Labor Draft," file 560; and Thatcher, *Planning,* pp. 102, 111–12. The OASW's initial search was incomplete. By 1930, the Legislative Appendix to the Industrial Mobilization Plan enumerated many pieces of legislation passed between 1916 and 1920 that were relevant to industrial mobilization. The 1933 and 1936 plans expanded this limited purview to one that included the entire American constitutional process as it related to the warmaking powers of the state.

44. War Department–American Legion relations will be fully analyzed and documented in chapter 13.

45. Weeks to Chairman, House Committee on Military Affairs, 2/9/23, file 374, PB, ASW, OSW.

46. From Saunders's assignment came his valuable history of Section 5a of the National Defense Act, 1920, "National Defense Act: Legislative History of Industrial Mobilization Clauses," 10/11/23, file 628, PB, ASW, OSW; and Thatcher, *Planning,* pp. 111–21.

47. Thatcher, *Planning,* pp. 111–21.

48. Since the "Basic Procurement Plan, 1928" contained no Legislative Appendix, these bills are contained in the Legislative Appendix to the "Industrial Mobilization, the Assistant Secretary of War, Basic Plan," 1924, and were not added to this plan until 1928. See "Legislative Appendix-1, 1924 to Industrial Mobilization Plan," file 107; "A Bill to Provide for the National Security and Defense" (Proposed Industrial Mobilization Act)" by Col. Walton, 7/19/24, and *"A Bill to Provide for the National Security and Defense"* by Col. Ferguson, 12/5/27, file 560; and Quartermaster General memo, "Legislation-Industrial War Plan," 4/11/24, and other documents, file 562, PB, ASW, OSW.

49. Scott, "How the United States Should Plan for Industrial Mobilization," 12/16/27, file 345 A-9, AWC; Hugh S. Johnson to Baruch, 5/29/29, with enclosure, draft of letter to Chamber of Commerce, and Baruch to McSwain, 6/15/35, Selected Correspondence, Baruch Papers; Scott to Col. Vestal, 6/18/29, file, "War Dept.-AWC, 1928–1929, Box 4; and Scott to Wainwright, 6/27/23, Newton D. Baker to Scott, 6/27/23, Major Somers to Scott, 1/23/23, Scott to Jamison, 11/9/23, and Jamison to Scott, 11/11/23, file, "War Dept., Preparedness Program, 1921–1928, file folder 1 to 1923," Scott Papers; AWC, Rept. of Comm. no. 3, "Economic and Industrial Support of War," 12/5/38, file A-1939-3A and B, G-4, no. 16, 1939; and Baruch, "War Preparations," 2/2/38, file CofW no. 4, 1938, AWC. See also Paul A. C. Koistinen, "The 'Industrial-Military Complex' in Historical Perspective: World War I," *Business History Review* 41 (Winter 1967): 398–99, 402–3.

50. For contrasting positions on proposed legislation, see *ARSW,* 1925, p. 28, and *ARSW,* 1930, p. 9. See also Thatcher, *Planning,* pp. 97–98, 126–28. The War Department's legislative activity is analyzed in chapter 13.

51. This theme is examined in detail in chapter 13.

52. War Department relations with capital and labor are examined in chapter 13.

53. *ARSW,* 1925, p. 27; *ARSW,* 1927, p. 32; Smith, *Army and Economic Mobilization,* pp. 96–97; and Thatcher, *Planning,* pp. 74–78.

54. *ARSW,* 1927, pp. 32–33; *ARSW,* 1928, p. 53; *ARSW,* 1929, p. 69; *ARSW,* 1930, p. 38; *ARSW,* 1940, pp. 6–7; and Smith, *Army and Economic Mobilization,* pp. 95–96.

55. *ARSW,* 1931, p. 25. See also Col. Hasson to All SA&S, 9/20/30, file 145, PB, ASW, OSW.

56. By late 1930 Moseley had been promoted to major general and appointed a deputy chief of staff to Chief of Staff MacArthur. In 1935 Moseley and his supporters launched an aggressive campaign to have him appointed chief of staff as successor to MacArthur. Besides being a dynamic, talented officer, Moseley, even while on active duty, displayed many of the attributes of the superpatriot. Upon retirement from the

army in the late 1930s, he became active in radical-right group activities involving the Knights of the White Camellia and other such organizations. In 1939 Moseley came under congressional scrutiny for his right-wing political activity. See U.S. Congress, House, Special Committee on Un-American Activities, *Hearings, Investigation of Un-American Propaganda Activities in the United States,* 76th Cong., 1st sess. (1939), vol. 5, pp. 3545–703. See also Rodney G. Minott, *Peerless Patriots: Organized Veterans and the Spirit of Americanism* (Washington, DC: Public Affairs Press, 1962), pp. 63, 132; Thatcher, *Planning,* pp. 84–85, 153–54; Asst. Sec. of War Payne, "Mobilization of Industry," 10/29/33, AWC; and George Armsby to Baruch, 11/18/35, Selected Correspondence, Baruch Papers.

57. Johnson to Baruch, 11/29, Selected Correspondence, Baruch Papers. Johnson and Moseley at one time had been close friends. See Johnson, *Blue Eagle,* pp. 33, 91.

58. "Plan for Governmental Organization for War," 11/12/29, file 109, and "November 12, 1929 Draft of Industrial Mobilization Plan," file "War Plans," file 90, PB, ASW, OSW; and Moseley to Baruch, 11/29/29, Selected Correspondence, Baruch Papers.

59. Major General Gibbs, Chief Signal Officer, "Comments on IMP, 1930," 1/30/31, and other documents, file 381/116.4, PB, ASW, OSW; AWC, Supplement no. 2 to Rept. of Comm. no. 6, "Adequacy of the Plan for Industrial Mobilization," 11/14/31, file 384-6, G-4, no. 14, AWC; and Thatcher, *Planning,* pp. 89–90.

60. Johnson to Baruch, 11/29, Selected Correspondence, Baruch Papers.

61. The unsigned, undated, but identified letter of Baruch to Moseley is included with the 1929 plan, on which Baruch has also written marginal notes, file 109, PB, ASW, OSW. See also Moseley to Baruch, 11/27/29, 12/20/29, and Baruch to Moseley, 12/21/29, Selected Correspondence, Baruch Papers; and Baruch address, "Economic Mobilization of the United States," 3/6/30, file 364-A-17, G-4, no. 17, AWC.

62. Moseley to Baruch, 1/9/30, 2/1/30, 2/13/30, and Baruch to Moseley, 2/2/30, 2/18/30, Selected Correspondence, Baruch Papers. The various revisions of the original Hurley Plan are in file 110, PB, ASW, OSW. See also Thatcher, *Planning,* pp. 90–94.

63. The WPC is covered in depth in chapter 13.

64. Industrial Mobilization Plan, 1930, file 110, PB, ASW, OSW. A published version of this plan is conveniently available in the printed hearing of the WPC. See "Message from the President . . . Transmitting Report of the War Policies Commission," H. Doc. 163, 72d Cong., 1st sess., 1931, pp. 395–477 (hereafter cited as WPC, *Hearings).* The entire War Department presentation of its IMP and the testimony of various of its members is contained in pp. 351–93. For purposes of convenience and clarity, any future references to the pagination of the IMP will involve the published version.

65. IMP, 1930, file 110, PB, ASW, OSW. The Selective Service and Public Relations Administrations were more mentioned than developed in the plan because the General Staff was to be the architect of these organizations, and it had not completed plans for them; see nn. 12, 71, and 93–95 on this subject.

66. Ibid., and WPC, *Hearings,* pp. 354–56, 365–66, 371–73, 376–77.

67. IMP, 1930, file 110, PB, ASW, OSW. The selective service law actually first appeared in the Hurley Plan of late 1929.

68. Like other important aspects of the IMP, the subject was introduced in the

plan and then MacArthur provided a more detailed, graspable explanation in his testimony, which was prepared by the OASW (see ibid.); and WPC, *Hearings,* p. 370. The idea of the OASW serving as a nucleus and transitional mobilization agency was first introduced in the "Basic Procurement Plan–1928–Revised 1929, 1930." It was further developed and elaborated on in the Hurley Plan of 1929. See "Plan for Governmental Organization for War," file 109, PB, ASW, OSW, and Moseley to Baruch, 2/1/30 and 2/13/30, Selected Correspondence, Baruch Papers.

69. IMP, 1930, file 110, PB, ASW, OSW (relations between organized labor and the War Department and labor's place in the OASW plans will be analyzed in chapter 13).

70. Ibid., p. 411.

71. Ibid., p. 418. General Staff dominance of the Public Relations Administration is clearly evident in the appendix for that agency in the IMP, 1933; see also nn. 12, 65, and 93–95 on General Staff authorship of portions of the industrial mobilization plans.

72. IMP, 1930, p. 419, file 110, PB, ASW, OSW.

73. Baruch to Moseley, 2/4/30, Selected Correspondence, Baruch Papers. See also War Policies Commission, "Documents by War Policies Commission," H. Doc. 271, 72d Cong., 1st sess., 1932, pp. 1–71 (hereafter cited as WPC, *Documents*).

74. Moseley to Baruch, 2/1/30, Selected Correspondence, Baruch Papers.

75. Baruch's views are stated fully in his testimony before the Commission, WPC, *Hearings,* pp. 30–72, 794–841. See also Baruch, untitled address to AWC, 11/16/31, file, "Address-AWC," Unit 8, Box 4, Special Memoranda, Baruch Papers, and Baruch, "Control of Civilian Activities in War," 2/23/33, file 325-F-6, AWC.

76. "Message from the President . . . War Policies Commission . . . Final Recommendations," H. Doc. 264, 72d Cong., 1st sess., 1932, pp. 2–5. See also WPC, *Documents,* pp. 1–71. The WPC findings and recommendations will be discussed and analyzed more fully in chapter 13. See also Asst. Sec. of War Payne, "Mobilization of Industry," 10/29/32, file 394-A-3, G-4, no. 3, AWC.

77. IMP, 1933, file 112, PB, ASW, OSW. The Nye Committee published this plan. See *Industrial Mobilization Plan, Revised 1933,* Senate Committee Print no. 2, 74th Cong., 1st sess., 1935, pp. i–xi, 1–102 [Special Senate Committee Investigating the Munitions Industry]. All further citations giving pagination will refer to this published edition.

78. Ibid., p. 17.

79. Ibid., Appendix 6.

80. Ibid., Appendix 3. The significance of this administration will be treated in greater detail in chapters 13–15. See also Hugh S. Johnson to Asst. Sec. of War Johnson, 8/24/37, file 381/116.4b, PB, ASW, OSW.

81. IMP, 1933, p. 14, file 112, PB, ASW, OSW.

82. Ibid., Appendix 7.

83. See chapter 1.

84. See n. 68.

85. IMP, 1933, and Appendix 7, file 112, PB, ASW, OSW.

86. Ibid., Assistant Secretaries of War and Navy to Joint Board, 7/19/34, and Capt. Farber and Lt. Col. Harris to Executive Committee, 7/19/34. See also Capt.

Jennings to Lt. Col. Harris, 10/19/33, and Capt. Jennings to Capt. Pence, 9/7/32, file 145.

87. Ibid., Farber and Harris to Executive Committee, 7/19/34, file 112.

88. The military's changing approach to legislation for economic mobilization will be discussed in fuller detail in chapter 13. See Thatcher, *Planning*, pp. 208–9.

89. IMP, 1933, Appendix 8, file 112, PB, ASW, OSW.

90. IMP, 1930 (quotation, p. 404) [WPC, *Hearings*]; IMP, 1933, file 112, PB, ASW, OSW; and Thatcher, *Planning*, pp. 192–93. For the AWC response to the IMP, 1933, see AWC, Rept. of Comm. no. 1, "Economic and Industrial Support of Supplies," 11/14/33, file 404-1, G-4, no. 10, and Rept. of Comm. no. 3, "Industrial Mobilization Plan, 1933 and Related War Department Plans," 11/26/34, file, 4-1935-3, G-4, no. 12, 12A, AWC.

91. Industrial Mobilization Plan, Revised-1936, file 120, and "Notes on the Press Conference of the Secretary of War," 12/10/36, file 381/116.4b, PB, ASW, OSW.

92. "Notes on the Press Conference of the Secretary of War," 12/10/36, file 381/116.4b, PB, ASW, OSW.

93. Ibid., Chief of Staff Malin Craig to Asst. Sec. of War, 4/8/36, file 381/116.4b. The origins and nature of the informal agreement between the OASW and the General Staff involving selective service and public relations are obscure. Much more information is available on the former than on the latter. Selective service became inextricably combined with the extraordinary complex and controversial subject of trade unions and military-organized labor relations involving economic mobilization planning. Since 1931 the AWC had been pressing, first, for the details on the structure of the Public Relations Administration and, second, for more effective measures for propaganda and censorship during wartime situations. See AWC, Supplement no. 2 to Rept. of Comm. no. 6, "Economic and Industrial support of War," 11/14/31, file 384-6, G-4, no. 14, and Rept. of Comm. no. 1, "Economic and Industrial Support of War Procurement of Supplies," 11/14/33, file 404-1 G-4, no. 10, AWC. See nn. 12, 65, 71, 94–95 on the General Staff and the selective service and public relations agencies.

94. Asst. Sec. of War to Chief of Staff, 4/17/36, file 381/116.4b, PB, ASW, OSW. It is not clear from other documents if the General Staff agreed to relinquish review rights over just the 1936 industrial mobilization plan or over all existing and future plans (see nn. 12, 65, 71, 93, and 95 on the General Staff and the IMPs).

95. IMP, 1936, pp. 74–75, file 120; Col. Rutherford to Capt. Allen, 7/16/38, Subcommittee, Joint Planning Committee to Selective Service Committee, 8/2/38, file 381/116.4c; Capt. Battley to Col. Rutherford, 10/18/39, file 381/169; Lt. Col. Burns, Sept. 1939, file 344.8/172; and file 381/116.4b, PB, ASW, OSW. For further discussion of this matter, including brief descriptions of the Joint Army-Navy Board and Joint Planning Committee, see n. 12; see also nn. 65, 71, and 93–94. An AWC study of the IMP, 1936, stated that selective service and manpower control measures were intentionally left out of the principal proposed bill for implementing the IMP because they were so "charged with political dynamite that their inclusion in the bill would surely prevent its peacetime passage" (see AWC, Rept. of Comm. no. 2, "Industrial Mobilization Plan, 1936," 12/12/36, file 4-1937-2, G-4, no. 12, 12A, 1937, AWC).

96. IMP, 1936 (direct quotation, p. 101), file 120, PB, ASW, OSW.

97. This subject will be covered more fully in chapters 14 and 15. For the response of the SA&S to the IMP, 1936, see Col. Jordan to Director, Planning Branch, 4/8/36, and other documents, file 1401. For the response of the secretary of war and the chief OASW spokesman on key aspects of the IMP, 1936, including an example of the War Department again supporting the passage of legislation, see "Notes on the Press Conference of the Secretary of War," 12/10/36, file 381/116.4b. See also the extensive exchange of correspondence between Assistant Secretary of War Louis Johnson, Hugh S. Johnson, and Baruch in August through October 1937, file 381/116.4b, all in PB, ASW, OSW, and Selected Correspondence, Baruch Papers. For the response of the AWC to the IMP, 1936, see Rept. of Comm. no. 2, "Industrial Mobilization Plan," 12/12/36, file 4-1937-2, G-4, no. 12, 12A, 1937; Rept of Comm. no. 3, "Economic and Industrial Support of War," 12/17/37, file 4-1938-3; Rept. of Comm. no. 3, "Economic and Industrial Support of War," 12/5/38, file A-1939-3A and B, G-4, no. 16, 1939; and Baruch, "War Preparedness," 2/2/38, file CofW no. 4, 1938, AWC.

98. Industrial Mobilization Plan, Revision of 1939, file 334/117.3, PB, ASW, OSW. A published version of the plan appears in the volume of Harold J. Tobin and Percy W. Bidwell, *Mobilizing Civilian America* (New York: Council on Foreign Relations, 1940), appendix, pp. 237–57. The volume was sponsored by the Council on Foreign Relations, and the authors received the full cooperation of the OASW as an effort to facilitate preparedness (see also chap. 1, n. 46 for reference to another published version).

99. Col. Hines to Asst. Sec. of War, 10/3/39, file 381/116.4c, PB, ASW, OSW, and *ARSW,* 1939, p. 20.

100. IMP, 1939, file 334/117.3 (direct quotation, p. 13); see also "Administrative Annex to Operating Plan, WRA-(Draft Copy), [circa] 1938, file 004.7/239.10, and Col. Rutherford speeches, 11/9/38, 5/11/39, and 9/12/40, file 020.4/114.8, all in PB, ASW, OSW.

101. Ibid., IMP, 1939, War Trade Board Annex, file 334/117.3.

102. IMP, 1939, file 334/117.3.

103. Ibid.; Col. Hines to Asst. Sec. of War, 10/3/39, file 381/116.4c, PB, ASW, OSW; and Thatcher, *Planning,* pp. 244–45.

104. Col. Hines to Asst. Sec. of War, 10/3/39, and Col. Rutherford to Wescott, 7/12/39, file 381/116.4c, PB, ASW, OSW.

105. See the various annexes to the IMP for the three-stage approach, ibid., file 334/117.3. See also Thatcher, *Planning,* pp. 277–79. The OASW had been aware of the need for flexible economic mobilization plans since 1925. See Baruch, "War Industries Board," 1/15/25, file 011.2, WPB.

106. This subject is analyzed in chapter 1.

107. Kreidberg and Henry, *History of Military Mobilization,* p. 536. Roosevelt did not seem to be fully aware of the OASW work as late as November 1938. See Ogburn to Delano, 11/22/38, Roosevelt to Delano, 12/1/38, Johnson to Delano, 12/5/38, file 381/116.4b, PB, ASW, OSW.

108. IMP, 1939, Annexes, file 334/117.3, PB, ASW, OSW. Commentaries about and analyses of the Annexes to the IMP, 1939, as well as the plan itself, are found in file 011.2, WPB.

109. Price Control Annex to the IMP, 1939, file 334/117.3, PB, ASW, OSW.

110. Ibid., Power and Fuel Annex to the IMP, 1939.

111. Ibid., Transportation Annex to the IMP, 1939.
112. Ibid., Labor Annex to the IMP, 1939.
113. Ibid., War Trade, War Finance, and Price Control annexes.
114. Ibid., Col. Rutherford to Wescott, 7/12/39, file 381/116.4c; Col. Rutherford to Asst. Sec. of War, 9/26/38, file 381/169; and War Finance and Price Control Annexes, file 334/117.3; AWC, Rept. of Comm. no. 3, "Economic and Industrial Support of War," 12/5/38, file A-1939-3A and B, G-4, no. 16, 1939; and AWC, Rept. of Comm. no. 3, "Economic and Industrial Support of War," 12/4/39, file 4-1940-3A and B, G-4, no. 15, 1940, AWC; and Thatcher, *Planning*, pp. 261–67, 288–89 (this subject will be covered more fully in chapter 14).
115. IMP, 1939, file 334/117.3; see also Col. Hines to Asst. Sec. of War, 10/3/39, file 381/116.4c; Administrative Annex to Operating Plan, WRA-(Draft Copy), [circa] 1938, file 004.7/239.10; Col. Rutherford speeches, 11/9/38, 5/1/39, and 9/12/40, file 020.4/114.8, all in PB, ASW, OSW; Col. Rutherford to Sec. of the Treasury Morgenthau, 5/22/40, file 471/231/2-13-1; and Lt. Col. Charles Hines, "The Army and Navy Munitions Board," 3/29/39, file 370/200-18.00, ANMB. The history and evolution of the ANMB can be readily traced through the board's reports: "Annual Reports of the Executive Committee of the Army and Navy Munitions Board," 1932–1939, small gray box, ANMB. For the AWC critique of the 1939 plan, see Rept. of Comm. no. 3, "Economic and Industrial Support of War," 12/4/39, and Supplement no. 2 to the Rept. "Provisions of the Industrial Mobilization Plan," 12/4/39, file 4-1940-3A and B, G-4, no. 15, 1940, AWC.
116. Annexes to the IMP, 1939, file 334/117.3, PB, ASW, OSW. A Transition Annex was being prepared or revised to rationalize the nation's entry into war. The three-stage mobilization arrangement probably would have been standardized in that document.
117. Ibid., War Trade Annex to the IMP, 1939.
118. On this development, see chapter 15.
119. War Finance Annex to the IMP, 1939, file 334/117.3, PB, ASW, OSW.
120. Ibid., Facilities Annex to the IMP, 1939.
121. See n. 113.
122. Fuller information on the Scott versus the Baruch group is presented in chapter 13; chapter 3 also has relevant information.

CHAPTER THREE. MILITARY-BUSINESS RELATIONS

1. Alfred D. Chandler, "The Structure of American Industry in the Twentieth Century: A Historical Overview," *Business History Review* 63 (Autumn 1969): 255–98, and Thomas R. Navin, "The 500 Largest American Industrialists in 1917," *Business History Review* 64 (Autumn 1970): 360–86. Many of the sources cited in Paul A. C. Koistinen, *Mobilizing for Modern Warfare: The Political Economy of American Warfare, 1865–1919* (Lawrence: University Press of Kansas, 1997), chap. 2, n. 4, and chap. 6, n. 1, are also relevant to the structure of the interwar economy.

2. Paul A. C. Koistinen, "The 'Industrial-Military Complex' in Historical Perspective: World War I," *Business History Review* 61 (Winter 1967): 392 and n. 29. See also, Koistinen, *Mobilizing for Modern War*, chap. 9, n. 18.

3. See the sources on Hoover, the 1920s, and the New Deal cited in chapter 11, nn. 9 and 10. Agriculture and labor are covered in these citations.

4. The Ordnance Department, Quartermaster Corps, and other bureaus were called "supply branches" in the 1920s, "supply arms and services" in the 1930s, and finally "technical services" during World War II. I will refer to them either as bureaus or supply arms and services throughout the period under discussion.

5. Frank A. Scott to Colonel Carr, 4/3/28, file, "War Department, Army Industrial College, 1924–1928"; James L. Walsh to Scott, 8/16/24, file, "War Department, Preparedness Program, 1921–1928"; and Major Pringer, Bulletin no. 21, 8/20/35, file, "Commencement: The Army Industrial College-6/22/35," Frank A. Scott Papers, Princeton University, Princeton, NJ (hereafter cited as Scott Papers); U.S. Congress, Senate, Special Committee Investigating the Munitions Industry, *Hearings, Industrial Organization in War—Continued*, 73d, Cong., 1934, Part 16, pp. 4016, 4148–52 (hereafter cited as Nye Committee [after the committee chair, Sen. Gerald P. Nye, R-ND], *Hearings*. Insight into the operations of the Ordnance Districts can be acquired from "Minutes of the Eighth Meeting of the Ordnance District Chiefs, October 4, 5, 1927," and Scott to E. F. Carter, 12/1/27, file, "War Department-Cleveland Ordnance District-1927"; Major Borden, "Monthly Report of Activities for the Month of April, 1929," 5/7/29, file, "War Department Cleveland-Ordnance District-1928"; "The Cleveland Ordnance District," 1/28/26, file, "War Department-Cleveland Ordnance District-1926," Scott Papers; and Nye Committee, *Hearings*, Part 16, pp. 3996–4002, 4148–52.

6. Walsh to Scott, 7/20/20, and numerous other correspondence and documents, file, "Army Ordnance Association, 1920–1922," Scott Papers; Minutes of "Industrial Preparedness Dinner of the New York Sections of the Army Ordnance Association," 2/5/24, file 1206, Planning Branch (PB), Assistant Secretary of War (ASW), Office of the Secretary of War (OSW), RG 107, National Archives, Washington, DC (hereafter cited as PB, ASW, OSW); Nye Committee, *Hearings*, Part 16, pp. 4121–41, and Part 37, pp. 12399–405; and Lt. Gen. Levin H. Campbell, Jr., *The Industry-Ordnance Team* (New York: McGraw-Hill, 1946), pp. 17–34.

7. The role of the executive secretaries from Walsh through Codd can be traced and analyzed in the "Minutes of the Annual Meeting, Officers and Directors," and in numerous other documents and correspondence in these files: "Army Ordnance Association, 1920–1922," "Army Ordnance Association, 1923–1924–1925," "Army Ordnance Association, 1926–1927," "Army Ordnance Association, 1928–1929," and "Army Ordnance Association 1929–1931," Scott Papers; Nye Committee, *Hearings*, Part 37, pp. 12399–443, 12501–28; Campbell, *Industry-Ordnance Team*, p. 81; Constance McLauglin Green, Harry C. Thomson, and Peter C. Roots, *The Ordnance Department: Planning Munitions for War* (Washington, DC: Office of the Chief of Miliary History, 1955), p. 103. There is no scholarly work on the Army Ordnance Association. Codd wrote a volume that is useful but limited because the author was an important participant in the organization and an intense partisan—*The American Ordnance Association, 1919–1969* (Richmond, VA: William Byrd Press, 1969). An invaluable source on the association is its publication, *Army Ordnance*. From the outset, the magazine was high quality and professional. Through *Army Ordnance* it is possible to trace the major developments in the association, the Ordnance Districts, the AOA Local Posts, the Ordnance Department, and external developments affecting

these institutions. I have researched the publication from 1920 through 1941. With a few exceptions, I have not cited *Army Ordnance* in subsequent notes. However, I have depended on it to check data in the primary and secondary sources that are undeveloped, unclear, or contradictory and to determine if the magazine confirms the interpretation I have derived from other sources.

8. See sources cited in n. 7.

9. Ibid.

10. See ibid. and also Cobb to Scott, 6/1/21, file, "Army Ordnance Association, 1920–1922"; Little to Scott, 11/8/23, file, "Army Ordnance Association, 1923–1924–1925"; Major Baxter to Scott, 3/2/27, file "Army Ordnance Association, 1926–1927"; and Scott to Sparks, 1/14/29, file, "Army Ordnance Association, 1928–1929," Scott Papers.

11. Major Rose to Scott, 10/10/25, Lt. Whitney to Major Rose, 10/23/25, Scott to Dillard, 4/22/26, Robinson to Dalton, 6/8/26, Dalton to Dillard, 6/10/26, Dillard to Scott, 6/22/26, Scott to Major Rose, 7/8/26, Major Rose to Scott, 7/19/26, file "War Department-Cleveland Ordnance District-1926"; "Minutes of the Eighth Meeting of the Ordnance District Chiefs, October 4–5, 1927," file, "War Department-Cleveland Ordnance District-1927"; and General Ruggles to Scott, 6/6/28, file, "War Department-Cleveland Ordnance Department-1928," Scott Papers.

12. "Minutes of the Eighth Meeting of the Ordnance District Chiefs, October 4–5, 1927," file, "War Department-Cleveland Ordnance District-1927"; Scott to General Ruggles, 6/9/29, General Ruggles to Scott, 6/15/27, General Ruggles to Scott, 6/29/27, Captain Dillon, "Monthly Report covering course of instruction at the American Multigraph Company and the Industrial Brownhoist Corporation, Cleveland Ohio," 4/30/28, and General Ruggles to Scott, 5/16/28, file, "War Department-Cleveland Ordnance District-1928"; and Captain Dillon, "Monthly Report covering course of instruction in the plant of the American Multigraph Company, Cleveland Ohio," 4/2/28, file, "Cleveland Ordnance District, 1927–1928," Scott Papers.

13. "Minutes of the Eighth Meeting of the Ordnance District Chiefs, October 4–5, 1927," file, "War Department-Cleveland Ordnance District-1927," Scott Papers.

14. Pierce to Scott, 1/13/22, and numerous other correspondence, file, "War Department-Preparedness Program-1921–1928," and Pierce to Scott, 6/4/25, file, "Army Industrial College-4/30/25-Development of the General Munitions Board"; see also "Minutes of Meeting, Board of Directors," 1/6/21, file, "Army Ordnance Association, 1920–1922"; Little to Scott, 11/8/23, file, "Army Ordnance Association, 1923–1924–1925"; and Major Baxter to Scott, 3/2/27, file, "Army Ordnance Association, 1926–1927," all in Scott Papers.

15. Major Brett to Scott, 12/27/21, and numerous other correspondence, file, "War Department-Preparedness Program, 1921–1928," and Major Brett to Scott, 3/10/25, file, "Army Industrial College-1/15/25-Organization of the WIB," Scott Papers.

16. Brett to Baker, 4/10/24, file, "War Department-Army Industrial College," Scott Papers; see also the citations on the AIC in chap. 1, nn. 14 and 15.

17. Harold W. Thatcher, *Planning for Industrial Mobilization, 1920–1940* (Washington, DC: Office of the Quartermaster General, 1943), pp. 23–27.

18. Numerous addresses of Scott and Baruch delivered to the AIC are contained in

the Baruch and Scott Papers, various War Department files, files of the Army War College, and elsewhere. Many of these addresses have been cited in chapters 1 and 2, and others are cited subsequently. Nye Committee, *Hearings,* Part 16, pp. 4146–47, includes an extended list of speakers appearing before the AIC.

19. War Department, *Report of the Secretary of War to the President,* 1926 (Washington, DC: U.S. Government Printing Office, 1927), pp. 30–31 (hereafter cited as *Annual Report of the Secretary of War [ARSW]; ARSW,* 1929, pp. 35–65; Davis to Scott, 4/6/25, and Scott to Davis, 4/8/25, file, "War Department-General-1922–1926," Scott Papers; and Paul A. C. Koistinen, "The 'Industrial-Military Complex' in Historical Perspective: The Interwar Years," *Journal of American History* 56 (March 1970): 826–27.

20. Davis and Weeks are discussed in chapter 1.

21. The information relating to Davis's elevation to the office of secretary of war is taken from letters, telegrams, and other documents, beginning with Dravo to Scott, 5/1/25, file, "War Department-General-1922–1926"; see also Walsh to Scott, 11/14/24, file, "General Correspondence, 1914–1931, P-Z," and Colonel Hunt to Scott, 5/14/26, file, "War Department-Army Industrial College-1924–1928," all in Scott Papers.

22. The General Ruggles imbroglio is covered in elaborate detail in the numerous documents starting with General Williams to the Adjutant General of the Army, 12/10/26, file, "Correspondence with the War Department (Ordnance), 1927–1931," Scott Papers. Letters and memorandums of Ruggles, other Ordnance officers, and the Ordnance District chiefs set forth forcefully the consequences of Davis's proposed new policy for the SA&S in general, Ordnance in particular, and Ruggles as a special case. These documents also provide background on the intricacies of the War Department's promotion policies. Numerous documents scattered throughout the Scott Papers illustrate Ruggles's capabilities as an assistant chief of ordnance and as the director of the Ordnance Districts. For example, see "Minutes of the Eighth Meeting of the Ordnance District Chiefs, October 4–5, 1927," file, "War Department-Cleveland Ordnance District-1927." AOA and Ordnance District leaders later made an unsuccessful attempt to persuade the War Department to allow General Williams to continue as chief of ordnance once his tour of duty was up and his retirement from active duty expected.

23. Nye Committee, *Hearings,* Part 37, pp. 12420–24, 12508–17.

24. Ibid., pp. 12424, 12515.

25. Ibid., p. 12425. The entire Nye Committee hearings and exhibits involving the AOA are found in ibid., pp. 12399–443, 12501–28. The AOA appeared in a more negative light from information contained in the Nye Committee hearings (covering principally the 1930s) than from the Scott Papers (dealing mostly with the 1920s). Nye, his associates, and staff, however, turned up little hard evidence of questionable action or wrongdoing by the AOA, even though the committee appeared to be straining to do so and, uncharacteristically, attempted to treat the AOA witness rather unfairly. For further documentation on the AOA and its influence in reserve officer affairs, see Scott to Secretary of War, 4/7/26, and Secretary of War to Scott, 4/14/26, file, "War Department-General-1922–1926"; Walsh to Scott, 10/15/24, file, "Army Industrial College, 1/15/25-Organization of the WIB"; General Williams to Scott, 11/29/24, file, "War Department, General Correspondence, 1914–1931, A-N"; and Scott to Walsh, 11/4/24, file, "General Correspondence, 1914–1931, P-Z," Scott

Papers. Only a few instances of outright influence-peddling by the AOA over military contracts were exposed by the Nye Committee or are evident in the Scott Papers (see preceding references on the Nye Committee). See also chairman, Creditors' Committee to Assistant Secretary of War, 2/5/27, and other correspondence, file, "War Department-Cleveland Ordnance District-1927," also in Scott Papers.

26. See chapter 1, particularly n. 6, for further discussion, cross references, and citation of other sources on this subject. See also Scott to Dravo, 4/19/26, and numerous other correspondence, file, "War Department-Army Industrial College-1924–1928"; Scott, "Industrial Mobilization"; 3/19/27, and Colonel Carr to Scott, 9/19/27, file, "Quartermaster Convention-Washington, DC-Industrial Mobilization"; and Scott, "Industrial Mobilization for a Great War," 12/26/26, file, "Army War College-12/16/26-Industrial Mobilization for a Great War," Scott Papers.

27. For a fuller discussion of these themes, see chapter 1.

28. The information on educational orders is drawn from Jones to General Ruggles, 10/20/27, and numerous other correspondence and documents, file, "War Department-Preparedness Program-1921–1928"; "Minutes of the Eighth Meeting of the Ordnance District Chiefs, October 4–5, 1927," file, "War Department-Cleveland Ordnance District-1927"; and Davis to Chairman, Senate Military Affairs Committee, 9/24/27, with enclosures, and other documents, file, "War Department-Cleveland Ordnance District-1928," Scott Papers; Nye Committee, *Hearings,* Part 37, pp. 12399–443, 12501–28; Col. Harry K. Rutherford, "Educational Orders: Peace Time Training for Industry in Arms Manufacture," *Army Ordnance* 20 (November–December 1939): 162–71—this issue also contains a copy of the statute authorizing educational orders, enacted in 1938 along with some additional background information; Peter M. Abramo, "The Economic and Military Potential of the United States: Industrial Mobilization Planning, 1919–1945" (Ph.D. diss., Temple University, 1995), pp. 82–91; and Koistinen, "Industrial-Military Complex," p. 838, and n. 58.

29. Walsh to Scott, 7/2/26, and Scott to Walsh, 7/8/26, file, "War Department-Cleveland Ordnance District-1926"; "Comments of District Chiefs on Basic Charts for District Office, 11/18/24," file, "War Department-Cleveland Ordnance District-1925"; and Franklin to General Williams, 2/17/27, file, "War Department-Cleveland Ordnance District-1927," Scott Papers.

30. Scott to General Williams, 4/5/27, General Williams to Scott, 4/12/27, and Scott to General Williams, 4/15/27, file, "War Department-Cleveland Ordnance District-1927," and General Ruggles to Scott, 3/12/28, file, "War Department-Cleveland Ordnance District-1928," Scott Papers.

31. Scott to General Williams, 2/12/26, and other correspondence, file, "War Department-Cleveland Ordnance District-1926"; "Minutes of the Eighth Meeting of the Ordnance District Chiefs, October 4–5, 1927," file, "War Department-Cleveland Ordnance District-1927"; and General Ruggles to Scott, 3/26/25, and other correspondence and documents, file, "Cleveland Ordnance District-1925," Scott Papers.

32. Franklin to Davis, 1/10/27, file, "Correspondence with War Department (Ordnance), 1927–1931," Scott Papers.

33. Ibid.

34. AOA attitudes and activities in general and the annual meetings specifically can be traced from the documents in "Army Ordnance Association-1920–1922," "Army Ordnance Association-1923–1924–1925," "Army Ordnance Association-1926–1927,"

"Army Ordnance Association-1928–1929," and "Army Ordnance Association-1929–1931," Scott Papers. See also Nye Committee, *Hearings*, Part 37, pp. 12399–443, 12501–28, and *Army Ordnance*, 1920–1941.

35. Little to Scott, 11/8/23, file, "Army Ordnance Association, 1923–1924–1925," Scott Papers.

36. Crowell to Hurley, 2/1930, file 334.8/246.2, PB, ASW, OSW.

37. "Minutes of Meeting of the Board of Directors of the Army Ordnance Association, 1/23/23," file, "Army Ordnance Association, 1923–1924–1925," and "Minutes of a Meeting of the Trustees and Directors, Army Ordnance Association," January 1930, file, "Army Ordnance Association, 1929–1931," Scott Papers; Delafield to Davis, 1/6/25, file, 1241; and "Industrial Preparedness Dinner of the New York Sections of the Army Ordnance Association," 2/5/24, file 1206, PB, ASW, OSW.

38. Major Brett to Scott, 10/30/22, and other correspondence and documents, file, "War Department-Preparedness Program-1921–1928," Scott Papers.

39. Ibid., Walsh to Scott, 8/16/24.

40. Ibid., Scott to Walsh, 9/19/24, and other correspondence.

41. Walsh to Scott, 3/19/25, file, "General Correspondence, 1914–1931, P-Z"; for other examples of Gary's efforts in behalf of industrial preparedness, see Walsh to Scott, 11/6/24, and Gary to Scott, 3/18/25, file, "Army Industrial College-1/15/21-Organization of the WIB," all in Scott Papers; and Major Hardigg to OASW, 9/9/25, file 292, PB, ASW, OSW.

42. "Industrial Preparedness Dinner of the New York Sections of the Army Ordnance Association," 2/5/24, file 1206, PB, ASW, OSW.

43. The information on the ASME is based on Colonel Ferguson to Rice, 6/13/23, and numerous other correspondence and documents, file 1201; Colonel Ferguson Memorandum to Chiefs of all Supply Branches, 3/5/25, and other correspondence and documents, file 1202; and Major Pettis to Dr. Green, 12/23/24, file 1203, PB, ASW, OSW; Bullock, "National Defense Division-Minutes of Meeting," 12/10/24, and numerous other correspondence and documents, file, "General Correspondence, 1914–1931, A-N"; Walsh to Scott, 1/26/26, file, "General Correspondence, 1914–1931, P-Z"; Major Hobley to Scott, 5/25/25, file, "War Department-General-1922–1926"; Baur to Scott, 6/3/24, file, "War Department-Preparedness Program-1921–1928"; "The Cleveland Ordnance District," 1/28/26, file, "War Department-Cleveland Ordnance District-1926," Scott Papers; and Colonel Ferguson, "Industrial Mobilization," file, 215-114, 228-50, Army War College Collection, Carlisle Barracks, Carlisle, PA (hereafter cited as AWC Collection). Bruce Sinclair's *A Centennial History of the American Society of Mechanical Engineers, 1880–1980* (Toronto: University of Toronto Press, 1980) is a useful history of the society, which includes background information helpful to understanding the ASME's preparedness programs and proposals. The *Proceedings* of the ASME conventions and meetings are included in whole or in part in the trade publication *The Iron Age* during the 1920s and into the 1930s. Howard E. Coffin is discussed in Koistinen, *Mobilizing for Modern War*, chaps. 7 and 8.

44. Scott to Assistant Secretary of War, 11/9/25, file, "General Correspondence, 1914–1931, A-N," Scott Papers. Scott proposed that Baruch be included among the event's notables, but his name is missing from the list. Almost a year earlier, Walsh had

requested that Baruch serve on the advisory board of the New York Ordnance District. Baruch declined, indicating that he should sit on a national, not a regional, advisory board, if one were established. Rivalries among wartime mobilization figures seemed to be involved in Baruch's absence from AOA–Ordnance District affairs. Whether Baruch was being aloof, the Ordnance group standoffish, or a combination of the two is difficult to discern. See Walsh to Scott, 8/16/24, file, "War Department-Preparedness Program-1921–1928," also in Scott Papers.

45. General Ruggles to Bruce, 11/1/26, file, "War Department-Preparedness Program-1926–1928," and Scott to Durand, 12/22/24, file, "General Correspondence 1914–1931, A-N," Scott Papers.

46. Some information concerning the counterparts of the AOA for the other SA&S is available in "Proceedings of the Quartermaster Convention held in Washington, DC, March 18–19, 1927," and in other documents, file, "Quartermaster Convention-Washington, DC, Industrial Mobilization," and "Joint Memorandum of suggested amalgamation of the Society of Military Engineers and the Army Ordnance Association," 7/29/21, file, "Army Ordnance Association, 1920–1922," Scott Papers; and in "Signal Corps Industrial Defense Association, New York City, New York, Minutes of Meeting, April 23rd, 24th, 1925," and other documents, file 1242, PB, ASW, OSW.

47. The analysis of the AIME and its work with the War Department is based on the entire file, beginning with Major Ramsey to Colonel Saltzman, 1/18/22, file 1192, PB, ASW, OSW; entire file, beginning with memorandum, "History of the Mineral Advisory Committee to the Assistant Secretary of War," 10/7/38, file 370.26/213.0, Records of the Joint Army and Navy Boards and Committees, RG 225, National Archives, Washington, DC (hereafter cited as ANMB); Colonel Ferguson to Dwight, 10/12/23, and other documents, file 285, PB, ASW, OSW; and Colonel Ferguson, "Industrial Mobilization," 5/26/22, file 215-114, 228-50, AWC Collection. Several secondary sources are relevant to the work of the AIME and related institutions: Brooks Emeny, *The Strategy of Raw Materials: A Study of America in Peace and War* (New York: Macmillan, 1937); G. A. Roush, *Strategic Mineral Supplies* (New York: McGraw-Hill, 1939); Stephen D. Krasner, *Defending the National Interest: Raw Materials Investments and U.S. Foreign Policy* (Princeton, NJ: Princeton University Press, 1978); Alfred E. Eckes, *The United States and the Global Struggle for Minerals* (Austin: University of Texas Press, 1979); and Sylvia W. McGrath, *Charles Kenneth Leith, Scientific Adviser* (Madison: University of Wisconsin Press, 1971). The Emeny and Roush volumes draw directly upon studies done for or by the OASW. The work of the AIME and the Mining and Metallurgical Society of America in behalf of the OASW actually began earlier as part of an effort to establish international control over all raw materials in order to advance the cause of peace and to reduce the possibility of war.

48. Dwight to Ferguson, 8/14/22, file 1192, PB, ASW, OSW.

49. Lieutenant Colonel Hines to Colonel Rutherford, 6/1/39, file 370.26/213.0, ANMB.

50. Major Pettis to Colonel Ferguson, 2/24/22, with attached address, file 1192, PB, ASW, OSW.

51. Ibid., quotations from Jordan to Johnson, 3/9/38, file 334.8/246.2. For further information about the NICB, see Robert H. Wiebe, *Businessmen and Reform: A*

Study of the Progressive Movement (Cambridge: Harvard University Press, 1962), pp. 31, 32–33, 39, and 178.

52. General Ruggles to Bruce, 11/1/26, file, "War Department-Preparedness Program-1921–1928," Scott Papers.

53. Ibid., Scott to General Ruggles, 11/12/26.

54. Alexander to Payne, 5/6/30, file 334.8/246.2, PB, ASW, OSW.

55. The information on the NICB comes from Alexander to Scott and numerous other correspondence, file, "War Department-Preparedness Program-1921–1928," Scott Papers, and entire file, beginning with Alexander to Payne, 5/6/30, file 334.8/246.2, PB, ASW, OSW. See also the sources cited in note 51.

56. Colonel Saltzman Memorandum, 5/17/23, file 1226, PB, ASW, OSW.

57. "Preliminary Report, Committee on Industrial Preparedness, National Association of Manufacturers," 12/15/26, file, "War Department-Preparedness Program-1921–1928," Scott Papers.

58. The analysis of the NAM and its interaction with the War Department involving industrial preparedness is based on National Association of Manufacturers, *Proceedings of the Twenty-Eighth Annual Convention*, 1923, pp. 278–79, and *Proceedings of the Thirty-first Annual Convention*, 1926, pp. 52–54, 275–93 (*Proceedings* of the annual conventions and meetings throughout the 1920s are significant for what they contain and omit about national defense and subjects related to it); entire file beginning with MacNider to Walker, 12/6/26, file 334.8/246.2, and Colonel Saltzman memorandum and other documents, file 1226, PB, ASW, OSW; "Minutes, Annual Meeting, Board of Directors, Army Ordnance Association, February 1928," file, "Army Ordnance Association, 1928–1929," and Benton to Scott, 11/15/26, with enclosures, and numerous other documents, file, "War Department-Preparedness Program-1921–28," Scott Papers. See also the sources on the NAM cited in Koistinen, *Mobilizing for Modern War*, chap. 7, n. 3.

59. Fuller to Patterson, 8/26/41, file 334.8/246.2, PB, ASW, OSW.

60. These themes will be explored further and documented in the forthcoming volume four of this series.

61. The role of the Chamber of Commerce in mobilizing the World War I economy is analyzed in Koistinen, *Mobilizing for Modern War*, chaps. 7–10.

62. The information on and analysis of the Chamber of Commerce–War Department relations are based on the entire file, beginning with Lt. Col. Burton memorandum, 5/8/26, file 334.8/246.2, and entire file, beginning with C. R. P. to Colonel Ferguson, 5/11/23, file 1211, PB, ASW, OSW; and Fitzpatrick to Pierce, 2/15/30, with enclosures, file, "Aftermath-1930 through 1940," Scott Papers. See also the analysis of and documentation concerning the Chamber of Commerce in Koistinen, *Mobilizing for Modern War*, chap. 7.

63. Fitzpatrick to Pierce, 2/15/30, with attached, "Summary of Report on Work of Special Committee on National Defense," 1/24/30, file, "Aftermath-1930 through 1940," Scott Papers.

64. Major Wilkes to Executive, Office of the Assistant Secretary of War, 2/17/30, file 334.8/246.2, PB, ASW, OSW.

65. Ibid., General Simonds to Chief of Staff, 11/18/33, and also Colonel Voris to General Drum, 11/13/33.

66. Ibid., Colonel Voris to General Drum, 12/20/33.

CHAPTER FOUR. COMMODITY COMMITTEES

1. Commodity committees and their operations have been introduced and explicated in chapter 1.
2. The commodity committee activity as outlined in the six categories includes most but not all of the OASW's work in this area. Commodity committees were also created for products like abrasives, automobiles, fibers such as jute, foodstuffs, paints and pigments, and refractories. Such committees, however, were never activated, only briefly activated, or remained relatively inactive throughout the interwar period. The OASW did not consider these products to be of pressing importance, or it believed commodity committees inappropriate for handling them. Information on those commodity committees that received little attention is available in files 151–365, Planning Branch (PB), Assistant Secretary of War (ASW), Office of the Secretary of War (OSW), RG 107, National Archives, Washington, DC (hereafter cited as PB, ASW, OSW).

The OASW had other means for gaining information about and making contacts with business America. Almost all strategic and critical materials, and many essential ones as well, were the subject of Resource Studies—brief to extended monographlike analyses of various products written by army officers or government agencies such as the U.S. Geological Survey, the U.S. Bureau of Mines, and the Department of Agriculture. These studies were carried out in the 1920s, and most were completed before 1928. The Resource Studies are contained in files 1018-1109, PB, ASW, OSW.

Additionally, between 1926 and 1928, the OASW had the supply bureaus complete Organizational Surveys of corporations with which they dealt or would deal in the future. These studies usually turned out to be quite superficial and were halted as a result of loud protests from the supply arms and services about their uselessness. Only in instances where officers spent a great deal of time studying or visiting a business or both and became privy to confidential information were the efforts worthwhile. This was the case with the Aluminum Company of America (Alcoa), American Telephone and Telegraph Company (ATT), and some machine tool firms. The Organizational Surveys are in files 632–96, PB, ASW, OSW. The army's study of ATT is covered in these files. For Alcoa and machine tool firms, see chapters 6 and 8.

The OASW also maintained files on almost all trade associations and professional groups involved in World War I mobilization and interwar planning, plus other organizations relevant to its work, such as the American Federation of Labor and the Carnegie Endowment for International Peace. Technical societies and associations are covered in files 1185–1247, PB, ASW, OSW. Further, through studies of and plans written for power, fuel, transportation, labor, and finance, the military worked closely with many economic groups and numerous government agencies. These efforts were supplemented by War Department Mobilization Monographs, written in the 1920s by army officers on subjects such as allocations and conversion. The mobilization monographs are in files 1418–46, PB, ASW, OSW.

3. The classification of commodities tended to be somewhat erratic and unreliable. By definition, most products were at least essential and certainly so if a commodity committee was established to study them. If a product does not appear on a strategic/critical/essential list but had a commodity committee (active or inactive) appointed to study it, then that commodity will be classified as essential, for purposes of discussion.

CHAPTER FIVE. STEEL

1. See chapter 4, Table 4.1.
2. See chapter 3.
3. See Paul A. C. Koistinen, *Mobilizing for Modern War: The Political Economy of American Warfare, 1865–1919* (Lawrence: University Press of Kansas, 1997), chaps. 8–10.
4. Davis to Bonner, 7/17/23, and numerous other correspondence, file 90, and Whelan, "Minutes of the War Department Commodity Committee on Steel and Non-Ferrous Metals," file 282, Planning Branch (PB), Assistant Secretary of War (ASW), Office of the Secretary of War (OSW), RG 107, National Archives, Washington, DC (hereafter cited as PB, ASW, OSW); Grosvenor B. Clarkson, *Industrial American in the World War: The Strategy Behind the Line, 1917–1918* (Boston: Houghton Mifflin, 1923), p. 537.
5. See Koistinen, *Mobilizing for Modern War,* chap. 12.
6. Nix to Clark, 8/11/26 (quotation), and Nix memorandum, "Conference with J. B. Bonner," 12/19/24, file 90, PB, ASW, OSW.
7. Ibid., Davis to Bonner, 7/17/23, and other correspondence, file 90, and Nix to Ferguson, 6/3/27, and other correspondence, file 91.
8. For an explanation of these terms, see chapter 1.
9. Nix, "Work of War Department Commodity Committee no. 45, Iron and Steel," 5/7/28, file 91 and other correspondence in that file and file 90, PB, ASW, OSW.
10. Ibid., Nix memorandum, 12/23/25, and other documents, file 90, and Bonner to Ferguson, 6/7/27, and other documents, file 91.
11. Ibid., Nix memorandum, 12/19/24 (quotations), and other correspondence, file 90, and Nix to Assistant Secretary of War, 8/23/28, and other correspondence, file 91.
12. Ibid., Nix to Bonner, 12/19/24 (quotation), and Nix to Clark, 8/11/26, file 90, and Ferguson to Chiefs All Supply Branches, 11/1/27, file 91. For bureau complaints, see Williams to Assistant Secretary of War, 5/14/29, and other correspondence, file 470.1/129.5, and Nix to Hobley, 8/14/28, file 91.
13. Ibid., Nix, "Work of War Department Commodity Committee no. 45, Iron and Steel," 5/7/28, file 91.
14. Ibid., Davis to Bonner, 7/17/23, file 90.
15. The transformation in steel-military relations can be traced in ibid., 470.1/129.5 files series. Good information on the dynamics of the steel industry is available in Robert Hessen, *Steel Titan: The Life of Charles M. Schwab* (New York: Oxford University Press, 1975), pp. 267–69, 279–81. A fine, brief study of the steel industry is offered by Walter Adams, "The Steel Industry," in *The Structure of American Industry: Some Case Studies,* ed. Adams, pp. 144–84, 3d ed. (New York: Macmillan, 1961). See also Melvin I. Urofsky, *Big Steel and the Wilson Administration: A Study in Business-Government Relations* (Columbus: Ohio State University Press, 1969); Robert D. Cuff and Melvin I. Urofsky, "The Steel Industry and Price-Fixing During World War I," *Business History Review* 44 (Autumn 1970): 291–306; William T. Hogan, *Economic History of the Iron and Steel Industry in the United States,* 5 vols. (Lexington, MA: DC Heath, 1971); Kenneth Warren, *The American Steel Industry, 1850–1970: A Geographical Interpretation* (Oxford: Clarendon Press, 1973); Richard

A. Lauderbaugh, *American Steel Makers and the Coming of the Second World War* (Ann Arbor: UMI Research Press, 1980); and Philip E. Brown, "The American Steel Industry: An Analysis of Its History, Strategies, and Market Control" (Ph.D. diss., Union Institute, 1994). Thomas J. Misa, *A Nation of Steel: The Making of Modern America, 1865–1925* (Baltimore: Johns Hopkins University Press, 1995), analyzes the American steel industry in an imaginative way. In chapter 3 he focuses on the making of armor for the navy in the late nineteenth and early twentieth centuries, which adds some new information and insight to my analysis of the subject in Koistinen, *Mobilizing for Modern War*, chap. 3.

16. Bonner to Robbins, 4/11/28, and other correspondence, file 91, PB, ASW, OSW.

17. Ibid., Wooten to Chiefs of All Supply Branches, 4/13/29, Hobley to Knapp, 10/27/31, and other correspondence, file 470.1/129.5.

18. Ibid., Nickerson to Hobley, 2/24/32 (quotations), and other documents.

19. Ibid. For the writing of the first IMP and its review by the WPC, see chapters 2 and 13. War Department–steel relations were no doubt slow to be reestablished after the break in 1929, partly because during the years from 1929 to 1932 the OASW became almost totally absorbed in writing the IMP, 1930, and in the operations of the WPC.

20. Hobley to Knapp, 10/27/31, and other correspondence, file 470.1/129.5, PB, ASW, OSW.

21. Change within the OASW and its new start in the 1930s are clearly evident in ibid., Voris to Tower, 2/28/34.

22. Minton prepared a document in 1934 that summarizes the contents of the OASW files on steel from 1923 to 1934. This summary is particularly valuable since some documents are missing from the existing files. See ibid., Minton, "Digest of O.A.S.W. Files, Commodity Committee no. 45, Iron and Steel, July 5, 1934," file 470.1/129.5.

23. Ibid., Minton, "Proposed Revisions of 1927 Steel Plan," 7/17/34, and Voris to Tower, 2/28/34; writing the Steel Plan, 1936, as opposed to proposals for doing so, is covered in the 470.1/129.5 file series.

24. Ibid., Minton to Director, Planning Branch, 7/9/35, Minton to Harris, 12/14/36, *O.A.S.W.—1936 Revision of Steel Plan*, and numerous other documents, file 470.1/129.5.

25. Ibid., Minton to Office of the Assistant Secretary of War, 11/7/34, Minton to Harris, 7/5/35, and numerous other documents.

26. Ibid., Rutherford to Perry, 1/21/39, Becker to Director, Planning Branch, 1/22/40, Rutherford to Johnson, 1/3/39, and numerous other documents.

27. Ibid., Tower to Rutherford, 6/27/40 (documentation on the AISI's role in the 1940 plan is included in n. 26).

28. Ibid., Harmon to Chief of Ordnance, 9/30/34, with enclosure, Rose to McFarland, 1/13/36, Harris to Schwartz, 3/3/38, and numerous other correspondence.

CHAPTER SIX. ALUMINUM AND RUBBER

1. It is unclear from the records whether the study was a seminar report, a thesis for a degree, or part of some larger project because references to it are both vague and

contradictory. No Harvard University library currently catalogs the work. See also Brooks Emeny, *The Strategy of Raw Materials: A Study of America in Peace and War* (New York: Macmillan, 1937), consult index; G. A. Roush, *Strategic Mineral Supplies* (New York: McGraw-Hill, 1939), pp. 200–237; Charlotte F. Muller, *Light Metals Monopoly* (New York: Columbia University Press, 1946); Louis Marlio, *The Aluminum Cartel* (Washington, DC: Brookings Institution, 1947); Robert F. Lanzillotti, "The Aluminum Industry," in *The Structure of American Industry: Some Case Studies*, ed. Walter Adams, pp. 185–232, 3d ed. (New York: Macmillan, 1961); Alfred E. Eckes, Jr., *The United States and the Global Struggle for Minerals* (Austin: University of Texas Press, 1979), consult index; George D. Smith, *From Monopoly to Competition: The Transformation of Alcoa, 1888–1986* (New York: Cambridge University Press, 1988); and Margaret B. W. Graham and Bettye H. Pruitt, *R&D for Industry: A Century of Technical Innovation at Alcoa* (New York: Cambridge University Press, 1990).

2. Harris to Chiefs, Supply Arms and Services, 8/22/34, file 470.1/129.2, Planning Branch (PB), Assistant Secretary of War (ASW), Office of the Secretary of War (OSW), RG 107, National Archives, Washington, DC (hereafter cited as PB, ASW, OSW).

3. Ibid., Woodring to Hobley, 4/4/34, file 268, Hobbs to Hobley, 1/20/34, Harris to Assistant Chief of Staff, G-4, 12/7/36, and other correspondence. A copy of Hobley's report was not located in the files, perhaps for reasons to be explained, but an outline of the report's contents is provided in "Memorandum for Colonel Rutherford," 4/29/38. The 470.1/129.2 file series also include documents that constantly refer to the nature and content of Hobley's work.

4. Ibid., Hobbs to Hobley, 1/29/34, and other documents, file 268; Wagner, "Report of Meeting of Commodity Committee no. 34-Non-Ferrous Metals," 11/14/33, file 282; and Harris to Chief of Staff, 4/15/35, Johnson Memorandum, "Aluminum and Aluminum Alloys-Productive Capacity of the Aluminum Company of America," 4/18/35, and other documents, file 470.1/129.2.

5. Ibid., Harris to the Assistant Chief of Staff, G-4, 12/7/34 (quotation), and Crom, "Minutes of Meeting of Commodity Committee no. 34-Non-Ferrous Metals," 2/30/36.

6. Ibid., Hopkins to Ramsey, 1/19/37, and numerous other documents.

7. Ibid., Rutherford to Hill, 5/25/40.

8. Ibid., Hopkins to Ramsey, 1/19/37, Hopkins to Logan, 3/36/38, Hopkins to Rogers, 2/25/37, Rogers to Hopkins, 3/31/39, and numerous other documents.

9. Ibid., Cummings to Secretary of War, 1/3/38.

10. Ibid., Harris Memorandum, 1/12/38.

11. Ibid., Secretary of War to Attorney General, 1/13/38, Gibbons to Woodring, 4/29/38, and numerous other documents.

12. Ibid., Rogers to Harris, 4/22/38.

13. Ibid., W. R. W. to Harris, 5/13/38.

14. Ibid., Gibbons to Woodring, 4/6/34, file 268.

15. The discussion on rubber is based on an excellent collection of memorandums and studies made by or presented to the OASW, including Rogers to Assistant Secretary of War, 8/1/22, Hunt to Ferguson, 1/29/23, McCain, Memorandum for File, 1/15/25, Assistant Secretary of War to the Secretary of Agriculture, 9/23/25, file 336; Stanley and Evans, "Monthly Report, Commodity Committee no. 42 (Rubber),"

3/31/26, Hardman, "Regular Meeting War Department Commodity Committee no. 42, Rubber and Rubber Goods," 9/27/28, Sadler, "Report of War Department Commodity Committee no. 42 (Rubber)," 4/29/31, with enclosure, Braden, "Minutes of Meeting of Commodity Committee no. 42-Rubber," 3/6/34, file 340, and Rogers and King, "Minutes of Meeting of Army and Navy Munitions Board Commodity Committee no. 42-Rubber," 11/3/36, file 400/129.18, PB, ASW, OSW. See also Brooks Emeny, *Strategy of Raw Materials*, pp. 132–38; Stephen D. Krasner, *Defending the National Interest: Raw Materials Investments and U.S. Foreign Policy* (Princeton, NJ: Princeton University Press, 1978), pp. 98–106; and Austin Coates, *The Commerce in Rubber: The First 250 Years* (Singapore: Oxford University Press, 1987).

16. McCain, Memorandum for File, 10/1/24, and other correspondence, file 340, and Assistant Secretary of War to Secretary of Agriculture, 9/23/25, and other correspondence, file 336, PB, ASW, OSW; Carnahan to Baruch, 9/27/27, with attached correspondence, and Carnahan to Baruch, 3/28/30, with attachment of numerous exchanges with Edison, Selected Correspondence, Bernard M. Baruch Papers, Princeton University, Princeton, NJ (hereafter cited as Baruch Papers).

17. Carnahan to Hurley, 5/4/32, file 336, PB, ASW, OSW.

18. For the information on guayule rubber, see Carnahan to Baruch and Baruch to Carnahan with various attachments, Selected Correspondence for the years 1927, 1928, 1930, and 1934, Baruch Papers; Carnahan to Huston, 1/2/30 and numerous other correspondence, file 336; and Sadler, "Report of Commodity Committee no. 42 (Rubber)," 3/24/30, and numerous other documents, file 340, PB, ASW, OSW.

19. Rogers to Assistant Secretary of War, 8/1/22, file 336, and Crom, "Minutes of Meetings of Commodity Committee no. 42-Rubber," 3/6/34, file 340, PB, ASW, OSW; Carnahan to Baruch, 3/28/30, with enclosure, Selected Correspondence, Baruch Papers.

20. Secretary of Commerce to Secretary of Agriculture, 8/10/26, which is an enclosure from McCain from Cook, 10/8/26, file 336; see also McCain, Memorandum for File, 1/15/25, PB, ASW, OSW.

21. Ibid., I. L. H., "Conference with Agriculture Department on Rubber," 6/3/28, and numerous other documents, file 336, and McCain, Memorandum for File, 10/1/24, and numerous other documents, file 340; Baruch and Carnahan correspondence with enclosures, Selected Correspondence for the years 1927, 1928, 1930, and 1934, Baruch Papers.

22. The quotations are from Browne to Colonels Rutherford, Hines, and others, 11/16/39, file 470.1/203.2-18.2, Records of the Joint Army and Navy Boards and Committees, RG 225, National Archives, Washington, DC (hereafter cited as ANMB).

23. Ibid., Howard to Stettinius, 6/11/40.

24. On synthetic rubber, see Casey to OASW, 11/30/31, and numerous other documents, file 336; Sadler, "Report of War Dept. Commodity Committee no. 42 (Rubber and Rubber Goods)," 12/16/31, and numerous other documents, file 340; and Baker, "Memorandum for the Assistant Secretary of War," 9/2/38, and numerous other documents, file 400/129.18, PB, ASW, OSW; and Hines to Howard, 11/16/39, and numerous other documents, file 470.1/203.2-18.2, ANMB. See also U.S. Cong., Senate, Subcommittee on Patents, Trademarks, and Copyrights of the Committee on the Judiciary, *Synthetic Rubber: A Case Study in Technological Development Under Government Direction*, Study no. 18, by Robert A. Solo, 85th Cong., 2d

sess., 1959, pp. 1–69; Solo, "Research and Development in the Synthetic Rubber Industry," *Quarterly Journal of Economics* 68 (February 1954): 61–82; Paul Wendt, "The Control of Rubber in World War II," *Southern Economic Journal* 13 (January 1947): 203–27; William M. Tuttle, Jr., "The Birth of an Industry: The Synthetic Rubber 'Mess' in World War II," *Technology and Culture* 22 (January 1981): 35–67; Vernon Herbert and Attilio Bisio, *Synthetic Rubber: A Project That Had to Succeed* (Westport, CT: Greenwood, 1985); David R. B. Ross, "Patents and Bureaucrats: U.S. Synthetic Rubber Development Before Pearl Harbor," in *Business and Government: Essays in Twentieth-Century Cooperation and Confrontation,* ed. Joseph R. Frese and Jacob Judd, pp. 119–55 (Tarrytown, NY: Sleepy Hollow Press, 1985); and Peter T. Morris, *The American Synthetic Rubber Research Program* (Philadelphia: University of Pennsylvania Press, 1989). Synthetic rubber immediately before and during World War II will be analyzed at length in the forthcoming volume 4 of this series.

25. Kelley to Assistant Secretary of War, 1/28/29, file 340, PB, ASW, OSW.

26. For OASW planning for rubber, see ibid., Stanley and Evans to Chief, Procurement Division, 3/16/25, and numerous other documents, file 340; Stanley and Evans to the Chief of Procurement Division, 6/15/25, and numerous other documents, file 336; and Harris to the Quartermaster General, 7/22/35, and numerous other documents, file 400/129.18.

27. Industry's motivation for participating in the planning is addressed in the PB, ASW, OSW files cited. See also ibid., Sprowls to McKay, 10/1/24, and numerous other correspondence, file 336; Stanley to Chief, Procurement Division, 2/16/25, and numerous other correspondence, file 340; and Ingels to Harris, 3/12/37, and other correspondence, file 400/29.18.

CHAPTER SEVEN. PETROLEUM, COPPER, AND LEAD

1. The American Institute of Mining and Metallurgical Engineers and the Mining and Metallurgical Society of America studied and reported to the OASW on nonferrous metals and other commodities in the 1920s. This work led to the organization of the Mineral Advisory Committee, which advised the OASW in the 1920s and 1930s and later served under the Army-Navy Munitions Board.

2. See Chapter 5 for steel.

3. Foley to Ferguson, 2/14/27, file 317, Planning Branch (PB), Assistant Secretary of War (ASW), Office of the Secretary of War (OSW), RG 107, National Archives, Washington, DC (hereafter cited as PB, ASW, OSW).

4. Ibid., Ferguson to Foley, 2/25/27.

5. Ibid., Paris to Dunn, 6/14/29.

6. Ibid., Crom, "Minutes of the Meeting of Commodity Committee no. 38-Petroleum and Products," 2/6/34, and Kelton, "Monthly Activities of the W.D.C.C. no. 38, Petroleum and Petroleum Products," 6/6/27, file 322.

7. For the discussion and analysis of oil and the OASW planning for it, see ibid., Nix, "Memorandum for the Files, O.A.S.W.," 7/17/26, and numerous other documents and correspondence, file 317; Kelton memorandum for the ASW, 11/30/25 and numerous other documents and correspondence, file 322; Moran to Woodring, 3/4/35, and other correspondence, Rogers and King, "Minutes of Meeting of Army

and Navy Munitions Board Commodity Committee no. 38-Petroleum and Petroleum Products," 11/3/36, and Sadler to Wesson, 11/2/39, and other correspondence, file 470.1/129.8; see also Austin to Mason, 3/17/38, and other correspondence, file 470.1/203.2-16.1, Records of the Joint Army and Navy Boards and Committees, RG 225, National Archives, Washington, DC (hereafter cited as ANMB). Secondary sources on petroleum are numerous. For some of the better ones, see U.S. Cong., Senate, Subcommittee on Monopoly of the Select Committee on Small Business, Staff Report to the Federal Trade Commission, *The International Petroleum Cartel*, 82d Cong., 2d sess., Committee Print no. 6, 1952; Joel B. Dirlam, "The Petroleum Industry," in *The Structure of American Industry: Some Case Studies*, ed. Walter Adams, pp. 277–310, rev. ed. (New York: Macmillan, 1961); Harold F. Williamson et al., *The American Petroleum Industry*, vol. 2, *The Age of Energy, 1899–1959* (Evanston, IL: Northwestern University Press, 1963); Gerald D. Nash, *United States Oil Policy, 1890–1964: Business and Government in Twentieth-Century America* (Pittsburgh, PA: University of Pittsburgh Press, 1968); Mira Wilkins, *The Maturing of Multinational Enterprise: American Business Abroad from 1914–1970* (Cambridge: Harvard University Press, 1974), consult index; Anthony Sampson, *The Seven Sisters: The Great Oil Companies and the World They Made* (New York: Viking Press, 1975); John M. Blair, *The Control of Oil* (New York: Pantheon Books, 1976); Norman E. Nordhauser, *The Quest for Stability: Domestic Oil Regulation 1917–1935* (New York: Garland Publishing, 1979); Michael B. Stoff, *Oil, War, and American Security: The Search for a National Policy on Foreign Oil, 1941–1947* (New Haven: Yale University Press, 1980); and David S. Painter, *Oil and the American Century: The Political Economy of U.S. Foreign Oil Policy, 1941–1954* (Baltimore: Johns Hopkins University Press, 1986).

8. Victor S. Clark, *History of Manufactures in the United States*, vol. 3, *1893–1928* (Washington, DC: Carnegie Institution of Washington, 1929), pp. 310–11, 325–26, and Alfred D. Chandler, Jr., *The Visible Hand: The Managerial Revolution in American Business* (Cambridge: Harvard University Press, 1977), pp. 362, 508–9. Consult also the indexes of Brooks Emeny, *The Strategy of Raw Materials: A Study of America in Peace and War* (New York: Macmillan, 1937); Stephen D. Krasner, *Defending the National Interest: Raw Materials Investments and U.S. Foreign Policy* (Princeton, NJ: Princeton University Press, 1978); and Alfred E. Eckes, Jr., *The United States and the Global Struggle for Minerals* (Austin: University of Texas Press, 1979).

9. Johnson to Woodring, 2/9/37, file 470.1/129.6, PB, ASW, OSW.

10. Ibid., Guthrie to Chief Signal Officer, 7/11/25, and other correspondence and documents, file 273, and Bricker, "Progress Report, W.D.C.C. no. 34, Non-Ferrous Metals," 4/10/33, file 272.

11. Ibid., Wagner, "Report of Meeting of Commodity Committee no. 34-Non-Ferrous Metals," 11/14/33, file 282, and G.A.M., "Commodity Survey-Copper-Non-Strategic Commodity," 4/37, file 470.1/129.6.

12. Ibid., Harris to Leith, 5/6/35, and other correspondence and documents, file 470.1/129.6, and Edwards to Crain, 11/9/33, and other correspondence and documents, file 273.

13. Clark, *Manufactures*, 3: 311; Chandler, *Visible Hand*, pp. 327, 334, 367, 374–75, 506–7. Consult also the indexes of Emeny, *Strategy of Raw Materials*, and Eckes, *Global Struggle for Minerals*.

14. Wagner, "Report of Meeting of Commodity Committee no. 34-Non-Ferrous

Metals," 11/14/33 (quotation), file 282, and Crom, "Minutes of Meetings of Commodity Committee no. 34-Non-Ferrous Metals," 2/20/36, file 470.1/129.6, PB, ASW, OSW.

15. Ibid., Dooley to Harris, 3/22/38 (quotation), and numerous other correspondence, file 470.1/179.6.

16. For brief summaries of OASW evaluation of nonferrous metals, see ibid., Wagner, "Report of Meeting of Commodity Committee no. 34-Non-Ferrous Metals," 11/14/33, file 282, and Crom, "Minutes of Meeting of Commodity Committee no. 34-Non-Ferrous Metals," 2/20/36, file 470.1/129.6, PB, ASW, OSW. See also correspondence on zinc in file 292.

CHAPTER EIGHT. MANGANESE, TIN, MICA

1. The discussion of manganese is based on "Report of the Sub-Committee on Manganese of the Committee on Industrial Preparedness of the American Institute of Mining and Metallurgical Engineers to the United States War Department," February 1932, and numerous other correspondence and documents, file 207, Planning Branch (PB), Assistant Secretary of War (ASW), Office of the Secretary of War (OSW), RG 107, National Archives, Washington, DC (hereafter cited as PB, ASW, OSW); Bernard M. Baruch, *American Industry in the War: A Report of the War Industries Board* (Washington, DC: Government Printing Office, 1921), pp. 142–44; Grosvenor B. Clarkson, *Industrial America in the World War: The Strategy Behind the Line, 1917–1918* (Boston: Houghton Mifflin, 1923), pp. 376–86; and Alfred E. Eckes, Jr., *The United States and the Global Struggle for Minerals* (Austin: University of Texas Press, 1979), pp. 7–8, 12–25.

2. For a discussion of the role of the AIME and the Mining and Metallurgical Society of America in OASW planning, see chapter 3. See also Eckes, *Global Struggle for Minerals*, pp. 16–55, and Sylvia W. McGrath, *Charles Kenneth Leith: Scientific Adviser* (Madison: University of Wisconsin Press, 1971), pp. 95–110, 160–219, for more detailed information on the mining societies, government agencies, and their wartime and postwar efforts involving raw materials.

3. "Report of the Sub-Committee on Manganese of the Committee on Industrial Preparedness of the American Institute of Mining and Metallurgical Engineers to the United States War Department," 1/29/24, file 207, PB, ASW, OSW.

4. Ibid., AIME, "Report of the Sub-Committee on Manganese," February 1932.

5. The information on the national and international nature and operation of the manganese industry is based on ibid., Gale to Director of Naval Intelligence, 7/17/31, Furness to Hunt, 1/23/25, and numerous other correspondence and documents, file 207; and Rose to Assistant Secretary of War, 3/16/25, Walker to Assistant Secretary of War, 4/1/29, and other documents and correspondence, file 205; Eckes, *Global Struggle for Minerals,* pp. 32–33; Brooks Emeny, *The Strategy of Raw Materials: A Study of America in Peace and War* (New York: Macmillan, 1937), pp. 42–56; and G. A. Roush, *Strategic Mineral Supplies* (New York: McGraw-Hill, 1939), pp. 31–69.

6. "Statement to the Press by J. Carson Adkerson, President, American Manganese Producers Association, National Press Building, Washington, DC," 12/5/35, McFarland Memorandum, 2/2/35, and numerous other correspondence and docu-

ments, file 470.1/129.3, and Nickerson to Hobley, 2/24/32, and numerous other correspondence, file 207, PB, ASW, OSW.

7. Ibid., MacNider to Adkerson, 10/3/27, Taylor to Chief, Planning Branch, 8/4/27, and numerous other correspondence and documents, file 207, and Furness to Ferguson, 9/15/26, and other correspondence, file 209.

8. Ibid., Gale to Director of Naval Intelligence, 7/16/31, file 207.

9. Ibid., McCain to Chief, Planning Branch, 9/23/26, file 209.

10. Ibid., Good to American Iron and Steel Institute, 4/9/29, file 207.

11. Ibid., Taylor to Fife, 4/5/29, McFarland to Bomar, 2/27/33, Secretaries of Interior, War, and Commerce to the President, 5/25/34, and other correspondence, file 207, and MacArthur to Adkerson, 8/7/34, and other correspondence, file 470.1/129.3.

12. Ibid., Payne to Grace, 2/12/32 (this letter is not dated, but other attached correspondence indicates that the letter or one very similar to it was sent out to Bethlehem and U.S. Steel on this date), Mettler to Hof, 8/12/32, Clement to Williams, 10/21/24, Voris Memorandum, "Policies in Connection with Securing National Defense Reserves of Manganese Ore," 2/3/34, and numerous other correspondence and documents, file 207; and McFarland to Dunn, 11/27/34, and other correspondence, file 470.1/129.3; U.S. War Department, *Report of the Secretary of War to the President,* 1927, pp. 32, 37 (hereafter cited as *Annual Report of the Secretary of War [ARSW],* 1927); *ARSW,* 1928, pp. 52–53; *ARSW,* 1929, pp. 68–69; *ARSW,* 1930, pp. 38–39; *ARSW,* 1938, pp. 22–23; *ARSW,* 1940, p. 77; Eckes, *Global Struggle for Minerals,* pp. 57–119 (intermittent); and R. Elberton Smith, *The Army and Economic Mobilization* (Washington, DC: Office of the Chief of Military History, 1959), pp. 68, 602–10.

Congress in the Naval Appropriations Act of 1937 included a modest $3.5 million for stockpiling purposes. In June 1939 the nation's legislators passed the Strategic and Critical Materials Stockpiling Act, which authorized the Army-Navy Munitions Board to determine stockpiling policies and practices, with Congress to make appropriations later. Though the board wanted $200 to $600 million for this purpose in 1940, it received only $10 million. Even then, the Buy-American provisions of the Treasury-Post–Office Appropriations Act of 1933 put severe limitations on what could be done. The legislation provided that in the case of strategic materials, domestic producers, acting without bond for delivery, had to be allowed a year to develop and produce the desired commodity before foreign purchases could be made. The American Manganese Producers Association had tried to use this act to force the steel firms to use only domestic manganese for steel sold to the federal government or to buy a comparable amount of domestic manganese, but the War Department exempted steel from the bill's provisions because such a small amount of manganese went into steel production. See Smith, *Army and Economic Mobilization,* pp. 68, 602–10; David E. Lockwood, *The Stockpiling of Strategic and Critical Materials: Legislative History and Analysis of Pertinent Developments, 1919–1973* (Washington, DC: Foreign Affairs Division, Congressional Research Service, Library of Congress, 1974), pp. 1–2; Adkerson to Roosevelt, 3/25/33, and other correspondence, file 207; and MacArthur to Adkerson, 8/7/34, and other correspondence, file 470.1/129.3, PB, ASW, OSW. For the OASW's complicated relations with the steel industry in the interwar years, see chapter 5.

13. AIME, "Report of the Sub-Committee on Manganese," February 1932, file 207, PB, ASW, OSW.

14. Ibid., Hobley to Carr, 1/14/31, Nickerson to Executive, OASW, 5/5/33, and other correspondence, file 207.

15. Ibid., Nickerson to Executive, OASW, 10/18/32, and numerous other documents and correspondence, file 207, and Harris to Chief of Engineers, 7/1/36 and other correspondence, file 470.1/129.3; Russell H. Bennett, *Quest for Ore* (Minneapolis: T. S. Denison, 1963), pp. 321–61, and U.S. Congress, House, Committee on Military Affairs, "Supplies for the Armed Forces in Time of an Emergency," *Hearings*, 75th Cong., 1st sess., 1937, pp. 1–94.

16. For nickel, see MacNider to the International Nickel Co., 11/3/25, and numerous other correspondence, file 213; Walker, "Progress Report, W.D.C.C. no. 19, Ferro-Alloys," 3/28/28, and other documents, file 205; and Crom, "Minutes of Meeting of Commodity Committee no. 19-Ferro-Alloys," 1/23/36, file 470.1/129.3, PB, ASW, OSW; Baruch, *American Industry in the War*, p. 152; Clarkson, *Industrial America in the World War*, pp. 361–62; Eckes, *Global Struggle for Minerals*, chaps. 1–3 (intermittent); Emeny, *Strategy of Raw Materials*, pp. 69–76; and Roush, *Strategic Mineral Supplies*, pp. 70–96.

17. "American Institute of Mining and Metallurgical Engineers Committee on Industrial Preparedness, Report of Sub-Committee on Chrome," 6/29/23, file 206; Dwight to Davis, 6/23/25, and other correspondence and documents, file 216; Clement for Files, 6/1/25, and other correspondence, and Rose to Assistant Secretary of War, 10/16/24, and numerous other correspondence and documents, file 205; and Crom, "Minutes of Meeting of Commodity Committee no. 19-Ferro Alloys," 1/23/36, and other documents, file 470.1/129.3, PB, ASW, OSW.; Baruch, *American Industry in the War*, pp. 142–46; Clarkson, *Industrial America in the World War*, pp. 376–84; Eckes, *Global Struggle for Minerals*, chaps. 1–3 (intermittent); Emeny, *Strategy of Raw Materials*, pp. 56–69, 76–84; and Roush, *Strategic Mineral Supplies*, pp. 97–161.

18. Ferguson to Chairman of All War Dept. Commodity Committees, 12/8/24, and numerous other correspondence and documents, file 203; Rose to Assistant Secretary of War, 10/16/24, and numerous other correspondence and documents, file 205; and Crom, "Minutes of Meeting of Commodity Committee no. 19-Ferro Alloys," 1/23/36, and other documents, file 470.1/129.3, PB, ASW, OSW.

19. Ibid., Clement to Fife, 6/18/25, and other documents and correspondence, file 289; and Williams to Stettinius, 9/15/39, and other correspondence, file 470.1/129.6; Baruch, *American Industry in the War*, pp. 146–48; Clarkson, *Industrial America in the World War*, pp. 365–69; and Eckes, *Global Struggle for Minerals*, chaps. 1–3 (intermittent).

20. Clement to Fife, 6/18/25, and numerous other documents and correspondence, file 289, and Henderson to Secretary of War, 11/5/35, and other correspondence, file 470.1/129.6, PB, ASW, OSW; Eckes, *Global Struggle for Minerals*, chaps. 1–3, especially p. 35.

21. Crom, "Minutes of Meeting of Commodity Committee no. 34-Non-Ferrous Metals," 2/20/36, file 470.1/129.6; Falk to Connatser, 4/5/26, and other correspondence and documents, file 291; Hildreth to McAdoo, 8/15/37, and other correspondence, file 470.1/129.6, PB, ASW, OSW; and Eckes, *Global Struggle for Minerals*, pp. 72–78.

22. Dern to Sheppard, 4/25/34, Caldwell to Dern, 4/30/34, and numerous other documents and correspondence, file 289, and Johnson to McReynolds, 12/28/38, and numerous other documents and correspondence, file 470.1/129.6, PB, ASW, OSW.

23. Ibid., Hilgard to Chairmen, War Department Commodity Committees, 12/18/25, file 291.

24. Ibid., Woodring to Tin Investigating Committee, House of Representatives, 7/31/34, and other correspondence, file 289, and Crom, "Minutes of Meeting of Commodity Committee no. 34-Non-Ferrous Metals," 2/20/36, file 470.1/129.6.

25. On OASW planning for tin, see ibid., Fife to the Quartermaster General, 6/2/25, and numerous other documents and correspondence, file 291; Whelen, "Minutes of the War Department Commodity Committee on Steel and Non-Ferrous Metals," 4/25/24, and numerous other documents and correspondence, file 282; Merrill, "Memorandum on the Procurement Plan for Tin," February 6–19, 1933, and other documents and correspondence, file 289; and MacKay to Director, Planning Branch, 9/11/37, and other documents and correspondence, file 470.1/129.6.

26. For the four metals, see ibid., documents in files 282, 284, 285, 292, and 470.1/129.6. Emeny, *Strategy of Raw Materials*, and Roush, *Strategic Mineral Supplies*, cover these metals in addition to tin; consult their indexes.

27. Shearer, "Bimonthly Report of the War Department Commodity Committee no. 32-Mica, October, 1930," 10/6/30, file 265, PB, ASW, OSW; Baruch, *American Industry in the War*, pp. 201–3; Clarkson, *Industrial America in the World War*, p. 385; Eckes, *Global Struggle for Minerals*, chaps. 1–3 (intermittent); Emeny, *Strategy of Raw Materials*, pp. 121–26; and Roush, *Strategic Mineral Supplies*, pp. 339–76.

28. Watts, "Report on Commodity Committee on Mica," 12/20/24, and numerous other correspondence and documents, file 265, and Watts to Storrs, 2/16/25, and numerous other correspondence and documents, file 264, PB, ASW, OSW.

29. Ibid., Watts, "Report of Commodity Committee on Mica," 2/16/25, file 265.

30. Ibid., Shearer to Assistant Secretary of War, 10/6/30.

31. Ibid., Harris, "Minutes of Meeting of Commodity Committee no. 32-Mica," 1/9/34, and numerous other documents and correspondence, file 265, and Coles to Chief of Finance, 11/1/28, and numerous other documents and correspondence, file 264.

32. For the Commodity Committee on Mica and its operations, see ibid., Watts, "Report on Commodity Committee on Mica," 12/30/24, and numerous other documents and correspondence, file 265, and Watts to Storrs, 2/16/25, and numerous other documents and correspondence, file 264.

33. Ibid., Crom, "Minutes of Meeting of Commodity Committee no. 54-Wool," 3/20/34, file 365.

34. Ibid., Arthur Besse, "The Problems and Trends of the Woolen Industry," address to the AIC, 11/4/36, file 400/129.22; Baruch, *American Industry in the War*, pp. 231–38; Clarkson, *Industrial America in the World War*, pp. 439–51; and Emeny, *Strategy of Raw Materials*, pp. 147–52.

35. For the information on wool, see Crom, "Minutes of Meeting of Commodity Committee no. 54-Wool," 3/20/34 (quotation), and numerous other correspondence and documents, file 365; Harry B. Williams, "Wool as a Strategic Commodity," 1/30/29, and numerous other correspondence and documents, file 363; and Besse,

"Problems and Trends of the Woolen Industry," 11/4/36, and numerous other correspondence and documents, file 400/129.22, PB, ASW, OSW; Mahoney to Hines, 6/20/39, and other correspondence, file 470.1/203.2-23.2, Records of the Joint Army and Navy Boards and Committees, RG 225, National Archives, Washington, DC (hereafter cited as ANMB).

36. On the planning for wool, see Davis to Wood, 12/26/24, and numerous other correspondence and documents, file 363; Stanley and Howard to Chief, Procurement Division, 1/12/25, and numerous other correspondence and documents, file 365; and Besse, "Problems and Trends of the Woolen Industry," 11/4/36, and numerous other correspondence and documents, file 400/129.22, PB, ASW, OSW; and Mahoney to Hines, 6/20/39, and other correspondence, file 470.1/203.2-23.2, ANMB.

37. See n. 36.

38. MacNider to Wendt, 1/19/26, and numerous other documents and correspondence, file 348, and Hardigg to Assistant Secretary of War, 3/23/25, and numerous other correspondence and documents, file 350, PB, ASW, OSW. See also Baruch, *American Industry in the War,* 241–42; Emeny, *Strategy of Raw Materials,* pp. 138–42; and Clarkson, *Industrial America in the World War,* pp. 442n, 450, 506, 541.

39. Rodgers to Burns, 9/23/39, file 400/129.19, and Woodring to Edison, 7/22/39, and other correspondence, PB, ASW, OSW.

40. Ibid., Howard to DeShields, 1/13/25, and numerous other documents and correspondence, file 345; Fife to Gardner, 12/17/25, and numerous other documents and correspondence, file 346; and Howard, "Schedule of Accomplishments," [circa] September 1924, and numerous other documents, file 347. See also Baruch, *American Industry in the War,* p. 190, and Emeny, *Strategy of Raw Materials,* pp.158–61.

41. For the Commodity Committee on Shellac and attitudes of the industry advisers, see Howard to DeShields, 1/13/25, and numerous other documents and correspondence, file 345; Fife to Gardner, 12/17/25, and numerous other documents and correspondence, file 346; and Howard, "Schedule of Accomplishments," [circa] September 1924, and numerous other documents, file 347, PB, ASW, OSW.

42. On World War I, see Baruch, *American Industry in the War,* pp. 259–69, and Clarkson, *Industrial America in the World War,* pp. 452–58. The documentation on the planning of the interwar years contains some excellent information on World War I. For the early nineteenth-century antecedents for the modern machine tool industry associated with small arms, see Paul A. C. Koistinen, *Beating Plowshares into Swords: The Political Economy of American Warfare, 1601–1865* (Lawrence: University Press of Kansas, 1996), chap. 4. For a general treatment of the machine tool industry, see Harless D. Wagoner, *The U.S. Machine Tool Industry from 1900 to 1950* (Cambridge, MA: MIT Press, 1968). See also Wayne G. Broehl, Jr., *Precision Valley: The Machine Tool Companies of Springfield, Vermont* (Englewood Cliffs, NJ: Prentice-Hall, 1959).

43. Dunbar, "The Machine Tool Industry," address to AIC, 11/4/37, file 470.1/203.2-13, ANMB.

44. Excellent information on the machine tool industry is provided in the addresses of the NMTBA's officers to the AIC. See Lind, "The Machine Tool Industry," 11/28/36, file 334.8/129.23, PB, ASW, OSW; Dunbar, "The Machine Tool Industry," 11/4/37; and Lovely, "The Machine Tool Industry," 11/27/39, file 470.1/203.2-13, ANMB.

45. Ferguson to Saltzman, 12/19/21, and Wooten to Chief of Ordnance et al., 10/17/28, file 246, PB, ASW, OSW.
46. Ibid., Davis to Fife, 10/9/28, file 246.
47. Ibid., Crom, "Minutes of Meeting to Commodity Committee no. 30-Machine Tools," 2/27/34, file 249.
48. For additional information on the AOA and its relations to military planning and other groups involved in it, see chapter 3.
49. Berna to Jordan, 7/31/37, file 334.8/129.23, PB, ASW, OSW.
50. Ibid., "Minutes of Meeting of Commodity Committee no. 30-Machine Tools," 2/27/36.
51. Ibid., "Report of Ordnance Machine Tool Conference, Held in the Cincinnati Ordnance District Office, Cincinnati, Ohio, October 5th, 6th, and 7th, 1937," Harris to Minton, 1/21/38, and Berna to Harris, 1/21/38.
52. Ibid., Harrison to Rutherford, 11/23/38 (quotations), and 12/20/38, and Rutherford to Harrison, 12/20/38.
53. The information on the machine tool industry is based on ibid., Ferguson to Saltzman, 12/19/21, and numerous other documents and correspondence, file 246; Clark to Assistant Secretary of War, 2/26/26, and numerous other correspondence, file 249; Doan to Crom, 5/17/33, and numerous other documents and correspondence, file 434.8/129.23; Harris to Harrison, 1/29/38, and other correspondence, file 334.8/246/2 (Hydraulic Machinery Manufacturers' Association), and Burns to Berna, 5/17/39, and other correspondence, file 334.8/246.2 (National Machine Tool Builders' Association); and Rutherford to Chief, Signal Officer, 5/18/38, and numerous other documents and correspondence, file 470.1/203.2/13, ANMB.
54. On the engineering societies and their role in interwar planning, see chapter 3.
55. Johnson and Henning to Berna, 8/19/40, and other documents and correspondence, file 470.1/203.2/13, ANMB.
56. Machine tools during World War II will be analyzed in the forthcoming volume 4 of this series.
57. MacNider to the National Hardware Association of the United States, 3/2/26, and other correspondence, file 238, and Schrackenberg, "Hand Tools," 4/15/24, and other documents, file 239, PB, ASW, OSW.
58. Ibid., Bausch, "The Industrial War Load As It Relates to the Optical Industry," 1/14/37, file 470.6/129.13; Baruch, *American Industry in the War*, pp. 68–69; and Clarkson, *Industrial America in the World War*, pp. 470–71.
59. Bausch to Wilbur, 1/25/27, file 308, PB, ASW, OSW.
60. Ibid., Bausch, "The Industrial War Load As It Relates to the Optical Industry," 1/14/37, file 470.6/129.13.
61. Ibid.
62. Ibid., Colladay to Executive, OASW, 10/17/32, file 308.
63. Ibid., Harris to Minton, 11/19/37, file 470.6/129.13.
64. Ibid., Eisenhart to OASW, 4/26/32, file 308.
65. For the analysis of the optical glass industry, see ibid., Ferguson to Beardsley, 10/7/25, and numerous other correspondence and documents, file 308, and "Minutes of Meeting, Optical Glass Conference," 10/19/34, and numerous other correspondence and documents, file 470.6/129.13; and Hines to Roberts, 7/12/39, and other correspondence, file 470.1/203.2-15, ANMB.

66. Mixter to McAfee, 3/5/26, file 263, PB, ASW, OSW.

67. For the analysis of the surgical instruments industry, see ibid., Hefleblower to Assistant Secretary of War, 1/15/25, and McAfee to Chief of the Planning Branch, 12/17/25, file 254; Ireland to the Assistant Secretary of War, 9/6/22, and numerous other documents and correspondence, file 263; and Reeves to Shook, 11/10/39, file 470.6/129.14; Baruch, *American Industry in the War,* pp. 204–7; and Clarkson, *Industrial America in the World War,* pp. 472–73. For further information on the medical profession and mobilization for World War I, see Paul A. C. Koistinen, *Mobilizing for Modern War: The Political Economy of American Warfare, 1865–1919* (Lawrence: University Press of Kansas, 1997), chaps. 7 and 8.

CHAPTER NINE. LUMBER, COAL AND COAL PRODUCTS

1. For information on lumber and related products during the war years, see Bernard M. Baruch, *American Industry in the War: A Report of the War Industries Board* (Washington, DC: U.S. Government Printing Office, 1921), pp. 211–27, and Grosvenor B. Clarkson, *Industrial America in the World War: The Strategy Behind the Line, 1917–1918* (Boston: Houghton Mifflin, 1923), pp. 420–31, 497, 505, 538, and 543.

2. For a discussion of the army's wartime building programs, see chapter 12.

3. Crom, "Minutes of Meeting of Commodity Committee no. 8-Building Materials," 12/5/33, file 185, Planning Branch (PB), Assistant Secretary of War (ASW), Office of the Secretary of War (OSW), RG 107, National Archives, Washington, DC (hereafter cited as PB, ASW, OSW).

4. Ibid., Compton to Woodring, 5/31/40, and Rutherford to Compton, 6/6/40, file 334.8/246.2 (National Lumber Manufacturers' Association).

5. Ibid., "News Release, Department of Commerce, National Committee on Wood Utilization," April 11, 1932, and April 5, 1933, file 179. For a discussion of the Commerce Department and the National Committee on Wood Utilization, see Ellis Hawley, "Three Facets of Hooverian Associationalism: Lumber, Aviation, and Movies, 1921–1930," in *Regulation in Perspective: Historical Essays,* ed. Thomas K. McCraw, pp. 95–123, 221–33 (Boston: Harvard Business School, 1981).

6. Davis et al. to Assistant Secretary of War, 3/4/27, file 185, PB, ASW, OSW.

7. Ibid., Hanley to Coordinator of Commodity Committees, 12/1/26.

8. Ibid., Hanley to Horkan, 8/15/27, file 179.

9. Ibid., Wilkes to Fife, 2/1/30.

10. For interwar planning for lumber and building materials, see ibid., Hanley to Planning Branch, 5/14/26, and other correspondence, file 173; Hanley to Sadler, 2/11/25, and other correspondence, file 177; Davies to Davis, 10/16/25, and other correspondence, file 179 (1924–1925); Horkan to Hanley, 4/29/26, and numerous other correspondence and documents, file 179 (1926–1928–1934); Wilkes to Worthington, 6/21/28, file 181; Wilkes to Oxholm, 8/1/29, and other correspondence, file 182; Wheaton, "Monthly Report of War Department Commodity Committee no. 29 Lumber," 2/5/26, and numerous other correspondence and documents, file 185; Rutherford to Porter, 9/12/39, and other correspondence, file 400/129.16; Oxholm to Harris, 3/12/38, and other correspondence, file 400/129.16-A; and Compton to

Woodring and other correspondence, file 334.8/246.2 (National Lumber Manufacturers' Association); and Brooks Emeny, *The Strategy of Raw Materials: A Study of America in Peace and War* (New York: Macmillan, 1937), pp. 34–35, 188.

11. For information on the coal industry before, during, and after World War I, see Kelton, "Some of the Difficulties of the United States Fuel Administration—Synopsis of Talk by James H. Allport," and other documents and correspondence, file 188, PB, ASW, OSW; James B. Hendry, "The Bituminous Coal Industry," in *The Structure of American Industry: Some Case Studies,* ed. Walter Adams, pp. 74–112 (New York: Macmillan, 1961); William Franklin Willoughby, *Government Organization in War Time and After: A Survey of the Federal Civil Agencies Created for the Prosecution of the War* (New York: D. Appleton, 1919), pp. 293–315; Emeny, *Strategy of Raw Materials,* pp. 17, 20, 21, 23, 30–31, 42, 59, 161, 169, 172, and 177; Clarkson, *Industrial America in the World War,* pp. 29, 43, 49n, 50n, 60, 68, 91, 128, 146, 167, 167n, 184, 459, 460, 482; Alfred E. Eckes, Jr., *The United States and the Global Struggle for Minerals* (Austin: University of Texas Press, 1979), pp. 8–9, 11, 41, 51–52, 121, 124, 126, 178, 182, 257, 260; Alfred D. Chandler, Jr., *The Visible Hand: The Managerial Revolution in American Business* (Cambridge, MA: Belknap Press, 1977), pp. 52, 76–77, 153–54, 157, 244–45, 259, 503–4; Ellis W. Hawley, "Secretary Hoover and the Bituminous Coal Problem, 1921–1928," *Business History Review* 62 (Autumn 1968): 247–70; John R. Bowman, *Capitalist Collective Action: Competition, Cooperation, and Conflict in the Coal Industry* (New York: Cambridge University Press, 1989).

12. Gandy to Weeks, 8/14/24, file 1231 (National Coal Association), PB, ASW, OSW.

13. For further background on efforts to regulate the coal industry, see n. 11. Additional information on Hoover's efforts at rationalizing the economy are discussed in chapter 11.

14. For OASW planning for coal, see Gandy to MacNider, 3/17/26, and numerous other correspondence and documents, file 188; Maddox and duRell, "Coal," 12/13/25, file 189; Gandy to Davis, 12/17/25, and other correspondence, file 191; "A Study of the Functions of the War Industries Board with Special Reference to Toluol," 7/14/30, and other correspondence, file 194; Gandy to Weeks, 8/14/24, file 1231 (National Coal Association); Schulz to Assistant Secretary of War, 1/18/39, and numerous other correspondence and documents, file 470.6/129.11; and Hilgard to Ferguson with enclosures, 1/15/26, file 334.8/256.2, PB, ASW, OSW.

15. On the cotton textile industry and knit goods, see ibid., George A. Sloan, "Problems and Trends in the Cotton Textile Industry," address to the AIC, 10/28/35, file 400/129.21; Baruch, *American Industry in the War,* pp. 228–31, 236–38; Clarkson, *Industrial America in the World War,* pp. 439–42, 446–51, 534; Emeny, *Strategy of Raw Materials,* pp. 17, 21, 34–35, 145–47, 169, 172, 188; and Louis Galambos, *Competition and Cooperation: The Emergence of a National Trade Association* (Baltimore: Johns Hopkins University Press, 1966). Galambos's work is an excellent study of the cotton textile industry and its trade associations, particularly the Cotton-Textile Institute.

16. For cotton goods and military planning, see Tiffany to Assistant Secretary of War, 7/12/27, and other correspondence, file 197; McCain to file with W.D.C.C. no. 15, no. 28, no. 54, 3/15/26, and numerous other correspondence, file 199; Cheney to Wainwright, 3/9/23, and other correspondence, file 245; and Elgin to OASW,

7/9/37, and numerous other correspondence and documents, file 400/129.21, PB, ASW, OSW.

17. For World War I mobilization and some general information on the leather industry, see Baruch, *American Industry in the War,* pp. 247–54; Clarkson, *Industrial America in the World War,* pp. 432–36; Emeny, *Strategy of Raw Materials,* pp. 147–52; and Chandler, *Visible Hand,* p. 508. See also Paul A. C. Koistinen, *Mobilizing for Modern War: The Political Economy of American Warfare, 1865–1919* (Lawrence: University Press of Kansas, 1997), chaps. 8–10.

18. "Notes of Conference Between Representatives of the Hide and Leather Industry and This Office," December 2, 1925, file 240, and Crom, "Minutes of Meeting of Commodity Committee no. 27-Hides," February 13, 1934, file 242, PB, ASW, OSW.

19. For OASW planning in the interwar years, see ibid., Koenig, "Notes on Conference with Mr. Stout," [circa] June 1924, and numerous other correspondence, file 240; Sadler, "Report of Commodity Committee no. 27 (Hides and Leather), 4/16/30, and other correspondence and documents, file 242; Stanley and Mitchell to Chief of Procurement Division OASW, 3/16/25, and numerous other documents and correspondence, file 243; and Crom, "Minutes of Meeting of Commodity Committee no. 27-Hides and Leather," 10/17/35, and other correspondence and documents, file 400/129.17.

CHAPTER TEN. EXPLOSIVES AND AIRCRAFT

1. See Paul A. C. Koistinen, *Mobilizing for Modern War: The Political Economy of American Warfare, 1865–1919* (Lawrence: University Press of Kansas, 1997), chaps. 6 and 8–10 for background on this subject.

2. For prewar and wartime developments of the chemical industry, see Roberts to McMullen, 3/15/22, and other documents, file 161; Parsons to Wainwright, 10/10/22, and other correspondence, file 160; Koenig, "Chemical Commodity Committee" Minutes, 10/30/22, and other documents, file 154, Planning Branch (PB), Assistant Secretary of War (ASW), Office of the Secretary of War (OSW), RG 107, National Archives, Washington, DC (hereafter cited as PB, ASW, OSW); Bernard M. Baruch, *American Industry in the War: A Report of the War Industries Board* (Washington, DC: U.S. Government Printing Office, 1921), pp. 157–95; and Grosvenor B. Clarkson, *Industrial America in the World War: The Strategy Behind the Line, 1917–1918* (Boston: Houghton Mifflin, 1923), pp. 387–419.

3. On the chemical industry in the postwar world, see Koenig, "Chemical Commodity Committee" Minutes, 10/30/22, and other documents, file 154, and Roberts to McMullen, 3/15/22, and other documents, file 161, PB, ASW, OSW; Alfred E. Kahn, "The Chemical Industry," in *The Structure of American Industry: Some Case Studies,* ed. Walter Adams, pp. 233–76 (New York: Macmillan, 1961); Alfred D. Chandler, *The Visible Hand: The Managerial Revolution in American Business* (Cambridge, MA: Belknap Press, 1977), pp. 375, 376, 416–17, 438–50, 452, 456–59, 463, 473, 474–75; Ralph L. Nelson, *Merger Movements in American Industry, 1895–1956* (Princeton, NJ: Princeton University Press, 1959), pp. 48–49; and Victor Perlo, *The Empire of High Finance* (New York: International Publishers, 1957), pp. 189–211.

Various volumes on Du Pont have already been cited in Paul A. C. Koistinen, *Beating Plowshares into Swords: The Political Economy of American Warfare, 1606–1865* (Lawrence: University Press of Kansas, 1996), chap. 3, n. 90. The most important volumes not previously cited include Alfred D. Chandler, Jr., and Stephen Salsbury, *Pierre S. Du Pont and the Making of the Modern Corporation* (New York: Harper and Row, 1971); Graham D. Taylor and Patricia E. Sudnik, *Du Pont and the International Chemical Industry* (Boston: Twayne, 1984); and David A. Hounshell and John K. Smith, Jr., *Science and Corporate Strategy: Du Pont R&D, 1902–1980* (New York: Cambridge University Press, 1988). See also Norman B. Wilkinson, *Lammot Du Pont and the American Explosives Industry, 1850–1884* (Charlottesville: University Press of Virginia, 1984); Robert F. Burk, *The Corporate State and the Broker State: The Du Ponts and American National Politics, 1925–1940* (Cambridge: Harvard University Press, 1990); Joseph F. Wall, *Alfred I. Dupont: The Man and His Family* (New York: Oxford University Press, 1990); Charles W. Cheape, *Strictly Business: Walter Carpenter at Du Pont and General Motors* (Baltimore: Johns Hopkins University Press, 1995); Max Dorian, *The du Ponts: From Gunpowder to Nylon* (Boston: Little, Brown, 1961); and Arthur P. Van Gelder and Hugo Schlatter, *History of the Explosives Industry in America* (New York: Columbia University Press, 1927).

4. Wagner, "Report of Meeting of Commodity Committee no. 39-Power and Explosives," 11/21/33, file 327, PB, ASW, OSW.

5. Ibid., Ferguson to Assistant Secretary of War, 2/5/24, file 331.

6. The Nye Committee and its investigation and findings will be taken up more fully in chapter 14.

7. For Universal Oil and its relations with the OASW, see chapter 9 and n. 14 of that chapter.

8. For military planning for explosives and powder, see Wainwright to Chief, Chemical Warfare Service, 9/23/22, and numerous other documents and correspondence, file 154; Wainwright to Parsons, 11/28/22, and numerous other documents and correspondence, file 160; Roberts to McMullen, 3/15/22, and numerous other documents and correspondence, file 161; Armstrong to Moxham, 11/7/27, and other correspondence, file 171; Smith to Walker, 3/1/29, and numerous other documents and correspondence, file 325; Hardigg to Assistant Secretary of War, 8/3/25, and other correspondence, file 327; Dupont to Williams, 11/3/21, and other correspondence, file 331; Robinson to Commodities Division, 7/12/39, and other correspondence, file 470.6/129.10; and Warfield to Assistant Secretary of War, 1/18/39, and other correspondence, file 470.6/129.11, PB, ASW, OSW; and Hines to Kimball, 1/22/40, and other correspondence, file 471.213.2-13, Records of the Joint Army and Navy Boards and Committees, RG 225, National Archives, Washington, DC (hereafter cited as ANMB).

9. Alex Roland, "The National Advisory Committee for Aeronautics," *Prologue* 10 (Summer 1978): 71. Roland subsequently published a full-scale study of NACA, *Model Research: The National Advisory Committee for Aeronautics, 1915–1958*, 2 vols. (Washington, DC: National Aeronautics and Space Administration, 1985).

10. Elsbeth E. Freudenthal, *The Aviation Business: From Kitty Hawk to Wall Street* (New York: Vanguard Press). Freudenthal's information and statistics are impressive, but the quality of the analysis is uneven; however, this does not detract from the general value of the book.

11. Ibid., p. 98.
12. Ibid., pp. 228–29.
13. Ibid., pp. 246–47.
14. Irving Brinton Holley, Jr., *Buying Aircraft: Material Procurement for the Army Air Forces* (Washington, DC: Office of the Chief of Military History, 1964), p. 11.
15. Secondary sources on the wartime aircraft production record vary considerably. John B. Rae, *Climb to Greatness: The American Aircraft Industry, 1920–1960* (Cambridge, MA: MIT Press, 1968) paints a positive picture, Freudenthal, *Aviation Business*, a negative one. Primary sources support Freudenthal more than Rae, and most authors on the subject follow the line of the former rather than the latter.
16. Leighton W. Rogers, "Functions of the Aeronautical Chamber of Commerce," *Journal of Air Law* 6 (October 1935): 554–55.
17. The airplane had nearly unique qualities as a weapon of war. The railroads, as demonstrated in the Civil War and World War I, had a very important military function. With few exceptions such as railroad artillery, however, they served logistical purposes within an existing transportation system, used, adapted, or extended for military purposes. They were not a weapon of war itself, as was the case with the airplane. In this instance, the airplane was closer in its relationship to military usage to the nineteenth-century revolution in naval technology involving ships of steel, steam, and screw propeller. Those basically civilian advances had a profound military significance when used to build ships of war and combined with armor and modern ordnance. Nonetheless, the emergence and impact of air power on the conduct of war was much faster and greater than that involving sea power.
18. The Nye Committee and its predecessors investigating the political economy of warfare during the interwar years are analyzed in chapters 12 through 14.
19. For Air Corps procurement planning, see chapter 1.
20. Besides the preceding citations on aviation, the discussion and analysis are based on Somervell, "War Time Aircraft Production," 12/24/25, Burleson, "The Airplane Industry," 12/24/25, and Wilson, "The Airplane Industry," 12/24/25, file 313A-16; Fickel, "Bearing of Development of Commercial Aviation on the Peace-time Programs of the Army and Navy," 2/28/31, file 377-22; Report of Committee no. 5, AWC, "Aviation," 9/27/33, file 403-5A G-3, no. 10; Copthorne, "Ability of the Airplane Industry to Meet the Losses of Airplanes in War," 12/10/38, file 7-1939-50; and Ruddell, "Airplanes for War Reserve," 12/9/39, file 7-1940-58, Army War College Collection, Carlisle Barracks, PA; Robert R. Russell, "Expansion of Industrial Facilities Under Army Air Force Auspices, 1940–1945," (1945), Army Air Force Historical Studies no. 40, Historical Office, Air Technical Service Command; and Jerold E. Brown, "Where Eagles Roost: A History of Army Air Fields Before World War II" (Ph.D. diss., Duke University, 1977).

For published sources, see David A. Anderton: *Sixty Years of Aeronautical Research, 1917–1977* (Washington, DC: National Aeronautics and Space Administration, 1978); Marylin Bender and Selig Altschul, *The Chosen Instrument: Pan Am's Juan Trippe: The Rise and Fall of an American Entrepreneur* (New York: Simon and Schuster, 1982); Roger E. Bilstein, *Flight in America: From the Wrights to the Astronauts*, rev. ed. (Baltimore: Johns Hopkins University Press, 1994); Peter W. Brooks, *The Modern Airliner: Its Origins and Development* (London: Putnam, 1961); Lester H. Brune, *The Origins of American National Security Policy: Sea Power, Air Power and Foreign Pol-*

icy, 1900–1941 (Manhattan, KS: Military Affairs/Aerospace Historian, 1981); Joseph J. Corn, *The Winged Gospel: America's Romance with Aviation, 1900–1950* (New York: Oxford University Press, 1983); Wesley Frank Craven and James Lea Cate, eds., *The Army Air Forces in World War II*, vol. 6, *Men and Planes* (Chicago: University of Chicago Press, 1955); R. E. G. Davies, *Airlines of the United States Since 1914* (London: Putnam, 1972), and Davies, *A History of the World's Airlines* (London: Oxford University Press, 1964); Burke Davis, *The Billy Mitchell Affair* (New York: Random House, 1967); John L. Frisbee, ed., *Makers of the United States Air Force* (Washington, DC: Office of Air Force History, 1987); George W. Gray, *Frontiers of Flight: The Story of NACA Research* (New York: Alfred A. Knopf, 1948); Thomas H. Greer, *The Development of Air Doctrine in the Army Air Arm, 1917–1941* (rpt.; Washington, DC: Office of Air Force History, 1985); Alfred Goldberg, ed. *A History of the United States Air Force, 1907–1957* (Princeton, NJ: D. Van Nostrand, 1957); Richard P. Hallion, *Legacy of Flight: The Guggenheim Contribution to American Aviation* (Seattle: University of Washington Press, 1977); T. A. Heppenheimer, *Turbulent Skies: The History of Commercial Aviation* (New York: John Wiley and Sons, 1995); Robin Higham, *Air Power: A Concise History*, 3d ed., rev. (Manhattan, KS: Sunflower Press, 1988), Higham, "Government, Companies, and National Defense: British Aeronautical Experience, 1918–1945 as the Basis for a Broad Hypothesis," *Business History Review* 39 (Autumn 1965): 323–47, and Higham, "Quantity vs. Quality: The Impact of Changing Demand on the British Aircraft Industry, 1900–1960," *Business History Review* 42 (Winter 1968): 443–66; I. B. Holley, Jr., *Ideas and Weapons: Exploitation of the Aerial Weapon by the United States During World War I; A Study in the Relationship of Technological Advance, Military Doctrine, and the Development of Weapons* (New Haven: Yale University Press, 1953); J. C. Hunsaker, "Forty Years of Aeronautical Research," Annual Report of the Board of Regents of the Smithsonian Institution for 1955 (Washington, DC: Smithsonian Institution, 1956), pp. 241–71; Alfred F. Hurley, *Billy Mitchell: Crusader for Air Power* (Bloomington: Indiana University Press, 1964, 1975); Edward C. Johnson, *Marine Corps Aviation: The Early Years, 1912–1940*, ed. Graham A. Cosmas (Washington, DC: History and Museums Divisions, Headquarters, U.S. Marine Corps, 1977); Benjamin S. Kelsey, *The Dragon's Teeth? The Creation of United States Air Power for World War II* (Washington, DC: Smithsonian Institution Press, 1982); Lee Kennett, *The First Air War, 1914–1918* (New York: Free Press, 1991); Nick A. Komons, *Bonfires to Beacons: Federal Civil Aviation Policy Under the Air Commerce Act 1926–1938* (Washington, DC: U.S. Department of Transportation, Federal Aviation Administration, 1978); W. David Lewis and Wesley Phillips Newton, *Delta: The History of an Airline* (Athens: University of Georgia Press, 1979); Lockheed Aircraft, *Of Men and Stars* (New York: Arno Press, 1980); Maurer Maurer, *Aviation in the U.S. Army, 1919–1939* (Washington, DC: Office of Air Force History, 1987); Stephen L. McFarland, *America's Pursuit of Precision Bombing, 1910–1945* (Washington, DC: Smithsonian Institution Press, 1995); F. Alexander Magoun and Eric Hodgins, *A History of Aircraft* (New York: McGraw-Hill, 1931); Ronald Miller and David Sawers, *The Technical Development of Modern Aviation* (New York: Praeger, 1970); Lloyd Morris and Kendall Smith, *Ceilings Unlimited: The Story of American Aviation from Kitty Hawk to Supersonics* (New York: Macmillan, 1953); John H. Morrow, Jr., *The Great War in the Air: Military Aviation from 1909–1921* (Washington, DC: Smithsonian Institution Press, 1993); various essays in Williamson Murray and

Allan R. Millett, eds., *Military Innovation in the Interwar Period* (New York: Cambridge University Press, 1996); John Niven, Courtland Canby, and Vernon Welsh, eds., *Dynamic America: A Study of General Dynamics Corporation and Its Predecessor Companies* (New York: General Dynamics Corporation and Doubleday, 1958); Edwin H. Rutkowski, *The Politics of Military Aviation Procurement, 1926-1934: A Study in the Political Assertion of Consensual Values* (Columbus: Ohio State University Press, 1966); Robert Schlaifer and S. D. Heron, *Development of Aircraft Engines and Development of Aviation Fuels: Two Studies of Relations Between Government and Business* (Boston: Division of Research, Graduate School of Business Administration, Harvard University, 1950); G. R. Simonson, ed., *The History of the American Aircraft Industry: An Anthology* (Cambridge, MA: MIT Press, 1968); Henry Ladd Smith, *Airways: The History of Commercial Aviation in the United States* (New York: Alfred A. Knopf, 1942); William F. Trimble, *High Frontier: A History of Aeronautics in Pennsylvania* (Pittsburgh, PA: University of Pittsburgh Press, 1982), Trimble, "The Naval Aircraft Factory, the American Aviation Industry, and Government Competition, 1919-1928," *Business History Review* 60 (Summer 1986): 175-98, and Trimble, *Admiral William A. Moffett: Architect of Naval Aviation* (Washington, DC: Smithsonian Institution Press, 1994); Richard H. K. Vietor, "Contrived Competition: Airline Regulation and Deregulation, 1925-1988," *Business History Review* 64 (Spring 1990): 61-108; Jeffrey S. Underwood, *The Wings of Democracy: The Influence of Air Power on the Roosevelt Administration, 1933-1941* (College Station: Texas A&M University Press, 1991); F. Robert van der Linden, *The Boeing 247: The First Modern Airliner* (Seattle: University of Washington Press, 1991); Jacob Vander Meulen, *The Politics of Aircraft: Building an American Military Industry* (Lawrence: University Press of Kansas, 1991); Bill Robie, *For the Greatest Achievement: A History of the Aero Club of America and the National Aeronautic Association* (Washington, DC: Smithsonian Institution Press, 1993); Robert Wohl, *A Passion for Wings: Aviation and the Western Imagination, 1908-1918* (New Haven: Yale University Press, 1994); and William M. Leary, ed. *From Airships to Airbus: The History of Civil and Commercial Aviation*, vol. 1, *Infrastructure and Environment*, and William F. Trimble, ed., vol. 2, *Pioneers and Operations* (Washington, DC: Smithsonian Institution Press, 1995).

CHAPTER ELEVEN. OASW PLANNING

1. The opening of the Hoover Papers in 1966 and various ideological and historiographical trends in the nation and the scholarly profession in the past twenty-five years have produced virtually a cottage industry dedicated to interpreting Hoover. Historians have applied all sorts of labels in attempts to categorize or understand Hoover, including "corporatism," "modified pluralism," "guildism," "statism," "syndicalism," "associational progressivism," "corporate liberalism," "mutualism," the "American System," and others. One of the best, clearest, and most jargon-free discussions of Hoover's approach as a political leader is found in James Stuart Olson, *Herbert Hoover and the Reconstruction Finance Corporation, 1931-1933* (Ames: Iowa State University Press, 1977), pp. 14-23. Some of the more important "new era historiography" on Hoover includes William A. Williams, *The Contours of American History* (Cleveland, OH: World Publishing, 1961), pp. 425-38; Joseph Brandes, *Herbert Hoover and Eco-*

nomic Diplomacy: Department of Commerce Policy, 1921-1928 (Pittsburgh, PA: University of Pittsburgh Press, 1962); Edwin T. Layton, Jr., *The Revolt of the Engineers: Social Responsibility and the American Engineering Profession* (Cleveland, OH: Press of Case Western Reserve University, 1971); Murray N. Rothbard, "Herbert Hoover and the Myth of Laissez-Faire," in *A New History of Leviathan,* ed. Ronald Radosh and Rothbard (New York: E. P. Dutton, 1972), pp. 111-45; J. Joseph Huthmacher and Warren I. Susman, eds., *Herbert Hoover and the Crisis of American Capitalism* (Cambridge, MA: Schenkman, 1973); Craig Lloyd, *Aggressive Introvert: A Study of Herbert Hoover and Public Relations Management, 1912-1932* (Columbus: Ohio State University Press, 1972); Martin L. Fausold and George T. Mazuzan, eds., *The Hoover Presidency: A Reappraisal* (Albany: State University of New York Press, 1974); Gary Dean Best, *The Politics of American Individualism: Herbert Hoover in Transition, 1918-1921* (Westport, CT: Greenwood Press, 1975); Edgar Eugene Robinson and Vaughn Davis Bornet, *Herbert Hoover: President of the United States* (Stanford, CA: Hoover Institution Press, 1975); Joan Hoff Wilson, *Herbert Hoover: Forgotten Progressive* (Boston: Little, Brown, 1975); Robert F. Himmelberg, *The Origins of the National Recovery Administration: Business, Government, and the Trade Association Issue, 1921-1933* (New York: Fordham University Press, 1976); Robert D. Cuff, "Herbert Hoover, the Ideology of Voluntarism, and War Organization During the Great War," *Journal of American History* 64 (September 1977): 358-72; David Burner, *Herbert Hoover: A Public Life* (New York: Alfred A. Knopf, 1979); and Lawrence E. Gelfand, ed., *Herbert Hoover: The Great War and Its Aftermath, 1914-1923* (Iowa City: University of Iowa Press, 1979).

For another anthology on Hoover, see Ellis W. Hawley, ed., *Herbert Hoover as Secretary of Commerce: Studies in New Era Thought and Practice* (Iowa City: University of Iowa Press, 1981). Hawley's essay in this collection, pp. 1-16, contains an extensive bibliography on Hoover. A few additional titles of relevance have appeared since Hawley's volume was published, with its cutoff date of 1978 for revisions. See Ellis W. Hawley, *The Great War and the Search for a Modern Order: A History of the American People and Their Institutions, 1917-1933* (New York: St. Martin's Press, 1979); Gary Dean Best, *Herbert Hoover: The Post Presidential Years, 1933-1964,* 2 vols. (Stanford, CA: Hoover Institution Press, 1983); George H. Nash, *The Life of Herbert Hoover: The Engineer, 1874-1914* (New York: W. W. Norton, 1983), Nash, *The Life of Herbert Hoover: The Humanitarian, 1914-1917* (New York: W. W. Norton, 1988), and Nash, *The Life of Herbert Hoover: Master of Emergencies, 1917-1918* (New York: W. W. Norton, 1996); Richard Norton Smith, *An Uncommon Man: The Triumph of Herbert Hoover* (New York: Simon and Schuster, 1984); Guy Alchon, *The Invisible Hand of Planning: Capitalism, Social Science, and the State in the 1920s* (Princeton, NJ: Princeton University Press, 1985); William J. Barber, *From New Era to New Deal: Herbert Hoover, the Economists, and American Economic Policy, 1921-1933* (New York: Cambridge University Press, 1985); Julie Z. Strickland, "War Making and State Building: The Dynamics of American Institutional Development, 1917-1935" (Ph.D. diss., Stanford University, 1988); Neil L. Mitchell, *The Generous Corporation: A Political Analysis of Economic Power* (New Haven: Yale University Press, 1989); Morton Keller, *Regulating a New Economy: Public Policy and Economic Change in America, 1900-1933* (Cambridge: Harvard University Press, 1990); William G. Scott, *Chester I. Barnard and the Guardians of the Managerial State* (Lawrence: University Press of Kansas,

1992); and Robert F. Himmelberg, ed., *Antitrust and Regulation During World War I and the Republican Era, 1917–1932* (New York: Garland, 1994), and Himmelberg, ed., *Business-Government Cooperation, 1917–1932: The Rise of Corporatist Policies* (New York: Garland, 1994). *Business History Review* 64 (Spring 1990): 1–149, includes four articles analyzing government-business relations in the 1920s and after. Mary M. Dodge, ed., *Herbert Hoover and the Historians* (West Branch, IA: Herbert Hoover Presidential Library Association, 1989), includes the most up-to-date bibliography on Hoover by Richard Dean Burns, pp. 117–41.

The scholarship on Hoover is related to another trend principally among historians and economists who have focused on the institutional adjustments required by the "new, industrial" society. Although this group has attempted to treat with most major institutions, the important work has been done on the modern corporation and appropriately is called the New Business History. The best example of this work is Alfred D. Chandler, Jr., *The Visible Hand: The Managerial Revolution in American Business* (Cambridge, MA: Belknap Press, 1977). *Business History Review* 52 (Autumn 1978) published a Special Issue on Corporate Liberalism, which illuminates aspects of the subject that Chandler examines. Louis Galambos also focuses on institutional adjustments in several articles. See "The Emerging Organizational Synthesis in Modern American History," *Business History Review* 44 (Autumn 1970): 279–90, and "Technology, Political Economy, and Professionalization: Central Themes of the Organizational Synthesis," *Business History Review* 57 (Winter 1983): 471–93. My analysis of the New Business History is included in "Warfare and Power Relations in America: Mobilizing the World War II Economy," in *The Home Front and War in the Twentieth Century*, ed. James Titus, pp. 239–40, n. 20 (Colorado Springs, CO: United States Air Force Academy, 1984).

2. Concerning the discussion of the New Deal, fifteen army officers served on seventeen different code authorities in the NRA and two additional officers were assigned full-time to the Office of Administrator, NRA. Colonel Charles T. Harris, Jr., in his testimony before the Nye Committee gave some insight into the importance of the NRA in the eyes of the military planners. See U.S. Congress, Senate, Special Committee Investigating the Munitions Industry, 73d and 74th Cong., 1934–1936, *Hearings*, Part 17, pp. 4292–93, 4307–8, 4319–20, and 4444–45. See also Peter M. Abramo, "The Economic and Military Potential of the United States: Industrial Mobilization Planning, 1919–1945 (Ph.D. diss., Temple University, 1995), pp. 158–67. The OASW records in the 1930s are replete with references to the NRA and documents on the OASW's analysis of it. On the military planners' proposals for handling labor relations in an emergency, see Paul A. C. Koistinen, *The Hammer and the Sword: Labor, the Military, and Industrial Mobilization, 1920–1945* (New York: Arno Press, 1979), pp. 28–60. The review of the OASW planning by the War Policies Commission and the Nye Committee is covered in chapters 13 and 14, as is the impact on the planning of the peace and isolationist movements and antimilitary attitudes in the 1930s.

The relevant bibliography on the New Deal of course is enormous. Ellis W. Hawley, *The New Deal and the Problem of Monopoly: A Study in Economic Ambivalence* (Princeton, NJ: Princeton University Press, 1966), remains the best volume for this study. Otis L. Graham, Jr., "The Age of the Great Depression, 1929–1940," in *The Reinterpretation of American History and Culture*, ed. William H. Cartwright and Richard L. Watson, Jr., pp. 491–508 (Washington, DC: National Council for the Social

Studies, 1973), presents a full and perceptive analysis of literature on the New Deal. For a provocative discussion of the New Deal and scholarly work on it from a New Left orientation, as opposed to the liberal position of Graham, see Ronald Radosh, "The Myth of the New Deal," in Radosh and Rothbard, eds., *New History of Leviathan*, pp. 146–87. See also Alan Brinkley, "Prosperity, Depression, and War, 1920–1945," in *The New American History*, ed. Eric Foner, pp. 119–41 (Philadelphia: Temple University Press, 1990), and Brinkley's latest publication, *The End of Reform: New Deal Liberalism in Recession and War* (New York: Alfred A. Knopf, 1995); Leon Fink, "American Labor History," in Foner, ed., *New American History*, pp. 243–50; Steve Fraser and Gary Gerstle, eds., *The Rise and Fall of the New Deal Order, 1930–1980* (Princeton, NJ: Princeton University Press, 1989); Robert M. Collins, *The Business Response to Keynes, 1929–1964* (New York: Columbia University Press, 1981); Mark A. Leff, *The Limits of Symbolic Reform: The New Deal and Taxation, 1933–1939* (New York: Cambridge University Press, 1984); Michael A. Bernstein, *The Great Depression: Delayed Recovery and Economic Change in America, 1929–1939* (New York: Cambridge University Press, 1987); Fred Block, *Revising State Theory: Essays in Politics and Postindustrialism* (Philadelphia: Temple University Press, 1987); Anthony J. Badger, *The New Deal: The Depression Years, 1933–40* (New York: Hill and Wang, 1989); Lizabeth Cohen, *Making a New Deal: Industrial Workers in Chicago, 1919–1939* (New York: Cambridge University Press, 1990); Mark J. Gobeyn, "The Rise and Fall of Liberal Corporatism: Economic Transformation and the Decline of Corporatist Political Structures in Advanced Industrial Societies" (Ph.D. diss., Washington State University, 1990); Alan Dawley, *Struggles for Justice: Social Responsibility and the Liberal State* (Cambridge, MA: Belknap Press, 1991); Stephen Skowronek, *The Politics Presidents Make: Leadership from John Adams to George Bush* (Cambridge, MA: Belknap Press, 1993), pp. 260–324; Robert F. Himmelberg, ed., *Survival of Corporatism During the New Deal Era, 1933–1945* (New York, Garland, 1994), and Himmelberg, ed., *The New Deal and Corporate Power: Antitrust and Regulatory Policies During the Thirties and World War II* (New York: Garland, 1994); William E. Leuchtenburg, *The FDR Years: On Roosevelt and His Legacy* (New York: Columbia University Press, 1995); David Plotke, *Building a Democratic Political Order: Reshaping American Liberalism in the 1930s and 1940s* (New York: Cambridge University Press, 1996); Theda Skocpol, "Political Response to Capitalist Crisis: Neo-Marxist Theories of the State and the Case of the New Deal," *Politics and Society* 10 (1980): 155–201; and Kenneth Finegold and Theda Skocpol, *State and Party in America's New Deal* (Madison: University of Wisconsin Press, 1995); William J. Barber, "Government as a Laboratory for Economic Learning in the Years of the Democratic Roosevelt," in *The State and Economic Knowledge: The American and British Experiences*, ed. Mary O. Furner and Barry Supple, pp. 103–37 (New York: Woodrow Wilson International Center for Scholars and Cambridge University Press, 1990); Richard P. Adelstein, "'The Nation as an Economic Unit': Keynes, Roosevelt, and the Managerial Ideal," *Journal of American History* 78 (June 1991): 160–87; Colin Gordon, *New Deals: Business, Labor, and Politics in America, 1920–1935* (New York: Cambridge University Press, 1994); Gary Gerstle, "The Protean Character of American Liberalism," *American Historical Review* 99 (October 1994): 1043–73; and Richard H. K. Vietor, *Contrived Competition: Regulation and Deregulation in America* (Cambridge, MA: Belknap Press, 1994). David Lynch's study of the Temporary National Economic Committee,

The Concentration of Economic Power (New York: Columbia University Press, 1946), remains exceptionally valuable for analyzing the New Deal years and the World War II economy. For an introduction to economic planning in the interwar years, see John D. Millett, *The Process and Organization of Government Planning* (New York: Columbia University Press, 1947); Otis L. Graham, Jr., *Toward A Planned Society: From Roosevelt to Nixon* (New York: Oxford University Press, 1976), pp. 1–68; Jean Christie, *Morris Llewellyn Cooke: Progressive Engineer* (New York: Garland, 1983); Anthony S. Campagna, *U.S. National Economic Policy, 1917–1985* (New York: Praeger Publishers, 1987), and other sources cited in Paul A. C. Koistinen, *Mobilizing for Modern War: The Political Economy of American Warfare, 1865–1919* (Lawrence: University Press of Kansas, 1997), chap. 11, n. 20.

3. The chemicals/explosives and aircraft industries are treated in chapter 10.

4. Baruch's fears are discussed and documented in chapters 2, 3, 13, and 14.

5. See the Bibliographic Essay.

6. War Department politics in the late 1930s and early 1940s, along with other matters relevant to economic mobilization, will be discussed at length in chapter 15. They will also be analyzed in greater depth in the forthcoming volume four of this series.

7. See the Bibliographic Essay.

8. See chapter 2 for changes of the M-Day concept in the IMP, 1939.

CHAPTER TWELVE. THE GRAHAM COMMITTEE

1. The various authors and their arguments will be discussed in the text, in the notes of chapters 13 and 14, or in both. Suffice it to say at this point that Clarkson in his testimony before the Graham Committee in mid-1919 was much more candid and direct about wartime mobilization patterns than is the case in his volume on the subject. See U.S. Congress, House, Select Committee on Expenditures in the War Department, *Hearings, War Expenditures,* Serial 1, 66th Cong., 1921, pp. 333–402 (hereafter cited as Graham Committee, *Hearings*), and Grosvenor S. Clarkson, *Industrial America in the World War: The Strategy Behind the Line, 1917–1918* (Boston: Houghton Mifflin, 1923).

2. Congressional hearings and their results are cited in chapter 1 and in Paul A. C. Koistinen, *Mobilizing for Modern War: The Political Economy of American Warfare, 1865–1919* (Lawrence: University Press of Kansas, 1997), chaps. 7–10.

3. The one work of substance is chapter 5 in Virgil Calvin Stroud, "Congressional Investigations of the Conduct of War" (Ph.D. diss., New York University, 1954). Stroud's work contains basic information about the committee and compares it with other investigating bodies. He accurately reflects the negative attitude of scholars toward the committee.

4. Information about the committee, its membership, and its mode of operation is found in the *Hearings* and *Reports,* many of which will be cited. Stroud, "Congressional Investigations," contains some good information on the topic. Wayne S. Cole, *Senator Gerald P. Nye and American Foreign Relations* (Minneapolis: University of Minnesota Press, 1962), is particularly good in analyzing the rural response to twentieth-century American foreign policy and warfare, both of which had definite urban emphases.

5. U.S. Congress, House, Select Committee on Expenditures in the War Department, "Expenditures in the War Department—Camps," *Report* no. 816, 66th Cong., 2d sess., 1920, pp. 1–174 (the reports hereafter are cited as Graham Committee, *Report*). The Graham Committee reports have been conveniently gathered in one volume: Graham Committee, *Hearings*, Serial 1, vol. 3, Reports of the Committee, 1921, pp. 1–771, Index, pp. i–ii. For the hearings, see Graham Committee, *Hearings*, Camps, Serial 3. The Graham Committee hearings have been cataloged according to their own serial set, which is rather unusual for the time and can be confusing. The breakdown is as follows: Serial 1, 13 parts, 3 vols., consists of general testimony on economic mobilization in addition to the consolidated reports; Serial 2, 3 vols., deals with aviation; Serial 3, 37 parts, 2 vols., covers "Camps"; Serial 4, 78 parts, 4 vols., focuses on foreign expenditures; Serial 5, 1 vol., treats with the Quartermaster Corps; and Serial 6, 70 parts, 4 vols., involves Ordnance. For purposes of simplicity and economy of citation, in the discussion and analysis of the Graham Committee I will cite the report that deals with a subject, only the appropriate serial number of hearings if essential, and a serial number and pagination only if a quotation is involved or imperative need exists. Some of the reports are based on material taken from hearings and exhibits ranging throughout all or much of the committee's work.

6. The Subcommittee on the Quartermaster Corps never made any reports. The most detailed report involving the Committee on Supplies was done by the Ordnance Subcommittee on leather and leather goods. See Graham Committee, *Report* no. 1307, 66th Cong., 3d sess., 1921, pp. 1–26. The operations of the Committee on Supplies and related mobilization agencies were treated extensively in the Graham Committee's hearings and will be cited.

7. Graham Committee, *Report* no. 1400, 66th Cong., 3d Sess., 1921, pp. 1–111. For the contrasting versions of Baruch and Clarkson, see Bernard M. Baruch, *American Industry in the War: A Report of the War Industries Board* (Washington, DC: Government Printing Office, 1921), pp. 130–37, and Clarkson, *Industrial America in the World War*, pp. 345–53.

8. Graham Committee, *Report* no. 1400; *Report* no. 998, Parts 1 and 2, 66th Cong., 2d sess., 1920, pp. 1–122; and *Report* no. 1307.

9. Graham Committee, *Report* no. 637, 66th Cong., 2d sess., 1920, Part 1, pp. 1–128, Part 2, 1–71 (quotations, p. 6).

10. Graham Committee, *Report* no. 1410, 66th Cong., 3d sess., 1921, pp. 1–59.

11. Ibid. Information on, analysis of, and judgments about property disposal, reconversion, and the like are scattered throughout the various reports, including Graham Committee, *Report* no. 171, 66th Cong., 1st sess., 1919, pp. 1–35; *Report* no. 441, 66th Cong., 1st sess., 1919, p. 1; Report no. 463, 66th Cong., 1st sess., 1919, Part 1, pp. 1–2, Part 2, pp. 1–7; *Report* no. 487, 66th Cong., 2d sess., 1919, pp. 1–4; *Report* no. 1307; and *Report* no. 1400.

12. See Koistinen, *Mobilizing for Modern War*, chaps. 7–10.

13. Some of this information is contained in a fragmentary way in various reports cited in nn. 5–11. The most important data and analysis are contained in the hearings. However, it is impossible to distinguish clearly between the evolution of the War Department's wartime supply system and the civilian economic apparatus created between 1915 and 1918, since the military and civilian systems were very close and interacting. For the most significant testimony of key military and civilian economic

mobilization participants, see Graham Committee, *Hearings*, Serial 1, Gen. H. M. Lord, pp. 205–303; Col. J. L. Schley, pp. 303–32, 447–49; Clarkson, pp. 333–402; Charles Eisenman, pp. 403–47; Gen. William Crozier, pp. 451–516; Gen. George W. Goethals, pp. 517–57; and Bernard M. Baruch, pp. 1793–1858; and Graham Committee, *Hearings*, Serial 3, Walter S. Gifford, pp. 869–79; Hollis Godfrey, pp. 880–90; and Frank A. Scott, pp. 987–1019. The hearings also contain some important documents related to the establishment and operation of the Purchase, Storage, and Traffic Division. See Graham Committee, *Hearings*, Serial 1, pp. 34–35, 128–54, 180–87.

14. See chapter 1. Investigation by the Senate Military Affairs Committee during World War I also carried out some important preliminary work in this area. See Koistinen, *Mobilizing for Modern War*, chaps. 8–10.

15. For the key witnesses, see n. 13.

16. Graham Committee, *Report* no. 1307, p. 26; no. 1400, p. 83, no. 1410, pp. 27–28, and Graham Committee, *Hearings*, Serial 1, 559–61.

17. Bad judgment, questionable assertions, contradictory conclusions, and the like abound throughout the *Hearings* and *Reports*. I am citing just the few examples provided in the text. See Graham Committee, *Reports* no. 816, pp. 23–36; no. 998, Parts 1 and 2; and no. 1400, pp. 1–2, 68, 82, 93, and Graham Committee, *Hearings*, Serial 1, pp. 544–45.

18. These points, conclusions, and judgments are scattered throughout the *Hearings* and *Reports* and are addressed most directly in the one place that Graham and his colleagues came closest to rendering final conclusions. A good example of committee observations along the lines discussed occur in Graham Committee, *Report* no. 1400, pp. 69–71, 84, and 94. For the Nye Committee's observations on the lack of data to evaluate many facets of the World War I economic mobilization effort, see chapter 14. Gerald T. White, *Billions for Defense: Government Financing by the Defense Plant Corporation During World War II* (University: University of Alabama Press, 1980), at least indirectly, makes the same point about the operations of the Defense Plant Corporation during World War II. The significance of White's analysis will be addressed in the analysis of World War II in the forthcoming volume 4 of this series.

19. Rather characteristically, the overall majority report, to the degree that one was made, was included with the findings and recommendations involving military camps. The minority confined its remarks largely to the issues concerning the construction of the cantonments. The Graham Committee as a whole never made a final report from or recommendations based on its two-year study. On this last point, see Stroud, "Congressional Investigations," pp. 247–48, 255–56.

20. This recommendation was specifically aimed at construction. However, from the committee's overall approach and attitude, it clearly intended the recommendation to apply to all wartime contracting. In the account of the majority's recommendations, I have shifted information about slightly and excluded some points but not in a way that alters significantly the majority's point of view.

21. Graham Committee, *Report* no. 816, pp. 145–48 (quotation, p. 145). A member of the Graham Committee, John C. McKenzie (R-IL), introduced a bill in the House of Representatives in November 1921 incorporating most of the recommendations of this report. See U.S. Congress, House, Committee on Military Affairs, *Hearings, Universal Mobilization for War Purposes*, 68th Cong., lst sess., 1924, pp. 481–83.

CHAPTER THIRTEEN. THE AMERICAN LEGION,
THE OASW, AND THE WPC

1. The secondary literature on the American Legion is quite extensive. Some of the better work includes Roscoe Baker, *The American Legion and American Foreign Policy* (New York: Bookman Associates, 1954); Dorothy Culp, *The American Legion: A Study in Pressure Politics* (Chicago: Private Edition, distributed by the University of Chicago Libraries, 1942); Marcus Duffield, *King Legion* (New York: Jonathan Cape and Harrison Smith, 1931); William Gellermann, *The American Legion as Educator* (New York: Teachers College, Columbia University, 1938); Justin Gray with Victor H. Bernstein, *The Inside Story of the Legion* (New York: Boni and Gaer, 1948); Richard Seelye Jones, *A History of the American Legion* (Indianapolis, IN: Bobbs-Merrill, 1946); Rodney G. Minott, *Peerless Patriots: Organized Veterans and the Spirit of Americanism* (Washington, DC: Public Affairs Press, 1962); David B. Truman, *The Governmental Process: Political Interests and Public Opinion*, 2d ed. (New York: Alfred A. Knopf, 1971); William Pencak, *For God and Country: The American Legion, 1919-1941* (Boston: Northeastern University Press, 1989); and Jennifer Diane Keene, "Civilians in Uniform: Building an American Mass Army for the Great War" (Ph.D. diss., Carnegie-Mellon University, 1991). Duffield, Gellermann, and Minott are the most useful for this study.
2. See n. 1, particularly Duffield, Gellerman, and Minott.
3. Most of the volumes cited in n. 1 cover the universal service movement.
4. Ferguson to Planning Branch, 6/1/22, and other documents, file 44; Fife to Wooten, 1/26/29, and other correspondence and documents, file 374; and MacNider to Weeks, 1/21/22, and other correspondence and documents, file 560, Planning Branch (PB), Assistant Secretary of War (ASW), Office of the Secretary of War (OSW), RG 107, National Archives, Washington, DC (hereafter cited as PB, ASW, OSW); U.S. Congress, House, Committee on Military Affairs, *Hearings, Universal Mobilization for War Purposes*, 68th Cong., 1st sess., 1924, pp. 447-67 (hereafter cited as HMAC, *Hearings*, 1924); U.S. Congress, Senate, Military Affairs Committee, *Hearings, To Provide for the National Security and Defense*, 68th Cong., 1st sess., 1924, pp. 3-7 (hereafter cited as SMAC, *Hearings*, 1924); U.S. Congress, Senate, Military Affairs Committee, *Hearings, To Provide for the National Defense*, 69th Cong., 1st sess., 1926, pp. 1-98; U.S. Congress, House, Military Affairs Committee, *Hearings, Universal Draft, Conscription of Man Power, Wealth, and Industrial Resources in Time of War*, 70th Cong., 1st sess., 1928, pp. 1-35 (hereafter cited as HMAC, *Hearings*, 1928); and Harold W. Thatcher, *Planning for Industrial Mobilization, 1920-1940* (Washington, DC: Office of the Quartermaster General, 1943), pp. 97-111. Chapter 2 deals with proposed legislation for economic mobilization as it involved the OASW's planning. This analysis is indispensable for understanding how the subject was treated in and outside of Congress.
5. Planning Branch, "Mobilization of Manpower and Industrial Resources, Legislative History," 2/18/37, file 010/178, PB, ASW, OSW. This document provides a valuable summary of all measures introduced in Congress dealing with wartime economics and their disposition between 1920 and 1937. The various bills, resolutions, and the like on which Congress held hearings are contained in the hearings cited in n. 4.

6. HMAC, *Hearings,* 1924, pp. 458–67, 473–80; SMAC, *Hearings,* 1924, pp. 3–7, 9–12, 25–33; and HMAC, *Hearings,* 1928, pp. 1–35.

7. HMAC, *Hearings,* 1924, pp. 456–57, 467–72, 513–22; SMAC, *Hearings,* 1924, pp. 20–25; and HMAC, *Hearings,* 1928. Hull, Garrett, and others were members of the House committee and made their views known through participation in the hearings rather than through formal testimony. For Hull's proposed legislation and responses to it, see "General Memorandum no. 73, Re: *Hull Bill,*"and other correspondence and documents, file 374, PB, ASW, OSW.

8. HMAC, *Hearings,* 1924, pp. 486–92; and HMAC, *Hearings,* 1928. McSwain testified even though he was a member of the committee. The views of McKensie, Wainwright, and others as members of the committee are scattered throughout the hearings. Baruch also corresponded with McSwain and others who shared the latter's thinking (see the citations, n. 9).

9. HMAC, *Hearings,* 1924, pp. 562–90. Baruch's ideas are more fully developed in Baruch, Lecture to the Army War College, 4/8/22, Baruch, Lecture to the Army War College, 1/19/23, Baruch, "The War Industries Board," 2/11/24, Baruch, "The War Industries Board," 1/15/25, Baruch, "Address to Meeting of the American Society of Mechanical Engineers," 5/28/24, Baruch, "The Control of Our Economic and Industrial Resources and Activities in War," 12/13/27, Baruch, "The Economics of Modern War," 4/22/29, and Baruch, "Economic Mobilization of the United States," 3/6/30, file "Address, AWC, 3/6/30," Unit 8, Box 3, Special Memoranda, Bernard M. Baruch Papers, Princeton University, Princeton, NJ (hereafter cited as Baruch Papers); 1921 article for the *Army and Navy Journal,* Johnson address, "Industrial and Manpower Mobilization," 12/22, 1923 correspondence with Brisbane and Davis, 1924 correspondence with Capper, Clarkson, Ely, Garrett, Gompers, and McSwain, 1925 correspondence with Capper, Ely, Johnson, McSwain and Scott, 1926 correspondence with Ballou, Coolidge, Davis, Ely, Garfield, Legge, McSwain, and Scott, and 1929 correspondence with Connor, Johnson, Legge, and Moseley, Selected Correspondence, Baruch Papers (the Selected Correspondence contains enormous amounts of material on industrial mobilization with these citations including only some of the more significant items); Baruch, "Control of Our Economic and Industrial Resources in War," 2/28/29, file 353-A-24, G-4, no. 24, and Baruch, "Economic Mobilization of the United States," 3/6/30, file 364-A-17, G-4, no. 7, Army War College Collection, Carlisle Barracks (hereafter cited as AWC); and Baruch, "Taking the Profits Out of War," *Atlantic Monthly* 137 (January 1926): 23–29. For the Johnson quotations, see Johnson, "Industrial and Man-Power Mobilization," 12/11/22, file 250-10, AWC, and Johnson, "Notes on 'Draft of Industry and Labor'—submitted November 29, 1922," file 555, PB, ASW, OSW.

Baruch claimed that he originated the concept, "Taking the Profits Out of War," with his final report on the WIB to the president (Bernard M. Baruch, *American Industry in the War: A Report of the War Industries Board* [Washington, DC: U.S. Government Printing Office, 1921]). Grosvenor B. Clarkson encouraged Baruch to claim credit for the idea and tried to validate it in his volume, *Industrial America in the World War: The Strategy Behind the Line, 1917–1918* (Boston: Houghton Mifflin, 1923). See Clarkson to Baruch, 3/31/24, and unlabeled memorandum in 1926 "B" category, Selected Correspondence, Baruch Papers. Baruch's relations with the OASW are discussed in detail with full documentation in chapter 2. The analysis is important for understanding the viewpoint and action of the former chairman of the WIB.

10. HMAC, *Hearings*, 1924, pp. 493–13 (quotation, p. 504).
11. Ibid., pp. 527–62, 665–83.
12. Ibid., pp. 645–61; SMAC, *Hearings*, 1926, pp. 7–9, 12–20; and HMAC, *Hearings*, 1928, pp. 43–55. Good insight into the War Department's thinking and action on varying bills for wartime economics are contained in Ferguson to Planning Branch, 6/1/22, and other documents and correspondence, file 44; Lassiter to Chief of Staff, 2/3/22, and other documents, file 62; Hasson to Carr, 2/5/31, and other correspondence, file 72; Hunt to Planning Branch, 9/20/22, file 90; "Plan for Governmental Organization for War," 11/12/29, and other documents, file 109; E. M. R. to Stoddard [circa] 2/1928, file 274; "Notes on Conference with Mr. Baruch and Mr. Summers-February 14th, 1923," and other documents, file 371; Davis to Morin, 2/27/28, and other documents and correspondence, file 374; Sep to Tom, 4/3/22, and numerous other documents and correspondence, file 555; Saltzman to All Officers, 2/7/22, and other documents and correspondence, file 560; Griffin et al. to Chief Signal Officer, 4/19/24 and other documents, file 562; Fife to Ferguson, 5/17/23, and other correspondence, file 612; and "Minutes of Meeting of Orientation Conference no. 9, Subject, Labor . . . , October 30, 1934," file 049.12/175, and other documents, PB, ASW, OSW. Numerous documents from the 1920–1930 period in the Army War College Collection are also useful. Some of them are cited in the discussion of interwar military planning and proposed legislation concerning it in chapter 2. The analysis in that chapter provides an indispensable background for the subject of this chapter. For a discussion of War Department interwar planning with particular attention paid to labor, see Paul A. C. Koistinen, *The Hammer and the Sword: Labor, the Military, and Industrial Mobilization, 1920–1945* (New York: Arno Press, 1979), chap. 1.
13. Scott to Vestal, 6/18/29, file "War Dept.-Army War College-1928–1929"; Scott to Wainwright, 6/27/22, and Pierce to Scott, 4/3/22, file "War Department-Preparedness Program 1921–1928-File Folder 1 to 1923"; Appendix "A," The Proposed Scheme, undated [circa 1922], file "War Dept.-Preparedness Program 1921–1928-Folder 2-1924–1928"; Scott address, "Industrial Mobilization for a Great War," 12/16/26, file, "Army War College"; and Scott address, "The Development of the General Munitions Board," 4/30/25, file "Army Industrial College," Frank A. Scott Papers, Princeton University, Princeton, NJ; and "Minutes of Meeting . . . Mr. Frank A. Scott," 1/14/22, file 371, PB, ASW, OSW. Scott generally looked upon proposals for drafting capital and labor as a grave threat. However, at times he wavered and appeared to consider national service for the working population as a possibility.
14. HMAC, *Hearings*, 1924, pp. 522–27; HMAC, *Hearings*, 1928, pp. 35–43; and newsclip from *Christian Science Monitor*, 5/8/24, file 520, PB, ASW, OSW. On the general topic of labor, unions, and interwar industrial mobilization planning, see Koistinen, *Hammer and Sword*, chap. 1.
15. Weeks to Chairman, House Judiciary Committee, Jan. 17 and 19, 1923, and Fife to Moseley, 1/18/30, file 374, PB, ASW, OSW.
16. HMAC, *Hearings*, 1924, pp. 661–65, and SMAC, *Hearings*, 1924, pp. 1–3. The views of Capper and Johnson are also manifested in correspondence with the War Department and Baruch in the preceding citations. Johnson appeared to be closer to the true believers' camp in the War Policies Commission hearings than in the hearing under consideration. His rambling, unfocused style always distracted from his presentation; at times, he comes across as senescent.

17. Thatcher, *Planning for Industrial Mobilization*, pp. 98–100.
18. For Hoover, see HMAC, *Hearings*, 1924, pp. 639–45.
19. HMAC, *Hearings*, 1924; SMAC, *Hearings*, 1924; HMAC, *Hearings*, 1928; and "Statement of Col. Ferguson Before Senate" on S 2561, 1924, file 374, PB, ASW, OSW.
20. Planning Branch, "Mobilization of Manpower and Industrial Resources: Legislative History," 2/18/37, file 010/178, PB, ASW, OSW.
21. The joint resolution creating the WPC is reproduced in many places but is most readily available in the interim report of the WPC to the president. See "Message from the President . . . Transmitting Report of the War Policies Commission," H. Doc. 163, 72d Cong., 1st sess., 1931, p. vi (hereafter cited as WPC, *Interim Report*). Attempts to explain why Congress excluded a labor draft from the WPC's purview recur throughout the documents and hearings of the WPC. The most direct statement occurs in an exchange between Congressmen Ross A. Collins and Fiorello H. LaGuardia, WPC, *Hearings*, pp. 668–69 (the *Hearings*, along with the *Minutes*, are included as part of the interim report just cited). See also Planning Branch, "Mobilization of Manpower and Industrial Resources, Legislative History," 2/18/37, file 010/178, PB, ASW, OSW.
22. WPC, *Interim Report*, p. vi, and Seymour Waldman, *Death and Profits: A Study of the War Policies Commission* (New York: Brewer, Warren, and Putnam, 1932), p. 9.
23. WPC, *Interim Report*, p. vi.
24. Eisenhower to Moseley, 2/25/31 and other documents, file 7, WPC, 1930–1932, PB, ASW, OSW (see n. 26 concerning this document collection); WPC, *Minutes*, 1/21/31, 1/28/31, 2/11/31, and 3/5/31, pp. xv–xix (the typed version of these minutes is in file 146). For additional background information on Hurley, see chapters 1 and 2. See also Stephen E. Ambrose, *Eisenhower*, vol. 1, *Soldier, General of the Army, President-Elect, 1890–1952* (New York: Simon and Schuster, 1983), pp. 88–93.
25. "Explanatory Statement to Accompany Chart Illustrating Organization of Proposed Secretariat," file 5; Montgomery to England, 3/4/31 and other documents, file 7B; Eisenhower to Moseley, 2/17/31, and other documents, file 31; Carr to Director, Planning Branch, 2/17/31, and other documents, file 38; and Moseley to Assistant Secretary of War, 6/25/30, file 68, WPC, 1930–1932, PB, ASW, OSW. The response, or more correctly, the lack of response of most departments to the WPC can be traced in the records of the OASW and of those departments. The OASW had no meaningful files on the attorney general and the secretary of agriculture. For the secretaries of navy, labor, and commerce, see files 15, 16, 19, WPC, 1930–1932, PB, ASW, OSW. For records in other departments, see file 9-03-1, Department of Justice, RG 60, National Archives, College Park, MD (hereafter cited as Department of Justice); War Policies Commission, General Correspondence of Robert P. Lamont, Secretary of Commerce, 1929–1932, General Records of the Department of Commerce, RG 40, National Archives, College Park, MD; Hurley to Hyde, 7/24/30, and other documents, War Policies Commission, Correspondence Files of the Secretary of Agriculture, 1906–1956, RG 16, National Archives, College Park, MD; and War Policies Commission, Records of the Secretary's Office, Navy Department, RG 80, National Archives, Washington, DC (hereafter cited as Navy Department). No files were located

in the Labor Department collection, RG 174, National Archives, College Park, MD. See also WPC, *Minutes,* 1/21/31, pp. xv–xvii.

26. The observations can be validated only by studying the WPC, *Minutes,* and more important, the *Hearings.* Also helpful is the one substantial record collection on the WPC in the OASW files, held as a separate entity under the label "War Policies Commission, File, 1930–1932," consisting of around 213 folders in about fifteen boxes; the rather meager files in the other departments are cited in n. 25. Besides the OASW collection, only the Justice Department files are in any way substantial.

27. Vandenberg to Hurley, 8/5/30, file 30, WPC, 1930–1932, PB, ASW, OSW.

28. For Baruch's testimony before the commission, see WPC, *Hearings,* pp. 29–72, 794–841 (hereafter only quotations will be cited for Baruch). For Baruch and Johnson's close ties and working relations with members and staff of the WPC, see Eisenhower to Moseley, 2/25/31, file 7; Montgomery to Baruch, 3/20/31, file 73; Hartrick to Hurley, 5/19/31, file 17; Moseley to Baruch, 5/22/31, file 31; Montgomery's secretary to Baruch, 11/26/31, file 79; Montgomery to Baruch, 3/13/31, file 67; and Johnson to Montgomery, 3/12/31, and other correspondence, file 95, WPC, 1930–1932, PB, ASW, OSW; Baruch to Robinson, 3/13/31, and 5/11/31, and Robinson to Baruch, 3/11/31, Selected Correspondence, Baruch Papers (Baruch's Selected Correspondence for 1931 and 1932, and especially the first year, contains a great deal of correspondence about or related to the WPC, which provides additional insights concerning the attitudes of Baruch and others on the political economy of warfare); and Holtzoff, Hill, and Lavender, "Preliminary Observations In Reference to Mr. Baruch's Plan for Fixing Prices," [circa May 1931] and numerous other documents, file 9-03-1, Department of Justice. See also John K. Ohl, *Hugh S. Johnson and the New Deal* (DeKalb: Northern Illinois University Press, 1985), pp. 70–91.

29. WPC, *Hearings,* pp. 49–50.

30. Ibid., p. 53.

31. Ibid., p. 34.

32. Ibid., pp. 30–31.

33. Baruch to Baker, 3/13/31, Selected Correspondence, Baruch Papers.

34. See chapter 2.

35. The entire IMP, 1930, was incorporated into the WPC, *Hearings,* pp. 395–477. The testimony of Payne, MacArthur, and Moseley is found on pp. 351–93.

36. See chapter 2 for a full description and analysis of the IMP, 1930.

37. WPC, *Hearings,* p. 355. See also Moseley to Collins, 3/7/31, and other documents and correspondence, file 22, WPC, 1930–1932, PB, ASW, OSW.

38. WPC, *Hearings,* pp. 479–80; Adams to Hurley, 2/28/31, and numerous other correspondence and documents, War Policies Commission, Navy Department; and Hurley to Adams, 8/16/30, file 15, WPC, 1930–1932, PB, ASW, OSW.

39. WPC, *Hearings,* pp. 169–90, 218–52, 315–23, 481–88, 787–90. See also Peek to Baruch, 3/8, 3/11, and 3/19/31, and Baruch to Peek, 3/11/31, Selected Correspondence, Baruch Papers.

40. Montgomery to Baruch, 3/20/31, file 78, WPC, 1930–1932, PB, ASW, OSW. Some insight into the Baruch-Legge relationship is provided by the correspondence between the two and related parties in Selected Correspondence, 1923, 1926, and 1929, Baruch Papers. John Kenneth Galbraith, *A Life in Our Times: Memoirs* (Boston: Houghton Mifflin, 1981), pp. 130–31, claims Legge was the true genius of

World War I economic mobilization, an assertion I question in Paul A. C. Koistinen, *Mobilizing for Modern War: The Political Economy of American Warfare, 1865–1919* (Lawrence: University Press of Kansas, 1997), chap. 8, n. 15.

41. WPC, *Hearings,* pp. 308–15, 502–35, 687–721, 791–94, and Eisenhower to Swope, 3/11/31, file 118, WPC, 1930–1932, PB, ASW, OSW. Writing plans for public relations as an aspect of economic mobilization generated a great deal of tension between the OASW and the General Staff in the 1930s (see chap. 2).

42. See chapter 2. World War I rivalries carried over into the interwar planning and are evident throughout the text and notes on the 1920s and 1930s. Pierce, who earlier supported OASW planning, albeit never uncritically, turned against it during the WPC deliberations and rejected some of Baruch's key ideas as well. Pierce's resentment of Baruch appeared to be critical in his reversal. See Pierce to Montgomery, 3/17/31, and Montgomery to Pierce, 3/20/31, file 109, WPC, 1930–1932, PB, ASW, OSW.

43. WPC, *Hearings,* pp. 113–69, 283–309, 776–87, 854–75. Baruch's correspondence with Baker involving the WPC deliberations is especially good and revealing; see Selected Correspondence, 1931, Baruch Papers.

44. Baruch's contacts with Baker are referred to in n. 43. Baruch addressed the position of Baker et al. in his rebuttal, WPC, *Hearings,* pp. 794–841, and Montgomery did so in his report. See also Moseley to Baker, 3/7/31, and other correspondence and documents, file 75; Montgomery to Gifford, 3/19/31, file 66; and Gifford to Montgomery, 3/23/31 and other correspondence, file 90, WPC, 1930–1932, PB, ASW, OSW.

45. WPC, *Hearings,* pp. 7–29.

46. Ibid., pp. 205–18.

47. Ibid., pp. 252–65.

48. Ibid., pp. 2–7.

49. Montgomery to Leach, 4/6/31, file 7B, Leach to Montgomery, 3/30/31, file 136; Montgomery to Hurley, 11/25/31, file 17; McSwain to Montgomery, 3/13/31, file 25; Montgomery to Bethea, 3/17/31, file 59; and Montgomery to past Commanders of the American Legion, [circa] March 1931, and other correspondence, file 58, WPC, 1930–1932, PB, ASW, OSW; Ralph T. O'Neil, Paul V. McNutt, and Charles B. Robbins, *The American Legion Presents to the War Policies Commission a Plan to Perpetuate Peace by Equalizing the Burdens of and Eliminating the Profits from War,* [circa] 11/5/31, file 9-03-1, Department of Justice; and the foregoing document reproduced in "Documents by the War Policies Commission," H. Doc. 271, 72d Cong., 1st sess., 1932, pp. 55–71 (hereafter cited as WPC, *Documents*).

50. WPC, *Hearings,* pp. 73–85, 850–52.

51. Ibid., pp. 555–92.

52. Ibid., pp. 612–66.

53. Ibid., pp. 85–113.

54. Ibid., pp. 266–83.

55. Ibid., pp. 750–59, 853–54 (quotation, p. 756).

56. Ibid., pp. 727–33.

57. Ibid., pp. 678–87.

58. Ibid., pp. 733–50.

59. Collins to Montgomery, 4/23/31, file 22; McSwain to Hurley, 5/5/31, file 25; and Hartrick to Montgomery, 5/2/31, file 7. In the last letter, the former—an

OASW Ordnance officer—noted to the latter that "the witnesses are lining up OK with the exception of the pacifists and it wont [sic] make any difference if we never [sic] hear from them" (WPC, 1930–1932, PB, ASW, OSW).

60. WPC, *Hearings*, pp. 323–43, 852–53.
61. Ibid., pp. 722–27, and Waldman, *Death and Profits*, pp. 101–3.
62. WPC, *Hearings*, pp. 666–77, 759–76 (Frear is cited in n. 51).
63. WPC, *Hearings*, pp. 535–55 (LaGuardia is cited in n. 62).
64. WPC, *Hearings*, pp. 592–611, 842–49 (March has been cited in n. 60; Thomas in n. 61).
65. WPC, *Hearings*, p. 611.
66. Ibid., p. 766.
67. Waldman, *Death and Profits*, pp. v–vii. See also pp. 71, 147–56, and the typed copy of a news story from the *Washington Times*, 3/20/31, on Collins's charges that the IMP was proposing to militarize industry, file 22, WPC, 1930–1932, PB, ASW, OSW.
68. Montgomery to Hurley, 3/28/31, file 7B, and McSwain to Montgomery, 3/13/31, file 25, WPC, 1930–1932, PB, ASW, OSW; WPC, *Minutes*, May 14, 1931, pp. xxi–xxii.
69. WPC, *Minutes*, November 5 and 24, pp. xxiii–xxiv.
70. Eisenhower to Montgomery, 11/11/31, and other correspondence and documents, file 7; Montgomery to Hurley, 3/28/31, file 7B; and Hurley to Doak, 11/25/31, file 16, WPC, 1930–1932, PB, ASW, OSW.
71. Ibid., "Tentative Draft for Consideration by Members of the Commission Created By Public Resolution no. 98, 71st Congress," file 210.
72. Ibid. To avoid needless complexity, I have incorporated into this draft some of the more minor changes made in a later version.
73. Attendance at the WPC executive and business sessions is easily traceable through the WPC, *Minutes*, as printed or in the typed version, file 146, WPC, 1930–1932, PB, ASW, OSW.
74. Ibid., Eisenhower to Montgomery, 12/8/31, and other correspondence and documents, file 7; Robinson to Hurley, 12/7/31, and other correspondence, file 17; and Robinson to Hurley, 12/7/31, and other correspondence, file 28, WPC, 1930–1932.
75. Ibid., Montgomery to Holtzoff, 4/15/31, and other documents, file 7B; Montgomery to Hurley, 12/2/31, and other correspondence and documents, file 17; McSwain to Hurley, 5/5/31, and other correspondence, file 25; Montgomery to Holtzoff, 3/18/31, and other correspondence and documents, file 38; and Montgomery to Johnson, 12/2/31, file 95, WPC, 1930–1932; Griswold to Solicitor General, 1/27/32, and numerous other correspondence and documents, file 9-03-1, Department of Justice. This last file is a very large and rich one, containing numerous legal opinions, correspondence, and memorandums circulated among the legal section, Johnson, and other parties.
76. McSwain to Eisenhower, 3/1/32, with three-page enclosure, file 25, WPC, 1930–1932, PB, ASW, OSW.
77. Waldman, *Death and Profits*, pp. 131–33 and n. 116.
78. WPC, *Interim Report*, pp. i–xii, and Waldman, *Death and Profits*, p. 131 and n. 116.
79. Montgomery to Hurley, 12/2/31, with enclosures and other correspondence

and documents, file 17; Eisenhower to Montgomery, 12/8/31, and other correspondence and documents, file 7; and "First Revision of Tentative Draft for Consideration by Members of the Commission Created by Public Resolution no. 98, 71st Congress," file 211, WPC, 1930–1932, PB, ASW, OSW.

80. Ibid., Eisenhower to Montgomery, 12/18/31, and 2/26/32, file 7.

81. William D. Mitchell, Attorney General, "Memorandum for the War Policies Commission on the Power to Fix Prices in War Time," with four related or supporting memorandums, WPC, *Documents*, pp. 34–53. The originals are in file 9-03-1, Department of Justice. Baruch managed to have a letter included in the set of published documents in which he argued, with bewildering logic, that the attorney general's findings were consistent with his and those of Hugh S. Johnson (p. 53).

82. Eisenhower, "Report to War Policies Commission," 3/3/32, file 146; Hurley to Reed, 2/27/32, file 27; and Vandenberg to Hurley, 2/29/32, file 30, WPC, 1930–1932, PB, ASW, OSW; the published *Minutes* contain no mention of this voting or its outcome. See "Message from the President . . . War Policies Commission . . . the Final Recommendations," H. Doc. 264, 72d Cong., 1st sess., 1932, pp. 5–6 (hereafter cited as WPC, *Final Recommendations*).

83. The nature of this compromise and how it was achieved must be reconstructed from fragmentary records of the WPC documents in the OASW collection, some material in the Justice, Commerce, Agriculture, and Navy Department records, and Waldman, *Death and Profits*. Crucial information about the commission's operations was left out of the published *Minutes* and other documents. Other important decisions were not recorded, and documents concerning them have been lost or were destroyed. Evidence suggests destruction. On December 18 and 31, Eisenhower and an office assistant refer to "condensing" the files so that they could be included in the OASW collection (Eisenhower to Montgomery, 12/18/31, and Walsh to Montgomery, 12/31/31, file 7, WPC, 1930–1932, PB, ASW, OSW). The files may have been sanitized. On a copy of Montgomery's First Revision of Tentative Draft report, there is attached a note: "Mrs. Stege— All copies except these were destroyed. Major Eisenhower felt that *all* should be destroyed, but to complete the record these few were kept. They should not be distributed and it may be you will wish to destroy them. R. D." (file 211, WPC, 1930–1932, PB, ASW, OSW). Throughout the WPC's existence, the OASW seemed exceptionally sensitive to anything going awry and adversely affecting its planning and plans.

84. WPC, *Final Recommendations*, pp. 1–5.

85. U.S. *Congressional Record*, 72d Cong., 1st Sess., vol. 75, part 5, p. 5557; WPC, *Documents*, pp. 1–33; WPC, *Final Recommendations*, p. 2; and Waldman, *Death and Profits*, pp. 131–34. The OASW had some difficulty in having Montgomery's report published (see Eisenhower to Vandenberg, 3/12/32, file 30, and Eisenhower to Hadley, 3/21/32, file 23, WPC, 1930–1932, PB, ASW, OSW).

86. Hurley to Barnes, 3/6/31, and Barnes to Hurley, 3/6/31, file 77, WPC, 1930–1932, PB, ASW, OSW.

CHAPTER FOURTEEN. THE NYE COMMITTEE

1. The Nye Committee's official name changed even in its own publication, including "Special Committee to Investigate" and "Special Committee on Investiga-

tion of." For purposes of consistency and clarity I will use in the text and the notes the form introduced in the text. After the initial citing of a committee document, the shorthand "Nye Committee" will be used in subsequent citations.

2. Scholarship on the American peace movement has come of age. The most important collection of work has been and continues to be done by a group of historians who founded the Conference on Peace Research in History (now the Peace History Society) in 1964, arranged for the reprint series under the title *The Garland Library of War and Peace* starting in 1971, began publication of *Peace and Change: A Journal of Peace Research* in 1972, and initiated and helped publish the *Biographical Dictionary of Modern Peace Leaders*, ed. Harold Josephson (Westport, CT: Greenwood, 1985). The *Dictionary*, the numerous issues of *Peace and Change*, and the Garland reprints are an invaluable source for studying the peace movement.

An extensive and thorough bibliographic essay on the peace movement is found in Charles Chatfield, *For Peace and Justice: Pacifism in America, 1914–1941* (Knoxville: University of Tennessee Press, 1971), pp. 345–69, which is made more current by the author in a later work, *The American Peace Movement: Ideals and Activism* (New York: Twayne, 1992), pp. 191–214. Another quite lengthy and useful essay is in Charles DeBenedetti, *Origins of the Modern American Peace Movement, 1915–1929* (Millwood, NY: KTO Press, 1978), pp. 253–67. DeBenedetti updates his earlier essay in a brief bibliographic note in *The Peace Reform in American History* (Bloomington: Indiana University Press, 1980), pp. 201–2. The best introduction to the bibliography and the subject matter of the peace movement is Charles F. Howlett, *The American Peace Movement: References and Resources* (New York: G. K. Hall, 1991). See also Howlett and Glen Zeitzer, *The American Peace Movement: History and Historiography*, AHA Pamphlet 261 (Washington, DC: American Historical Association, 1985), and Blanche W. Cook, *Bibliography on Peace Research in History* (Santa Barbara, CA: ABC–Clio, 1969). I have drawn also upon other scholarly publications to enhance my understanding of this rich and complex subject: Merle Curti, *The American Peace Crusade, 1815–1860* (Durham, NC: Duke University Press, 1929), and Curti, *Peace or War: The American Struggle, 1636–1936* (New York: W. W. Norton, 1936); Arthur A. Ekirch, Jr., *The Civilian and the Military* (New York: Oxford University Press, 1956); Peter Brock, *Pacifism in the United States: From the Colonial Era to the First World War* (Princeton, NJ: Princeton University Press, 1968), and Brock, *Studies in Peace History* (York, England: Ebor Press, and Syracuse, NY: Syracuse University Press, 1991); Robert H. Ferrell, "The Peace Movement," in *Isolation and Security*, ed. Alexander DeConde, pp. 82–106 (Durham, NC: Duke University Press, 1957); John K. Nelson, *The Peace Prophets: American Pacifist Thought, 1919–1941* (Chapel Hill: University of North Carolina Press, 1967); Robert L. Beisner, *Twelve Against Empire: The Anti-Imperialists, 1898–1900* (New York: McGraw-Hill, 1968); John Milton Cooper, Jr., *The Vanity of Power: American Isolationism and World War I, 1914–1917* (Westport, CT: Greenwood, 1969); Sondra R. Herman, *Eleven Against War: Studies in American Internationalist Thought, 1898–1921* (Stanford, CA: Hoover Institution Press, 1969); Warren F. Kuehl, *Seeking World Order: The United States and International Organization to 1920* (Nashville, TN: Vanderbilt University Press, 1969); Frederick J. Libby, *To End War: The Story of the National Council for Prevention of War* (Nyack, NY: Fellowship Publications, 1969); Lawrence S. Wittner, *Rebels Against War: The American Peace Movement, 1941–1960* (New York: Columbia University Press,

1969); Charles Chatfield, ed., "Peace Movements in America," *American Studies* 13 (Spring 1972): 5–209; Michael A. Lutzker, "The Formation of the Carnegie Endowment for International Peace: A Study of the Establishment-Centered Peace Movement, 1910–1914," in *Building the Organizational Society: Essays on Associational Activities in Modern America,* ed. Jerry Israel, pp. 143–62, 282–88 (New York: Free Press, 1972); Roland Marchand, *The American Peace Movement and Social Reform, 1898–1918* (Princeton, NJ: Princeton University Press, 1972; Charles Chatfield, ed., *Peace Movements in America* (New York: Schocken Books, 1973); David Clifton Lawson, "Swords into Plowshares, Spears into Pruninghooks: The Intellectual Foundations of the First American Peace Movement, 1815–1865" (Ph.D. diss., University of New Mexico, Albuquerque, 1975); David S. Patterson, *Toward a Warless World: The Travail of the American Peace Movement, 1887–1914* (Bloomington: Indiana University Press, 1976); Ernest C. Bolt, Jr., *Ballots Before Bullets: The War Referendum Approach to Peace in America, 1914–1941* (Charlottesville: University Press of Virginia, 1977); Michael Howard, *War and the Liberal Conscience* (New Brunswick, NJ: Rutgers University Press, 1978); Solomon Wank, ed., *Doves and Diplomats: Foreign Offices and Peace Movements in Europe and America in the Twentieth Century* (Westport, CT: Greenwood, 1978); Ronald A. Mulder, *The Insurgent Progressives in the United States Senate and the New Deal, 1933–1939* (New York: Garland, 1979); Paul F. Diehl, "Arms Races and the Outbreak of War 1816–1980" (Ph.D. diss., University of Michigan, 1983); Bradley D. Martin, "Weapons Innovation and the Course of Interstate Rivalries: 1870–1976" (Ph.D. diss., University of Michigan, 1983); Charles DeBenedetti, ed., *Peace Heroes in Twentieth-Century America* (Bloomington: Indiana University Press, 1986); James T. Johnson, *The Quest for Peace: Three Moral Traditions in Western Cultural History* (Princeton, NJ: Princeton University Press, 1987); Charles Chatfield and Peter Van Den Dungen, eds., *Peace Movements and Political Cultures* (Knoxville: University of Tennessee Press, 1988); James C. Schneider, *Should America Go To War: The Debate over Foreign Policy in Chicago, 1939–1941* (Chapel Hill: University of North Carolina Press, 1989); John Whiteclay Chambers II, ed., *The Eagle and the Dove: The American Peace Movement and United States Foreign Policy, 1900–1922,* 2d ed., rev. (Syracuse, NY: Syracuse University Press, 1991); Emily O. Goldman, *Sunken Treaties: Naval Arms Control Between the Wars* (University Park: Pennsylvania State University Press, 1994); Richard W. Fanning, *Peace and Disarmament: Naval Rivalry and Arms Control, 1922–1933* (Lexington: University Press of Kentucky, 1995); and Robert D. Johnson, *The Peace Progressives and American Foreign Relations* (Cambridge: Harvard University Press, 1995). Modern isolationism, as part of or related to the peace movement, began before World War I. Progressive complexities involving isolationism, nationalism, internationalism, and war and preparedness, along with bibliographic sources, are analyzed and cited in Paul A. C. Koistinen, *Mobilizing for Modern War: The Political Economy of American Warfare, 1865–1919* (Lawrence: University Press of Kansas, 1997), chap. 6.

    3. John E. Wiltz, *In Search of Peace: The Senate Munitions Inquiry, 1934–36* (Baton Rouge: Louisiana State University Press, 1963), pp. 24–37; Wayne S. Cole, *Senator Gerald P. Nye and American Foreign Relations* (Minneapolis: University of Minnesota Press, 1962), pp. 65–71; Dorothy Detzer, *Appointment on the Hill* (New York: Henry Holt, 1948), pp. 151–71; and Matthew W. Coulter, "The Franklin D. Roosevelt Administration and the Special Committee on Investigation of the Muni-

tions Industry," *Mid-America* 67 (January 1985): 23–35, and Coulter, *The Senate Munitions Inquiry of the 1930s: Beyond the Merchants of Death* (Westport, CT: Greenwood Press, 1997), pp. 19–33. See also Robert J. Leonard, "The Nye Committee: Legislating Against War," *North Dakota History* 41 (Fall 1974): 20–28. Negative views of the committee are presented in Robert H. Ferrell, "The Merchants of Death, Then and Now," *Journal of International Affairs* 26, no. 1 (1972): 29–39; and Stuart D. Brandes, *Warhogs: A History of War Profits in America* (Lexington: University Press of Kentucky, 1997), chap. 9. Ellis N. Livingston, "Senate Investigating Committees, 1900–1938" (Ph.D. diss., University of Minnesota, 1953), pp. 103–67, 322, also falls into the negative category, despite some effort on his part to treat the committee in an evenhanded way. Agnes Anne Trotter, "The Development of Merchants of Death Theory of American Intervention in the First World War, 1914–1937" (Ph.D. diss., Duke University, 1966), more successfully finds middle ground in evaluating the committee, although her work in primary sources on the Nye investigation is rather thin. According to the author (p. 229 n. 2), Nye told her in an interview that Detzer, contrary to common belief, did not play a key role in creating the committee he headed.

4. U.S. *Congressional Record*, 73d Cong., 2d sess. (1934), vol. 78, part 6, p. 6485 (hereafter cited as *Cong. Rec.*).

5. Indeed, to picture the Nye Committee in this light, as too often has been the case, involves not only a gross disservice to the committee and its accomplishments, but it also gravely distorts the environment in which Nye and his colleagues operated. The Nye Committee in part grew from and in part helped to feed a movement intended to better understand modern warfare so as to try to avoid another catastrophe. In an earlier publication, *The Military-Industrial Complex: A Historical Perspective* (New York: Praeger, 1980), pp. ix–x, 105–6, I pointed out that World War I had generated numerous studies by scholars and other analysts designed to grasp more securely the dynamics of modern warfare and its impact on society. In this regard, a direct line can be traced, as I briefly demonstrated, from these interwar efforts to the present-day analyses of the military in modern society, the military-industrial complex, nuclear war, and the like. These studies begun in the interwar years, however, were interrupted for a time by the Cold War consensus operating within society and the scholarly community from World War II into the 1960s.

The literature on war and its consequences is related to but distinct from the studies of peace and its advocates, which have been raised in the text and in the bibliography in n. 2. Those studying warfare, rather than its avoidance, came close to perceiving the emergence of a military-industrial complex in this nation and other industrial societies. Some warfare literature deals specifically with the munitions trade. In this category are such works as George Seldes, *Iron, Blood and Profits; An Exposé of the World-Wide Munitions Racket* (New York: Harper and Brothers, 1934), and Helmuth C. Engelbrecht and Frank C. Hanighen, *Merchants of Death: A Study of the International Armament Industry* (New York: Dodd, Mead, 1934). Others were based directly on the Nye Committee investigation: e.g., Engelbrecht, *"One Hell of A Business"* (New York: Robert M. McBride, 1934), and Charles A. Beard, *The Devil Theory of War: An Inquiry into the Nature of History and the Possibility of Keeping Out of War* (New York: Vanguard Press, 1936). Still others dealt with more specific subjects, such as the Industrial Mobilization Plans. This was the case with Harold J. Tobin and Percy W. Bidwell, *Mobilizing Civilian America* (New York: Council on Foreign Relations, 1940). The most interesting and significant literature went beyond a narrow focus to study the broadest possible implications of warfare for modern society. Like the Nye Committee itself, these authors attempted to embrace and grasp the national and international implications of the political economy of warfare and what would later come to be called the military-industrial complex. Along these lines, the best contemporary analysis of the Nye Committee work within the larger context of history is presented by Charles A. and Mary R. Beard, *America in Midpassage* (New York: Macmillan, 1939), chapter 9, "Exploring Domestic Sources of Foreign Policies," pp. 381–433. Among the better publications dealing exclusively with war and its repercussions is Pendleton Herring, *The Impact of War: Our American Democracy Under Arms* (New York: Farrar and Rinehart, 1941). Herring had directed the preparation of a bibliography for the Social Science Research Council, *Civil-Military Relations,* 1940. In *Impact of War,* Herring includes in his bibliography some of the key interwar publications on warfare, including Harold J. Lasswell's provocative and influential article, "The Garrison State," published along with other related essays in the *American Journal of Sociology* 66 (January 1941): 431–590 (Lasswell's is on pp. 455–68).

The principal point here is that the Nye Committee operated in and contributed to a serious environment for studying warfare and its real and possible effects. Both the committee and the scholarly world anticipated in stark ways the "warfare state"–world that emerged after World War II but that seems somewhat less threatening in today's post–Cold War atmosphere. The committee's contribution was profound rather than in any way simplistic and crude.

6. Wiltz, *Search of Peace,* pp. 72–91. See also John E. Wiltz, "The Nye Munitions Committee 1934," in *Congress Investigates 1792–1974,* ed. Arthur M. Schlesinger, Jr., and Roger Burns, pp. 249–83 (New York: Chelsea House Publishers, 1975). Coulter, *Senate Munitions Inquiry,* pp. 35–65, is more impresssed with the Nye Committee's work in this regard, and he presents its findings in detail.

7. U.S. Congress, Senate, Special Committee Investigating the Munitions Industry, *Report on Activities and Sales of Munitions Companies,* 74th Cong., 2d sess., 1936, Senate Report no. 944, Part 3, pp. 1–275, plus appendix and other backmatter. The report is based on U.S. Congress, Senate, Special Senate Committee Investigating the Munitions Industry, 73d and 74th Cong., 1934–1936, *Hearings,* Parts 1–12, 37, 38, and 39 (hereafter cited as Nye Committee, *Hearings*).

8. Wiltz, *Search of Peace,* pp. 54–55, 69–71. Even today, critical material on the arms trade can be gathered only orally and without revealing the identity of the sources. On this point, see George Thayer, *The War Business: The International Trade in Armaments* (New York: Simon and Schuster, 1969), p. 10.

9. Thayer, *War Business,* pp. 23–35.

10. See Koistinen, *Mobilizing for Modern War,* chap. 3, for the rise and impact of the modern navy.

11. U.S. Congress, Senate, Special Senate Committee Investigating the Munitions Industry, *Naval Shipbuilding,* 74th Cong., 1st sess., 1935, Senate Report no. 944, Part 1, pp. 1, 222. The report in its entirety is based on Nye Committee, *Hearings,* Parts 18–21, 23, 24, and 36.

12. Wiltz, *Search of Peace,* pp. 114–15.

13. Nye Committee, Report no. 944, Part 1, pp. 18, 42. The committee addresses directly and indirectly the collusion issue throughout the report.

14. Ibid. (quotation, p. 5).
15. Ibid., p. 3.
16. Ibid., pp. 159–62.
17. Ibid., pp. 323–89. Information of this subject is scattered throughout this almost 400-page report and its appendixes.
18. Ibid., the entire report; Nye Committee, *Hearings,* Part 2, pp. 475–87; and Part 7, 1696–700; Nye Committee Minutes, 6/5/35, Executive File, U.S. Senate, Special Committee Investigating the Munitions Industry, RG 46, National Archives, Washington, DC (hereafter cited as "Nye Committee, Senate Records"). This citation and all subsequent ones from this record collection are contained in one of these boxes: 20, 156, 157, 160, 162.
19. For the quotations, see Nye Committee, Report no. 944, Part 1, pp. 18, 223, and 258.
20. Ibid., pp. 223–318. For the investigation of the Shearer affair, see U.S. Congress, Senate, Subcommittee of the Committee on Naval Affairs, "Alleged Activities at Geneva Conference," *Hearings,* 71 Cong., 1st and 2d sess., 1929–1930, pp. 1–699.
21. Nye Committee, Report no. 944, Part 1, pp. 15–16, 223–318, and Nye Committee, Report no. 944, Part 3, pp. 11, 208–17.
22. Nye Committee, Report no. 944, Part 1, pp. 1–9, 175–318.
23. Ibid., p. 1.
24. Nye Committee, Report no. 944, Parts 1 and 3. These themes are scattered throughout these two reports. Part 3 contains various summaries involving the nation's major munitions makers and their organization, evolution, and operation. The compilation of this information is often exceptionally useful and almost unique in nature. The committee files include a list of Ordnance reserve officers, their assignments, and their occupations and affiliations; see Executive File, Nye Committee, Senate Records.
25. Nye Committee, Report no. 944, Part 3, p. 161.
26. Ibid., p. 12.
27. Nye Committee, Report no. 944, Part 1, pp. 11–14, and Wiltz, *Search of Peace,* pp. 115–16. Coulter, *Senate Munitions Inquiry,* pp. 67–87, presents a perceptive analysis of the committee's investigation of the shipbuilding industry and its results.
28. Nye Committee, Report no. 944, Part 3, pp. 15–17 (quotation, p. 17); U.S. Congress, Senate, Special Senate Committee Investigating the Munitions Industry, *Report on Government Manufacture of Munitions,* 74th Cong., 2d Sess., 1936, Senate Report no. 944, Part 7, pp. 1–123 (these reports are based on the hearings cited in nn. 7 and 11).
29. U.S. Congress, Senate, Special Committee Investigating the Munitions Industry, *Report on War Department Bills S. 1716–S. 1722 Relating to Industrial Mobilization in Wartime,* 74th Cong., 2d sess., 1936, Senate Report no. 944, Part 4, p. 7, and Nye Committee, Report no. 944, Part 3, p. 3.
30. The committee's insights concerning the operations of the World War I economy are scattered throughout its hearings and reports. A brief summary of the salient features of economic mobilization for World War I is presented in U.S. Congress, Senate, Special Committee Investigating the Munitions Industry, *Preliminary Report on Wartime Taxation and Price Control,* 74th Cong., 1st sess., 1935, Senate Report no. 944, Part 2, pp. 73–79.
31. Ibid., p. 19.

32. Ibid., p. 38.

33. Nye Committee, Report no. 944, Part 1, p. 345, and Nye Committee, Report no. 944, Part 7, p. 13.

34. Nye Committee, Report no. 944, Part 1, pp. 345–89, and Robert Hessen, *Steel Titan: The Life of Charles M. Schwab* (New York: Oxford University Press, 1975), pp. 235–44, 259–65.

35. Nye Committee, Report no. 944, Part 2, p. 17.

36. The committee covered World War I taxation and proposals for taxation in a future war in great detail (ibid., pp. 8–53 and the appendixes). The report is based on Nye Committee, *Hearings*, Parts 13–16, 21, 22, and 24, as well as on the work on munitions makers and shipbuilding previously referred to. The committee minutes, which are scattered throughout the committee's internal records, also provide good insight concerning its typically methodical work on wartime taxes and its attitudes about the subject. The correspondence is also helpful in this regard. See Raushenbush, "Status of Work on War Profits, July 24/34," and other documents, Administrative Files and Memorandum, "Income and Excess Profits Tax Data for Nineteen Corporations," [circa] April 1935, and other documents, Executive File, Nye Committee, Senate Records.

37. Nye Committee, Report no. 944, Part 2, pp. 73–74.

38. The Nye Committee's analyses of wartime pricing, past and future, which are summarized here, are presented fully in ibid., pp. 55–130 and the appendixes.

39. Ibid. See also Nye Committee, *Hearings*, Part 22, pp. 6259–643 (intermittent). This includes the testimony and statements of Baruch that deal extensively with World War I price policy and procedures.

40. The committee's analysis and judgment about the operations of the World War I economy are scattered throughout the report. However, many of its introductory and concluding remarks are especially helpful for understanding the committee's thinking. See Nye Committee, Report no. 944, Part 2, pp. 1–7, 111–30.

41. Wiltz, *Search of Peace*, pp. 117–19.

42. Copies of these bills, an explanation of how they were assigned to the committee, and the committee's brief analysis of them are located in Nye Committee, Report no. 944, Part 4, pp. 1–5, 62–76.

43. Nye Committee, Report no. 944, Parts 2 and 4 relate most directly to OASW plans and planning and contain most of the documents that are reproduced. The Industrial Mobilization Plan, the minutes of various World War I mobilization agencies, and the unpublished War Industries Board history edited and introduced by Hugh S. Johnson were published separately, although still under the committee's imprimatur. These are listed in Nye Committee, *Hearings*, Part 40, pp. iv–v. For the most relevant portion of the hearings relating to the OASW work, see Nye Committee, *Hearings*, Parts 15, 16, and 17.

44. U.S. Congress, Senate, Subcommittee of the Committee on Finance, *Hearings to Prevent Profiteering in War*, 74th Cong., 2d sess., 1936, pp. 40–43 (hereafter cited as SFC, *Hearings*, 1936); Nye Committee, *Hearings*, Part 22, p. 6646; Ronald Radosh, *Prophets on the Right: Profiles of Conservative Critics of American Globalism* (New York: Simon and Schuster, 1975), pp. 197–229; Michele Flynn Stenehjem, *An American First: John T. Flynn and the America First Committee* (New Rochelle, NY: Arlington House, 1976); and Wiltz, *Search of Peace*, pp. 47 and 53. See also Eugene

M. Tobin, *Organize or Perish: America's Independent Progressives, 1913–1933* (Westport, CT: Greenwood Press, 1986), and Geoffrey S. Smith, *To Save a Nation: American Countersubversives, the New Deal, and the Coming of World War II* (New York: Basic Books, 1973). After a considerable period of study, Flynn's bill was written within a few weeks. The fact that the Nye Committee had a bill prepared for wartime mobilization so early in its proceedings and while still investigating the subject was quite unusual. A competing bill designed to outmaneuver the committee's partly accounts for this development. But more was involved. Flynn had urged this approach in 1934, arguing that congressional committees too often exhausted their energy and resources on investigating a subject, leaving little time or energy for legislative solutions. A great deal of insight concerning the origins, evolution, and response to the Flynn bill is found in the Senate records. See Flynn to Raushenbush [circa] 1934 and numerous other documents and correspondence, Executive File, Nye Committee, Senate Records.

45. The Flynn bill was directly or indirectly the subject of numerous congressional *Hearings*, reports, and like considerations between 1935 and 1938; these sources will be discussed and cited, but for now, only the principal sources will be included. The Nye Committee issued a report on the Flynn bill that was totally separate from its regular report series: U.S. Congress, Senate, Special Committee Investigating the Munitions Industry, *To Prevent Profiteering in War*, 74th Cong., 1st sess., 1935, Senate Report no. 577, pp. 1–35 (quotation, p. 9). The plan was also explained, criticized, and analyzed by the committee and Baruch in the committee hearings: Nye Committee, *Hearings*, Part 22, pp. 6179–651.

46. Nye Committee, *Hearings*, Part 22, p. 6243.

47. Wiltz, *Search of Peace*, pp., 119–22 and n. 6, chap. 6, pp. 248–49, says that he can locate no documents on Roosevelt's motives in appointing the Baruch-Johnson Committee. Actually, the sources are not that bare. Documents reveal enough to warrant my analysis, in addition to several other points. First, Baruch attempted to manipulate cabinet members appointed to the committee he headed, such as Secretary of Agriculture Henry A. Wallace and Secretary of the Navy Claude A. Swanson, in order to get them to do his will. These efforts failed dismally, indicating that the president's ploy was not enthusiastically approved within the cabinet. Second, Baruch claimed that he had made a report to the president on economic mobilization, but it was nothing more than a memorandum serving up some warmed-over ideas he had been advocating for years and hence was of no significance. Actually, Baruch began supporting the McSwain bill as his main contribution to matters involving industrial mobilization at this time. Last, White House advisers were seriously divided over how to handle the Nye Committee. Secretary of State Cordell Hull wanted to bargain and compromise with the committee, which up to a point the Roosevelt administration did. Others thought that the president should use the touchy issues of war and peace to maneuver the Nye Committee into an unfavorable corner. Another set of White House analysts rather dispassionately saw that whatever the Nye Committee did would embarrass the government because the munitions trade was basically so tarnished and unsavory. These individuals also began to appreciate, as did the Nye Committee itself, that the issues involved in the political economy of warfare were so complex as to be nearly insoluble. Some of these advisers also believed that Baruch was too closely associated with the politically vulnerable aspects of profiteering, conflicts of interests, and the like during World War I to do anything but harm the administration, rather than

helping it, on the matter of economic mobilization. When the Nye Committee rather quickly began to level charges about Baruch's World War I income tax records, this move seemed to touch the sensitive political nerve that many feared. Looking at the Nye Committee from these angles, the most astute White House advisers had no particular suggestions to make to the president except to warn him that whatever was done or not done concerning the Nye Committee could have fateful consequences. Hence, those advising the president were as divided on the issues with which the Nye Committee was wrestling as the committee itself. In such a situation, the president was bound to hold off on hard decisions and keep his options open.

Concerning this information, see newsclip, the *State*, Columbia, SC [circa] 12/27/34; Baruch to Howe, 12/18/34, with enc., Roe to Howe, 12/20/34; Baruch, "Memorandum for Industrial Mobilization to Prevent Profiteering in War," 12/7/34 and 7/16/35; Roosevelt, Memorandum, 12/1934; Baruch to McIntyre, 12/26/34, and McIntyre to Baruch, 12/27/34; McSwain to Baruch, 12/20/34; Baruch to Swanson, 12/10/34, and Swanson to Baruch, 12/20/34; Baruch to Wallace, 12/10/34; Baruch-Byrnes exchanges, 1/24/35–4/18/35; Byrnes to Schwartz, 4/8/35; Baruch to Gonzales, 1/7/35; and Baruch to McIntyre, 1/3/35, Selected Correspondence, Bernard M. Baruch Papers, Princeton University, Princeton, NJ (hereafter cited as Baruch Papers); Baruch to Roosevelt, 1/25/35, and other documents, OF 178, and Roosevelt to Hull with enc., 2/23/35, and numerous other correspondence and documents, OF 1672, Franklin D. Roosevelt Papers, Hyde Park, NY (hereafter cited as FDR Papers); and Nye Committee, *Hearings*, Part 22, pp. 6648–51. Coulter, *Senate Munitions Inquiry*, throughout his study systematically examines the usually conflicted and tense relations between the Nye Committee and the Roosevelt administration.

48. The bill introduced by McSwain is included in the hearings involving it. See U.S. Congress, House, Committee on Military Affairs, Hearings, *Taking the Profits Out of War*, 74th Cong., 1st sess., 1935, pp. 1–2 (hereafter cited as HMAC, *Hearings*, 1935). Some modifications of the bill are covered in the hearings, others in the House debate on the bill: *Cong. Rec.*, 74th Cong., 1st sess. (1935), vol. 79, Part 5, pp. 4953–5329 (intermittent).

49. HMAC, *Hearings*, 1935, p. 107. In private, Raushenbush was even less generous, referring to past efforts to take the profits out of war as "fake and phoney [*sic*]." Less judgmentally, Nye labeled these earlier labors as "a pious wish"; see Raushenbush to Maverick, 12/2/35, and Nye to Maverick, 12/16/35, Administrative Files, Nye Committee, Senate Records.

50. The discussion of the McSwain bill is covered in HMAC, *Hearings*, 1935, pp. 1–334. See also Byrnes to Baruch, 1/24/35, and Baruch-McSwain exchanges, 1/7/35—6/17/35, Selected Correspondence, and Baruch Memorandum, 3/20/35, file "Re: McSwain Bill-for Taking Profits Out of War," Unit 8, Box 8, Special Memoranda, Baruch Papers.

51. *Cong. Rec.*, 74th Cong., 1st sess. (1935), vol. 75, part 5, pp. 4953–5329 (intermittent), and Planning Branch, "Mobilization of Manpower and Industrial Resources, Legislative History," 2/18/37, file 010/178, Planning Branch (PB), Assistant Secretary of War, (ASW), Office of the Secretary of War (OSW), RG 107, National Archives, Washington, DC (hereafter cited as PB, ASW, OSW).

52. Nye Committee, Report no. 577, pp. 1–35.

53. Flynn testified before and worked with other congressional committees on

his bill. However, his initial and most extended analysis and the most thorough, critical examination of the bill occurred before the Nye Committee. See *Hearings*, Part 22, pp. 6179–257, 6643–48. See also Nye Committee, Report no. 577, which Flynn obviously wrote.

54. Nye Committee, *Hearings*, Part 22, p. 6342.

55. Ibid., p. 6341.

56. Ibid., pp. 6421–22.

57. Ibid., p. 6638 (the entire Baruch statement is on pp. 6633–43).

58. Ibid., p. 6640.

59. Baruch to Sheppard, [circa] 1937, file, "Misc. Memos re Taking Profits Out of War," Unit 8, Box 8, Special Memoranda, Baruch Papers.

60. Baruch to Kent, 5/8/35, Selected Correspondence, Baruch Papers.

61. Ibid.

62. Flynn's rejoinder to Baruch's rejoinder and the staff analysis of Baruch's claims are located in Nye Committee, *Hearings*, Part 22, pp. 6643–51. Baruch's statement, testimony, and rejoinder are in ibid., pp. 6259–643 (intermittent). Baruch's Papers contain much correspondence and many documents that provide good insights into his views, the issues of economic mobilization, and the Nye Committee. See Baruch to Carroll, 12/22/34; Daniels to Baruch, 12/17/34, with enc.; Baruch-Du Pont exchanges, 7/13–10/6/34; Baruch-McSwain exchanges, 12/20/34–6/17/35; Baruch-Byrnes exchanges, 1/24/35–4/18/35; Baruch-Carpenter exchanges, 3/28/35–4/5/35; Baruch-Churchill exchanges, 4/13/35–5/12/35; Baruch-Clark exchanges, 4/3/35–8/15/35; Garfield to Baruch, 1/21/35; Glass to Baruch, 3/29/35; Baruch-Halsey exchanges, 4/9/35–6/13-35; Baruch to Harrison, 6/18/35; Howell to Baruch with enc., 4/3/35; Robinson to Boyle, 5/16/35; Baruch-MacDowell exchange, 4/6/35–4/8/35; Replogle to Baruch, 4/12/35; Baruch-Robinson exchange, 6/18/35–6/26/35; Baruch-Sheppard exchange, 6/15/35–6/17/35; Lee to Swope, 4/15/35; Baruch to Swope, 4/18/35; and Watson to Baruch, 4/6/35, Selected Correspondence; Baruch Memorandum, 3/20/35, and other documents, file "re, McSwain Bill for Taking Profits Out of War," and Baruch Comments, Nye Committee, Report no. 577, 6/13/35, and other documents, file "re: Senator Nye's Report to Committee," Unit 8, Boxes 8 and 10, Special Memoranda, all in Baruch Papers. See also in the Roosevelt Papers McSwain to Roosevelt, 3/13/36, and other correspondence and documents, OF 1672; newsclip of Lippmann column, "Today and Tomorrow," 4/9/35, PPF 1820; and various memorandums on the White House involvement in the Nye Committee investigation and letters from the public concerning the matter in OF 178.

63. Nye Committee, *Hearings*, Part 15, pp. 3540–718 (intermittent), Part 16, pp. 3932–4030 (intermittent), Part 17, pp. 4166–349 (intermittent), Part 21, pp. 5987–6062, and Part 24, 7077–469 (intermittent). Harris also testified in Parts 13 and 14.

64. The OASW is constantly referred to in this discussion because it was the active participant. Navy Department representatives were present but played a passive role, basically following the War Department's lead and endorsing its position.

65. U.S. Congress, Senate, Subcommittee of the Committee on Military Affairs, *Hearings, to Prevent Profiteering in War*, 74th Cong., 1st sess., 1935, pp. 1–66; U.S. Congress, Senate, Committee on Military Affairs, *To Prevent Profiteering in Time of War*,

Senate Report 889, 74th Cong., 1st sess., 1935, pp. 1–43; Harris, "Memorandum on Conference on H.R. 5529," 5/24/35, file 1401; Harris to Cain, 6/10/36, and numerous other correspondence and documents, file 010/178.1A, PB, ASW, OSW; and Baruch to Johnson, 6/16/36, and numerous other pieces of correspondence, Selected Correspondence, Baruch Papers. The negotiations with the military are also covered in the committee minutes. The War Department early in the committee operations unsuccessfully attempted to use the national defense rationale to withhold critical information and documents from Nye and his colleagues. See the committee minutes contained in the Administrative, Executive, and Raushenbush, Stephen Files, Nye Committee, Senate Records. For the sensitive issue of labor and controls over it, which were a constant source of friction for the Nye Committee and its predecessor bodies, a full and elaborate analysis is presented in Paul A. C. Koistinen, *The Hammer and the Sword: Labor, the Military, and Industrial Mobilization, 1920–1945* (New York: Arno Press, 1979), pp. 8–27.

66. Industrial Mobilization Plan, 1936, pp. 99–122 (quotations, pp. 108 and 113, file 120, PB, ASW, OSW).

67. SFC, *Hearings*, 1936, p. 27. The listed questions are exact quotations. I have rearranged their sequences slightly to facilitate analysis.

68. Ibid., pp. 1–151.

69. Planning Branch, "Mobilization of Manpower and Industrial Resources, Legislative History," 2/18/37, file 010-178, PB, ASW, OSW; U.S. Congress, Senate, Military Affairs Committee, *Hearings, To Prevent Profiteering in Time of War,* 75th Cong., 1st sess., 1937, p. 5 (hereafter cited as SMAC, *Hearings,* 1937).

70. Nye Committee, Report no. 944, Part 2, pp. 3–7.

71. Ibid., p. 6 (quotation).

72. The findings and recommendations are summarized in ibid., pp. 3–7 and then further elaborated and developed throughout that report and Report no. 944, Part 4.

73. Nye Committee, *Hearings,* Part 22, pp. 6179–257, 6277–78.

74. SFC, *Hearings,* 1936, p. 31.

75. Wiltz, *Search of Peace,* intermittently between pp. 32–47, treats extensively and sensitively with Vandenberg's character and leadership qualities.

76. Nye Committee, *Hearings,* Part 17, p. 4314.

77. Vandenberg to Baruch, 4/23/35, Selected Correspondence, Baruch Papers. Barbour was not lightweight as is often supposed. At times he made meaningful contributions to and intelligent observations about the committee's work, as are recorded in the committee's minutes and especially those in the Administrative and Executive Files, Nye Committee, Senate Records.

78. Vandenberg to Baruch, 1/15/37, Selected Correspondence, Baruch Papers (emphasis is Vandenberg's).

79. U.S. Congress, House, Military Affairs Committee, Hearings, *Taking the Profits Out of War,* 75th Cong., 1st sess., 1937, pp. 123–48 (hereafter cited as HMAC, *Hearings,* 1937). Raushenbush manifested at least ambiguity about the Flynn bill almost as soon as it was written. See Raushenbush to Flynn, 3/8/35, and other documents, Executive File, Nye Committee, Senate Records. The Nye Committee's proposal for a referendum on selective service, as was true with all findings and most recommendations, was unanimously adopted and is included in Report no. 944, Part 4, p. 5. This provision was, of course, related to the constitutional amendment proposed by Cong. Louis Ludlow (D-IN), which would have required a referendum on war. Peace advo-

cates had been promoting such an approach for years. Nye joined others of like thinking in the Senate to sponsor measures similar to Ludlow's. The proposal for limits on American soldiers and draftees serving outside the continental United States also had a long history. These matters were part of the neutrality drive of the 1930s. The voluminous work on the peace movement (see n. 2) deals with the Ludlow amendment and other such measures. For an intelligent and informed discussion of the Nye Committee and the Ludlow amendment, see Cole, *Senator Nye*, pp. 120–23.

80. The matter of access to documents and the difficulties involved are discussed by Wiltz, *Search of Peace*, pp. 53–71. See also Nye Committee Minutes, 8/14/35 and other dates, and memorandum, "Statement on Morgan Subpoena," 8/13/35, Executive File, Nye Committee, Senate Records.

81. American pre–World War I policies are covered in detail and fully documented in Koistinen, *Mobilizing for Modern War*, chap. 6. See also, Coulter, *Senate Munitions Inquiry*, pp. 107–25.

82. U.S. Congress, Senate, Special Committee Investigating the Munitions Industry, *Supplementary Report on the Adequacy of Existing Legislation*, Senate Report no. 944, Part 6, 74th Cong., 2d sess., 1936, p. 1.

83. U.S. Congress, Senate, Special Committee Investigating the Munitions Industry, *Report on Existing Legislation*, Senate Report no. 944, Part 5, 74th Cong., 2d sess., 1936, p. 8. The committee's full analysis of the so-called neutrality years and developments during them are covered in full in Report no. 944, Parts 5 and 6. These reports are based on Nye Committee, *Hearings*, Parts 25–35.

84. *Cong. Rec.*, 76th Cong., 1st sess. (1939), vol. 84, part 10, pp. 10, 406.

85. HMAC, *Hearings*, 1937, pp. 125–26.

86. As quoted in Wiltz, *Search of Peace*, p. 187.

87. Ibid., pp. 165–220, 227–231; and Cole, *Senator Nye*, pp. 60–235. The latter volume deals with this subject in much greater depth and detail and, more important, with greater sophistication. The most recent publication on the Nye Committee—Coulter, *Senate Munitions Inquiry*, pp. 89–146 (intermittent)—also takes middle ground concerning the committee and neutrality legislation. The same is true for Trotter, "Merchants of Death Theory," pp. 309–27. Many other volumes relevant to the issue have appeared since the publications of Wiltz and Cole, but none, with the exception of Coulter and Trotter, has addressed the issue as directly as these do, nor have they added anything particularly new where the Nye Committee is involved. Nonetheless, several volumes should be consulted on isolationism: Wayne S. Cole, *Roosevelt and the Isolationists, 1932–1945* (Lincoln: University of Nebraska Press, 1983); Thomas N. Guinsburg, *The Pursuit of Isolationism in the United States Senate from Versailles to Pearl Harbor* (New York: Garland, 1982); Richard J. Barnet, *The Rockets' Red Glare: When America Goes to War, the Presidents and the People* (New York: Simon and Schuster, 1990), chap. 8; and Johnson, *Peace Progressives*. Clyde P. Weed, *The Nemesis of Reform: The Republican Party During the New Deal* (New York: Columbia University Press, 1994), provides valuable information on progressive Republicans during the 1930s. The Senate records provide insight into this matter. See Raushenbush to Nye, 11/23/35, Administrative File, and various committee minutes, Executive File, Nye Committee, Senate Records.

88. *Cong. Rec.*, 74th Cong., 2d sess. (1936), vol. 80, part 1, pp. 501–657 (intermittent), quotation, pp. 568–69, and Cole, *Senator Nye*, pp. 89–90.

89. The Roosevelt Papers that I have researched contain little that relates directly to this topic. However, the Baruch Papers show that key Roosevelt legislative allies and workhorses, such as Senators James F. Byrnes (D-SC) and Joseph T. Robinson (D-AR)—who were also conservative allies and friends of Baruch—were hostile toward the committee from the outset. They were determined to undermine the committee when possible. Biding their time for the right opportunity, they were in on the kill when the occasion arose. Most of the significant correspondence and documents in this regard have already been cited (see nn. 47 and 62). See additionally Baruch to Gerry, 1/24/36 and 6/16/36; Baruch to Harrison, 11/6/36; Baruch-McSwain exchanges 3/10/36–6/18/36; McSwain to Roosevelt, 3/13/36; Baruch to Sheppard, 3/31/36 and Sheppard to Baruch, 4/8/36; Hugh S. Johnson radio address, 12/27/37; Baruch to Louis Johnson, 9/20/37; Krock to Baruch, 1/2/37; and Baruch-Vandenberg exchanges, 1/14/37–1/22/37. Robinson, like McSwain, had played a much more balanced or ambiguous role, or both, concerning the political economy of warfare during the War Policies Commission hearings. Why Robinson changed is not explained in the documents. However, since the Nye Committee so clearly represented the dissident position concerning war and economic mobilization, and at a time when the likelihood of war was becoming increasingly a reality instead of just a possibility, Robinson, McSwain, and others, as basically traditional people and politicians, rather naturally took a defensive and hostile stance toward Nye and his colleagues. By comparison with the Nye Committee, the WPC was a conservative, nonthreatening body. Partisan politics, of course, were also involved.

90. Nye Committee, Report no. 944, Part 7, pp. 1–123, and Nye Committee Minutes, 3/26/36, and other minutes, Executive File, Nye Committee, Senate Records. Wiltz, *Search of Peace*, pp. 202–10, relates the last days of the Nye Committee.

91. Beard, *Devil Theory of War*, p. 12.

92. *Cong. Rec.*, 74th Cong., 1st sess. (1935), vol. 79, part 13, p. 13779.

93. SMAC, *Hearings*, 1937, pp. 4–5, 40–41.

94. Ibid., pp. 1–36; memorandum, "Points for discussion with Col. Johnson," 8/16/37, file 020.2/113.6; speech for Rutherford, prepared by Jones, 12/1/38, file 029.2/113.1; Johnson to Johnson, 9/2/37, file 381/116.4b, PB, ASW, OSW; and citations from Baruch's Selected Correspondence in n. 89.

95. HMAC, *Hearings*, 1937, pp. 1–2.

96. Contrary to the line he took in the hearings, Baruch argued to Assistant Secretary of War Louis A. Johnson privately in September 1937, "There are too many fiery declarations being made against war and in favor of peace. What I want to know is, what are we going to do about it? There is one thing certain—we have to be well armed or we will not be able to do anything about it" (9/20/37, file 381/116.4b, PB, ASW, OSW).

97. Early in 1937 the Labor Department of the National Council for the Prevention of War published a blistering critique of the Industrial Mobilization Plan and the Sheppard-Hill bill, *A Blueprint for Fascism—An Analysis of the Industrial Mobilization Plan* (a reproduced version is available in SMAC, *Hearings, 1937*, pp. 175–86). The OASW responded to this attack both hostilely and defensively. A more moderate and informed analysis of the IMP appeared about the same time by Rose M. Stein, *M-Day, the First Day of War* (New York: Harcourt, Brace, 1936). In a sense, the OASW saw this volume as more damaging since Stein had worked with the Nye Committee,

knew what she was talking about, and was less inflammatory than the pamphlet, and, thus, was more credible. See Harris to Winningstad, 1/11/37, and other correspondence and documents, file 049.12/175, and *A Blueprint for Fascism* and other documents, file 381/116.4b, PB, ASW, OSW.

98. SMAC, *Hearings*, 1937, pp. 169–70.

99. The matters about the Sheppard-Hill bill, unless otherwise noted, are based on the hearings; see HMAC, *Hearings*, 1937, pp. 1–163, and SMAC, *Hearings*, 1937, pp. 1–197.

100. U.S. Congress, House, Military Affairs Committee, *Hearings, Supplies for the Armed Forces in Time of an Emergency*, 75th Cong., lst sess., 1937, and U.S. Congress, Senate, Subcommittee of the Committee on Military Affairs, *Hearings, To Draft the Use of Money in Time of War*, 75th Cong., 3d sess., 1938.

CHAPTER FIFTEEN. THE WAR RESOURCES BOARD

1. The analysis of the War Resources Board concludes the analysis of interwar planning. Since the WRB also began the process of mobilizing the economy for World War II, it will be examined further in the forthcoming volume 4 of this series. The most extensive and broad-based account of the War Resources Board is that of Albert A. Blum, "Birth and Death of the M-Day Plan," in *American Civil-Military Decisions*, ed. Harold Stein, pp. 61–96 (University: University of Alabama Press, 1963). (For an interesting critique of an unpublished version of Blum's essay, see Emmerich to Bock, 1/11/56, file U.S. Industrial Mobilization; Office for Emergency Management, 1940–1956, Box 30, Papers of Herbert Emmerich, University of Virginia Library, Charlottesville, VA.) Blum affirms the correctness of his interpretation in "Roosevelt, the M-Day Plans, and the Military-Industrial Complex," *Military Affairs* 36 (April 1972): 44–46. For other accounts, see Paul A. C. Koistinen, *The Hammer and the Sword: Labor, the Military, and Industrial Mobilization, 1920–1945* (New York: Arno Press, 1979), pp. 60–73, and Koistinen, "The 'Industrial-Military Complex' in Historical Perspective: The Interwar Years," *Journal of American History* 56 (March 1970): 835–39; Civilian Production Administration, *Industrial Mobilization for War* (Washington, DC: Civilian Production Administration, 1947), pp. 3–11; Eliot Janeway, *The Struggle for Survival: A Chronicle of Economic Mobilization in World War II* (New Haven: Yale University Press, 1951), pp. 19–101; Jordan A. Schwarz, *The Speculator: Bernard M. Baruch in Washington, 1917–1965* (Chapel Hill: University of North Carolina Press, 1981), pp. 356–63; R. Elberton Smith, *The Army and Economic Mobilization* (Washington, DC: Office of the Chief of Military History, 1959), pp. 98–103; Robert Connery, *The Navy and Industrial Mobilization in World War II* (Princeton, NJ: Princeton University Press, 1951), pp. 46–53; Keith D. McFarland, *Harry H. Woodring: A Political Biography of FDR's Controversial Secretary of War* (Lawrence: University Press of Kansas, 1975), pp. 172–73; Troyer S. Anderson, "Introduction to the History of the Under Secretary of War's Office (1914–1941)," (ms., U.S. Army Center of Military History, 1947), chap. 4; and Peter M. Abramo, "The Economic and Military Potential of the United States: Industrial Mobilization Planning, 1919–1945" (Ph.D. diss., Temple University, 1995), pp. 195–205. Most secondary works dealing with economic mobilization for World War II at least touch upon the

WRB. Other relevant sources will be cited here and in the forthcoming volume 4 of this series.

2. Blum, "M-Day Plan," pp. 79–83. On executive reorganization, see Barry D. Karl, *Executive Reorganization and Reform in the New Deal* (Cambridge: Harvard University Press, 1963); Richard Polenberg, *Reorganizing Roosevelt's Government* (Cambridge: Harvard University Press, 1966); and Peri E. Arnold, *Making the Managerial Presidency: Comprehensive Reorganization Planning 1905–1980* (Princeton, NJ: Princeton University Press, 1986), pp. 81–117. Executive reorganization and its effect on economic mobilization for war will be analyzed at greater length in the forthcoming volume 4 of this series. Many of the secondary sources relevant to rearmament in the 1930s have been cited in Paul A. C. Koistinen, *Mobilizing for Modern War: The Political Economy of American Warfare, 1865–1919* (Lawrence: University Press of Kansas, 1997), chap. 3, n. 1, and chap. 4, n. 1; other sources will be cited in the forthcoming volume 4 of this series. The latest bibliography on the army is Marvin Fletcher, *The Peacetime Army, 1900–1941: A Research Guide* (Westport, CT: Greenwood, 1988). Other secondary sources include Elias Huzar, *The Purse and the Sword: Control of the Army by Congress Through Military Appropriations 1933–1950* (Ithaca, NY: Cornell University Press, 1950); John W. Killigrew, "The Impact of the Great Depression on the Army, 1929–1936" (Ph.D. diss., Indiana University, 1960); Vincent David, *The Admirals Lobby* (Chapel Hill: University of North Carolina Press, 1967), pp. 3–153; Elmer H. Harrelson, "Roosevelt and the United States Army, 1937–1940: A Study in Challenge-Response" (Ph.D. diss., University of New Mexico, 1971); William A. Weinrich, "Business and Foreign Affairs: The Roosevelt Defense Program, 1937–1941" (Ph.D. diss., University of Oklahoma, 1971); Robert C. Ehrhart, "The Politics of Military Rearmament, 1935–1940: The President, the Congress, and the United States Army" (Ph.D. diss., University of Texas at Austin, 1975); Gerald J. Kennedy, "United States Naval War College, 1919–1941: An Institutional Response to Naval Preparedness" (Ph.D. diss., University of Minnesota, 1975); Malcolm Muir, Jr., "The Capital Ship Program in the United States Navy, 1934–1945" (Ph.D. diss., Ohio State University, 1976); Robert H. Levine, *The Politics of American Naval Rearmament, 1930–1938* (New York: Garland, 1988); Mark M. Lowenthal, *Leadership and Indecision: American War Planning and Policy Process, 1937–1942*, 2 vols. (New York: Garland, 1988); Robert G. Kaufman, *Arms Control During the Pre-Nuclear Era: The United States and Naval Limitation Between the Two World Wars* (New York: Columbia University Press, 1990); and Erik Goldstein and John Maurer, eds., *The Washington Conference, 1921–22: Naval Rivalry, East Asian Stability, and the Road to Pearl Harbor* (Portland, OR: Frank Cass, 1994). Kenneth S. Davis, *FDR: Into the Storm, 1937–1940. A History* (New York: Random House, 1993), provides a thorough albeit intensely critical account of the Roosevelt administration's policies in the late 1930s. Frank Freidel, *Franklin D. Roosevelt: A Rendezvous with Destiny* (Boston: Little, Brown, 1990), is less judgmental.

3. The conflict within the War Department and Woodring's differences with the White House are at the center of McFarland, *Woodring*. The War Department "mess" is the source of comment in most accounts of the period and is reflected in numerous document collections, some of which will be cited.

4. U.S. War Department, *Report of the Secretary to the President*, 1938, pp. 19–27 (hereafter cited as *Annual Report of the Secretary of War [ARSW]* and *ARSW*, 1939, pp. 15–22.

5. Johnson-Baruch exchanges, 8/19/37–10/21/37, and Johnson to Johnson, 7/19/37, and numerous other documents and correspondence, file 381/116.4b, Planning Branch (PB), Assistant Secretary of War (ASW), Office of the Secretary of War (OSW), RG 107, National Archives, Washington, DC (hereafter cited as PB, ASW, OSW). Baruch had proposed almost the same approach to Assistant Secretary of War Dwight F. Davis in 1923 with exactly the same negative results (see chap. 2).

6. Baruch to Johnson, 9/20/37, and other documents, file 381/116.4b, PB, ASW, OSW; Baruch to Edison, 3/22/37; Baruch-Johnson exchanges, 12/24/37–11/12/38; Johnson to President, 5/18/38–11/12/38; Kennedy to Baruch, 3/28/38–5/31/38; Baruch to Byrnes, 9/18/39; Baruch to Clark, 1/26/39; Baruch to Cohen, 8/23/39; Drum to Baruch, 8/17/39 and 10/20/39; Early to Baruch, 1/18/39; Heppelheuser to Baruch, February, 1939; Baruch-Johnson exchanges, 1/4/39–4/28/39; Johnson to Chief of Staff, 12/13/39; Baruch-Marshall exchanges, 7/19/39–12/28/39; Baruch to Peek, 3/17/39; Baruch to Pershing, 8/29/39, and 10/19/39; Baruch to Sadler, 12/12/39 and Sadler to Baruch, 12/14/39; elaborate exchanges between Baruch and Byrnes, 1/29/40–6/16/40; and numerous correspondence with other individuals in 1940 and 1941, Selected Correspondence, Bernard M. Baruch Papers, Princeton University, Princeton, NJ (hereafter cited as Baruch Papers); Baruch to LeHand, 4/29/38, with enc. and other documents, OF 178; Baruch to Early, 10/28/40, with enc. and other documents and correspondence, PPF 88 Baruch; newsclip, *Boston Post,* 10/16/38, OF 335, Franklin D. Roosevelt Papers, Hyde Park, New York (hereafter cited as FDR Papers); and Schwarz, *Speculator,* pp. 329–88.

7. Baruch to Missy, January 1938, and also McIntyre to Roosevelt, 6/1/38, Selected Correspondence, Baruch Papers. Howard E. Coffin, characteristically, had made similar recommendations to the White House late in 1936; see Coffin to Early, 12/21/36, OF 172, FDR Papers.

8. Baruch-Sloan exchanges, 5/12/38–6/2/38; Baruch-Grace exchange, 10/31–11/1/39; Baruch to Howard, 2/23/39; and Baruch-Sloan exchange, 11/1/39–11/9/39, Selected Correspondence, Baruch Papers.

9. This topic is covered in part in chapter 1 and can be traced in detail in the *ARSW,* 1937–1941.

10. Baruch's ambitions for leading the efforts for economic mobilization are discussed and documented here. Harold G. Moulton of the Brookings Institution believed that Baruch wanted to be secretary of state. All the evidence I have reviewed indicates Baruch would have welcomed heading the War Department as well. On Moulton's view, see Wiltse to Fesler, 7/19/46, file 011.2, Records of the War Production Board, RG 179, National Archives, College Park, MD (hereafter cited as WPB).

11. Ogburn to Delano, 11/22/38, and other correspondence, file 381/116.4b, PB, ASW, OSW; Epstein Memorandum on Defense Coordination Board with enc., 11/14/52, Baruch to President, 9/3/38, Otis-Baruch exchange, 4/7–4/11/39, Baruch to Peek, 3/17/39, Selected Correspondence, Baruch Papers; Roosevelt to Johnson, 11/26/37 and other documents, OF 335; and R. B. to McIntyre, 12/20/37, and other documents, 12/20/37, OF 813, FDR Papers. In October 1940, Basil Brewer, publisher of the Bedford, Massachusetts, *Standard-Times Mercury,* in a series of pieces on national defense, included two articles excoriating the Roosevelt administration's refusal to prepare for war despite war's certainty. Brewer also lauded Baruch's consistent warnings of the need for preparedness based on visits

to Europe, inside information, and the like. The articles claimed that New Deal insiders had checkmated Baruch's influence in the White House at every turn and had been the chief culprits in torpedoing the Roosevelt-Baruch Defense Coordination Board. Had the board been created, Brewer argued, the nation would have been prepared and the efforts for industrial mobilization would not have been in the state of chaos that then existed. Brewer claimed he had had personal interviews with Baruch and that he had been granted access to Baruch's papers for these articles. This caused quite a stir in the White House. Baruch insisted (disingenuously so) that he had not violated confidentiality, and he persuaded the publisher to print a retraction of sorts. The White House was only partly mollified by Baruch's claimed innocence in the whole affair. The Brewer incident is traceable in PPF 88-Baruch, FDR Papers. See also Baruch-Brewer exchanges, 9/16-10/30/40, and Baruch to Benet, 7/24/40, Selected Correspondence, Baruch Papers.

12. Harold L. Ickes, *The Secret Diary of Harold L. Ickes,* vol. 2, *The Inside Struggle* (New York: Simon and Schuster, 1954), pp. 526-27, 536-39, 552-53, 628-29 (quotation, p. 629), and McFarland, *Woodring,* pp. 138-234.

13. Johnson to Crowell, 8/9/39, and other correspondence and documents, file 011.27C, WPB; Hines to Hancock, 8/11/39, and other correspondence, file MB-223-23.1, Records of the Joint Army and Navy Boards and Committees, RG 225, National Archives, Washington, DC (hereafter cited as ANMB); and Johnson to Roosevelt, with enc., 8/9/39, OF 25, FDR Papers.

14. War Resources Board, Minutes, August 17, 1938, file 011.25, and Wiltse to Fesler, 7/19/46, file 011.2, WPB.

15. Memo., re: War [Resources] Board, undated, PPF 702, FDR Papers. Baruch's Selected Correspondence is strangely limited on comments involving the WRB. For the correspondence that is germane, see Burwell-Cohen exchanges, 8/15-8/23/39; Pershing to Baruch, 8/26/39; Replogle to Stettinius, 9/7/39; and Stettinius-Baruch exchanges, 9/6/39-11/27/39, Selected Correspondence, Baruch Papers.

16. Johnson to Stettinius, 8/21/39, file 011.27C, WPB.

17. Johnson's clipped columns of August and September 1939 are in ibid., usually attached to memorandums. See also Prudence to Hassett, 8/10/39, and other documents, OF 200 XXX; and Johnson to Watson, 8/25/39 OF 3759, 1939, FDR Papers. The minutes of the WRB from August 17, 1939, to October 12, 1939, which are quite detailed with numerous key documents attached, carefully trace the role of Hancock in the board's proceedings and the consultation with Baruch, his coterie, and war mobilizers such as Crowell and Scott. See file 011.25 and file 011.2, WPB.

18. Eaton to President, 9/12/29, and numerous other memorandums, documents, and correspondence, PPF 5344; Perkins to Roosevelt, 12/2/38 and other correspondence, file OF 25; and Perkins to Roosevelt, 8/11/39, and other documents, file OF 3759, 1939, FDR Papers; Koistinen, *Hammer and Sword,* pp. 68-70; and Blum, "M-Day," p. 77.

19. Ickes, *Secret Diary,* 2: 716-20, quotation, p. 716. See also E. M. W. to the President, 3/30/39, OF 3759, 1939, FDR Papers.

20. For some details on the ANMB in this period, see Rogers and King, "Report of the Army and Navy Commodities Division," 4/24/39, and numerous other documents, file 370.26/200-18, ANMB, and *ARSW,* 1938, 1939, 1940, 1941.

21. "Memorandum for the Secretary of War," 8/9/39, 334/117.3, PB, ASW,

OSW (this file contains numerous crucial documents concerning the War Resources Board).

22. Joint Release, War and Navy Departments, August 17, 1939, WRB Minutes, file 011.25, WPB.

23. IMP, 1939, file 381/116.4C, PB, ASW, OSW (for published versions of the plan, see chap. 1, n. 46). Evidence of the ambiguity about the military's role in proposed economic mobilization is scattered throughout the records pertaining to the WRB and especially those of the OASW; the memorandum cited in n. 21 is just one example. Another one is Rutherford to Stettinius, 8/28/39, file 011.27C, WPB, in which the head of the OASW planning tells the chairman of the WRB, "Perhaps the most important general function of the War Resources Board is to assist the armed services in obtaining supplies they need to carry on a war."

24. WRB Minutes, August 17, 1939, August 23–25, 1939, August 29–31, 1939, September 6, 1939, and September 13–14, 1939, file 011.25; Memo. of A. B. Anderson, 9/1/39, Rutherford to Stettinius, 9/4/39, and Wiltse to Fesler, 7/19/46, file 011.2; for the fourteen-page list of the names of individuals selected to staff the mobilization agencies, see file 011.27c, all in WPB.

25. WRB Minutes, September 6, 1939, file 011.25, WPB; Johnson and Edison to President, 9/6/39, with enc., "Memorandum for Departments and Executive Agencies, Federal Government," from the President, file 334/117.3, PB, ASW, OSW. On the disposition of these key documents, see HKR memo, 10/23/39, and Sears to Frank, undated, also in PB, ASW, OSW.

26. Currie to President, 9/5/39, and President to Secretaries of War and Navy, 9/6/39, OF 3759, 1939, Roosevelt Papers. Early in 1939, the OASW engaged the Brookings Institution to study the economics of warfare. This arrangement accounts for Moulton's appointment to the WRB. (He had also served on the Advisory Board to the Nye Committee, but more ceremoniously than actually.) The Brookings Institution was a traditional, nonpartisan policy research organization at odds with major trends of the later New Deal. By acting as the WRB's basic agency for research and study, the Brookings Institution could help portray the board as a nonpartisan, professional body on economic mobilization, a goal sought by members of the board and by the OASW. More important, the Brookings Institution could serve to remove the WRB from dependence upon, and hence control from, government sources for information, analysis, policy recommendations, and the like, thus allowing the World War I practice of voluntary, nongovernmental sources for economic mobilization to continue. Such circumstances were not particularly welcomed by many members of the Roosevelt administration. See Woodring to Harrison, 5/15/39, file 010.178.1A, PB, ASW, OSW; Johnson and Edison to Wood, 8/10/39, file 011.27c; WRB, Minutes, August 17–September 21, 1939, file 011.25, WPB; and *ARSW*, 1939, p. 20. Some of the studies of the Brookings Institution for the WRB are included in the WRB Minutes previously cited. Much more elaborate ones are located in files 011.2, 011.25, and 011.27c, WPB, and are included with other analyses and memorandums by the OASW in its files. For additional information on Currie and the Brookings Institution, see Roger J. Sandilands, *The Life and Political Economy of Lauchlin Currie: New Dealer, Presidential Adviser, and Developmental Economist* (Durham, NC: Duke University Press, 1990, and Donald T. Critchlow, *The Brookings Institution, 1916–1952: Expertise and the Public Interest in a Democratic Society* (DeKalb, IL: Northern Illinois Uni-

versity Press, 1985)—the author's specific observations about Moulton and the WRB on pp. 136–37 are off the mark.

27. Newsclip, *Milwaukee Sentinel,* OF 3759, 1939, FDR Papers.

28. Johnson to President, 8/22/39, and other documents, file OF 3759, 1939, FDR Papers; note, "Space," on OASW expansion, undated, and other documents, file 011.27c, Johnson, "Office Order," file 011.25, WPB; and Johnson to Director of the Budget, 9/2/39, file 334/117.3, PB, ASW, OSW.

29. Johnson and Edison to President, 6/30/39, and other documents, OF 3716, FDR Papers. This topic is complicated but is treated fully and in all its complexity by McFarland, *Woodring,* pp. 160–234.

30. WRB, Minutes, August 29–31, 1939, and September 13–14, 1939, file 011.25, WPB; Johnson and Edison to President, 9/6/39, file 334/117.3, PB, ASW, OSW; and Blum, "M-Day," pp. 79–85.

31. "Report of the War Resources Board," 10/12/39, file 011.28. This file also contains a summary of the report in addition to preliminary and modified drafts. The minutes of the WRB, file 011.25, are also helpful in tracing the report's authorship and evolution. On the antitrust issue, further insight is provided by "Conference with T. Arnold, 3 P.M., September 14, '39, file 011.27c, all in WPB.

32. Wiltse to Fesler, 7/19/46, file 011.2, WPB; and Leo M. Cherne, *Adjusting Your Business to War* (New York: Tax Research Institute of America, 1939), foreword, pp. ix–x. Cherne's volume and the marketing of it were extremely irresponsible and abusive of OASW trust, given that the office had aided the author immeasurably and reviewed the final product. The dedication page was made up to appear as if the volume was an official publication of the Army-Navy Munitions Board. Moreover, to sell the volume, advertisement went out that, in effect, said that the nation was about to go to war, that the New Deal would be shelved because of the war effort, and that every business needed Cherne's volume to know how to prepare for and deal with the impending crisis. At the insistence of the OASW, this advertisement was later repudiated by Cherne. Perhaps because Assistant Secretary of War Johnson was so eager to publicize the IMP and curry favor with business though, the OASW was uncharacteristically tolerant of Cherne's opportunistic and exploitative ways. The latter appeared impervious to rebuff or embarrassment. From late 1939 on, declaring his innocence of any wrongdoing and insisting that all had been set right, Cherne constantly bombarded the OASW with offers of his help, requests for assistance, and like moves that would give him an inside track on the economic mobilization front. The incident is covered in Thomas to Secretary of War, 9/18/39, and numerous other documents and correspondence, file 334/8/246.2, PB, ASW, OSW. See also Cherne, *Your Business Goes to War* (Boston: Houghton Mifflin, 1942).

33. President to Stettinius and others, 11/24/39, file 370.26/110.B, PB, ASW, OSW. The OASW tried to keep up its hope for the WRB long after its demise was certain. See Johnson to President, 11/21/39, and other correspondence and documents, OF 25, FDR Papers; and Rutherford to Wood, 11/3/39, and other correspondence and documents, file 334/117.3, PB, ASW, OSW. The division of labor among the WRB members is set forth in "Assignments and Studies Given Each Member of the Board," 9/20/39, file 011.27c; even more helpful is War Production Board, "War Resources Board: Chronology and Document List," 4/20/44, file 011.2, WPB.

34. On Roosevelt's activity involving a possible war council or war cabinet, see

Paul A. C. Koistinen, "Warfare and Power Relations in America: Mobilizing the World War II Economy," in *The Home Front and War in the Twentieth Century: The American Experience in Comparative Perspective*, ed. James Titus, pp. 91–110, 231–43 (Colorado Springs, CO: Office of Air Force History, 1984). See also Koistinen, "Toward a Warfare State: Militarization in America During the Period of the World War," in *The Militarization of the Western World*, ed. John R. Gillis, pp. 47–64, 175–79 (New Brunswick, NJ: Rutgers University Press, 1989).

35. On this point, see Koistinen, *Mobilizing for Modern War*, chaps. 7–10.

BIBLIOGRAPHICAL ESSAY

PART ONE—PLANNING WAR

The records of the Planning Branch, Assistant Secretary of War [Under Secretary of War in December 1940], Office of the Secretary of War, RG 107, National Archives, Washington, DC, are the principal primary source on the War Department's interwar procurement and industrial mobilization planning. Other primary source collections include Records of the Joint Army and Navy Boards and Committees, RG 225, National Archives, Washington, DC; Records of the War Department General and Special Staffs, General Staff–Purchase, Storage, and Traffic Division, Record Group 165, National Archives, Washington, DC; the Army War College Collection, Carlisle Barracks, Carlisle, PA; and Records of the War Production Board, RG 179, National Archives, College Park, MD. The Bernard M. Baruch Papers and the Frank A. Scott Papers, Princeton University, Princeton, NJ, and the Franklin D. Roosevelt Papers, Franklin D. Roosevelt Library, Hyde Park, NY, are of critical importance.

The annual *Reports of the Secretary of War to the President* (Washington, DC, 1919–1940) are of enormous help in dealing with interwar planning. Numerous Senate and House of Representatives hearings, investigations, and reports cited throughout the notes are indispensable for understanding the political economy of the interwar years. *U.S. Statutes at Large* have been cited where appropriate.

Secondary sources on the Office of the Assistant Secretary of War's (OASW) planning are limited. Most publications are part of the Office of the Chief of Military History's (now the U.S. Army Center of Military History) *United States Army in World War II* series. R. Elberton Smith, *The Army and Economic Mobilization* (Washington, DC: Office of the Chief of Military History, 1959), pp. 35–112, provides a valuable overview of procurement planning. His work must be supplemented by those on the various supply arms and services, which vary in quality: Constance McLaughlin Green, Harry C. Thomson, and Peter C. Roots, *The Ordnance Department: Planning Munitions for War* (Washington, DC: Office of the Chief of Military History, 1955), pp. 14–64, and Harry C. Thomson and Linda Mayo, *The Ordnance Department: Procurement and Supply* (Washington, DC: Office of the Chief of Military History, 1960), pp. 1–23; Levin H. Campbell, Jr., *The Industry-Ordnance Team* (New York: McGraw-Hill, 1946); Chester Mueller, *New York Ordnance District in World War II* (New York: New York Post, Army Ordnance Association, 1947); Dulaney Terrett, *The Signal Corps: The Emergency (to December 1941)* (Washington, DC: Office of the Chief of

Military History, 1956); Irving Brinton Holley, Jr., *Buying Aircraft: Materiel Procurement for the Army Air Forces* (Washington, DC: Office of the Chief of Military History, 1964), pp. 3–193; Erna Risch, *The Quartermaster Corps: Organization, Supply, and Services,* 2 vols. (Washington, DC: Office of the Chief of Military History, 1953), 1: 4–9, 56–57, 208–12, 243–65, 323–29; Risch's one-volume history of the Quartermaster Corps, perhaps because it is briefer and written after the World War II volumes, presents many of the corps' operations and problems in a clearer fashion: *Quartermaster Support of the Army: A History of the Corps, 1775–1939* (Washington, DC: Office of the Quartermaster General, 1962); Thomas M. Pitkin and Herbert R. Rifkind, *Procurement Planning in the Quartermaster Corps, 1920–1940* (Washington, DC: Office of the Quartermaster General, 1943); Blanche D. Coll, Jean E. Keith, and Herbert H. Rosenthal, *The Corps of Engineers: Troops and Equipment* (Washington, DC: Office of the Chief of Military History, 1958), pp. 88–108; Lenore Fine and Jesse A. Remington, *The Corps of Engineers: Construction in the United States* (Washington, DC: Office of the Chief of Military History, 1972), pp. 65–77; Leo P. Brophy and George J. B. Fisher, *The Chemical Warfare Service: Organizing for War* (Washington, DC: Office of the Chief of Military History, 1959), pp. 30–38; Brooks E. Kleber and Dale Birdsell, *The Chemical Warfare Service: Chemicals in Combat* (Washington, DC: Office of the Chief of Military History, 1966), pp. 24–30; and Clarence McKittrick Smith, *The Medical Department: Hospitalization and Evacuation, Zone of Interior* (Washington, DC: Office of the Chief of Military History, 1956).

No volume deals with commodity committee planning. Two authors, however, had access to OASW commodity committee files or to studies the office drew upon: Brooks Emeny, *The Strategy of Raw Materials: A Study of America in Peace and War* (New York: Macmillan, 1934), and G. A. Roush, *Strategic Mineral Supplies* (New York: McGraw-Hill, 1939). Several other volumes relate directly to commodity committee work: Alfred E. Eckes, Jr., *United States and the Global Struggle for Minerals* (Austin: University of Texas Press, 1979), and Stephen D. Krasner, *Defending the National Interest: Raw Materials and U.S. Foreign Policy* (Princeton, NJ: Princeton University Press, 1978). In the notes for chapters 5–10, I have cited at length numerous other published sources critical for understanding commodity committee activity.

Scholars have paid more attention to the Office of the Secretary of War's industrial mobilization planning. The most thorough study is by Harold W. Thatcher, *Planning for Industrial Mobilization, 1920–1940* (Washington, DC: Office of the Quartermaster General, 1943). Thatcher reliably summarizes documents on the subject. This enhances the value of his work since various Planning Branch documents have been lost, misplaced, or removed since Thatcher did his research. Marvin A. Kreidberg and Merton G. Henry, *History of Military Mobilization in the United States Army, 1775–1945* (Washington, DC: Department of the Army, 1955), pp. 377–540, provide a much briefer and more interpretive account of economic planning. Troyer S. Anderson's, "History of the Office of the Under Secretary of War (1914 to 1941)," 1947, U.S. Army Center of Military History, Washington, DC, is a much admired assessment of the OASW. The most recent account is that of Peter M. Abramo, "The Economic and Military Potential of the United States: Industrial Mobilization Planning, 1919–1945" (Ph.D. diss., Temple University, 1995). In its coverage and approach it resembles an earlier work: James L. Abrahamson, *The American Home Front: Revolutionary War, Civil War, World War I, World War II* (Washington, DC: National Defense University, 1983). Robert H. Connery, *The Navy and Industrial Mobilization in World War II* (Princeton, NJ: Princeton University Press, 1951), pp. 31–53, is the one volume treating the navy's interwar planning with sophistication and insight. See also Roderick L. Vawter, *Industrial Mobilization: The Relevant History,* rev ed. (Washington, DC: National Defense University Press, 1983), and Harry F. Ennis, *Peacetime Industrial Preparedness for Wartime Ammunition Production* (Washington, DC: National Defense University Research Directorate, 1980).

The preceding authors either withhold judgment about the Office of the Assistant Secretary of War's industrial mobilization planning or look upon it favorably. Other scholars are critical, viewing the planning at best as fundamentally flawed, at worst as useless. These authors include Harry B. Yoshpe, "Economic Planning Between the Two World Wars," *Military Affairs* 15 (Winter 1951): 199–204, and 16 (Summer 1952): 71–83, and Yoshpe, "Bernard M. Baruch: Civilian Godfather of the Military M–Day Plan," *Military Affairs* 30 (Spring 1965): 1–15; Albert A. Blum, "Birth and Death of the M–Day Plan," in *American Civil-Military Decisions: A Book of Case Studies,* ed. Harold Stein, pp. 61–96 (University: University of Alabama Press, 1963), and Blum "Roosevelt, The M–Day Plans, and the Military-Industrial Complex," *Military Affairs* 36 (April 1972): 44–46; Blum's 1953 Columbia Ph.D. dissertation, "Deferment from Military Service: A War Department Approach to the Solution of Industrial Manpower Problems," was published as *Drafted or Deferred: Practices Past and Present* (Ann Arbor: Bureau of Industrial Relations, University of Michigan, 1967); and Terrence J. Gough, "Soldiers, Businessmen and U.S. Industrial Mobilization Planning Between the World Wars," *War and Society* 9 (May 1991): 63–98. See also Gough's related article, "Origins of the Army Industrial College—Military-Business Tensions After World War I," *Armed Forces and Society* 17 (Winter 1991): 259–75. The interwar years are also treated briefly in James S. Nanney and Terrence J. Gough, "U.S. Manpower Mobilization for World War II," September 1982, U.S. Army Center of Military History, Washington, DC.

Most authors or studies analyzing economic mobilization for World War II at least mention the Industrial Mobilization Plan, 1939. Judgments vary from the tepid to the damning. For representative examples, see Bureau of the Budget, *The United States at War: Development and Administration of the War Program by the Federal Government* (Washington, DC: Bureau of the Budget, 1946), pp. 16, 23–24, 129–30; Civilian Production Administration, *Industrial Mobilization for War: History of the War Production Board and Predecessor Agencies, 1940–1945* (Washington, DC: Civilian Production Administration, 1947), pp. 3–18; Donald M. Nelson, *Arsenal of Democracy: The Story of American War Production* (New York: Harcourt, Brace, 1946), pp. 87–92; and Eliot Janeway, *The Struggle for Survival: A Chronicle of Economic Mobilization in World War II* (New Haven: Yale University Press, 1951), pp. 19–101.

Secondary sources on War Department planning as it relates to the Republican administrations in the 1920s and the Franklin D. Roosevelt administration in the 1930s are covered at length in chapter 11, notes 1 and 2. Numerous other secondary sources relevant to the political economy of the interwar years are cited throughout the notes.

PART TWO—PURSUING PEACE

The best sources on the House Select Committee on Expenditures in the War Department are its extensive hearings and reports, all of which are cited in the notes of chapter

12. Only one secondary source spends any time on the committee—Virgil Calvin Stroud, "Congressional Investigations of the Conduct of War" (Ph.D. diss., New York University, 1954), chapter 5—and the author's purview is rather limited.

The War Policies Commission's (WPC) hearings, reports, and documents, fully cited in chapter 13, provide excellent primary sources for analyzing its work. However, published material must be supplemented by document collections. The holdings of the War Department are the most extensive. They are cataloged as "War Policies Commission, File, 1930–32," with the records of the Planning Branch, Assistant Secretary of War, Office of the Secretary of War, RG 107, National Archives, Washington, DC. Other document collections are sparse but crucial: file 9-03-1, Department of Justice, RG 60, National Archives, College Park, MD; War Policies Commission, General Correspondence of Robert P. Lamont, Secretary of Commerce, 1929–1932, General Records of the Department of Commerce, RG 40, National Archives, College Park, MD; War Policies Commission, Correspondence Files of the Secretary of Agriculture, 1906–1956, RG 16, National Archives, College Park, MD; and War Policies Commission, Records of the Secretary's Office, Navy Department, RG 80, National Archives, Washington, DC. Other document collections listed in Part One are also relevant to the WPC. Various Senate and House hearings and reports in the 1920s that relate to the WPC's work are also cited fully in the notes to chapter 13.

Seymour Waldman's *Death and Profits: A Study of the War Policies Commission* (New York: Brewer, Warren, and Putnam, 1932), though spotty in coverage is insightful and provides valuable information on the commission unavailable elsewhere. His is also the only work of any substance on the commission. The American Legion played a leading role in creating the commission. See chapter 13, note 1 for the most important secondary sources on the legion.

The voluminous and fully indexed hearings and reports of the Senate Special Committee Investigating the Munitions Industry (Nye Committee) are the best primary source on the subject and are cited in the notes to chapter 14. In addition, the papers of the committee are valuable: U.S. Senate, Special Committee Investigating the Munitions Industry, RG 46, National Archives, Washington, DC. Other document collections cited in Part One are also essential for analyzing the committee's work.

Secondary sources on the Nye Committee exist but nowhere in proportion to the committee's significance. John E. Wiltz, *In Search of Peace: The Senate Munitions Inquiry, 1934–36* (Baton Rouge: Louisiana State University Press, 1963), is the first full-scale study of Sen. Gerald P. Nye, his colleagues, and staff. Despite its narrow focus, it is essential reading. Wayne S. Cole, *Senator Gerald P. Nye and American Foreign Relations* (Minneapolis: University of Minnesota Press, 1962), does less with the committee but is broader and more perceptive in his analysis. The best study to date is the most recent one: Matthew W. Coulter, *The Senate Munitions Inquiry of the 1930s: Beyond the Merchants of Death* (Westport, CT: Greenwood Press, 1997). For negative views of the committee, see the citations in chapter 14, note 3.

There is a vast literature on the modern peace movement that relates to the Nye Committee and its predecessors. Numerous studies are cited in chapter 14, note 2. In note 5 of that chapter I assess and cite a host of works on the impact of modern warfare on society that relates closely to the Nye Committee investigation. Other volumes relevant to the Nye Committee are cited throughout chapter 14's notes, as are the hearings and reports of other congressional committees that occurred simultaneously with or followed the Nye Committee work.

The primary sources involving the War Resources Board are listed in Part One. Most of the secondary sources are also included. However, additional volumes on the board and related topics are included in chapter 15, notes 1 and 2. Other relevant studies are also recorded in the notes.

INDEX

Aberdeen Proving Grounds (Md.), 77, 82–83
Adams, Charles F., 250
Adjusting Your Business to War (Cherne), 314
Adkerson, J. Carson, 141
Advisory Council on Legislation, 8
Advisory Defense Council, 60
Advisory National Economic Council proposal, 247, 250
Advocate of Peace, 239
AEF (American Expeditionary Forces), 213, 216, 218
Aeronautical Chamber of Commerce, 192
AFL. *See* American Federation of Labor
Africa, 140
Agrarian sector, 209
Agriculture, Department of, 121, 122, 123
  Fixed Nitrogen Research Laboratory, 175
  secretary, 250
Agriculture Marketing Act (1929), 148
AIC. *See* Army Industrial College
AIME. *See* American Institute of Mining and Metallurgical Engineers
Air Commerce Act (1926), 180, 181–82, 193
Air Corps, 15, 17, 95, 180, 182–84, 331(n64)
  chiefs, 31
  Industrial Planning Section (IPS), 196–97
  Material Division, 118, 195–96
  and Nye Committee, 195
  Procurement Districts, 197
  procurement planning, 28, 31, 100, 101, 116, 183, 184, 195–96, 199
  Supply Division, 24, 27
  See also Air Power; *under* Roosevelt, Franklin D.
Air Corps Act (1926), 180, 182–83, 184, 193
Aircraft engines, 186, 189, 190
Aircraft industry, 3, 91, 99(table), 101, 102, 179–82, 183, 187–93, 203–4
  and Great Depression, 179
  investigations, 192–93, 215–16
  mergers, 187, 188–89
  power relations, 190
  production, 27, 31, 180, 215
  production (1914), 179
  research, 184, 185
Airframes, 186–87, 189
Air Mail Act
  1925, 180, 189, 193
  1934, 181, 189
Airplanes, 4, 27, 170
  costs, 191
  exports, 191
  fuel, 131
Airports, 182
Air power, 194–95, 372(n17)
Air Service. *See* Air Corps
AISI. *See* American Iron and Steel Institute
Aitchison, Clyde B., 236
Alaska, 115
Alcoa (Aluminum Company of America), 116, 117
  antitrust suit, 118, 120
  and OASW, 118–20
  report, 116–17, 118–19
Alexander, W. W., 90
Alien Property Custodian, 173
Aluminum, 23, 101, 103, 116
  commodity committee, 99(table), 100, 104, 117, 118
  and OASW, 117–20
  as strategic material, 117, 128
American Airlines, Incorporated, 189
American Association of Railway Executives, 54
American Chemical Society, 175, 176
American Expeditionary Forces (AEF), 213, 216, 218
American Federation of Labor (AFL), 75, 226, 239, 282

415

American Institute of Chemical Engineers, 178
American Institute of Mining and Metallurgical Engineers (AIME), 21, 86–88, 96, 139, 142
American Iron and Steel Institute (AISI), 82, 100, 105, 106, 107, 109, 110, 111, 112, 113, 114, 115, 268
American League Against War and Fascism, 303, 304
American Legion, 51, 52, 53, 81, 94, 220, 221, 243, 271, 275, 282, 302, 304
  membership, 220–21, 305
  and OASW, 221, 222, 226
  universal service proposal, 221–26, 227, 237, 277
  and WPC, 237–38, 245
American Manganese Producers Association, 141, 363(n12)
American Peace Society, 239
American Petroleum Institute (API), 130, 132, 133
American Railway Association, 164
American Smelting and Refining Company, 134, 144
American Society of Mechanical Engineers (ASME), 72, 82, 84–87, 162
  National Defense Division, 84–85
American Telephone and Telegraph Company, 79, 309
American Tin Trade Association, 136
American Wholesale Coal Association, 164
American Woolen Company, 148
Ammonium nitrate, 171
AMPA (American Manganese Producers Association), 141, 363(n12)
Anaconda Copper Corporation, 134
ANMB. *See* Army-Navy Munitions Board
Antibusiness attitudes, 202, 209, 254
Antielite attitudes, xvi, 318
Antimilitary sentiments, xvi, 29, 202, 242–43, 318
Antimony, 136, 144, 145–46
Antitrust law, 118, 132, 170, 218, 224
Antiwar sentiment, xvi, 47, 202, 211, 251, 307, 318, 320–21
AOA. *See* Army Ordnance Association
API (American Petroleum Institute), 130, 132, 133
Appalachian Coals, Incorporated, 164
Apparel industry, 73
Armor, xiv
Armour and Company, 73
Armour Fertilizer Works, 172
Army
  air wing (World War I), 331(n64) (*see also* Air Corps)
Center of Military History, 204
chief of staff, 5, 6, 7, 8, 9, 10, 34, 36, 38, 39, 40, 55 (*see also* General Staff)
  and commodity committees, 21
  in industrial stage, xiv
  interwar manpower, 24–25, 37
  military technology, xiv
  planning, xvii, 1–2, 13–14
  professionalization, xiii, xiv
  purchases, 25, 162
  as rank-conscious, 8
  regular, 25
  Section I procurement lists, 22–23
  supply preparedness for World War II, 32
  in transitional stage, xiii
  war plans, 14
  and WIB, 5
  World War I purchased products, 22
  See also Army-Navy Munitions Board; War, Department of; *under* Procurement planning
Army and Navy Joint Board (1903), 11, 65, 336(n12)
Army Industrial College (AIC) (OASW), 7, 12, 13, 28, 34, 47, 79, 162
  advisers, 79, 149
Army-Navy Munitions Board (ANMB), 11–12, 16, 19, 26, 59, 61–62, 66, 69, 92, 118, 131, 153
  and aluminum, 117–18
  and industrial mobilization, 88, 154, 229
  and NAM, 92
  reorganization (1931), 19, 61–62, 88, 229
  Transition Plan, 62, 63, 64
  and WRB, 311, 312, 314
Army Ordnance (AOA), 77
Army Ordnance Association (AOA), 2, 3, 28, 45, 71, 72, 76, 77–84, 91, 96
  and industry, 78, 105, 152
Army Service Forces (1942), 33
Army War College (AWC), 12, 38
  Assistant Secretary of War Division (1924–1928), 44
  commandant, 44
  and industrial mobilization, 44–45, 47–49
  and OASW, 44–45, 48, 336(n12)
Articles of Confederation, xii
Artificial dyes, 172–73
Asheville Mica Company, 146
ASME. *See* American Society of Mechanical Engineers
Associative state, 200
Atlantic Monthly, 46
Atlantic Transport Company, 236
Atlas Powder Company, 175
Attorney general, 246
Austin, Warren R., 304

Australia, 148
Automobile industry
  and aircraft industry, 187, 197
  conversion possibility, 31
Aviation Corporation (AVCO), 188, 189, 190
AWC. *See* Army War College
Ayers, Leonard P., 79, 236

Bain, H. Foster, 87
Baker, Newton D., 6, 7, 45, 48, 50, 79, 215, 232, 236
Ballantine, Arthur N., 236
Baltimore Sun, 46
Banking, xiii
Bank of America, 79
Barbour, W. Warren, 255, 265, 290
Baruch, Bernard M., 2, 42, 43
  and AIC, 79
  and AWC, 44, 47–49
  Baruch-Johnson Committee, 274, 275, 276, 395(n47)
  and corporate capitalism, 47
  and economic mobilization, 45–46, 47, 48, 50, 56, 211, 224, 227, 231, 245, 271, 278, 279, 288, 289, 302, 306–7, 352(n44)
  and Graham Committee, 214
  and IMP, 306
  influence, 46–47
  and the media, 46–47
  on MIC, 204
  and NDAC, 171, 214
  and Nye Committee, 279–82
  and OASW, 45–46, 48–49, 50, 56, 94, 233, 235, 303
  as WIB chairman, 45, 47, 214
  and WPC, 230–33, 235, 236, 245, 251, 252
  and WRB, 308, 309
Bausch, Carl L., 156
Bausch and Lomb Optical Company, 155, 156–57, 158, 159
Beard, Charles A., 211, 299
Becker, W. E., 113, 114
Bell Aircraft Corporation, 189
Bethlehem Shipbuilding Company, 259
Bethlehem Steel Corporation, 83, 109, 268
Boeing, William E., 188
Boeing Airplane Company, 179, 189, 190
Bone, Homer T., 255, 265, 287, 289, 296
Bonner, James B., 79, 105–6, 108–9, 110
Booz, Fry, Allen, and Hamilton (management consultant firm), 34
Borah, William E., 296
Bradley, Samuel S., 192
Brandeis, Louis D., 272

Bransten, Louise, 303
Brass, 87
Brazil, 123, 140–41
Brett, Morgan L., 79
Bridgeport Ordnance District, 82
Brookhart, Smith W., 242
Brookings, Robert S., 79, 224–25, 236
Brookings Institution, 309, 312
Brotherhood of Locomotive Firemen and Engine Men, 239
Brown, Walter Folger, 189
Brown and Sharpe Company, 151
Buna (synthetic rubber), 124–26
Bureaucracy, 202, 263
  and government economic regulation, xiv
Bureau of Standards, 147, 149, 156, 157
Burns, James H., 27–28
Business. *See* Corporations; Economy; Federal government, –business alliance; Heavy industry; Manufacturing; Merchants; Military, –business relations; Oligopolistic industries
Business Council. *See under* War, Department of
Butyl (synthetic rubber), 126
Buy American, 363(n12)
Byrnes, James F., 46

Cadmium, 136
Cage, H. K., 235
Call, Arthur Derrin, 239–40
Campbell, Levin H., Jr., 28–29, 77
Canada, 146, 168
Cantonment construction, 214, 380(n19)
Capital, 52, 221, 245
Capper, Arthur, 222, 227, 296
Capper-Johnson bill, 222, 223, 226–27, 275
Carey, Robert D., 283
Carnahan, George H., 121, 122
Carnegie Institution, Geophysical Laboratory, 155
Carr, Irving J., 30
Cartels, 174
Carty, John J., 79
Census, Bureau of the, 16, 179
Chamberlain (S.Dak.) manganese reserves, 142
Chamber of Commerce, U.S., 82, 89, 93–95, 203, 244, 251, 312
  Special Committee on National Defense, 93–94, 95
Chase National Bank, 187
Chemical Foundation, Incorporated, 173
Chemicals, 1, 73, 170, 172
  commodity committee, 19, 175 (*see also under* Great Britain)
Chemical Warfare Service, 15, 17, 27, 124

418   Index

Cherne, Leo M., 314
Chief of staff. *See under* Army, Department of
Chile, 172
Chlorine, 19
Christian Science Monitor, 223
Chrome, 87
Chromium, 143
Cincinnati Milling Machine Company, 152
Civil Aeronautics Board, 181
Civilian Conservation Corps, 161, 201
Civilian district advisory boards, 26
Civil-military relations
  in industrial stage, xiv, xv (*see also* Federal government, –business alliance)
  interwar period, 3–4, 29, 86, 203, 206
  and merchants, xii
  and planning, 2–3, 21, 72, 207, 317, 320
  in preindustrial stage, xii, xv
  in transitional stage, xv
  and World War I, 1, 202
  See also Army, chief of staff; Constitution; Industrial Mobilization Plans, and warmaking powers; Military, –business relations; National Defense Act; Warmaking powers
Civil War, xii, 372(n17)
  in transitional stage, xiii
Clark, Bennett Champ, 255, 265, 285, 296, 297
Clarkson, Grosvenor B., 46, 211, 214, 289
Cleveland Ordnance District, 76
Cleveland Trust Company, 79
Clientelism, 263
CND. *See* Council of National Defense
Coal, 129, 163–66, 169
  commodity committees, 99(table), 101, 164
  mechanization, 163
Coal tar, 172, 173
Coast Artillery Corps, 15, 27
  absorbed by Ordnance Department (1940s), 32
Cobalt, 193
Codd, Leo A., 77, 80, 81
Coffin, Howard E., 84, 91, 187, 236
Cohen, Benjamin V., 307
Cold War (1945–1991), xv, 170, 211, 255
Cole, Wayne S., 292, 295
Collins, Ross A., 230, 238, 241, 242, 243, 244, 247, 248, 249, 250, 252
Colver, William B., 225
Commerce, Department of, 16, 43, 75, 122, 140, 162, 200, 264, 312
  Bureau of Air Commerce, 181–82, 187
  Bureau of Foreign and Domestic Commerce, 122, 152, 175
  Chemical Division, 175

  and OASW, 200–201
  secretary, 250
Committee on Industrial Preparedness, 87
  subcommittees, 87, 140
Committee on Militarism in Education, 240
Commodity committees (OASW), xvii, 2, 18, 19, 42, 150, 311
  classifications, 2, 97, 98, 99(table), 160
  lists, 19, 22
  planning, 18, 98, 100–103
  procuring and control plans, 18–19, 20
  reorganization, 19
  role, 20, 97, 104, 328(n38)
  and supply bureaus, 20
  and World War II, 19
  See also specific commodities; under Army; Ordnance Department; Quartermaster Corps; Signal Corps
Commodity section–war service committee system (WIB), 1, 2, 75, 97, 199, 217
Communications, 182
Confederacy (Civil War mobilization), xiii
Conflict of interest, 214
Congressional Record, 250
Congress of Industrial Organizations, 75
Connally, Thomas T., 287, 298
Conscription, 52, 53, 94, 238, 291, 292. *See also* American Legion, universal service proposal; Civil-military relations; Deferments; Selective Service Administration; Universal service concept; Work or fight program
Conservatism, 255
Consolidated Aircraft Corporation, 47
Constitution, xii, 238, 239, 242, 249, 287–88
Construction, 161, 214, 380(n19)
Contracts, 17, 76, 181, 218, 259–60
Controlled Materials Plan, 104
Conversion for warfare. *See under* Economy
Coolidge, Calvin, 54, 80, 91
Copper, 87, 103, 214–15, 279
  commodity committee, 99(table), 101, 104, 135
  source, 134
Corcoran, Thomas G., 307, 312
Cordiner, David C., 33
Corporate capitalism, 47
Corporations, xiii–xiv, xv, 202, 317
  decentralization, 74
  diversification, 74
  economic power, 4, 74, 130, 207
  as exploitative, 102–3, 135, 203
  growth, 74
  management, 74
  as military suppliers, 16, 17, 98, 102, 254–67

multinational, 128
and wartime control, 272, 284, 291
See also Business
Corporatism, 164
Corps of Engineers, 15, 27, 54, 165
Cotton, 103, 166–67, 169
   commodity committees, 99(table), 101, 166
   See also Textile industry
Cotton Linter Pool, 172
Cotton linters, 172, 178
Cotton-Textile Institute, 166, 167
Council of National Defense (CND), 43, 217, 218, 236, 266, 307, 312. *See also* National Defense Advisory Commission
Craig, Coulter, 86
Craig, Malin, 38, 39, 40
Critical materials, 16, 18, 19, 97, 134, 135, 146, 178
Crom, William H., 147
Crowell, Benedict, 5, 6, 7, 8, 45, 50, 71, 72, 77, 83, 89, 95, 235, 308, 325(n7)
Crowley, Patrick E., 83
Crozier, William B., 28
Cryolite, 136
Cummings, Homer S., 118, 119
Current Procurement Branch (OASW), 25
Current Procurement News Digest, 25
Currie, Lauchlin, 312
Curtiss, Glenn H., 187
Curtiss Aeroplane and Motor Company, Incorporated, 179, 187, 188
Curtiss-Wright Corporation, 189, 190, 197, 262

Davis, Dwight F., 13, 28, 49, 50, 80, 84, 85, 108, 324(n6)
Dayton Wright Airplane Company, 187
DC-3, 186–87
Decentralization, 272. *See also under* Corporations; Ordnance Department; War, Department of
Deeds, Edward A., 187, 192
Defense appropriations (1940), 26
Defense Coordination Board, 307
Deferments, 234. *See also* Selective Service Administration
Delafield, Edward C., 79
Delafield, John Ross, 83, 236
Delco (Dayton Engineering Laboratories), 187
Demobilization, 216
Democratic ideology, contradictions, xvi
Democrats, 49, 73, 104, 212–13, 255
Dern, George H., 305
Detroit Aircraft Corporation, 188
Detzer, Dorothy, 240, 243, 254, 256

Dewey, John, 241
Diesel fuel, 129
Dillard, James B., 85
Disabled American Veterans, 238, 277
Diversion from civilian to military use. *See under* Economy
Doak, William N., 249
Dollar-a-year service, 1
Dollar Decade (1920s), 206
Dooley, John J., 136
Douglas Aircraft Company, Incorporated, 180, 186, 189, 190
Douhet, Giulio, 194
Dow Chemical Company, 124, 126, 174
Draft. *See* Conscription
Du Pont de Nemours, E. I., Powder Company, 73, 74, 79, 101, 124, 125, 170, 171, 172, 174, 175, 176–78, 257, 262, 270
Duprene (synthetic rubber), 124
Durand, William F., 80
Dwight, Arthur S., 86–87
Dyes. *See* Artifical dyes

Eastern Air Lines, 189
Eastman Kodak Company, 16, 174
Eaton, Cyrus S., 310
Economic elite, xv, xvi, 4. *See also* Business
Economic mobilization for defense and war, xi, xiii, xv, 212–19, 305
   agencies, 55
   critics, 211 (*see also* Graham Committee; Neo-Jeffersonians; Nye Committee; War Policies Commission)
   and elites, xv–xvi, 1, 211
   factors, xii–xiii (*see also* Civil-military relations; Economy; Federal government; Military technology)
   legislation, 51–54, 222, 271, 277
   logistics, xi
   planning, xvi–xviii, 1–2, 5, 9, 10, 12, 21–22, 319
   stages, xii (*see also* Industrial stage; Preindustrial stage; Transitional stage)
   See also Industrial mobilization; Industrial Mobilization Plans; Political economy of warfare; War mobilization; World War I, mobilization planning; *under* Baruch, Bernard M.; Federal government; War, Department of; Wilson, Woodrow; World War II
Economic war game, 83
Economy
   and conversion for warfare, xii, xiv, 17, 197
   crash (1929), 152 (*see also* Great Depression)

420 Index

Economy *(continued)*
  and diversion from civilian to military use, xii, xiii
  and Great Depression, 3, 73
  in industrial stage, xiii–xiv
  interwar years, 73–76, 206
  and market forces, xiii, xiv, xvi *(see also* Business)
  in preindustrial stage, xii
  productive capacity, xiii, xiv, 6, 16, 166
  reconversion, 216
  recovery, 3
  regulation, xiv
  total product value, 73
  in transitional stage, xii
  wartime production, 16
  and World War I planning and procurement, 209–10
Edison, Charles, 308
Edison, Thomas A., 121
Edison Botanic Research Corporation, 121
Eisenhower, Dwight D., 122, 229, 244, 248, 388(n83)
Electrical industry, 146
Electrical machinery, 73
Electric Boat Company, 257
Electro Manganese Corporation, 142–43
Elites, xiv–xvi, 4, 317
  and democratic ideology, xvi
  See also Economic elite; Military elite; Political elite; *under* Economic Mobilization for defense and war; Political economy of warfare
Ely, Hanson E., 44, 221, 227
Emergency Fleet Corporation, 111, 113, 268, 270
Engineering and Mining Journal, 87
Engineering societies, 2, 84–89, 200. *See also specific names*
Essential materials, 19, 97, 100, 134, 135, 146, 167, 178
Esso Laboratories, 131
Evans, John M., 223
Excise tax, 134
Explosives, 99(table), 101, 102, 170–78
  commodity committee, 175, 176
Export-Import Bank, 67

Farm Credit Administration, 148
Favoritism, 214
Federal Bureau of Investigation, 119
Federal government, xii, 317
  –business alliance, xiv, xv–xvi, 1, 21, 26, 44, 50, 59, 74–75, 126, 180–81, 184, 202, 269–71, 312, 317 *(see also* Military, –business relations)
  debt, 266
  and economic mobilization, 44
  and economic regulation, xiv, xv, 4, 164, 165, 180–83, 193–94, 202, 206, 207 *(see also* Bureaucracy; National Recovery Administration)
  factions, xii–xiii
  in industrial stage, xiii–xiv
  leadership, 317
  in preindustrial stage, xii–xiii
  research subsidies, 186
  and social welfare, 4, 202
  in transitional stage, xii
  and wartime control, 272
Federalist party, xii
Federal Reserve Board, 67
Federal Trade Commission, 164, 215, 270
Fellowship of Reconciliation, 241
Ferguson, Harley B., 10, 32, 165, 221, 331(n65)
Ferguson, Homer L., 235, 261
Ferroalloys, 100, 143
Finance, 21, 76, 187, 256
Finished goods, 2, 17, 150, 167
Firestone Tire and Rubber Company, 123, 124, 125, 126
Fitzpatrick, James F., 277
Fixed Atmospheric Nitrogen Corporation, 175
Fletcher, Frank F., 172
Flood, Henry, 213
Flynn, John T., 272, 274, 277–78, 282, 288, 300, 317
Flynn Plan, 272–73, 278–79, 281, 282, 283, 284, 286–87, 302, 304
Foley, Paul, 132
Food industry, 73
Ford Motor Company, 73, 123
Forest Service, U.S., 162
Forrestal, James, 310
France, 294
Franklin, B. F., 82
Franklin, Philip A. S., 235–36
Fraud, 214, 215
Frear, James A., 238–39, 242
Freudenthal, Elsbeth E., 190
Fuel, 21, 68, 129, 163
  standardization, 132
  See also Coal; Petroleum
Furness, J. W., 88
Furniture industry, 73

Garrett, Daniel E., 223
Gary, Elbert H., 79, 80, 83, 84, 85, 89, 105, 109
Gas masks, 26
General Electric Company, 16, 20, 73, 74, 76, 79, 146, 174, 262

General Manganese Corporation, 142
General Motors Corporation, 74, 188, 190, 309
General Staff (Army), 6, 7, 8, 9, 10, 34, 35, 55, 205, 226
  General Mobilization Plans (1924, 1928), 14, 37, 38, 333(n84)
  General War Plan (1933), 38
  G-1 (Personnel) Division, 38
  G-3 (Operations and Training) Division, 36, 38
  G-4 (Supply) Division, 36, 38, 45
  and manpower, 37, 38
  and OASW, 35–41, 44, 65, 70–71
  planners, 37
  and procurement planning, 14, 37–38, 40, 333(n84)
  Purchase, Storage, and Traffic Division, 5–6, 9, 34
  war plans, 11, 14, 37, 38–39, 40 (*see also* War Plans Division)
  and WPC, 229
  See also Army; War, Department of
General Standardization Conference (Commerce Department), 162
Geneva Naval Conference (1927), 262
Geological Survey, U.S., 87, 140
George, Walter F., 255, 265, 296, 298, 300
Germany, 155, 158, 172–75. *See also* Nazi Germany
Gibbons, George R., 120
Gifford, Walter S., 79, 236, 309
Gilded Age (1865–1899), xi
Glass, Carter, 298
Goethals, George W., 5
Gompers, Samuel, 224
Goodrich, B. F., Company, 73, 121, 124, 125, 174
Goodyear Tire and Rubber Company, 121, 123, 125
Grace, Eugene G., 91, 307
Graham, William J., 212, 213, 217
Graham Committee (House Select Committee on Expenditures in the War Department), xvii, 209, 212–19, 316, 320
  subcommittees, 214–16
Graphite, 19, 87
Great Britain, 294
  chemicals, 174, 257
  and mica, 146
  munitions firms, 257, 258
  Navy structure, 263
  rubber supply, 120
  tin supply, 144
  Treasury, 310
  wool, 148

Great Depression, 3, 103, 104, 109, 179, 188, 201, 202, 206, 229, 230. *See also under* Economy
Great Power status, 318
Green, William, 239
Griswold, Augustus H., 235
Guayule (rubber source), 121–22
Guggenheim, Daniel, Fund for the Promotion of Aeronautics, 185–86

Hadley, Lindley H., 230, 244, 246, 248, 250
Haiti, 122
Hancock, John M., 236, 306, 309, 313
Harbord, James G., 10, 83, 85
Harbord Board, 10, 44
Harding, Warren G., 227
Hare, Ray M., 92–93
Harriman, W. Averell, 188
Harris, Charles T., Jr., 27, 110, 111, 117, 136, 162, 201, 271, 276, 283, 290
Harrison, R. E. W., 152, 154
Harvard University, 118, 119, 120
Hauseman, D. N., 153
Heavy industry, 98, 99(table), 116, 129
Henderson, Francis R., 127
Henry, Merton G., 39
Hercules Powder Company, 171, 174, 175
Hevea tree, 121–23
High, Stanley, 223
Hill, George P., 246
Hill, Lister, 275, 301
Hippelheuser, Richard H., 47
Hobley, Alfred H., 116–17, 118, 119, 147
Holaday, William P., 230, 249, 250
Holley, Irving Brenton, Jr., 191
Holtzoff, Alexander, 246
Hook, Charles R., 92
Hoover, Herbert, 54, 75, 122, 134, 164, 200–201, 227
Hopkins, H. V., 118
House, Edward M., 292
House Military Affairs Committee, 6, 52, 217, 222, 275, 295, 301
House Select Committee on Expenditures in the War Department. *See* Graham Committee
Huddleston, George, 228
Hudson Motor Car Company, 187
Hughes, Charles Evans, 192, 215
Hull, Morton D., 223
Hurley, Patrick J., 13, 54–55, 83, 228, 229, 230, 233, 234, 235, 237, 239, 242, 243, 244, 246, 250
Hurley Plan (1929), 56
Hyde, Arthur M., 250

422 Index

Hydraulic Machinery Manufacturers' Association, 152, 153
Hydroelectric power, 163
Hy-Grade Manganese Company, 141

Ickes, Harold L., 307, 312
I. G. Farbenindustrie A.G. (I. G. Farben), 124, 125, 128, 174
Imperial Chemical Industries, Limited, 174, 257
IMPs. *See* Industrial Mobilization Plans
Independent Petroleum Association of America (IPA), 130
India, 140, 146
Industrial America in the War: The Strategy Behind the Line, 1917–1918 (Clarkson), 46
Industrial Defense Association (Signal Corps), 135
Industrialization, xiv, xvi
Industrial mobilization, 23, 26, 27, 46, 319
  advisers, 44, 79, 94 (*see also* Baruch, Bernard M.)
  and AWC, 48
  civilian agencies, 43, 45, 51, 54, 72
  and Congress, 43, 274–75
  legislation, 301–2
  See also Economic mobilization for defense and war; Graham Committee; Industrial Mobilization Plans; Nye Committee; War Policies Commission; *under* Army War College; Roosevelt, Franklin D.
Industrial Mobilization Plans (IMPs) (OASW), 2, 21, 23, 50–54, 201, 222, 230, 233, 250, 276, 305, 320
  Annexes, 67–68, 69–70
  civilian review, 71
  Legislative Appendix, 51, 57–58, 59, 62–63, 65, 235, 341(n43)
  and military influence, 58–59
  1930, 42, 56–59, 234
  1933, 59–63, 196, 272, 341(n43)
  1936, 63–66, 284, 303, 341(n43)
  1939, 66–70, 92, 206, 311, 313, 314, 315
  and Nye Committee, 271–72
  and procurement, 63
  and warmaking powers, 67, 341(n43)
  See also Army-Navy Munitions Board; Industrial mobilization; Navy, Department of the; *under* War Policies Commission
Industrial Preparedness Dinner (1924), 84
Industrial production, 6
Industrial stage, xii, xiii–xiv, xv, xvi, xvii
Industrial Strategy Board proposal, 43, 50
Industrial technology, 102, 111, 121–23, 124–27, 174–75, 178, 183

Industry Board (Commerce Department) (1919), 43
Inflation, 266, 281
Influence peddling, 262, 263
Institute of Scrap Iron and Steel, Incorporated, 115
Institutional structures, xi, 263
  and Cold War, xv
  and modern war, 242–43
  reorganization, 19, 32, 331(n64)
  and World War I, 3, 219, 300–301
Intercontinental Rubber Company, 121, 122
Interest groups, xvi, 3, 75, 181, 202
Internal Revenue, Bureau of, 267, 288
International Harvester Company, 174
Internationalism, 213, 218, 253, 255
International Mercantile Marine Company, 235
International Nickel Company, 143
International Tin Executive (London), 144
International Tin Research and Developmental Council, 136
Interstate Commerce Commission, 61
Interventionists, 297
Interwar years (1919–1939), xv, xvii, 1, 27, 174, 319
  procurement costs, 24–26
  supply and mobilization problems, 41, 103, 135, 143–44, 198, 205, 211, 320 (*see also* Graham Committee; Nye Committee; War Policies Commission)
  war mobilization and peace movement, 253–54
  See also Army, interwar manpower; Industrial Mobilization Plans; Procurement planning; *under* Economy; Military technology
IPA (Independent Petroleum Association of America), 130
IPS. *See* Air Corps, Industrial Planning Section
Iron, 19, 115
  commodity committee, 20, 110
  See also Steel
Iron and Steel Works Directory of the United States and Canada (AISI), 112, 113
Isolationists, 202, 209, 213, 253, 255, 296, 297, 307. *See also* Neo-Jeffersonians; Neutrality; Peace

James, Marquis, 46
Japan, 11, 131, 158
Jessup, Philip C., 295
Johns Hopkins University, Walter Hines Page School of International Relations, 46
Johnson, Alvin S., 46
Johnson, Hiram, 296
Johnson, Hugh S., 46, 48, 49, 55, 224, 231,

232, 266, 274, 275, 281, 302, 303, 304, 306, 309–10
Johnson, Louis A., 13, 48, 119, 123, 305–6, 307, 308, 309, 310, 312
Johnson, Royal C., 222, 227, 239
Johnston, Mercer G., 242, 243
Joint Army-Navy-Industrial Proposal for National Organization in War, 40
Joint Committee on Internal Revenue Taxation, 285
J. P. Morgan and Company, 171, 292–93, 310
and Nye Committee, 254–56
Judge Advocate General's Office, 52
Justice, Department of, 118, 119

Kelly Act. *See* Air Mail Act
Kennecott Copper Corporation, 134
Kent, Frank, 46
Kettering, Charles F., 187
Keys, Clement M., 188
Kirby, Thomas, 238
Koroseal (synthetic rubber), 124
Kreidberg, Marvin H., 39
Krock, Arthur, 46

Labor, 17, 21, 221
control of, 52, 53–54, 68–69, 222, 224, 228, 276, 291, 303
in mass production industries, 75
Labor, Department of, secretary, 249
Labor Administration (OASW), 57, 68
Labor unions, 54, 58, 75, 163, 202, 226, 239, 282
La Follette, Robert M., 242
La Follette, Robert M., Jr., 296
LaGuardia, Fiorello H., 242
Lamont, Robert P., 250
Landowners, xv
Langley Field (Va.), 185
Lansing, Robert, 292, 298
Latin America, 121, 122–23, 160, 191
Lavender, Robert A., 246
Lawrence, David, 46
Lead, 87, 103, 135–37
commodity committee, 99(table), 101, 136–37
supply, 136
League for Industrial Democracy, 241
League of Nations, 240, 258
Leather and hides, 20, 73, 103, 167–69, 214
commodity committee, 99(table), 101, 102, 168, 199
sources, 167, 168
Legge, Alexander, 49, 224, 235
Lehman Brothers, 188
Leith, Charles K., 87

Lewis Flight Preparedness Field (Cleveland), 185
Libby, Frederick J., 275
Liberals, 255, 256
Liberia, 123
Lindbergh, Charles A., Atlantic crossing, 186, 188
Lobbying, 262
Lockheed Aircraft Corporation, 188, 190
Lovell, Arthur J., 239
Lovett, Robert M., 242
Lubell, Samuel, 46
Lubricants, 132
Lumber, 23, 73, 103, 160–63
commodity committees, 99(table), 101, 161, 162
prices, 161

MAA (Manufacturers Aircraft Association), 192
MacArthur, Douglas, 39, 40, 56, 57, 234, 334(n100)
MacDowell, Charles H., 172, 175
Mace, W. A., 109
McFarland, Earl, 27
McGowan, Samuel, 238
Machine industry, 73
Machine tools, 2, 17, 137, 150–55
commodity committee, 19, 99(table), 152
producers, 16, 101, 102, 151
McKensie, John C., 223
MacNider, Hanford, 24, 79, 85
McNutt, Paul V., 237
McRoberts, Samuel, 76, 77
McSwain, John J., 46, 222, 223, 227, 230, 238, 241, 244, 246, 247, 248, 249, 250, 252, 274–75, 276
McSwain bill, 275–76, 277–78, 283, 301–2
Malaya, 144
Management consultants, 34
Management draft, 272, 284, 291
Manganese, 2, 21, 87, 88, 103, 137, 159
alloys, 139
commodity committee, 99(table), 100, 104
sources, 139, 140, 141, 142
strategic importance, 138–39, 142
Manufacturers Aircraft Association (MAA), 192
Manufacturers Trust Company, 187
Manufacturing, xiii. *See also* Business
Marine Engineering Corporation, 259
Marines, 12
Maritime Commission, 113
Marketing, xiii
Markey, D. John, 222
Marsh, Benjamin C., 241, 242, 243

Martin, Glen L., Company, 187
Massachusetts Institute of Technology, 309
May, Andrew J., 275
M-Day. *See* Mobilization Day
Medical Department, 15, 27
  Section I articles, 22–23
Medical supplies, commodity committee, 99(table), 158
Merchant fleet, 106
Merchant marine, 95
Merchant Marine Act (1928), 262
Merchants, xii, xv. *See also* Business
Mercury, 87, 144, 145–46
Merger movement (1897–1903), 73. *See also* Aircraft industry, mergers
Metal products industry, 73
Metals, 73
  substitutes, 146
Mexican War (1846–1848), in transitional stage, xiii
Mexico, 122, 129
Meyer, Eugene, Jr., 235, 279
Mica, 146–47, 159
  commodity committee, 99(table), 100, 104, 147
  sources, 146
Militarism, 265, 294, 301, 318. *See also* Military-industrial complex
Military
  budget, 3, 8, 103–4, 112, 114
  –business relations, 72–73, 76, 79–80, 81–84, 89–95, 98, 104, 119–20, 123, 191, 195, 234, 264, 316 (*see also* Commodity committees; *specific commodities*)
  construction corruption, 162, 214
  power in wartime, 236, 238, 251–52, 319, 320
  reserve officers, 81, 93, 105, 115, 153
  specialized goods, 26, 27
  See also Air Corps; Army; Military elite; Navy; Navy, Department of the; War, Department of
Military contractors, 16
Military elite, xv, xvi, xvii, 318
Military history, xi, 204
Military-industrial complex (MIC), 3, 170, 203, 204, 210, 230, 254, 257, 317, 321. *See also* Militarism; Nye Committee; *under* Baruch, Bernard M.
Military technology
  expenditures, 207
  in industrial stage, xiv, xv, xvi
  and industry, 186, 207
  in interwar years, 4, 102
  in preindustrial stage, xii, xiii
  production, xiv, 32
  in transitional stage, xiii

  See also Air Corps; Air power; Cold War; Munitions industry; Shipbuilding industry; *under* Navy
Minerals study (post–World War I), 139–40
Mines, U.S. Bureau of, 21, 87, 140, 142, 147
Mining and Metallurgical Society of America, 87, 139
Minton, H. C., 110, 111, 112–13
Mitchell, William (Billy), 31, 182, 195
Mitchell, William D., 246, 247, 248–49, 250
Mobilization Day (M-Day) plans, 26, 34, 45, 68, 205–6. *See also* Industrial mobilization; Industrial Mobilization Plans; Procurement planning
Moffett Field (Calif.), 185
Monel, 143
Monopolistic industries, 269–70
Monsanto Chemical Company, 174
Montgomery, Robert H., 228–29, 235, 236, 244, 245, 246, 248, 306
Moseley, George Van Horn, 55, 229, 233, 234, 342(n56)
Moulton, Harold G., 309, 313
Mount Wilson Observatory, 155
Munitions industry, xvii, 43, 215
  nationalization possibility, 254, 265–66
  and Nye Committee, 254, 257–58, 363–66
  production, 28
  See also Military technology; *under* Great Britain

National Advisory Committee for Aeronautics (NACA), 184–85, 186, 192, 193, 204
National Association of Manufacturers (NAM), 21, 72, 81, 89, 90–93, 96, 203, 312
  Industrial Preparedness Committee, 91
  National Defense Bureau, 92
National Association of Wool Manufacturers (NAWM), 148–49
National Bituminous Coal Commission, 165
National Bureau of Standards, 122
National City Bank of New York, 188
National Coal Association (NCA), 164, 165
National Committee on Wood Utilization (Commerce Department), 162
National Council for the Prevention of War, 275
National Council of American Shipbuilders, 260, 262
National Defense Act (1920), 5, 6, 7, 9, 10, 24, 25, 42, 217
  and presidential authority, 51, 62
  Section 5a, 7, 27, 30, 31
  Section 120, 62

National Defense Advisory Commission (NDAC), 43, 113, 126, 131, 133, 154, 160–61, 167, 171, 217, 236, 266, 307, 312
  Committee on Supplies, 214
  Energy Construction Committee, 214, 217
  See also Council of National Defense; *under* Baruch, Bernard M.
National Defense Day, 83
National Electrical Manufacturers Association, 146
National Electric Light Association, 54
National emergency (1930s), 19, 27
National Guard, 40
National Industrial Conference Board (NICB), 72, 89–90, 93, 203
National Industrial Recovery Act (1932), 142, 165. *See also* National Recovery Administration
National Labor Relations Act (1935), 75. *See also* Labor
National Lead Company, 135, 136
National Lumber Manufacturers' Association, 161, 162–63
National Machine Tool Builders' Association (NMTBA), 151, 152, 153, 154
National Malleable Casting Company, 76
National Munitions Control Board, 145
National Recovery Administration (NRA), 3, 44, 75, 130, 152, 177, 201, 283
  procurement purchases, 25, 259
  regulations, 134, 149, 191–92
National Resources Board (1934), 145
National Retail Coal Merchants Association, 164
National security, 128, 137, 253
National Service Corporations, 57
National Women's Trade Union League of America, 303
National Wool Growers Association, 148
National Wool Marketing Corporation, 148
National Wool Trade Association, 148
Natural gas, 163
Naval Aircraft Act (1926), 180, 182, 193
Naval Aircraft Factory (Philadelphia), 186
Naval Appropriations Act (1937), 363(n12)
Naval Consulting Board, 217
Naval Intelligence, 140
Navy
  and AIC, 12
  and army, joint structure, 11, 12
  chief of naval operations, 11, 55
  military technology, xiv, 186
  modern, 3, 317
  and Nye Committee, 195, 258–64
  oil use, 129
  planning, xvii
  professionalization, xiii, xiv
  in transitional stage, xiii
  See also Army-Navy Munitions Board; Shipbuilding industry
Navy, Department of the
  and ANMB, 62, 229
  assistant secretary, 308
  commodity plans, 19, 129
  in industrial stage, xvii
  and OASW, 25, 235
  planning and procurement, xvii, 2, 11, 25, 117, 152, 205, 260–61
  reorganization, 19
  secretary, 55, 250, 308 *(see also individual names)*
  Secretary, Office of the, 11
  strategy planning, 11
  in transitional stage, xii
  and War Department, 40, 64, 88, 229
  See also Navy; *under* War, Department of
Navy League, 262
NAWM (National Association of Wool Manufacturers), 148–49
Nazi Germany, 125, 127, 314. *See also* Germany
NCA (National Coal Association), 164, 165
NDAC. *See* National Defense Advisory Commission
Neo-Hamiltonians, 213
Neo-Jeffersonians, 209, 213, 223, 255, 256, 257, 318, 320, 321
Neoprene (synthetic rubber), 124. *See also* Graham Committee; Isolationists; Neutrality; Nye Committee; Pacifists; Peace; War Policies Commission
Neutrality, 256, 292–301, 303, 307. *See also* Neo-Jeffersonians; *under* Wilson, Woodrow
Neutrality Act (1935), 145
New Deal, 64, 75, 132, 255, 256, 313–14
New England, 166
Newport News Shipbuilding and Drydock Company, 259, 261, 267
New York Central Lines, 83
New York Ordnance District, 76, 83
New York Shipbuilding Company, 259
New York Times, 46, 47
New Zealand, 148
NICB. *See* National Industrial Conference Board
Nickel, 19, 143
  commodity committee, 100
Nitrates, 172, 175, 215
Nitric acid, 176
Nitrocellulose powder, 171
Nitrogen fixation plants, 171

Nix, R. R., 48
NMTBA. *See* National Machine Tool Builders' Association
Nonferrous metals, 21, 100, 136, 144, 146
  commodity committee, 101, 117
Nonstrategic industries, 98, 99(table), 105
Noris, George W., 254, 256
North American Aviation, Incorporated, 188, 189
NRA. *See* National Recovery Administration
Nye, Gerald P., xvii, 69, 255, 256, 265, 287, 290, 292, 294–95, 296, 300–301, 317, 321
Nye Committee (Senate Special Committee Investigating the Munitions Industry), xvii, xviii, 66, 177–78, 195, 209–10, 218, 316
  areas of investigation, 256 (*see also* Munitions industry; Shipbuilding industry; War mobilization; *under* Industrial Mobilization Plans)
  chief investigator, 254
  and constitutional amendments, 287–88
  critics of, 298–99
  members, 255–56
  and neutrality, 291–96
  records and reports, 254, 255, 266, 291–92, 299, 300
  significance, 253, 254, 255, 256, 318, 391(n5)
  subpoena powers, 255
  and WPC, 254
  See also Industrial mobilization; *under* Baruch, Bernard M.; Navy; Political economy of warfare; Roosevelt, Franklin D.; War mobilization; Wilson, Woodrow
Nylon, 150

OASW (Office of the Assistant Secretary of War). *See* War, Department of, Assistant Secretary, Office of the
Ohio Bell Telephone Company, 76
Oil. *See* Petroleum
Oligopolistic industries, 73, 74, 98, 99(table), 105, 129, 134, 174, 181, 187
  as opportunistic, 102–3
  See also Business
O'Neil, Ralph T., 237
Optical glass, 102, 151, 155–58, 159
  commodity committee, 99(table), 104, 156
Ordnance Department, 15, 16, 17, 35, 84
  chiefs, 28–29, 76, 77
  and commodity committees, 20, 98, 101, 102, 105, 152–53
  contracts, 26, 76
  decentralization, 28
  and industry, 20, 72, 76, 77, 91, 95–96, 153, 154, 172, 177–78
  investigation of, 214–15
  officer corps, 91
  Production Division, 76
  Section II articles, 22
  supply operations and planning, 26, 27, 28–29, 76, 84, 113, 144, 166
  See also Army; Army Ordnance Association; War, Department of, Ordnance Procurement Districts; War, Department of, supply bureaus
OUSW (Office of the Undersecretary of War). *See* War, Department of, Undersecretary, Office of the
Oxholm, Alex H., 162

Pacifists, 253, 255. *See also* Neo-Jeffersonians
Palmer, John McA., 221
Panama Canal Zone, 122
Paper industry, 73
Paris, William F., 133
Parker, Lovell H., 285, 286
Parsons, James K., 37
Patents, 174–75, 192
Patriotism, 288
Patterson, Robert P., 34, 92–93
Payne, Frederick H., 90, 234
PB. *See* Planning Branch
Peace, 228
  and elites, xvi
  movement, 202, 209, 239–40, 245, 253–54
  and war, 244, 253
  See also Neo-Jeffersonians
Pecora, Ferdinand, 272
Peek, George N., 49, 235, 306, 307
People's Legislative Service, 242
People's Lobby, 241
Pershing, John J., 6, 10, 47, 49, 129
Petroleum, 19, 21, 23, 73, 87, 101, 103, 129–33
  antitrust suits, 132
  commodity committee, 99(table), 100, 131, 133
  fraud and waste, 215
  prices, 130, 132
  production, 129, 130
PFC. *See* Price Fixing Committee
Phelps Dodge Corporation, 134
Phenol, 171, 172, 178
Philippines, 123
Phillips Petroleum Corporation, 126
Picatinny Arsenal (Del.), 177
Picric acid, 171, 178
Pierce, Palmer E., 27, 45, 79, 83, 95, 172, 236

Pittman, Key, 296
Pittsburgh Ordnance District, 112
Planning Branch (PB) (OASW), 10–11, 12, 13, 27, 28, 95, 118, 136, 147–48, 271
  directors, 32, 33, 110, 113
  See also Army-Navy Munitions Board; Industrial mobilization; Industrial Mobilization Plans; Procurement planning; War, Department of
Plant conversion, 17
Planters, xv
Platinum, 87, 146
PMP. See Protective Mobilization Plan
Political economy of warfare
  defined, xii
  and elites, xvi, 211, 316
  factors, xii, 201–2 (see also Civil-military relations; Economy; Federal government; Military technology)
  impact, xi, 73, 211–12
  and Nye Committee, 299–300
  stages, xvi (see also Industrial stage; Preindustrial stage; Transitional stage)
  See also Economic mobilization for defense and war
Political elite, xv, xvi
Political factor. See Federal government
Political parties, xii
Pope, James P., 255, 265, 287, 296, 298, 300
Post Office Department, 180, 181
Potash, 176
Potassium chlorate, 176
Potassium nitrate, 176
Power (energy), 17, 21, 54, 68
Power structure, xi, 41, 52, 236, 318. See also Warmaking powers
Pratt, John Lee, 309
Preindustrial stage (colonial period–1815), xii, xiii, xvi. See also under Economy; Federal government; Military technology
Price Control Agency, 68
Price Control Authority, 67
Price Control Committee, 60–61
Price controls, 231–32, 236, 238, 268, 269–70, 281–82
  bulk-line method, 268
Price fixing, 245, 249
Price Fixing Committee (PFC), 266, 268, 269, 270, 282
Price freeze, 235, 236, 238, 245, 249
Price stabilization, 52, 222
Primary requirements. See Finished goods
Procurement planning, xvii, 1–4, 9, 10, 12, 13–41
  accepted schedules of production, 17
  allocation, 16, 17

apportionment, 16, 17
army, 13–14, 22–23, 24–25
  authority, 9, 26, 35
  competitive bidding, 25
  and contracts, 17, 25, 26
  emergency (Sections I–III), 22, 43
  factory plans, 17
  general, 14
  interbureau and interdepartment buying, 25, 27
  lists, 22–23
  organizations, 2, 16, 21
  versus purchasing, 24, 26
  requirements, 2, 17, 22
  strategic, 14, 16, 18, 23
  survey, 17
  See also Army-Navy Munitions Board; Commodity committees; Planning Branch; War, Department of, planning in procurement and supply; War, Department of, supply bureaus; under General Staff; Quartermaster Corps; World War II
Profit rate, 284
Progressive Era, xi, xiv, 4
Propellants, 171
Protective Mobilization Plan (PMP) (1937–1939), 39, 40, 68, 113, 206
Public Relations Administration, 57, 58, 65, 70–71, 236
Public Works Administration, 183, 262, 264, 265
Publishing and printing industries, 73
Pure Oil Company, 131, 178

Quartermaster Corps, 15
  and commodity committees, 20, 21, 24, 98, 100, 101, 102, 127, 128, 131, 132, 133, 149, 199
  and construction, 214
  procurement planning, 27, 30–31, 32–33, 166, 168
  Section I articles, 23
  supplies for mobilization, 37, 214
  supply purchases, 25, 27, 28
  See also Army; War, Department of, supply bureaus

Radicalism, 255
Radio Corporation of America, 83
Railroads, 54, 129, 164, 372(n17)
Ramseyer, C. William, 242
Raushenbush, Stephen, 254, 255, 280, 288, 289, 290–91, 295, 300, 304, 317
Rauschenbusch, Walter, 254
Raw materials, 2, 17, 18, 19
  information, 88, 139–40

428   Index

Raw materials *(continued)*
  stockpiling, 43, 135, 140
  substitutes, 159
  See also Critical materials; Essential materials; Strategic materials; specific materials
Rayon, 150
Realism, 40
Rearmament, 29, 34
Reconstruction Finance Corporation, 67
Reconversion, 216
Red-baiting, 282, 304
Reed, David A., 229, 230, 249, 250
Remington Arms Company, 262
Rentschler, Frederick B., 188
Reorganization Act (1939), 307
Replogle, J. Leonard, 109, 235, 309
Republican administrations, 2–3, 44, 73, 74–75, 78, 103–4, 200, 319
Republican party, xii
  factions, 213
Republicans, 212–13, 255
Republic Aviation Corporation, 189
Requa, Mark L., 131
Requirements coordinator, 56
Reserve Officers Association, 81, 83, 277
Revolutionary War (1775–1783), xii, xiii, xv
Rhodium, 136
Rice, Calvin W., 84, 86
Richards, Charles L., 223
Rifles, 26
Robbins, Charles B., 237–38
Robinson, Joseph T., 46, 230, 246, 248, 249, 250, 252
Rochester Mechanics' Institute, 155
Rochester Ordnance District, 156
Rockwell, Fletcher W., 136
Rohm and Haas Company, 125
Roosevelt, Franklin D., 3, 11
  and Air Corps, 184
  on Bernard Baruch, 46
  and industrial mobilization, 68, 104, 123, 145, 201–2, 271, 307, 308, 314, 315, 319
  and Nye Committee, 297, 298–99, 395(n47), 400(n89)
  and war profit investigation, 274
  and WRB, 305, 309, 312–13, 314
Roosevelt, Theodore, 220
Roosevelt, Theodore, Jr., 220
Root, Elihu, 39, 220
Rubber, 2, 73, 103, 116, 272
  commodity committee, 99(table), 100, 102, 121, 127–28
  prices, 120, 123, 124
  reclaimed, 124
  sources, 120–21
  as strategic material, 19, 23, 120
  synthetic, 121–23, 124–27 (*See also under* Great Britain)
Rubber Manufacturers Association, Inc., 121, 127
Rubber Trade Association, 121
Ruggles, Colden L'H., 80, 85, 89–90
Rural districts, 213, 223, 320
Rutherford, Harry K., 28, 113, 136, 311

SA&S (supply arms and services). *See* War, Department of, supply bureaus
Saltzman, Charles McK., 30, 91
San Francisco Ordnance District, 79
Saunders, Edwin O., 52
Sayre, John Nevin, 241
Scarcity concept, 200, 201
Schwab, Charles M., 83, 109, 268
Scott, Frank A., 2, 29, 44, 45, 48, 50, 71, 76, 77, 79, 80, 82, 83, 84, 85, 86, 90, 91, 95, 226
Sears, Roebuck, and Company, 309
Secondary requirements. *See* Commodity committees; Finance; Fuel; Labor; Machine tools; Raw materials; Power (energy); Transportation
Securities Exchange Commission, 67
Security exchanges, 273
Selective Service Administration, 57
  system, 52, 57–58, 276, 291
  See also Conscription
Semifinished products, 2, 17, 134, 188
Senate Banking and Currency Committee, 272
Senate Finance Committee, 65, 285, 286, 287
Senate Foreign Relations Committee, 296
Senate Military Affairs Committee (SMAC), 6, 65, 215, 217, 222, 283, 285
Senate Naval Affairs Committe, 265
Senate Special Committee Investigating the Munitions Industry. *See* Nye Committee
Shastid, Thomas Hall, 238–39
Shearer, William B., 262
Shellac, 100, 150, 159
Shell Oil Company, 126, 132
Sheppard, Morris, 301
Sheppard-Hill bill, 301–3, 304
Shipbuilding industry, 3, 106, 170, 195
  and Nye Committee, 258–63, 265, 267–68
Shipstead, Henrik, 296
Shortridge, Samuel L., 262
Shortridge Committee, 262
Siberia, 218
Signal Corps, 15, 29–30, 35
  army air wing, 331(n64)
  commodity committees, 100, 147

and industry, 29, 30
procurement, 22, 24, 26
staff, 30
Silk, 103, 150, 159. *See also* Textile industry
Simplex Automobile Company, 187
Singer Sewing Machine Company, 174
Sloan, Alfred B., 307
SMAC. *See* Senate Military Affairs Committee
Small-to-medium-sized industries, 98, 99(table), 101, 137, 138, 159, 160
Smith, George Otis, 87
Smith, Tucker P., 240
Smokeless powder, 171, 175, 176, 177, 270
Snell, Bertrand H., 228
Snell resolution (1930), 228
Socialism, 241, 304
Somers, Richard H., 79
South, 166
and Civil War, xii
Soviet Union (Russia), 140, 141, 176, 240
Spafford, Edward E., 222, 227
Spanish-American War (1898), xiv
Spruance, William C., 79, 86
Spurr, Josiah Edward, 87
Standard Oil Company of New Jersey, 73, 124, 125, 126–27, 128, 130, 131, 132, 133, 165, 174, 178
Starett, William A., 214
State, Department of, 66, 264
Steam, xiv
Steamship Owners Association, 262
Steel, xiv, 1, 2, 102, 103
alloyed, 111, 145
carbon, 111
commodity committee, 20, 99(table), 104, 105, 110, 114–15
as essential material, 19, 23, 97
fraud and waste, 215
high-speed tool, 111
and manganese, 139
plans (1927, 1936, 1940), 106–7, 112–13, 114
prices, 109, 268
production, 112, 113
stainless, 111, 143
technology, 111
See also Iron
Stettinius, Edward R., 309
Stettinius, Edward R., Jr., 126, 309, 313
Stevenson, James, 120
Stevenson Plan, 120, 123
Stimson, Henry L., 7, 83, 220
secretary of war, 92, 93
Stockpiling, 43, 104, 122, 135, 142, 144, 363(n12)
Strategic and Critical Materials Stockpiling Act (1939), 363(n12)

Strategic industries, 98, 99(table), 105
Strategic materials, 16, 18, 21, 97, 100, 103, 117, 120, 138, 147, 151
stockpiling, 142, 144
Subcontracting abuses and waste, 214
Submarine, 4
Sugar, 272
Sullivan, Mark, 46
Sulphur, 115
Sulphuric acid, 176, 178
Summerall, Charles P., 39, 83
Summers, Leland L., 171, 192
Supply arms and services (SA&S). *See* War, Department of, supply bureaus
Surgical instruments, 151, 158–59
Surplus, disposal of, 216
Swanson, Claude A., 230, 243, 249, 308
Swope, Gerard, 79, 91
Swope, Herbert Bayard, 46, 231, 236
Synthetic materials, 121–23
Synthetic Organic Chemical Manufacturers Association, 175

Taft, William Howard, 129
Talbott, H. E., Senior and Junior, 187
Tangeman, Walter W., 152
Tanks, 4, 215
Tanners' Council of America, 168
Tariff protection, 134, 137, 141, 150, 158, 173
Taxation, 267, 272, 281, 284, 285–86, 287. *See also under* World War I
Taylor, John Thomas, 222, 275, 302, 304
Technology. *See* Industrial technology; Military technology
Temporary National Economic Committee, 132
Tetryl, 175
Textile industry, 73, 99(table), 101, 103, 199. *See also* Cotton; Silk; Wool
Thickol (synthetic rubber), 124
Thomas, Norman, 241, 242, 243
Tin, 19, 87, 136, 144–46, 159
commodity committee, 99(table), 104, 145
scrap, 145
source, 144
See also under Great Britain
Tires, 124
Titanium, 19
TNT (trinitrotoluene), 171, 175
Toluene, 178, 215
Toluol, 172, 178
Tower, Walter S., 111, 113
Trade associations, 3, 21, 72, 75, 89–95, 98, 99(table), 121, 136, 148, 151, 160, 175, 200
regional, 166
See also specific industries

Trading with the Enemy Act (1917), 173
Transitional stage (1816–1865), xii, xiii, xvi
Transportation, 17, 21, 54, 68, 164
  air, 180, 181, 236
  equipment and vehicles, 73
Treasury, Department of the, 67, 236, 260, 269, 285, 312
  Procurement Division, 25
  in transitional stage, xiii
Treasury–Post-Office Appropriations Act (1933), 363(n12)
Tripp, Guy E., 28, 29, 76, 83, 89, 91, 95
Tungsten, 87, 143
TWA (Transcontinental and Western Air), 189

Union (Civil War mobilization), xiii
Union Carbide and Carbon Corporation, 165, 174, 175
Union Oil Company, 132
United Aircraft and Transportation Company, 188, 189, 190
United Aircraft Corporation, 189, 190
United Airlines (company), 189
United Mine Workers of America (UMW), 163, 164
United Shoe Machinery Corporation, 174
United States Steel Corporation, 16, 73, 76, 79, 83, 100, 140, 267
  and AISI, 106, 109, 110
  and AOA, 105
  and OASW, 105, 106, 108, 110–12, 113
Universal Military Training, 243
Universal Oil Products Company, 126, 165, 178
Universal service concept, 53, 221–22, 230, 237, 277, 290–92. *See also* Conscription
University of Wisconsin, 87
Upper class, xv
Uranium, 136
U.S. Coal Commission (1922), 164
U.S. Fuel Administration (1917), 164
U.S. Rubber Company, 74

Vanadium, 19, 87, 143
Vandenberg, Arthur H., 46, 230, 249, 250, 252, 254, 317
  and Nye Committee, 255, 265, 273, 289, 290, 296
Venezuela, 129
Vertical integration, 74, 130, 135
Veterans of Foreign Wars, 238, 277, 282
Vickers-Armstrong (company), 257
Vinson-Trammell Act (1934), 260, 265
Voluntary organizations, 200

Wadsworth, James W., Jr., 49, 91
Wage controls, 276
Wage freeze, 238
Wage stabilization, 52, 222
Wainwright, J. Mayhew, 10, 19, 24, 49, 50, 223
Walsh, James L., 76, 77, 83, 84, 85, 91, 92
Waldman, Seymour, 211, 243
War, Department of
  assistant secretary, 5, 6, 7–9, 10, 12, 13, 24, 43–44, 48, 90, 305, 308 (*see also* individual secretaries)
  Assistant Secretary, Office of the (OASW), 7, 8, 10–13, 14–41, 42, 44, 45, 49–50, 76, 84, 95–96, 151, 154–55, 200–201, 204–6, 221–22, 225–26, 230, 256, 271, 310, 314, 324(n6), 336(n12) (*see also* Current Procurement Branch; Planning Branch; *subentry* Undersecretary, Office of the; *under* Alcoa; American Legion; Army War College; Baruch, Bernard M.; Commerce, Department of; General Staff; Navy, Department of the; United States Steel Corporation; War Industries Board)
  budget, 8, 28, 201
  Business Council, 79–80
  centralization, 217
  Commodities Division, 19, 20 (*see also* Industrial Mobilization Plans)
  and Congress, 6, 8–9, 20
  Contributory Division, 21
  decentralization, 15, 26, 27, 28, 217
  economic mobilization, 44–45, 48, 49, 50–56, 59, 70–71, 79, 84, 199, 253, 256, 310, 318, 320 (*see also* Economic mobilization for defense and war; Military, –business relations)
  Educational Orders, 26, 28, 31, 81, 91, 93, 197
  and Flynn bill, 284
  General Mobilization Plan (1924), 14, 37, 38, 333(n84)
  general orders, 10, 11
  General War Plan (1928, 1933, 1936), 38
  historian, 45
  Industrial Division (*see subentry* Contributory Division)
  in industrial stage, xvii
  Mineral Advisory Committee, 88
  and Navy Department, 40, 64
  Ordnance Procurement Districts, 15, 16, 17, 24, 26, 30, 45, 48, 71, 76, 77, 78, 79, 80, 81–82, 96, 105, 112, 136, 152, 156, 200 (*see also* Ordnance Department)
  planning in procurement and supply, xvii, 1–2, 10, 11, 12–13, 14–41, 42, 51, 71, 114, 133, 134–35, 153–55, 199, 204–6, 256, 264, 271, 318

Index 431

power relations, 41, 205, 336(n12)
reorganization (1942), 34
secretaries, 5, 6, 7, 13, 55, 80, 305 (*see also* individual secretaries)
supply bureaus (SA&S), 5–6, 7, 8, 9, 10, 14, 15, 16, 17, 18, 20, 23, 24, 29, 31–32, 33, 34–35, 48, 49, 71, 98, 109, 117, 132, 147, 155, 167
in transitional stage, xiii
undersecretary, 34 (*see also* Patterson, Robert P.)
Undersecretary, Office of the (OUSW), 34
and WIB, 1, 5, 70
and WPC, 228–29, 230
and WRB, 311
See also Army; Army-Navy Munitions Board; Commodity committees; Graham Committee; Military; Nye Committee; War Policies Commission; *under* Navy, Department of the
War avoidance, 291–92
War Council, 5, 55, 57, 60, 323(n2)
Warfare
and democratic ideology, xvi
and social patterns, xi, xvi
tendency towards, 256–57
twentieth century, xii, xiii–xiv, xvii
War Finance Administration, 67, 68, 70
War Finance Control Commission proposal, 284
War Finance Corporation proposal, 273
War Industries Administration, 60, 61, 62, 63
War Industries Board (WIB), xiv, xv, 1, 2, 3, 4, 47, 58–59, 75, 143, 144, 149, 151, 161, 167–68, 172, 217, 244, 266
centralization, 50, 156
chairmen, 45
Chemicals Division, 172, 175
critics, 47
and OASW, 49, 317, 320
objectivity, 282
See also under Army; Baruch, Bernard M.; War, Department of
War Industry coordinator, 56, 57
War Labor Administration, 61. *See also* Labor
Warmaking powers, 52, 53, 221–22, 227, 238, 247, 341(n43). *See also* Civil-military relations
War Minerals Stimulation Act (1918), 139
War mobilization, 253, 254
and Nye Committee, 266–71, 279
Warner and Swasey Company, 76, 78
War of 1812, xii, xiii
War Plan for Industrial Mobilization (1920s), 50. *See also* Industrial Mobilization Plans
War Plan Orange, 11

War Plans Division (General Staff), 10, 36
War Policies Commission (WPC) (1930), xvii, 13, 56, 59, 201, 209, 227–30, 251–52, 268, 289–90, 312, 316
critics, 242–43
hearings, 230–41, 243, 244
and IMP, 233–35
report, 244–51
See also under American Legion; Baruch, Bernard M.; General staff; War, Department of
War Production Board, 12, 19
Controlled Materials Plan, 18
War profiteering, 214, 234, 245, 259, 266
legislative proposals, 51, 53, 57, 222, 225–26, 273–74, 275, 277
tax proposal, 238, 273, 285–86, 287
War Resources Administration (WRA), 64, 66, 67, 69, 70, 313
Advisory Council, 67
War Resources Board (WRB), 71, 308, 309–13, 314–17
opposition to, 310, 312
See also under Baruch, Bernard M.; Roosevelt, Franklin D.; War, Department of
War service committees, 51. *See also* Commodity section–war service committee system
War trade, 66, 68, 295
War Trade Board, 67, 70
Waste, 266
Weaponry, xiii, xiv, 4. *See also* Military technology
Weather Bureau, 182
Weeks, John W., 13, 49, 80
Wesson, Charles M., 28, 81
Western Electric Company, 30
Westinghouse Electric and Manufacturing Company, 28, 30, 76, 262
Weyerhaeuser Timber Company, 73
Wheat, 272
WIB. *See* War Industries Board
Wilkes, Gilbert Van B., 122
Willard, Daniel, 79, 235
Williams, Clarence C., 28, 29, 77, 177, 236
Williams, William R., 325(n7)
Willys Car Company, 187
Wilson, Woodrow, 9, 49, 192, 218, 246, 292
and economic mobilization, 43, 129, 216
and neutrality, 292
and Nye Committee, 298
Wiltz, John E., 257, 295
Wolman, Paul C., 238
Women's International League for Peace and Freedom, 240, 254, 303
Wood, Robert E., 309
Woodin, William H., 89

Wood products. *See* Lumber
Woodring, Harry H., 13, 38, 39, 120, 184, 275, 276, 305, 308, 310
Wool, 101, 103, 147–50, 159
   commodity committee, 99(table), 102, 147
   See also Textile industry; *under* Great Britain
Work or fight program, 68–69, 228. *See also* Conscription
World Court, 240
World War I, xi, xii, xiv, xv, xvii, 103, 211, 314, 319
   airplane role, 193
   mobilization planning, 199–200, 209–10, 256, 318
   supply, 36, 101, 215
   taxation, 267–68
   See also Neo-Jeffersonians; Peace, movement; *under* Army
World War II, xii, xv, 211
   planning and procurement, xvii, 9

WPC. *See* War Policies Commission
WRA. *See* War Resources Administration
WRB. *See* War Resources Board
Wright, Theodore P., 197
Wright Aeronautical Corporation, 188
Wright brothers, 187
Wright Field (Dayton, Ohio), 24, 27, 118, 186
Wright-Martin Aircraft Corporation, 179, 187, 188

Yeatman, Pope, 87, 279
Yellow pine, 160
Yoshpe, Harry B., 45
Young, Owen D., 46

Zaharoff, Basil, 258
Zinc, 87, 136, 146
Zinsser and Company, 176
Zucker, J. S., 288, 289

www.ingramcontent.com/pod-product-compliance
Lightning Source LLC
Chambersburg PA
CBHW050133240426
43673CB00043B/1650